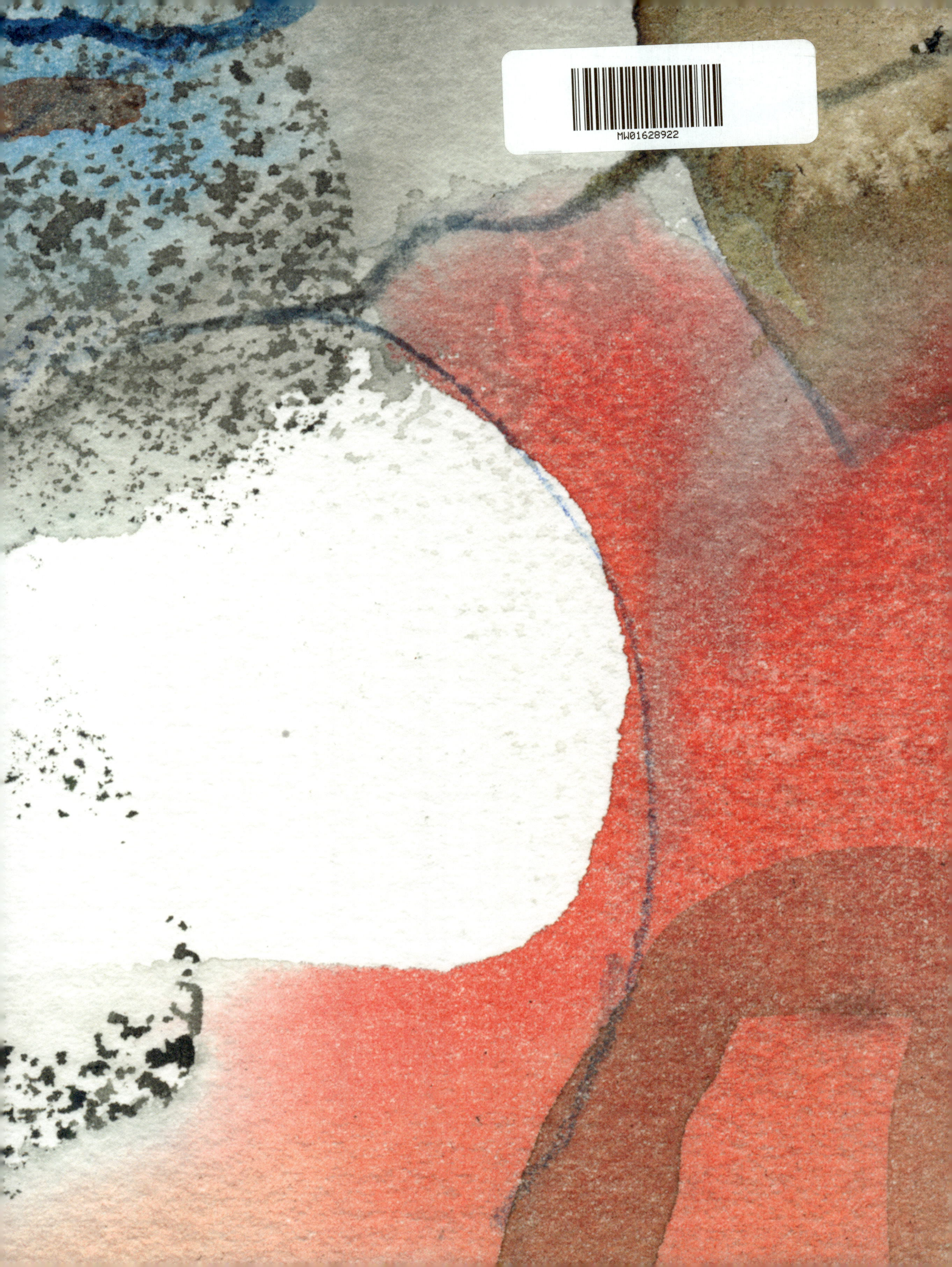
MW01628922

Thomas Schütte

THOMAS SCHÜTTE

Paulina Pobocha

THE MUSEUM OF MODERN ART, NEW YORK

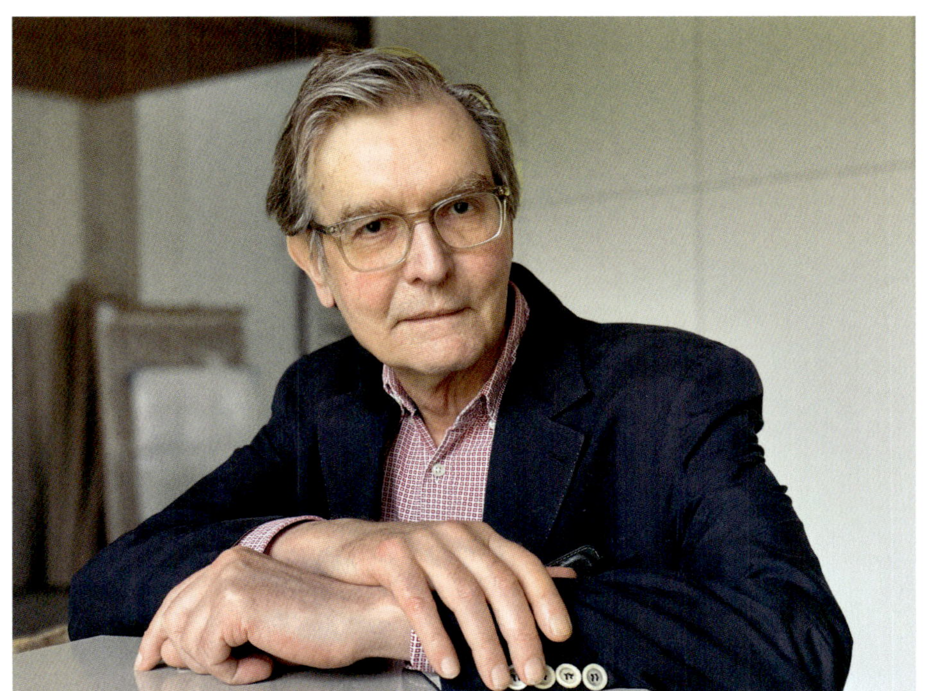

Contents

Foreword 7
Glenn D. Lowry

Alles in Ordnung 8
Paulina Pobocha

How do you tie a bronze knot? 22
Charles Ray

Permanent Provisionality: Notes on Thomas Schütte's Figures 26
André Rottmann

The Train at the End of the Tunnel 36
Marlene Dumas

Art Is a Capital Letter 38
Jennifer L. Allen

Plates 49

Chronology / *Caitlin Chaisson and Lydia Mullin* 198
Checklist of the Exhibition 202
Selected Exhibition History 206
Selected Bibliography 213
Acknowledgments 220
Trustees of The Museum of Modern Art 224

Hyundai Card

Hyundai Card is proud to support The Museum of Modern Art's exhibition *Thomas Schütte*, an ambitious retrospective spanning the fifty-year career of one of the most important artists working today. The first museum survey of Schütte's work in the United States in more than two decades, this exhibition provides an unparalleled view of the artist's practice, from imposing figurative sculptures to intimate watercolors to architectural models—including early works and rarely seen projects from Schütte's own collection. *Thomas Schütte* considers the common thread that connects these disparate objects and explores what they reveal about both art and the culture in which they were made.

Hyundai Card champions the work of contemporary artists such as Thomas Schütte, whose practice and actions challenge conventions and stimulate dialogue about art and artistic practice around the world.

As a leading Korean credit card company with expertise in data science, Hyundai Card provides customers with unparalleled access to premium products and digital and cultural services. Hyundai Card embraces the power of design, music, and the arts and believes in the capacity of creative endeavors to enrich everyday life. We are proud to partner with The Museum of Modern Art and support its mission to connect people with art in meaningful ways.

Foreword

The Museum of Modern Art is honored to present *Thomas Schütte*, an exhibition devoted to half a century of work by one of the most inventive artists of our time. Schütte's capacious practice encompasses a wide variety of disciplines: drawing, painting, sculpture (from metal to ceramic to glass and more), installation, printmaking, photography, design (from graphic works to furniture), and architecture. Born in West Germany in 1954, Schütte came of age as an artist during what he has called the "grey, square Seventies." Although influenced by Minimalism and Conceptualism, he turned to narrative and figuration, adopting a richly material approach to art making inspired by ancient Greek and Roman statuary, early modernist sculpture, postmodern architecture, and his own roving inquiries into artistic, personal, cultural, and political histories.

Schütte participated in more than a dozen solo and group exhibitions in Germany and throughout Europe before his work first appeared in the United States. One of his early presentations in this country took place in 1987 at MoMA PS1 (then known as the Institute for Art and Urban Resources). Three years later, in 1990, The Museum of Modern Art made its first acquisition of his work: a suite of seven watercolors titled *Sieben Felder* (*Seven Fields*, 1989). These spyglass-view drawings depict a motley array of motifs, including colorful circles, a figure with a bandaged head, and a black lemon, references to artworks Schütte had made, intended to make, or would soon make—including *Silberne Ringe* (*Silver Rings*, 1981), *Alain Colas* (1989), and *Schwarze Zitronen* (*Black Lemons*, 1990), all of which have been generously lent to the Museum for this retrospective. Today, MoMA has a robust holding of more than two dozen works by the artist, including several significant print portfolios and two major sculptures, acquired through the efforts of many dedicated supporters.

This ambitious exhibition and publication are the products of a committed, yearslong collaboration between the artist and Paulina Pobocha, Robert Soros Senior Curator at the Hammer Museum, Los Angeles, and former Associate Curator in the Department of Painting and Sculpture at MoMA. We are grateful to her and to Caitlin Chaisson, Curatorial Assistant, Department of Painting and Sculpture, and Lydia Mullin, Manager of Collection Galleries and former Curatorial Assistant, Department of Painting and Sculpture, who have been essential to this undertaking.

A project of this magnitude could not have been realized without the generosity of our donors. Major support for this publication was provided by Jo Carole and Ronald S. Lauder through The International Council of The Museum of Modern Art. Additional funding was provided by the Dale S. and Norman Mills Leff Publication Fund. The exhibition was made possible by MoMA's partner Hyundai Card. Leadership support was provided by the Eyal and Marilyn Ofer Family Foundation, the Xin Zhang and Shiyi Pan Endowment Fund, Eva and Glenn Dubin, and The International Council of The Museum of Modern Art. I also extend our sincere thanks to the institutions, galleries, and individuals who have allowed us to display artworks from their collections—including many complex objects, large and small—demonstrating these lenders' high regard for the artist as well as their understanding of the historic importance of this project. We are deeply appreciative of their trust.

Finally, we are profoundly indebted to Thomas Schütte himself, not only for his essential commitment to this exhibition and his expert counsel throughout its development but also for allowing us to present to our audiences a number of extraordinary works from his personal collection that have never before been seen in the United States. The mark that he has made on intellectual and aesthetic inquiry across disciplines has long been understood in Europe. It is our privilege at MoMA to bring his story to museumgoers in New York.

Glenn D. Lowry
The David Rockefeller Director
The Museum of Modern Art

Alles in Ordnung

PAULINA POBOCHA

In 1978, Thomas Schütte, a student at the Kunstakademie Düsseldorf, made a work entirely from language, *Alles in Ordnung*—a colloquial expression variously translatable as "All in order," "Just great," and "Everything's OK." The phrase is at once a common German saying and something borrowed from Jean-Luc Godard and Jean-Pierre Gorin's 1972 film *Tout va bien*, a portrayal of unfulfilled promise in the aftermath of the leftist utopian revolutions of May 1968. The filmmakers' use of the phrase satirically captures the sense of humdrum resignation that pervades the entirety of the film—life's not great, but it could be worse.

Detached from a narrative, an object, and any image other than itself, Schütte's *Alles in Ordnung* points in many directions. The words first appear painted directly on the bedroom wall of a classmate at the academy (fig. 1). Students lacked access to many official exhibition spaces and thus often installed work in each other's apartments and hallways as well as other interstitial areas. Despite its makeshift site, *Alles in Ordnung* was no improvisation. The letters were cut from stencils made by Schütte in the style of Volkswagen's typography from that decade, using the font VAG Rounded and painted in black in a location Schütte designated on a handmade, rigorously accurate floor plan of the apartment (fig. 2).[1] By invoking Volkswagen, Schütte positioned the work within a historical context. Volkswagen, the "people's car," was established in 1937 under the auspices of National Socialism; it was the car for every German family. After the war, it became something different, an emblem of the German "Economic Miracle." By the 1960s, it was synonymous

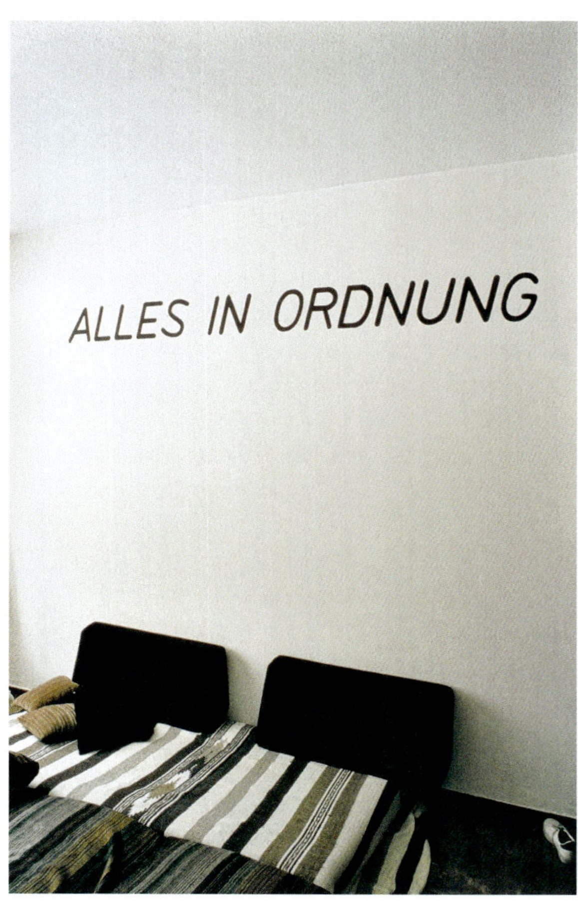

Fig. 1. Thomas Schütte. *Alles in Ordnung* (*All in Order*). 1978. Paint on wall, 7 ⅞" × 9' 2 ¼" (20 × 280 cm). Installation view, Düsseldorf, 1978

with youth and hippie culture, especially the Beetle (Volkswagen Type 1) and the van (Volkswagen Type 2). By the 1970s, it was a global company manufacturing and selling cars around the world. As far as Volkswagen was concerned, having ably buried its Nazi past and traded it for economic success built on affordability, reliability, and cheery jingles, everything was indeed OK. *Alles in Ordnung* was not an advertisement, of course, but an artwork, and one situated in a domestic setting. There, it can read as a daily mantra or affirmation. Despite evidence to the contrary—first and foremost the complicated history of postwar Germany, including the lingering aftereffects of the German Autumn as well as the general unease wrought by the Cold War—if one said it often enough, maybe it would be so: "Everything's OK."

Schütte explores the inherent tension between the phrase, the form it assumes, and the larger social and political context again a few years later. In 1981, the Walther König postcard shop in Cologne commissioned Schütte and Ludger Gerdes, his friend and fellow artist, to create a work in situ. In addition to painting the walls with a trompe l'oeil frieze, they painted *Alles in Ordnung* in white using stencils on a ceiling they had just colored blue (fig. 3; plate 16). This time, the words did not appear in the Volkswagen font but in an elegant and elaborate script, circling the ceiling in a half oval. A closer look revealed that Schütte and Gerdes designed it so that it appeared to be emanating from fighter jets, like skywriting.

These two iterations of *Alles in Ordnung*, a rare, text-based work in Schütte's oeuvre, offer a summation of his study at the academy. It was a period of crucial intellectual and artistic maturation. Moreover, its governing ideas, which span aesthetic, social, ideological, and historical registers, would form the conceptual bedrock of Schütte's practice going forward. If fighter jets are delivering the message that everything's OK, chances are that it is not.

DOCUMENTA

Schütte first encountered contemporary art in 1972 at age seventeen when he visited Documenta 5 in Kassel, Germany. An ambitious quinquennial art exhibition inaugurated in 1955, Documenta initially aimed to familiarize German audiences with the history of avant-garde art from the 1920s to the present, filling in a lacuna of knowledge that derived from the censorial policies of, first, the National Socialist Party and then the tumult of World War II. Documentas 2, 3, and 4 increasingly focused on contemporary art, overwhelmingly but not exclusively from Europe, the United Kingdom, and the United States. The fifth iteration, under the direction of Harald Szeemann, differed from the preceding ones. Documenta 5 privileged action and social engagement, with "programmed experiences, a space of interaction, [and] an accessible event structure with diverse action centers" taking precedence over the display of discrete artworks isolated from the world and one another in the museum.[2] Leveling hierarchies, Szeemann included painting, sculpture, film, and performance alongside objects and images from other fields of cultural production, among them advertising, architecture and urban

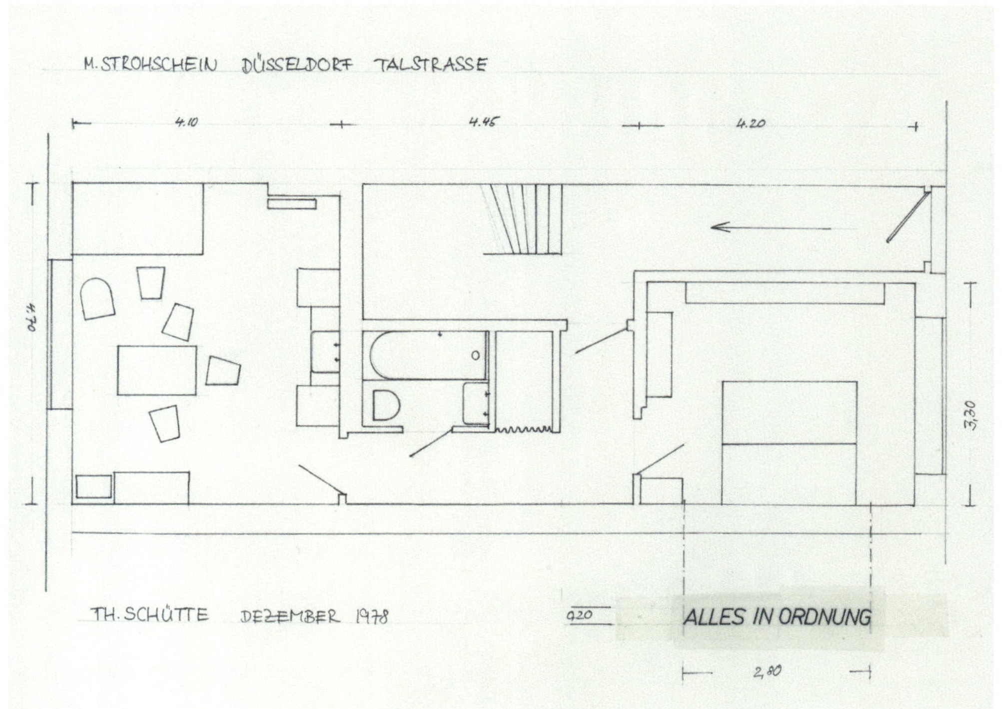

Fig. 2. Thomas Schütte. Drawing for *Alles in Ordnung*. 1978. Pen on paper, 8 ¼ × 11 ¹¹⁄₁₆" (21 × 29.7 cm). Collection the artist, Düsseldorf

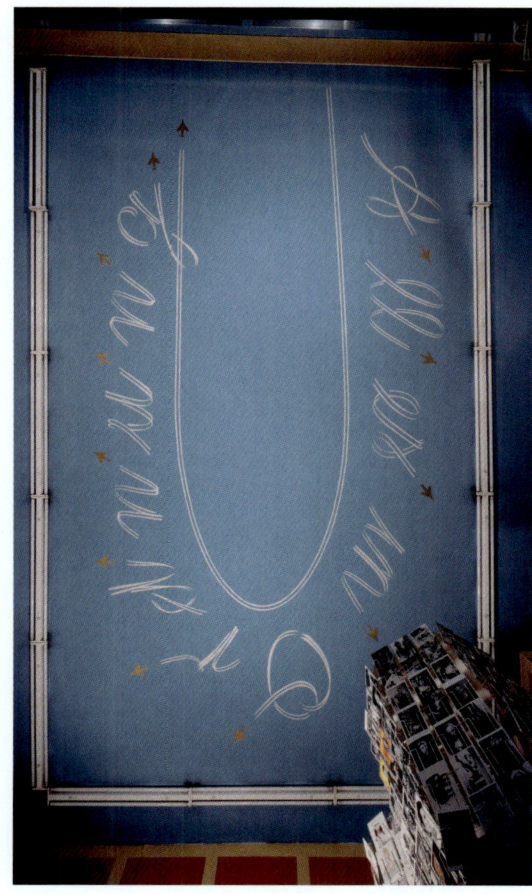

Fig. 3. Interior view of Postkartenladen Walther König, Cologne, with *Alles in Ordnung* (*All in Order*, 1981) visible on the ceiling, 1981

planning, and science-fiction illustration as well as "corporate iconography." As critic Harold Rosenberg summarized in the *New Yorker*, "Art has lost its definition, or is prepared to share it with things never before thought of as art. . . . All aesthetic standards have been discarded (as clues to reality, images that possess quality and those that lack it are equally significant)."[3]

Szeemann's unorthodox curatorial approach frustrated many artists, some of whom withdrew from participation. Others used the exhibition as a platform to levy criticism from within. For instance, the American artist Robert Smithson's sole contribution to Documenta 5 was an essay in the exhibition catalogue titled "Cultural Confinement." There, he elaborates the problem of institutional bureaucracy robbing an artwork of its "charge," whereby it becomes "disengaged from the outside world"—a complaint arising paradoxically from a show "postulated," by Szeemann, "as the conceptual interrogation of reality." The definition of "reality" itself was at issue, as Smithson's conclusion draws out: "The museums and parks are graveyards above the ground—congealed memories of the past that act as a pretext for reality."[4] While for Szeemann, Documenta 5 proposed an energetic challenge to staid presentations of contemporary art, to Smithson the gesture revealed only the subjective disposition of its curator, whose "congealed memories of the past" served as an artificial stand-in for the world beyond the walls of the exhibition's two venues, the Neue Galerie and the Museum Fridericianum. Or, as Daniel Buren put it, "*Documenta 5* is the art work of Harald Szeemann, and we, the artists, give him the materials to make it."[5]

What did this contested exhibition look like to a seventeen-year-old encountering contemporary art for the first time? Although Schütte's two visits to Documenta 5 are thoroughly integrated into his biography, the published interviews in which he mentions the show are few. To curator James Lingwood, his comments on the subject come as part of a larger discussion of the sculpture *Die Fremden* (*The Strangers*, plate 40), which Schütte installed in Kassel in 1992. "I knew the context well, particularly from my visit to Documenta 5," Schütte explains, recalling in particular a performance by James Lee Byars: "[He was] standing in a blue suit among the muses on the roof of the Fridericianum, holding a megaphone and shouting names to the crowd on the square. These allegorical figures on top of the building had stayed in my mind."[6] The work Schütte had seen was Byars's *Calling German Names* (1972, fig. 4), in which the artist enacted the title with the aid of a golden megaphone. It took place in the plaza in front of the Fridericianum before moving to the top of the building, an eighteenth-century neoclassical structure, where Byars positioned himself alongside the monumental figurative statues and continued his roll call. Byars's performance addressed Germany's history but not only that. On the one hand, a public calling of names evoked a military muster—a highly provocative gesture reminding audiences of World War II, in which some of them and many of their friends, neighbors, and family members had taken part, and so by extension recalling Documenta's foundational mission to fill the gap in information on contemporary art that the Nazi regime and the war's devastation had created. On the other hand, the action evoked the unremarkable task of taking attendance in grade school. Names

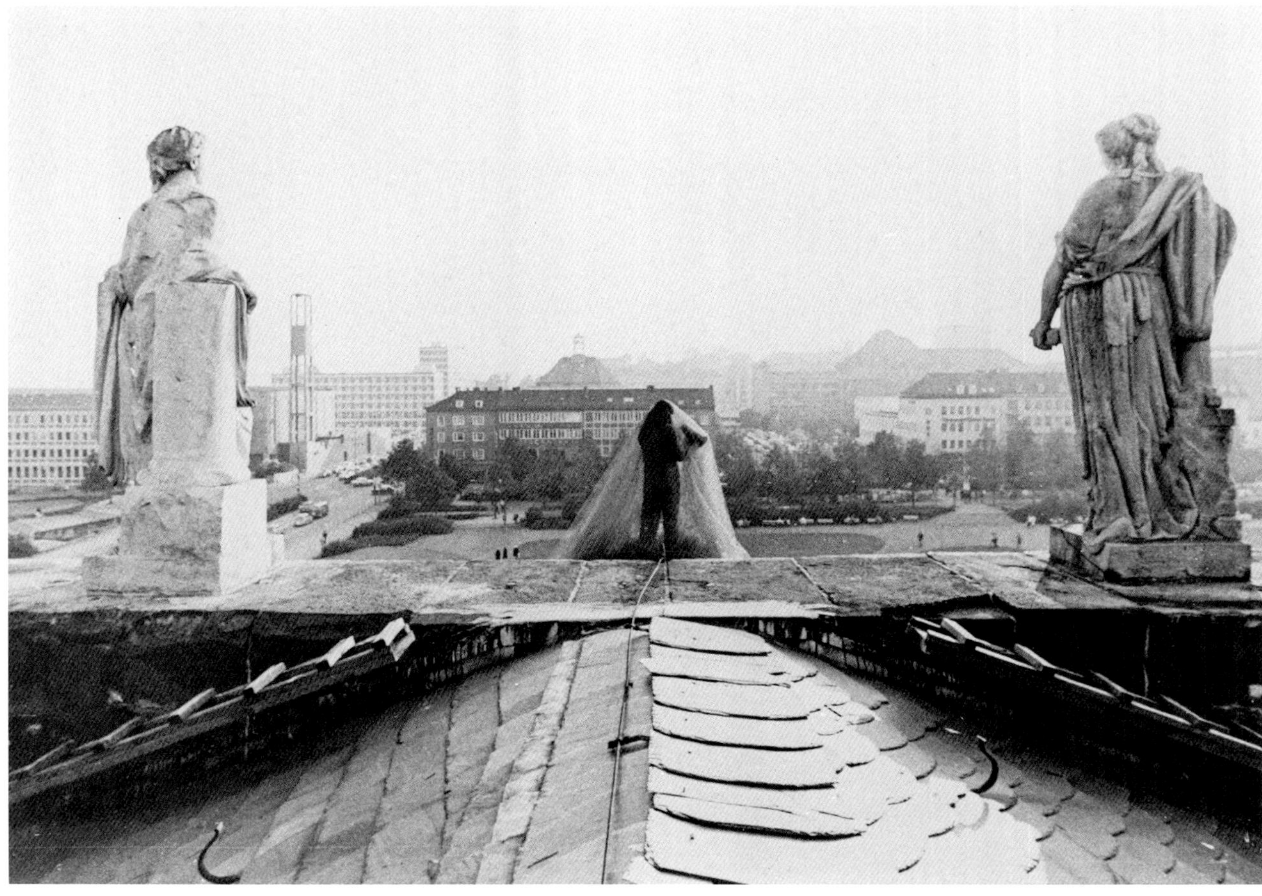

Fig. 4. James Lee Byars. *Calling German Names*. 1972. Performance view, Documenta 5, Kassel, Germany, 1972. University of California, Berkeley Art Museum and Pacific Film Archive. Bequest of James Elliott

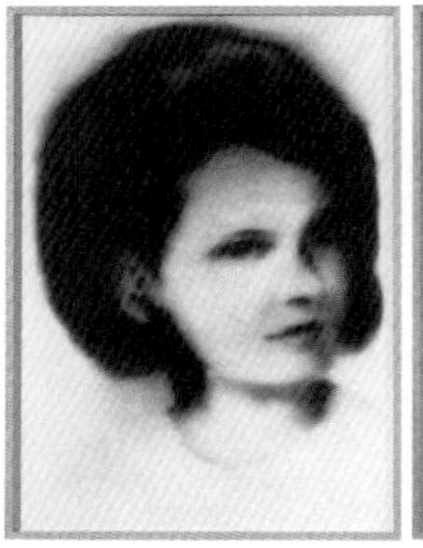
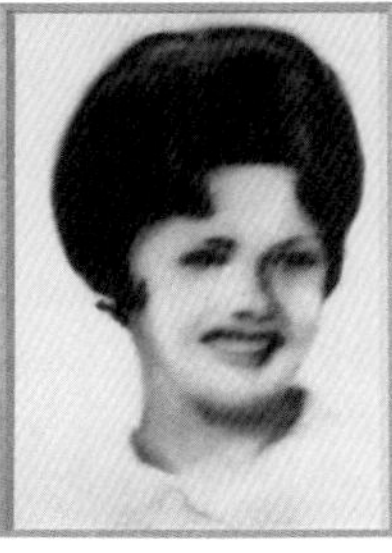
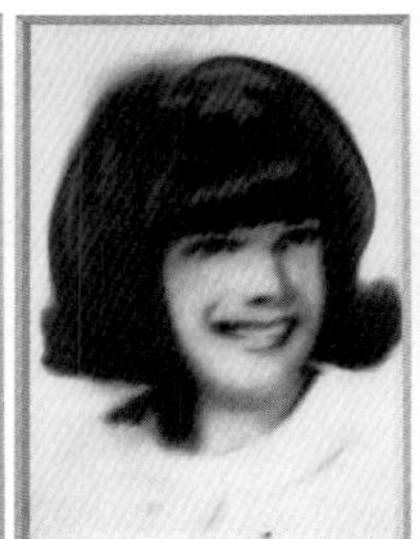
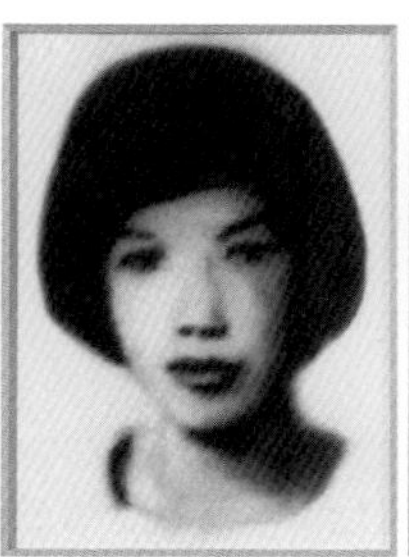
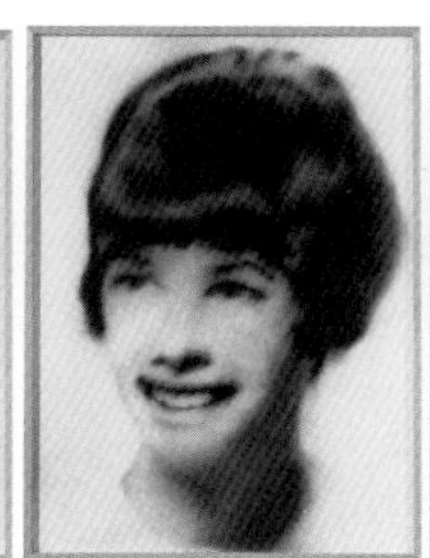
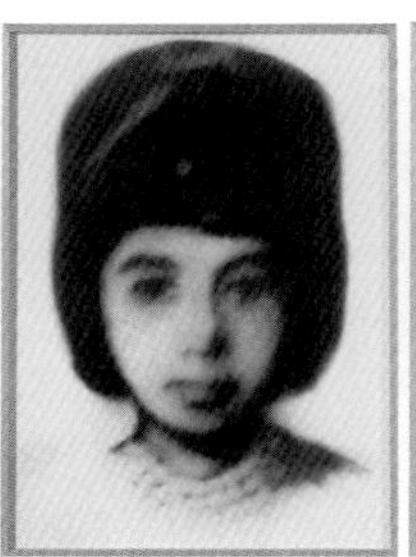
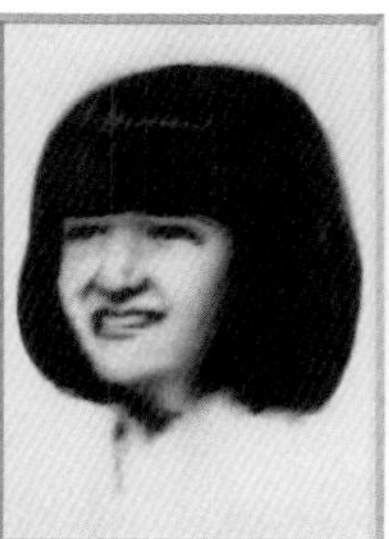
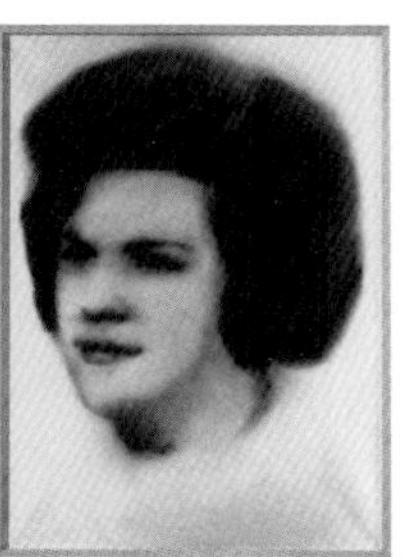

Fig. 5. Gerhard Richter. *Acht Lernschwestern* (*Eight Student Nurses*). 1966. Oil on canvas, eight parts, each 37 ⅜ × 27 ⁹⁄₁₆" (95 × 70 cm). Kunsthaus Zürich, Vereinigung Zürcher Kunstfreunde. Donated by Hans B. Wyss and Brigitte Wyss-Sponagel

are names, and many of those called by Byars were not particularly Germanic, the work's title notwithstanding. However you choose to interpret the piece, it dissolved the distinction between soldier and civilian. Everyone was implicated, he seemed to say; when that fateful roll was called, you were "here." The "allegorical figures on top of the building" that had stayed in Schütte's mind gained complexity against the backdrop of Byars's performance. An emblematic example of Schütte's ability to extract multiple readings from even the most straightforward bits of language, the figures can both lead back to the architectural sculptures *and* reference all those German names uttered by Byars—an allegory, perhaps, not of the horrors of war but of its workaday nature.

An oblique, if highly critical, address of history would become a hallmark of Schütte's mature sculpture. To argue that he learned it from Byars's performance assigns an inordinate amount of significance to the event. Nonetheless, *Calling German Names* did offer Schütte a model of political engagement from the side, so to speak, at a foundational moment in his intellectual and artistic maturation. It was sufficiently significant for him to publicly cite it more than twenty years later and effectively write Byars into his own artistic genealogy. The aforementioned *Die Fremden* offers one particularly relevant example of the work's influence. On a formal level, the architectural details of the museum would inform the piece, which was commissioned by a department store next door to the Fridericianum whose building preserved the surviving front portico of the Rotes Palais, an early nineteenth-century palace. Schütte installed *Die Fremden* in 1992 so that it coincided with Documenta 9 (pages 138–39). Initially it comprised twenty-five individual ceramic elements characterized by simple geometries and brightly colored surfaces, including ten figures with downcast eyes accompanied by fifteen containers of sorts, variably resembling urns, bags, stacks of crates, and a garbage can. The work is not cheery, but neither does it exude pathos. Like so much of Schütte's work, it is enigmatic. Rather than assuming an active ethical position, it asks questions and asks the audience to do the same—even when the artist's personal views on a situation may be very much resolved.

Schütte's earliest studies for *Die Fremden* date to 1991 (page 137), one year after the implementation of the unification treaty that officially ended the division of Germany into East and West. The year 1991 also witnessed the onset of wars in Yugoslavia, which were marked by genocide, ethnic cleansing, and mass rape, among a litany of crimes. By 1992, "foreigners" looking for greater economic opportunities—those from east of the Berlin Wall, including from the former German Democratic Republic (GDR) as well as from farther into the so-called Soviet sphere, and those from the south, both refugees and asylum seekers escaping the threat of violence or even death—were immigrating into the Federal Republic of Germany (FRG). Several years later, Schütte described the situation: "At a certain moment in Germany, after the unification . . . when housing problems and unemployment became more severe, the foreigners—the ones who had come from the East or from Yugoslavia or Africa—became the scapegoats. They were held responsible for everything." Then he asks, "What defines a German, the passport, the blood, the country of birth, the language or the mentality?"[7] The ghosts of World War II loom in these reflections, which also call to mind Byars's tacit indictment of the German people, many of whom had been willing to stand by as their fellow citizens were arrested, interned, and systematically exterminated.

Documenta 5 comprised thematic presentations that showcased the work of approximately 170 artists, not including the anonymous or unnamed makers of political propaganda posters, religious art and artifacts, printed advertisements, and a variety of everyday objects culled from popular culture. Schütte found the heterogeneity of art on view remarkable. In an interview with art historian Marta Gnyp, he remembers its impact: "I also saw photorealism, which is completely forgotten now and which was at the time the main public attraction, art brut, landscapes, objects, and so on. I was old enough to understand that even at that time, everything was possible. Every thinkable position was simply in this show."[8] In the exhibition, photorealist works were classified in a section simply called Realism. Paintings typically considered photorealist by artists such as Robert Bechtle and Richard Estes made up the core of the presentation, but the omission of the highly specific *photo-* prefix from the section's title opened the door to Jasper Johns, who exhibited his 1958 *Flag*, and Gerhard Richter, who showed *Acht Lernschwestern* (*Eight Student Nurses*, 1966; fig. 5) and four panels of *180 Farben* (*180 Colors*, 1971). Above all, the most conceptually provocative, if visually innocuous, presence in Realism was a wall of white-on-white stripes by Buren called *Exposition d'une exposition: Une pièce en sept tableaux* (*Exhibition of an Exhibition: A Piece in Seven Tableaux*, 1972). Painting vertical white stripes measuring 8.7 cm (approximately 3 ½ inches) wide on a variety of surfaces both inside and outside conventional art venues had been his signature since 1967. For Documenta, he presented white paper printed (not painted) with white stripes in seven locations across both venues. The paper covered certain walls top to bottom, and in some cases works by other artists hung atop Buren's, including paintings by Bechtle (fig. 6) and Johns. By drawing attention to the exhibition's literal supports, in this case the walls themselves, Buren's intervention offered a critique of the supposed neutrality of museum spaces (albeit at a cost to other artists, who may have preferred even a false neutrality to the subtly striped backdrop by which they found their works framed). The site-specific installation also challenged the dominance of the artist's studio as the site of production and, just as important, the portable and thus salable condition of art itself—in other words, the status of art as a commodity circulating through networks of exchange that include galleries, museums, and international exhibitions such as Documenta.

Yet for all this, Buren's white-on-white stripes exude a quiet elegance, quite different from his contemporaneous interventions in the city—hastily wheat-pasted stripes deployed to disrupt the visual language of the street with their repetitive, rectilinear patterning. To the uninitiated, *Exposition d'une exposition* may have seemed like a simple if wayward application of wallpaper. Its influence resonates across Schütte's work from the 1970s, perhaps most directly in a series of paintings on paper called *Tapetenmuster* (*Wallpaper Pattern*, fig. 7) from 1975, which feature delicately striped compositions in a variety of colors and thicknesses executed on small squares of kraft paper and pinned directly to the wall. The work situates Buren's radical gesture of institutional critique within the universe of decorative arts—itself an occasional vehicle for politics, best exemplified by the work of William Morris, whose ornate wallpapers encoded the artist's revolutionary socialist commitments.[9] Schütte's squares recall the swatches or samples used to help designers and decorators settle on a larger pattern. And, in fact, they functioned similarly for Schütte, who followed the *Tapetenmuster* with the larger *Große Tapeten* (*Large Wallpapers*, 1975; plate 1)—seven vertically striped paintings each measuring some four meters (twelve feet) high and one meter (three feet) wide. Conceptually positioned halfway between Buren's stripes and actual wallpaper, *Tapetenmuster* and *Große Tapeten* offer a pithy one-two punch—a tactic at which Schütte would become quite adept. The implicit critique landed, as evidenced by a droll mention in the *Düsseldorfer Stadtpost*: "Another [student] sits and paints patterns of stripes in order to calm himself after the frightening discovery: wallpaper is pictures and pictures are wallpaper."[10]

Many of Schütte's works from the late 1970s and early 1980s purposefully destabilize accepted and supposedly incommensurate categories of art. Like *Tapetenmuster* and *Große Tapeten*, *Kollektion* (*Collection*, 1980; plate 12), *Schwarze Girlande* (*Black Garland*, 1980; plate 14), *Rote Girlande* (*Red Garland*, 1979; page 82), and *Goldene Ringe* (*Golden Rings*, 1981; plate 17) swing back and forth between Conceptual art and decoration. Schütte returns to this strategy four decades later in a body of work he calls *Fake Flags* (2017–18; fig. 8 and plates 94–95). Every *Fake Flag* uses a tripartite composition common to the flags of many sovereign states. Their appearance in turn recalls the modernist monochrome, especially Aleksandr Rodchenko's 1921 trio of side-by-side canvases *Pure Red Color, Pure Yellow Color, Pure Blue Color* (fig. 9), with which the Bolshevik announced the death of painting. (By contrast, Schütte made his monochromes from glazed ceramic.) Schütte is not alone in exploiting the visual kinship between national flags and modernist paintings; the most obvious precedent is Johns, who decades earlier had understood flags to be both representational images and readymade abstractions.

Over time, *Große Tapeten*'s meanings have expanded. Significantly deteriorated, the work is today markedly different from its younger self. Over the course of fifty years, the emulsion paint Schütte used has flaked off to leave large swaths of the support visible, looking like "wallpaper" best suited to the parlor of Miss Havisham. In 1980, when Schütte held his first commercial exhibition, a collection of his riffs on decoration-cum-Conceptual art at a gallery in Munich, he announced the show with postcards of the reconstructed Baroque

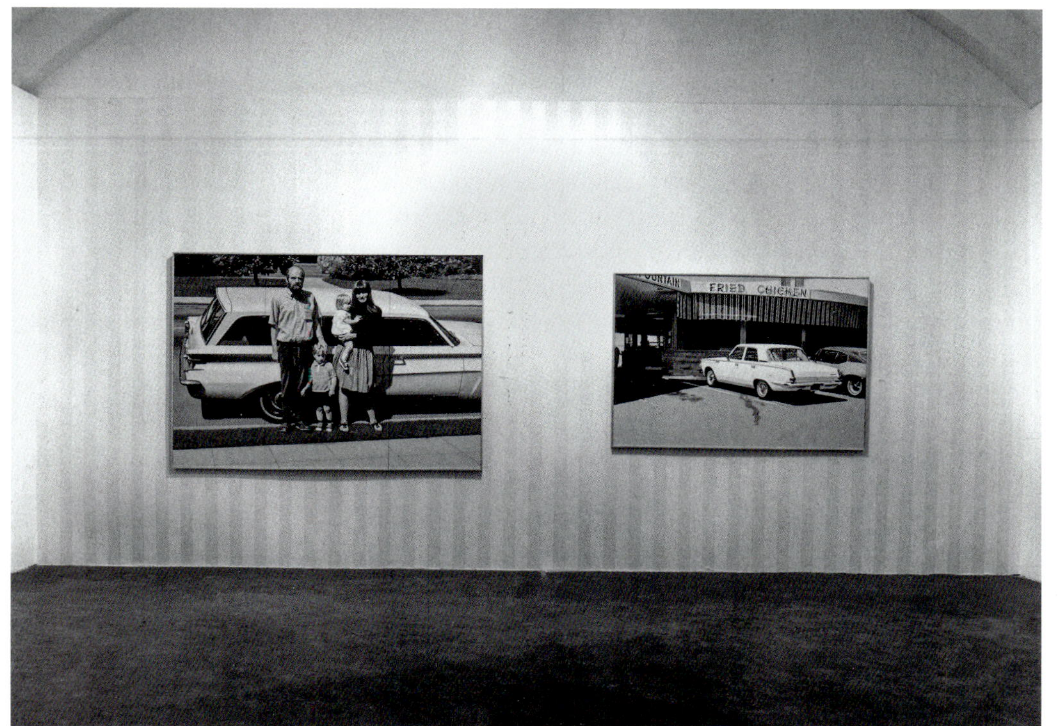

Fig. 6. Daniel Buren. *Exposition d'une exposition: Une pièce en sept tableaux* (*Exhibition of an Exhibition: A Piece in Seven Tableaux*). 1972. Detail of work with (left to right) *'61 Pontiac* (1968–69) and *'64 Valiant* (1971) by Robert Bechtle, Realism section, Documenta 5, Kassel, Germany, June 28–October 8, 1972

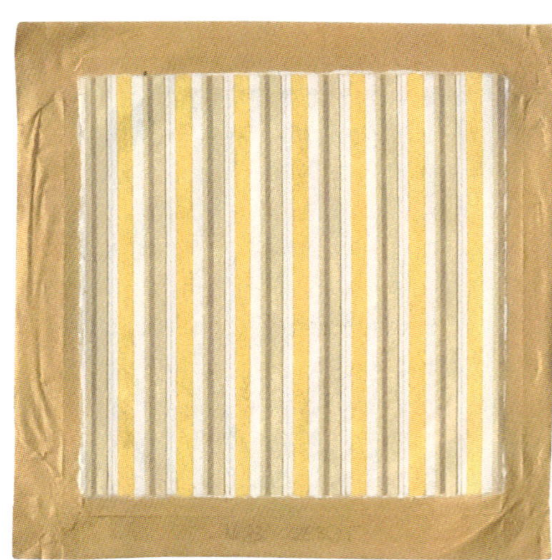

Fig. 7. Thomas Schütte. *Tapetenmuster* (*Wallpaper Pattern*). 1975. Emulsion paint on packing paper, one of 30 parts, each approx. 18 × 18" (45.7 × 45.7 cm). Collection the artist, Düsseldorf

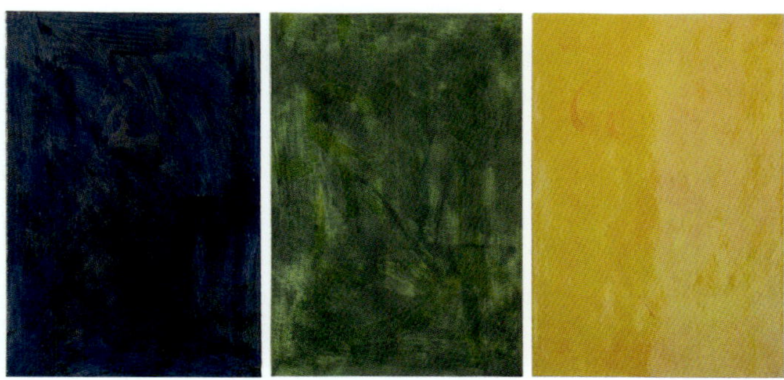

Fig. 8. Thomas Schütte. *Fake Flag A*. 2018. Glazed ceramic, three parts, overall 3' 1 13/16" × 6' 9 ½" × 1 9/16" (96 × 207 × 4 cm). Private collection, Switzerland

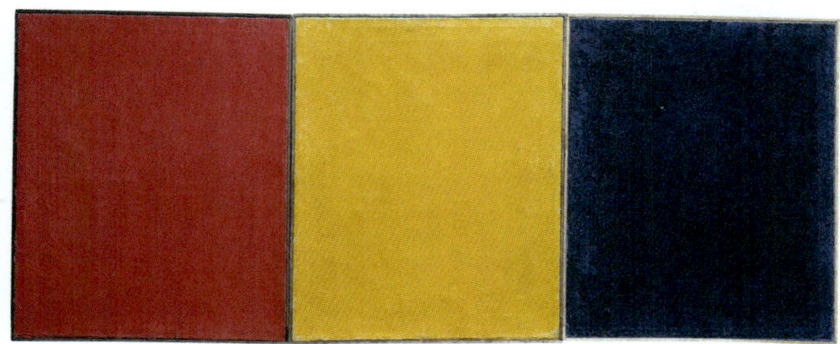

Fig. 9. Aleksandr Rodchenko. *Pure Red Color, Pure Yellow Color, Pure Blue Color*. 1921. Oil on canvas, three parts, each 24 ⅝ × 20 11/16" (62.5 × 52.5 cm). A. Rodchenko and V. Stepanova Archive, Moscow

and Rococo interiors of the city's Residenz München. It's almost as if the *Große Tapeten* were made to indict this sort of refusal to reckon with history and the passage of time. For an artist who values materiality, including durability, as primary, *Große Tapeten*'s state signals failure. Schütte was unaware of how the work would age when he made it, and it has not aged well. Yet it remains in circulation, having appeared in multiple exhibitions, emerging from storage first in 2007 for *Thomas Schütte: Fake/Function*—organized by the Henry Moore Institute in England—and then for several shows afterward. He shows it in its dilapidated state intentionally. Failure, in all its guises, inflects just about every work in Schütte's oeuvre. It may not be immediately perceptible, but it's almost always present. This failure, however, is not Schütte's—he finds it inherent in the genres his work inhabits and brings it to our attention. Within this universe, both Conceptual art and monumental sculpture are deficient and deeply flawed.

In the 2012 work *Krieger* (*Warriors*, plate 93), two figures carved from wood stand like sentinels nearly ten feet tall, helmeted and armed. Belonging to a body of monumental figurative sculpture for which Schütte is well known, including the bronze *Vater Staat* (*Father State*, 2010; plate 91) and *Wichte* (*Jerks*, 2006; plate 73), at a glance *Krieger* appears to reify the conventions of commemorative, public statuary that it in fact undermines. Mighty as the figures may seem, *Krieger* depicts "warriors" that are at once hideously and comically deformed. One stands on legs so spindly that only a feat of engineering allows them to support its torso puffed up with bravado.[11] The same sculpture is missing its right arm and left hand. Schütte depicts the second "warrior" more conventionally, with defined musculature and a stable stance. In his hands, he holds a staff or spear. But again, Schütte deviates from the heroism typical to the genre, reducing the left arm to a mangled stub. These distorted bodies are not the casualties of war. Instead, wearing bottlecaps as helmets, Schütte's warriors are dunces, clowns; they are the physical manifestations of the degenerate society that birthed them, grotesque and ineffectual to the point of hilarity. Like the damaged and degraded wallpaper, the warrior figures, usually symbols of militaristic strength and valor, are ugly actors in a satirical slapstick—a drama that, for Schütte, seems to be a stand-in for Western culture. Something is indeed rotten in the state of Denmark. Or, to extend the metaphor, perhaps Denmark has always been in decay.

KUNSTAKADEMIE DÜSSELDORF

Buren's *Exposition d'une exposition* was just one "thinkable position" of many from Documenta 5 that would impact Schütte for decades. Just as potent were Bruce Nauman's *Kassel Corridor* (1972), particularly as an example of architecture as a psychological space, and Claes Oldenburg's *Mouse Museum* (1965–72). (Oldenburg's importance to Schütte cannot be overstated. From his modest sculptural experiments using everyday objects on view in *Mouse Museum* to his contemporaneous Colossal Monuments, Oldenburg endowed representational sculpture with an incisive criticality—not to mention a dose of humor—that pointed a way around Minimal and Conceptual art without betraying either). For Schütte, an artist who throughout his more-than-fifty-year career has remained restless and refused to settle into a signature style, who may not have experimented with *every* thinkable position but who has tried out more than most, Documenta 5 provided not only a formidable introduction to contemporary art but also a glimpse into the vastness of its scope. The exhibition made evident both the heterogeneity of mediums available to artists and the variety of the intellectual, philosophical, and ethical positions they could assume and shift among. Presumably this boundlessness appealed to Schütte so much that, in 1973, he applied to and was accepted by the Kunstakademie Düsseldorf on the basis of approximately twenty Surrealist-inspired drawings.

Schütte spent his first three semesters, considered the orientation period, in the studio of Fritz Schwegler, a multidisciplinary artist who wrote poetry and made sculpture, painting, Conceptual art, and performance art, and whose work Schütte would have also encountered at Documenta 5. Though Schwegler taught no official courses or seminars, he was there almost daily, ready to advise his students. Schütte's interests were changing at a fast clip, and he used this time to experiment. Of the few works remaining from this period, the most notable are *Tapetenmuster* and *Große Tapeten*, among the last projects completed under Schwegler's tutelage, and a large-scale drawing called *Amerika* (*America*, plate 2) from earlier in 1975.

Schütte produced *Amerika* over the course of five days in February 1975 (fig. 10). Measuring two by two and a half meters (roughly six and a half by eight feet), the work takes the form of a large silvery gray rectangle inset from the paper's edges, with the title stenciled in the upper left-hand corner and the name of its maker and dates of execution inscribed at upper right. Compositionally, the drawing resembles an exhibition poster or announcement, though one of significantly larger size. The work was also a durational performative exercise; how it was made figures centrally in its conception. Rather than working in his studio, Schütte staged the action in an academy hallway during Rundgang, the annual student exhibition. He pinned the paper to a wall and worked in clear view of visitors and passersby. On these days, Schütte also documented his progress on a much smaller piece of paper, a timesheet of sorts that includes a "working" drawing mapping in miniature the surface area he covered with pencil over a given time. Below, he logged the hours spent on the piece, which reached thirty-one at the work's completion. To the right, a more cryptic calculation reveals that Schütte photographed himself once during every hour he spent drawing. As a final element, he hung pencil stubs (he used each pencil until he could no longer hold it), a bag of pencil shavings, and a chart noting the pencils' hardness alongside *Amerika* while he worked (pages 54–55). This focus on collateral documentation—evident by the attention given to accounting for the materials, labor, and time involved in the making of an artwork—takes inspiration from much process-oriented art made around this time. One needn't strain to find the influence of On Kawara and stanley brouwn in Schütte's recording of both time and distance. Sol LeWitt's 1971 *Wall Drawing #84: A 12" (30 cm) square filled in by using all of the Crayola crayons in the pack of 12*, a work that comes into being only by exhausting the materials of its making, and Michael Asher's graphite drawings on cardboard from the late 1960s, a little-known series in which Asher applied graphite until it transferred entirely to the support and ceased to exist as an independent object, offer compelling antecedents. Although Schütte may not have been aware of these specific works, he was certainly familiar with the practices of these artists. Kawara, brouwn, and LeWitt showed at Konrad Fischer Galerie in Düsseldorf, Asher at Galerie Heiner Friedrich in nearby Cologne.[12] Something was in the air, and Schütte picked up on it either firsthand or by reading art publications. Like many in his his cohort, he followed the goings-on in both *Artforum* and *Art in America* in addition to the German press. Indeed, the visual similarity between *Amerika* and advertisements for Leo Castelli's New York gallery may not be coincidental. The ads Castelli published in art journals at this time were often stark and sometimes used stencil-style lettering reminiscent of work by Johns, whom he represented (fig. 11). According to Schütte, however, the greatest influence on *Amerika* was Klaus Rinke, a professor at the academy. Rinke's photographs and drawings from the early 1970s explore sequencing and serial compositional strategies. In a 1974 review of his exhibition at the Clocktower Gallery in New York, Roberta Smith wrote, "Klaus Rinke is one of those artists whose use of systems often pushes his work toward the very decorativeness which such systems are generally intended to circumvent. This is probably because the systems and ideas which Rinke is involved with form the content of his work; they do not really determine its visual appearance as much as they are illustrated by it."[13] Smith might as well have been describing Schütte.

Beyond the echoes of other artists in Schütte's drawing, there is its subject matter. Schütte called the work *Amerika* after the brand of pencils he used to execute the piece—the cheapest he could find, each marked with an American flag. As James Lingwood explains, "The idea was to finish the work on the last day of the exhibition, sell it and go to America. He was successful only in the first of these aims."[14] Taking the interpretation one step further, art historian and curator Penelope Curtis suggests, "Underlying the whole project is the proposition that art is time, and that time is money. What was Schütte's labour worth, and was it sufficient to buy him a trip to the States?"[15] But what of the imposing gray rectangle the drawing leaves us with? It fills the field of vision, the paper rippled by the pressure of Schütte's hand and pocked by the pencils' sharpened tips, creating a highly textured expanse reflective of ambient light, much like the surface of water.[16] *Amerika* embraces ambiguity, a typical stance for Schütte. Yet the mere act of connecting an abstract form with a concrete (if complex) subject is the work's triumph.

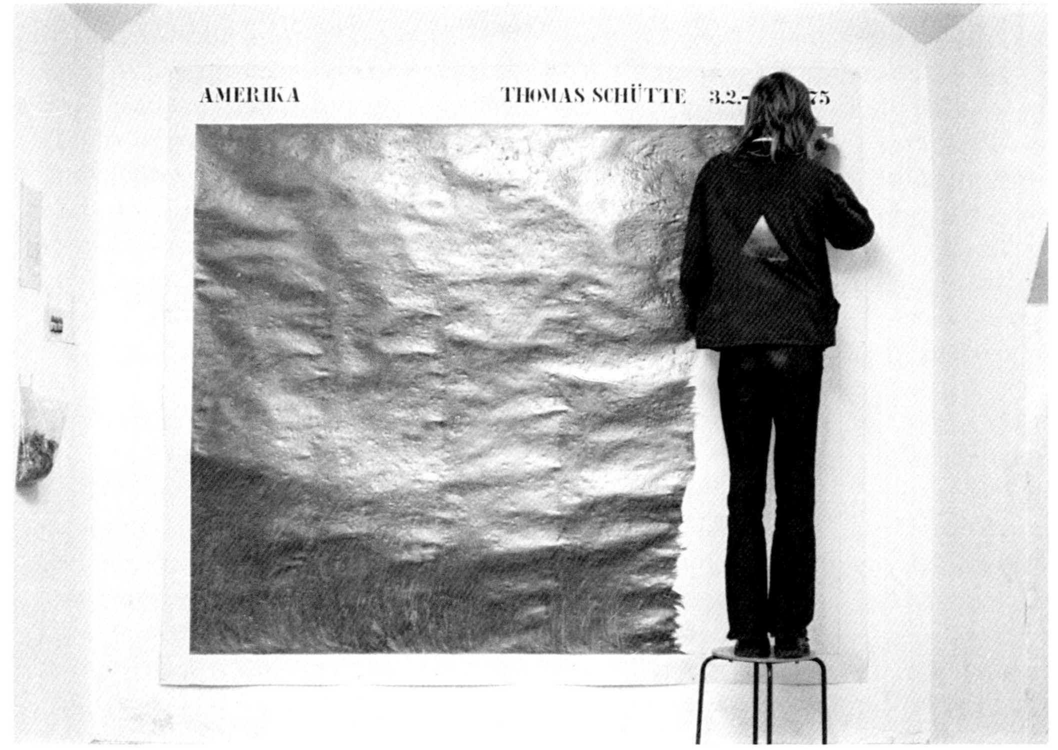

Fig. 10. Thomas Schütte working on *Amerika* (*America*, 1975), 1975

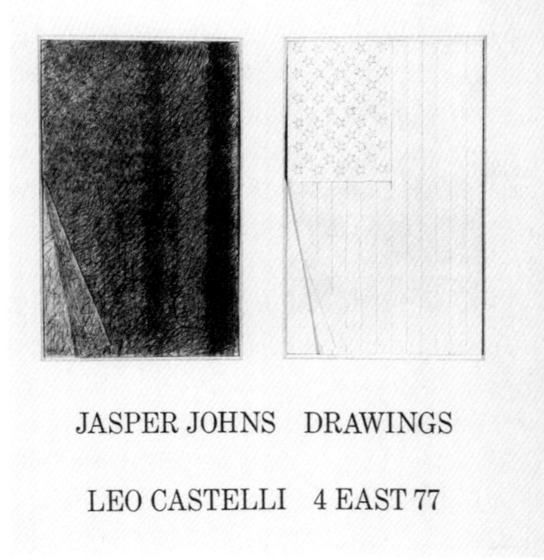

Fig. 11. Advertisement for *Jasper Johns: Drawings* at Leo Castelli Gallery, New York, in *Artforum* 8, no. 5 (January 1970)

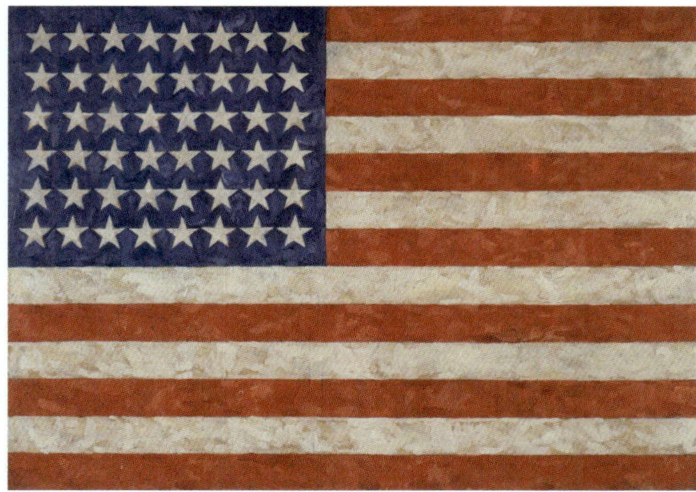

Fig. 12. Jasper Johns. *Flag*. 1958. Encaustic on canvas, 41 ¼ × 60 ¾" (104.8 × 154.3 cm). Private collection

Among other things, it suggests that art can no longer exist within a hall of mirrors, looking only at itself. The subjects of time, of material, of measure, and especially of labor are always specific, anchored in a world occupied by people and things, shaped by history, and governed by a range of ideologies that are propagated and administered by governments, social networks, and the many systems around and within them. Schütte's work from this point forward asserts this fact again and again with the persistence of a drumbeat. It largely sets aside engagement with art's supervening conditions and instead tackles contemporary and historical circumstance. *Amerika* invites us to consider the United States as an imposing monolith on the one hand—a fitting image, considering the heavy hand of US foreign policy in shaping Germany in the decades following World War II—and on the other, to imagine the unknown and maybe unknowable. If Johns pictures America as a flag (fig. 12), *Amerika* is perhaps a darkly humorous retort, with Johnsian stenciling and a visual similarity to Johns's nearly abstract, monochromatic drawings and prints of the American flag—a retort in which Schütte refuses to picture it at all.

This sort of operation extends to virtually all the works Schütte made at the academy. Reflecting on the period nearly two decades later, he bluntly lays out his position:

> I see only the official school of thought, which has been a tabula rasa for a hundred years. Always abstract, always the empty table with nothing on it. Art as science, as discourse, as analysis, corroded to the bone. . . . The method of nonobjectivity meanwhile preaches to the choir and comes to the conclusion that the black square, in its hundredth rehash, hangs somewhere and means nothing more. The metaphysics and ideology to which these are connected are lost. Suddenly it becomes clear how thoughtless this art is. With the loss of its object, it becomes decoration.[17]

For Schütte, this kind of "decoration" has little to do with aesthetics and a lot to do with function. The barest of gestures can be "decorative" if it only assumes the look of criticality; without criticality, art, no matter its look, becomes academic. Schütte's need for a new means of engagement with form brings forth in the 1970s an art that, rather than forsaking the "idea," submerges it in context and muddles it with contradictions fully manifest in the real world he inhabits. Or, as he is fond of saying, in his work he "brought the story in again." He has done so by taking an art that points to itself, its own materiality, spatial determinism, and circumstance, and transforming it into a recognizable object—whether it be wallpaper or a wall. These things invite real-world referents and the evocations they conjure; representation rules.

In May 1975, Schütte left Schwegler's studio for that of Richter, with whom he would continue to study until his graduation with a master's degree (*Meisterschüler*) in 1981.[18] That same month, he began a series of grayscale paintings, all self-portraits based on a black-and-white photograph whose image he transferred to canvas using a simple grid system (plates 3–4). This body of work is the only one that closely emulates the look of Richter's paintings,[19] and Schütte is the first to note that his professor was not particularly keen on training a generation of acolytes. Schütte made twenty of these paintings, each measuring 60 × 45 cm (some 24 × 18 inches). Only two are believed to have survived to today, but a contemporaneous photograph documents the other eighteen. As with *Amerika,* Schütte added a temporal component to his process: he had to make one painting a day. The painting stopped at day's end, regardless of the degree of finish. Predictably, a survey of the paintings reveals a great disparity with regard to the level of abstraction, or conversely, fealty to the source material. One canvas shows the figure only penciled in, as though Schütte had grown bored or exhausted before the brush could even touch the canvas; another hews so closely to the photograph that characterizing it as an example of photorealism wouldn't be a stretch. In addition to the black-and-white palette, which had been a hallmark of Richter's work since the early 1960s, the head shot is a format that Schütte would have associated with his instructor. At Documenta 5, Schütte had seen *Acht Lernschwestern,* and the epic *48 Porträts* (*48 Portraits*; page 29, fig. 6)*,* made for the German Pavilion at the 1972 Venice Biennale (which Richter painted, according to Schütte, at a rate of two portraits per day), was subsequently published in a catalogue, making it available to the young artist, who had not seen the presentation in situ. The chief distinctions between Schütte's grisaille self-portraits and Richter's paintings—apart from the divergence in facility with oil paint—are, first, the sheer fact that Schütte was painting himself and, second, his resistance as a subject, a refusal to reveal himself. In the works, he's shown wearing sunglasses with his head downturned, essentially evading identification, the raison d'être of the head shot, the signal genre of official photography. Richter also maintains a consistent mood from one work to the next in order to make each series a cohesive whole. In the case of *Acht Lernschwestern*, the images are united by a softness that comes from Richter's paint handling and his soon-to-be signature blur, which imparts a tenderness to the subjects, all victims of a serial killer. With *48 Porträts,* although the compositional strategy is nearly identical, the emotional register is wholly different. Colder, crisper, and nearly clinical, the work pictures men of renown (some more, some less) with a distance typically found in passport photos and other bureaucratic documents. By contrast, a formal *inconsistency* holds Schütte's group of paintings together—everyone is an outlier, suggesting the immense psychological difficulty of depicting oneself as constant and unchanging. In two paintings, his face is barely

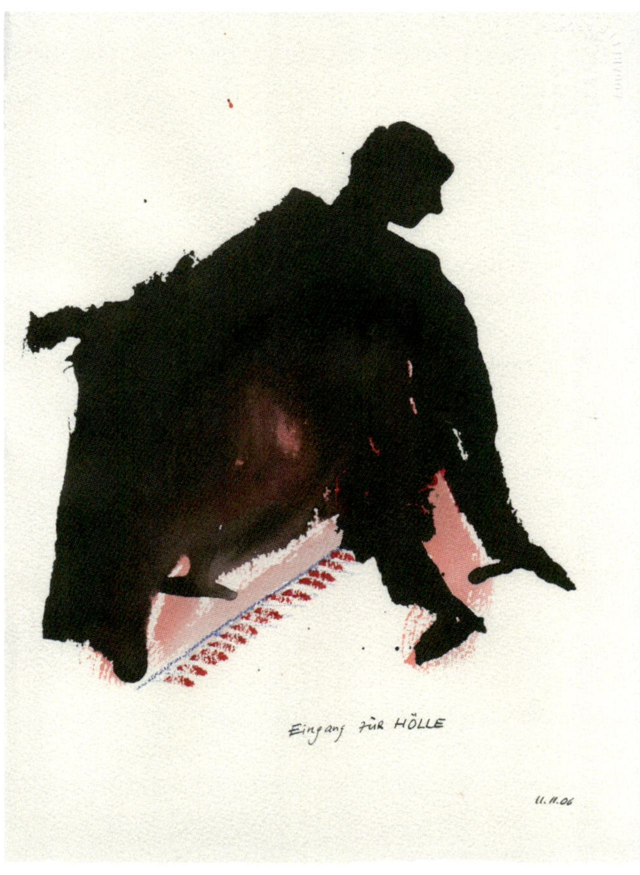

Fig. 13. Thomas Schütte. *Eingang zur Hölle* (*Entrance to Hell*) from *Deprinotes.* 2006. Watercolor and ink on paper, 14 15⁄16 × 11" (38 × 28 cm). Collection the artist, Düsseldorf

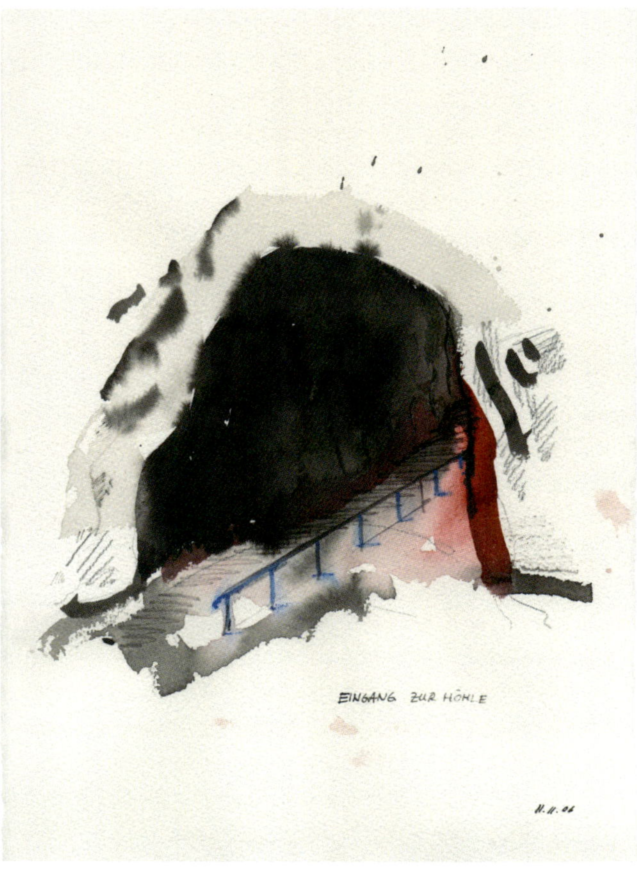

Fig. 14. Thomas Schütte. *Eingang zur Höhle* (*Entrance to the Cave*) from *Deprinotes.* 2006. Watercolor and ink on paper, 14 15⁄16 × 11" (38 × 28 cm). Collection the artist, Düsseldorf

visible, already signifying the poverty of portraiture. This series was Schütte's first sincere and sustained encounter with self-portraiture, an endeavor he took quite seriously, dating and documenting each canvas. Not long after, he deemed the works uninteresting and abandoned conventional oil painting entirely. Nonetheless, the self-portrait—could he overcome the impasse of picturing oneself?—would continue to hold Schütte's attention throughout his career.

The works most rooted in these thematics are Schütte's *Mirror Drawings* (plates 53–66), begun two decades later in 1998 and completed over the course of a year. Across the series, Schütte depicts himself in a round shaving mirror, alternately using watercolor, ink, pencil, and crayon, sometimes alone and sometimes in combination, resulting in an extraordinarily delicate body of work comprising eighty-seven individual self-portraits, each measuring 38 × 28 cm (15 × 11 inches). These are drawings made from life, the results of direct observation. They are self-reflexive by definition: the figure looks straight into the mirror and back out at us. On any given day, Schütte could vary the physiognomy of the face to such a degree that, at times, it seems as though he is depicting not one person but several. Moreover, the face not only changes shape from one work to another but also registers a change in mood. Pensive, ferocious, impassioned, drowning in sadness or melancholy, or simply detached, Schütte has mastered how to capture nearly every psychological state with directness and economy—a raised brow or a pursed lip can transform an expression of curiosity to one of resentment. (We never see the figure smiling.) Like the 1975 self-portraits, these drawings argue that only in multitude can we locate the self, though now Schütte is able to communicate this idea not only in how he paints the figure but also by choosing which self he paints.

The *Mirror Drawings* reveal how the caprice of the mind imprints itself on the body so strongly that locating oneself in a single image is not only insufficient but also deceptive. Any literal attempt at self-portraiture, therefore, must be multipart. But portraiture needn't be literal. In another group of drawings, collectively referred to as the *Deprinotes,* a neologism combining *depression* or *depressive* with *notes*, the self is once again the subject—though now self-portraiture presents itself wholly as an image of internal life, manifest sometimes in the quotidian, sometimes in the fantastic. Between 2006 and 2008, Schütte made at least six hundred *Deprinotes*. Like the *Mirror Drawings,* all the works in this series are intimately scaled, and each is dated. Though Schütte pictures himself on at least one occasion, in an untitled drawing from 2006, the vast majority of the works depict everyday objects, including a pair of broken scissors, flowers, teacups, apples and lemons; portraits of Schütte's children, his friends, his lovers; and abstract images, rudimentary symbols, and invented scenarios that border on the surreal. Within this panoply, some drawings are sweet, some maudlin, some banal, some goofy, and some grim, even hopeless. A watercolor-and-ink drawing from November 11, 2006, for example, is dominated by a dark shadow in the shape of a figure with arms asplay and legs straddling what seem to be diminutive train tracks. The train tracks in turn affect our understanding of the shadow, which begins to resemble the entrance to a cave or tunnel. Like many of the *Deprinotes*, the work bears a handwritten inscription that doubles as its title: *Eingang zur Hölle*, or, in English, "Entrance to Hell" (fig. 13). On the same day, Schütte made another drawing so compositionally close to *Eingang zur Hölle* that they can be considered a pair. The black stain in the center of this composition lacks the recognizable attributes that would allow us to read it as a figure; indeed, it is an image of a cave, confirmed by the title *Eingang zur Höhle*, or "Entrance to a Cave" (fig. 14). A characteristic example of Schütte's love of wordplay, the titles of the two works differ by only one letter. Everything can turn on a dime, the artist seems to say. Such disquieting imagery does not dominate the larger group, but neither is it an aberration. In a particularly unsettling drawing from December 17, 2006, Schütte draws the faintest of lines in the center of a field of paper otherwise marked only by text. Running vertically down the page, it ends in a loop in the shape of a teardrop. Barely there, the object is not easy to identify, but the text illuminates: *Wenn alle Stricke reißen—häng ich mich auf*, or "If all else fails, I'll hang myself." Gallows humor. If the *Mirror Drawings* suggest that a self-portrait must be multiple, the *Deprinotes* rid themselves of the mandate to depict physical likeness altogether. The self exists in the other and the other inhabits the self, whatever that other might be—the objects that surround us, the songs we hear, the people we visit, the images that float in and out of mind.

Often self-portraiture in Schütte's work exists only in a symbolic register. The most obvious example is the sculpture *Mann im Matsch (I. Version)* (*Man in Mud [1st. Version]*), made in 1982 (plate 19). Schütte initially created a freestanding wax figure; when it kept tipping over, he stabilized it by submerging its legs in more wax. The operation was intended to solve a technical problem, if crudely, but it also provided a visual metaphor: while the piece has been interpreted as an allegory of modernism and its failures,[20] it also presents a compelling vision of an artist paralyzed, unable to work. In the more than forty years since the first iteration of *Mann im Matsch*, Schütte has made no fewer than twenty variations on the subject (see, for example, plate 92), upending the very metaphor the work introduces—this symbol of inertia, paradoxically, proves to be among the most generative of Schütte's career.

GROßE MAUER (LARGE WALL)

Looking back at his early work, particularly at the 1975 self-portraits, Schütte realized that he was interested not in making things but rather in creating spaces. After a year away from Düsseldorf completing his mandatory civil service (*Zivildienst*), Schütte returned to the academy and to Richter's studio in October 1976, beginning work on an ambitious project that would result in *Große Mauer* (*Large Wall*, plate 7), a large-scale installation of painted "bricks" completed the following year and installed in the hallway of the academy in the summer of 1977 (fig. 15). His interest in bricks had been sparked during his year away. For the first six months, Schütte worked at a home for the aged, located in Brüggen near the Dutch border, an area surrounded by clay pits and known for brick production. He photographed the bricks at the brickworks as well as brick walls built using a range of masonry techniques. Later, in Düsseldorf, these images became the source material for dozens of preparatory sketches that pictured bricks in a variety of configurations as Schütte consulted dictionaries and encyclopedias to gain a greater familiarity with masonry. Drawings depicting a variety of bonding styles and techniques annotated by the artist to distinguish between types (e.g., Gothic, block, cross, and bandage) appear at the start of 1977.

Of course, the plan was never to fabricate real bricks. Instead, Schütte would paint panels to resemble them. Using the academy's wood shop, he cut thin chipboard into approximately 1,200 plates measuring 10 × 20 cm (approximately 4 × 8 inches), with some only 10 × 10 cm (4 × 4 inches). Because the board wouldn't take the oil paint well, he glued canvas to their surfaces, cutting up many of the 1975 self-portraits and using them as raw material; when that cache was depleted, he asked his friend and fellow Richter student Thomas Struth to donate his paintings to the project. He painted the panels loosely, mixing reds and oranges as though indiscriminately with ochers, browns, and blacks that together would read as brick red. All in all, it took Schütte just over a month to make the individual paintings and a few days to install them in the hallway of the academy. Each panel sat atop two barely visible nails, tilted ever so slightly to lean against the wall and positioned in rows that framed the existing architectural elements of the space. Schütte staggered each row off-center from the one above and the one beneath, leaving precisely 2 cm between each panel—a negative space that reads as mortar—to create the illusion of a brick wall.

Janice Guy, a friend and schoolmate of Schütte's who would go on in 1998 to open Murray Guy gallery in New York, remembers the installation well:

> I never knew if he talked to anyone about it beforehand, but it felt like a spontaneous act not quite of rebellion, but certainly one that flew in the face of authority—it was a guerrilla action of sorts. Thinking about the politics of the time, there was the unavoidable reference to the Berlin Wall, such a symbol of the Cold War—I remember how we sneered at America for its fear of nuclear war when *we* were at the edge, pushed up against the Warsaw Pact countries with missiles stationed on our territory. Apart from this unavoidable reference, the individual "bricks" were like mini Richters, poking fun at painting.[21]

Guy succinctly describes Schütte's ability to metabolize and consolidate competing sets of concerns and references within a single work.

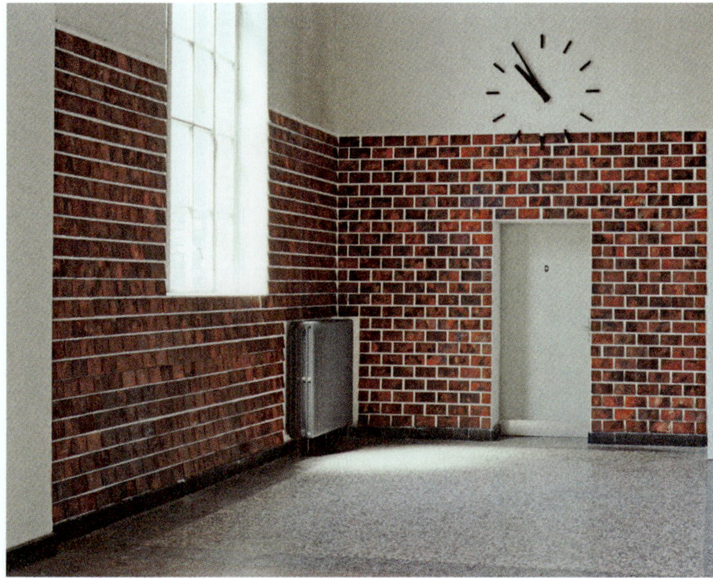

Fig. 15. Installation view of *Große Mauer* (*Large Wall*, 1977) in a student exhibition, Kunstakademie Düsseldorf, summer 1977

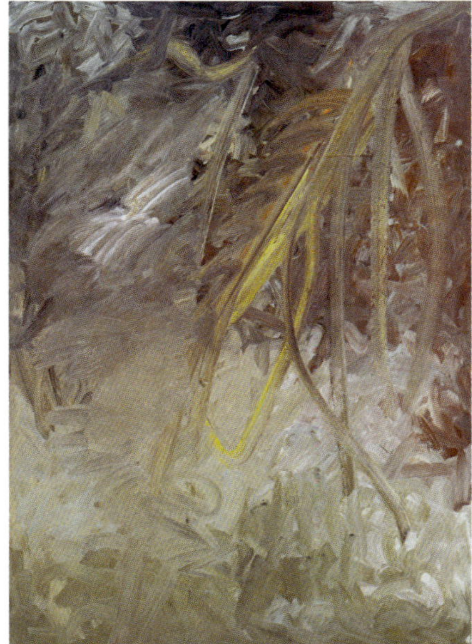

Fig. 16. Gerhard Richter. *Ohne Titel (Selbstportrait)* (*Untitled [Self-portrait]*). 1971. Oil on canvas, 68 ⅞ × 49 3⁄16" (175 × 125 cm). The Melissa and John Ceriale Family Collection, Palm Beach, Florida

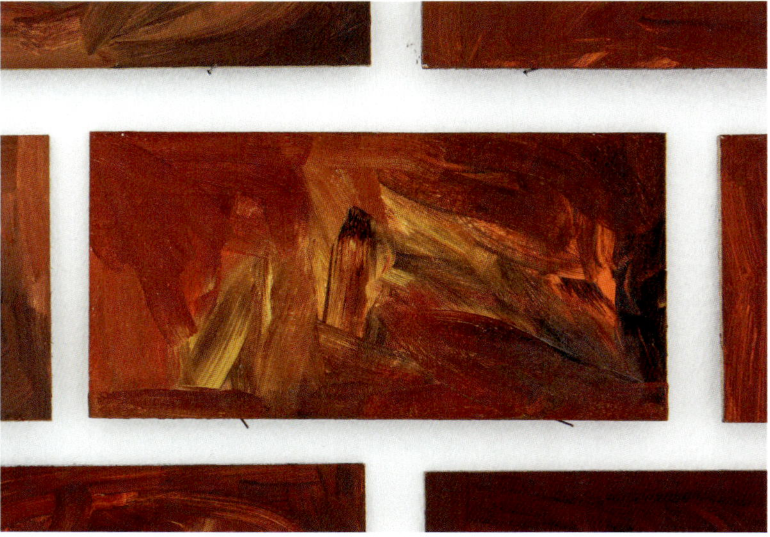

Fig. 17. Detail of *Große Mauer* (*Large Wall*). 1977

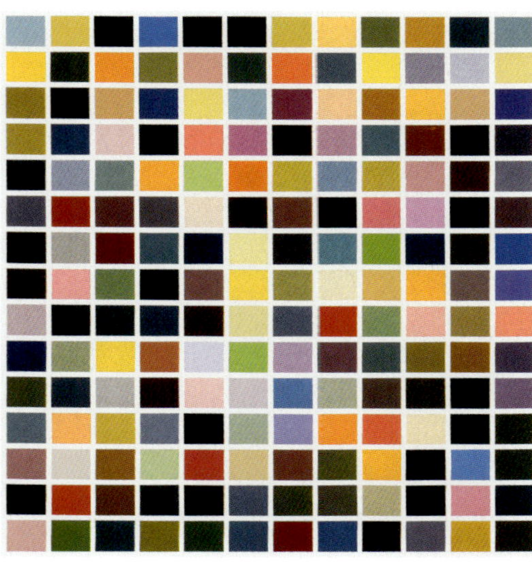

Fig. 18. Gerhard Richter. *180 Farben* (*180 Colors*). 1971. Enamel paint on canvas, 6' 6 ¾" × 6' 6 ¾" (200 × 200 cm). Philadelphia Museum of Art. Gift (by exchange) of Mrs. Herbert Cameron Morris, 1998

With *Große Tapeten*, Schütte had already engaged with the architecture of the exhibition space in a way that ably questioned the work's ontological status and, by extension, that of many works of this sort. (I.e., is this a painting or is it wallpaper, and what, after all, is the difference, as the *Düsseldorfer Stadtpost* columnist joked back in 1975?) *Große Mauer* ups the ante. Individually, as Guy points out and Schütte acknowledges, the canvases resemble abstractions by Richter, especially a 1971 group of nearly monochromatic paintings animated by lively brushwork, but at a fraction of the size (figs. 16–17). Their identity as bricks results entirely from their installation. A precisely rectilinear grid would have yielded a color chart of the sort made by Richter and others (fig. 18). But by leaning each canvas against the wall, leaving a bit of space between one painting and the next, and shifting each row 10 cm off center from the one above and the one below, Schütte immediately changes our perception. What could have been a cerebral abstraction transforms in Schütte's hands into a brick wall, albeit a fragile and precarious one, hanging atop plaster that conceals a structural wall beneath, thereby forming a miniature mise en abyme. He selected for its location two perpendicular walls along a hallway interrupted by a window, a radiator, a clock, and the door to the women's restroom, because the site was "more interesting" than a flat wall. The preexisting architectural elements made the installation more dynamic and heightened the trompe l'oeil quality that Schütte desired, so that, at a distance, the distinction between a brick and a painting of a brick became less clear (fig. 19).[22] The decision to turn a corner also made *Große Mauer* a sculpture. The bricks not only articulated the flat plane of a single wall, the domain of painting, but also delineated and activated the three-dimensional area between the walls: the space of sculpture.

Große Mauer also points to the physicality of the institution, which is far from neutral considering the histories of the prestigious school, some two hundred years old at the time; of Düsseldorf, a city battered during World War II and rebuilt thereafter; and of Germany in general. Constructed between 1875 and 1879, the building had been devastated by Allied bombings (fig. 20) and partially rebuilt. With this in mind, Schütte's bricks function as a mnemonic, pointing into the not-too-distant past. Alternately, perhaps they look to the future, as if buttressing the nineteenth-century architecture for posterity. Certainly they would have reminded Schütte's contemporary audiences of the massive reconstruction efforts that were newly completed or still underway across the republic. According to Struth—whose earliest photographs picture empty streets in Düsseldorf in black-and-white—for the generation of artists born in the aftermath of the war, architecture was an index of history, a much more reliable and different kind of truth than the potentially faulty memories of their parents or the whitewashed history found in schoolbooks. As he puts it, "Architecture didn't lie."[23] Context and historical circumstance were of paramount consequence to him, Schütte, and many other artists their age. Years later, the art historian and critic Benjamin H. D. Buchloh, who taught at the Kunstakademie during Schütte's time there, noted, "It takes incredible focus to immediately say, 'OK, this is where we are, this is who we are, this is what we live in.' The repressive dimension of German architecture, of postwar reconstruction architecture, has, of course, all of these features [reflecting] the actual social conditions: 'Small windows. No remembering. No thinking. No seeing. Just let's get a roof over our head and pretend nothing happened.'"[24] Or, to hear it from Struth:

> The individual in the public realm and responsibility—that's the main postwar question. As a student, I would walk around Düsseldorf and be informed by prewar buildings, by postwar buildings, by buildings that had been heavily damaged during air strikes and only the ground floor had remained to be used. Buildings from the 1950s were so bland compared to turn-of-the-century buildings; why? Thomas, I think, was in a very similar situation, as a human being. And, he played with conceptual work, with conceptual thinking, but also psychology, emotion, and theatrical elements.[25]

Schütte's attention to this kind of psychogeography, which extends throughout his career, found its first major expression in *Große Mauer*'s theatrically tinged reflections. In 2013, Schütte and curator Massimiliano Gioni discussed the piece. "Of course, in Germany when you make a wall, it's not just a wall," Gioni said, stating moments later that he sees the work as not just a "reflection on decoration" but also a "reflection on history and on Germany." Characteristically, Schütte replied by focusing on process: "It's an awful lot of work; it's a modernist one thousand little paintings. But because of this brick shift, it was immediately a story. If it's just a normal grid, there's no story. Because of this one shift . . . suddenly it was a stage design, and suddenly there was a story." Gioni then asked, "But it wasn't the story of the Berlin Wall or German history?" "No, not at all," replied Schütte. "You can see it afterwards, but not at that time."[26] Perhaps, though among the preparatory sketches for the installation found in the artist's archives is an encyclopedia entry for *Mauer*, at the end of which the reader is directed to both the Berlin Wall and the Great Wall of China.

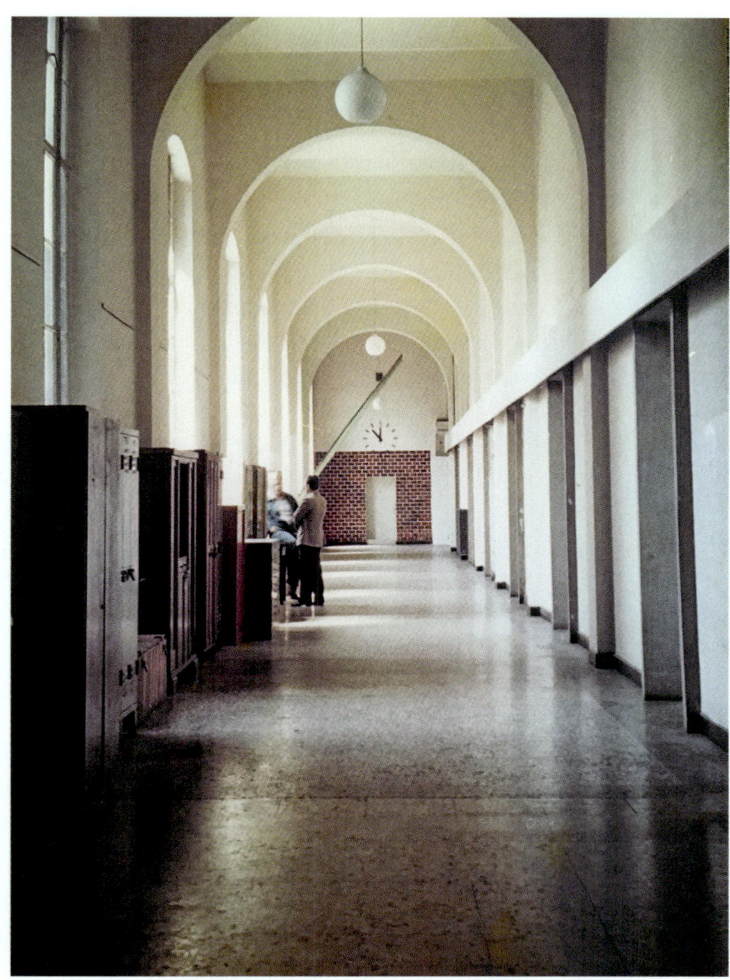

Fig. 19. Installation view of *Große Mauer* in a student exhibition, Kunstakademie Düsseldorf, summer 1977

Schütte's career-long reluctance to close down the understanding of his work by strictly defining or dictating its meaning—a tendency he shares with many artists—is also an act of generosity. He allows the viewer to draw their own conclusions. According to Struth, his friend learned this lesson from his gallerist Konrad Fischer (also known as the artist Konrad Lueg): "Don't give too much lest you reveal something. People should figure it out themselves."[27] Even if Schütte claims that he did not intend to evoke the Berlin Wall, the reference was all but inevitable, given how large the structure loomed (and continues to loom) in the popular imagination. Built in 1961 largely from concrete cinder blocks (rather than the red-clay bricks depicted in Schütte's work), the wall was not only symbolic of Berlin's, and by extension, Germany's, partition into East and West; it was also a functional ideological structure that divided space and separated people along a semi-arbitrary border. On one side Western capitalism ruled and on the other Soviet-style communism. In all but a few cases, who ended up where was largely a matter of circumstance.

Ideological architecture had reached a high point in Germany decades earlier, during the National Socialist period, with modest building campaigns beginning as early as 1933, the year Hitler was appointed chancellor, and accelerating throughout the decade until 1942, when major military setbacks forced a reallocation of resources from monumental architectural projects, such as the construction of the Party Rally Grounds in Nuremberg, to the wholesale support of munitions production and the military economy in general.[28] Overseen by architect Albert Speer, Nazi architecture was neoclassical in style, drawing heavily on Greek and Roman sources. As the architectural historian Paul B. Jaskot explains, "This conflation allowed for the competing and often contradictory claims made

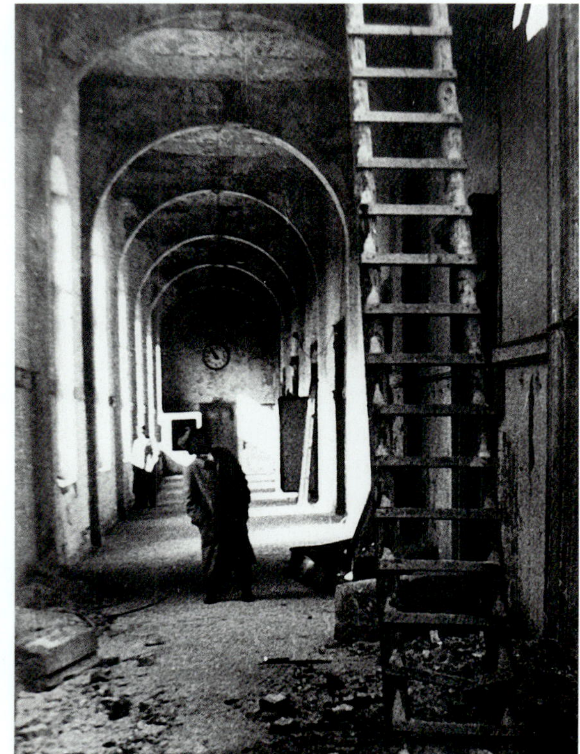

Fig. 20. Director Werner Heuser in the hallway of the Kunstakademie Düsseldorf, January 31, 1946

about monumental architecture by National Socialist cultural administrators: Greek to emphasize the supposed racial connections between contemporary Germany and its Aryan ancestors, Roman to buttress the claims of Nazi Germany as a new and powerful empire."[29] As important as the style were the materials from which these grand structures were built. Iron and cement, essential to most contemporaneous building projects, were allocated to the construction of factories, workers' barracks, and more ambitious but decidedly functional enterprises such as the expansion of the railroads and the creation of the Autobahn. With Hitler's approval, stone and brick became Speer's preferred building materials—stone for its perceived permanence and ties to empires past, brick for its association with a particular "German academic tradition (most notably, that of [Karl Friedrich] Schinkel)."[30] The SS established concentration camps near quarries and clay pits to expedite the procurement of stone and the production of brick. (As one bureaucrat mandated in a letter in April 1937, "The camp inmates should be occupied . . . with the production of bricks."[31]) All of which is to say that if Schütte's work allows and even invites story, this story holds significance not only for *Große Mauer*—with Schütte's offhand remark about the intense labor exerted during his own "brick" production gaining extra valence in this context—but also for the sculptures and architectural models he would make in the decades to come, which allude heavily to the long history of Germany. Above all, *Große Mauer* succeeds because Schütte's subjects, both wall and brick, are ubiquitous and banal, which renders them open to a vast range of meanings beyond those intended by their maker.

While the *Große Mauer* project was underway, in the winter semester of 1976, Buchloh arrived at the school and began teaching the first of three seminars focused on contemporary art, collectively titled Mythological and Phenomenological Aspects of Art in the Present. Attendance was small, Buchloh remembers, rarely exceeding twenty students, among them Isa Genzken (who had invited him to the academy), Harald Klingelhöller, Ludger Gerdes, Struth, and Schütte. The course's bibliography offered a combination of theoretical texts focused largely on semiotics and phenomenology; artists' writings and exhibition catalogues (of Marcel Broodthaers, Buren, Richter, Sigmar Polke, Hans Haacke, Dan Graham, Nauman, Lawrence Weiner, and Robert Barry, among others); and contemporary art criticism on topics such as Minimal and Conceptual art. While we can suppose that Buchloh presented the work of these artists through the neo-Marxist lens that he would begin to articulate in his writings around this time, we can equally imagine that the very construction of a critical apparatus through which to see art (regardless of its particularities) would itself have been impactful. Looking back at the seminar, Klingelhöller confirms just this: "Buchloh's sessions dealt with what we were seeing on a theoretical level. It was about systematic thinking, lines of development, and their ends."[32] Significantly, the art historian also often gave the (metaphorical) lectern over to artists passing through town, including Buren, Graham, Serra, Weiner, and others, allowing them to speak about their work with no guarantee that their views would align with his own. Schütte valued the direct access to relatively new information that the seminars provided, whether in the pages of *Artforum* and other publications or from the mouths of the artists themselves.[33] Before Buchloh's arrival in Düsseldorf, Schütte had already begun to stake a position in the discursive landscape, to "learn the grammar and the semantics [and] certain tricks."[34] His early student work espouses ambiguity as a critical position, enabling him to avoid reaching the series of dead ends that in his mind had confronted many artists of the previous generation. Buchloh, looking back, asks, "But where does he turn? What are the historical spaces to which you return when you abandon a radical position? You have understood Buren, you have understood [Niele] Toroni, you have understood Lawrence Weiner. *All of this, he understood everything*. Where do you turn then?"[35]

Radical positions are not singular or finite. The choice for Schütte is neither an affirmation nor a negation of the art that directly preceded his own but rather finding a way out of the binary altogether. "The real problem is knowing why you should continue, of trying to find something more interesting. . . . And I keep moving from one form across to another," Schütte has declared. "I'm against this mono-culture. I try to see one thing from five different viewpoints. And you keep moving and working around a central point, but what it is we don't know. Because as soon as you can define it, it's ended."[36]

VON HIER AUS (UP FROM HERE)[37]

In 1981, the year Schütte left the academy, he made one of his earliest architectural models: a red structure with a pitched roof measuring 63 cm in height, 53 cm in width, and 25 cm in depth (25 × 21 × 10 inches). It bears the inscription *Thomas Schütte / 16.11.1954 / 25.3.1996*, which identifies it as a gravestone, the supreme marker of finality. He called the work *Mein Grab* (*My Grave*, plate 18) and arrived at the death date by giving himself fifteen years to "make it" as an artist. It's 2024, and Schütte is very much alive and making art.

In the more than four decades since *Mein Grab*, Schütte has created hundreds of artworks that engage a bewilderingly broad range of genres. There are more architectural models, some simply sculptures, like *Mein Grab*, others depicting structures intended to be built. Among them is the model for Skulpturenhalle, Schütte's museum in Neuss, Germany, which opened in 2016. (Though the artist's body will not be interred there, his body of work will.) There are works on paper, ranging from deeply personal watercolors (*Mirror Drawings* and *Deprinotes*) to large and colorful woodblock prints (*Woodcuts*, 2011). There are installations large, like *Melonely* (1986, plate 24), and small, such as *Mohr's Life* (1988–99, plates 36–38), and at least one made from paper (*Wattwanderung*, 2001, called *Low Tide Wandering* in English; page 46). Figurative sculpture abounds—monumentally scaled bronzes that invoke public statuary, such as *Vater Staat*, *Große Geister* (*Large Spirits*, 1995–2004; plate 50), *United Enemies I* (2011, pages 146–47), and *Mann im Wind* (*Man in Wind*, 2018) as well as a group of eighteen reclining female nudes called *Frauen* (*Women*, plates 68–71), made between 1998 and 2006, each cast twice in steel, twice in bronze, and once in aluminum for a total of ninety sculptures overall. Most recently, Schütte has taken to making elegant busts in ceramic—some of which have collapsed under the heat of the kiln—and, in the same material, strange sculptures that resemble dogs or devils. Surveying his career, it can be difficult to believe that this multifarious body of work originated with one person. An attitude holds them together, one that developed over a crucial five-year period that began with a trip to Documenta in 1972 and reached full expression with 1977's *Große Mauer*.

This story finds significance beyond the particularities of one artist's career trajectory. Looking left and right, up and down, straight on and from the side, as Schütte has when determining what to do next, evinces a broad suspicion of not only teleology but of any tidy, linear construction of history. Asking where you turn after you've understood Buren, Toroni, Weiner, and others assumes there is somewhere to turn—a far-off finish line for some, a dead end for others. In "On the Concept of History," the German philosopher Walter Benjamin, writing in 1940, recognized the trouble to which a faith in progress can lead: "One reason why Fascism has a chance is that in the name of progress its opponents treat it as a historical norm." He continues, "The current amazement that the things we are experiencing are 'still' possible in the twentieth century is *not* philosophical. This amazement is not the beginning of knowledge—unless it is the knowledge that the view of history which gives rise to it is untenable."[38] In his work, Schütte has never moved in one direction. For him, "progress" is multidirectional: past, present, and future become tangled like a mishandled ball of yarn. We can try to follow a strand, but it will fall out of our hands or twist into a knot. The return to representation, in Schütte's case and in the case of so many artists of his generation, does not signal a retreat to the familiar or an espousal of convention. Schütte treats figurative sculpture just as he treats Buren's stripes and Toroni's brush marks—it is fertile ground for reinvention, a reinvestment of criticality in forms sometimes considered decorative. And decoration is "for the birds," he might say.[39]

---

1 Coincidentally, the font also resembles Normschrift DIN EN ISO 3098, which is frequently used by architects and engineers in technical drawings.
2 Harald Szeemann, "Documenta 5," Documenta Archiv, cited in Max Rosenberg, "Harald Szeemann and the Road Back to the Museum," *Getty Research Journal* 11 (2019), 114.
3 Harold Rosenberg, "The Art World. Enquiry '72: On the Edge," in *Biennials and Beyond—Exhibitions That Made Art History 1962–2002* (London: Phaidon, 2013), 172. Originally published in the *New Yorker*, September 9, 1972.
4 Robert Smithson, "Cultural Confinement," in *Biennials and Beyond*, 171. Originally published in 1971.
5 Daniel Buren, quoted in Lucia Pesapanc, "Interview with Co-Curators: Jean-Christophe Ammann, Bazon Brock, François Burkhardt, and Johannes Cladders," in *Harald Szeemann: Individual Methodology*, ed. Florence Derieux (Zurich: JRP Ringier, 2008), 135.
6 "James Lingwood in Conversation with Thomas Schütte," in Julian Heynen, James Lingwood, and Angela Vettese, *Thomas Schütte* (London: Phaidon, 1998), 13.
7 Ibid., 10 and 13.
8 Thomas Schütte, interview by Marta Gnyp, in *Made in Mind: Myths and Realities of the Contemporary Artist* (Stockholm: Art and Theory, 2014), 229.
9 See Kristin Ross, *Communal Luxury: The Political Imaginary of the Paris Commune* (Brooklyn: Verso, 2015).
10 Quoted in Penelope Curtis, *Thomas Schütte: Early Work* (Leeds: Henry Moore Institute, 2007), 92. Originally published in *Düsseldorfer Stadtpost*, June 12, 1975.
11 The figure in question features an internal metal scaffold into which the wood fits to strengthen the legs enough to prevent its toppling over.
12 As the chief proprietor of a small gallery with limited funds, Konrad Fischer invited artists to Düsseldorf to create work on-site rather than paying for crating and shipping from the place where the works would have otherwise been made, which is to say, with a handful of exceptions, the United States.
13 Roberta Smith, "Klaus Rinke, The Clocktower; Doug Davis, Fischbach Gallery; Elie Nadelman, Zabriskie Gallery; Hugo Robus, Forum Gallery; John McLaughlin, Emmerich Gallery; Moshe Kupferman, Rina Gallery," *Artforum* 12, no. 10 (Summer 1974), 73.
14 James Lingwood, "Amerika," in *Thomas Schütte: Public/Political*, ed. Ulrich Loock (Cologne: Walther König, 2012), 15.
15 Curtis, *Thomas Schütte: Early Work*, 88.
16 Schütte was likely aware of Richter's seascapes, which he made between 1968 and 1975 (he returned to the subject again in the 1990s). Likewise, he may have seen Vija Celmins's ocean drawings in pencil, also begun in 1968, reproduced in art publications.
17 All quotations in this paragraph are from Thomas Schütte, conversation with the author, March 2017.
18 Both *Tapetenmuster* and *Große Tapeten* were first exhibited in Room 43 of Richter's studio June 9–16, 1975.
19 It's worth noting that in 1976 Schütte's generational peer Martin Kippenberger embarked on a series of grisaille paintings also inspired by Richter, in the end producing one hundred works based on newspaper clippings. Like Schütte, Kippenberger set limits on this exercise. Rather than producing one painting a day, he intended to make enough paintings so that when stacked they would equal his height.
20 Ulrich Loock, "Thomas Schütte: A Rather Serious Game," in *Thomas Schütte*, ed. Dorothea Zwirner (Berlin: Friedrich Christian Flick Collection; Cologne: DuMont Literatur und Kunst, 2004), 24
21 Janice Guy, e-mail messages to the author, March 28 and April 2, 2020. The emphasis is Guy's.
22 Thomas Schütte, conversation with the author, June 16, 2020.
23 Thomas Struth, conversation with the author, April 2016.
24 Benjamin H. D. Buchloh, conversation with the author, March 6, 2020.
25 Thomas Struth, conversation with the author, February 3, 2020.
26 Thomas Schütte, "Conversations | Premiere | Artist Talk with Thomas Schütte," interview by Massimiliano Gioni, Art Basel, June 12, 2013, https://www.youtube.com/watch?v=sF02nI6Kt7Y.
27 Struth, conversation with the author, February 3, 2020.
28 A thorough account of the interrelations between forced labor and the monumental building economy in Nazi Germany can be found in Paul B. Jaskot, *The Architecture of Oppression* (New York: Routledge, 2000).
29 Ibid., 57.
30 Ibid., 29.
31 Quoted in ibid., 21.
32 "'Ich wollte eine künstlerische Position gewinnen und keine theoretische.' Brigitte Kölle im Gespräch mit Harald Klingelhöller," interview, in *Es geht voran: Kunst der 80er: Eine Düsseldorfer Perspektive* (Munich: Prestel and Kunstsammlung Nordrhein-Westfalen, 2010), 222.
33 "'In den Achtzigern waren alle munter.' Brigitte Kölle im Gespräch mit Thomas Schütte," interview, in *Es geht voran*, 193. Schütte remembers of Buchloh's class, "Buchloh photographed *Artforum*. . . . That was almost first-hand information. He also introduced us to the theories of the time. And he brought artists. . . . That was very important."
34 "James Lingwood in Conversation with Thomas Schütte," 17.
35 Buchloh, conversation with the author, March 6, 2020. The emphasis is Buchloh's.
36 "Thomas Schütte," interview by Iwona Blazwick and Andrea Schlieker, in *Possible Worlds: Sculpture from Europe* (London: Institute of Contemporary Art and Serpentine Gallery, 1990), 70.
37 This section borrows its title from the 1984 exhibition *Von hier aus,* organized by Kasper König in Düsseldorf, which surveyed contemporary German art and included work by Schütte.
38 "On the Concept of History," in *Walter Benjamin: Selected Writings, Volume 4: 1938–1940*, ed. Howard Eiland and Michael Jennings (Cambridge, MA: Harvard University Press, 2006), 392.
39 In 2007, Schütte exhibited *Model for a Hotel* on the Fourth Plinth in London's Trafalgar Square—a work that was initially to be titled *Hotel for the Birds*.

How do you tie a bronze knot?

CHARLES RAY

I know how to make a bronze knot. That's easy. You start with clay or wax and model it with a tool or your hands. You make a mold and pour molten metal into it and you create the image of a knot that is made in bronze. It's not so hard to tie a knot with a rope or sculpt a knot in a soft material like clay. But how do you tie a knot in bronze? Does this happen in the sculpting process? Is the sculptor a magician who knows how to manipulate hard metal and make it pliable and soft? Or does it happen in the viewer's or the sculptor's mind? Can a knot be so beautifully sculpted that it seems to have been tied after the metal that forms it was poured, cooled, and made hard? What would a metallurgist say? What would a perceptual psychologist or even a philosopher think?

Thomas Schütte's sculptures not only have such knots but are such knots. They maintain a fluid, malleable quality even after leaving clay and being made in bronze. The bronze *Mann ohne Gesicht* (*Man without Face*, 2018; fig. 1) is made of a material I think of as super clay. As a bronze, the form is more pliable than the clay the sculpture's mold was patterned on. This fluidness isn't just across the surface of the figure, but it is a form that exists between the artist, his sculpture, and the perception of the viewer. I think the elements of this equation exist in the past, present, and future. The surface of Schütte's sculpture is not a manifold of details, but when the topology of his figure's face, drapery, foot, or hand ripples across one's

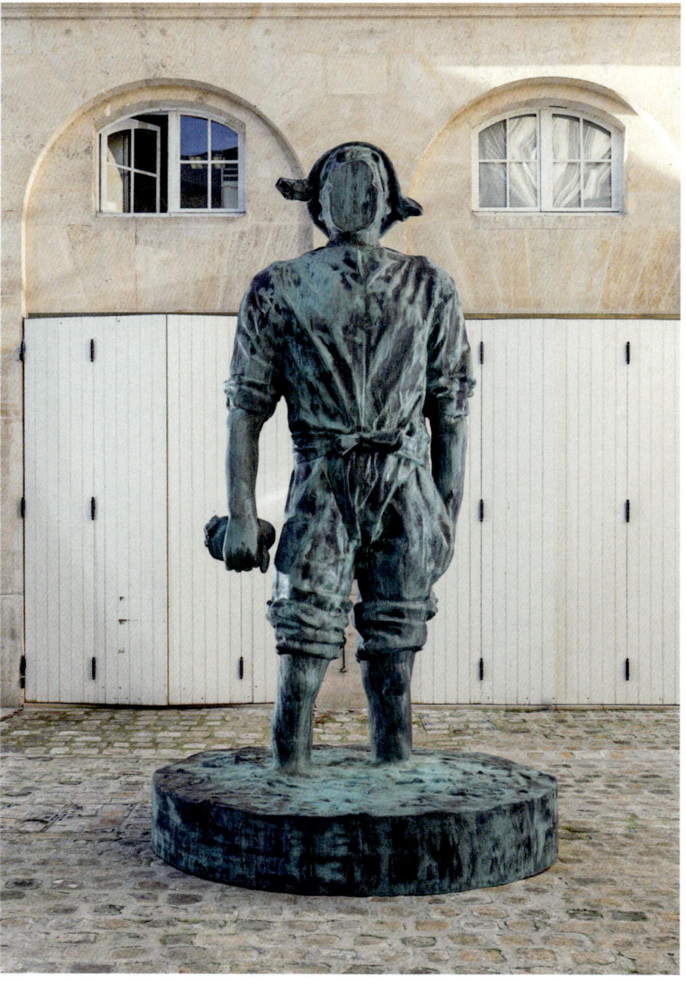

Fig. 1. Thomas Schütte. *Mann ohne Gesicht* (*Man without Face*). 2018. Patinated bronze, 14' 9 3⁄16" × 7' 10 ½" × 7' 10 ½" (450 × 240 × 240 cm). Thomas Schütte Stiftung, Neuss, Germany. Installation view, *Thomas Schütte: Trois Actes*, Monnaie de Paris, March 15–June 16, 2019

awareness of the surface, it creates a form that can only be sculpture. This modeling of the surface is not made simply from chunks of clay, as the space and place around the sculpture are modeled, too. The form of the figure, the surface of the sculpture, and the space it occupies are in the same equation to the extent that they become one and the same. It seems that an inward reverberation from the surface creates the gesture of the figure. Or is it the gesture of the figure that reverberates outward and creates the surface of the sculpture? Where does Thomas Schütte stand? I know he is the artist, and his touch is in the sculpture, but are his hands still as apparent to the viewer as they must have been to him? Is the fact that he made the sculpture and gave in to its gesture as important as the image of the sculpture is to us? Was the physicality of the work emergent from the image, or was the image emergent from the artist sculpting?

Schütte's sculptures have no debt to our present time. It's not that they're not part of the contemporary world. They emerge from it, but they weren't made with the need to be relevant. If he uses history as a pattern, the sculpture doesn't stand behind artists of the past. His works don't sit stably in my appreciation of Rodin, nor do they belong to Degas, although Degas also sculpted a figure in a tub of water. Degas's *Le Tub* (*The Tub*, modeled 1888–89, cast 1921–31; fig. 2) shows a lady in a bath with a sponge in her hand and a gesture that seems to spring forth from the artist's sculpture rather than his idea of the figure in a bath. This sculpture knots together the figure, Degas, and me. When I bend over to look down upon this work, it's hard to separate the activity of the bath, the water, and the bather. I am not a passive viewer, but my viewing has been sculpted, as I also form a gesture of bending over to look at the sculpture. I'm pulled in physically from my bent waist. This gesture necessary to view the sculpture is one strand of a string that ties a knot with the string of activity apparent in the sculpture. This sculpture exists in a matrix of a process of making and viewing that extends its contemporariness into the future. Schütte's sculpture not only is modeled in water-based clay but finds fluidness in the wetness of the clay and the wetness of our bodies and our minds. It's not to say his work is old fashioned or analog, but the digital retreats in the fluidness of looking and material. While Degas used wax, it too has a malleability that's translated up and out into the sculptor's world. Degas's bronzes were cast postmortem. Thomas Schütte's aren't. Great bronze figurative sculpture has a meaning that can be superimposed over the temporal qualities of culture. How do such works extend, both forward and backward in cultural or biological time? The modeling in Schütte's sculptures is not unlike the forces of geology. The geological has a different temporal register. Schütte's work, like a mountain or a desert, not only exists but shows evidence of the past and present, as well as projections into the future. There is a quickness and a looseness to the fluidity of Schütte's sculptures, but like the geology of a mountain, beach, or ocean, it couldn't be any other way.

Perhaps some of the artfulness in these works exists in another family of knots, tying effortlessness and exactitude together. In Schütte's portrait heads, the eyes are like bellybuttons, a remnant of an umbilical cord. There are both innies and outies in his sculpted heads (fig. 3). But what the innies and the outies have in common is that they puncture the image of the bust. It's not just physically; the eyes don't bulge out or open into a great hollow dark interior. Rather, both the innie and the outie eyes are like passages into a perceived soul of the portrait—not that one has to believe in god or a soul to pass through the eyes of these busts, but their made-ness in clay translated into the super-clay quality of his bronze superimposes through this passage the interior qualities of our mind into the physicality of the portrait bust. The metallic qualities of the bronze, the psychological geology of the modeling pass out of the eyes of the sculpture into the mind of the viewer. An animation exists between our eyes and the sculpted eyes. The eyes are only a catalyst for this process as the entire surface of the sculpture exchanges information in a dialogue with the viewer. Through form and surface and fluidity of material, Schütte's sculptures dissolve

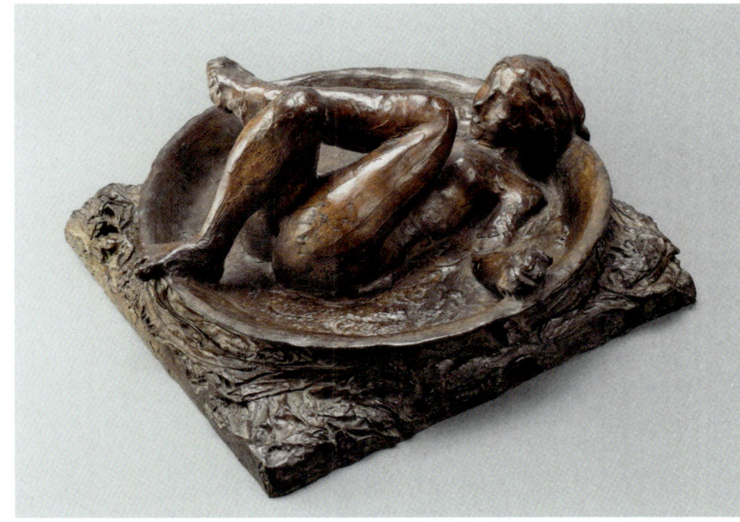

Fig. 2. Edgar Degas. *Le Tub* (*The Tub*). Modeled 1888–89, cast 1921–31. Patinated bronze, 8 ⅞ × 17 ¼ × 18 1/16" (22.5 × 43.8 × 45.8 cm). Musée d'Orsay, Paris. Acquired through the generosity of the artist's heirs and the Hébrards, 1931

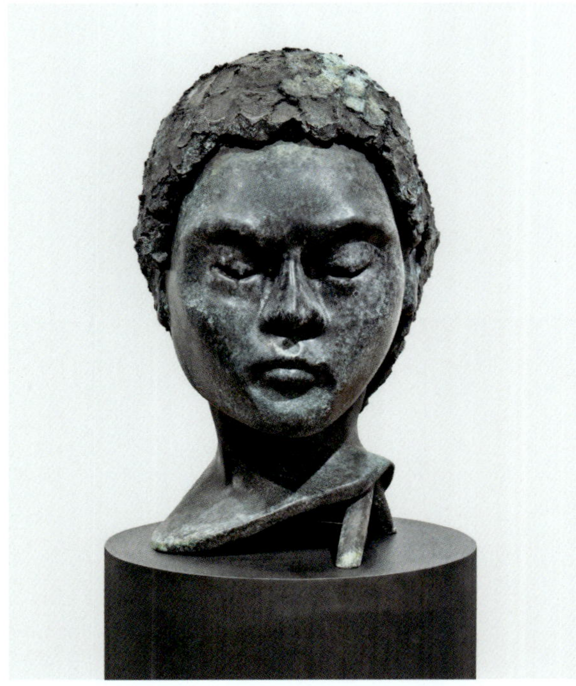

Fig. 3. Thomas Schütte. *Walser's Wife*. 2011. Patinated bronze on steel pedestal, bronze: 25 9/16 × 14 15/16 × 21 ¼" (65 × 38 × 54 cm), pedestal: 47 ⅜ × 17 11/16 × 17 11/16" (120.3 × 45 × 45 cm). Collection Anne Dias Griffin

a boundary between interior and exterior. If the surface emerges from the form or the form from the surface, we emerge from the sculpture as the sculpture emerges from us. There is no interior only because the exterior is the interior. The viewer and the sculpture exist in the same or an identical material world. The spatial reality that his art exists in is the same spatial reality that we create for our own existence.

Recently I had a conversation with a young artist without much money looking for ways to work while she couldn't afford a studio. I told her to look at Schütte's heads, his portrait busts; they're monumental yet they fit upon a kitchen table. It's like the saying "All that glitters isn't gold" has a sculptural equivalent in "All that's big is not monumental." I don't measure a sculpture such as the man with his face in his hand with a physical or even a psychological yardstick. It simply exists in a scale that is not big or small. The model of *Mann ohne Gesicht* (2018, fig. 4) is not a small version of the larger version. To me, it's not a study of the bigger version. In a sense, the bigger version could be a study of the smaller version. Perhaps scale is an idea of inside and outside that the two sculptures can be placed in. Is one sculpture a reference to the individual viewer and the other to the greater public that wanders in a public space that the work is placed in? Perhaps the larger of the two sculptures not only embeds itself in a public space but also embeds itself in the public itself. The sculpture needs the crowd, as it is part of the crowd even if the plaza is empty. Meanwhile the smaller sculpture is quietly embedded in the history of sculpture yet has a special relationship to the individual in the present moment. Here—and I am speaking strictly for myself—I find beauty, in that the sculptures, both the model and the one outside, are two completely different sculptures rather than two versions of one and the same. The big and the small, the model and the real dissolve or lose importance when placed in the indoors and the outdoors. This embedment is something Thomas Schütte may not necessarily think about, but the effortlessness of the perception of his work brings it forth.

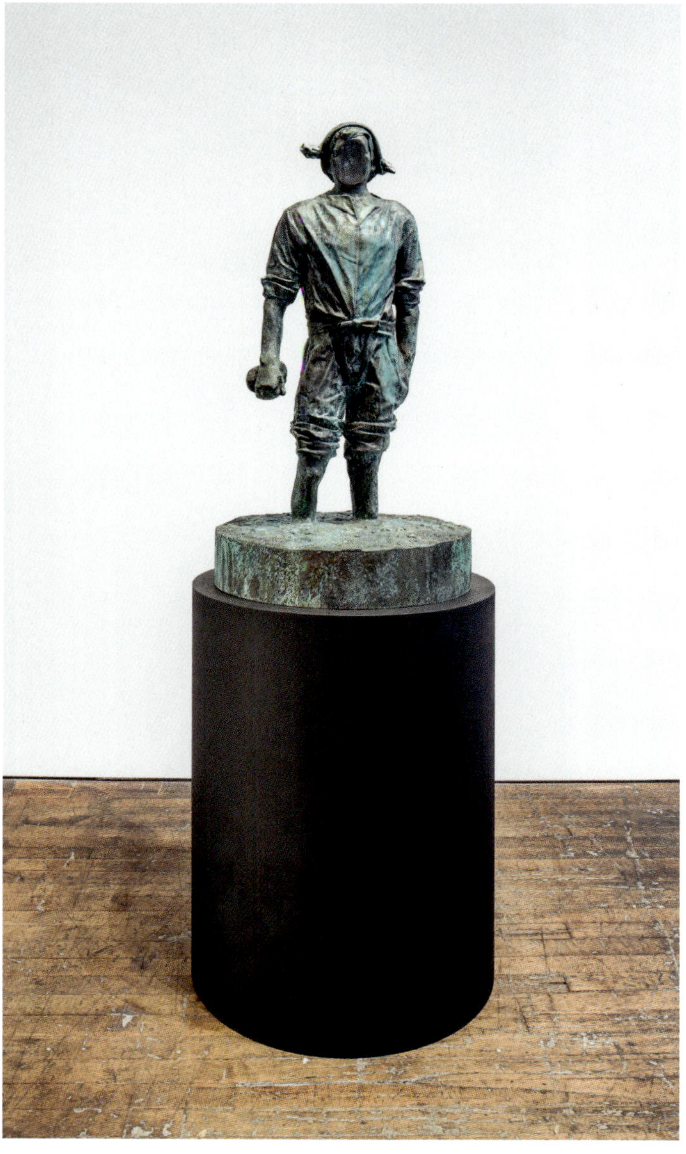

Fig. 4. Thomas Schütte. *Mann ohne Gesicht (Modell 1:5)* (*Man without Face [Model 1:5]*). 2018. Patinated bronze on steel pedestal, bronze: 48 ⅜ × 26 ⅝ × 26 ⅝" (123 × 67.5 × 67.5 cm), pedestal: 39 ⅜ × 31 ½ × 31 ½" (100 × 80 × 80 cm). Pinault Collection

But what of the image itself? How does the image of a man with his face in his hand standing in muck or water bring meaning to the perception of the sculpture? Was the image of the sculpture thought of and then made? Did the image of a man with his face in his hand start out as an idea for Schütte to sculpt? I'm not saying that he didn't see the image first in his head and then set upon the activity of sculpting to bring it forth, but somehow it ends up, this image, as a compositional part of the larger mechanics of this project. How could he sculpt this sculpture? How did he sculpt the sculpture? How could the face of the figure be in the figure's hand yet the head of the figure still be completely and totally complete? The facet left where the face is missing doesn't function as a meta-face. It creates a face of another part of ourselves. It's as if I'm looking at myself as a kind of centaur or other creature. But this image of the man with the face in the hand doesn't create a Surrealist window where I am on one side and the image is on the other. It's not dreamlike, though I imagine it could appear to you in a dream. The sculpture itself is active. It's not stable enough to become an image on the other side of the line between reality and unreality. That is to say, the sculpture is completely and totally, in image and physicality, real. Its physicality and its made-ness bring a reality to the object that has to be dealt with and pondered if you want to look at the sculpture not as a photograph but as an object in front of you.

When I first saw the model of the man with his face in his hand, it was in Francois Pinault's collection at the Bourse de Commerce in Paris. It was over in the corner of the room, but that didn't matter. I remember liking the pedestal, but that also maybe didn't matter. I first saw the facet left by the missing face. In the hand of the figure, I didn't see a face but a sponge. Perhaps because the figure was standing in muck or water. If in the hand I saw a sponge, a split second later I saw it as a face, the face of the figure. The magic of this sculpture is that the face never seems to be missing. It was sculpted in such a powerful relation to the totality of the sculpture that in this context it almost seems to have been left in its correct anatomical position. The figure being in the water in a kind of barrel or tub that is missing its sides is what perhaps brought the first impression of the face as a sponge. It's an impression that I have no need to correct, even after connecting the face to the identity of the subject. The surface of the liquid that the man is standing in is modeled not like a rough sea or even wind on water but more like a bog. But the bogginess is a kind of meta-liquid, the water or wind we exist in.

My perception of the face as a rag or sponge of the figure standing in the bronze, waterlike fluid is what brought me in the first instance of viewing to Degas's *Le Tub*. I do see this as a relationship between the two artists, as a temporal vibration between the past, present, and future. How could Degas's sculpture of the bather surface in the now, so present and powerfully? Schütte's relationship to history is not anachronistic, even if the dress and drapery of his sculptures appear so. His relationship to history springs out of a figurative tradition, like if we could dive on a diving board into the future. I think our experience of the sculpture is the meaning of the work. I can write about it and put my thoughts to pen and paper, but the experience of its embeddedness in the space and time of culture springs from a language not of words but of form, surface, and material. You may tell me that everything is embedded in the world and that would be true. A car, the space shuttle, an apple, a tree, or a shoe—they are all artifacts of the beehive. But Schütte's work and its embedment is different because the embedment is not a function of the object but is central to the experience of the object. Somehow it is the experience itself rather than the object alone that finds embedment in space and time. You don't drive his sculpture on errands through the town. You don't pick a hybrid apple from its branches. No, the sculpture affects you in a different way. It's a work of art. Look closely at the figure, the image of the figure, and what the figure is doing, the narrative of the figure. However understandable, however masterfully rendered, it exists in a fluid. The fluidity of culture, space, and time don't matter. What matters to me is that the figure and the nature of fluidity are somehow completely one and the same. This figurative sculpture, with his face in his hand, is embedded or standing in the muck. It is an image or a juxtaposition of an internal sculptural structure superimposed on our human condition. In other words, it is a metaphor. But if this figure is embedded in the muck of its imagistic environment, the larger idea of the sculpture itself is embedded in the cultural muck existing all around us. That is to say, the sculpture of this embedded figure is embedded in a larger matrix of our condition. If you walk into a room and say, "Who put that here? How long is that going to be here?" Or in a city plaza, where one sculpture can be replaced with another. Or when the crowds of people rise up against an old hero and topple his or her bronze edifice for whatever sins they may have committed in the past. If this happens before, after, and during the experience of looking, the game is over. The art has collapsed. But if a sculpture is complete, it is never standing in the way. The complexity of the artfulness of a sculpture embedded in space and time is both physical and cultural. Schütte's sculpture of a man can withstand or at least gives the perception of withstanding disruptions geological and cultural. The weight of the sculpture's ground is both physical and mental. The flat facet left from a displaced face is one and the same as the flat unseen facet under the volume of water, the round wheel of liquid whose flatness and weight stabilize the sculpture. It will not gravitationally topple in the physical and popular culture of human activity.

I would like to end with this thought about knots. The knot that ties the shirt ends of Schütte's bronze sculpture *Mann ohne Gesicht* looks to me like the looping tail ends of looking, thinking, and making. A mathematician will tell you that if you remove from the world the space that a knot exists in, each and every kind of knot with the space removed will open to a new dimensional domain. Perhaps this is what happens when looking at the knot Schütte's sculpture ties.

Permanent Provisionality: Notes on Thomas Schütte's Figures

ANDRÉ ROTTMANN

Since Thomas Schütte began making art as a student at the renowned Kunstakademie Düsseldorf in the mid-1970s, his work has been peculiarly "postconceptual." Conceptual art, as the aspiring artist first encountered it—for instance, in the works of Sol LeWitt, Blinky Palermo, and Daniel Buren, during two trips from his hometown of Oldenburg to Documenta 5 in Kassel in the summer of 1972[1]—at the time undoubtedly conveyed, even determined, the dominant terms and methods of approaching art. In Düsseldorf (where Schütte still lives and works today), Konrad Fischer Galerie had begun to show American artists such as Carl Andre, Bruce Nauman, and Lawrence Weiner as early as 1967. More important, perhaps, starting in 1975, Schütte studied in the studio of painter Gerhard Richter and attended classes with art historian Benjamin H. D. Buchloh, both of whom (albeit to different degrees and in distinct ways) were engaged with the impact and the impasses of the Conceptualist assault on certain tenets of the aesthetic (e.g., medium, genre and object, authorship, originality and value, contemplation and context). In the aftermath of Minimalist sculpture and its abstract and phenomenological emphasis on place, space, and time (in the work and writing of Andre, Donald Judd, and Robert Morris, among others), Conceptualism had emerged in the mid-1960s. Rejecting and upending modernist claims for medium specificity and concomitant ideals of self-reflexivity, which supposedly would help separate art from mere consumption and kitsch,[2] it radically redefined the object of art in terms of linguistic propositions and intentionally prosaic black-and-white photographic records, diagrams, notations and scores, permutational systems, bureaucratic files, and commercial contracts. By applying these methods and means, it resolutely sought to enact a deskilling of aesthetic practice with the aim of altering, even emancipating, modes of spectatorial address beyond the realms of taste and expertise and art's established markets and conduits of distribution (most notably

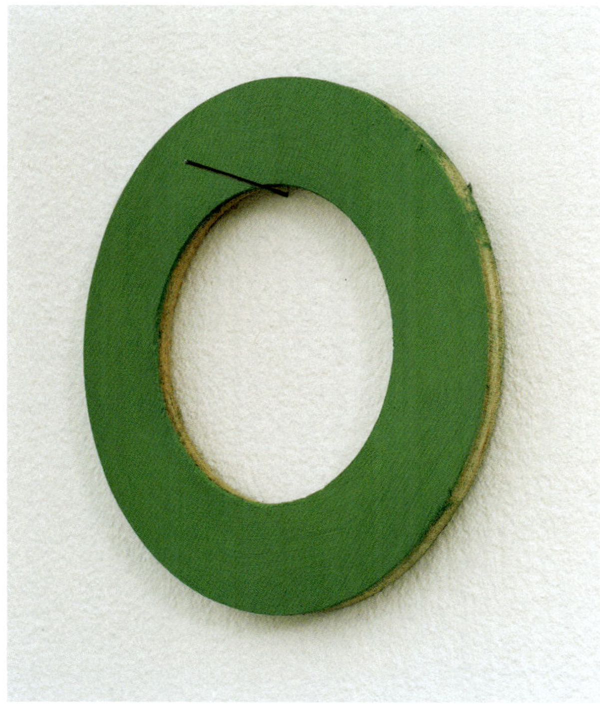

Fig. 1. Thomas Schütte. *Ringe* (*Rings*, detail). 1977. Paint on wood, 500 parts, each ring 4 ⅛" (10.5 cm) diam. Installation dimensions variable. Museo d'Arte della Svizzera Italiana, Lugano, Switzerland. Collection Cantone Ticino. Donation Panza di Biumo

by making works circulate in journals and books beyond the spaces of museums and galleries).[3] As art historian David Joselit has remarked, the "equation of art with information"—traversing the varied practices of Weiner, LeWitt, Douglas Huebler, Mel Bochner, and others—according to which "objects exist in a transactional relation with text," constituted a "profound ontological challenge to the work of art."[4] It is against this backdrop that, with hindsight, Peter Osborne could put forward a "single and simple, speculative proposition: *contemporary art is postconceptual art*."[5] But even if Schütte's oeuvre has been mainly organized (and is increasingly so), as the British philosopher has observed for contemporary art at large, in the logical form of "distributive unities," i.e., groups of works to be revisited recursively, and hence time and again has mediated between individual works and the universality of "Art" through the principle of the series,[6] the young artist's reaction to the interpellations and implications of the conceptual was far more complex and complicated than such a general proposition may capture.

In opposition to the doxa rampant at the Kunstakademie and elsewhere, Schütte defiantly based his earliest works, which mainly confronted painting, on a dialectic of decoration and demarcation. Using habitually overlooked architectural fixtures such as wallpaper, friezes, and garlands, he altered the margins of mundane public or private spaces, of corridors and passageways. The poles of abstraction and ornamentality are uneasily joined in these sardonic and unassuming installations. For *Tapetenmuster* (*Wallpaper Pattern*, page 50), first installed in a room at his university in June 1975, Schütte pinned unframed striped paintings resembling wallpaper samples directly onto a wall and arranged them to form a large grid,[7] blurring the distinctions between work and support, supplement and site, painterly idiom and design device. The pictures appear as sheets of wallpaper and vice versa.[8] Art historian Christine Mehring has convincingly characterized the artist's approach of the period as follows: "If Schütte seizes the space between world history and banality, between idealism and resignation, between public and private, that recourse to a disarming modesty, as it may be called, more often than not takes the form of a highly ambivalent use of design: somewhat functional and somewhat pointless, somewhat engaged and somewhat evasive, somewhat communal and somewhat intimate."[9] At the same time, Schütte's ambition exceeded the modesty of his means, for his ostentatiously "minor" wallpaper works equally commented on the major commitments and convictions of (post-)Conceptualism.

Buren's contribution to Documenta 5 may have served as a critical template for the driven student. For his *Exposition d'une exposition: Une pièce en sept tableaux* (*Exhibition of an Exhibition: A Piece in Seven Tableaux*, 1972), the French artist had covered the walls of the section of the exhibition devoted to Conceptual art (Idea and Idea/Light, organized by Klaus Honnef and Konrad Fischer) with his alternating white and colored vertical stripes of 8.7 cm (approximately 3 ½ inches) in width to critically reframe, even refuse, the exhibition as a site of curatorial control and institutional power.[10] In the hands of Schütte, contemporary art's purported critical, or even transgressive, aspirations were now programmatically undercut by the banality of pedestrian, petit bourgeois design.[11] For *Ringe* (*Rings*, figs. 1–2, plate 17), a work he has remade regularly since 1977, the walls of the "white cube" (as targeted by Buren and others since the mid-1960s) are covered with the titular objects, rings of wood or vinyl appliqué with a diameter of some four inches in a variety of colors. They take on the spare repetitiveness of painting conceived as a medium of "Institutional Critique"—apart from Buren's stripes, Niele Toroni's so-called *empreintes* of a no. 50 brush at unvarying intervals of 30 cm (11 13⁄16 inches) come to mind (fig. 3)—with an ironic exaggeration of the reversal of analytical markings into wall embellishment, of

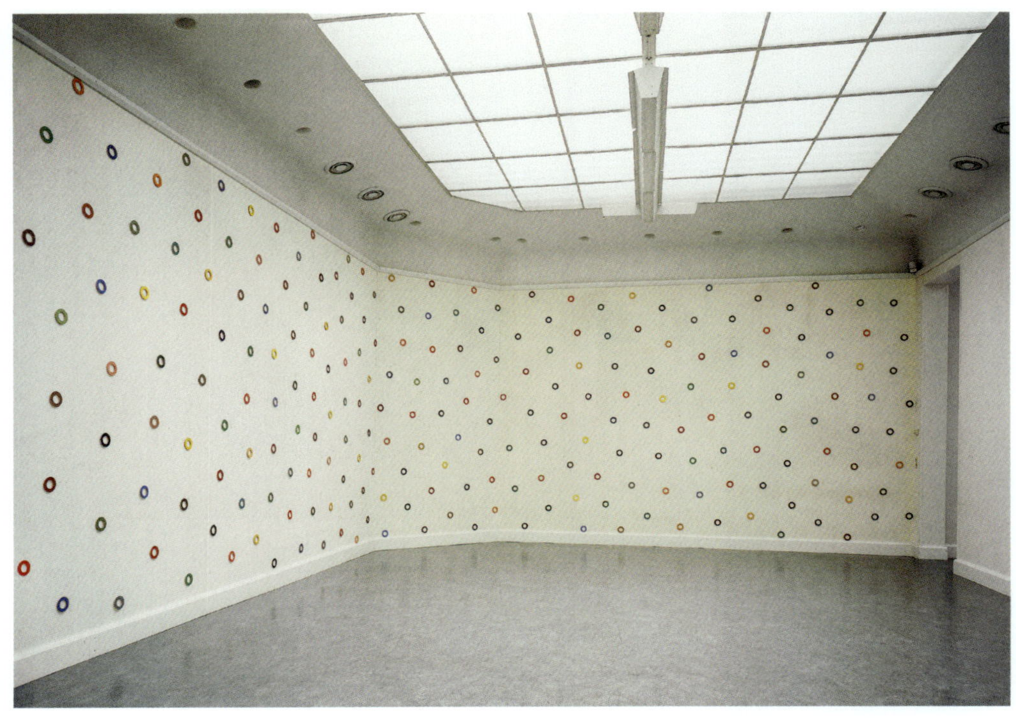

Fig. 2. *Ringe* (*Rings*). 1977. Installation view, *Sieben Felder*, Van Abbemuseum, Eindhoven, Netherlands, October 20, 1990–December 2, 1991

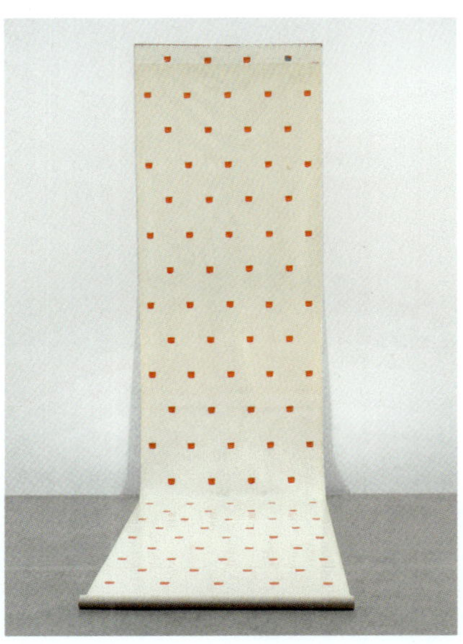

Fig. 3. Niele Toroni. *Empreintes de pinceau n° 50 répétées à intervalles réguliers de 30 cm* (*Imprints of a No. 50 Paintbrush Repeated at Regular Intervals of 30 cm*). 1969. Alkyd on vinyl-impregnated fabric, 33' 2" × 4' 7 ⅛" (1011 × 140 cm). The Museum of Modern Art, New York. Partial gift of the Daled Collection and partial purchase through the generosity of Maja Oeri and Hans Bodenmann, Sue and Edgar Wachenheim III, Agnes Gund, Marlene Hess and James D. Zirin, Marie-Josée and Henry R. Kravis, and Jerry I. Speyer and Katherine G. Farley

abstraction into decoration.[12] Typically, Schütte refrains from the strict systematicity of a Buren or Toroni and instead distributes the elements of his protosculptural wall installation in a manner that at first sight seems to suggest a consistent pattern but upon closer scrutiny reveals itself to be improvised or even erratic.

Although conceived much later, in 1986, in the context of his then increasingly predominant exploration of scale and monumentality in sculpture, the room-filling work *Melonely* (fig. 4; plate 24) similarly plays with the fraying of art and design, aesthetics and kitsch, sculpture and commodity, mediatization and literalness—while also retrospectively engaging with the syntax of historical Minimalism and the seriality of Pop Art.[13] Consisting of eleven painted-wood units each measuring over seven feet long (accompanied by fourteen exquisite small watercolors of the same motif), the piece surrounds viewers with gigantic slices of watermelon arranged on the gallery floor. The sections of fruit are standing in pairs, tilted and pushed together to form a circle, standing in splendid isolation as single pieces, or leaning in the corner. Reminiscent of both Morris's famous exhibition of painted plywood polyhedrons at Green Gallery in New York in 1964–65 and Andy Warhol's print portfolio *Space Fruit: Still Lifes* from 1979, which featured cantaloupes, Schütte's installation once again mobilizes banality to humorously fathom and subvert the aspirations and acuity of art. In so doing, Schütte was surely also informed by the sculptural ontology of consumption that Claes Oldenburg had developed beginning in the early 1960s; the food items made of painted plaster and canvas included in *The Store* from 1961 to 1964 (fig. 5), for instance, not only had mimicked the commodity-form in a site of commercial transaction but by the same token had presented (part) objects of expenditure that embodied and conveyed human drives and psychosexual impulses.[14] The wordplay of Schütte's title, which links the name of the fruit to the disposition of a perpetual attachment to a lost object of desire felt by a subject left to itself, is both poignant and pertinent with regard to this genealogy of sculpture after modernism.

Faced in his personal formation as an artist with the mandate of an anti-aesthetic point of no return—which was based, according to Buchloh's retrospective critique of Conceptualism, on the "purging . . . of imaginary and bodily experience, of physical substance and the space of memory" as well as on the effacement of "all residues of representation and style, of individuality and skill"[15]—the multifarious Schütte would seem to outright resist or fully repudiate the paramount challenge of an art of absences. Starting with his first public installations, such as *Große Tapeten* (*Large Wallpapers*, plate 1) and *Große Mauer* (*Large Wall*, plate 7), both debuted as part of the biannual students' show at the Kunstakademie in 1975 and 1977, respectively,[16] his multifaceted oeuvre has been provocatively, laconically rejecting Conceptualism's alleged "dematerialization of art."[17] Despite persistent signs of doubt and recalcitrance, he has almost reveled in the aesthetics and physicality of paintings and drawings, watercolors and engravings, architectural models and ceramics, bronzes, steel sculptures, and photographs. As he told curator Massimiliano Gioni in a conversation at Art Basel in 2013, the exigencies and evacuations

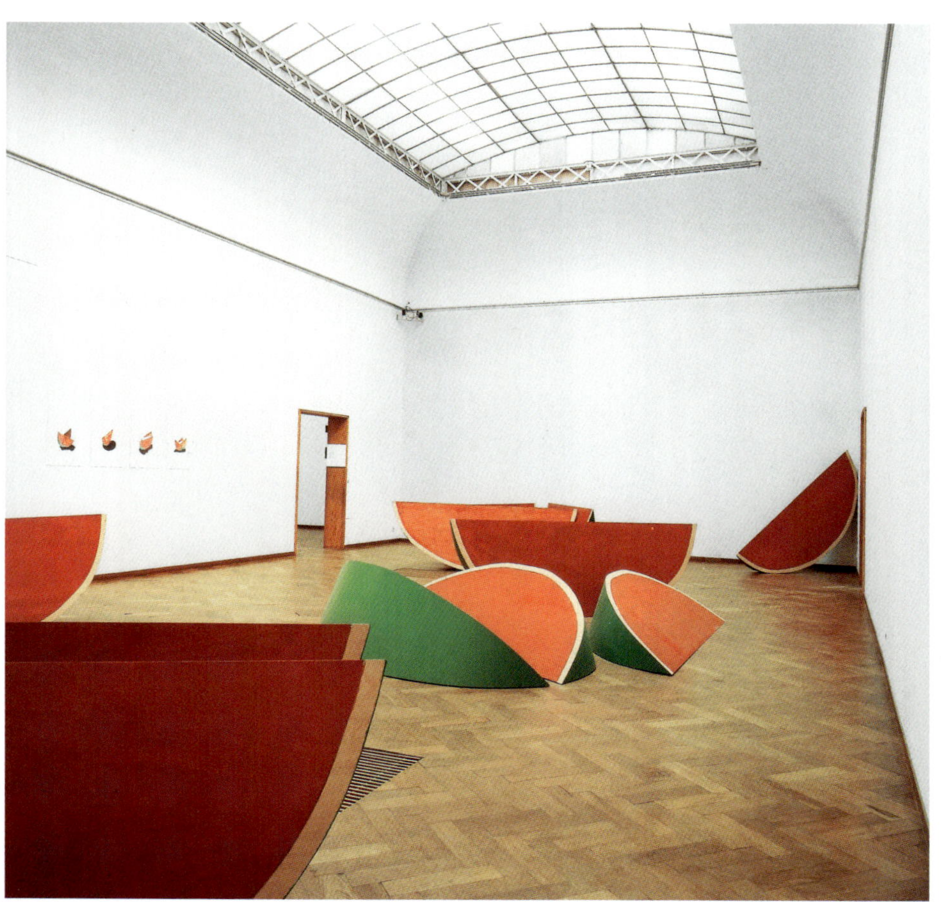

Fig. 4. Thomas Schütte. *Melonely*. 1986. Paint on wood, 11 parts, and gouache and watercolor on paper, 14 sheets; each wooden part 39 3/8 × 19 11/16 × 7' 6 9/16" (100 × 50 × 230 cm), each sheet 25 9/16 × 19 11/16" (65 × 50 cm). Installation dimensions variable. Private collection. Installation view, *Correspondentie Europa*, Stedelijk Museum, Amsterdam, September 20–November 2, 1986

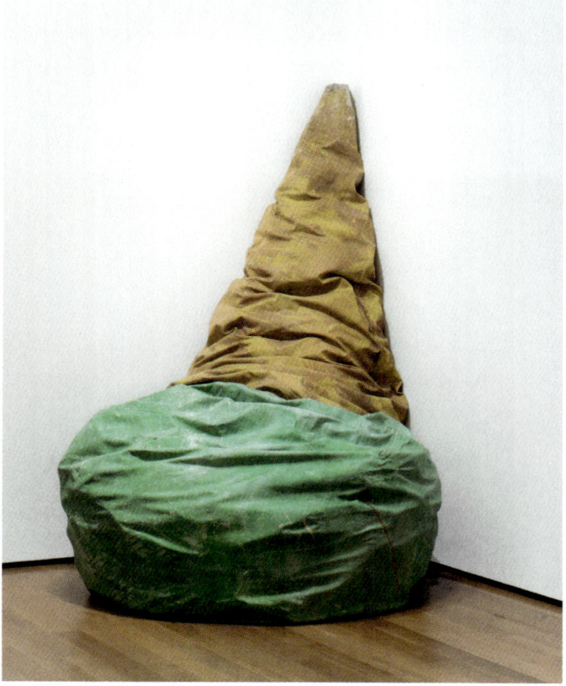

Fig. 5. Claes Oldenburg. *Floor Cone*. 1962. Synthetic polymer paint on canvas filled with foam rubber and cardboard boxes, 53 3/4" × 11' 4" × 56" (136.5 × 345.4 × 142 cm). The Museum of Modern Art, New York. Gift of Philip Johnson

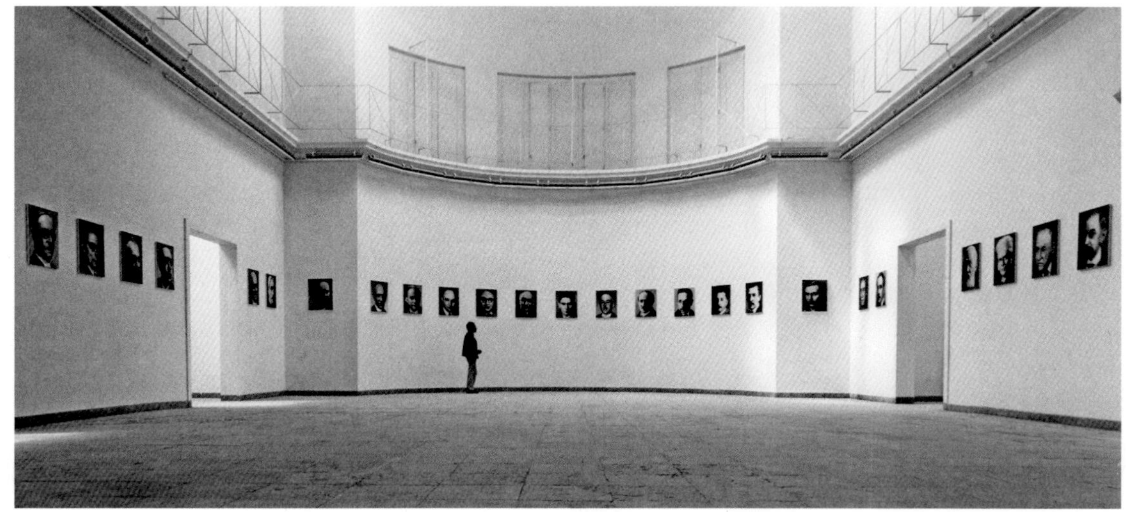

Fig. 6. Gerhard Richter. *48 Porträts* (*48 Portraits*). 1971–72. Oil on canvas, 48 paintings, each 27 9/16 × 21 11/16" (70 × 55 cm). Museum Ludwig, Cologne. Installation view, German Pavilion, 36th Venice Biennale, June 11–October 1, 1972

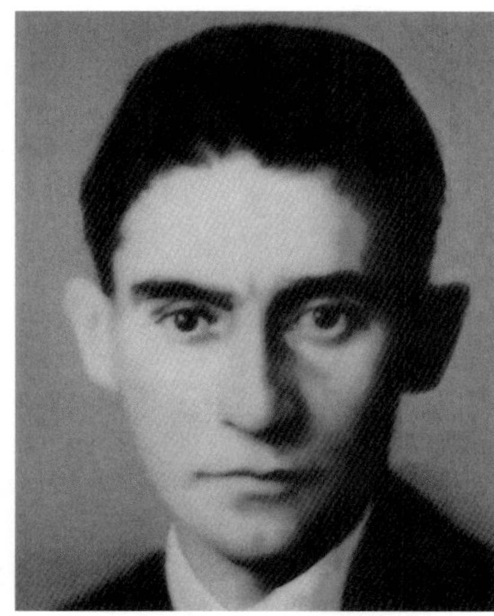

Fig. 7. Gerhard Richter. *Franz Kafka* from *48 Porträts* (*48 Portraits*). 1971–72. Oil on canvas, 27 9/16 × 21 11/16" (70 × 55 cm). Museum Ludwig, Cologne

of Conceptual art for him amounted to an "endgame" he needed to escape from.[18] Contrary to the withdrawal or even negation of visuality commensurate with a supposed "art as idea as idea" (as propagated, most notably, by the work of Joseph Kosuth), his half-century oeuvre variously presents human bodies and faces, animals and fruits, flowers and monuments, buildings and ornamental patterns in manifestly material forms ripe with mass and volume, texture and surface, that seriously toy with questions of scale and size. Apposite to this bewildering resuscitation of traditional motifs, Schütte has not only reinstated, in a highly individual, at times even idiosyncratic manner, the factors and forces of color and gesture, narrative and *Spiel*; he has simultaneously recalibrated the notions of manufacture, skill, and technique. After Conceptual art had supplanted the aesthetic with the informational, Schütte responded in myriad ways with a return to the figure as a preeminent subject and sustained attention to all matters of the figural as guiding principles of his practice.[19]

In his above-quoted classic essay on (the repercussions of) Conceptual art, Schütte's onetime instructor Buchloh concludes that the convergence of the movement's critical achievements and aspirations with an annihilation "of image and skill, of memory and vision" had two outcomes. Either it prompted a dialectic destined to make this purging more palpable as both an irretrievable loss and self-imposed erosion of aesthetic criteria with regard to the institutional and ideological sites of art, or it ignited "the ghostlike reapparitions of . . . displaced painterly and sculptural paradigms of the past" through which "the specular regime, which Conceptual art claimed to have upset, would be . . . reinstated with renewed vigor."[20] Schütte's immense and prolific body of work, and in particular his return to the figure, resides *between* these two alternatives of enlightened critique and the politics of retrospection. His figures are melancholic and maladroit, deconstructive and derisive, understated and uncanny, virtuosic and flawed, all at the same time. Far from being ideal forms or self-sufficient enclosed entities, they always describe, by way of their tangible dynamics and tendencies toward disfiguration, the position and status of the subject of representation vis-à-vis the fraught yet responsive milieu in which it is made to appear or in which it comes into existence. As French philosopher Gilles Deleuze would argue, there is no figure that could be fully abstracted or isolated from the "material structure" around it.[21] Schütte's early *Selbstportrait. 30/31.5.75* (*Self-portrait: 5/30–31/75*, 1975; plate 3), quickly executed in a photorealistic manner and in a variety of hues of gray oil paint on a midsize canvas (and in fact based on a black-and-white photograph), is indicative, perhaps even programmatic in this regard. With a downcast gaze partially hidden behind a pair of sunglasses, the young artist sports a white shirt, a dark jacket with an open collar, and long, wavy hair. He emerges from a vivid light-gray background; in the zones where his hair comes into contact with the undefined space around him (especially in the middle section on the left), small uneven white patches generate an impression of both disjunction and attraction between site and subject that prompts an altered rapport between figure and field. In the words of Deleuze, which strongly resonate with Schütte's contemporaneous approach to figuration, "It is no longer [only] the material structure that curls around the contour in order to envelop the Figure" but rather "the movement of the Figure toward the material structure, toward the field of color."[22] In redefining the venerable art-historical concept of "the Figure" in terms of the relationship between body, image, and context in his book *Francis Bacon: The Logic of Sensation* (1981), Deleuze argues that such a figure, which dissipates and delineates forms at the same time, results from an "intense movement [that] flows through the whole body, a deformed and deforming movement that at every moment transfers the real image onto the body in order to constitute the Figure."[23] The figure becomes an interface of a contentious exchange between the exterior and interior motivations shaping and enabling it. The poetics of Schütte's work in this configuration have been both dismissing and daring, tendered with great aplomb and ironic terseness, gauging and pressuring the polarity (as intimated by Buchloh vis-à-vis the aftermath of Conceptualism) between a critical investigation of art's own condition and a myopic and ahistorical recollection of tradition. It is hardly incidental therefore that the artist's *Selbstportrait. 30/31.5.75* appears indebted to his teacher Gerhard Richter's 1971–72 series *48 Porträts* (*48 Portraits*, figs. 6–7), in which the latter had created a melancholic mausoleum of modernity consisting of exclusively male figures, all given in photography-based pictures of the same size and format that oscillate between instant recognizability and painterly dissemblance, between the return of a classical genre and its concurrent deconstruction through sequence and seriality.[24] With an astute sense of irony, Schütte paints himself to proactively join this pantheon of a potentially forlorn past while by the same token attesting to inheriting and confronting the problematics of how to sustain its aesthetic continuity as a (re)source of *Weltbezug* (world relation). Schütte's two existing *Selbstportrait* works (plates 3–4) are in fact from a set of twenty variations, all based on the same image, executed in May–June 1975 and mostly later destroyed by Schütte so that he could reuse the canvas (pages 60–61).[25] The works offer a wide visual spectrum of the figure's obliteration as it is erased, blurred, smeared, overshadowed, defaced, hollowed out, blocked, fragmented, parcellated.

With reference and representation irrevocably under siege, the artist's more recent figures, often wrested from the history of modern sculpture and its repertoire of forms, genres, and techniques, find consistency only in their innate ambivalence.[26] Schütte's art is peculiarly "postconceptual" precisely because the rediscovery and gauging of the contemporary conditions of the figural and its materialities continuously propelling the artist's trajectory partake in "the dialectics of deskilling and reskilling" resulting from the impositions and provocations of Conceptualist negativity.[27] What makes Schütte's work so unique and influential is that from the outset he has recognized the fact that dismantling the premises of cultural representation and the mastery of skills was becoming untenable given "the expansion of an aesthetic of universal deskilling" in the newly afforded leisure time and the now-available "plenitude of object consumption" of liberal Western societies.[28] As can be discerned from his initial projects, Schütte would seem to have intuitively realized that, in order to secure the surplus value and the (however residual) critical, mnemonic, cognitive, and epistemic potentialities of art, it is not possible to further erode the constitutive and inexhaustible alterity of the aesthetic object and the reflexivity it might activate through the "unstable alliance of matter and image";[29] nor is it feasible to merely reinstate traditional criteria of virtuosity in a retrograde *retour à l'ordre*. In the vast array of shapes and features, of proliferations and saturations assembling this oeuvre with brio, his figures appear farcical, grotesque, inept, derailed, faceless, interchangeable, fragmented, distorted, or collapsed—yet also detailed, sanguine, humorous, refined, composed, alluring, seductive, calm, or reclusive. Schütte's figures do not mark the return of the integral individualist subject of humanism and anthropocentrism. As suggested by some of his most memorable and famous titles, they are specters (*Große Geister* [*Large Spirits*, 1995–2004; plate 50]) or foes (*United Enemies*, 1993–94; plates 43–48), or they are simply deflated (*Frauenkopf [implodiert]* [*Woman's Head (Imploded)*, 2020; plate 100]). In the aftermath of a pervasive denial of embodiment, memory, and substance in favor of the currencies of information and protocols of communication (which have only become more domineering), they rather may, in the poignant formulation of German media theorist Friedrich A. Kittler, solely "yield historical traces of the unknown called the body."[30]

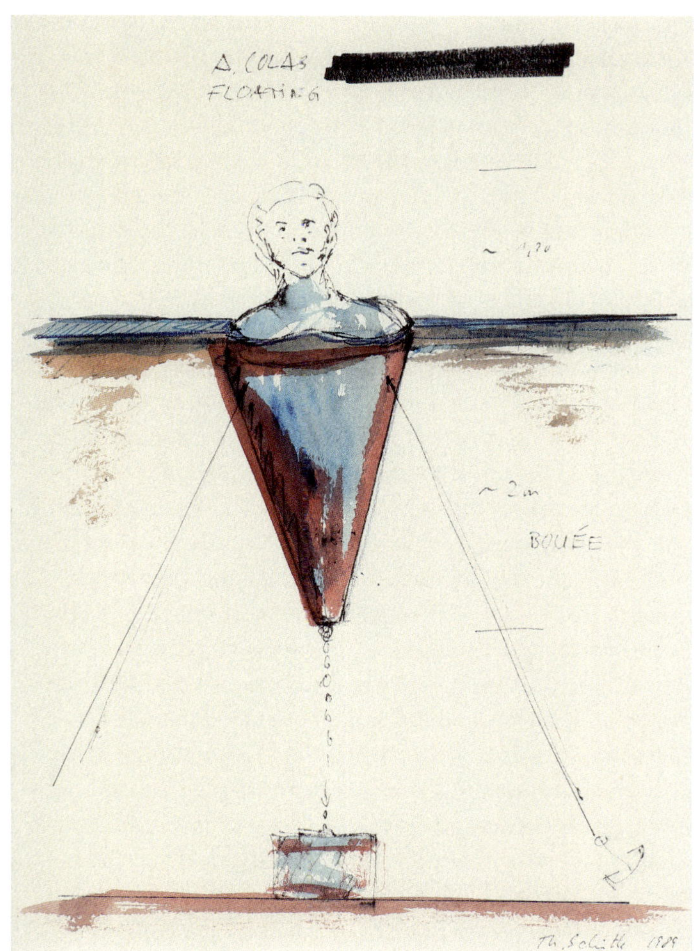

Fig. 8. Thomas Schütte. *A. Colas Floating* from *Étude pour la commune de Clamecy* (*Study for the Town of Clamecy*). 1989. Ink and watercolor on vellum paper, 12 ⅝ × 9 ¼" (32 × 23.5 cm). Centre National des Arts Plastiques, Paris

Schütte first fully conceived a sculptural figure, albeit a rigorously uncompleted one, in context of an ultimately failed commission by the French government for a monument in the city of Clamecy to the lost French sailor Alain Colas in 1989. Colas, the first man to complete a solitary round-the-world race in a multihull vessel, had disappeared near the Azores in 1978. His body was never found (which sparked rumors of his survival and secret life on a remote island).[31] Schütte's proposal centered on a model in which the artist imagined the injured adventurer literally resurfacing, like a swaying buoy, in the river of his hometown (fig. 8).[32] White polystyrene blocks, found at a brick factory and glued together with brownish foam, serve as the shoulders supporting a head modeled by Schütte out of fifty kilograms of clay (which to this day has not been properly fired, only eventually hardened on the surface by a gas flame).[33] The inert facial features of the unfortunate yachtsman, based on a photograph, are framed by a white bandage on his head and a red scarf around his neck and upper chest. Patches of pigment seeping through and beyond this defined area invoke wounds but also perseverance and stamina against all odds. After the proposal was rejected, the artist turned this model into a proper sculpture, exhibiting the work *Alain Colas* (1989, plate 34) as a ludic, oversize bust strapped with the help of wires onto two industrial wooden pallets. The sculpture remains deliberately stuck in the status of a suggestive sketch, its makeshift display emphasizing its permanent provisionality. It could therefore be said to epitomize Schütte's concept of the figure at large.

With *Alain Colas*, the figure unexpectedly (and allegorically) resurfaces from an unfathomable past, albeit damaged, poorly patched together, and far from glorious. In his book *Realism after Modernism*, literary scholar and cultural theorist Devin Fore argues that the interwar period of mechanization and urbanization (after the historical avant-garde's radical turn toward abstraction and montage) brought about a rediscovery of the human figure—but not in terms of the recomposition of a shattered wholeness that reinstated traditional representation. Rather, "within this countermouvement dwells a glaring paradox, for although the human body, as both subject matter and technical precondition, served as the guarantor of mimetic realism's validity, the reassertion of the human figure . . . was a deeply conflicted proposal, since the seemingly natural body had . . . become a thoroughly vexed construction."[34] Schütte's sculptural gambits like *Alain Colas* present equally vexed constructions, with verisimilitude and likeness in this paradoxical modality of mimesis appearing strained and pressured at best. In parallax view, the artist's figures may best be understood as a postmodern recalibration of the remnants of the figural after Conceptualism, which itself had misapprehended its complicity with "the laws of positivist instrumentality and the logic of administration" of the postwar period.[35] Over the course of his trajectory, this mode of refitting and rejoining forms, pieces, and volumes into figural entities would lose its initially contrarian stance and more and more oscillate between the poles of ambivalence and defiance, seriousness and satire, the sensuous and the grotesque, the melancholic and the monumental.

The curator of the present exhibition, Paulina Pobocha, clairvoyantly observed that the conflicted and complex return of the figure in Schütte's oeuvre was so closely tied to the architectural model as a concomitant new matrix of sculpture that together the two forms ultimately created "a single unit." The artist's model for the construction *Mann im Matsch (I. Version)* (*Man in Mud [1st Version]*, 1982/2014; plate 19)—which would serve Schütte as a creative wellspring for years to come, with the artist producing twenty iterations of the motif over the decades—most strikingly incorporates this intricate rapport.[36] A small wax figure stands alone on a large scaffold composed of four stacked and interlocking circular daises, with the overall assemblage suggesting, perhaps, a design for an antimonument to the grandiosity and totality of modernist aspirations. Despite, or rather due to, his vast ambitions, man is portrayed as stuck in the resulting proverbial mud of a modernity that apparently is messier than ideology could ever account for.[37] Two years prior to *Mann im Matsch*, Schütte's famous three *Westkunst Modelle* (*Westkunst Models*) had figuratively and literally set the stage for this allegorical exploration of the figure at loss. When, in 1980, curators Kasper König and Laszlo Glozer invited him to contribute to the large-scale exhibition *Westkunst. Zeitgenössische Kunst seit 1939* (*Art of the West: Contemporary Art since 1939*), slated to open at the Messehalle in Cologne the following year, Schütte conceived a series of painted-wood models of scenographic devices or situations. Documented in photographs by Candida Höfer, a fellow student at the Kunstakademie Düsseldorf, one of these works, *Bühne (Modell 1:20) (Stage [Model 1:20]*, 1980; fig. 9), presented viewers with a miniature oval-shaped stage elevated on three broad grayish tiers and encased by a curved, golden yellow wall with two red pilasters on each side and a black verso. At a scale of 1:20, the wall displays small-format photographs of lacquered paintings enigmatically showing the letter *H* in several variations of hue and typography, a device previously used in

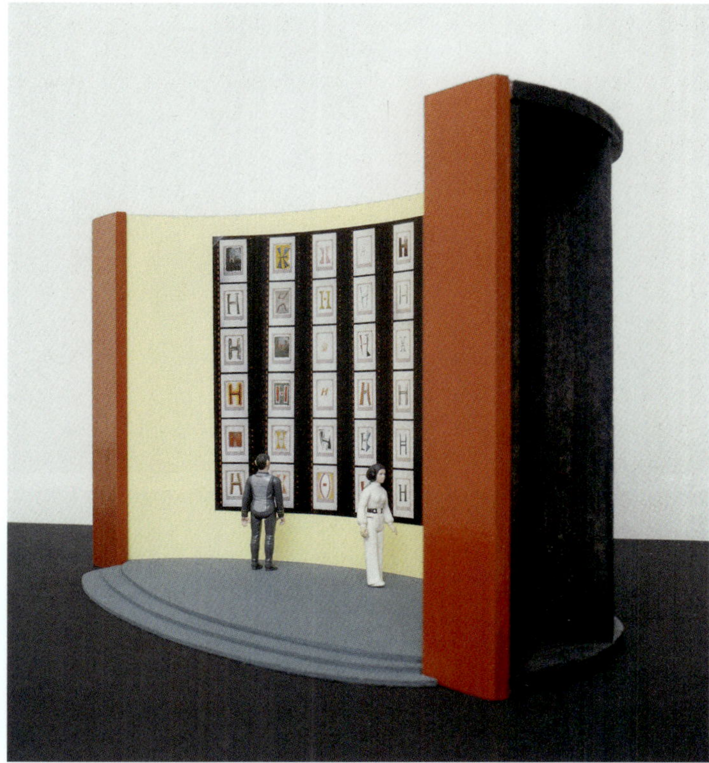

Fig. 9. Thomas Schütte. *Bühne (Modell 1:20)* (*Stage [Model 1:20]*). 1980. Wood, paint, and photographs with plastic figurines, 13 ¾ × 19 11/16 × 9 13/16" (35 × 50 × 25 cm). Private collection

Schütte's multipart work on paper *Hysterie* (*Hysteria*, 1979; plate 10). Two toy figures, a man and a woman, are installed within this open exhibition pavilion, and the personnel are not generic: they are in fact the popular sci-fi characters Princess Leia from the *Star Wars* franchise and Spock from *Star Trek* (both page 78, top), a comical pairing that fuses the futurity of the model with the fictional and futile. Acting as museum visitors, they perform under the gaze of us real, life-size visitors in a dizzying and ironic mirror effect.[38] Already in these early instances of the figure's reappearance, Schütte's sculpture was engaged with scenarios and structures of permanent provisionality that would provide an aperture for the entrance of all the new creatures and colossi, physiognomies and persona to this utterly unpredictable oeuvre.

Undoubtedly, Schütte's series *United Enemies* (1993–94, plates 43–48) ranks not only among the best-known but also most resonant of the artist's engagements with what Deleuze has pertinently called the "violent comedy" inherent to the dynamics of the figure enthralled in a conflict with itself and its vicinity.[39] Prompted by his everyday studies of the faces, heads, and necks of elderly men—abounding, according to his observation, in Rome (on public transport, for instance), where he spent a year during a residency at the Villa Massimo (home to the Deutsche Akademie Rom) beginning in the summer of 1992—the artist created a comprehensive series of sculptural pairings, each consisting of two small figures that are mainly distinguished by the detailed yet schematic rendition of their facial features and expressions.[40] Meticulously shaped in the open palm of the artist's hand using streaks and stripes of different-colored modeling clay (and then fired in a household oven) in a process that resembles an amateur pastime, these wrinkly and

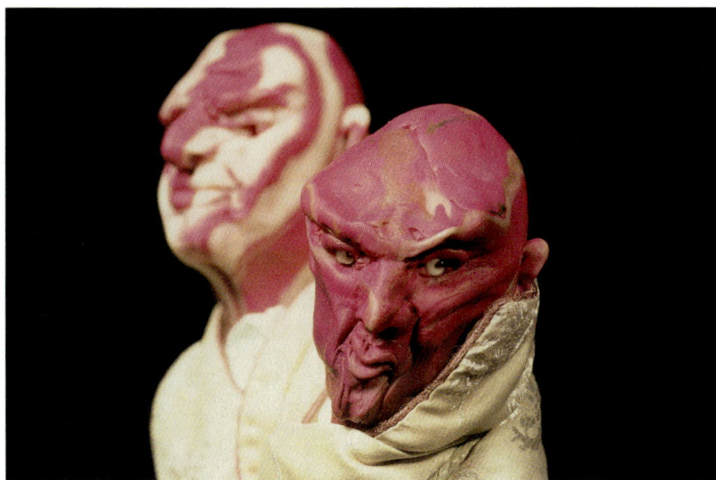

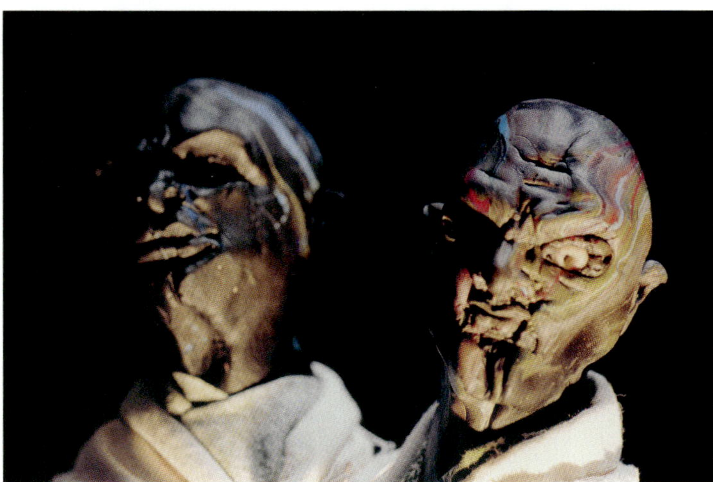

Figs. 10–11. Thomas Schütte. *United Enemies, A Play in Ten Scenes*. 1994. Offset lithographs, two of ten sheets, each 27 1⁄16 × 38 3⁄4" (68.8 × 98.4 cm). The Museum of Modern Art, New York. Committee on Prints and Illustrated Books Fund

contorted faces emerging from invariably bald (and actually hollow) heads with empty or deep-set eyes seem to grimace and stare, anguish and judge, condescend and grieve, contemplate and introspect. Taken together, they offer a rich panoply of the bleak and challenging side of human moods, impulses, and affects. While the physiognomy of these figures, which registers as both varied and stereotypical, is represented with palpable care and interest—and thus evokes the historical pseudoscience of "face reading" as it was advanced, most notably, by Johann Lavater in the eighteenth century, with repercussions in art ranging from Messerschmidt to Hogarth and Daumier[41]—their limbs and bodies are concealed by bulky swaddling garments made from pieces of cloth and textiles either found by the artist around the Deutsche Akademie Rom or taken from his own shirts and bathrobes. Like puppets, they stand on wooden dowels, suggesting a precarity and paucity peculiarly at odds with their comparatively solid faces and at times slightly deformed (fore)heads (figs. 10–11).[42] Obviously they are far from traditional representations of the human body as integral and sovereign. As suggested by the series title, these figures are finally brought into an apparently unwanted proximity through tightly knotted twine. This predicament might help explain their expressed emotions of remorse, defeat, regret, annoyance, repulsion, and so on. With their eyes never meeting and heads turning away from each other, these gnarled, grumpy figures appear doomed to cohabitate despite their egotistical wishes and individual desires. Beginning in 1994, these ill-fated or involuntary pairs of dissatisfied men were presented by Schütte under glass bell jars, adding to the sense of a sculptural taxonomy of specimen and states of mind.[43] Their many similarities (in size and shape, faciality and corporality, materiality and execution), however, would seem to imply that they are less apart than is intimated by their mutual antipathy, not only in terms of space but also with regard to identity; they might even be regarded as split images of the same embodied subject. Stasis and dynamism coincide in one configuration. Not surprisingly read at first as allegories of German reunification and its discontents, these theatrical and resolutely antiheroic doubles who resent and reject being bound together are pivotal and evocative figures in Schütte's oeuvre. In the words of Deleuze, "If there is an effort, and an intense effort, it is in no way an extraordinary effort, as if it were a matter of undertaking something above and beyond the strength of the body and directed toward a separate object. The body exerts itself in a very precise manner, or waits to escape from itself in a very precise manner. It is not I who attempt to escape from my body, it is the body that attempts to escape from itself."[44]

Since the early to mid-1990s, the sculptural work of Thomas Schütte has imagined and presented the human figure in terms of a body that palpably yet without pathos tries to "escape from itself." His famous group *Große Geister* confronts viewers with a veritable hauntology of the figural and its ancestral logic of commemoration. These specters appear as towering (though in most instances they are bending and bowing), ungendered corporeal emanations that, in the protracted process of their making, owe their bulbous shapes and steady circular contours to twine constricting a wax figurine that was subsequently enlarged and executed in polished cast aluminum, bronze, or steel. The shiny aluminum ones (see, for example, plate 50), which register as almost liquid, unite within themselves a struggle between morphological mutability and material permanence and hence simultaneously contradict and perform monumentality. Despite being laboriously crafted and industrially produced, from today's vantage point they seem prescient regarding the then newly emergent possibilities of digital technology to replicate and modulate forms.[45] Once more, Schütte's figures allegorically evoke and ludically defy their ambivalent status as anachronistic revenants in the field of the aesthetic contemporary.

It is with his vexingly disfigured and deformed *Frauen* (*Women*, 1998–2006; plates 68–71), however—Schütte's most challenging and provocative manifestation of the notion of the figure attempting to escape from itself—that the artist would fully embrace and enact the prevalent "athleticism" of his figures, to use Deleuze's term, which is caused by the singular conditions of their fabrication and formation. ("The source of the movement is not in itself," Deleuze writes; rather, from the outside it "envelops and imprisons the Figure."[46]) Given Schütte's return to the anachronistic genre of the female nude and its concomitant recourse to the sculptural tradition of Aristide Maillol, Henri Matisse, Pablo Picasso, and Henry Moore during the interwar period,[47] the very conception of the *Frauen*—all cast in steel, aluminum, or bronze at a larger-than-life scale and displayed on steel tables below eye level—cannot but prompt questions of gender politics in art and beyond. Seemingly, as if untouched by feminist critiques of the preceding decades, the male artist advances to (re) assume the old Promethean position of creating (the representation

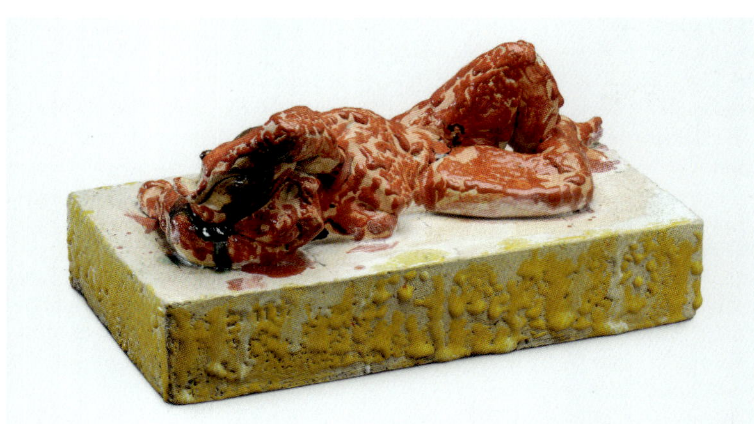

Fig. 12. Thomas Schütte. *Untitled (Ceramic Sketch)*. 1997. Glazed ceramic, approx. 9 13/16 × 13 × 7 7/8" (25 × 33 × 20 cm). Kunstsammlung Nordrhein-Westfalen, Düsseldorf

of) female subjects in his studio according to his will, needs, and desires. Too, the particular "athleticism" of the resulting figures—which are as curvaceous as they are disturbed vis-à-vis the conventions of naturalism—could even be (mis)read as manifestations of misogyny. These sculptures of lying, reclining, crouching, cowering, sitting, or kneeling feminine bodies appear not only voluptuous and vital but also fragmented, abstracted, dismembered, violently bent, mutilated, distorted, folded, or flattened and with formulaic (or even no) faces, closed or downcast eyes. More often than not, they are bereft of both anatomical coherence and (unlike the figures of *United Enemies*) individual traits, the latter lack exacerbated by their replication in various materials.

Yet first impressions might be misleading. Lynne Cooke has cautioned against too-sudden dismissals of the specific procedures and poetics of Schütte's monumental women; they are part and parcel of "a probing of the ways in which standard or normative modes may be used against themselves so that they prove revisionist rather than reactionary."[48] All sculptures in the series—the artist's largest, with each of the eighteen figures cast five times—are derived from Schütte's vast repertoire of *Ceramic Sketches* (1997–99; fig. 12, plate 67), which assembles seemingly the entire spectrum of the female nude's positions and poses. In the creation of these models, the artist strictly followed a self-imposed routine of forming figures by hand that allotted only one hour of labor to each block of clay, which were all the same size, with the result being the production of approximately one hundred twenty models over a period of nine months. The works were glazed by Schütte in one go before being fired, with the glazing unpredictably stagnating in blobs and patches on the surface and craters and holes left visible as a "production fault."[49] Rather than signifying ingenuity and inventiveness, these models are tangibly inept and imperfect. The restrictions inherent in the delimited process of their making programmatically facilitate the mistakes and errors, failures and acts of chance that mark the *Frauen* from their very inception.[50] It is from the flaws and defaults imbued into the ceramic sketches that Schütte further develops and determines his dramatically enlarged, metal female nudes. Thus the elusive materialities and elaborate manufacture involved in the production of the series dictate the forms and shapes devised by the artist. It is a continuous testament to a standoff in the studio (and later in the foundry) between his capacity to generate plastic figural entities and the resistance with which they are physically and

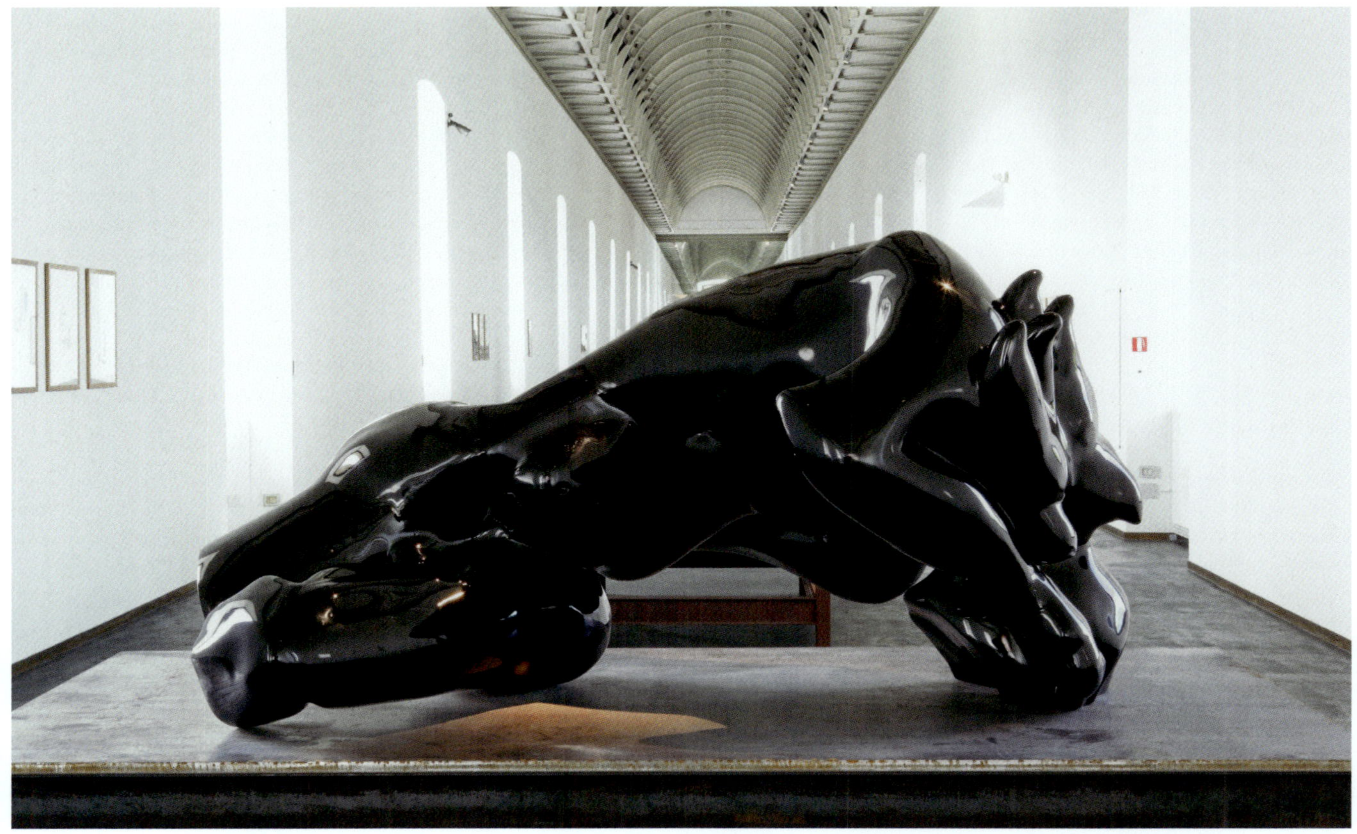

Fig. 13. Thomas Schütte. *Aluminiumfrau Nr. 6* (*Aluminum Woman No. 6*). 2001. Aluminum and lacquer on steel table, 5' 4 3/16" × 8' 2 7/16" × 4' 13/16" (163 × 250 × 125 cm). Thomas Schütte Stiftung, Neuss, Germany. Installation view, *Thomas Schütte: Frauen*, Castello di Rivoli, Rivoli/Turin, May 22–September 23, 2012

procedurally met at every turn. Rather than stemming from a unilateral assault on ultimately uncontrollable matter (as the legend of the male artist as sole and unimpeded demiurgical creator suggests), the body in each of Schütte's *Frauen* is subjected to exterior forces as much as it attempts to escape from itself (fig. 13). Suspended in an intense moment within a course of action that contains (but never sublates) the tension between the movement of the figure and its materiality, *Stahlfrau Nr. 1* (*Steel Woman No. 1*, 1998; plate 68), for instance, offers the puzzling sight of an odalisque who seems to be pushed down toward the platform her body rests on while her faceless head (marked by the imprint of a disc rather than facial features) is entwined by intimations of curls of hair and, most importantly, held and supported by her arms, which appear to be stretching up to lift her entire body out of its predicament. In this ambivalent configuration, the reclining figure is residual and resilient at the same time. The shape of Schütte's *Aluminiumfrau Nr. 6* (*Aluminum Woman No. 6*, 2001; plate 69) pushes this ambiguity to a distracting extreme: its treatment of bodily signifiers has led to an almost violently disfigured and contorted representation of the feminine. While the lower body registers as roughly naturalistic and thus legible, the upper part becomes contorted to the degree that the areas of the back and neck thrown into relief (at the cost of the head being pushed into the steel table and the left arm being painfully twisted backward) are covered by proliferations and protuberances. These spikes and jags read as an apotropaic armoring—aimed against the very forces that brought them into existence. Conflicted and confident at the same time, Schütte's *Frauen* epitomize and conclude his postconceptual return to the figure in its permanent provisionality: "The deformation takes place on the spot. Just as the effort of the body is exerted upon itself, so the deformation is static."[51]

---

1 Lynne Cooke, "Turning the Tables," in *Thomas Schütte: Hindsight*, ed. Cooke (Madrid: Museo Nacional Centro de Arte Reina Sofía, 2010), 13.

2 To some extent, these tenets had still guided the theory and practice of Minimalism. See Hal Foster, "The Crux of Minimalism" (1986), in *The Return of the Real: The Avant-Garde at the Turn of the Century* (Cambridge, MA: MIT Press, 1996), 5–70.

3 On the genealogies, paradigms, and fallacies of Conceptualism, see the influential essay by none other than Benjamin H. D. Buchloh called "Conceptual Art 1962–1969: From the Aesthetic of Administration to the Critique of Institutions," *October* 55 (Winter 1990), 105–43.

4 David Joselit, "Conceptual Art of the Press Release, or Art History without Art," *October* 158 (Fall 2016), 167.

5 Peter Osborne, *Anywhere or Not at All: Philosophy of Contemporary Art* (New York: Verso, 2013), 3. Emphasis in the original.

6 Ibid., 86.

7 See the excellent account of the work's creation in Penelope Curtis, *Thomas Schütte: Early Work* (Leeds: Henry Moore Institute, 2007), 92.

8 Christine Mehring, "Modest Abstraction: Thomas Schütte's Early Work," in Cooke, *Thomas Schütte: Hindsight*, 37. In this respect, Mehring relates Schütte's ambivalence and skepticism about abstraction's continued claims for supreme reflexivity, as evidenced by his use of wallpaper, to Richter's recourse to commercial color charts as a matrix of (increasingly aleatory) painting; see page 39. On Richter's color charts and use of grids, see also my "Randomizing Painting: Notes on Richter's Abstractions," in *Gerhard Richter: Painting After All*, ed. Benjamin H. D. Buchloh and Sheena Wagstaff with Brinda Kumar (New York: Metropolitan Museum of Art, 2020), S. 82–93, S. 258–60.

9 Mehring, "Modest Abstraction," 34.

10 For in-depth discussion of Buren's intervention, see Beatrice von Bismarck, "'The Master of the Works': Daniel Buren's Contribution to *documenta 5*, Kassel 1972," in "Documenta: Curating the History of the Present," ed. Nanne Buurman and Dorothee Richter, special issue, *On Curating* 33 (June 2017), 54–60.

11 With regard to the concept coined by French philosophers Gilles Deleuze and Félix Guattari, Schütte's early work arguably occupies a "minor" position; see Deleuze and Guattari, *Kafka: Toward a Minor Literature*, trans. Dana Polan (Minneapolis: University of Minnesota Press, 1986). This position is not in terms of historical significance but rather, as art historian Branden W. Joseph has phrased it, "on account of their relation of proximity to the movements and categories engendered by major history and because of the unceasing pressure that they exert upon them." Joseph, *Beyond the Dream Syndicate: Tony Conrad and the Arts after Cage—A Minor History* (New York: Zone Books, 2008), 51.

12 On *Ringe* (and the conceptually related *Punkte* [*Points*] from 1977), see Curtis, *Thomas Schütte: Early Work*, 94. For a discussion of an extension of the dialectics of demarcation and decoration in the most advanced practices of contemporary sculpture, see my "Nairy Baghramian: The Matrix of Sculpture," trans. Gerrit Jackson, in *Nairy Baghramian: Déformation Professionnelle*, ed. Vincenzo de Bellis and Martin Germann (New York: Prestel, 2018), 99–103.

13 In his survey of 1960s and 1970s sculpture, art historian Simon Baier assigns Donald Judd's "specific objects" and Andy Warhol's *White Brillo Boxes* (1964) to the same historical juncture; both, he argues, "cannot avoid also speaking of something that is [their] economic condition of possibility: industrial production and standardization as well as the luster of the fetish that this configuration of the commodity as the idol of sameness . . . bears on its surface." Baier, "Speaking without a Tongue," in *Sculpture on the Move: 1946–2016*, ed. Bernhard Mendes Bürgi (Ostfildern-Ruit, Germany: Hatje Cantz, 2016), 45.

14 See Claes Oldenburg and Emmett Williams, eds., *Store Days: Documents from "The Store" (1961) and "Ray Gun Theater" (1962)*, photographs by Robert R. McElroy (New York: Something Else Press, 1967). A year after *Melonely* was first shown at the Stedelijk Museum in Amsterdam, in 1987, Schütte would erect his famous *Kirschsäule* (*Cherry Column*) on Harsewinkelplatz as part of the second edition of Skulptur Projekte Münster. Permanently installed in the Westphalian city ever since, the work consists of a classic sandstone column topped by a bright and shiny red aluminum cherry that clearly pays tribute to the sculptures of Oldenburg and in this configuration satirically comments, with recourse to Pop art and postmodern architecture, on the predicaments of public monuments to serve as tokens of commerce and city marketing.

15 Buchloh, "Conceptual Art 1962–1969," 143.

16 See Cooke, "Turning the Tables," 13; and Mehring, "Modest Abstraction," 37.

17 Lucy R. Lippard and John Chandler, "The Dematerialization of Art" (1968), in *Conceptual Art: A Critical Anthology*, ed. Alexander Alberro and Blake Stimson (Cambridge, MA: MIT Press, 1999), 46–50.

18 "Conversations | Premiere | Artist Talk with Thomas Schütte," Art Basel, June 12, 2013, https://www.youtube.com/watch?v=sF02nI6Kt7Y&t=3475s.

19 Not surprisingly, perhaps, two large exhibitions by Schütte in the past programmatically carried the term in their titles: *Thomas Schütte (Figur)*, Hamburger Kunsthalle and Württembergischer Kunstverein Stuttgart, 1994; and *Thomas Schütte: Figur*, Fondation Beyeler, Riehen/Basel, 2013–14.

20 Buchloh, "Conceptual Art 1962–1969," 143. In this passage, Buchloh refers to the critical melancholy of Belgian artist Marcel Broodthaers and his status as a proponent of so-called Institutional Critique, and to the return of representation in European painting (for example in the work of German artists Markus Lüpertz, Georg Baselitz, and Anselm Kiefer). On the latter topic, see Buchloh, "Figures of Authority, Ciphers of Regression: Notes on the Return of Representation in European Painting" (1981), in *Formalism and Historicity: Models and Methods in Twentieth-Century Art* (Cambridge, MA: MIT Press, 2015), 115–72.

21 Gilles Deleuze, *Francis Bacon: The Logic of Sensation*, trans. Daniel W. Smith (New York: Bloomsbury, 2013), 6. In turn, for Deleuze, "painting has to extract the Figure from the figurative." Ibid., 8.

22 Ibid., 16, 18.

23 Ibid., 19. Accordingly, "the contour thus assumes a new function, since it no longer lies flat, but outlines a hollow volume and has a vanishing point." Ibid., 17. Art historian Alex Kitnick has summarized this concept, which would seem pertinent to the contemporaneous turn to the figure in Schütte's practice as follows: "To put it bluntly: body plus image equals Figure." Kitnick, "The Brutalism of Art and Life," *October* 136 (Spring 2011), 63–86, 85.

24 In conversation with Richter, Schütte has also pointed to the presence of photorealism in Documenta 5, which coincided with Richter's exhibition of *48 Porträts* in the German Pavilion of the Venice Biennale that year. See Theodora Vischer, "Gerhard Richter und Thomas Schütte: Ein Gespräch," in *Thomas Schütte: Figur*, ed. Theodora Vischer (Basel: Fondation Beyeler, 2013), 170–75, 173.

25 Ibid., 12–14.

26 In this regard in particular, Schütte has acknowledged the influence of Richter as a "master of ambivalence: it's from him that I learned that." Heinz-Norbert Jocks, "Thomas Schütte: 'Man kann auch schattenboxen oder weiter stochern im Nebel,'"

Kunstforum International 128 (October–December 1994), 257, quoted in Mehring, "Modest Abstraction," 39.
27 Benjamin H. D. Buchloh, "Introduction," in *Formalism and Historicity*, xv–xli, xxiii.
28 Ibid., xxiv.
29 David Joselit, *Art's Properties* (Princeton, NJ: Princeton University Press, 2023), 12. In his recent ruminations, Joselit has argued, "The history of art is drawn from . . . socially embedded performances of alterity. . . . The temporality of these effects is distinct from the rhythms of conventional politics. Alterity's elsewhere or otherwise does not take place in the exclusively human realm of the state, or civil society. Art's special capacity is to configure multiple registers of experience (the spiritual, the terrestrial, the abstract, and the material) rather than remaining embroiled in the ephemeral conflicts of day-to-day politics. Its power *is its capacity to activate alterities*." Ibid., 3; emphasis in the original. Schütte's brand of figuration undoubtedly acknowledges, articulates, and amplifies this basic and important alterity of the aesthetic.
30 Friedrich A. Kittler, *Gramophone, Film, Typewriter*, trans. Geoffrey Winthrop-Young and Michael Wutz (Stanford, CA: Stanford University Press, 1999), xl.
31 See *Thomas Schütte: Figur*, 27.
32 The proposal also included an accompanying installation comprising a large drawing that shows Colas's head on a submerged column; a figurine of modeling clay; and printed articles (plates 33 and 35). See Cooke, "Turning the Tables," 26.
33 See *Thomas Schütte: Figur*, 27.
34 Devin Fore, *Realism after Modernism: The Rehumanization of Art and Literature* (Cambridge, MA: MIT Press, 2015), 3–4.
35 Buchloh, "Conceptual Art 1962–1969," 143.
36 Paulina Pobocha, "Inhabitance," in *Thomas Schütte: Three Acts*, ed. Camille Morineau (Paris: Musée 11 Conti—Monnaie de Paris, 2019), 47. A version of *Mann im Matsch* was rendered and installed as a colossal bronze in front of Landessparkasse zu Oldenburg, Germany, in 2009. See page 38 in the present volume.
37 At the time, Schütte was loosely associated with a group of young local artists commonly referred to as the Düsseldorfer Modellbauer (Düsseldorf Model Makers), all of whom valued models "for the epistemological effects issued by miniaturization and scalar play, for their relation to architecture as a signifier of the social and public realm, and for their association with the private, memory, interiority, and the mind, all at the same time." Stefan Vervoort, *Models Beyond Sculpture: Architectural Objects in the Visual Arts in New York and Düsseldorf, 1966–1984* (Ghent: Universiteit Gent, Faculteit Letteren en Wijsbegeerte, 2020), 92. The "model makers" comprised artists like Ludger Gerdes, Harald Klingelhöller, and Reinhard Mucha as well as—or at least in close proximity to—Katharina Fritsch, Tony Cragg, Hubert Kiecol, Hermann Pitz, and Martin Kippenberger. Artist Isa Genzken, who had been a student at the Kunstakadamie Düsseldorf from 1973 to 1977 and soon thereafter started to devise architectural models in the development of her own post-Minimalist sculptural syntax of fragments, ruins, and shelters, was arguably informed by Schütte's work. See my *Isa Genzken: Fuck the Bauhaus*, Afterall One Work Series (Cambridge, MA: MIT Press, 2024), 37–39.
38 In an alternate version (with the same title and from the same year), the stage remains empty except for a large blue curtain thrown over the wall that partly conceals the backdrop of the vacated scene.
39 Deleuze, *Francis Bacon*, 15.
40 See *Thomas Schütte: Figur*, 50–53.
41 In addition to these rather obvious art-historical references from the history of caricature, Schütte has stressed the impact of coverage on Italian television at the time of (exclusively male) politicians charged with corruption. See ibid., 53.
42 Pobocha has emphasized the indebtedness of *United Enemies* to the *theatrum mundi* of Schütte's *Mohr's Life* series (1988–99, plates 36–38), which would seem to narrate, with the help of remotely architectural elements, light fixtures, boxed or hung pieces of life-size clothing like jackets and socks, and small-scale figures, the struggles of an artist's life. See Pobocha, "Inhabitance," 48.
43 In 2012, Schütte produced monumental bronze versions of *United Enemies*, one edition of which was shown in Kensington Garden next to the Serpentine Galleries in London as part of the exhibition *Thomas Schütte: Faces and Figures*. A year later, another edition was exhibited in Central Park in New York by the Public Art Fund (pages 146–47).
44 Deleuze, *Francis Bacon*, 15.
45 On the arguably protodigital nature of the series, see also *Thomas Schütte: Figur*, 78.
46 Deleuze, *Francis Bacon*, 14.
47 For an account of Schütte's sculptural precedents, see Penelope Curtis, "Reclining Sculpture," in *Thomas Schütte: Hindsight*, 53–64.
48 Cooke, "Turning the Tables," 29. Schütte's *Frauen* were first documented in *Thomas Schütte: Scenewright—Gloria in Memoria—In Medias Res*, ed. Lynne Cooke and Karen Kelly (New York: Dia Art Foundation, 2002).
49 See *Thomas Schütte: Figur*, 96.
50 See Linda Walther, *Schwebezustände: "Frauen" von Thomas Schütte* (Berlin: De Gruyter, 2020), 28–30.
51 Deleuze, *Francis Bacon*, 19.

The Train at the End of the Tunnel

MARLENE DUMAS

Art takes time. Endless back-and-forth wanderings through buildings, bungalows, basements, hotels, houses, homes, and graveyards literal and psychic.

In prison, people do time. Trying to find escape routes or places to stay.

Thomas Schütte and I are almost the same (biological) age. The same generation, so to speak. Often invited to participate in the same (thematic) group shows in the 1990s. It took various journeys through the years for me to appreciate his art.

October 1987 was the first time I saw his work in person, at Museum Overholland in Amsterdam. A solo show: *Aquarellen*. I did not know what to do with it. Here was a young, serious, German artist making sweet, colorful pictures of fruit. The black lemon was something I could understand, but pleasant slices of watermelons and potatoes? No.

Being familiar with the figurative drawings of the Italians of the Transavanguardia, like Francesco Clemente (shown at the Stedelijk Museum in Amsterdam in 1980), did not help me understand Schütte's aquarellen any better; instead, they put me on the wrong track. The Italians clearly wanted to seduce viewers with their elegance and charm. Thomas did not. Or did he? Perhaps he was like a child pulling a yellow daisy apart around its small dark heart, petal by petal, saying, "Love me, love me not."

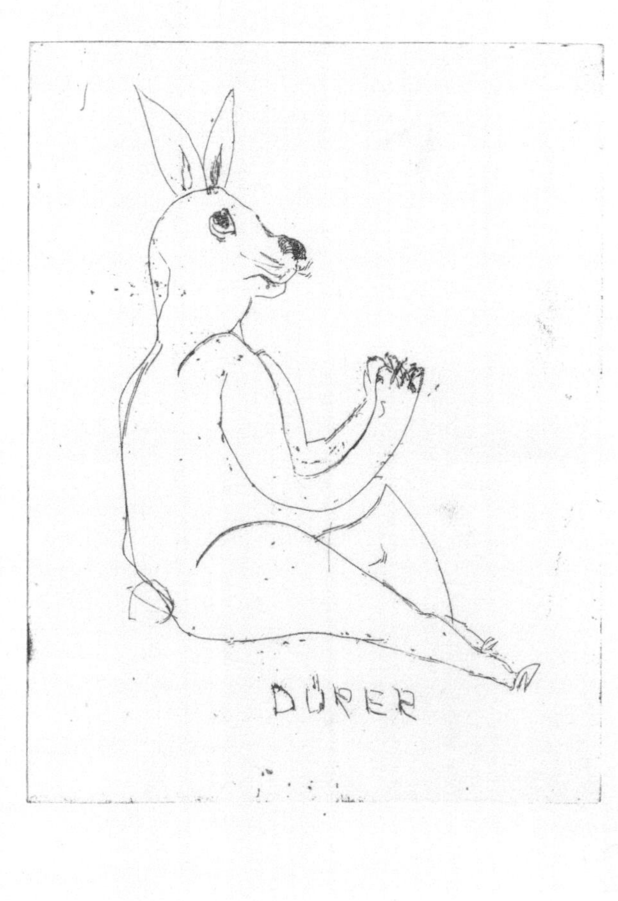

Fig. 1. Exhibition invitation for *Thomas Schütte: Dürer*, Galerie Nelson, Paris, September 21–November 8, 2002. Pictured: *Quengelware Nr. 40* from *Quengelware*. 2002. Etching on paper, one of 104 sheets, each 23 × 17" (58.4 × 43.2 cm)

In 1990, he had an exhibition titled *Jokes*. But Thomas does not want to make you laugh too loud.

Looking now at the invitation card for his show *Dürer* (at Galerie Nelson in Paris in 2002), so many years later, I smile with delight. Delicately etched lines forming a hare sit upright with the word *Dürer* below (fig. 1). The image is so simple in its linearity, yet it offers a pool of associations to drown in. There are the memories of Joseph Beuys performing *How to Explain Pictures to a Dead Hare* (1965). There is Dürer's *Hase* (1502), whose posture reminds me of the prints of Dürer's *Praying Hands* (1508) that were found in all the places with the wrong political views—and the power—in the South Africa I grew up in. There is Thomas Schütte himself, steeped in history of all kinds.

In December 1987, we were both in the group show called *Nachtvuur* (*Nightfire*) at De Appel, Amsterdam. Thomas showed three drawings titled *Weinende Frauen* (*Weeping Women*).

The first time I met Thomas Schütte was in 1991 in Kassel.

The Belgian Jan Hoet (1936–2014) had arranged a meeting with a group of artists to talk about their participation in Documenta 9, of which he was the director.

Looking back on these discussions, Hoet said that Thomas was the most difficult of those assembled, almost at times like a psychiatric case. In approaching his contribution, Thomas started not with the concept of the show, nor with the choice of artists, but rather with the building, as he said to Jan Hoet: "You have to understand that Documenta is a building. What is most important about a building? The entrance door. If you don't know what you want to do with the entrance, you should not want to make Documenta!"[1]

Hoet understood Schütte and appreciated him dearly. He felt that, like most of his favorite artists in the show, Schütte started with his own pathology and from there captured the melancholy of the whole universe. And like all good art, his work is more than mere sentiment. It is a complex embodiment of contradictions.

Thomas had his doubts and criticisms about the workings of these much-too-large art shows, but he did participate. In 1992, at Documenta 9, Thomas Schütte installed his now-famous forlorn-looking group of brightly colored ceramic figures *Die Fremden* (*The Strangers*, pages 138–39) above the entrance of the neoclassical former Rotes Palais building on the Friedrichsplatz. It set the tone for the whole exhibition, as if the fugitive or lost peoples of the world displaced the gods that once ruled here.

In 1996, Thomas and I met again, this time in the United States because of a group show called *Distemper: Dissonant Themes in the Art of the 1990s* at the Hirshhorn Museum in Washington. The American politics of the day were very present. Mike Kelley and Thomas eventually engaged in a lively late-night bar discussion on public sculpture. Kelley said it could not or should not be done anymore; Schütte disagreed. Unfortunately, due to too much drinking, I can't remember how the argument ended, but I believe it went unresolved.

It is worth noting, though, that in the year before he died, Kelley created *Mobile Homestead*, a near-exact replica of his childhood home in Detroit that was his first, last, and only public-art project.

Back to Washington, now in daytime, where Thomas answered some questions about his drawings from Rudolf Evenhuis, who was shooting a video.

Thomas: "If I draw, I draw much more traditional. Not from photos. I tried it with real people, which is very difficult."

Q: "Marlene told me once you had a discussion about working with water paint, aquarelle, that it's so nice and easy."

Thomas: "Yes, we used to work like the same, like making twenty, thirty drawings a day like a photocopy machine. But I stopped it. As soon as it gets successful you have to stop.

"I was painting this year, I was drawing a woman, and I draw her so much that I got emotional problems. We got too near and then we had to stop it."

Q: "She was a model?"

Thomas: "No, she was an artist, and I used her as a model. I was drawing her [pause] . . . and if you draw something carefully, you fall in love and then you get unhappy because you are married with somebody else. [Laughter.]"

Q: "Maybe that is why Marlene never uses models."

Thomas: "Yes, just photos to protect yourself."

Q: "Can you understand that?"

Thomas: "Yes, yes. To touch somebody with a pen, just to have the feeling that you are on the right way—that is something really interesting, very interesting. And I have to find a new way. I tried it with flowers last year. Very interesting. Very kitschy."[2]

How can I not like the work of an artist who can make fun of himself, which means also being able to embrace failure? An artist who is conceptually alert but can also lose himself working with his hands and listening to his materials?

Thomas is not alone in being a nonheroic male figurative artist.

To name just the first to come to mind, like the provocative yet vulnerable Mike Kelley, who wrote beautifully about Paul Thek, whom we must not forget in this context either, and Juan Muñoz . . . and yes, Maurizio Cattelan, who also displays that tragicomic focus, drawing on boyhood memories and fictional characters.

Note, too, that Thomas made works inspired by a Swiss writer he admired, of whom he said, "People never explore failure—except for Robert Walser who did it so wonderfully."[3] He made a sculpture called *Walser's Wife* (2011; page 23, fig. 3), depicting a spouse that the author never had.

That Thomas manages in this day and age to retain tenderness even in a heavy bronze sculpture while at the same time making sad, silly drawings must mean that he has something else that most of us have lost: innocence.

And never forget the humor.

Thomas: "I don't see light at the end of the tunnel.

"Well, I see some light, but it could be a train coming."

He laughs.[4]

---

1 Thomas Schütte, quoted in interview with Jan Hoet by Hans den Hartog Jager in his monograph *Jan Hoet* (Veurnes, Belgium: Hannibal, 2013), 87–89. Translation by the author.

2 Rudolf Evenhuis, "Thomas Schütte on Drawing, Photographs and Models," video shot at the Hirshhorn Museum and Sculpture Garden, Washington, DC, 1996. Courtesy Studio Dumas.

3 Thomas Schütte, quoted in Jackie Wullschlager, "Thomas Schütte: Faces and Figures, Serpentine Gallery, London," *Financial Times*, October 16, 2012.

4 Adrian Searle interviewed Thomas Schütte about *Model for a Hotel* (2007), his glass sculpture on Trafalgar Square in London, in "It Is Like a Jewel," *Guardian*, November 8, 2007.

Art Is a Capital Letter

JENNIFER L. ALLEN

Beginning in 1982, Thomas Schütte developed a series of artworks, each featuring a small figurine up to its knees in a large pool of some substance clearly unfriendly to forward motion. The *Mann im Matsch* (*Man in Mud*) works foregrounded the experience of being stuck, of going nowhere fast, a motif that lends itself to straightforward interpretations: most look unfavorably on encounters with impediments. And to read the representation of impediment as criticism would have made particular sense in the West Germany of the 1980s. The economy reeled from an oil crisis. Society reeled from confrontations with terrorism. The environmental movement gestured at a natural world in peril. And a new conservatism under the recently elected Chancellor Helmut Kohl seemed to stifle opportunities for expressions of difference. After the great hopes of the 1960s had been dashed, the 1970s and 1980s had yet to articulate compelling alternatives. The Federal Republic might well have seemed stuck.

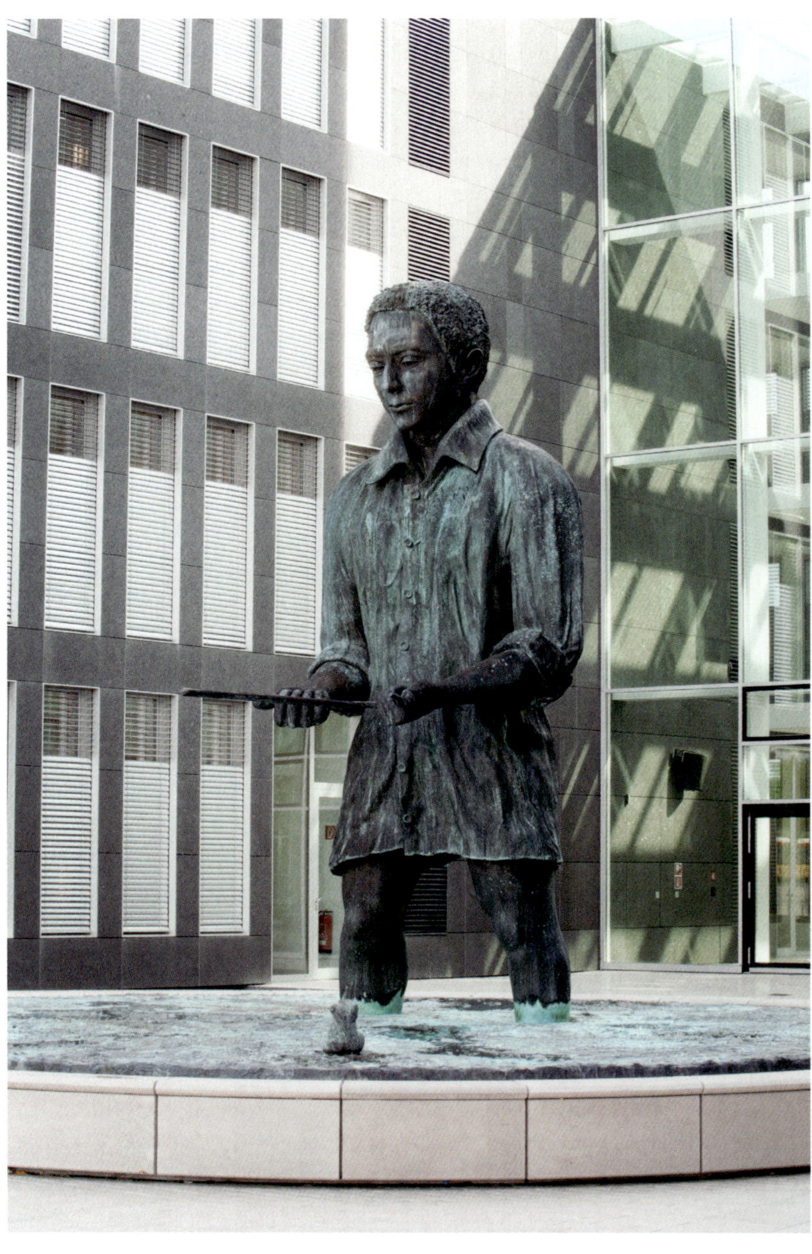

Fig. 1. Thomas Schütte. *Mann im Matsch—Der Suchende* (*Man in Mud—The Seeker*). 2009. Patinated bronze, 18' 4 ½" × 27' 10 ⅝" × 27' 10 ⅝" (560 × 850 × 850 cm). Landessparkasse zu Oldenburg, Germany

But Schütte's work demands we proceed with caution. As generations of German philosophers have been keen to remind us, obstacles can offer their own kind of liberation. We only truly come to understand the hammer once it has broken and no longer functions as it should, Martin Heidegger argued in 1927. And it is not, in fact, the victors who write history, Reinhart Koselleck contended, but instead the vanquished, who, in confronting their own failure, must creatively reconceptualize their master narrative.[1] Schütte, too, challenges us to recognize the many, sometimes contradictory meanings of being stuck. The concept speaks not only to an impasse; it also represents a state of potential, being on the way, rather than a preoccupation with the destination. In 2009, Schütte made this productive tension more explicit in a piece that monumentalized, immortalized, even celebrated the man in the mud (fig. 1). Here, in the plaza of an Oldenburg bank, a man stands knee deep in sludge. Every other feature of the piece, however, resists a pessimistic reading. At nearly six meters tall, the bronze figure's thick arms and broad shoulders suggest he would be up to the task of making his way forward. His downcast eyes and peaceful expression indicate concentration, not panic or defeat. That he holds a divining rod implies the optimism of a search for something. So, too, the work's title: *Mann im Matsch—Der Suchende* (*Man in Mud—The Seeker*). Whether he will find what he's after is immaterial. Instead, he urges us to approach Schütte's art with curiosity, creativity, skepticism, and the patience to view it not as punctuation at the end of a sentence but as a capital letter that starts one. Schütte's sensibility for art that exists more as solicitation than proclamation has led to a body of work that speaks powerfully to the political, social, cultural, and economic developments of the past five decades.

1: INTERSTICES

Skizzen zum Projekt Großes Theater (*Sketches for the Large Theater Project*, 1980) / *Alles in Ordnung* (*All in Order*, 1978)

Everything's OK. All's well. *Alles in Ordnung*. This casual expression is used to reassure, a kind of declarative exhale. On the surface, it seemed to fit the postwar West German context into which Thomas Schütte was socialized. Born in the city of Oldenburg in 1954, Schütte grew up in a Germany flourishing. The Allies had long since driven the final nail into the coffin of Nazism. The West German economy was riding the wave of the "economic miracle" brought about by Marshall Plan funding and the irresistible invasion of American consumer culture. Outside a Cold War raged, but inside West Germans sipped Coca-Cola, smoked Marlboros, and listened to Elvis. Even when youth activists took to the streets in the 1960s to protest nearly every facet of German life, a strong current of optimism about the possibilities the future held ran through their demonstrations. Viewing the situation at the right angle and in the right light, one could easily have declared *alles in Ordnung*.

By the late 1970s, however, when Schütte used this phrase in his art, its reassurance had become less convincing. West Germany's economy had tanked after the oil crises in 1973 and 1979. And while the politics of détente had begun to dial down the contrast in the Cold War's Manichaean international diplomacy, growing anxieties about domestic radicalism reproduced this climate of suspicion closer to home. It was a moment, in other words, in which one could at best declare that everything was "in order," *in Ordnung*, with a smirk and a dash of irony. It was only amid this uncertainty—amid the need to turn up the end of the sentence so that one queried whether everything was OK rather than proclaimed it—that Schütte's oeuvre could emerge.

Though he never directly thematized German division in his work and the Cold War appeared in it only implicitly, perhaps it was the experience of inhabiting a binary world that led Schütte to seek out blurred lines instead. Or perhaps it was his membership in a kind of liminal generation. Of those who came of age in the 1970s, Schütte explained, "Our generation falls precisely into the gap between the hippies and the punks. We weren't naïve enough to improve the world, and we weren't destructive enough to reduce everything to rubble."[2] Perhaps his generational in-betweenness led him to seek out interstices elsewhere. Schütte's work has nearly always played in some way with tensions: cautious nostalgic citations but also a strong forward orientation that foregrounds concepts like hope and the future; a skepticism toward political critique but also an inability to escape it; an acknowledgment of the weight of Germany's past but also a sense of humor; one hand on established art forms and the other reaching for new expressions.

Probing the limits of the claim that everything was alright—the moments in which it held and those in which it didn't—became a central motif in Schütte's early work. In 1977, a wave of terrorism that included the murders of several public figures by the militant leftists of the Red Army Faction and the hijacking of a commercial jetliner gripped the Federal Republic. On the heels of this chaos, in 1978, Schütte painted the phrase *Alles in Ordnung* on the wall above the bed in a friend's apartment like a wry wish for sweet dreams (page 8, fig. 1). But context mattered. With West Germany having quickly snuffed out terrorism's flame, the context for interpreting the phrase flattened, inadvertently permitting a simple, literal reading. When Schütte incorporated it into an image in his photographic series *Skizzen zum Projekt Großes Theater* (*Sketches for the Large Theater Project*, 1980; plate 13) a few years later, he built into the work itself an occasion to read the expression with nuance. Though the series surrounded the phrase with a buffer of optimism—companion images featured the words *Freiheit* (freedom), *Zukunft* (future), *Hoffnung* (hope), and *Frieden* (peace)—Schütte began the piece on high alert: the first image read *Achtung* (warning). In another, he clarified why we should be on the lookout: *Etwas fehlt* (something's missing). The idea that everything could be in order was at least a distraction if not a mirage. He tasked his audience with watching out for the missing pieces.

A year later, Schütte immortalized this skepticism in his first permanent work in public space. In 1981, he adorned the ceiling of Walther König's postcard shop in Cologne with the same phrase: *Alles in Ordnung* (plate 16). Its lilting white script suggested levity. But Schütte tempered this uplift with an accompanying series of fighter-jet silhouettes (pages 88–89). Contrails formed the looping white text, whose existence could, thus, at most be fleeting. But what exactly was impermanent? The presence of jets suggesting violence and war unsettled any reassurance one might derive from the insistence that all was well. But might causes for cynicism be just as impermanent? The onset of the administrations of Reagan, Thatcher, and, soon, Kohl implied, at least for some, modest optimism of the sort allowed by new political trajectories. For those inclined toward dissatisfaction with this new conservative turn, the Vietnam War had at least come to an end when Schütte created *Alles in Ordnung*.

The force of Schütte's experiments with the phrase *Alles in Ordnung* rests in these ambiguities. Riffing on the 1972 French film *Tout va bien*—including by appropriating the German translation of its title—in which directors Jean-Luc Godard and Jean-Pierre Gorin explored the texture of the world after the upheavals of 1968, Schütte's pieces tested the expression's strength a decade later.[3] Shaped by the burdens of Nazism but also by the dreams and defeat of the '68ers, Schütte's generation had settled into the pragmatism that followed the discrediting of grand utopias.[4] But it was not a despairing pragmatism, nor even a resigned pragmatism. The artist approached pragmatism with playfulness. He explained his work as a form of mimicry, the creation of simulacra. It was designed "not to shock people, but to express an idea of permanence and an ambition for a better life. Beauty was a subject, too." Here, Schütte deliberately set himself apart from his artistic forebears. "I think more ironically than the older generation do," he explained. "They really could believe in themselves." Schütte's position in a generational interstice had not led him to foreclose all hope, though: "I'm not thinking about the history," he clarified. "I'm thinking about the future." For Schütte's generation, this future, however, was no longer one of grand plans. "Utopia means a goal, and in our times," he clarified, "the path is the goal."[5]

For Schütte, the process of creating art yielded a space of experimentation, a means to test out new ideas or to practice new ethics. Even the final artwork refused to foreclose new possibilities. The dialogue, debate, or disagreement it generated with its viewing public made the art object essentially dynamic. This permanent state of becoming meant that the piece that hangs in the gallery or stands in the public square—in what art historian James Meyer has referred to as the artwork's "literal site"—mattered less than the ongoing process of constituting the work's meaning discursively.[6] In fact, Schütte saw art as "the only place where [one] can do work this way."[7]

2: MODELS
Ringe (*Rings*, 1977) / *Modell für ein Museum* (*Model for a Museum*, 1982)

The postwar process of transforming Germany from foe to friend unfolded with remarkable speed. Still three months away from the Second World War's conclusion in the European theater, the Allies had already begun to plan for the postwar occupation of Germany. And when the bifurcation of international geopolitics prompted a choosing of sides soon thereafter, occupation zones became blueprints for states. The Federal Republic of Germany (FRG, or West Germany) materialized first, officially founded in May 1949. The German Democratic Republic (GDR, or East Germany) made its way onto the map in October of the same year.

The project of building the Federal Republic was a peculiar one that demanded, on one hand, taking into account Germany's weighty past and, on the other, building a new state in some sense from scratch. Constructing a future that led away from authoritarianism into the arms of liberal democracy and capitalism involved the rapid integration of the FRG into the West. It accumulated memberships in a veritable alphabet soup of Western alliances, beginning in 1949, when West Germany joined the OEEC (Organization for European Economic Cooperation). In 1951, it joined the ECSC (European Coal and Steel Community); in 1955, NATO (North Atlantic Treaty Organization); and in 1957, the EEC (European Economic Community).[8]

Schütte's artistic trajectory in many ways reflects this same Western integration, with his works appearing over the course of his career in, among other places, Chicago, New York, Venice, London, Madrid, Antwerp, and Turin. By the last quarter of the century, which coincided with the start of Schütte's career, the Federal Republic was clearly no longer the empire of Hitler or even of Bismarck as it shook off the last remnants of its status as a provisional state and reentered the arena of continental and, eventually, global democratic power brokers. It had become what many dubbed Modell Deutschland (Model Germany).[9] But "model" in what capacity? A model stands, in one sense, as a thing to display. It might also be a thing to copy. Schütte, for whom the concept of the model became a muse and who might offer a rubric for analyzing the meaning of Germany as model, has treated the model in a third sense, however—as a proposal, a thing to experiment with, to amend. Schütte uses models not because they offer prescriptions but because they necessitate openness; they present one possible path forward but leave room for new diversions.

Experimentation requires flexibility, a quality that Schütte made a prominent feature of many of his early works (though, as he himself has admitted, it was often on account of his own impatience or boredom as much it was an intentional aesthetic choice). In *Ringe* (*Rings*, 1977; pages 26–27, figs. 1–2), hundreds of wooden rings—10.5 cm (4 ⅛ inches) in diameter, in a variety of colors—hung from the walls on tiny nails. What appeared to be an installation at measured intervals was, in fact, ever so slightly irregular. The artwork resisted issuing authoritarian imperatives for its display. It could be reassembled on different walls or in different arrangements, as in 1990, for example, when it was displayed at the Van Abbemuseum in Eindhoven, the Netherlands. It could be recreated with different materials, as in 1981 (and again in 2007 and 2022) when Schütte crafted *Goldene Ringe* (*Golden Rings*, plate 17) by sticking rings of barely there adhesive foil to the walls; the work's force relied on the light sources of the spaces in which it was installed. Or in 2004, when Schütte installed rings made varyingly of ceramic and platinum along the balcony of the RWE Pavillon of the Philharmonie in Essen.

Schütte created *Ringe* at a moment in which artists were launching a major reconsideration of the boundaries of the spaces in which art belonged and what it could do there. The nature of abstract art and its relationship to more mundane forms of design emerged as one facet of this conversation that preoccupied the young artist. What was *Ringe*, after all, if not a kind of wallpaper? Wallpaper—mass-produced art for display in our quotidian, often intimate spaces—served as an organizing principle in other of Schütte's early works, like *Rote Girlande* (*Red Garland*, 1979; page 82), *Schwarze Girlande* (*Black Garland*, 1980; plate 14), and *Sortiment* (*Assortment*, 1978). All three featured simple monochrome friezes: easily produced, essentially portable, and flexible enough to install in a wide range of possible locations from the public to the private. In fact, Schütte took advantage of that flexibility when he reconfigured *Sortiment* into *Lager* (*Storage*, 1980; plate 9) by leaning its component panels against the wall rather than attaching them to it.

Schütte's openness to displaying his art in mundane, personal, and otherwise unconventional spaces, such as a friend's bedroom wall and the ceiling of a postcard shop, drew momentum from a moment in which the gallery space had come under strong fire. Artists took aim at the authoritarian demands of what the Irish art critic Brian O'Doherty famously critiqued in 1976 as the "white cube." The gallery creates aesthetic sterility. It strictly regulates who or what may make contact with its spaces: objects, visitors, even light and sound. The museum's only context is itself.[10] Schütte participated in this anti-institutionalism when he conspicuously mobilized the form of the model in his 1982 work *Modell für ein Museum* (*Model for a Museum*, plate 20). Smokestacks and large furnaces glowing red—which, by the 1980s, could hardly escape associations with the violence of the death camps—revealed that the museum was a place where art goes to die. Or perhaps Schütte wanted viewers to think of factories, whose assembly lines churn out identical products. In this reading, the museum reinforces aesthetic standardization rather than encouraging innovation, becoming a place that throttles originality.

If Schütte understood models as offering just one rendering of a proposed solution to a problem that cleared the way for a range of possible future applications, *Modell für ein Museum* hardly indicated what form any final solution might take. (It should go without saying that gesturing at any kind of final solution—lowercase or otherwise—would also have been conspicuously problematic for a postwar German artist; that impulse has remained anathema in Schütte's oeuvre.) We might, however, consider the implications of another model. In 1987, Schütte drew inspiration from a frustration with the limited number of concession stands available at the international art exhibition Documenta in Kassel: "They all felt they were too posh to feed half a million people," Schütte charged. "Sausage stands just got in the way."[11] If food got in the way of the museum, and the museum got in the way of art, the resolution seemed to demand that art itself offer something to eat. *Eis* (*Ice Cream*, 1987; figs. 2–3) was born of this inference. The temporary pavilion, located in front of the Orangerie in Karlsaue Park, satisfied these needs by selling ice cream and coffee while transplanting the artwork beyond the museum's walls and mostly out of reach of its imperatives. With *Eis*, Schütte's use of the model changed qualitatively. No longer simply an experiment in miniature, a piece that began as a series of sketches and models (the first of which was an upside-down paint bucket) transformed a fantasy into a real structure performing consequential functions in the world. *Eis* took seriously its efforts to critique both the museum and the artwork without taking itself too seriously. In a sober and earnest country where making art could rarely just involve making art, Schütte's models often emphasize the benefits of lightening up just a bit.

3: RESPONSIBILITIES

Wo ist Hitlers Grab? (*Where Is Hitler's Grave?*, 1991) / *Die Fremden* (*The Strangers*, 1992)

If Schütte understood himself as a member of an uneasily liminal generation, caught between the main acts, so to speak, he nevertheless witnessed one of the most important transformations of the German state in its modern history: in November 1989, he saw the Berlin Wall open, an event followed less than a year thereafter by

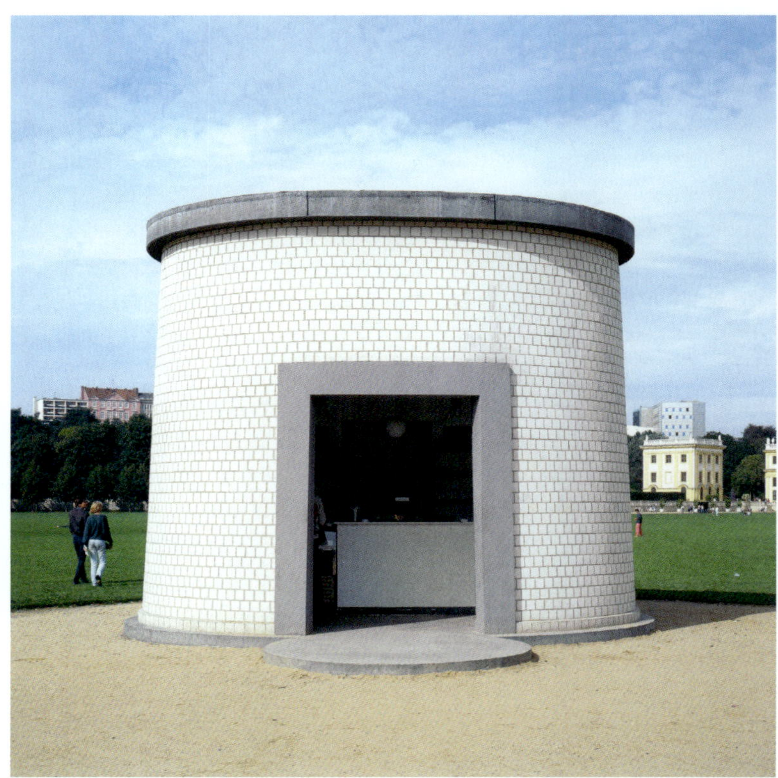

Fig. 2. Thomas Schütte. *Eis* (*Ice Cream*). 1987. Brick, mortar, and concrete, 12' 1 5/8" × 16' 4 7/8" × 21' 7 7/8" (370 × 500 × 660 cm). Exterior view, Documenta 8, Kassel, June 12–September 20, 1987

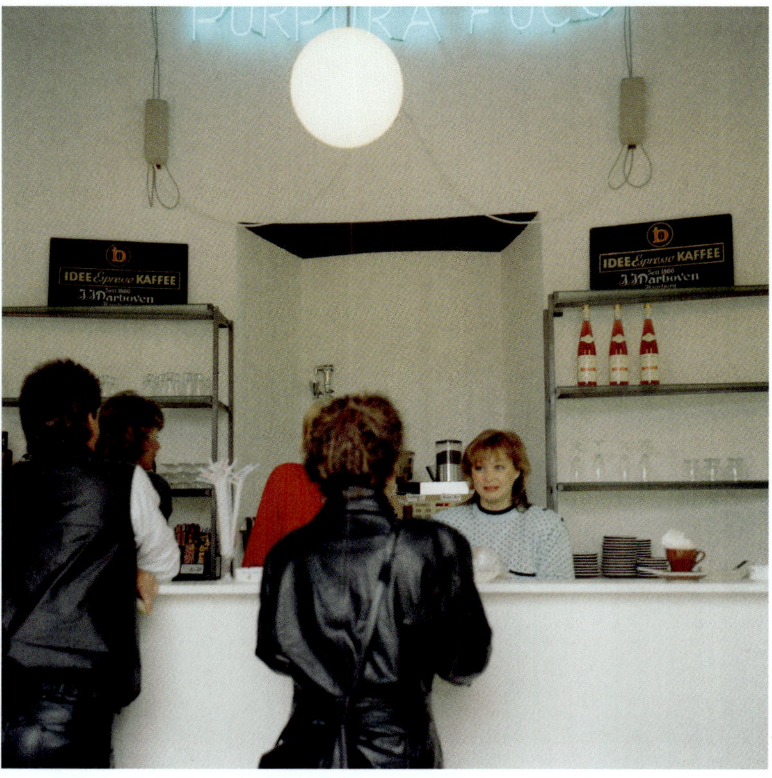

Fig. 3. Interior view of *Eis*

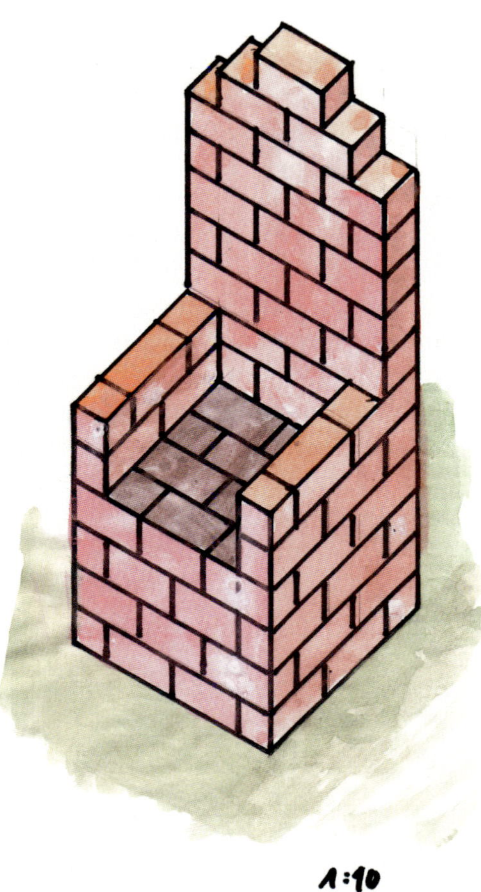

Fig. 4. Thomas Schütte. Drawing for *Tisch* (*Table*). 1984. Watercolor, felt-tipped pen, and pencil on paper, 11 11⁄16 × 8 1⁄4" (29.7 × 21 cm). Collection the artist, Düsseldorf

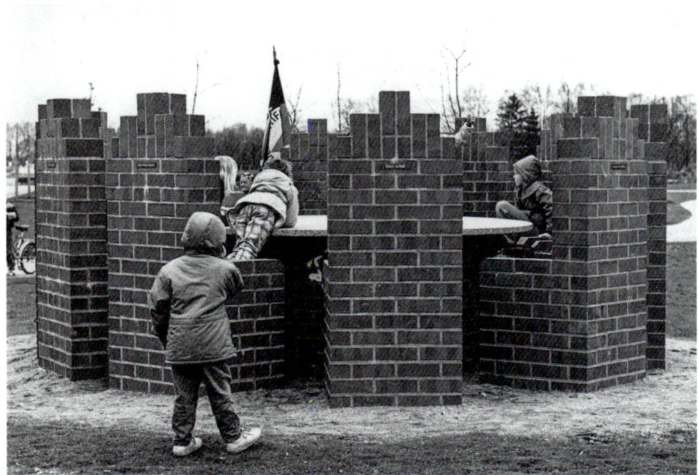

Fig. 5. Thomas Schütte. *Tisch*. 1985. Bricks, marble, and brass, 5' 3" × 16' 4 7⁄8" × 22' 11 5⁄8" (160 × 500 × 700 cm). Commissioned by the Kulturbehörde Hamburg, permanently installed in Niendorf-Nord, Hamburg, Germany. Installation view, c. 1987

German reunification, in October 1990. One might have expected that the ambiguous nature of the intervening ten months would have appealed to an artist with an affinity for the indefinite. And one could certainly find a resonance with Schütte's longstanding interest in walls, which stretched back to his years studying at the Kunstakademie Düsseldorf. *Große Mauer* (*Large Wall*, 1977; plate 7) and *Grüne Kacheln* (*Green Tiles*, 1980), for example, consisted of small, individually painted panels propped up on nails against a wall and arranged to resemble a brick wall. The illusion of the wall as artwork suggested the impermanence of walls as physical objects. These links aside, however, the watershed events of 1989–90 figured relatively minimally in Schütte's work, as was the case with many artists and intellectuals of his generation. One group of works seemed explicitly to point to the unease of this moment: *United Enemies* (1993–94, plates 43–48), which paired mixed-media figures with strained expressions and tied them together under bell jars. The idea that the pairs might represent East and West forced back together seems self-evident. For his part, however, whether in earnest or out of a passion for provocation, Schütte dismissed the association. "Somebody told me they were about the German unification," he noted several years later, "but I couldn't really follow that."[12]

Schütte opted to foreground a different set of political debates in his work at the time. The artist belonged to that group of Germans whom Chancellor Kohl, in 1984, described as enjoying the "blessing of a late birth": although their lives were deeply shaped by the Nazi period, they were too young to have participated in its violence or thus to bear direct responsibility for the regime. Though the Kohl administration took considerable strides to effect a "spiritual-moral transformation" in German society that would shore up conservative values and fashion a new, post-Nazi German identity, many Germans struggled to shed the weight of fascism's legacies so easily. Pressure to atone appropriately for Nazi brutality, to "master the past"—an unwieldy imperative captured by the equally unwieldy German term *Vergangenheitsbewältigung*—became pervasive. It shaped the firestorm that erupted around President Reagan's botched 1985 visit to a cemetery that housed Waffen-SS members. And it helped to launch an energetic dispute among leading historians and public intellectuals in West Germany's most prominent newspapers, the so-called Historians' Debate (*Historikerstreit*), around the question of whether Germany's past—meaning not simply Nazism as a subject of historical study but also Germany's ongoing self-flagellation for that moral catastrophe—was, in fact, "a past that would not pass."[13]

From the 1980s through the turn of the millennium, the Federal Republic witnessed the onset of what historian Jay Winter has called a "memory boom," during which artists and scholars alike began to explore what forms a more effective commemoration of the Nazi past might take.[14] They experimented with uncovering traces, honoring social voids, and resisting traditional commemorative forms via what came to be called countermonuments.[15] Schütte was not terribly inclined toward generosity to many of these efforts. Reflecting on an invitation he received to help shape a commemoration for the fiftieth anniversary of the end of the Second World War at the site of the former Neuengamme concentration camp near Hamburg, he grumbled about "people who had done nothing for the past fifty years suddenly [deciding] to do something."[16]

Schütte himself participated in the mid-1980s experimentation with new mnemonic forms in his permanent installation *Tisch* (*Table*,

1985; figs. 4–5), in which twelve brick chairs surround a round table in a residential area of Hamburg. In response to the local government's commission for the work, eleven chairs bear a label, each with the name of one anti-Nazi resister who was captured and killed. One seat without a name prompts guests both to honor the countless unnamed resisters—to honor the memory of those who go unremembered—and to imagine themselves into this history. Bucking many of the conventions of traditional memorials, *Tisch* invites visitors not simply to reflect upon history with distance but rather to understand themselves as sitting at the table alongside it.

Over the next few years, as Germany's engagement with Nazi history and memorialization intensified, Schütte grew frustrated: frustrated with the pressure of the responsibility to remember but also frustrated that those who left behind this legacy approached it with relative silence. In 1991, that frustration boiled over when he posed a question one dared not ask: Where is Hitler's grave? In *Wo ist Hitlers Grab?* (fig. 6), Schütte used the question as a springboard for exploring the opportunities and limits of commemorative culture. The absence of a grave eliminated a key site for neo-Nazi gatherings, but it also made for open-ended commemoration. With no burial site, Nazism's ghosts could never be put to rest; they were left to haunt. The notion of hauntings would become a central motif in Schütte's later series *Große Geister* (*Large Spirits*, 1995–2004; plate 50).

Wo ist Hitlers Grab? confronted both the incomprehensible extent of Nazi violence and the practical limits on honoring its victims. Schütte set out to document all the deaths of the Second World War, victim and perpetrator, Ally and Axis. The immensity of this task reduced the artist to a tabulator; it asked him to assume an uncomfortable stance not entirely unlike the so-called desk murderers (*Schreibtischmörder*) among the Nazis. Schütte calculated how many individuals died each hour of the war, and using a small stamp of a cross (fig. 7), he inked six tables to signify the dead. Doomed to inadequacy, the artist noted he would need some one hundred thousand tables to finish the task. What marked Schütte as a member of his generation, though, was that this aesthetic equivalent of throwing one's hands up at the impossibility of creating an adequate memorial was not an assertion of the uselessness of trying.

Even in the absence of Hitler's burial site, however, the far right seemed to do fine in rallying on its own. In the early years after reunification, Germany witnessed an explosion of agitation and violence from a resurgent far right. As the onset of the Gulf War (1990–91) sent a wave of refugees and asylum seekers into the Federal Republic, some German extremists read their presence—the conspicuous presence of difference—as an invitation to violence. They attacked foreigners and burned down their living spaces in scores of cities, such as Hoyerswerda (1991), Rostock (1991), Mannheim (1992), Mölln (1992), and Solingen (1993). Neo-Nazi ideas and practices, in other words, looked frighteningly similar to Nazi ideas and practices, and the frequency of these attacks suggested they might not be one-off imitations but rather an ideology that was there to stay. In this context, it was not enough to excavate and remember the horrors of the past. In the imperative never to forget his country's history, Schütte also recognized the imperative to excavate the racism and xenophobia of the present.

Schütte staged his own reckoning with this violence in the city of Kassel in 1992. The colorful, stylized, life-size ceramic figures he installed on the portico of a department store clearly represented people on the move (pages 138–39). Like the refugees and asylum seekers who had made their way into West Germany, the figures, three of which remain in place today, invite questions: Are they

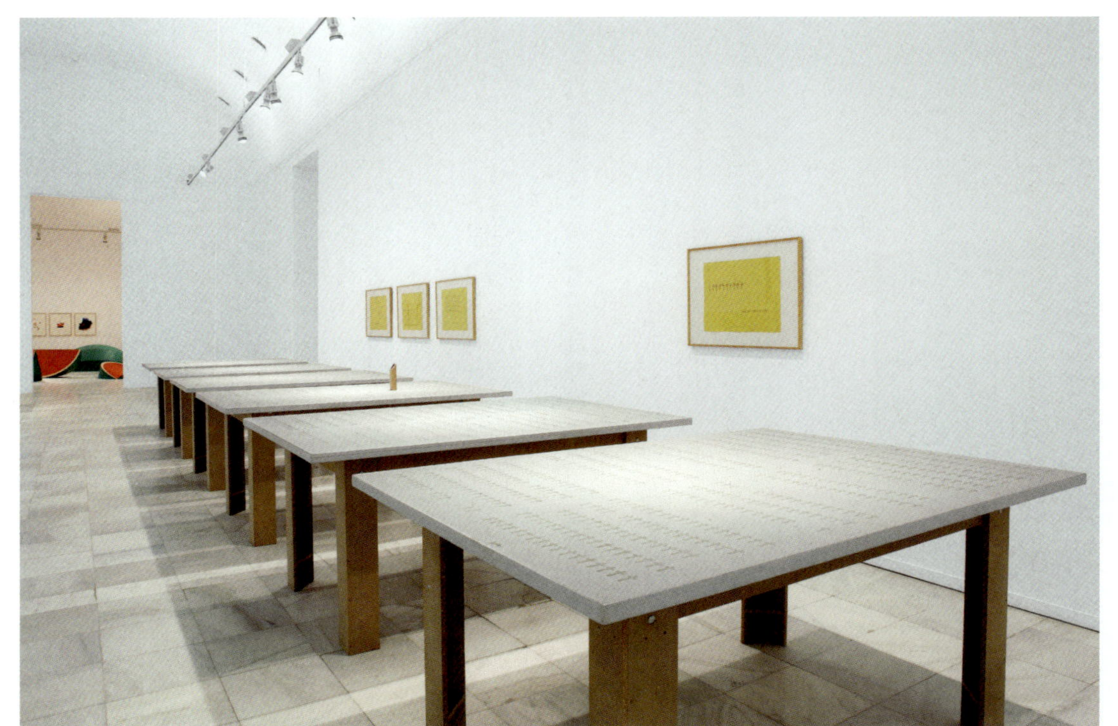

Fig. 6. Thomas Schütte. *Wo ist Hitlers Grab?* (*Where Is Hitler's Grave?*). 1991. Paint on wood, six parts, and ink on paper, four sheets; each table 59 1/16 × 78 3/4 × 39 3/8" (150 × 200 × 100 cm), each sheet 19 11/16 × 27 9/16" (50 × 70 cm). Sprengel Museum, Hannover, Germany. Sammlung Niedersächsische Sparkassenstiftung. Installation view, *Thomas Schütte: Hindsight*, Museo Nacional Centro de Arte Reina Sofía, Madrid, February 17–May 17, 2010

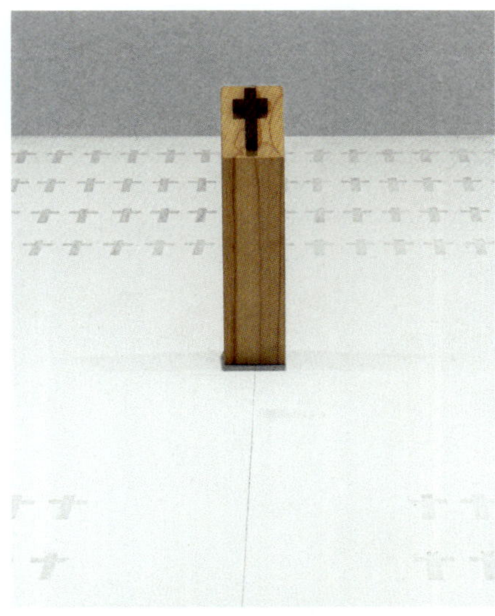

Fig. 7. Detail of *Wo ist Hitlers Grab?*

coming to stay or just passing through? What's in the boxes and bags they carry? Are they bringing things or taking things away? Are they like us, or are they different? As they look out over the plaza in front of the Fridericianum—one of Germany's most historic museums—the figures witness the thousands of visitors to Documenta as they ponder answers to these questions at a distance. Schütte was careful to highlight, however, that it was really the media that formalized the piece's meaning, even its name. *Die Fremden* appeared frequently in the press, where it was read as a commentary on the politics of migration.[17] If one could speak of a New Germany after reunification, contending with its own unique expressions of alterity and exclusion became an urgent responsibility.

4: SHELTERS

Schutzraum (*Shelter,* 1986) / *Ferienhaus für Terroristen* (*Vacation Home for Terrorists,* 2009)

Over the course of his career, Schütte has made dozens of models for various types of structures. When he embarked on his first set, the *Westkunst Modelle* (*Westkunst Models*, page 31) in 1980, he intended to use them as mockups for eventual production at 1:1 scale. After failing to secure the necessary funding, however, he had to downsize his ambitions. For several years thereafter, Schütte opted to create smaller models that would exist only in and for themselves; they made no promise of a subsequent full-scale usable adaptation. Gradually, as Schütte cemented his place in the international art world, he found himself better positioned, and it became possible for him to make models not only at tabletop scale but also as full-scale structures—and to make them functional buildings as well. Consistently across these works, Schütte has aimed to create architecture with characteristically various, often ambiguous uses.

Among the earliest and most legible of these full-scale architectural pieces was *Schutzraum* (*Shelter*, 1986; plate 29), which confronted the desire for spaces of protection in Cold War Germany. The late twentieth century had served up a buffet of threats, of which a dogged past and a resurgent far right were only two courses. Just as consequential were those looming disasters that emerged amid new postwar environmental and geopolitical constellations. The formation of the German Green Party in 1980 created a new mouthpiece for those concerned about these issues. The party built a platform around more than its attempts to curtail the effects of acid rain and forest dieback. The newly vibrant environmentalist movement in the Federal Republic also took aim at the construction of nuclear power plants on German soil. Even more menacing was a rapidly accelerating nuclear arms race. Though détente between the West and the Soviet Union in the 1970s had appeared to pump the brakes on the drive toward mutually assured destruction, NATO's 1979 Double-Track Decision, which positioned hundreds of missiles in Central Europe, put any real reassurance out of reach. West Germans registered their objections in loud protest. Those disinclined to heed protesters or a new political party found it hard to ignore the physics of fusion, especially when it went awry. When the nuclear power plant on Pennsylvania's Three Mile Island experienced a partial meltdown in 1979, it set the world on edge. The catastrophic meltdown of the Soviet Union's Chernobyl nuclear plant in Ukraine in 1986 brought the crisis closer to home and into clearer focus.

Anxieties about the threat of nuclear destruction—whether through scientific misstep or as a tool of war—appeared conspicuously in several of Schütte's works of the 1980s. From 1981 to 1987,

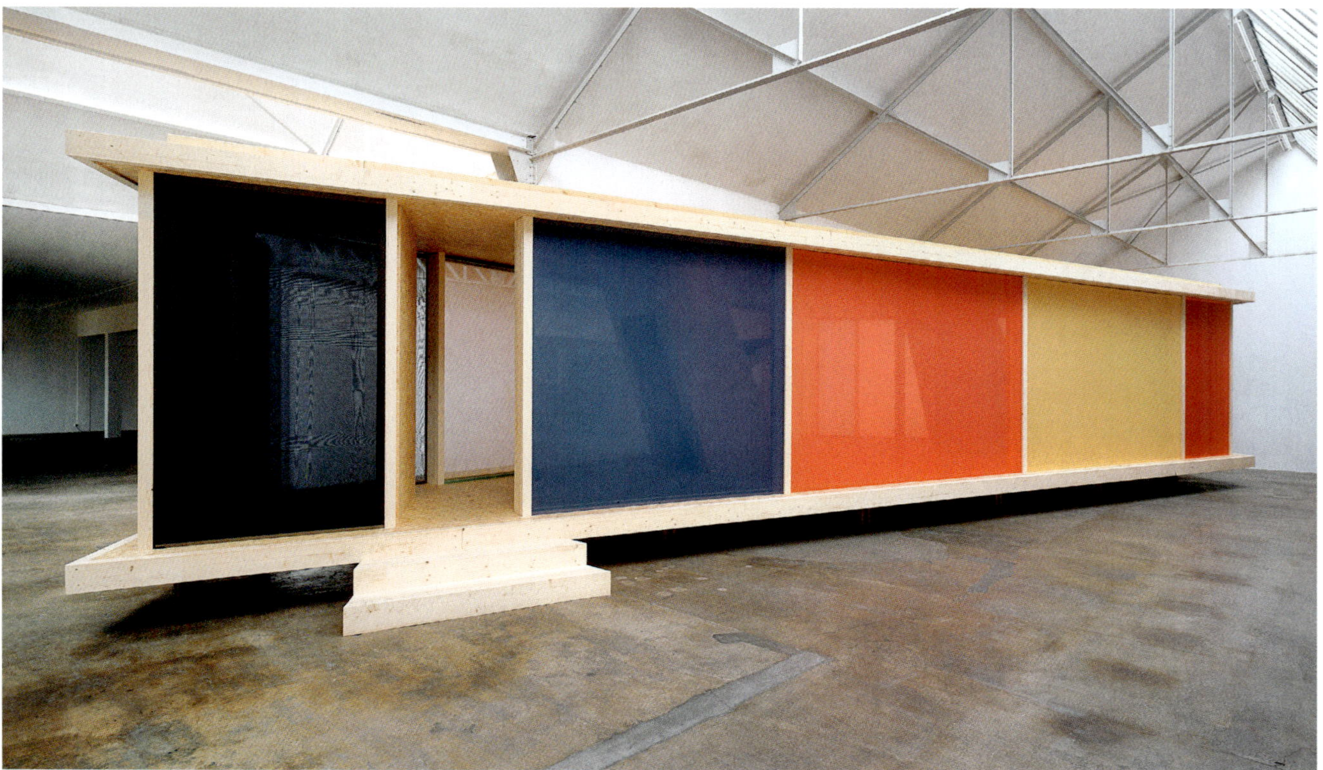

Fig. 8. Thomas Schütte. *Ferienhaus für Terroristen I (Modell 1:1)* (*Vacation Home for Terrorists I [Model 1:1]*). 2009. Wood and fabric, approx. 11' 5 13/16" × 59' 11/16" × 26' 2 15/16" (350 × 1800 × 800 cm)

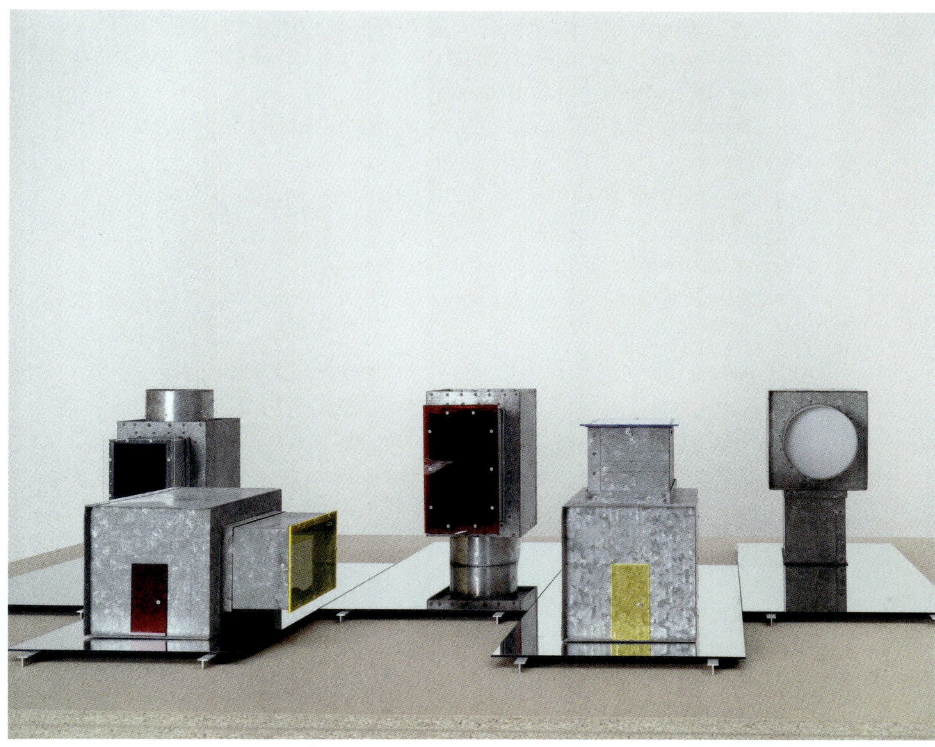

Fig. 9. Thomas Schütte. *One Man Houses*. 2003. Metal, mirrored glass, and acrylic sheeting on fiberboard pedestal, 4' 7 ⅞" × 5' 6 15⁄16" × 7' 2 ⅝" (142 × 170 × 220 cm). Collection the artist, Düsseldorf

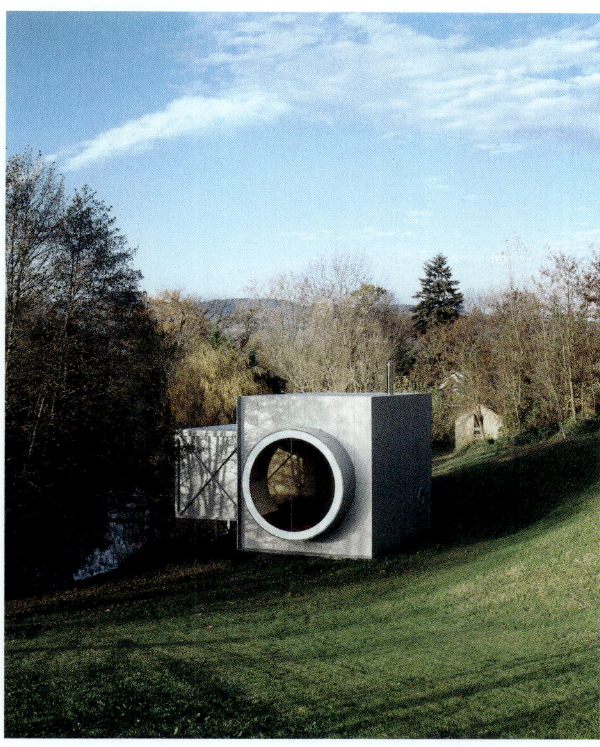

Fig. 10. Thomas Schütte. *One Man House II*. 2007–9. Steel, wood, glass, and paint, 16' 4 ⅞" × 26' 3" × 26' 3" (500 × 800 × 800 cm). Collection Marc and Anne Marie Robelin. Exterior view, Roanne, France

he produced a series of small-scale crude plaster models of bunkers. They mimicked caves and earthworks or took the form of simple geometrical structures, as much as possible stripped of the discernable architectural designs that humanity had developed to resist nature's constraints. Taking shelter from the *effects* of human intervention in the world seemed to demand a retreat from the very *forms* of human intervention. Moving away from the model, Schütte's *Schutzraum* gave him a chance to work on a 1:1 scale. (Increasing scale corresponded to the increasing proximity of nuclear catastrophe, though it remains unclear whether one can attribute this correlation to chance, intention, or more mundane factors like finances.) *Schutzraum* also allowed Schütte to play with the limits of the notion of shelter. Tucked away in a forest in Sonsbeek Park in Arnhem, in the Netherlands, a cool gray cylinder of concrete and steel seemed worthy of its name. Large enough for at least a couple of inhabitants, surely it could protect them against nuclear fallout. But, destined to offer only false hope, *Schutzraum*'s door was welded shut. Never actually inhabitable, the bunker's titular promise was a fantasy: one way or another, one would always be left out in the open. Though it is less conspicuous in the piece's final form, one of Schütte's preliminary drawings for the structure (page 114, top) underscores this point clearly: there, *Schutzraum* was shaped not as a cylinder but as an omega, the last letter of the Greek alphabet. The building itself would have signaled an ending—including all apocalyptic implications.

In subsequent decades, the theme of shelter would continue to surface in Schütte's work. As companions to pieces exploring protection for those who sought to escape disaster, he made artworks that explored the idea of refuge for those who create it—as well as the relationship between the two. Working again in the form of a model, Schütte completed *Ferienhaus für Terroristen I, II,* and *III* (*Vacation Home for Terrorists I, II*, and *III*) in 2002 against the backdrop of a world reeling from the terrorist attacks of September 11. Made of wood and pieces of clear, colorful acrylic sheeting, Schütte's designs posed a host of probing questions. Do terrorists take vacations? If they do, where do they go? Where do they sleep? How do they live (with themselves)? Seven years later, as several members of the Red Army Faction were released from prison on parole to live normal lives decades after their guerilla campaigns, Schütte created a full-scale rendering of *Ferienhaus für Terroristen* (2009, fig. 8), which led the art dealer Rafael Jablonka to commission a functional version for his personal use in the Austrian Alps. Located on the edge of a ski resort, this vacation home brought another set of questions more clearly into relief—questions that interrogated the relationship between wealth, power, and violence. Who counts as a terrorist? Who gets to make those designations? What factors determine who possesses the power to dictate the boundaries between criminal and innocent, good and evil? What began as an investment in an abstract idea of shelter, in other words, evolved into a more nuanced exploration of power and the conditions that protect it.

Not all of Schütte's studies on the meaning of sanctuary have elicited such sobering treatment. Concurrent with his explorations of refuge for criminality, for example, Schütte developed a series that plays with the idea of home itself. He began by creating small-scale models, titled *One Man Houses* (2003–5), of metal and acrylic sheeting (fig. 9). Several years later, a private commission allowed him to build *One Man House II* (2007–9, fig. 10) at full scale overlooking an idyllic estate in France. The elegant if spartan design of the interior stood in contrast to the lush landscape that the structure, like the aperture of a camera, framed for the house's imagined inhabitant. In this relatively innocuous piece, and much more so

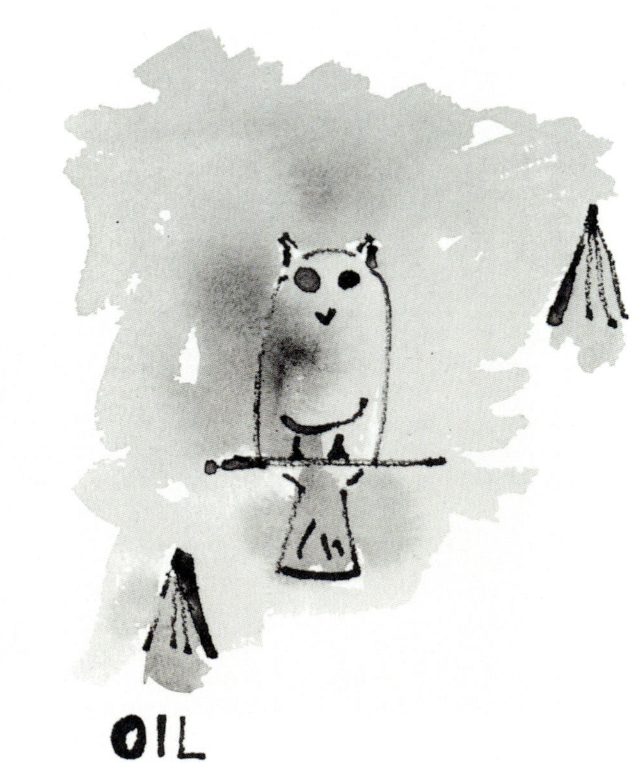

Fig. 11. Thomas Schütte. *Aufzeichnungen aus der 2. Reihe Nr. 55* (*Notes from the 2nd Row No. 55*). 1991. Ink and watercolor on paper, 10 ⅝ × 7 ⅞" (27 × 20 cm). Droege Art Collection, Germany

in *Ferienhaus für Terroristen* and *Schutzraum*, one gets the sense that Schütte wanted his audience to ask what it might mean to make oneself "at home" in a world whose military, economic, environmental, religious, and political practices often render it complicated to do so.

5: HEROICS

Aufzeichnungen aus der 2. Reihe (*Notes from the 2nd Row*, 1991) / *Wattwanderung* (*Low Tide Wandering*, 2001)

Beginning in the late 1970s, the historian Martin Broszat undertook a monumental project on a micro scale: he sought to uncover the daily life of a Bavarian mining village during the entire Nazi era. Over six volumes, Broszat attempted an act of reconstruction that would piece together mundane moments of solidarity, spontaneity, conflict, critique, and compromise. In place of histories of great men, military strategy, abstract social phenomena, or large-scale demographic shifts, Broszat's work helped to kindle in the 1980s an affinity for the history of everyday life (*Alltagsgeschichte*). But this interest in the ordinary did not confine itself to ivory-tower scholarship. Inspired by similar movements in England and Sweden, local Germans banded together to form "workshops" that would peel back the layers of the present to expose the residue of the past—initially meaning Nazism but increasingly interpreted more capaciously—that lingered even in their own communities. History was not something that happened far away and to other people; it

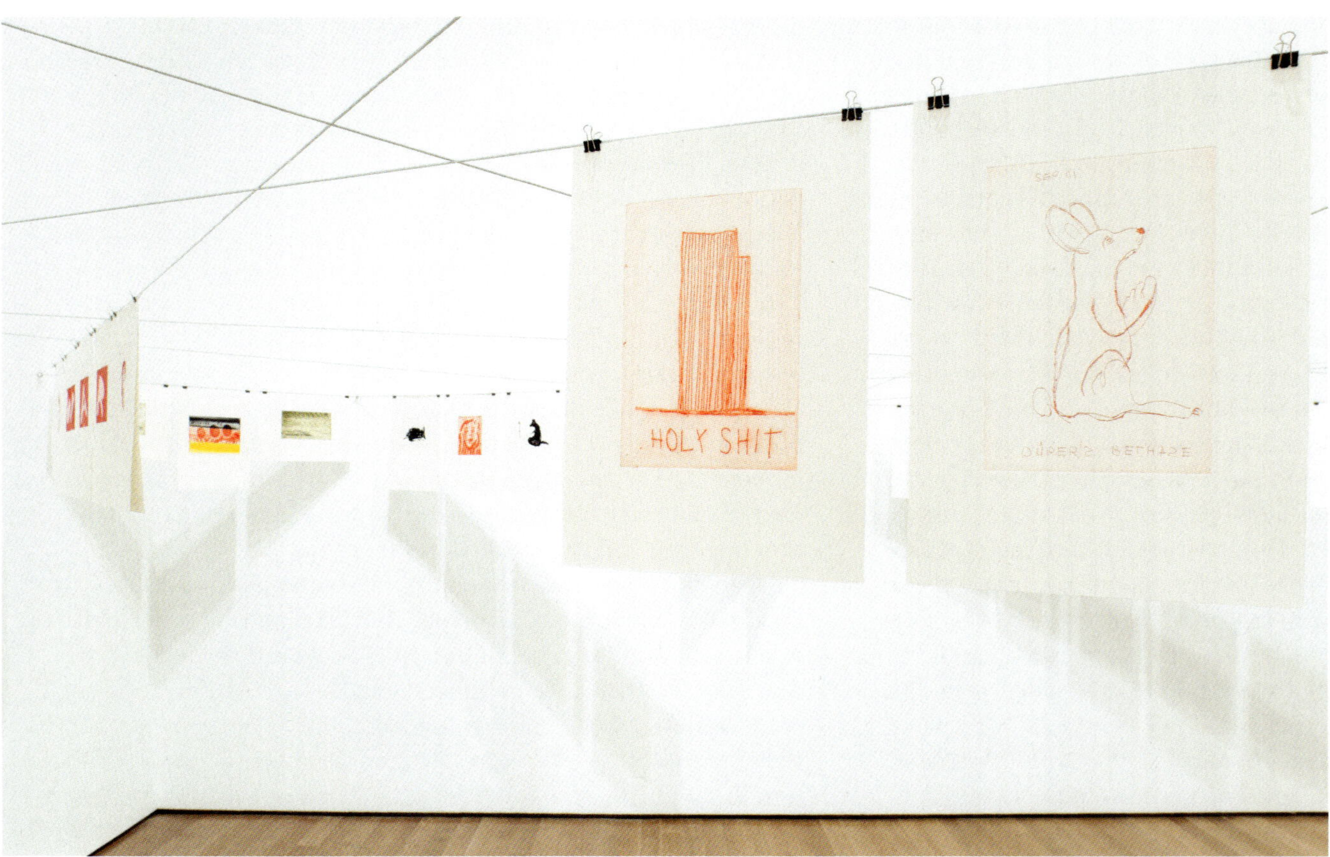

Fig. 12. Thomas Schütte. *Wattwanderung* (*Low Tide Wandering*, detail). 2001. Etching on paper, 139 sheets, each approx. 12 ¹¹⁄₁₆ × 17 ⅝" (32.2 × 44.7 cm) or 17 ⅝ × 12 ¹¹⁄₁₆" (44.7 × 32.2 cm). The Museum of Modern Art, New York. Sue and Edgar Wachenheim III Fund and Gift of the Contemporary Arts Council of The Museum of Modern Art. Installation view, *Print/Out*, The Museum of Modern Art, New York, February 19–May 14, 2012

was proximate, familiar, and personally relevant. They adopted the imperative "Dig where you stand." Suddenly everyone became a documentarian. Schütte, too. And there was much to document.

Those who watched the Federal Republic's main public-television stations, ARD and ZDF, were promised premium access to history in the making: "With us," their slogan went, "you sit in the front row." As the shocking events of the Gulf War unfolded, Schütte recognized the power of television to mediate current events, but he also saw the constraints of tidy, prepackaged presentation. "You have limited awareness of what you are confronted with on television," he explained. "It passes through the person."[18] *Aufzeichnungen aus der 2. Reihe* (*Notes from the 2nd Row*, 1991) emerged out of Schütte's discontent with the passivity television permitted of its viewers. Riffing on the television slogan, the artist gave up his front-row seat for a bit more perspective. On a daily basis, he registered the news—especially the war—in the form of a small drawing that often featured a word or phrase. Schütte's function, however, was not primarily interpretive: "I've mentioned repeatedly for some time that I'm just the seismograph," he clarified. His drawings generally bear out this stance. Some approach their themes more explicitly. The words *No*, *Rache* (vengeance), and *Ekel* (disgust) make clear his aversion to bombing, for example, as do several scatological motifs, such as two anuses (*A Holes*) or a person on a toilet (*Teilnehmer*, or "participant"). But most rest on their essential ambiguity to demand the viewer assume an interpretive stance. A drawing of an owl—wisdom, perhaps?—sits perched above the English word *oil*, a near-homonym with the German word for owl, *Eule* (fig. 11). Is this just wordplay? Is there wisdom in oil? Have we misunderstood oil's promise? In another image, four musical notes hover over the word *Nöte*, or "hardships." Are these just notes? Are they pointing to the coexistence of beauty alongside pain? Is there music in suffering, or vice versa? "By writing and reformulating things, breaking them down into diagrams," Schütte said, he took it as his task to make the news "enjoyable" (*genießbar*), perhaps even "something beautiful" (*etwas Schönes*).[19] In this regard, he joined a broad milieu of artists, intellectuals, and ordinary Germans intent on granting the value of the quotidian and resisting the impulse to offer conclusive interpretations.

A decade later, Schütte presciently reprised this project in *Wattwanderung* (*Low Tide Wandering*, 2001). Over the course of 139 etchings, Schütte's seismograph registered the rumblings of the year, as global watersheds wove in and out of the rhythms of his ordinary life: five sketches in a group labeled *Ebbe* (low tide); a series of sketches of flowers; several drawings of a mouse, one tucked between the letters of the word *Ich*, or "me"; a series of self-portraits. Nestled among these images is a rough sketch of two tall rectangles in red. In all-caps beneath them appears the phrase *Holy Shit* (fig. 12). The simplicity of Schütte's reaction to the attack on the Twin Towers reminds us of the double meaning of the profane: both obscenity and that which is not sacred. The mundane documentary impulses of *Wattwanderung* underscore Schütte's commitment to both the power and the limits of the artist. "I have no ambition to turn from the weak position of art towards the politics of the day," he emphasized, or to "take up the power of mass media in order to enhance my status."[20] As Schütte argued pointedly in a 1998 interview, the artist is not heroic.[21]

---

1 See Martin Heidegger, *Being and Time*, trans. John Macquarrie and Edward Robinson (Oxford: Blackwell, 1962), 102–4; and Reinhart Koselleck, "Transformations of Experience and Methodological Change: A Historical Anthropological Essay," in *The Practice of Conceptual History: Timing History, Spacing Concepts*, trans. Todd Samuel Presner (Stanford, CA: Stanford University Press, 2002), 45–83.

2 "Conversation: Ulrich Loock with Thomas Schütte," in *Thomas Schütte: Public/Political*, ed. Ulrich Loock (Cologne: Walther König, 2012), 206.

3 Hans Rudolf Reust, "Alles in Ordnung (mit Ludger Gerdes)," in *Thomas Schütte: Public/Political*, 25.

4 Jennifer L. Allen, *Sustainable Utopias: The Art and Politics of Hope in Germany* (Cambridge, MA: Harvard University Press, 2022).

5 Heinz-Norbert Jocks, "Thomas Schütte: 'Man kann auch schattenboxen oder weiter stochern im Nebel,'" interview, *Kunstforum International* 128 (October–December 1994), 249. Translation by the author. See also Christine Mehring, "Modest Abstraction: Thomas Schütte's Early Work," in *Thomas Schütte: Hindsight*, ed. Lynne Cooke (Madrid: Museo Nacional Centro de Arte Reina Sofía, 2009), 51.

6 James Meyer, "The Functional Site; or, The Transformation of Site-Specificity," in *Space, Site, Intervention: Situating Installation Art*, ed. Erika Suderburg (Minneapolis: University of Minnesota Press, 2000), 23–37.

7 Thomas Schütte, "Interview," by James Lingwood, in Julian Heynen, James Lingwood, and Angela Vettese, *Thomas Schütte* (London: Phaidon, 1998), 20–21, 24.

8 See Kiran Klaus Patel, *Project Europe: A History* (Cambridge: Cambridge University Press, 2020); and Axel Schildt, "Fünf Möglichkeiten, die Geschichte der Bundesrepublik zu erzählen," *Blätter für deutsche und internationale Politik* 44 (1999), 1234–44.

9 See Andreas Wirsching, *Abschied vom Provisorium: Geschichte der Bundesrepublik Deutschland 1982–1990* (Stuttgart: Deutsche Verlags-Anstalt, 2006); and Thomas Hertfelder and Andreas Rödder, eds., *Modell Deutschland: Erfolgsgeschichte oder Illusion?* (Göttingen, Germany: Vandenhoeck and Ruprecht, 2007).

10 Brian O'Doherty, *Inside the White Cube: The Ideology of the Gallery Space* (San Francisco: Lapis Press, 1976).

11 "Conversation: Ulrich Loock with Thomas Schütte," 210.

12 Schütte, "Interview," 28.

13 Ernst Nolte, "Vergangenheit, die nicht vergehen will. Eine Rede, die geschrieben, aber nicht gehalten werden konnte," *Frankfurter Allgemeine Zeitung*, June 6, 1986.

14 Jay Winter, "The Memory Boom in Contemporary Historical Studies," *Raritan* 21, no. 1 (2001), 52–66.

15 See Rudy Koshar, *From Monuments to Traces: Artifacts of German Memory, 1870–1990* (Berkeley: University of California Press, 2000); Andreas Huyssen, "The Voids of Berlin," *Critical Inquiry* 24, no. 1 (1997), 57–81; and James E. Young, "The Counter-Monument: Memory against Itself in Germany Today," *Critical Inquiry* 18, no. 2 (1992), 267–96.

16 Schütte, "Interview," 8.

17 Ibid., 13.

18 "Conversation: Ulrich Loock with Thomas Schütte," 204.

19 Ibid., 204–5.

20 Ibid., 205.

21 Schütte, "Interview," 36.

Plates

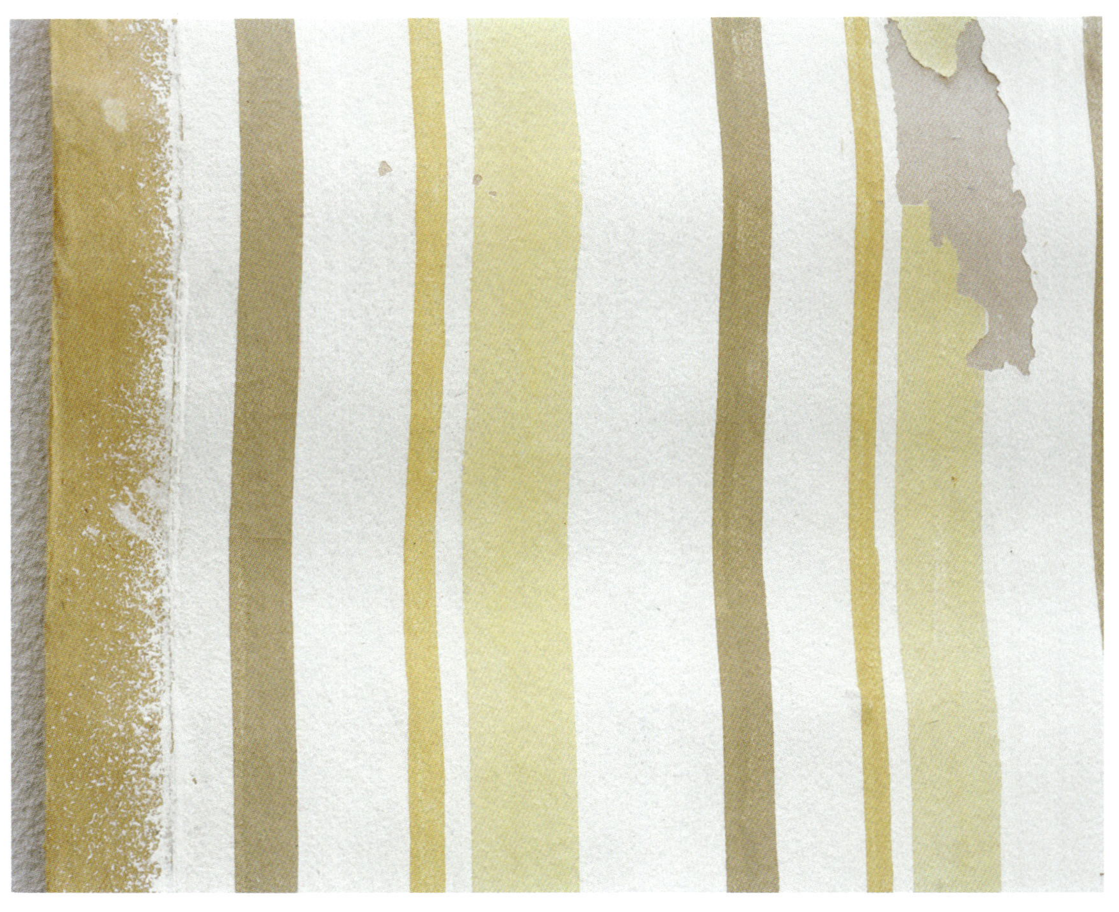

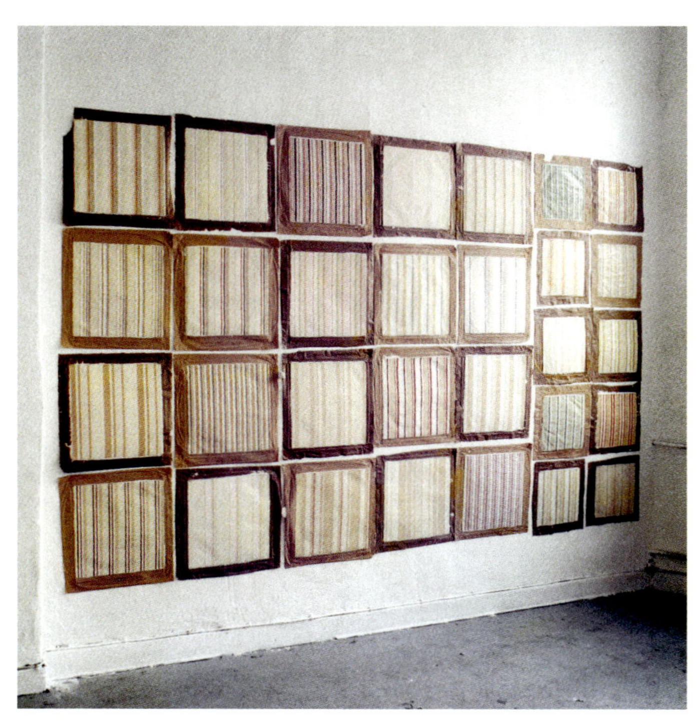

1
Große Tapeten (*Large Wallpapers*). 1975. Emulsion paint on packing paper, seven parts, each 12' 7 ⁹⁄₁₆" × 3' 1" (385 × 94 cm). Installation view, *Thomas Schütte: Early Works*, Kunstmuseum Liechtenstein, Vaduz, February 1–April 20, 2008

Above:
Detail of *Große Tapeten*

Right:
Thomas Schütte. *Tapetenmuster* (*Wallpaper Pattern*). 1975. Emulsion paint on packing paper, 30 parts, each approx. 18 × 18" (45.7 × 45.7 cm). Collection the artist, Düsseldorf

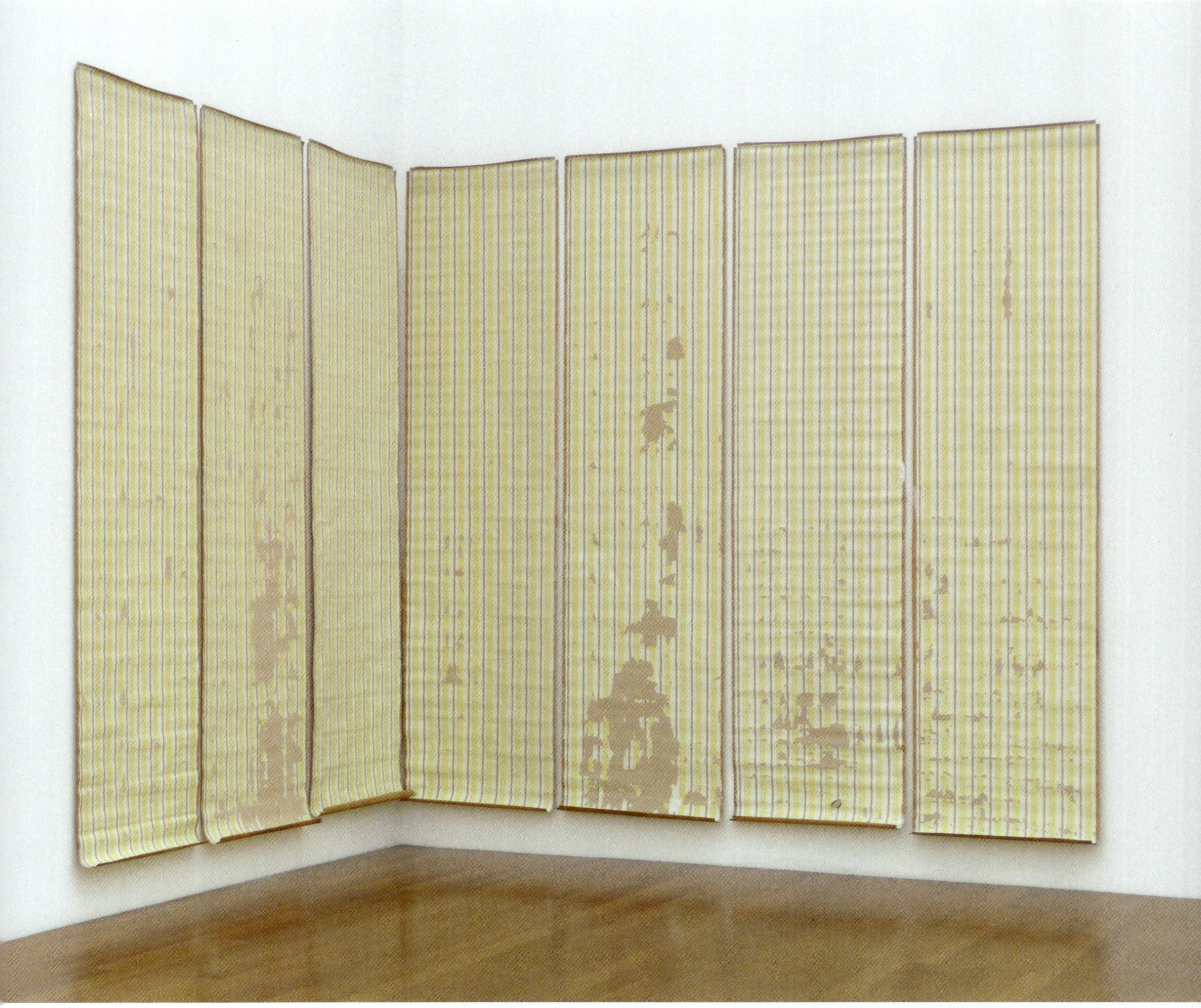

1

2
Amerika (*America*). 1975. Pencil on paper, 6' 10 11⁄16" × 7' 10 ½" (210 × 240 cm)

Below:
Schütte seated in front of the partially completed *Amerika*, 1975

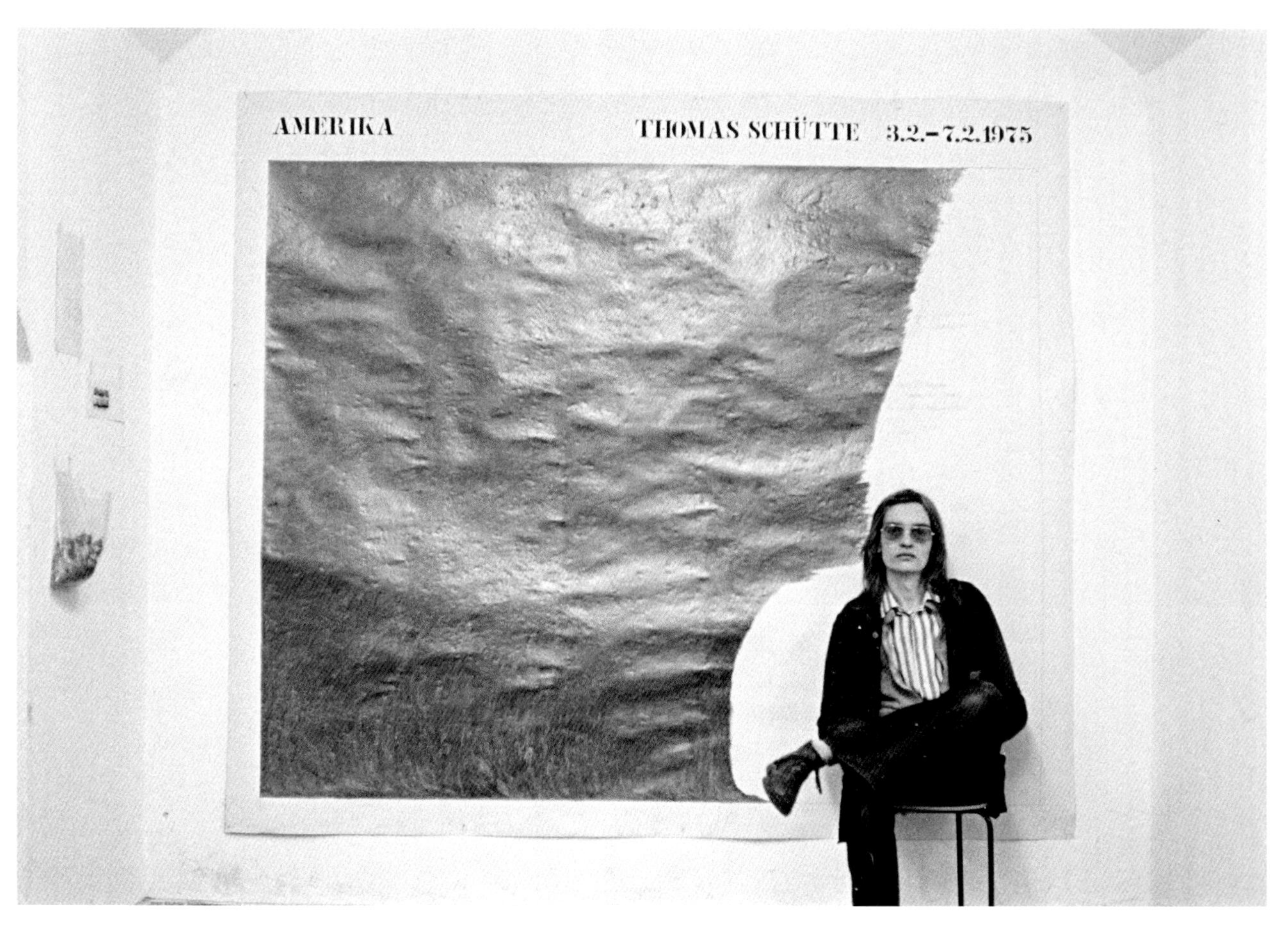

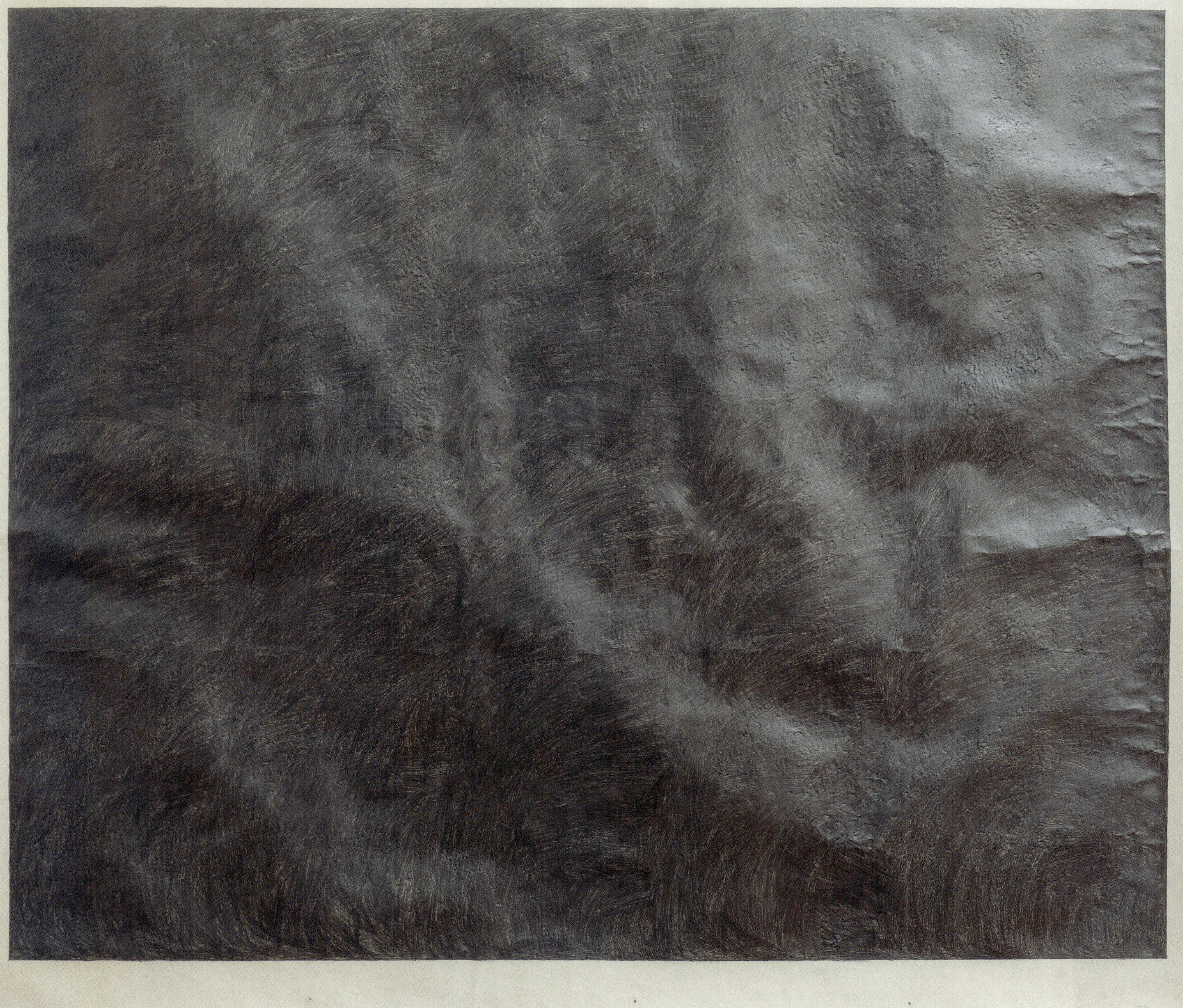

2

Skizze für Amerika (*Sketch for America*). 1975. Typewritten text on paper with photograph, 11 11⁄16 × 8 ¼" (29.7 × 21 cm). Collection the artist, Düsseldorf

AMERIKA THOMAS SCHÜTTE 3.2.-7.2.75

3.2.	1o.oo - 13.3o
	14.oo - 16.oo
	17.oo - 19.3o
4.2.	1o.oo - 13.3o
	14.oo - 16.oo
	17.15 - 19.15
5.2.	1o.oo - 13.3o
	14.oo - 16.3o
6.2.	1o.oo - 13.3o
	14.oo - 16.3o
7.2.	1o.oo - 13.3o
	14.oo - 14.3o

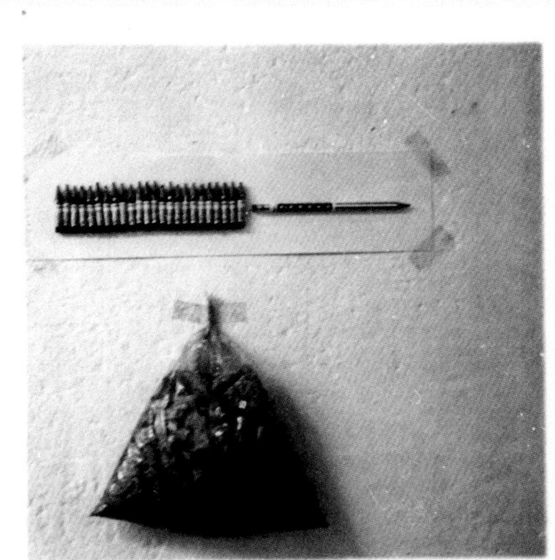

Größe: 2x2,5m
Tage: 5
Stunden: 31
Verbrauch: 25 Bleistifte
Photos: stündlich

AMERIKA - ein Reizwort,Irritation,eine absichtlich geschaffene Unklarheit,um Fragen zu provozieren!

AMERIKA neu entdecken.
ALLES muß neu entdeckt werden:das MALEN,die "KUNST", SICH SELBST allererst!
Zu einer Maschine werden,um den Kopf freizumachen.
Keine Bilder malen WOLLEN,sondern nur MALEN!
Bilder entstehen immer.
Keine KUNSTFERTIGKEITEN,die verschleiern nur alles.
Von ganz vorn anfangen: NEUGIERIG UND STUMPFSINNIG HARTNÄCKIG!
Alte Bilder zerstören,besonders die im KOPF.
Die Grenzen erforschen und überschreiten.
Das entdecken,aufdecken,erfahren ein Selbstzweck.
Nach der Entdeckung die Traurigkeit,weil alles immer wieder neu entdeckt werden muß!

Als ästhetisches Phänomen ist uns das Dasein immer noch erträglich,und durch die Kunst ist uns Auge und Hand und vor allem das gute Gewissen dazu gegeben,aus uns selber ein solches Phänomen machen zu können. Nietzsche

Skizze für Amerika (*Sketch for America*). 1975. Typewritten text and pencil on paper, 11 ¹¹⁄₁₆ × 8 ¼" (29.7 × 21 cm). Collection the artist, Düsseldorf

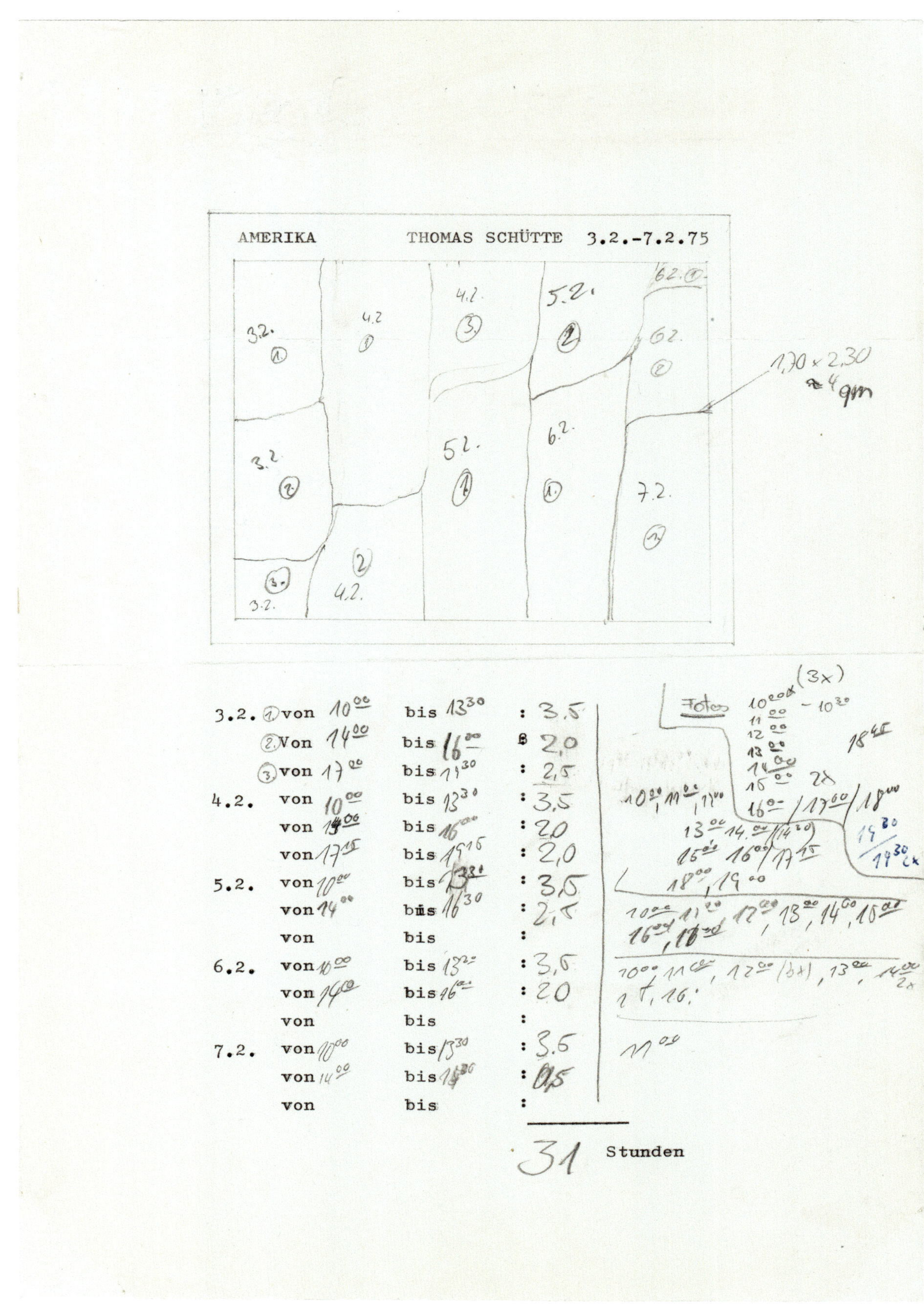

3
Selbstportrait. 30/31.5.75 (*Self-portrait: 5/30–31/75*). 1975. Oil on nettle cloth, 23 ⅝ × 17 ¹¹⁄₁₆" (60 × 45 cm)

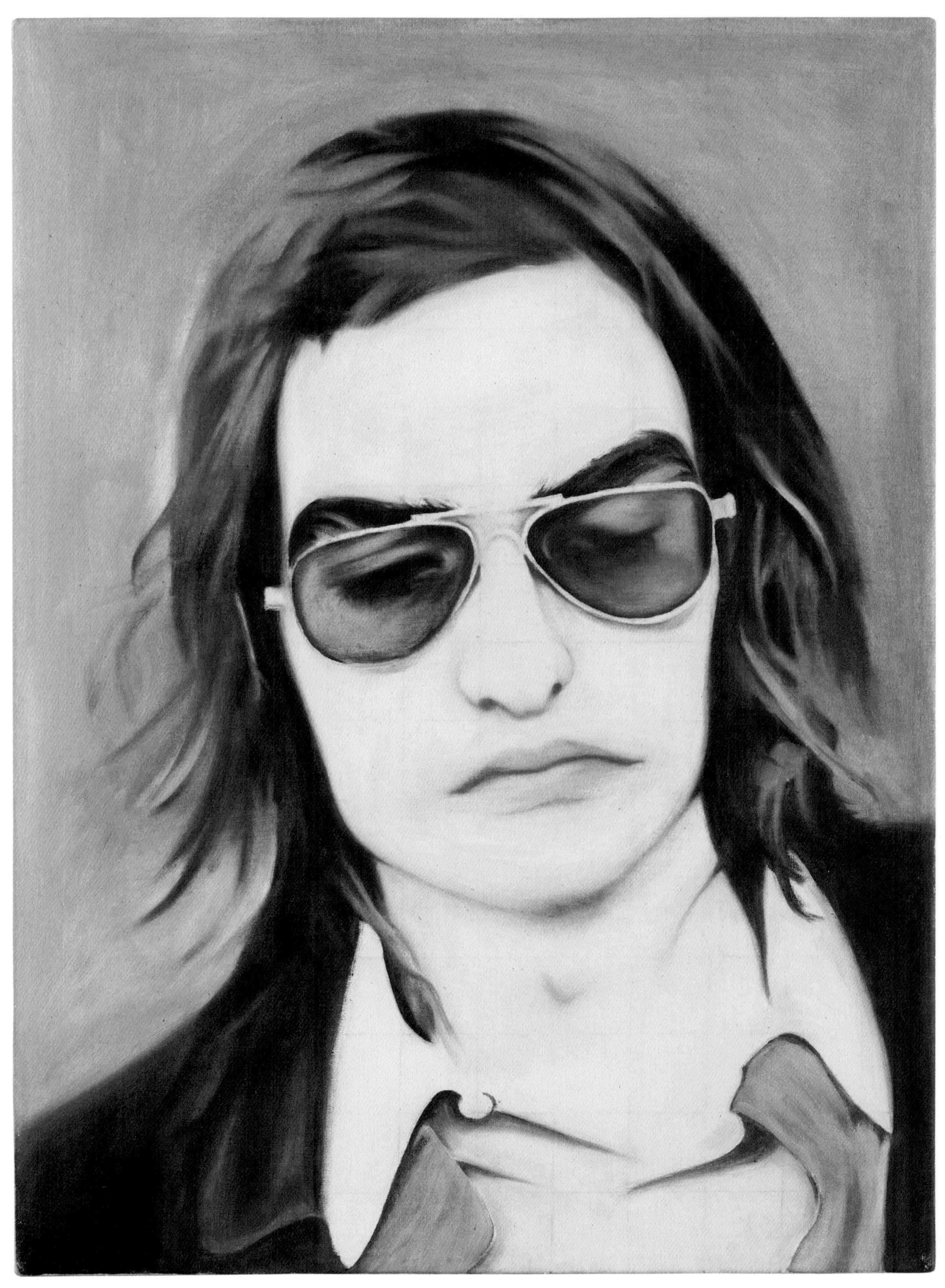

4
Selbstportrait. 29.5.75 (*Self-portrait: 5/29/75*). 1975.
Oil on nettle cloth, 23 ⅝ × 17 $^{11}/_{16}$" (60 × 45 cm)

Below:
Photograph of Schütte by Joachim Tiffert with grid used as a template for the *Selbstportrait* series, 1974

Next spread:
Eighteen *Selbstportrait* works. 1975. Destroyed

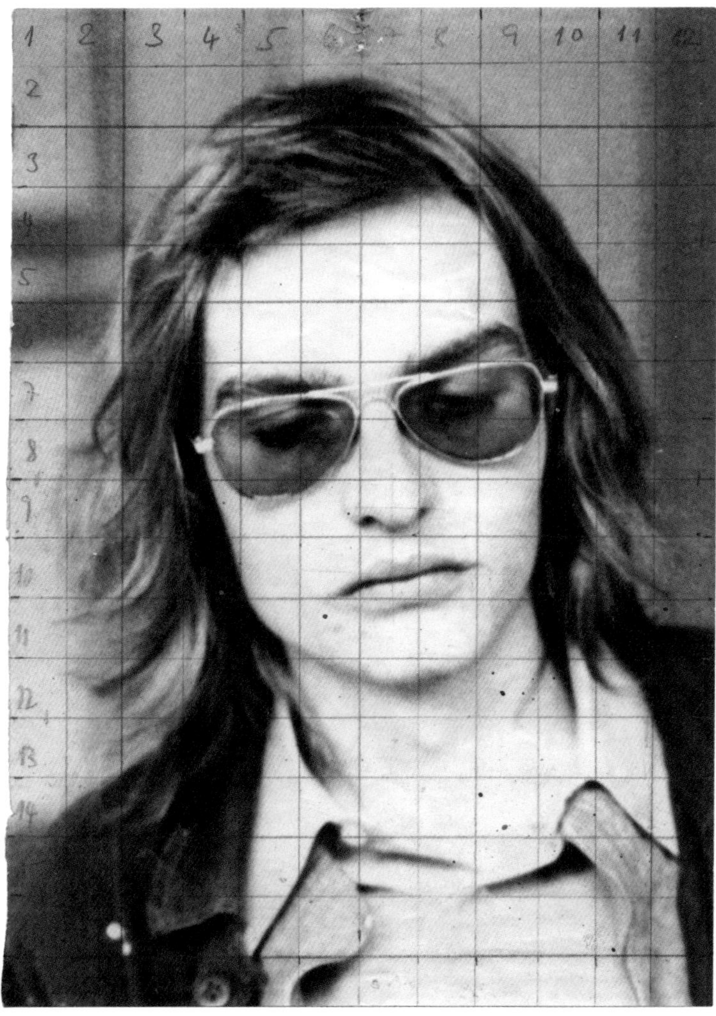

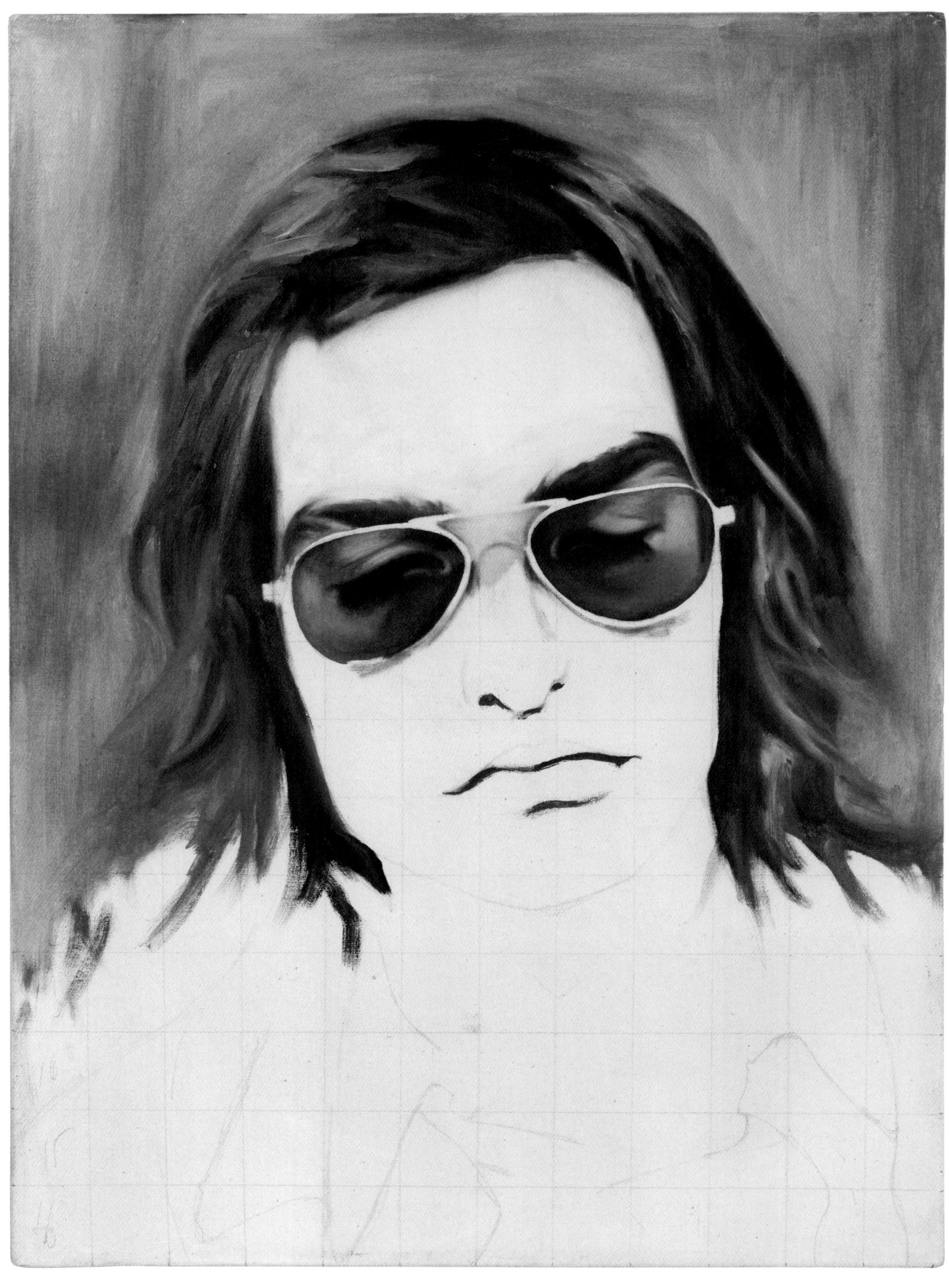

4

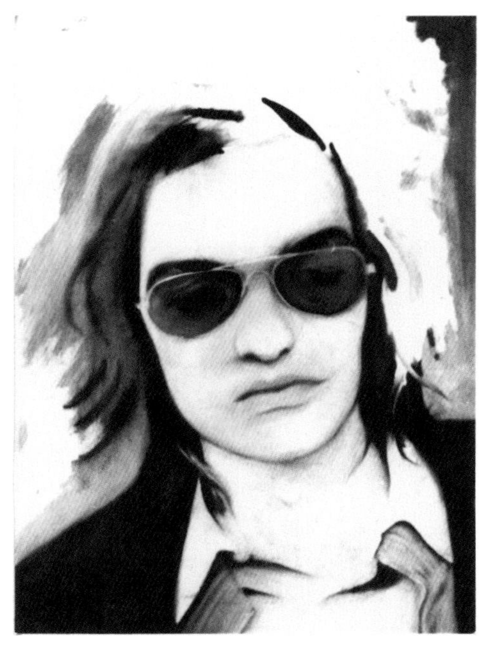
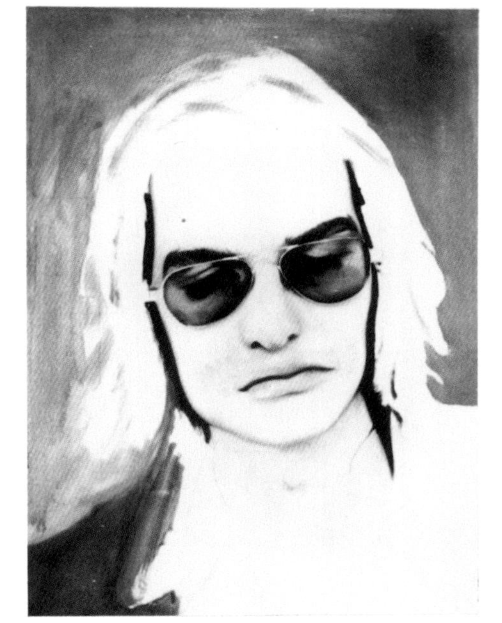
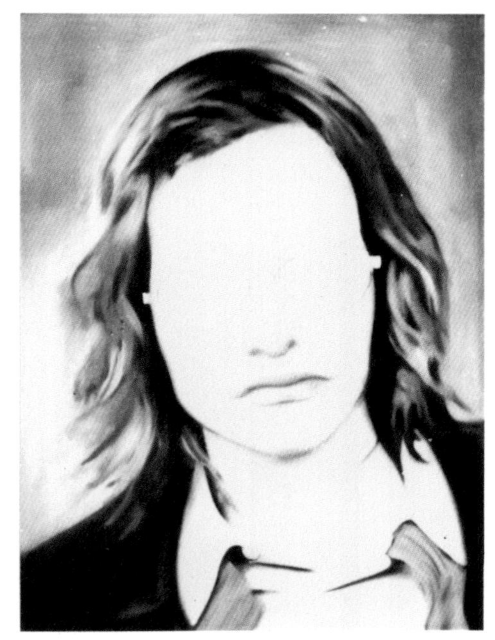
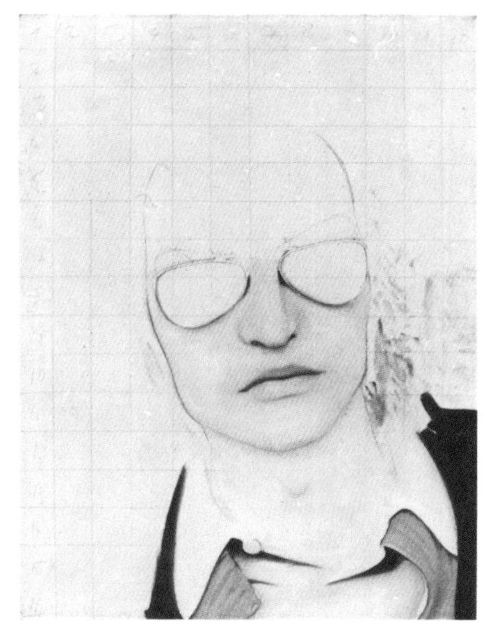
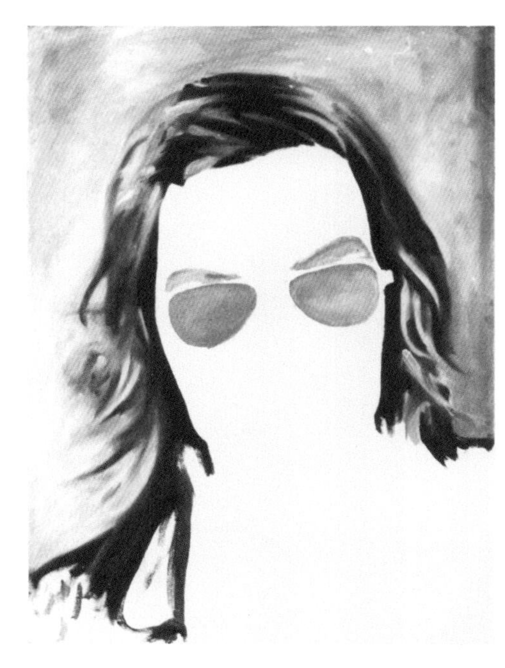
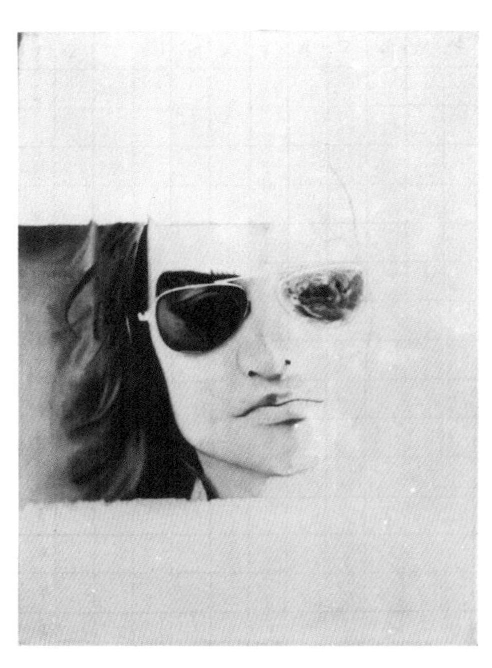
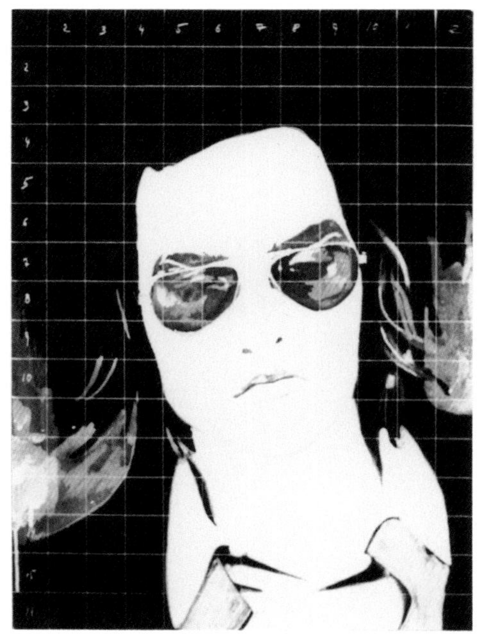
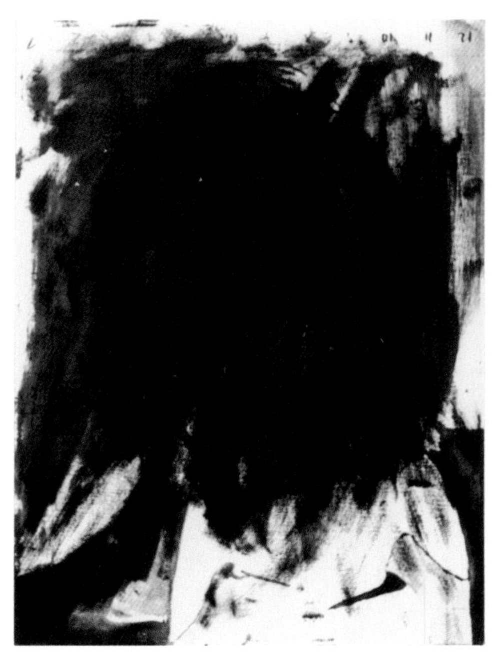
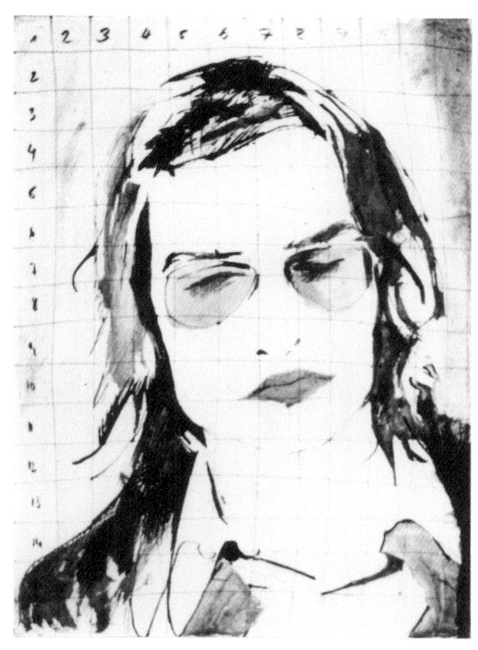

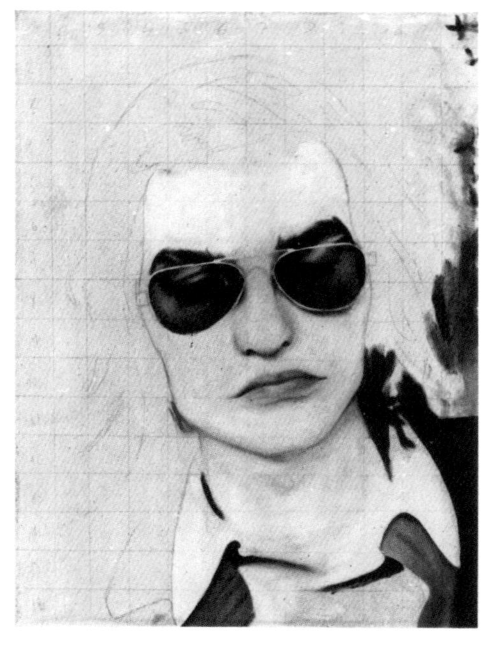
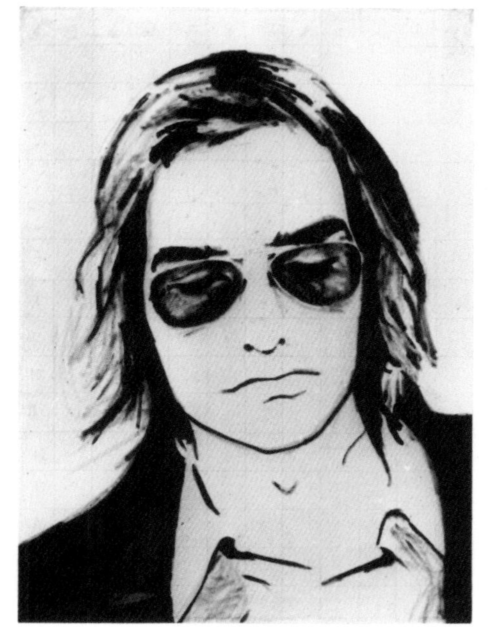
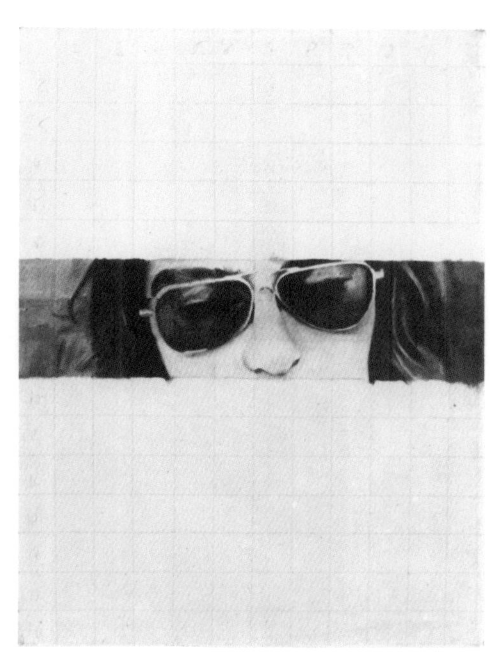
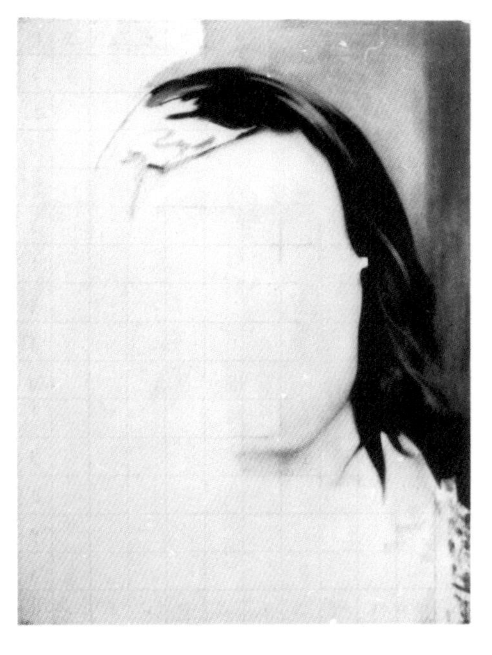
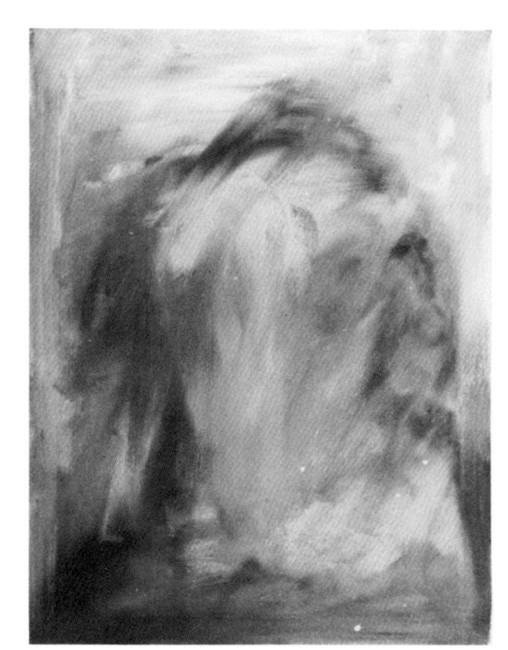
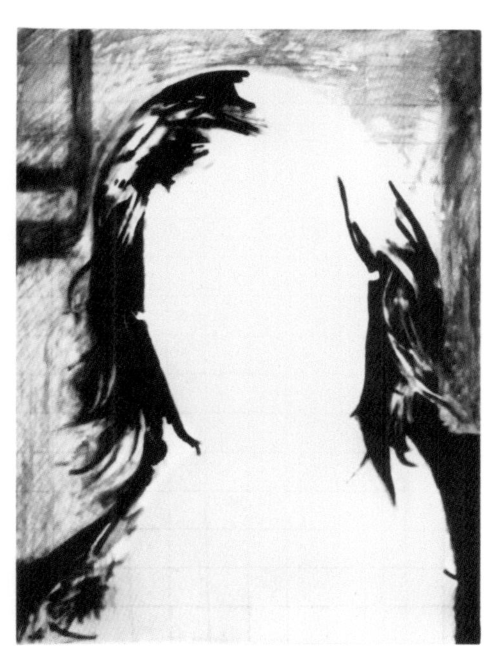
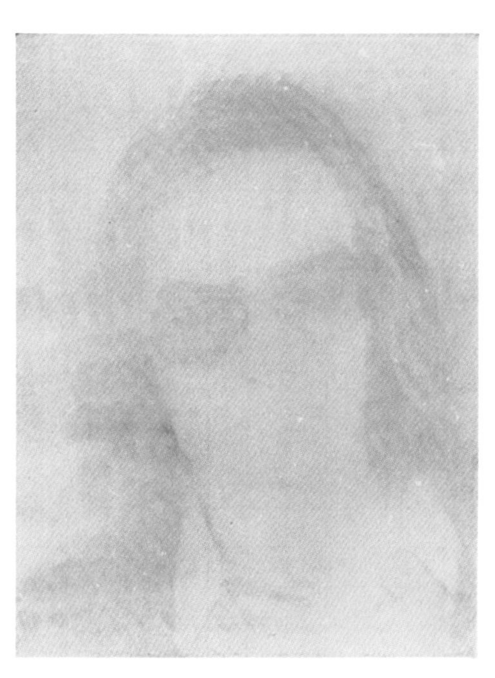
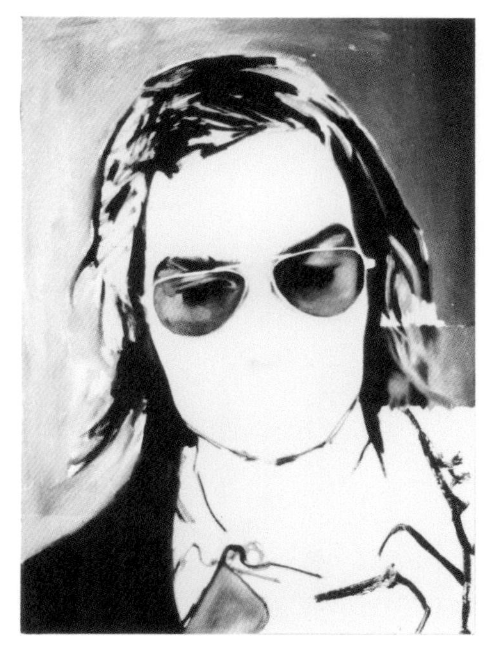
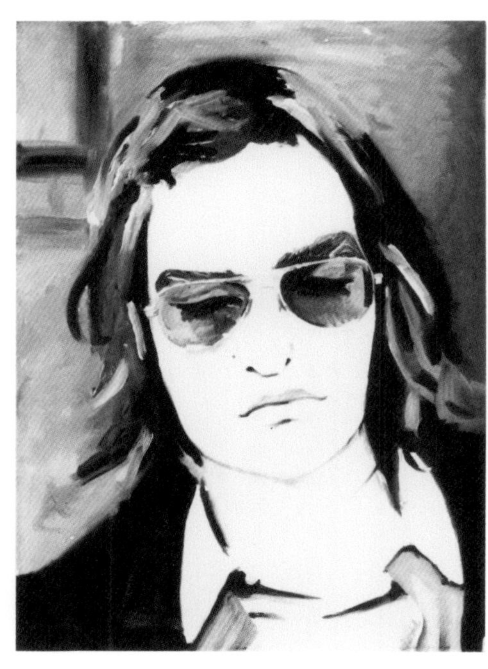

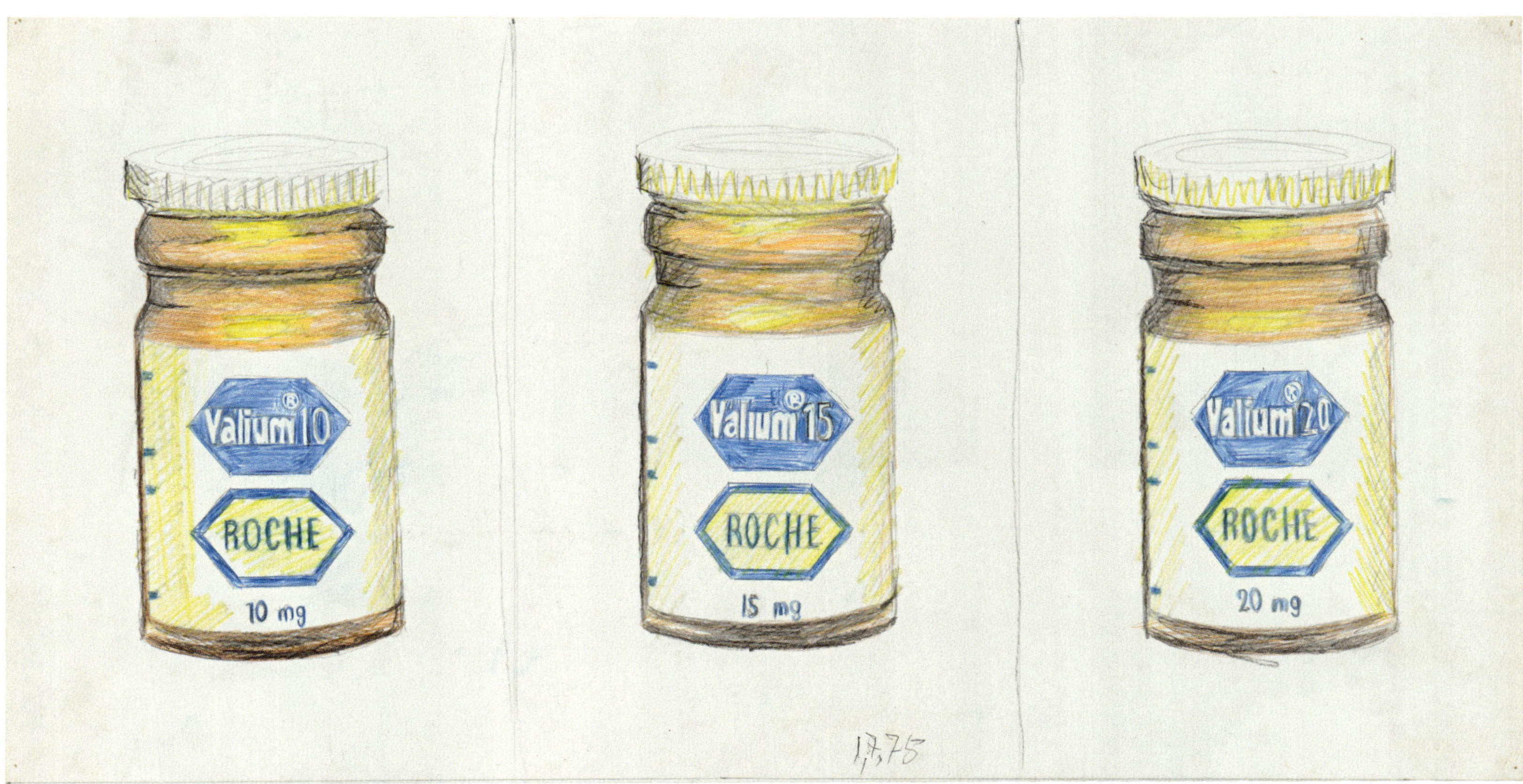

5

5
Valium. 1975. Crayon on paper, 11 13⁄16 × 23 5⁄8" (30 × 60 cm)

6
Valium. 1975. Watercolor and pencil on paper, 22 13⁄16 × 15 3⁄4" (58 × 40 cm)

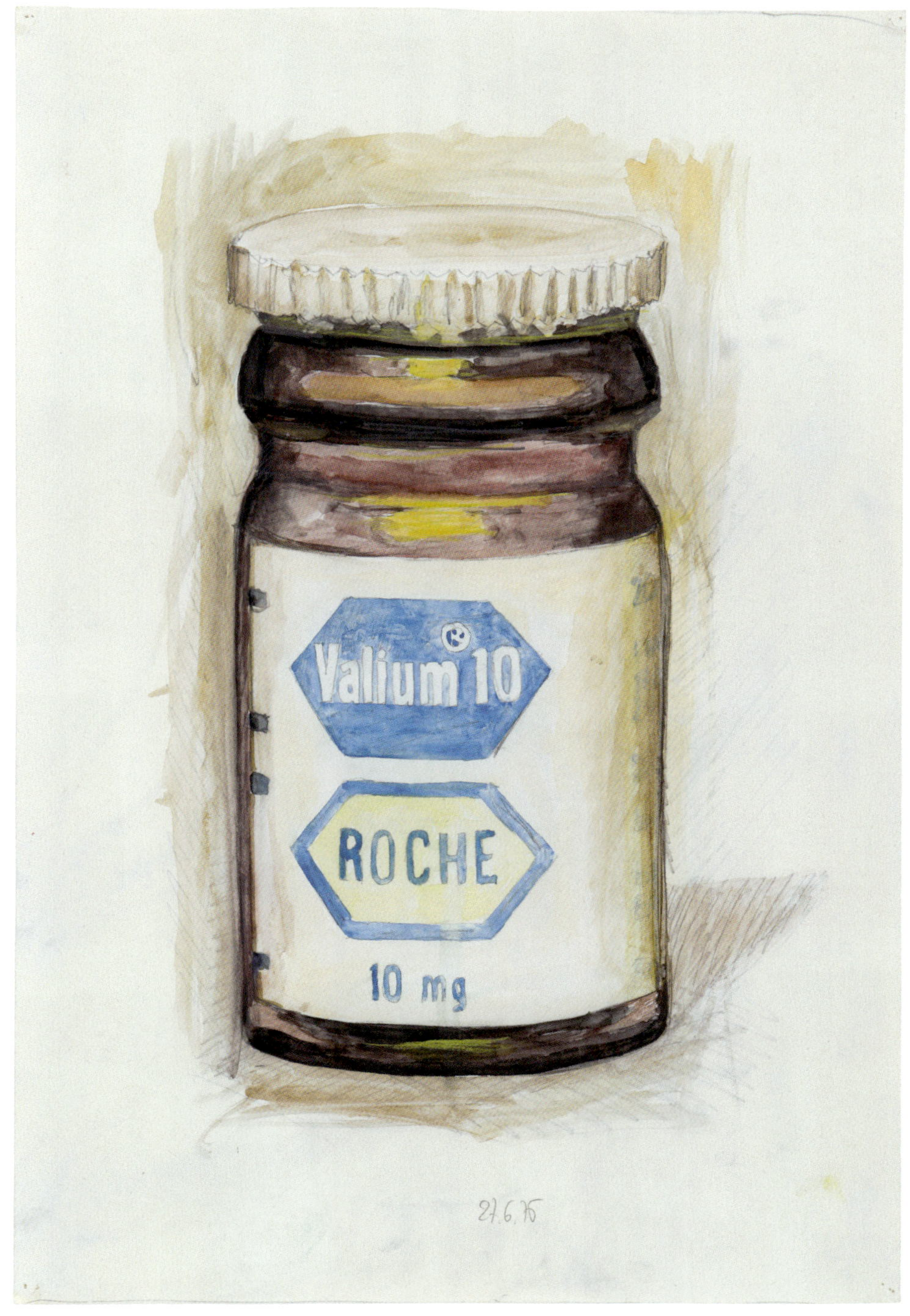

6

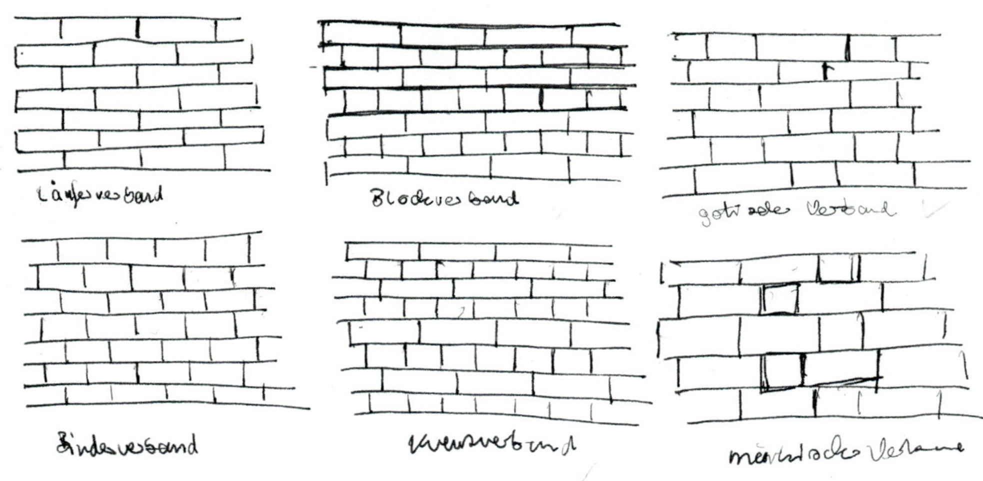

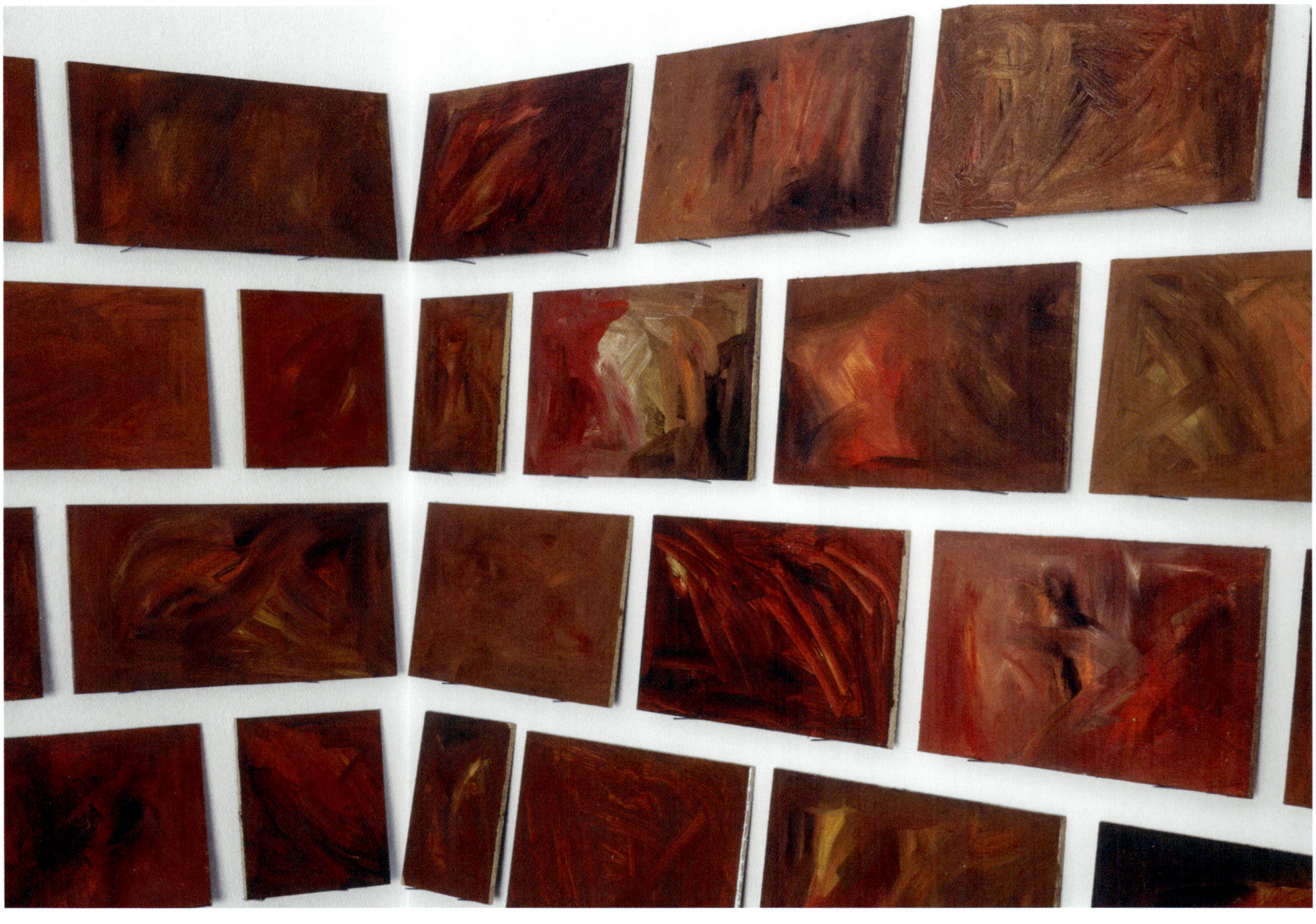

7
Große Mauer (*Large Wall*). 1977. Oil on hardboard, 1,200 parts, each 3 15⁄16 × 7 7⁄8" (10 × 20 cm). Installation dimensions variable. Installation view, *Wände/Walls*, Kunstmuseum Stuttgart, September 26, 2020–May 30, 2021

Left, top:
Drawing for *Große Mauer* (detail). 1977. Pen and pencil on paper, 11 11⁄16 × 8 1⁄4" (29.7 × 21 cm). Collection the artist, Düsseldorf

Left, bottom:
Detail of *Große Mauer*

7

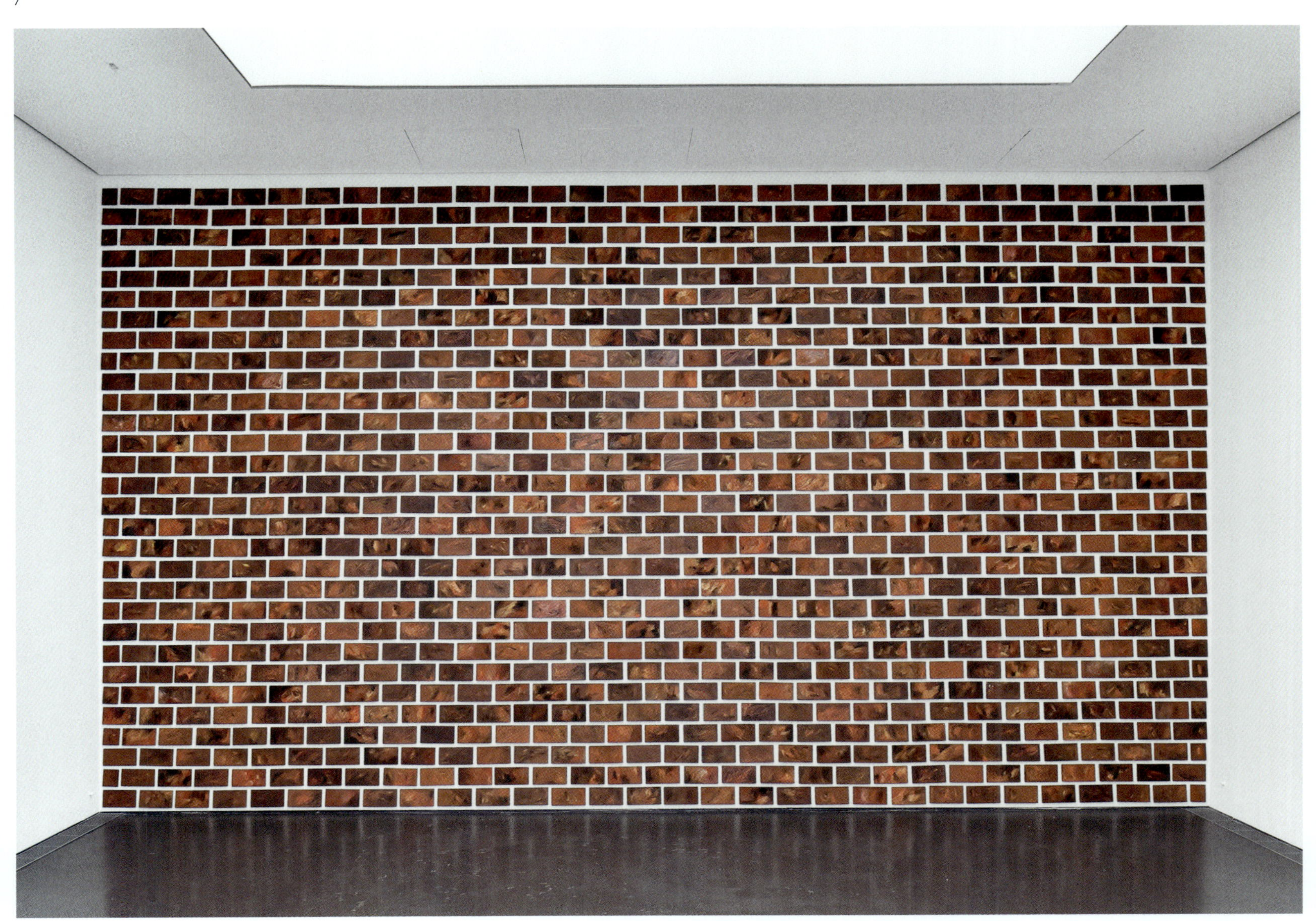

8
Schwäbisch Hall. 1980. Lacquer on plastic, four parts, each 3 15⁄16 × 7 7⁄8" (10 × 20 cm), overall 13 3⁄8 × 16 9⁄16" (34 × 42 cm)

Below:
Logo for Schwäbisch Hall, the largest building society in Germany, and logo on corporate headquarters

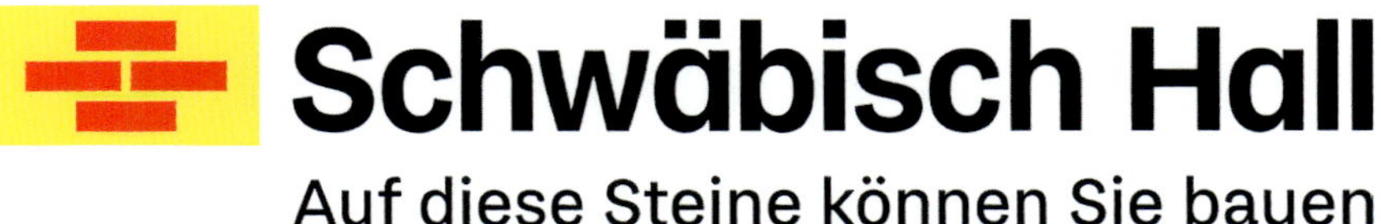

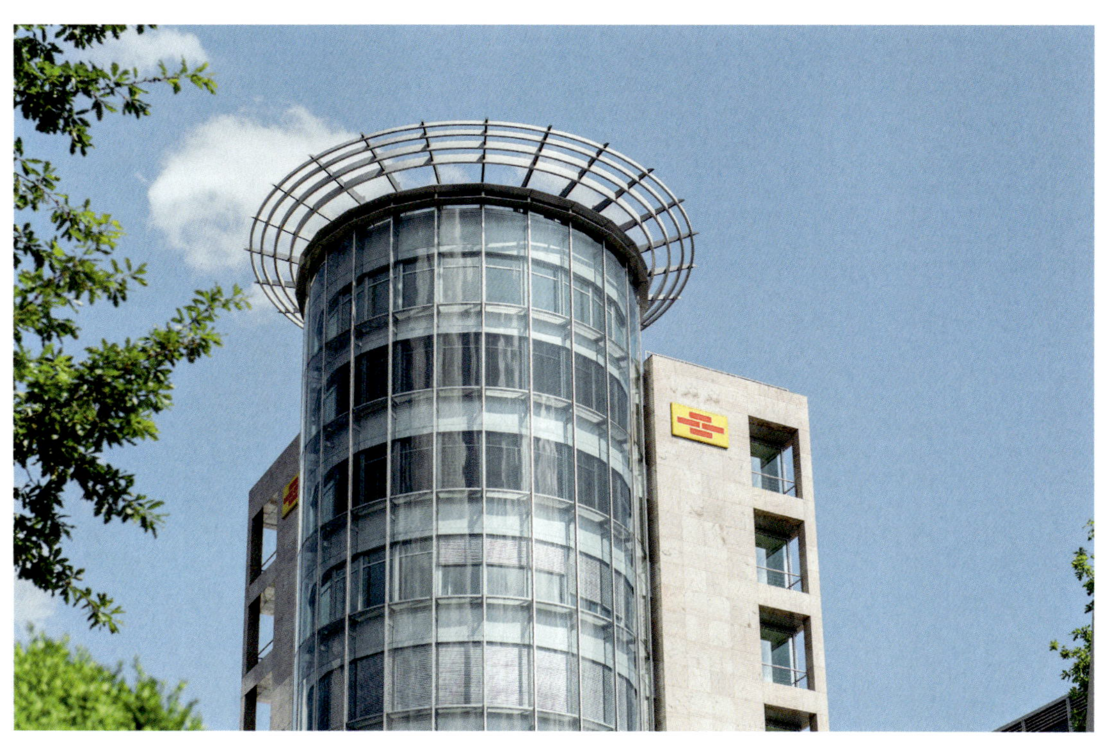

8 >

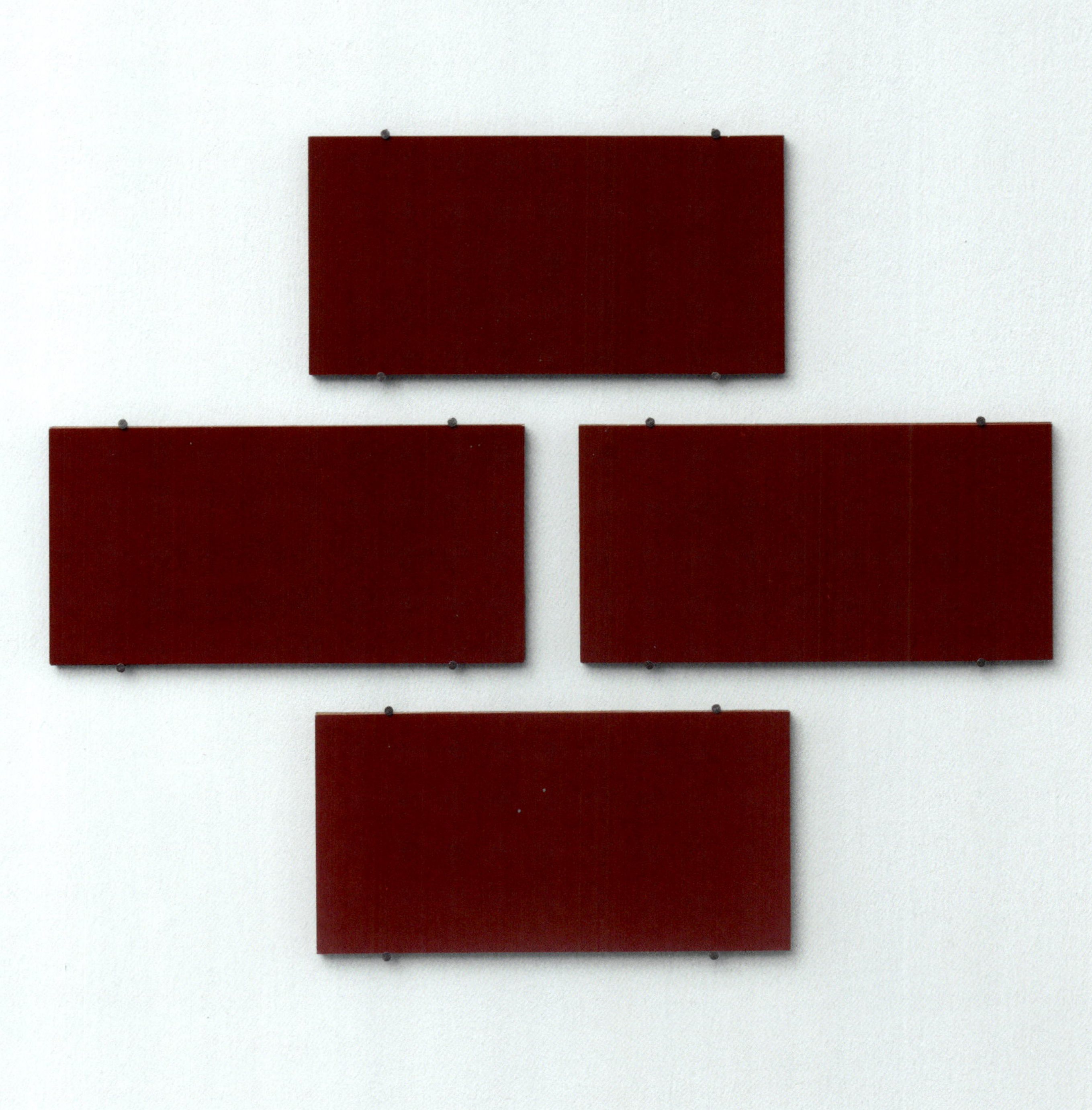

9

Lager (*Storage*). 1978. Paint and varnish on wood, 144 parts, various dimensions from 11 7/8 × 6 7/8" (30 × 17.5 cm) to 53 15/16 × 26 5/8" (137 × 67.7 cm). Installation dimensions variable. Installation view, *Thomas Schütte: Hindsight*, Museo Nacional Centro de Arte Reina Sofía, Madrid, February 17–May 17, 2010

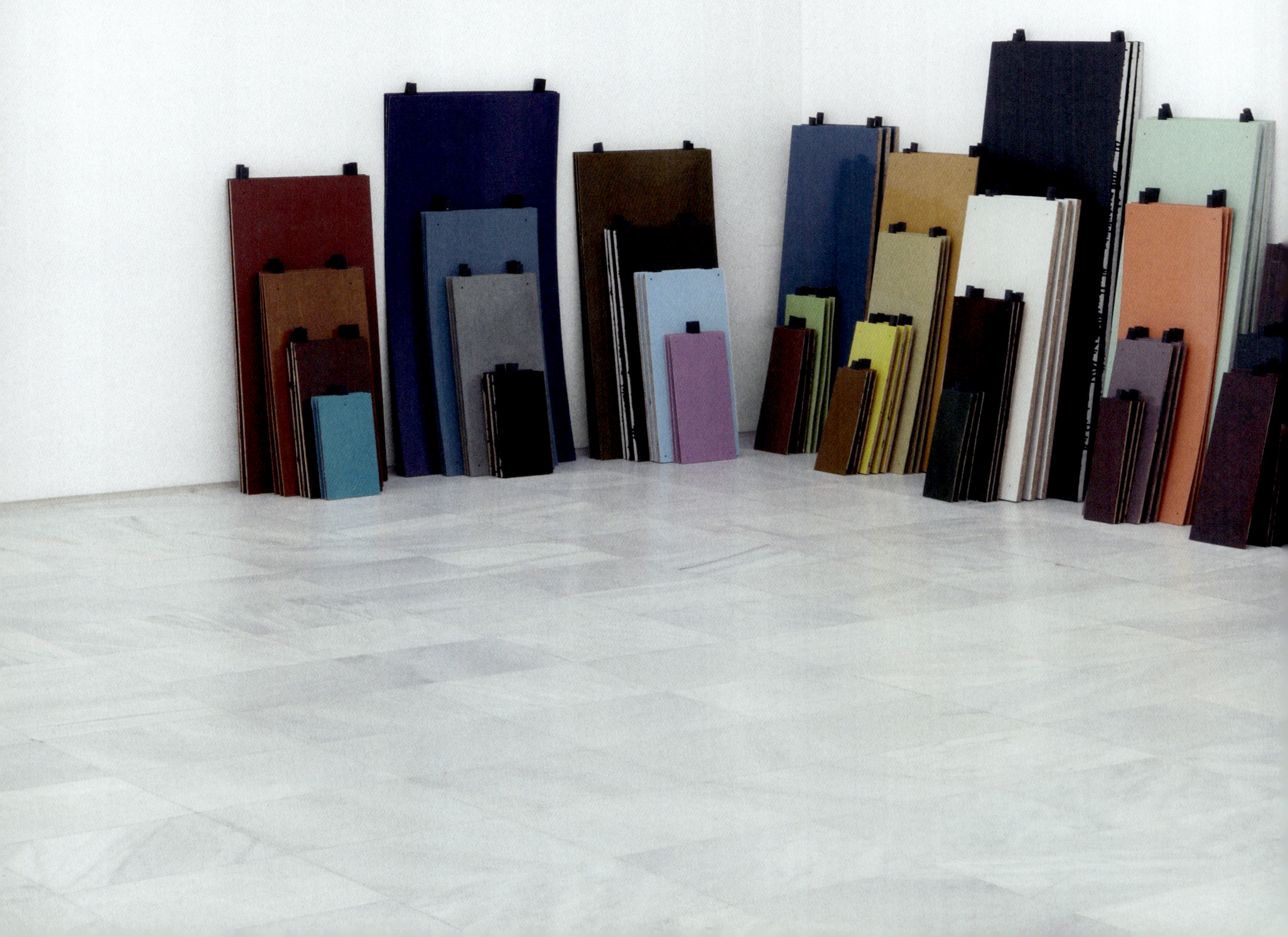

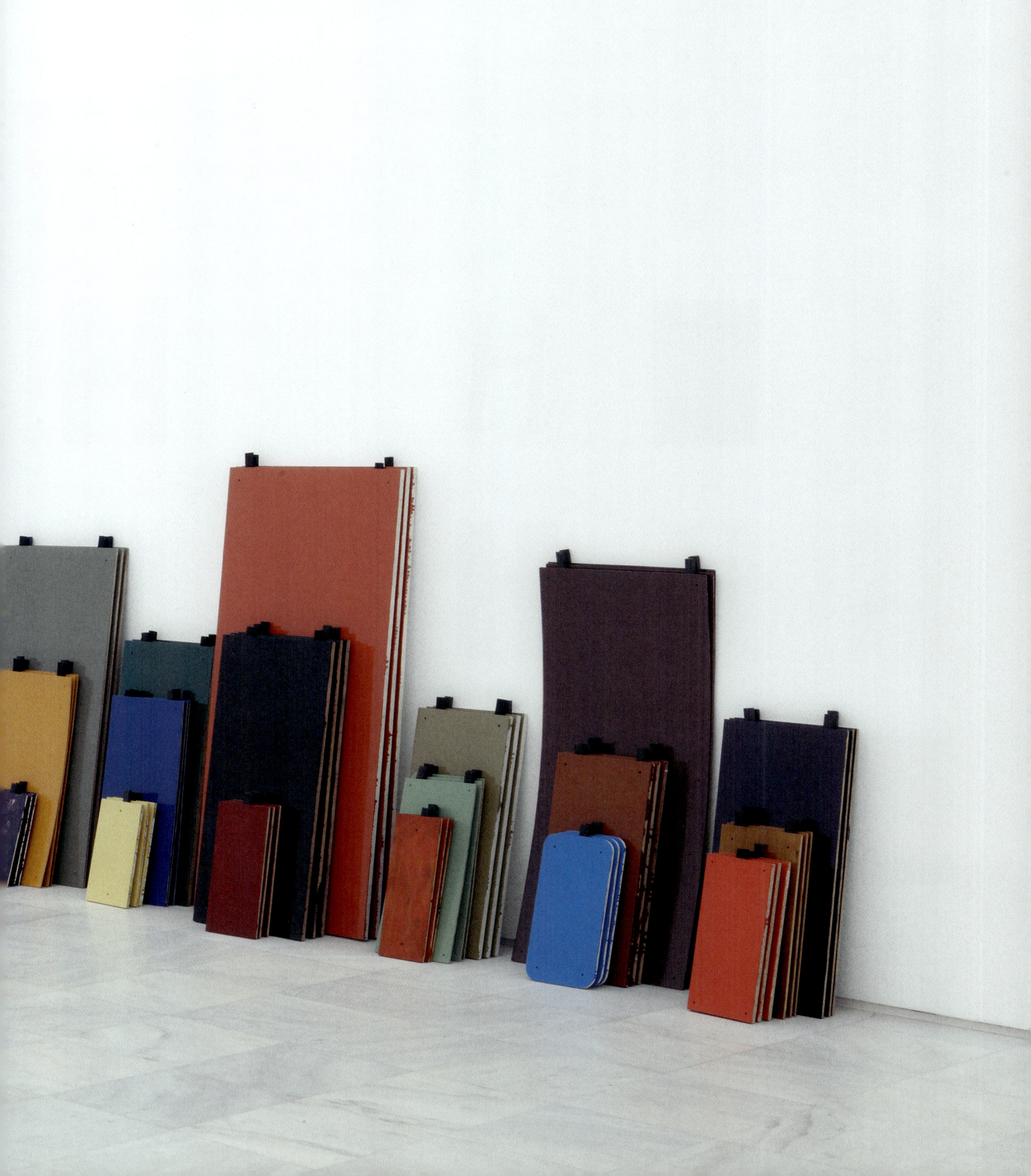

This spread and next:

10
Hysterie (*Hysteria*). 1979. Lacquer on paper, 100 of 105 sheets. Each 27 15⁄16 × 20 1⁄16" (71 × 51 cm)

Right:
Installation view, *Skulpturen* (*Sculptures*), Skulpturenhalle, Neuss, Germany, January 13–July 30, 2023

10

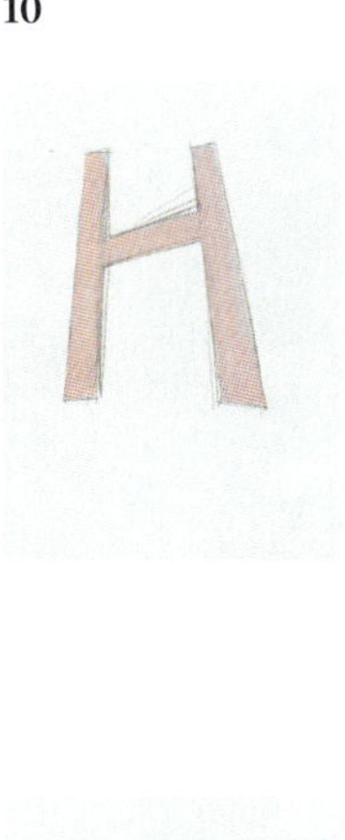
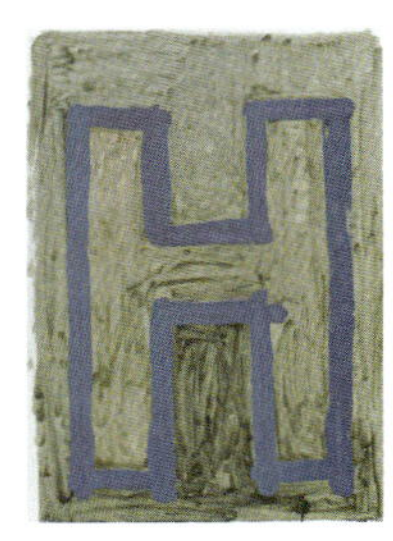
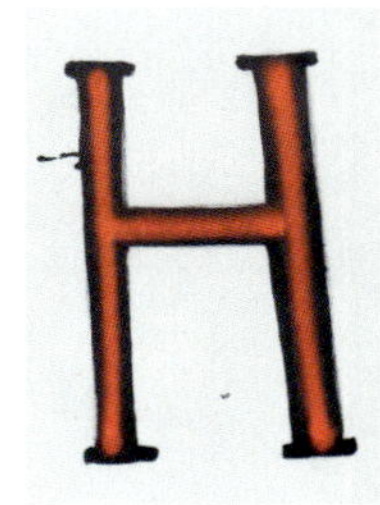
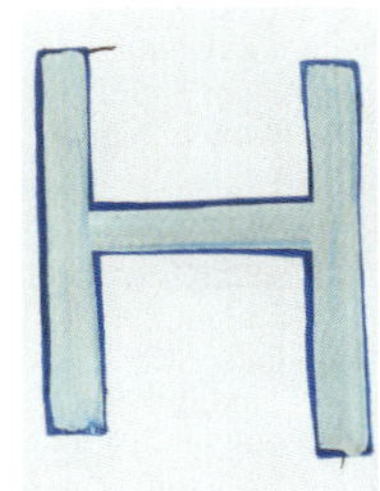
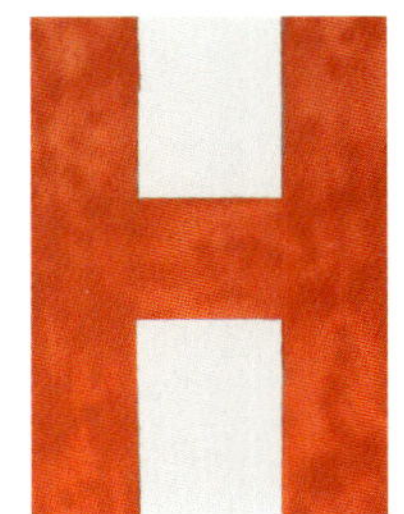
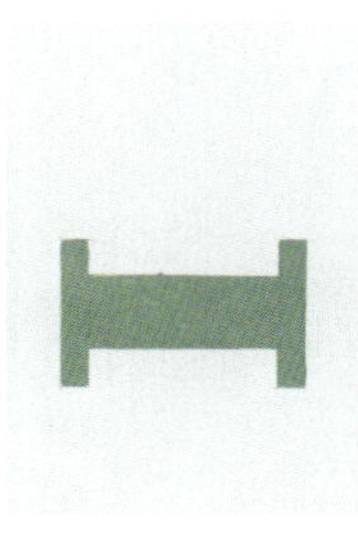
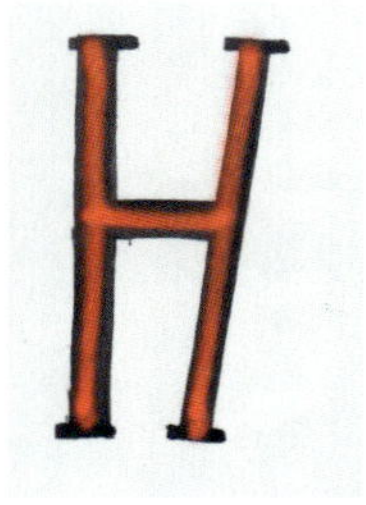
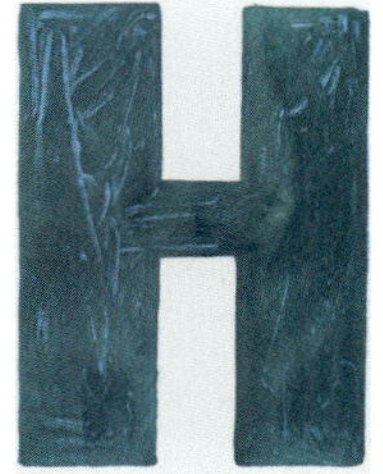
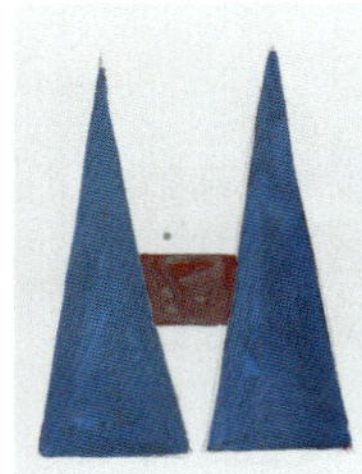
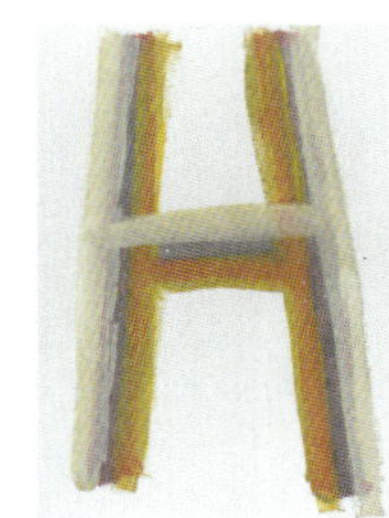
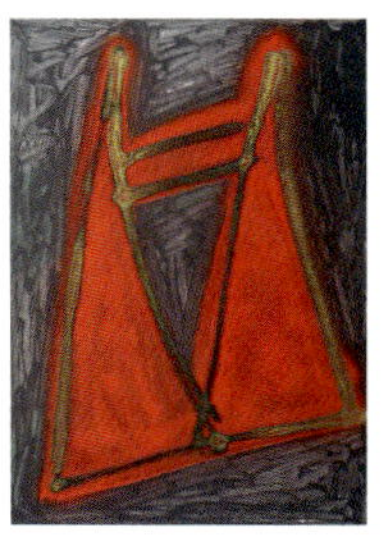
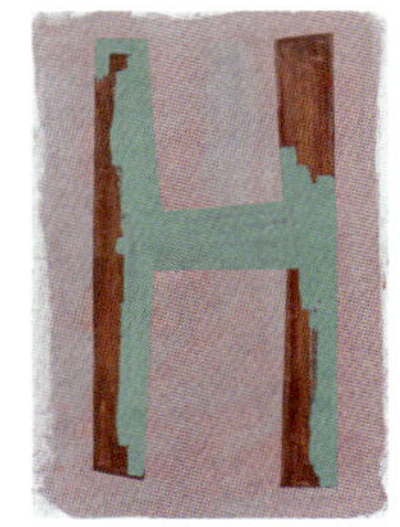
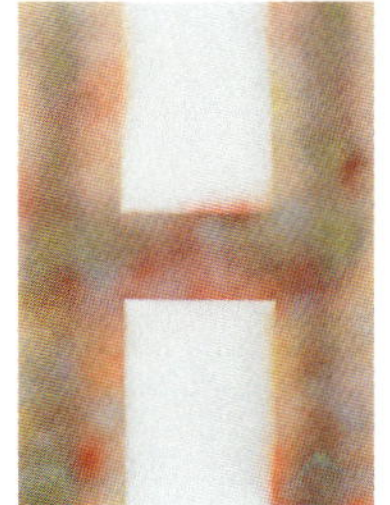
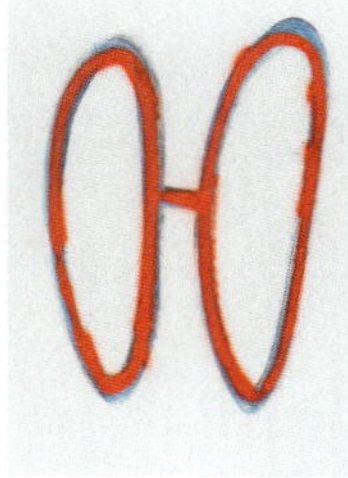
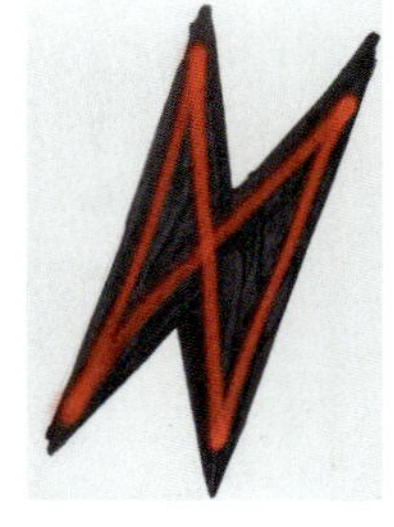
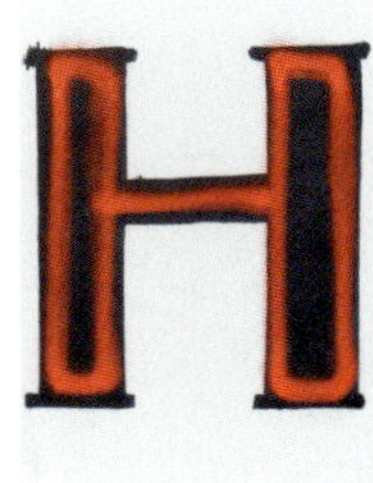
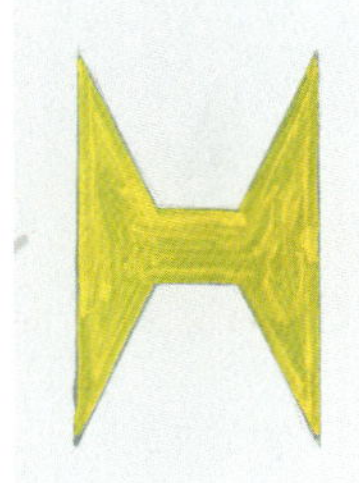
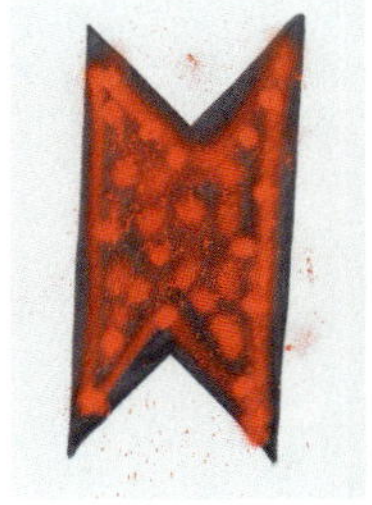
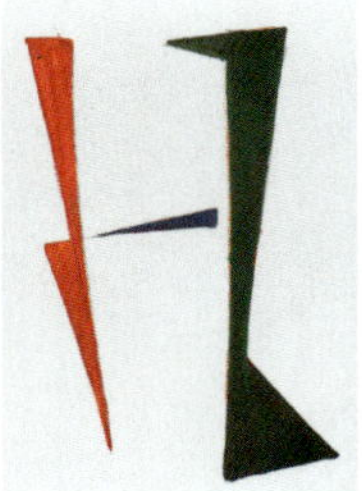
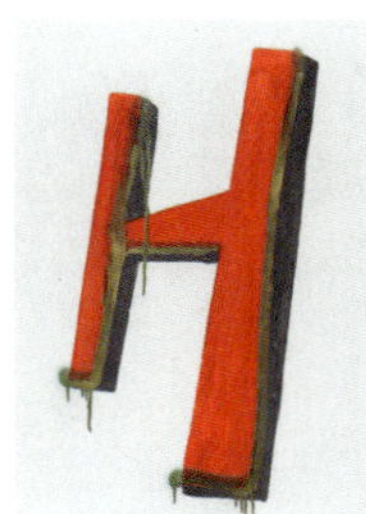

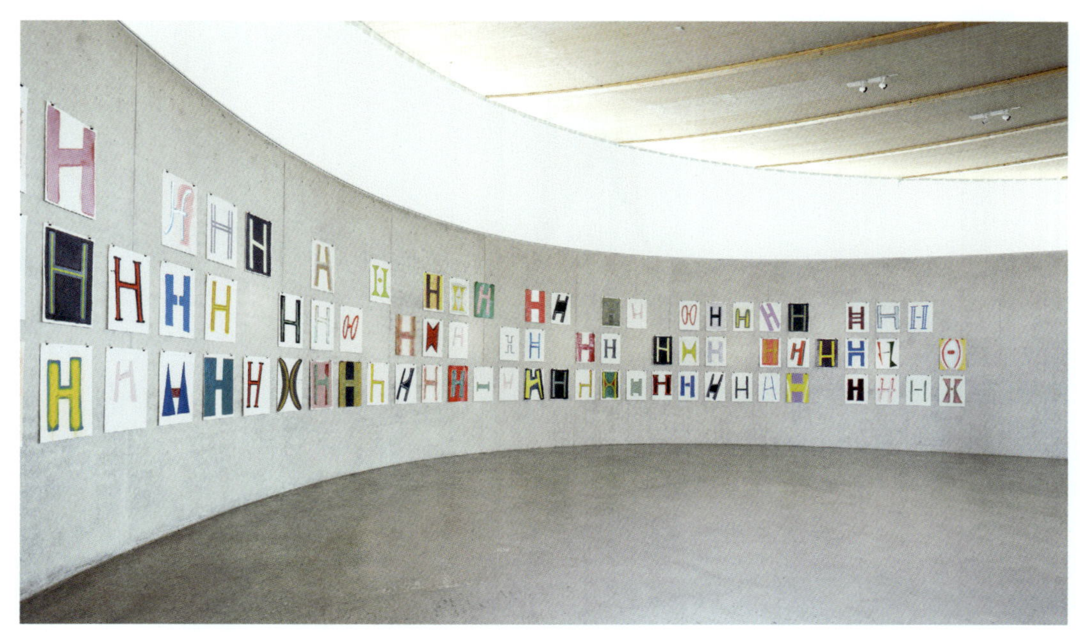

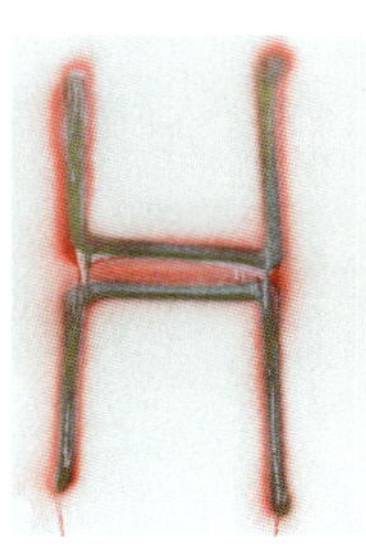
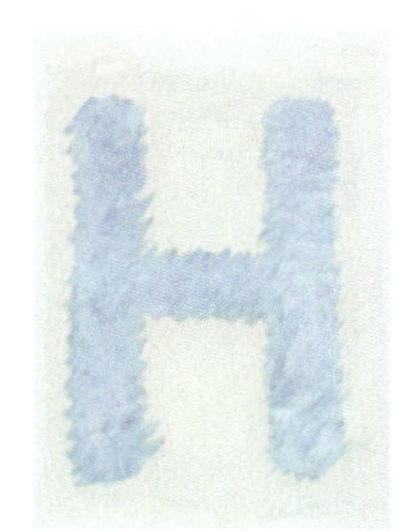
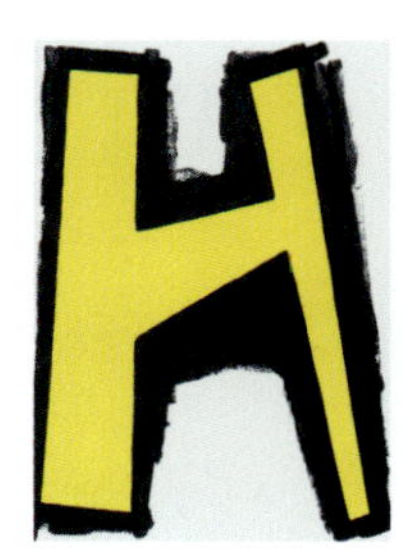
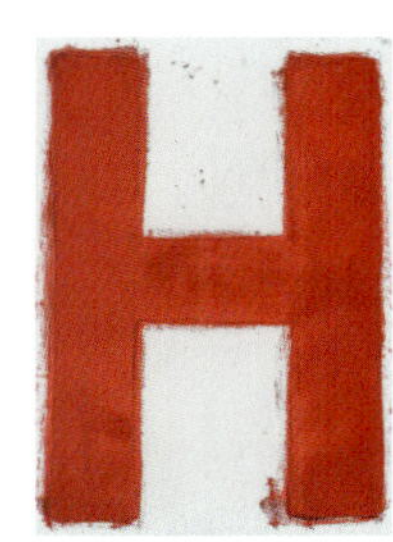
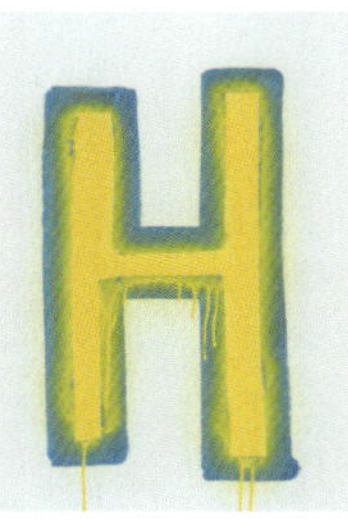
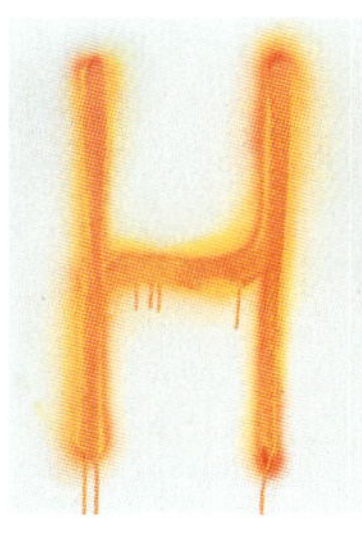
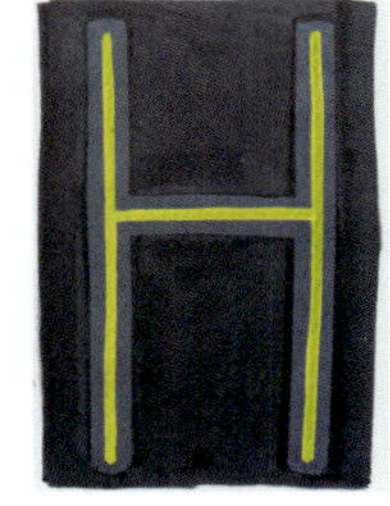
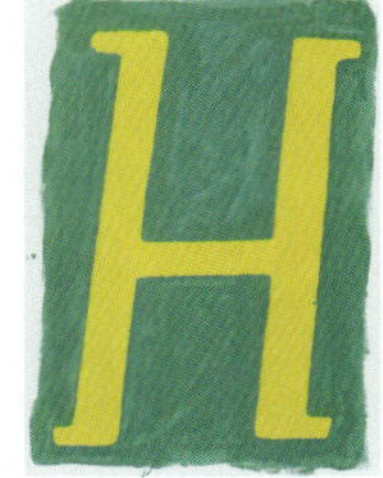
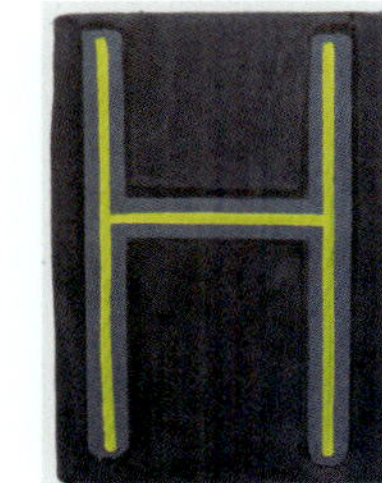
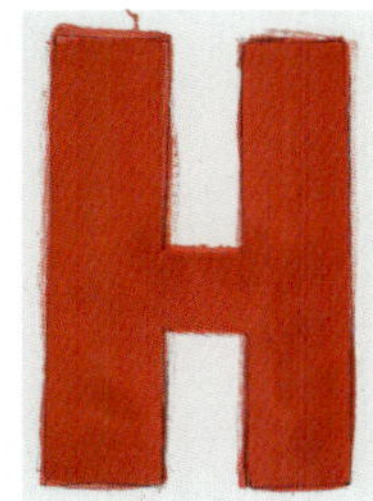
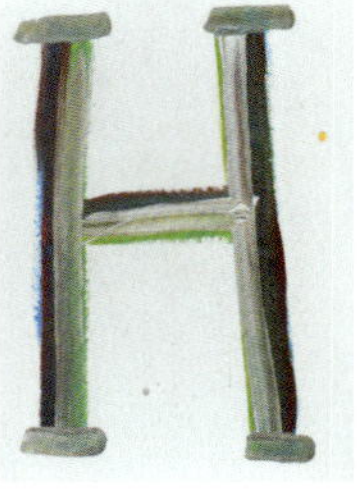
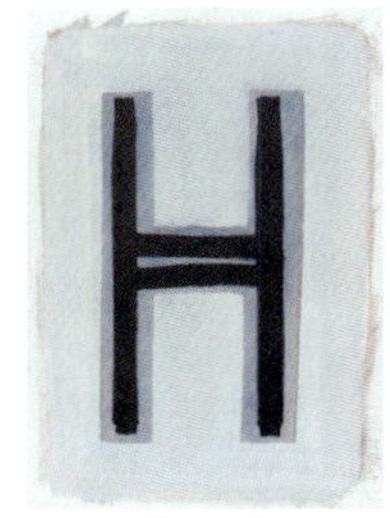
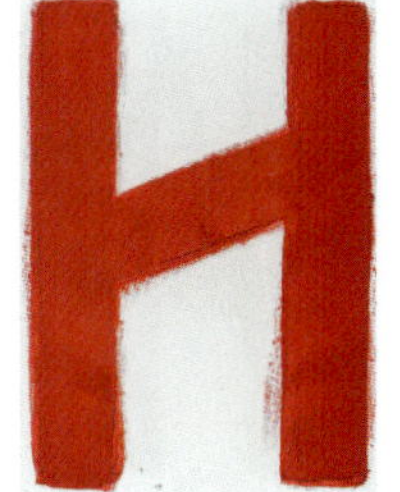
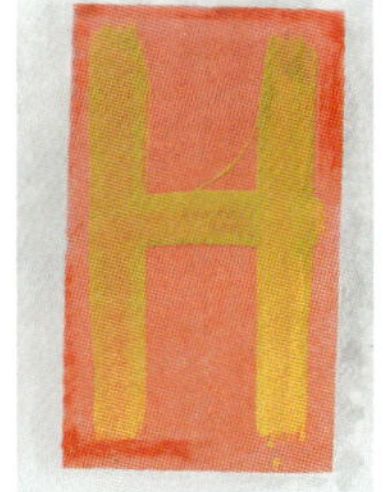
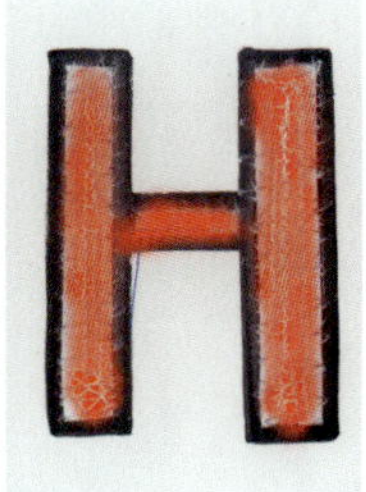
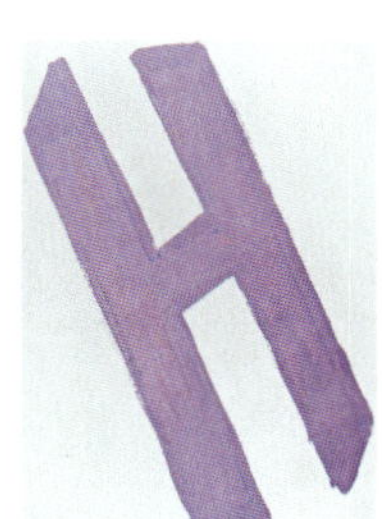
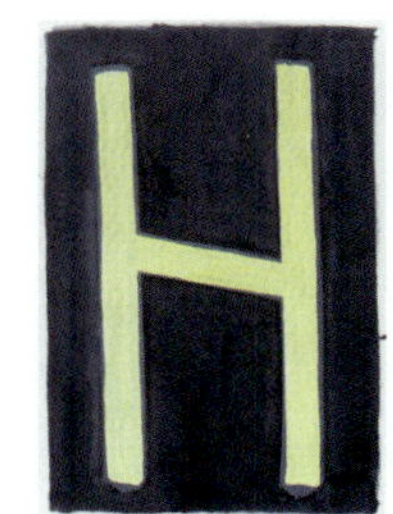
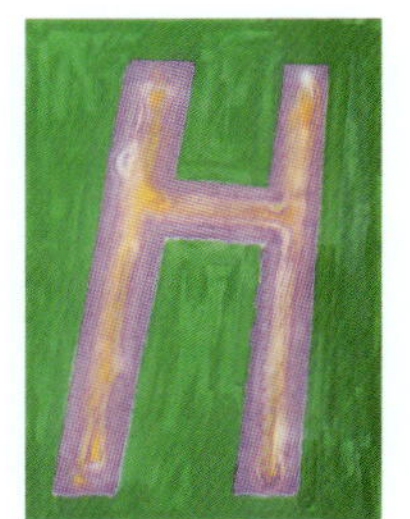
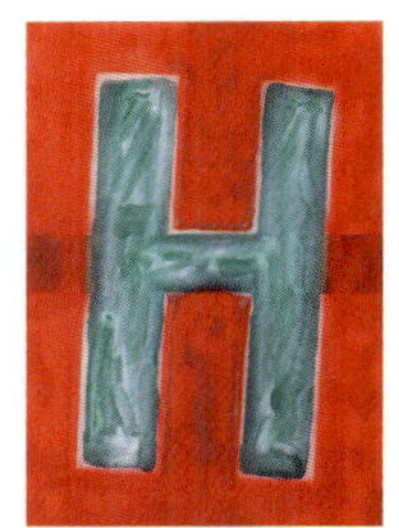
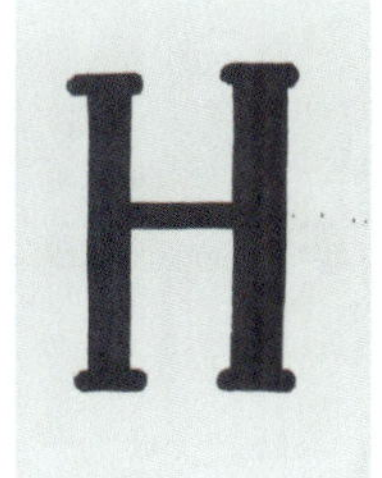

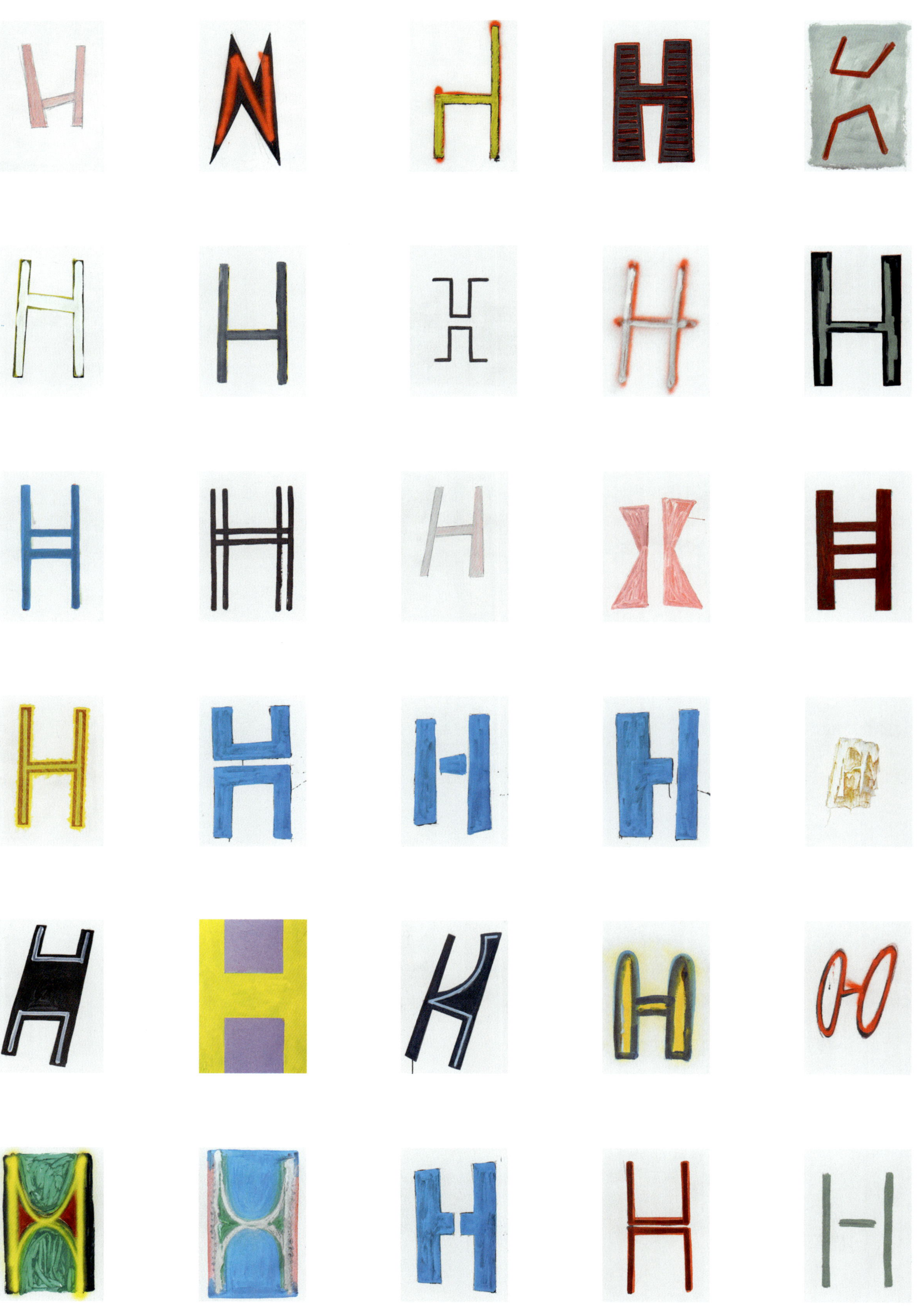

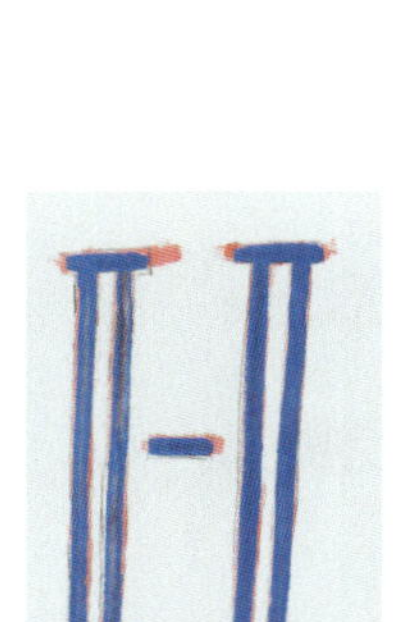
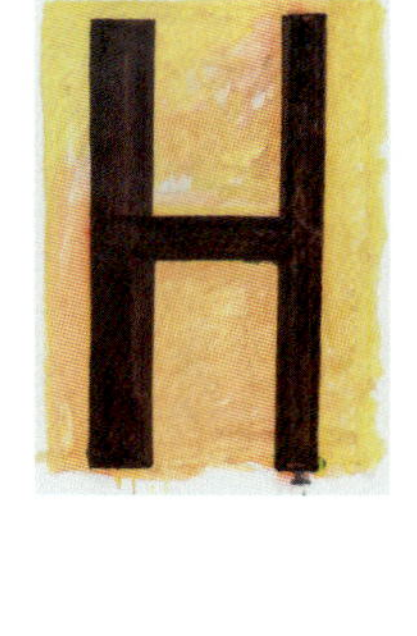
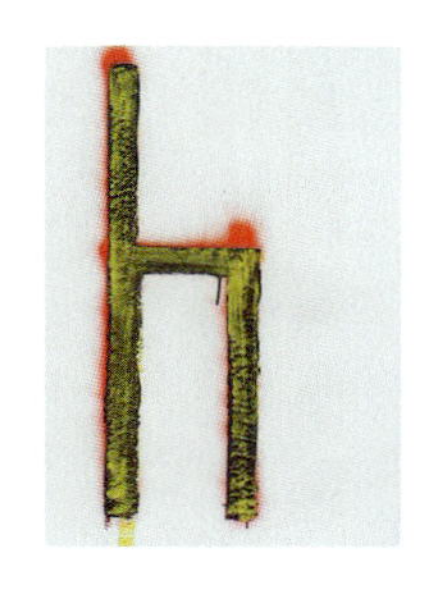
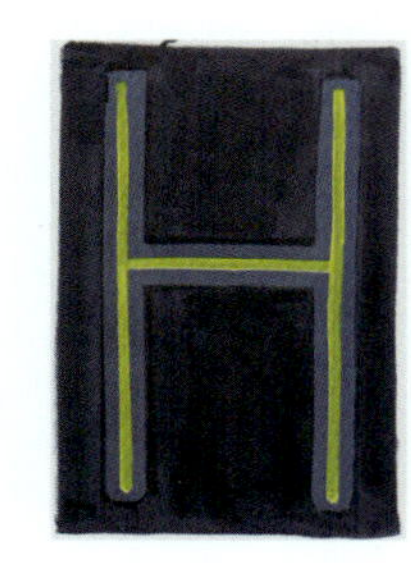
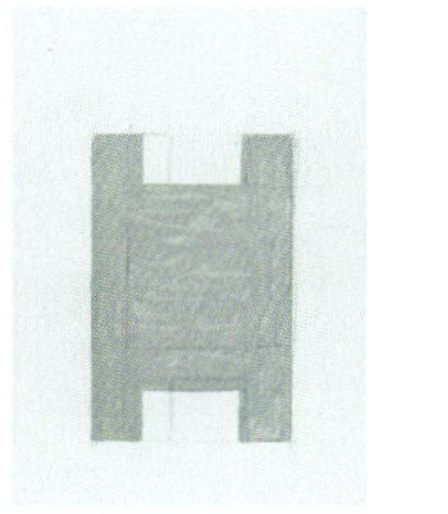
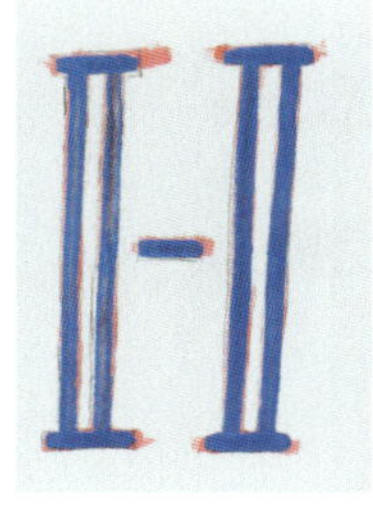
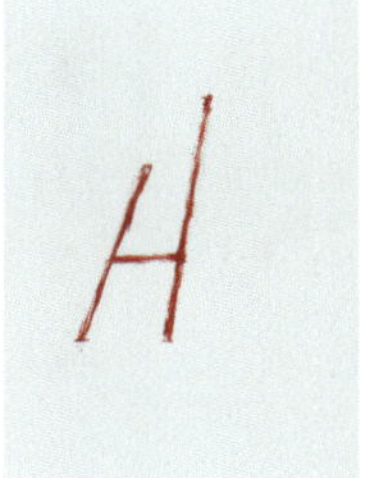
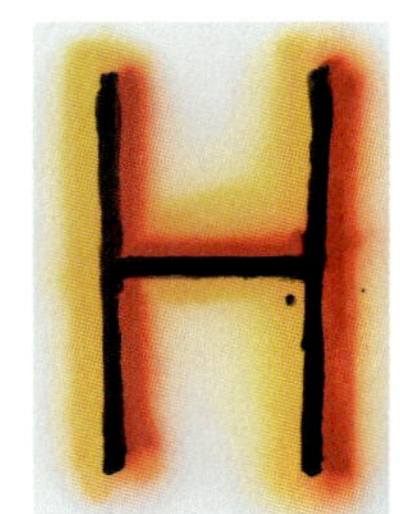
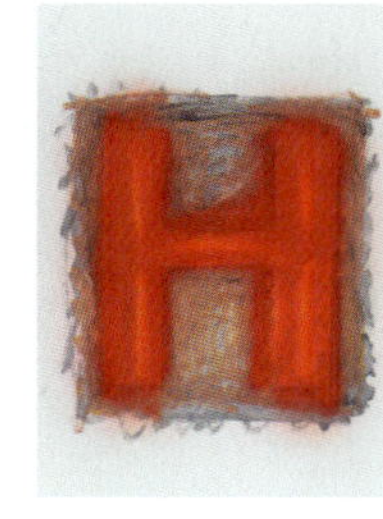
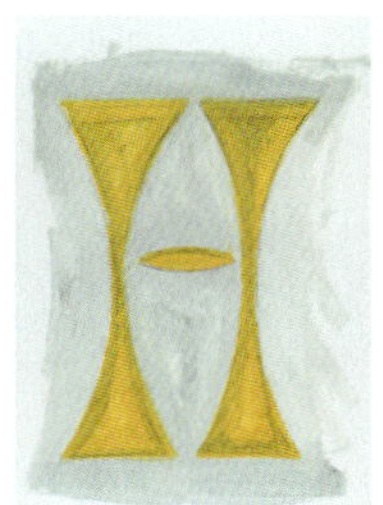
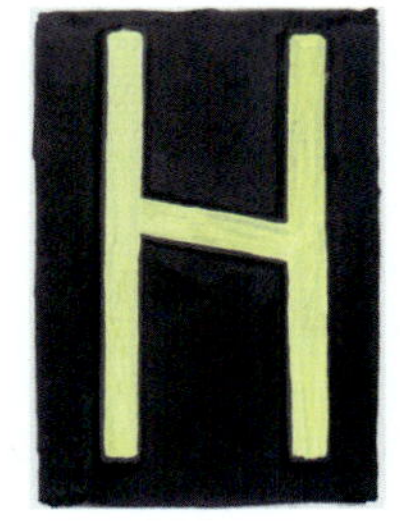
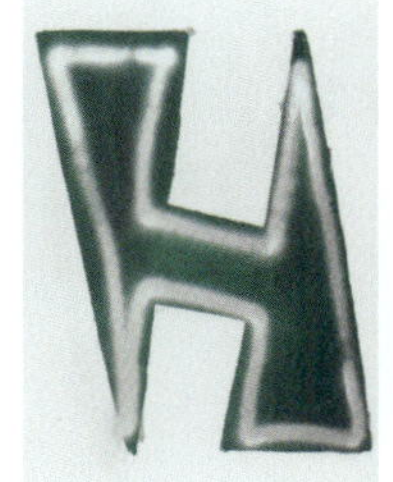
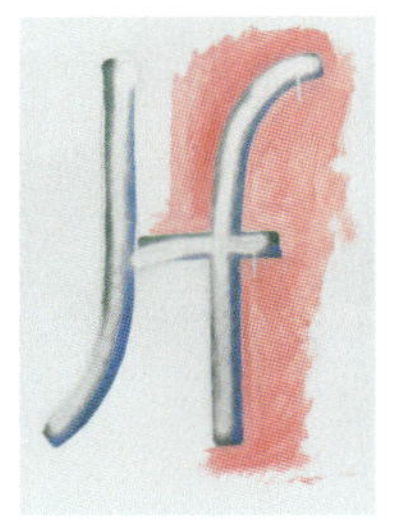
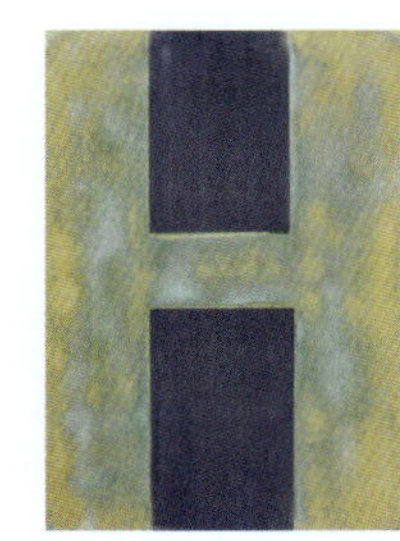
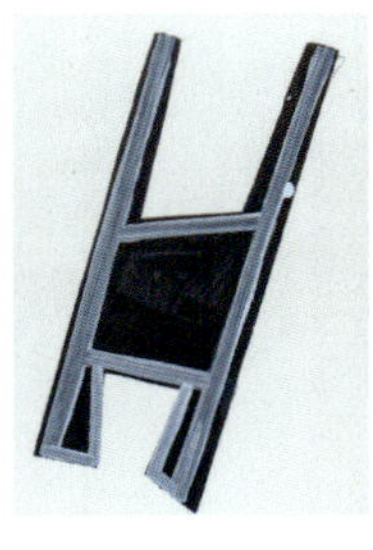
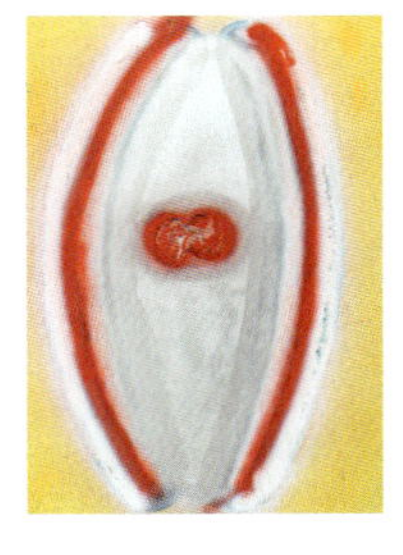
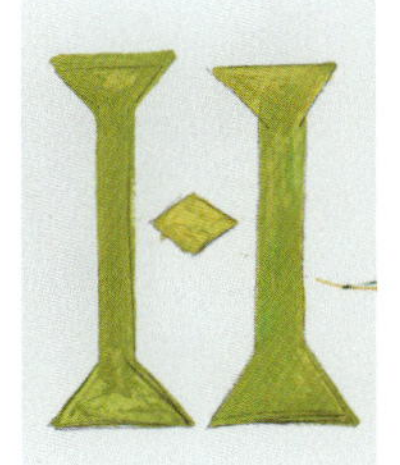
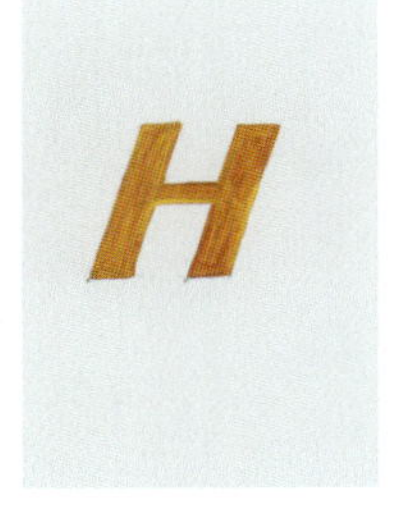
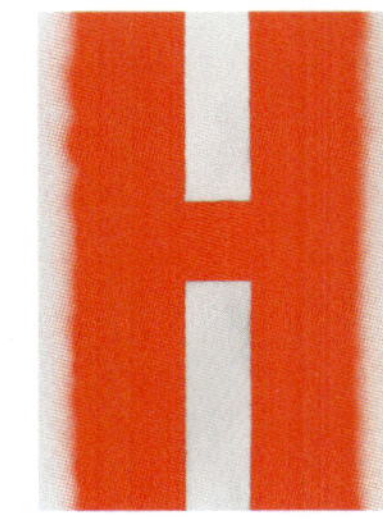
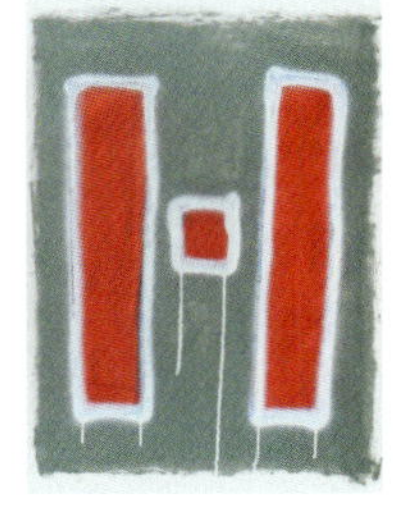
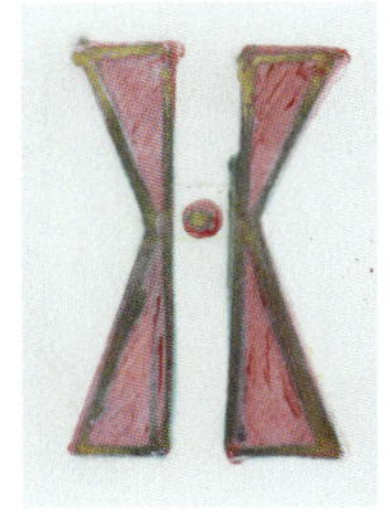
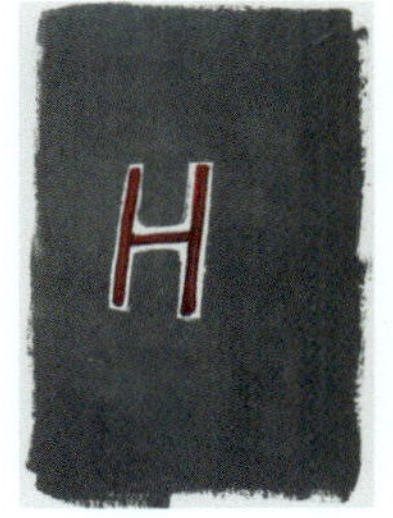
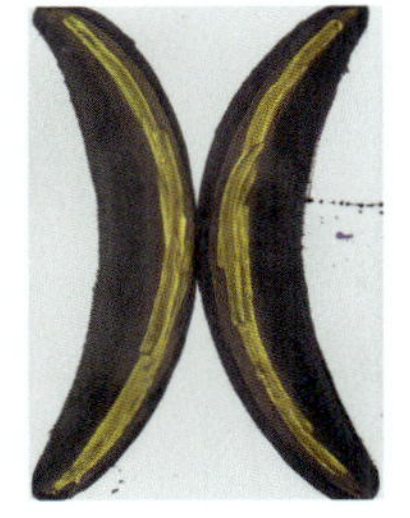
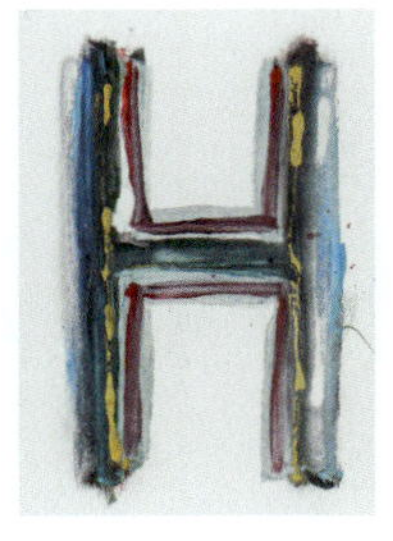
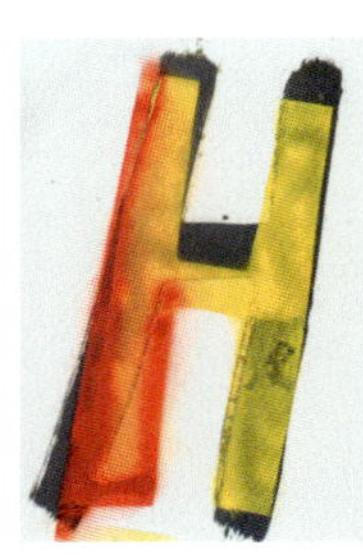
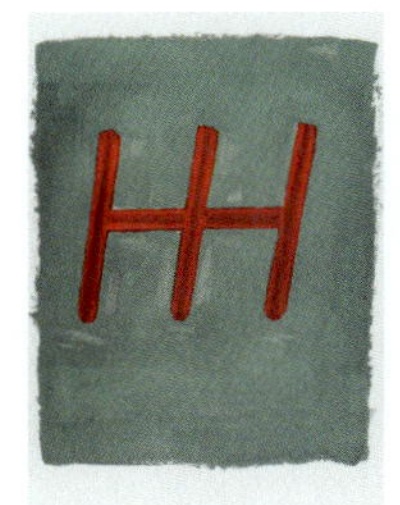
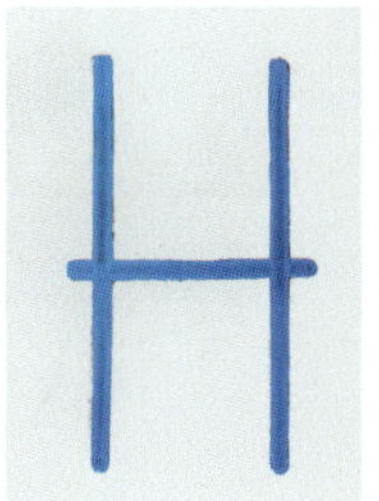
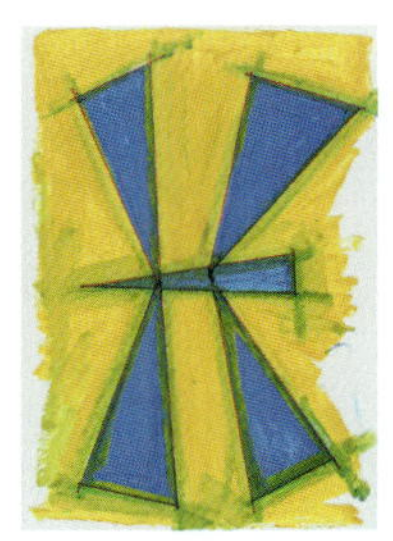
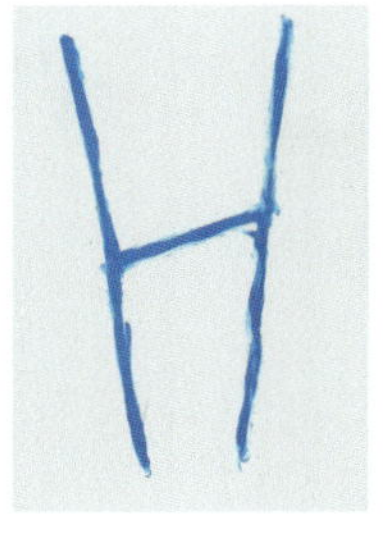

11
In Arbeit seit Juli 74 (*In Progress since July '74*). 1980.
Pencil and primer on nettle cloth, 23 ⅝ × 23 ⅝"
(60 × 60 cm)

IN ARBEIT SEIT JULI 74

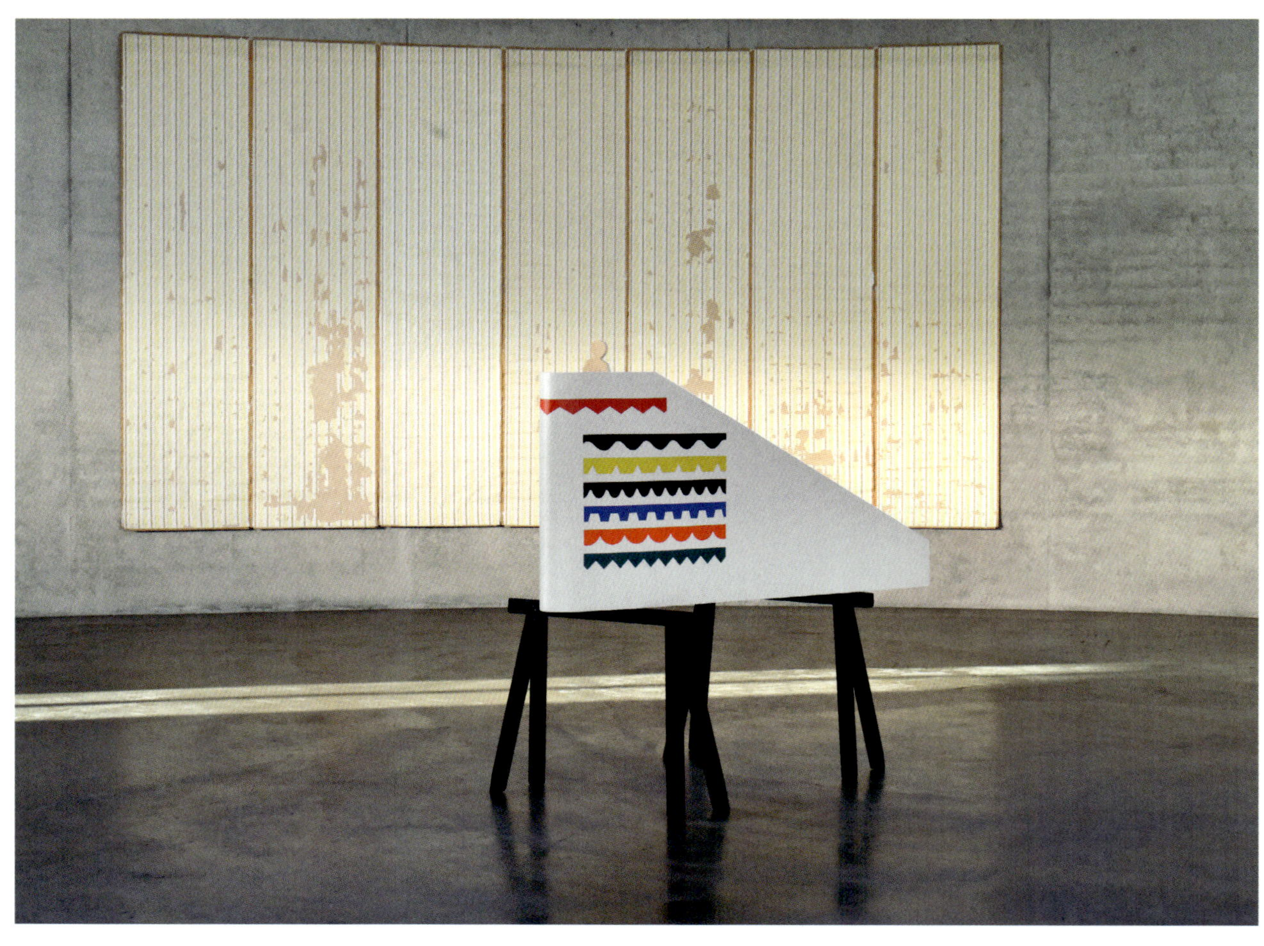

12
Kollektion (*Collection*). 1980. Fabric, eight parts, various lengths from 6' 11" (211 cm) to 10' 7 ⅜" (323.5 cm), overall 10' 4" × 10' 7 9⁄16" (315 × 324 cm)

Above:
Miniature version of *Kollektion* on the side of *Schiff (Modell 1:5)* (*Ship [Model 1:5]*). 1980. Wood, paint, and color adhesive film on sawhorses, 36 ⅝ × 77 15⁄16 × 39 ⅜" (93 × 198 × 100 cm). Kunstsammlung Nordrhein-Westfalen, Düsseldorf. Donation of Dorothee and Konrad Fischer 2015. Installation view, *Arbeiten 1975–1981* (*Works 1975–1981*), Skulpturenhalle, Neuss, Germany, January 14–March 13, 2022. Background: *Große Tapeten* (*Large Wallpapers*, 1975)

12>

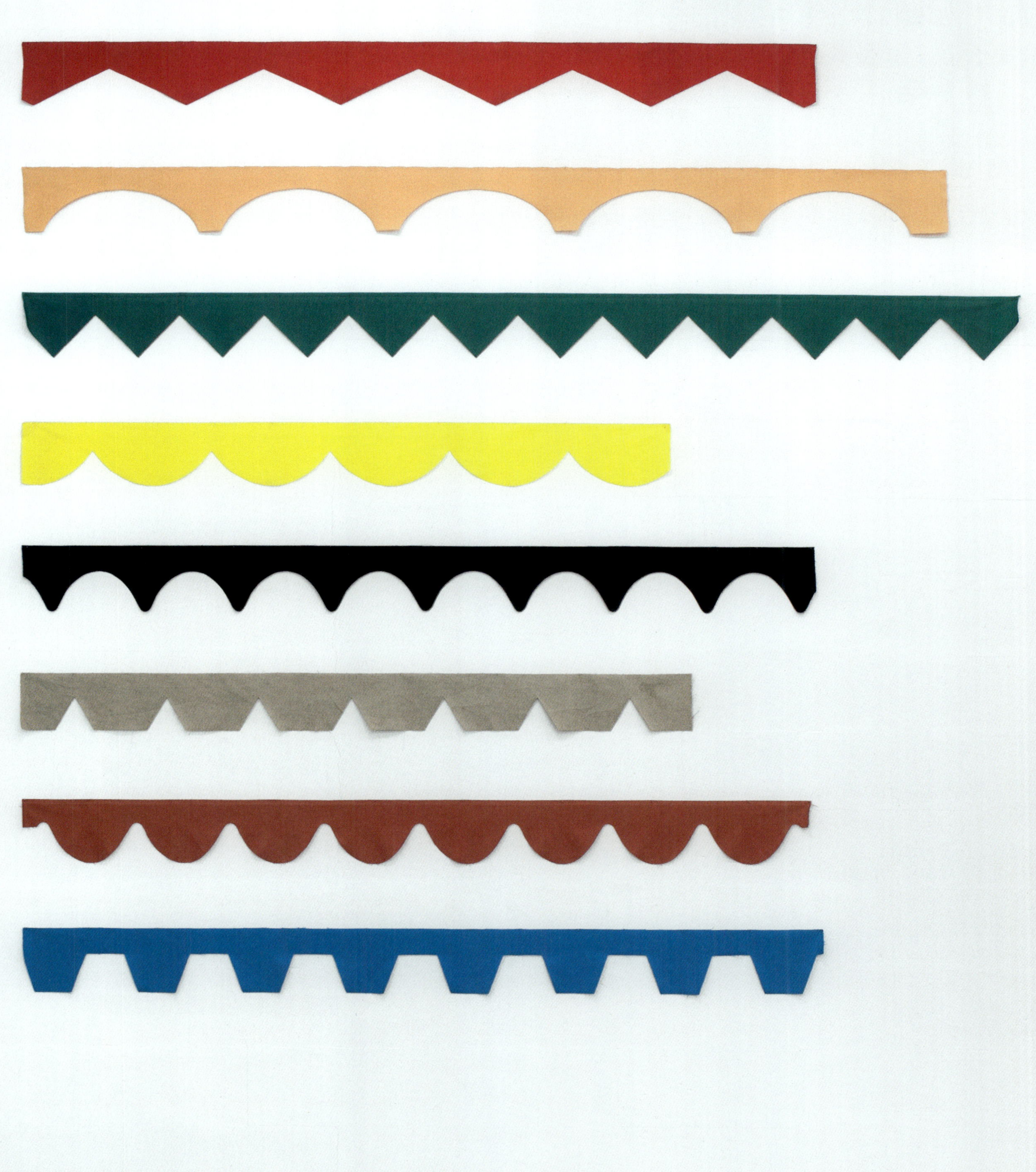

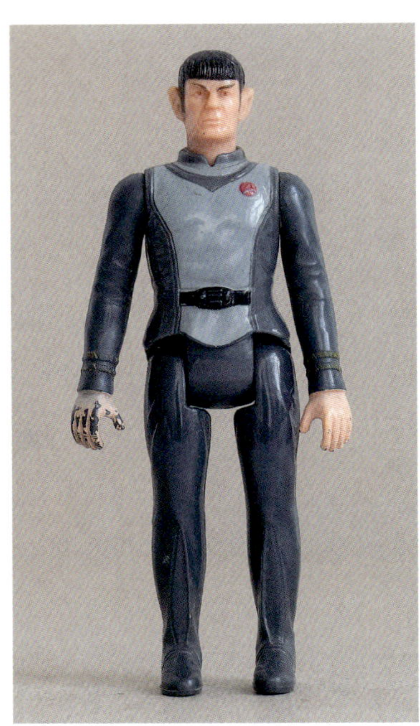

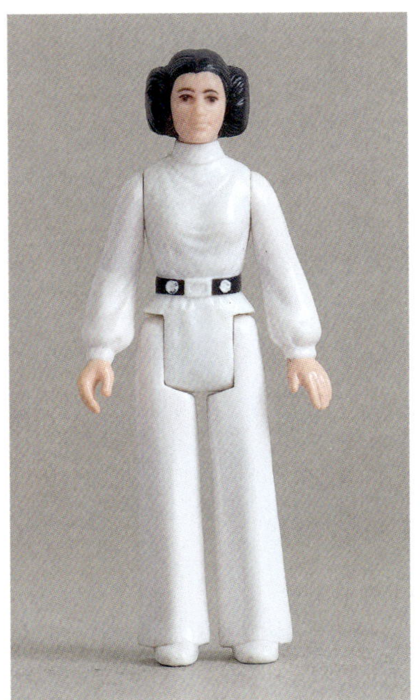

13

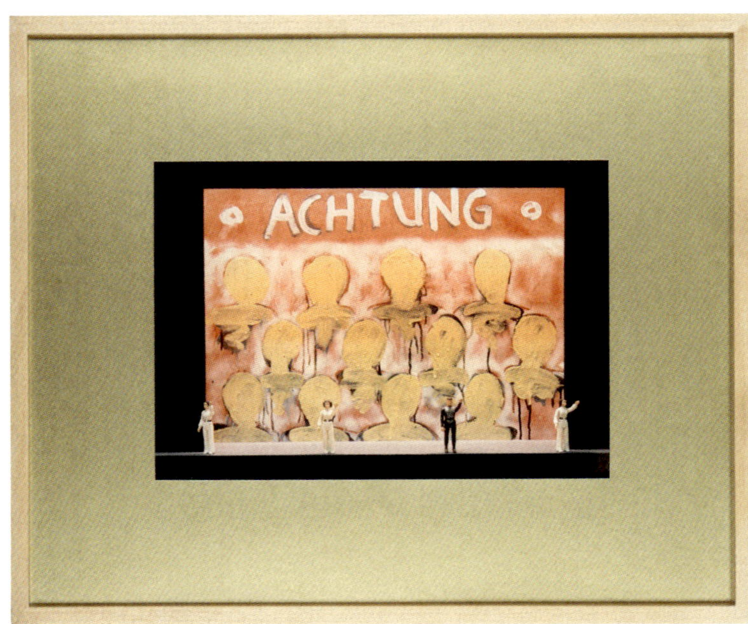

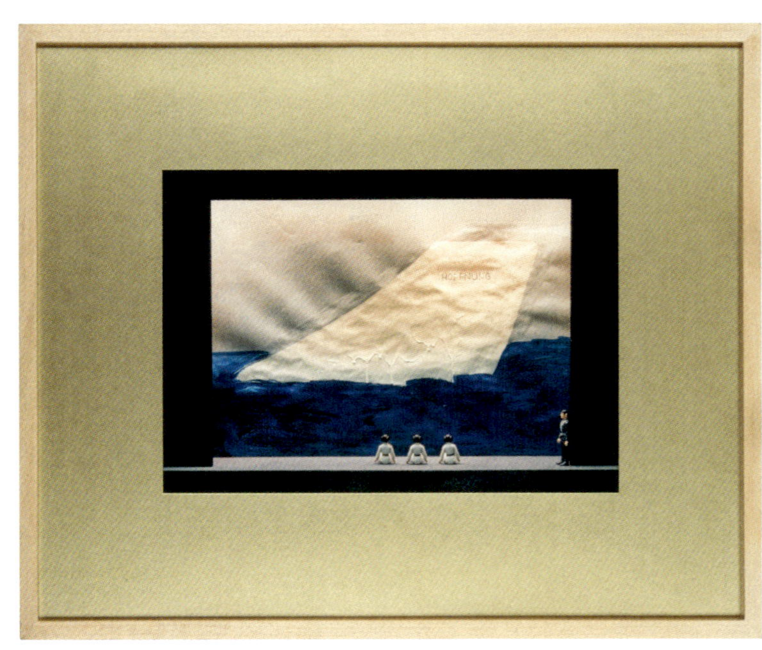

This spread and next:

13
Skizzen zum Projekt Großes Theater (*Sketches for the Large Theater Project*). 1980. Chromogenic color prints, 14 sheets, each 15 ¾ × 19 ¹¹⁄₁₆" (40 × 50 cm)

Left:
Spock and Princess Leia figurines from *Skizzen zum Projekt Großes Theater*

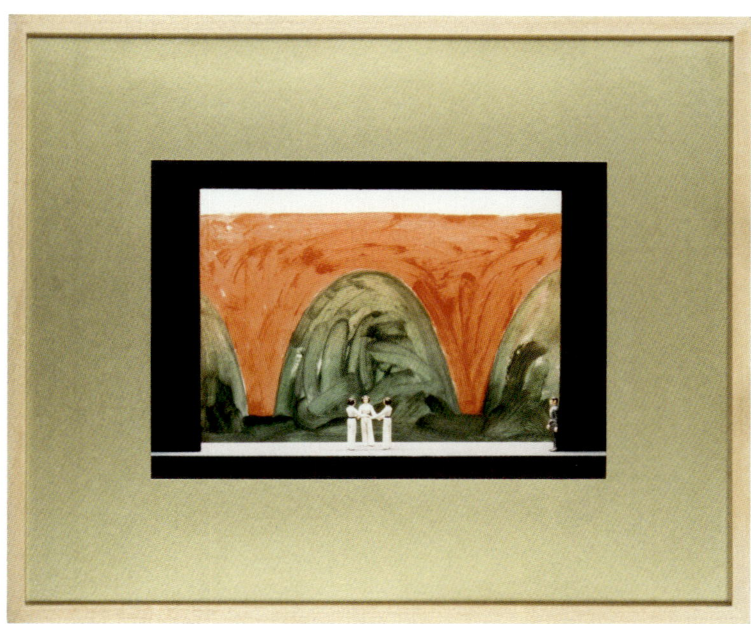

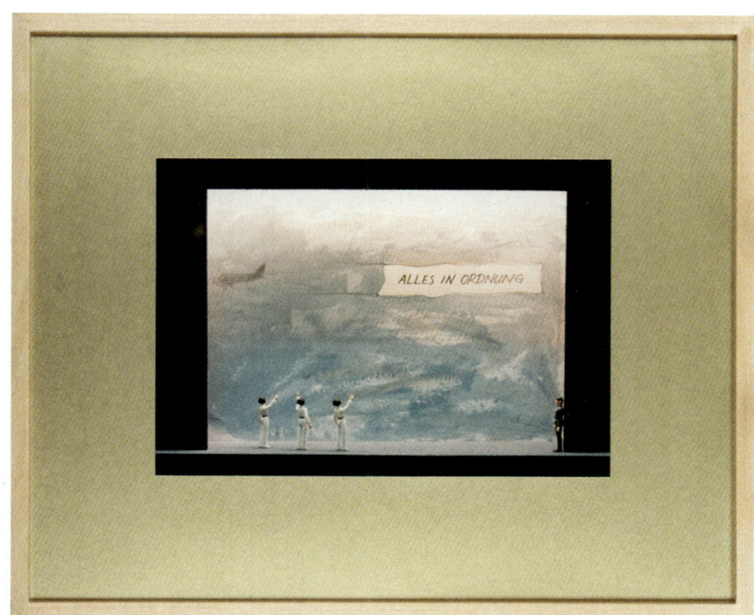

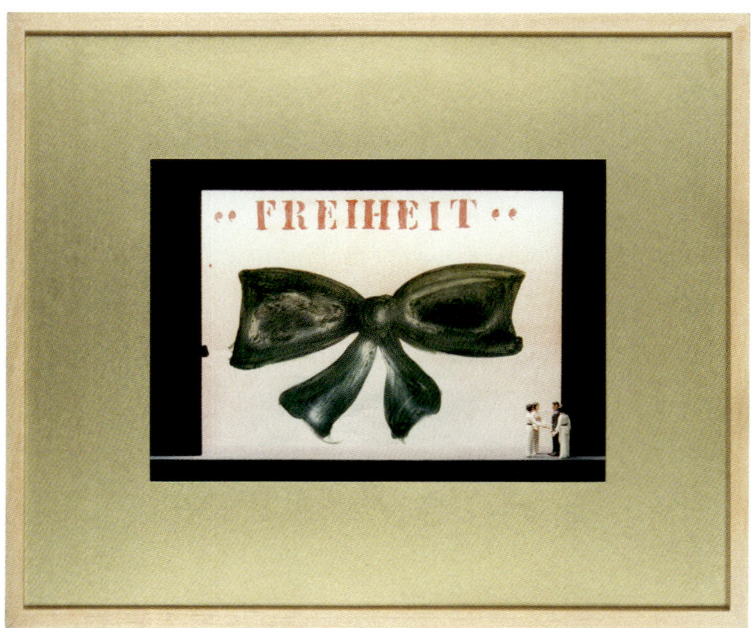

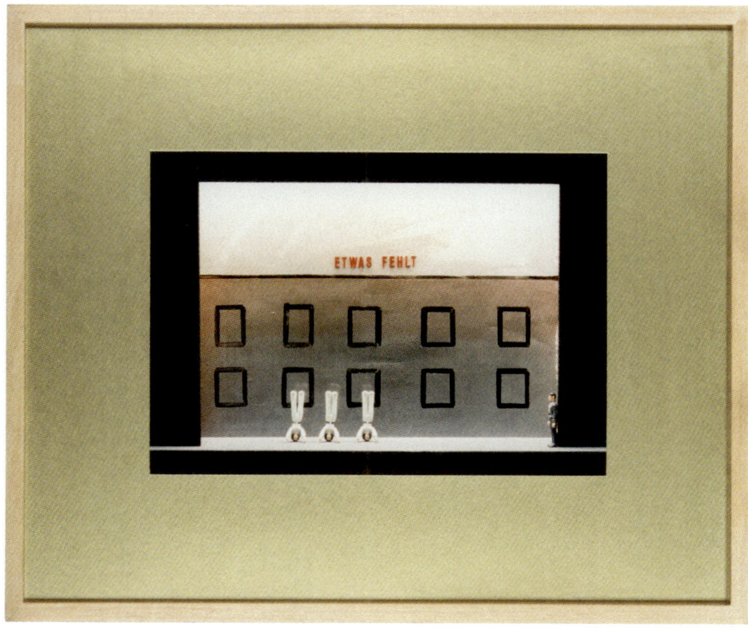

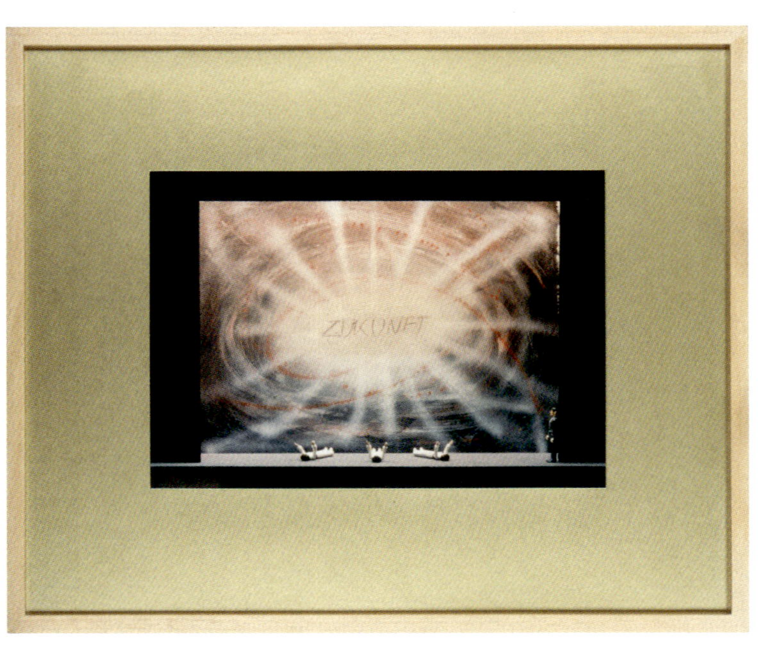
ZUKUNFT

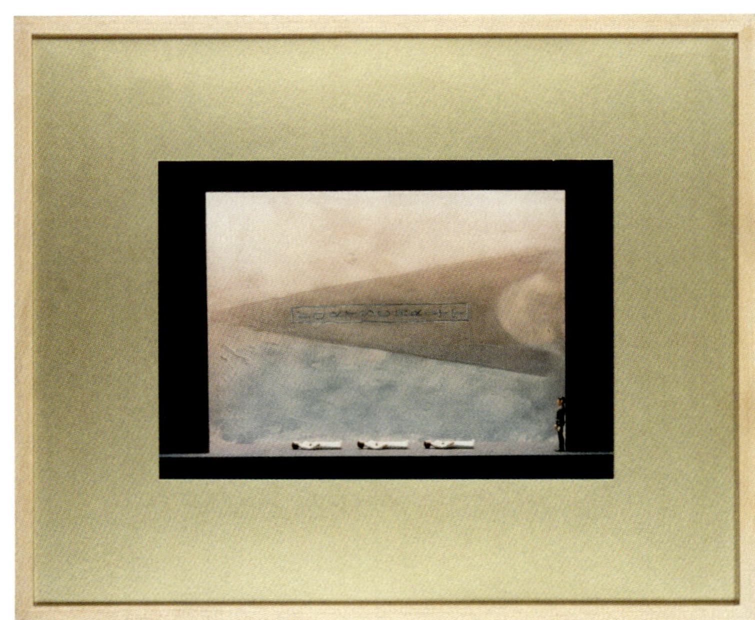

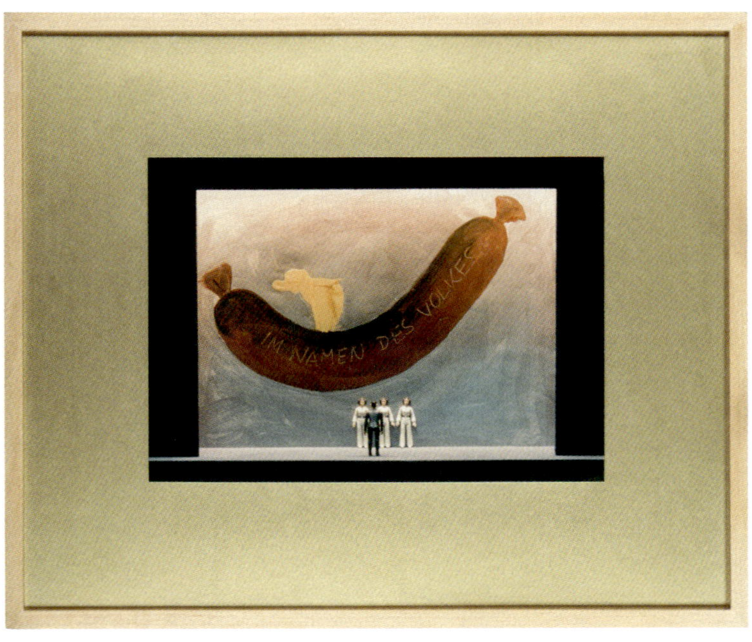
IM NAMEN DES VOLKES

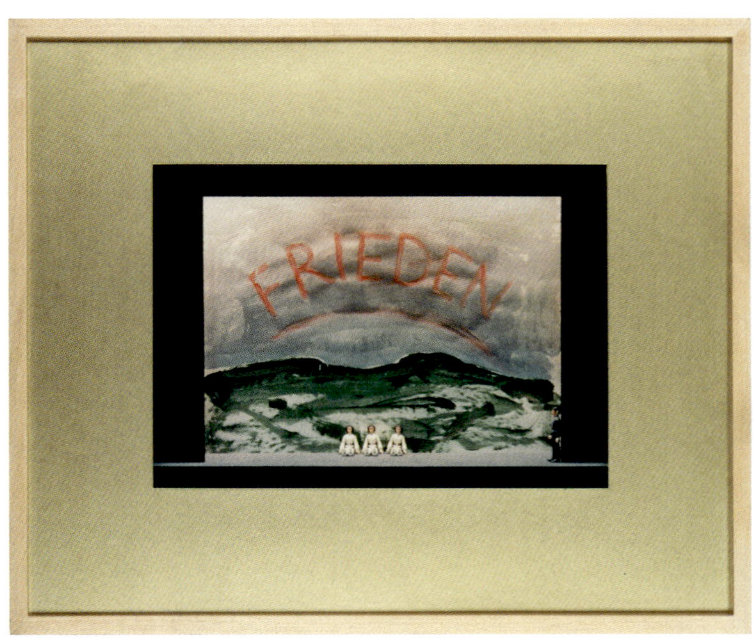
FRIEDEN

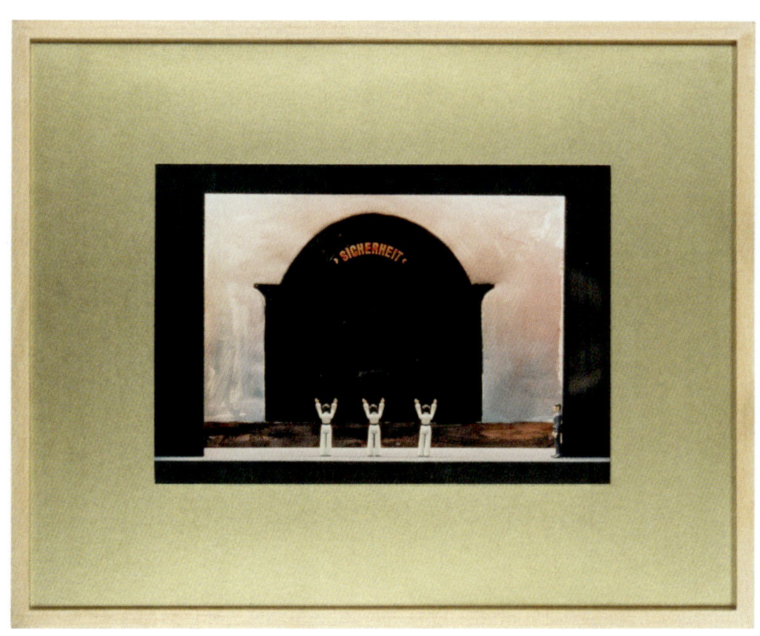
SICHERHEIT

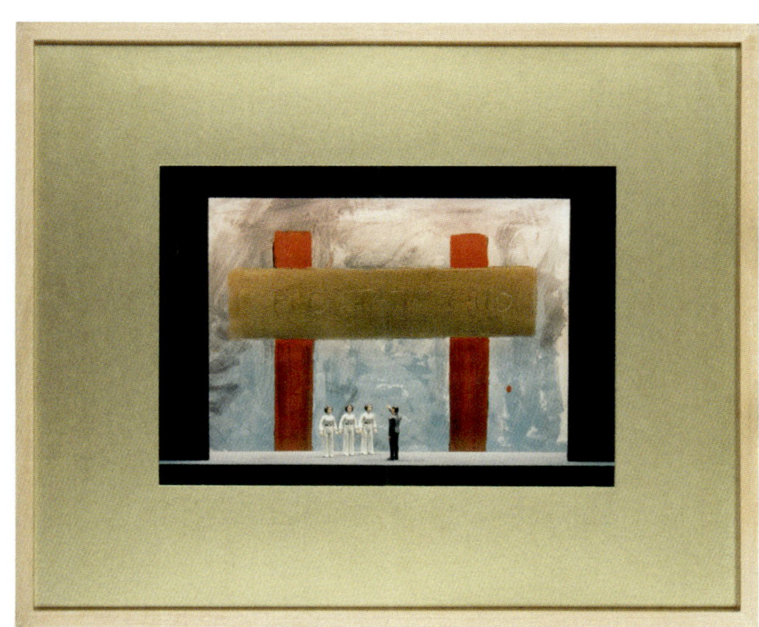

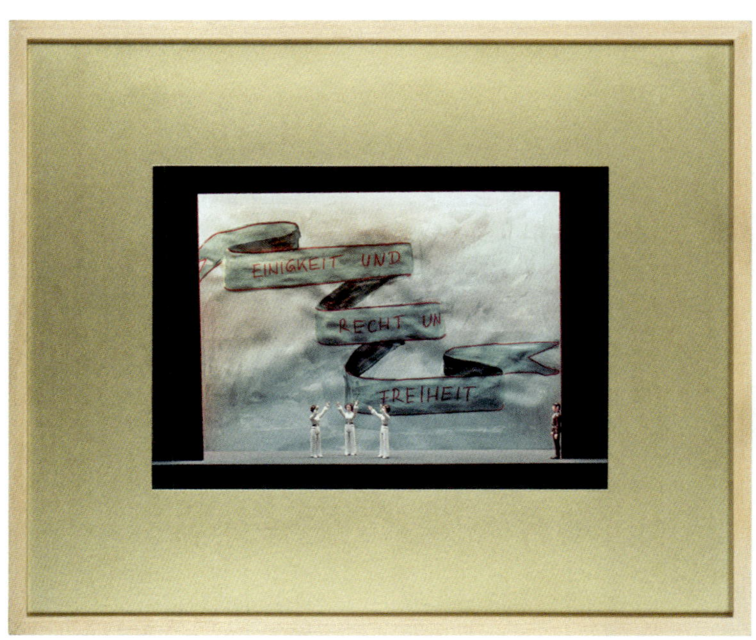
EINIGKEIT UND
RECHT UN
FREIHEIT

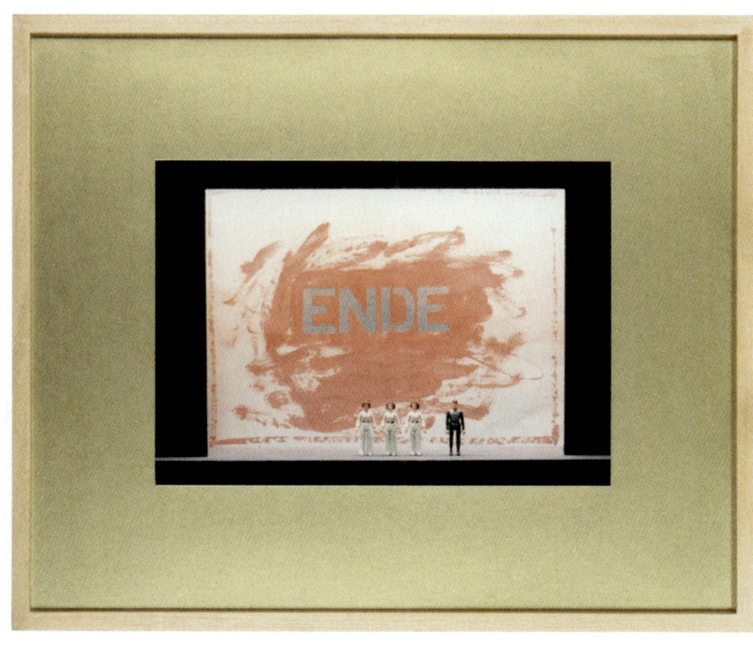
ENDE

14
Schwarze Girlande (*Black Garland*). 1980. Fabric, seven parts. Various lengths from 11' 9 ¾" (360 cm) to 13' 3 7⁄16" (405 cm). Installation dimensions variable. Installation view, *Ruhe vor dem Sturm: Postminimalistische Kunst aus dem Rheinland* (*The Calm before the Storm: Post-Minimalist Art from the Rhineland*), Museum Morsbroich, Leverkusen, Germany, September 13, 2015–January 10, 2016

This page:
Two views of *Rote Girlande* (*Red Garland*). 1979. Fabric, five parts, various lengths from 12' 5 ⅝" (380 cm) to 35' 9 ½" (1091 cm). Collection Kasper König. Installation view, curatorial office for *Westkunst: Zeitgenössische Kunst seit 1939* (*Art of the West: Contemporary Art since 1939*), Cologne, 1979. Pictured: Kasper König

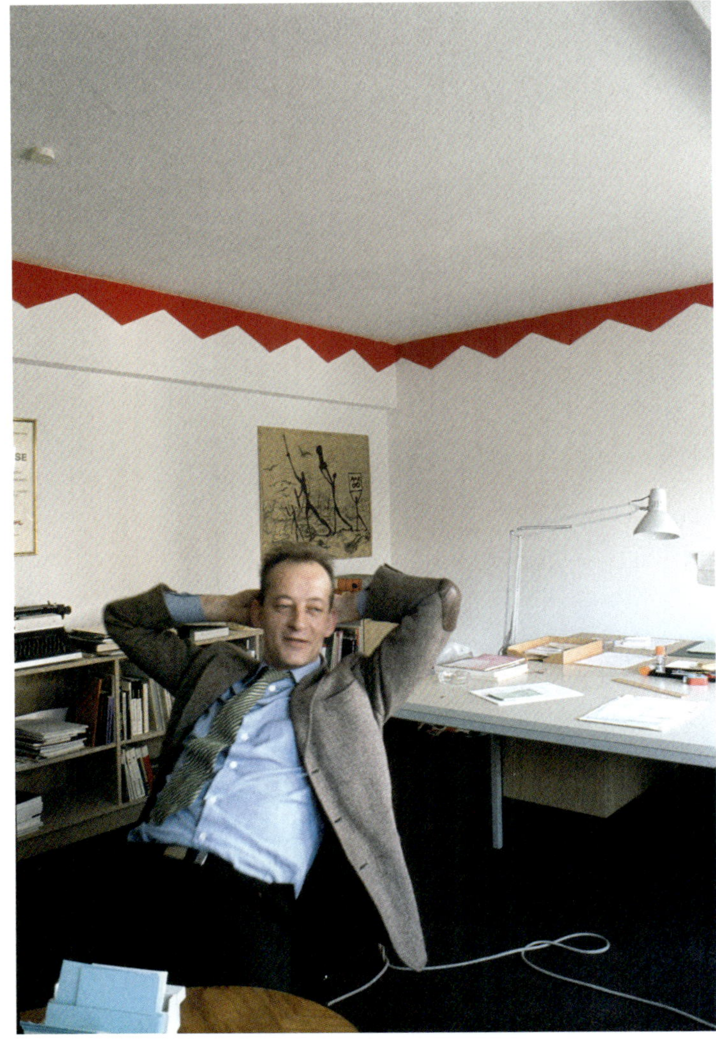

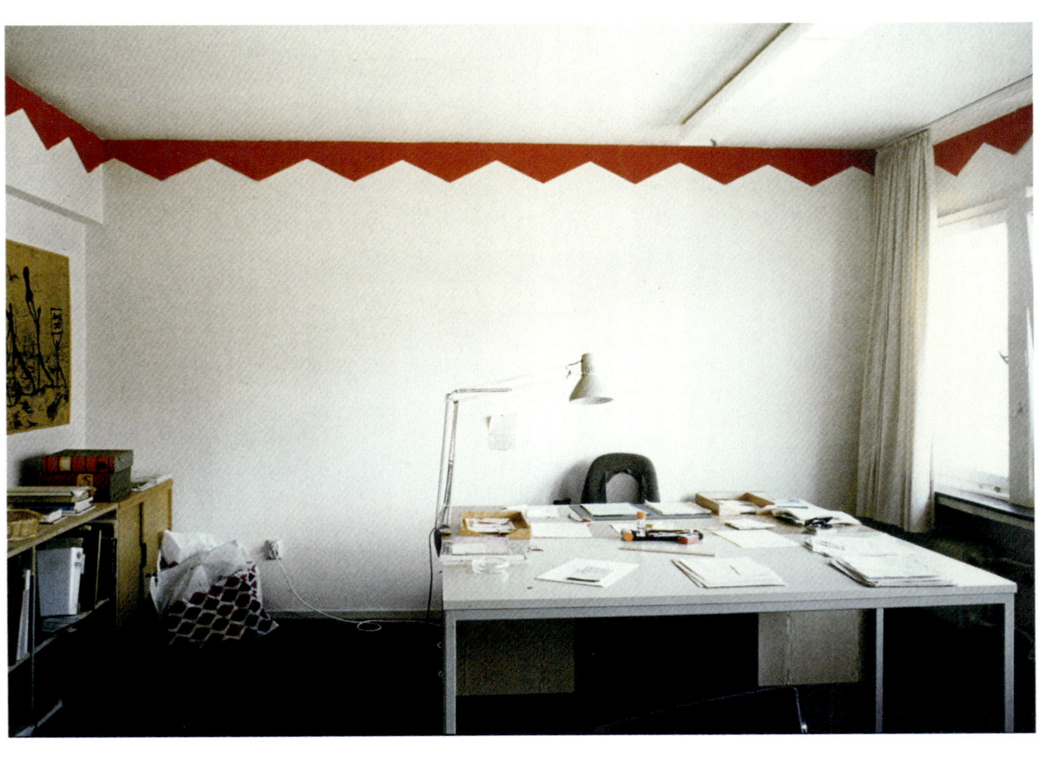

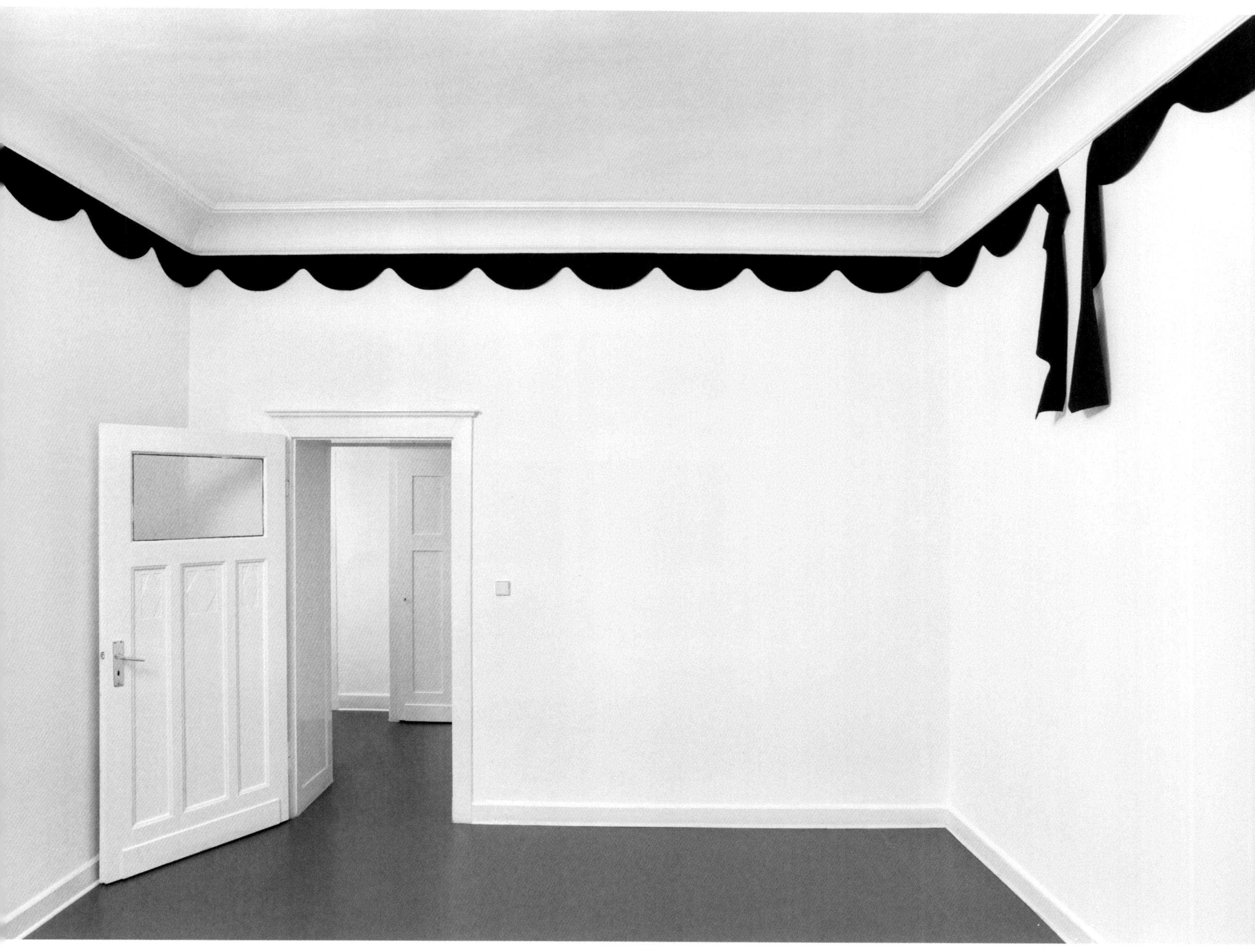

14

15
Postkarten, München (*Postcards, Munich*). 1980. Postcards mounted on paper, four sheets, each 22 × 32" (55.9 × 81.3 cm)

Right:
Exhibition invitation (recto and verso) for *Thomas Schütte: Arbeiten 1977–80* (*Thomas Schütte: Works 1977–80*), Galerie Rüdiger Schöttle, Munich, May 10–June 10, 1980

15

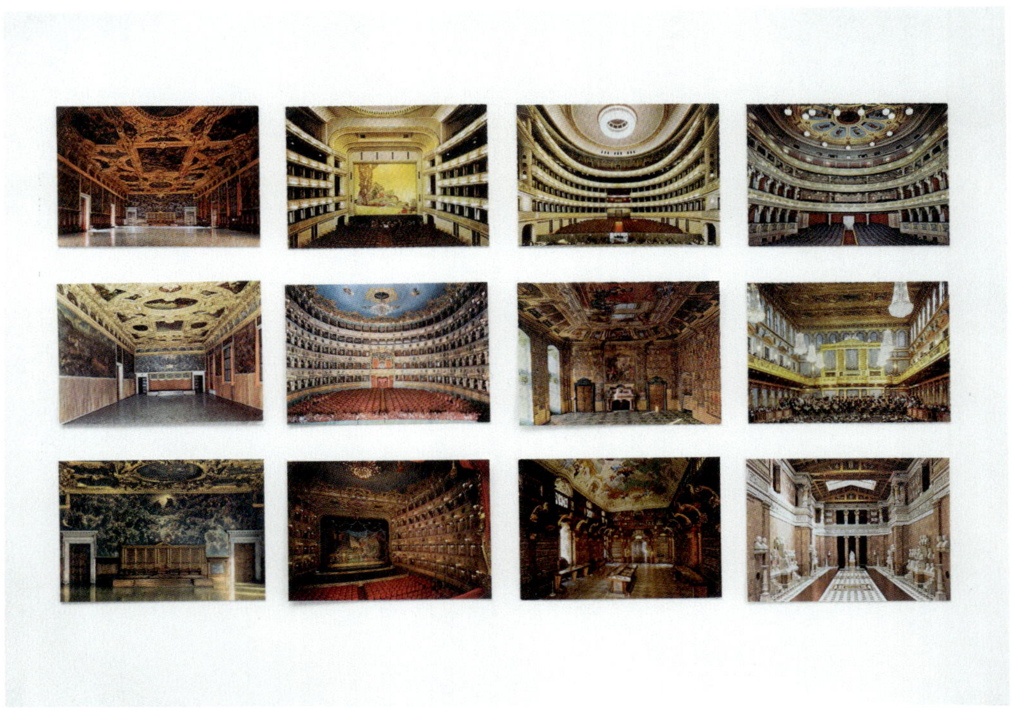

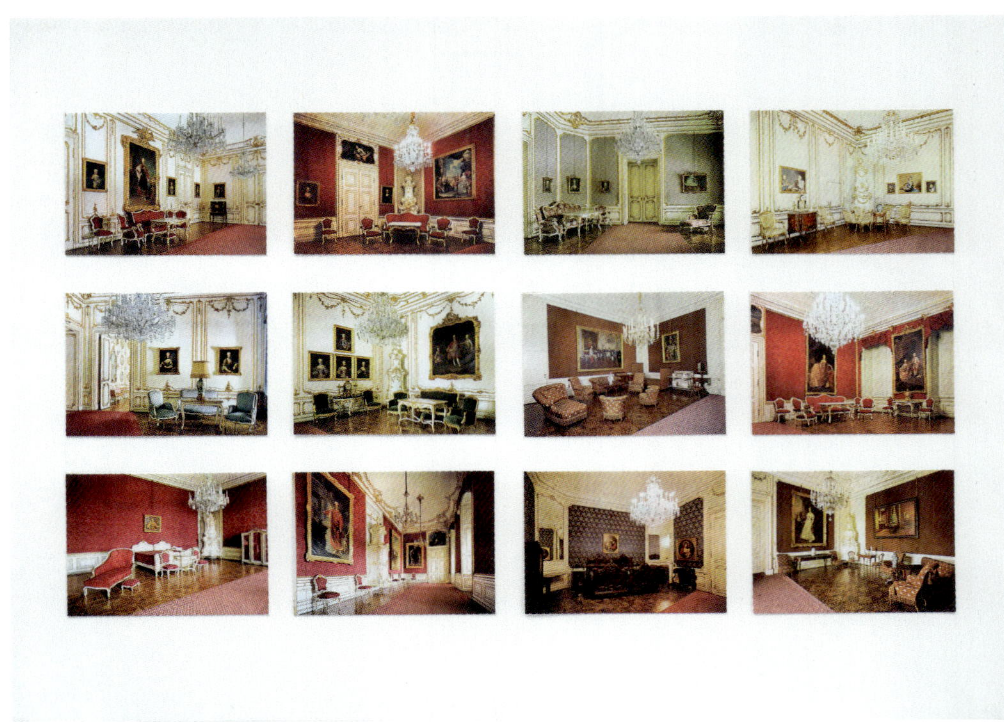

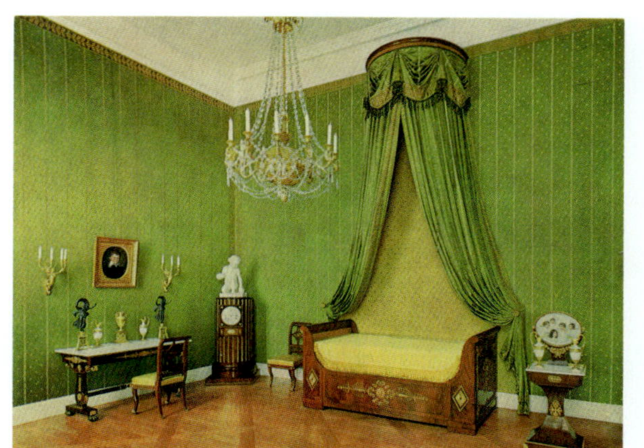

Residenzmuseum München
»Charlottenzimmer«
Schlafzimmer, um 1810-20

THOMAS SCHÜTTE

Arbeiten 1977-80

gezeigt vom 10.5.80 - 10.6.80

Eröffnung:

Freitag, 9.5.80, 19 - 21 h

RÜDIGER SCHÖTTLE
Martiusstraße 7
München 40
Tel: 33 36 86

Orig.-Aufn. J. Härtl – Verlag M. Herpich – München 54

DRUCKSACHE

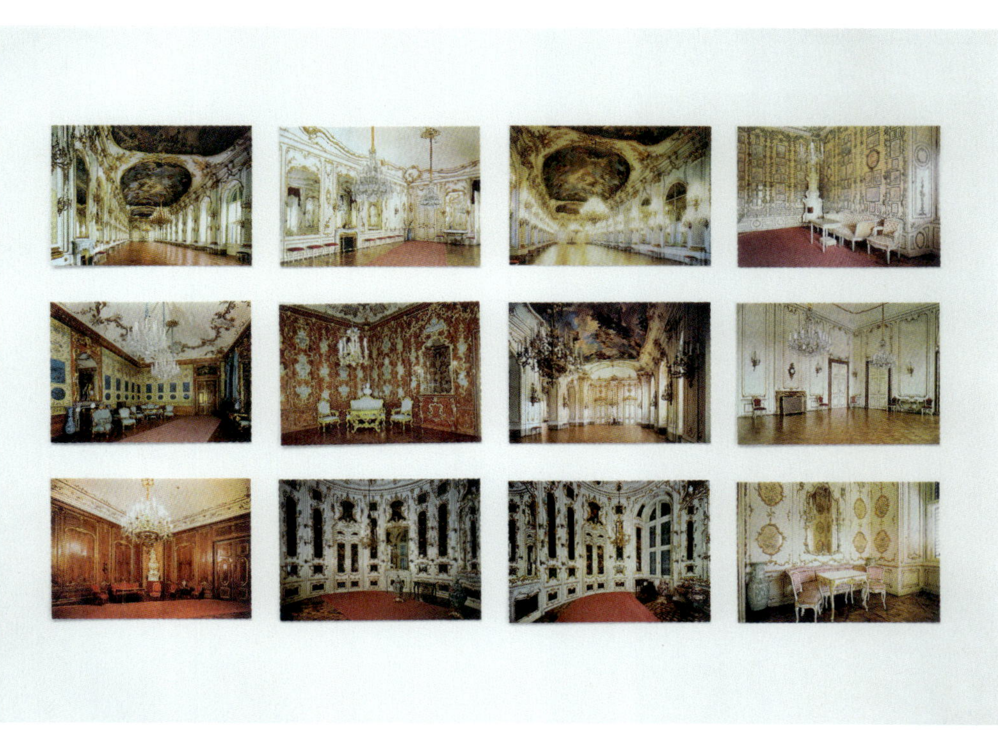

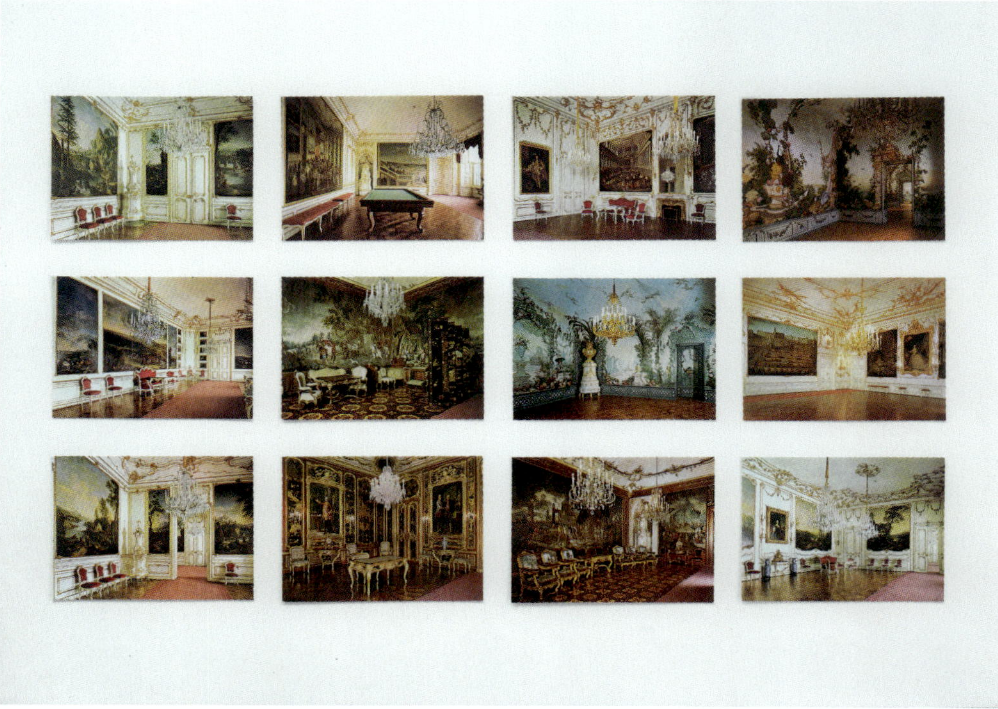

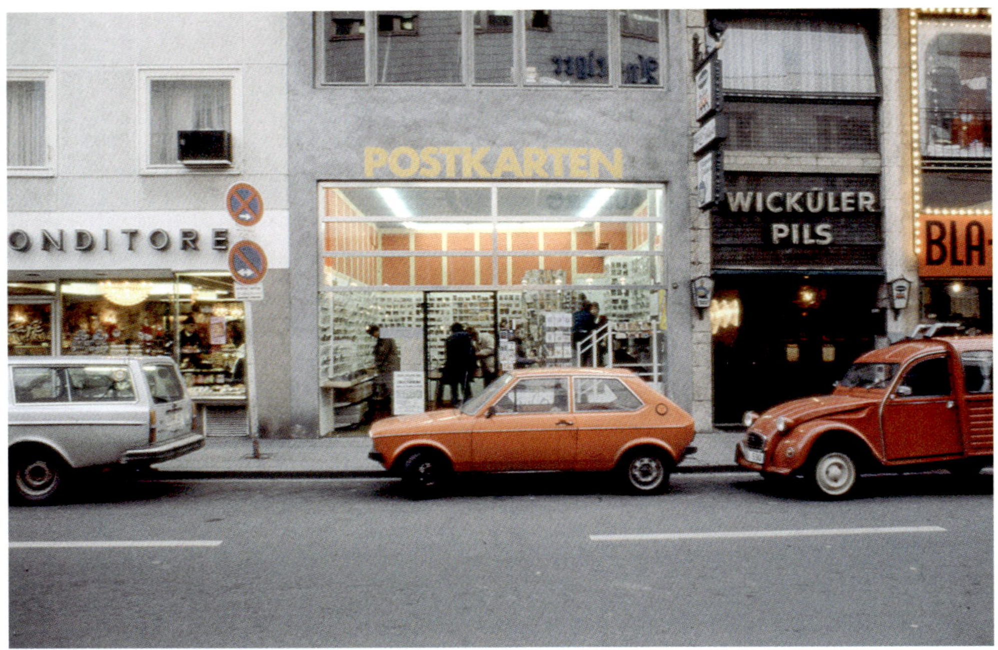

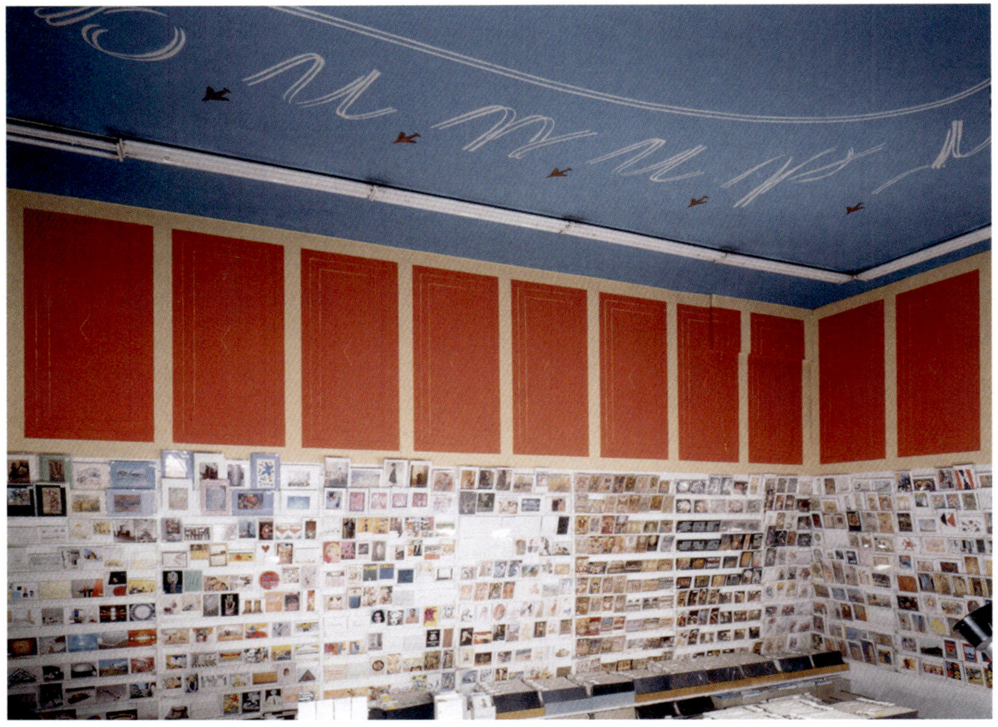

16
Alles in Ordnung (*All in Order*). 1981. Paint on ceiling, 22' 11 9/16" × 18 9/16" (700 × 550 cm). Installation view, Postkartenladen Walther König, Cologne, 2024

This page:
Exterior and interior views of Postkartenladen Walther König, Cologne, 1981

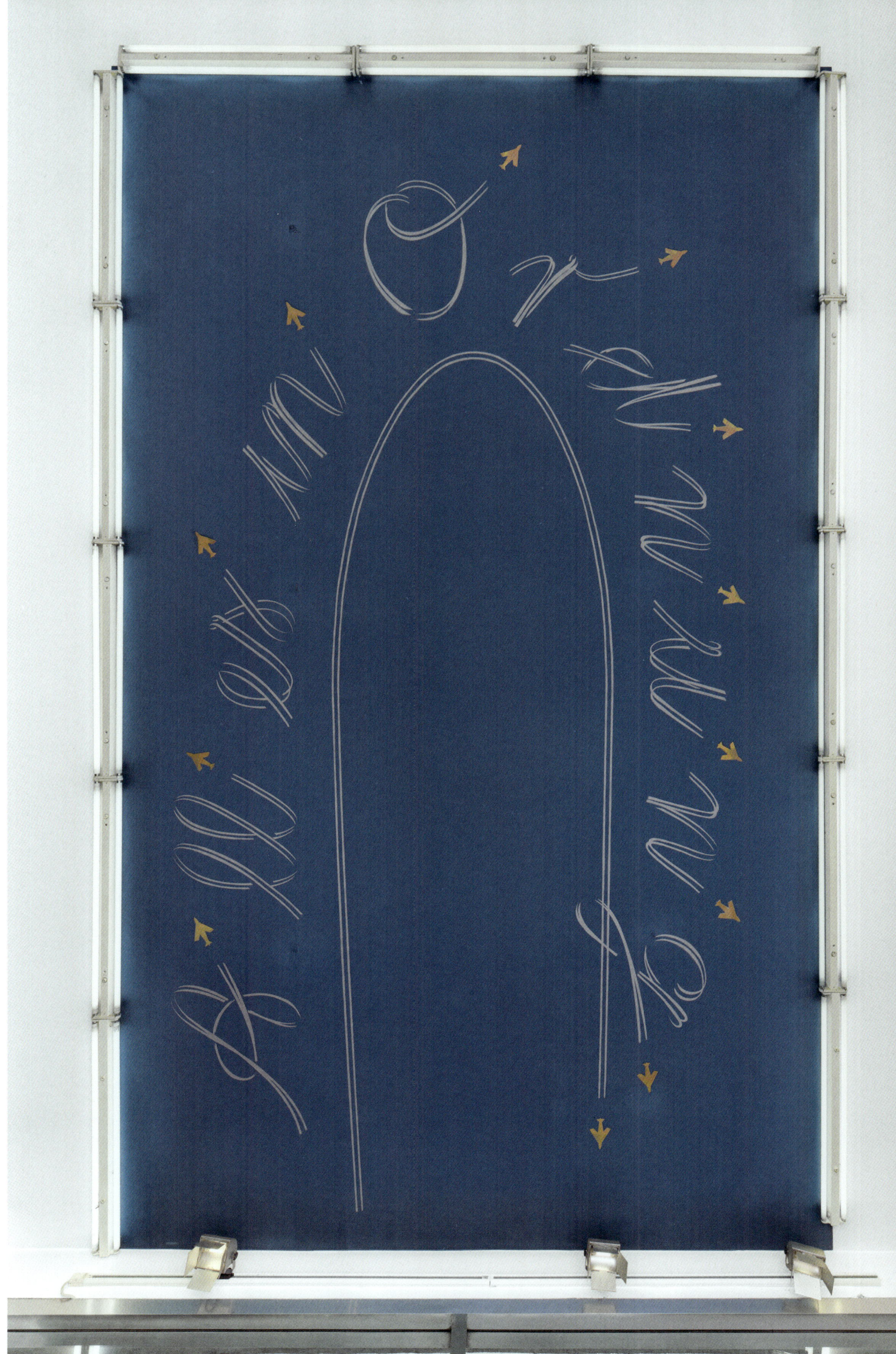

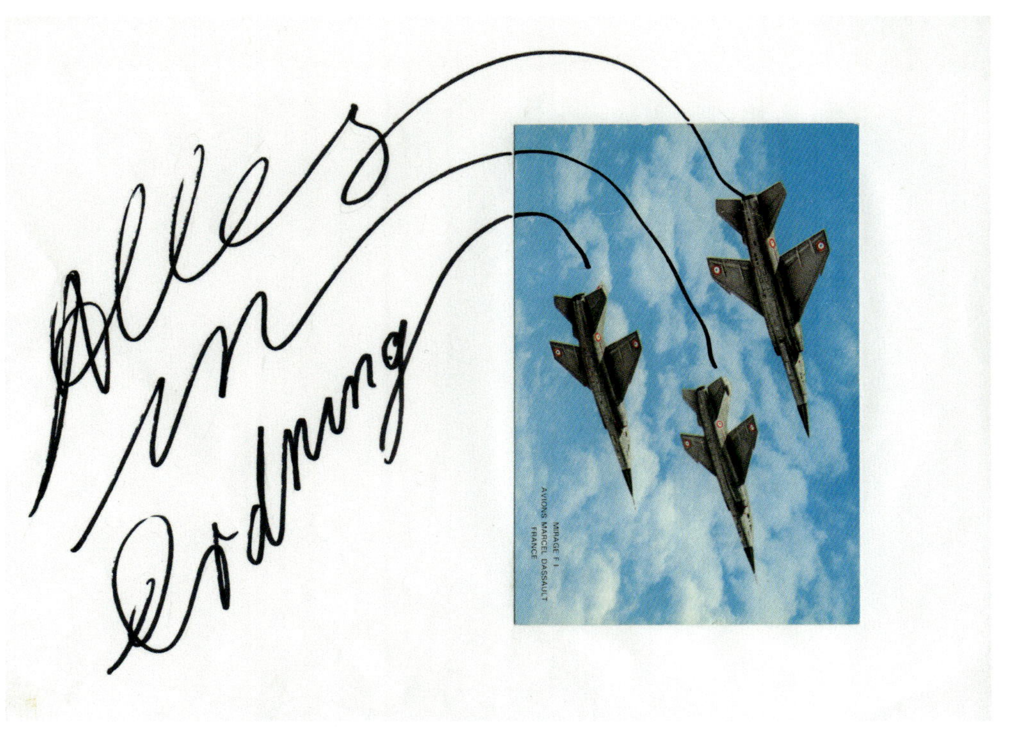

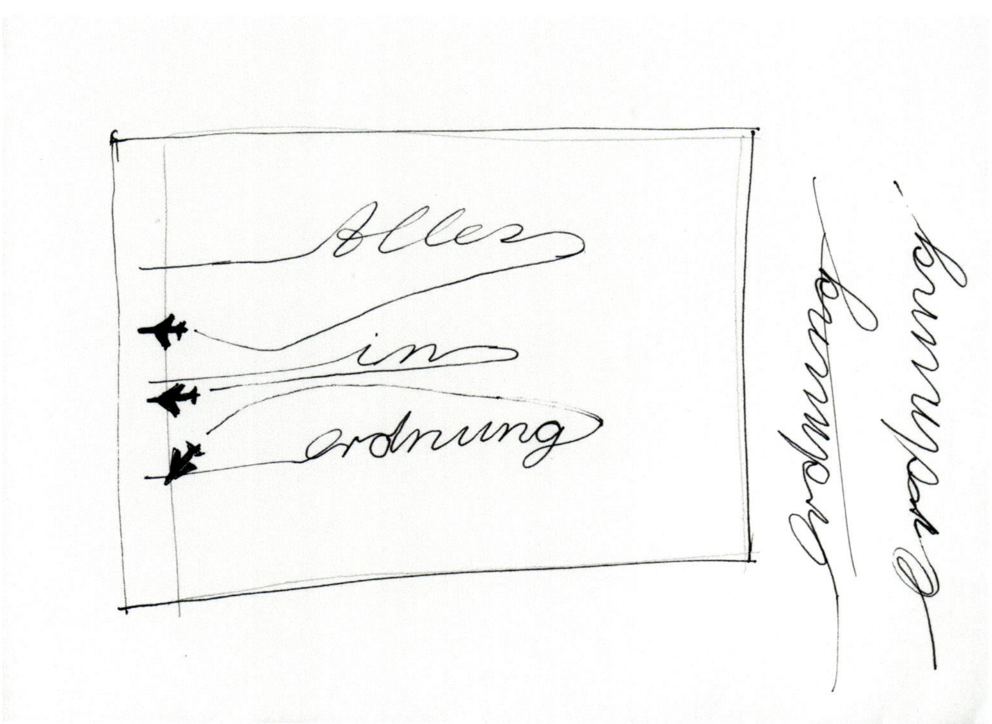

This page, from top:

Drawing for *Alles in Ordnung* (*All in Order*). 1981. Collage with pen on paper, 8 ¼ × 11 ¹¹⁄₁₆" (21 × 29.7 cm). Collection the artist, Düsseldorf

Drawing for *Alles in Ordnung*. 1981. Pen on paper, 8 ¼ × 11 ¹¹⁄₁₆" (21 × 29.7 cm). Collection the artist, Düsseldorf

Opposite page:
Three drawings for *Alles in Ordnung*. 1981. Pen on paper, 11 ¹¹⁄₁₆ × 8 ¼" (29.7 × 21 cm). Collection the artist, Düsseldorf

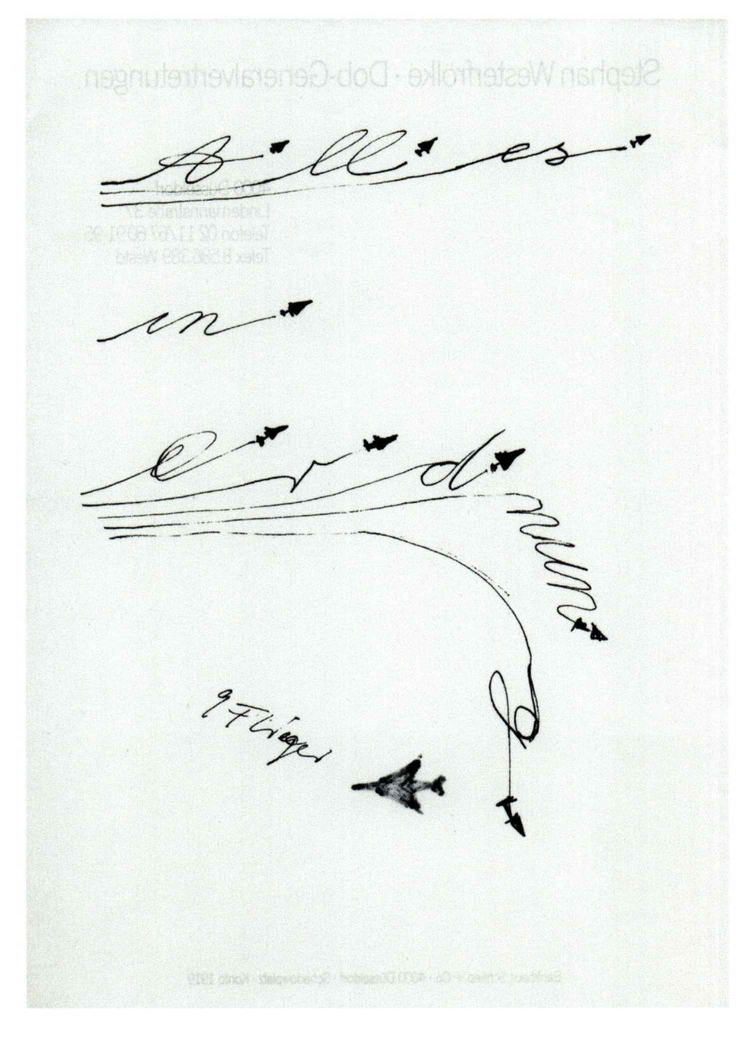

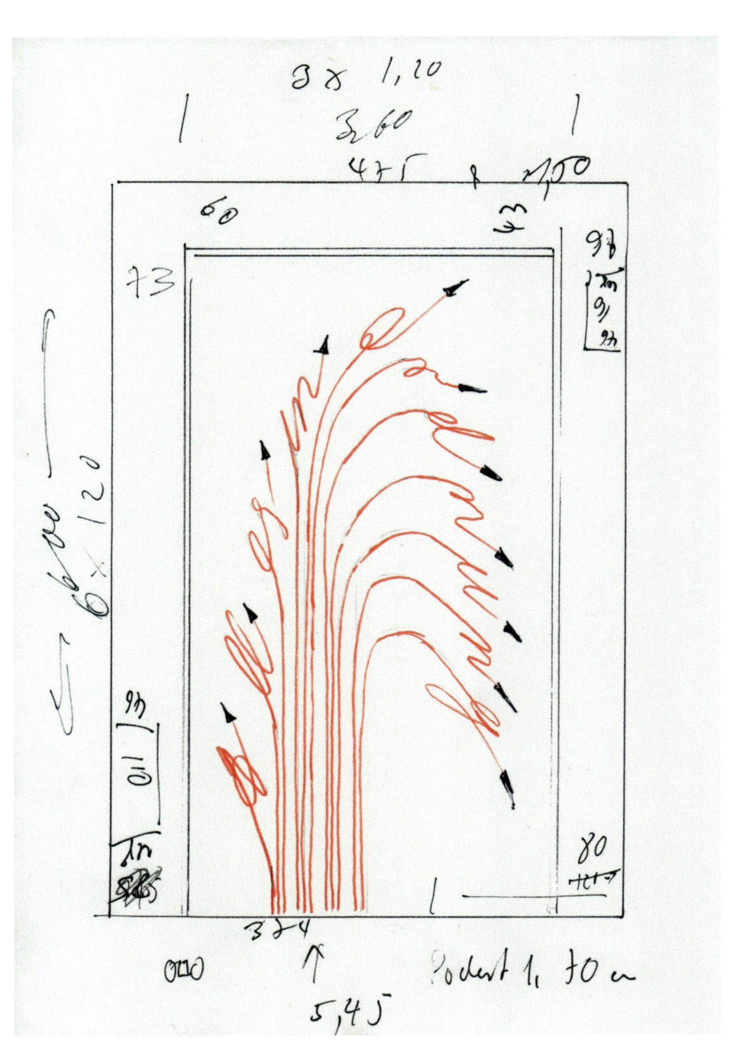

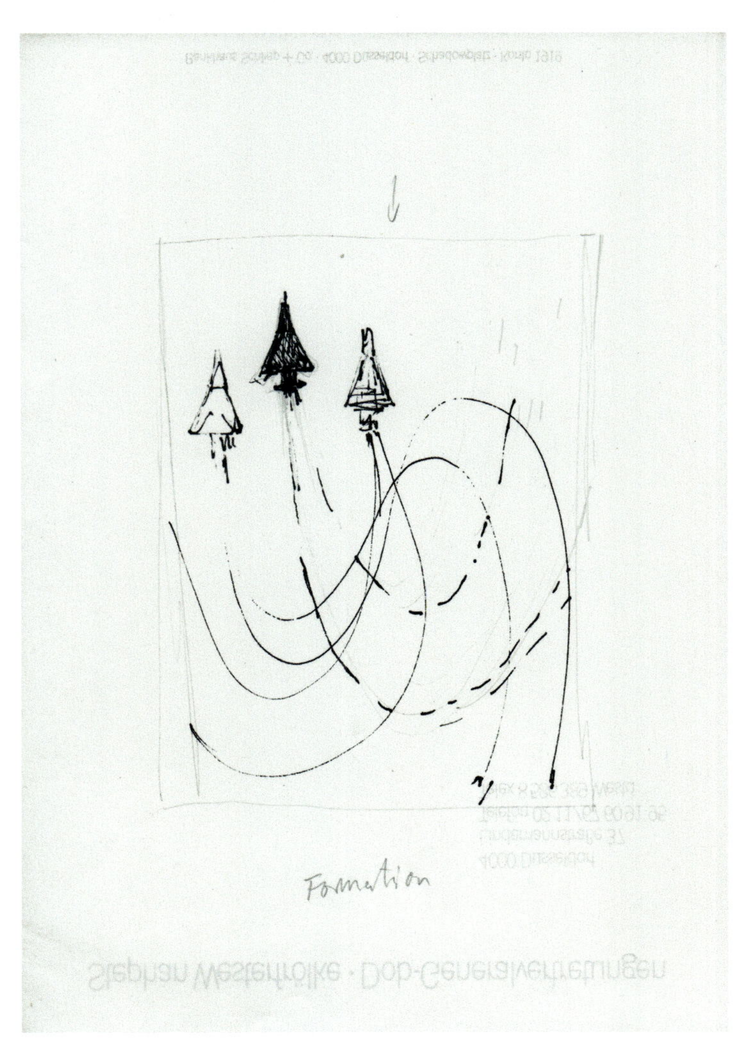

17
Goldene Ringe (*Golden Rings*). 1981. Adhesive vinyl, each ring 4 ⅛" (10.5 cm) diam. Installation dimensions variable

Right:
Installation view, *Arbeiten 1975–1981* (*Works 1975–1981*), Skulpturenhalle, Neuss, Germany, January 14–March 13, 2022

17

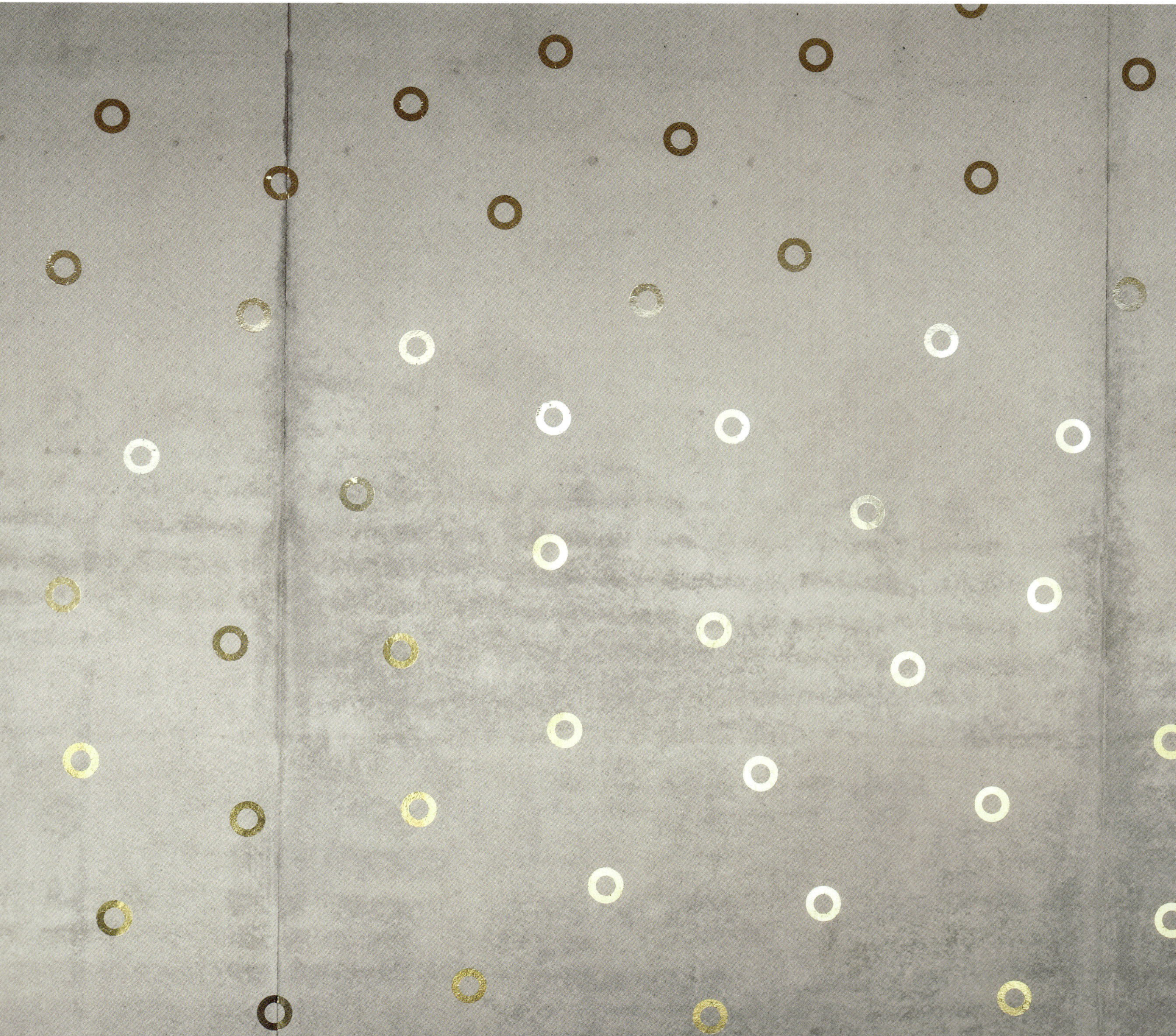

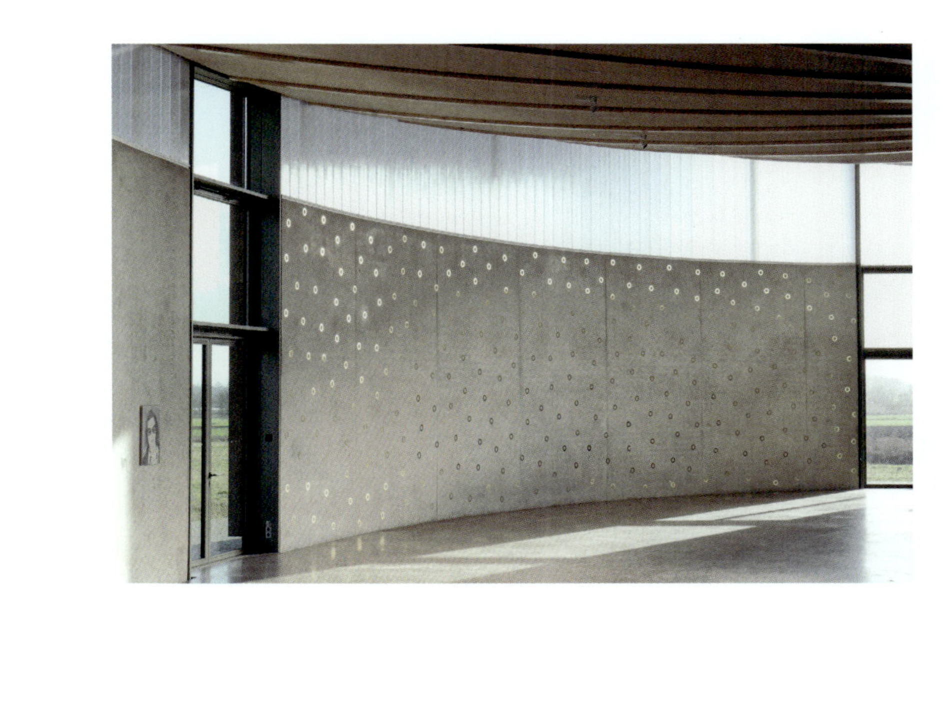

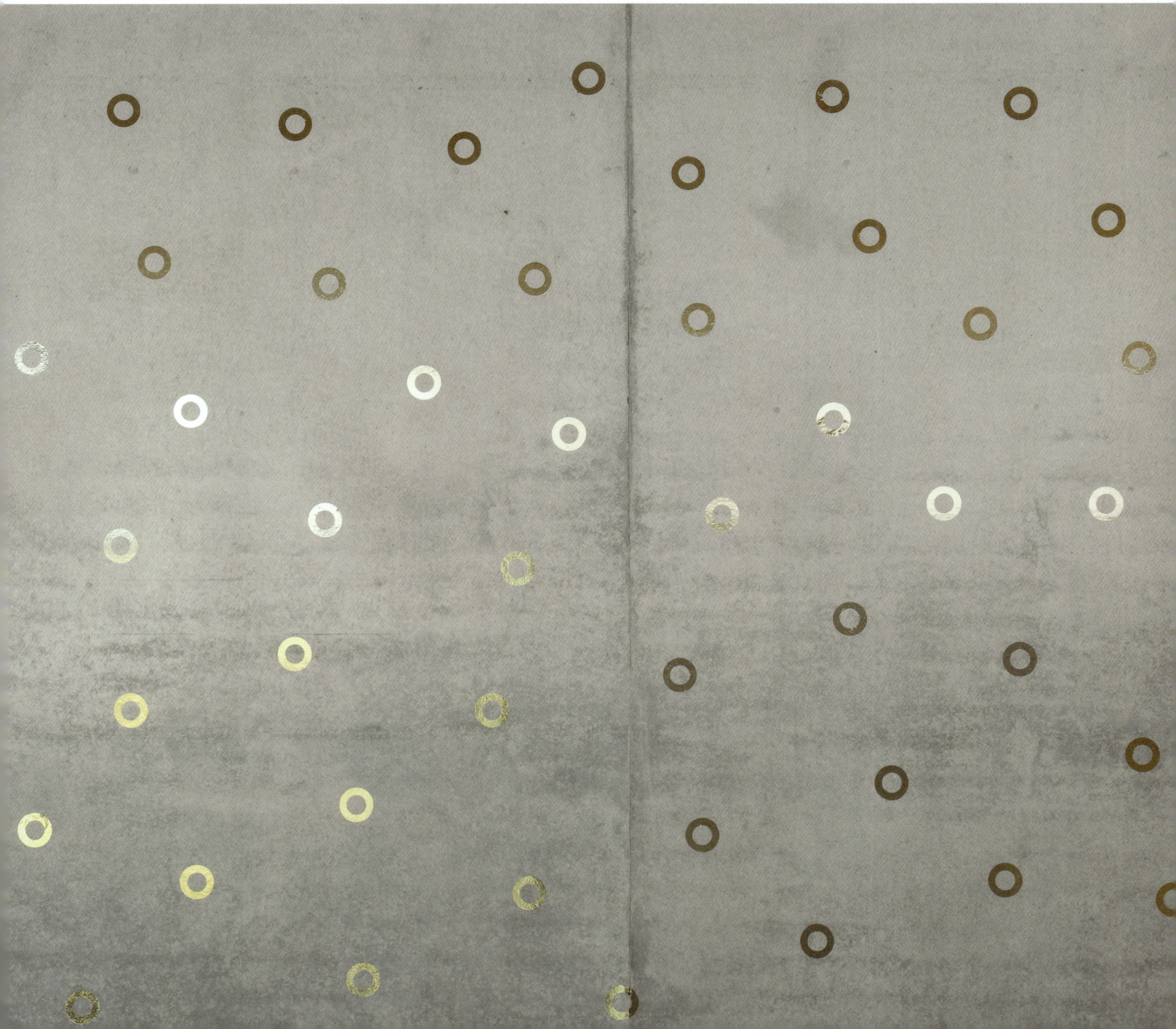

18
Foreground: *Mein Grab* (*My Grave*). 1981. Lacquer on wood on fiberboard pedestal, model: 20 ½ × 24 13/16 × 9 13/16" (52 × 63 × 25 cm), pedestal: 45 11/16 × 29 ½ × 13 ¾" (116 × 75 × 35 cm). Background: *Mein Grab* (*My Grave*). 1981. Lacquer on paper, 51 3/16 × 43 5/16" (130 × 110 cm). Installation view, *Thomas Schütte*, Kunsthaus Bregenz, Austria, July 13–October 6, 2019

Below:
Drawing for *Mein Grab*. 1981. Lacquer, pencil, pen, and crayon on paper, 11 11/16 × 8 ¼" (29.7 × 21 cm). Collection the artist, Düsseldorf

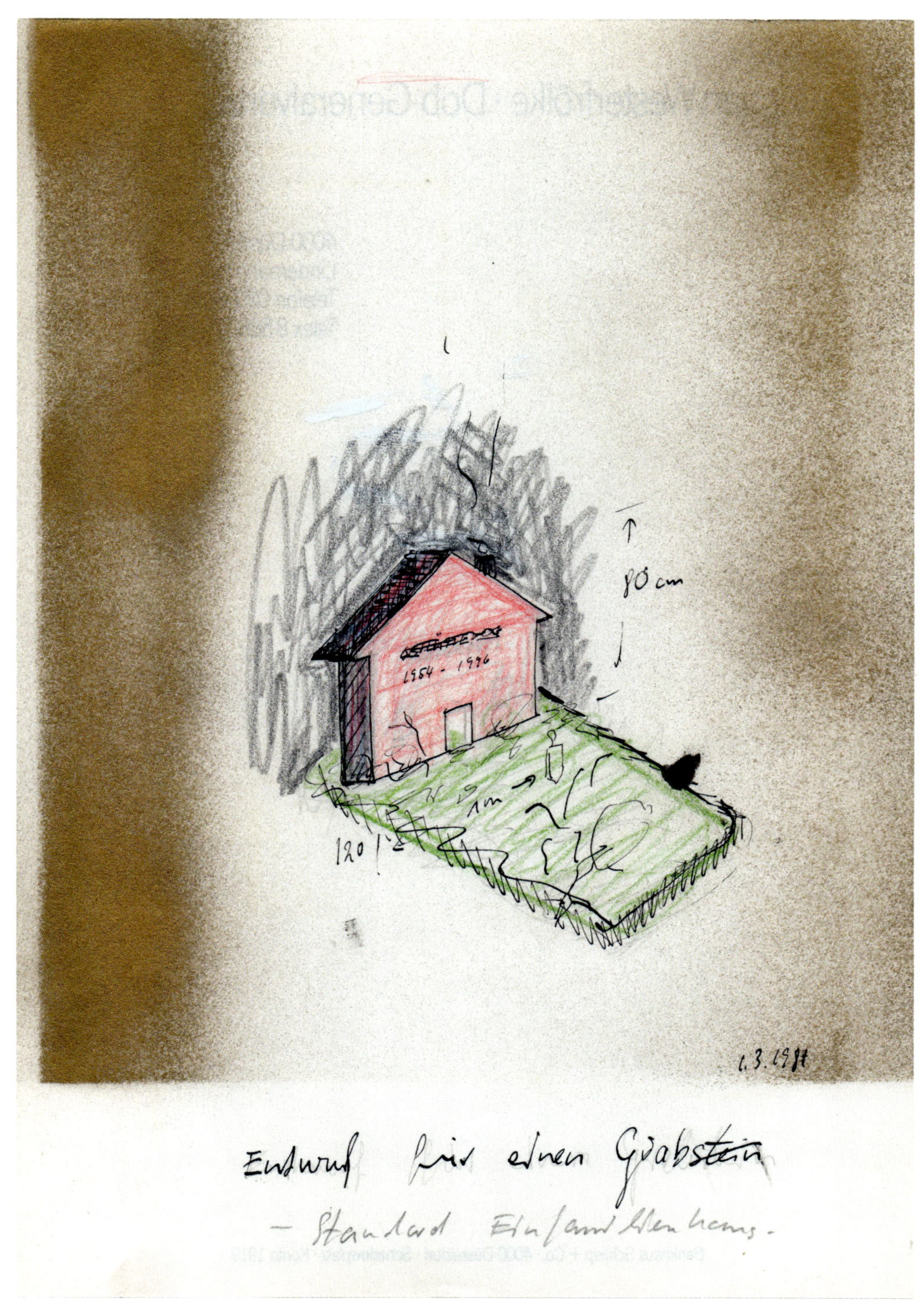

18>

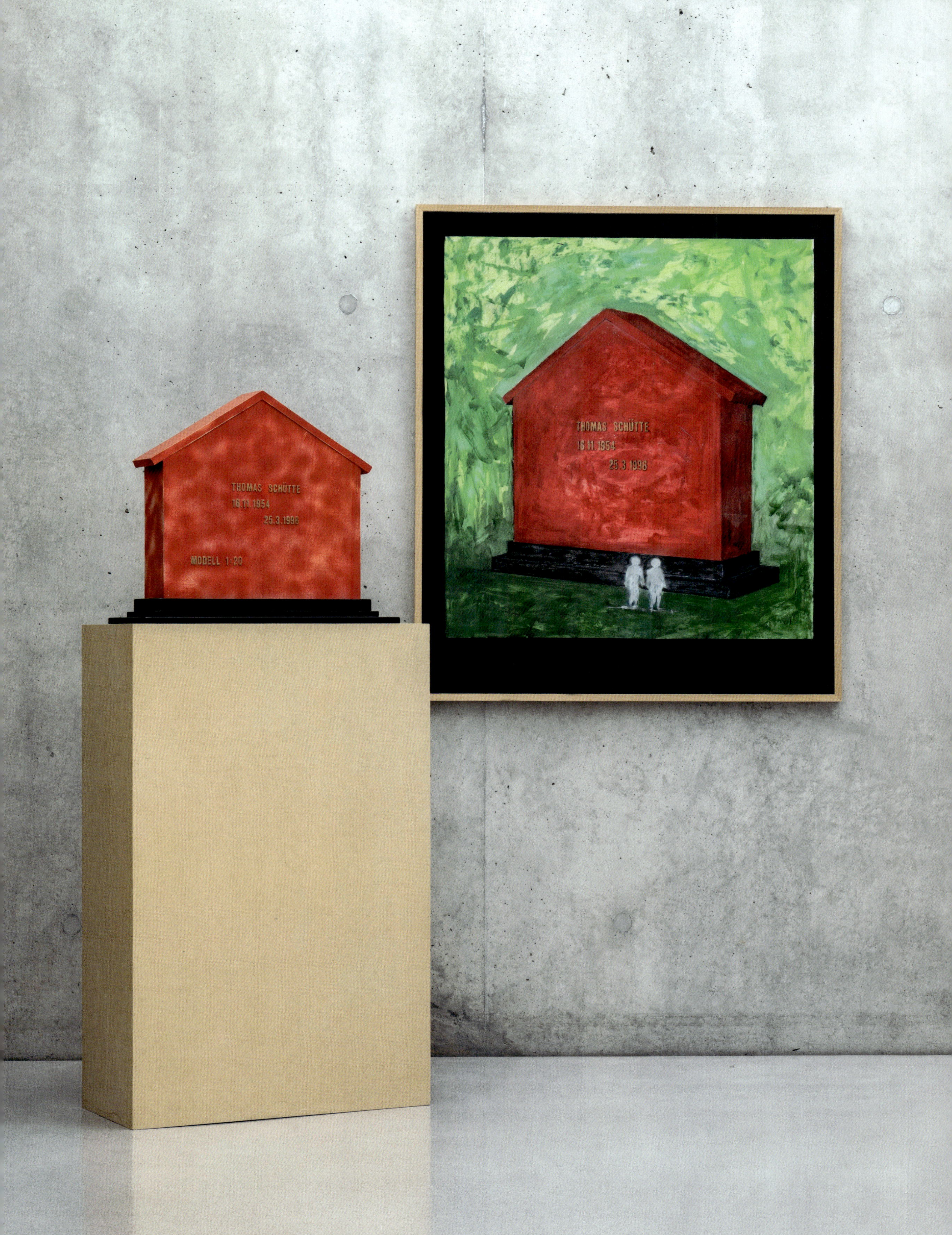
THOMAS SCHÜTTE
16.11.1954
25.3.1996
MODELL 1:20
THOMAS SCHÜTTE
16.11.1954
25.3.1996

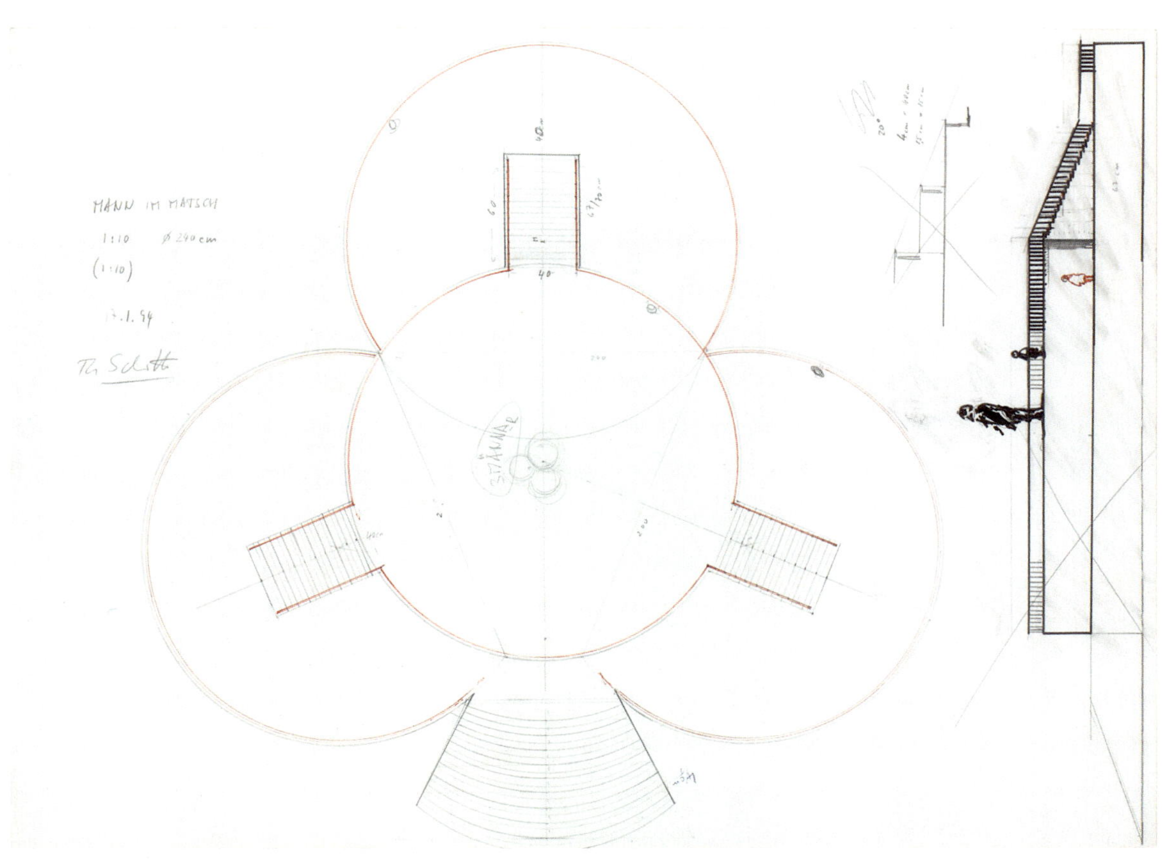
MANN IM MATSCH
1:10
13.1.94
Th. Schütte

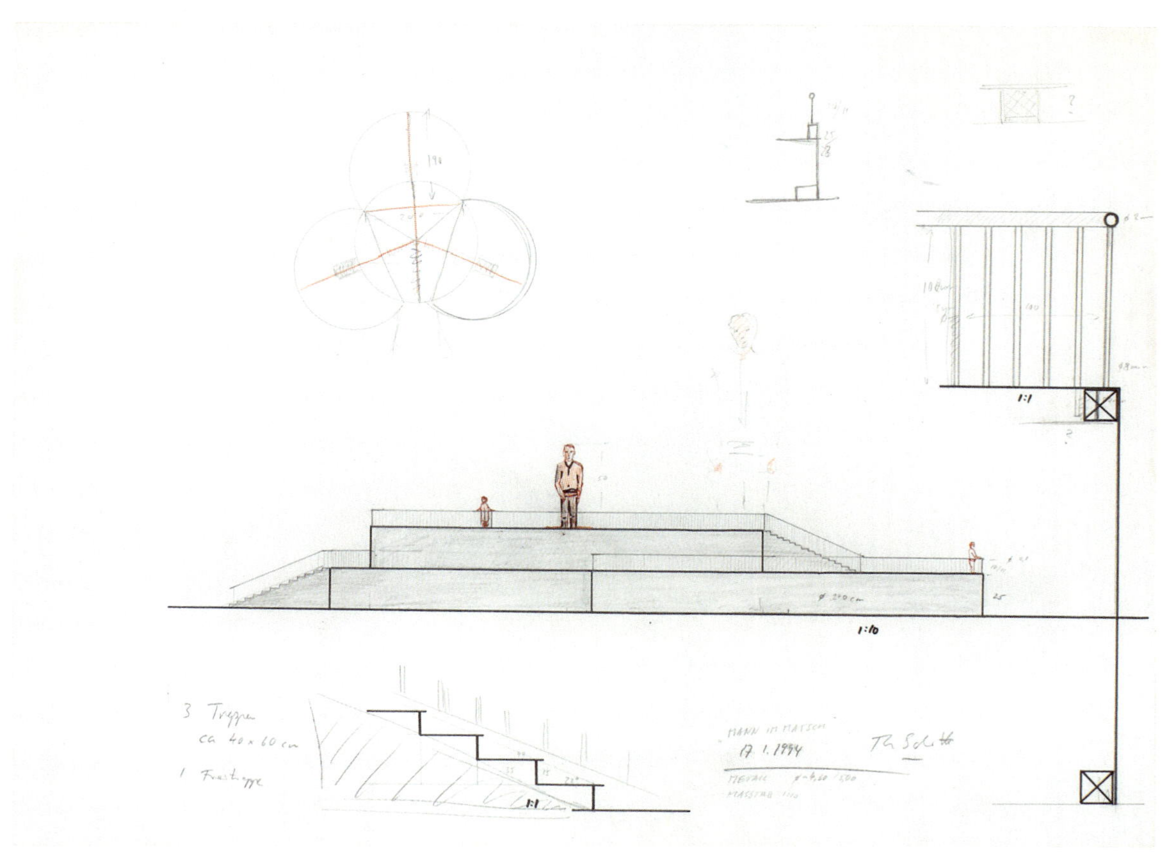
1:1
1:10
3 Treppen
ca. 40 x 60 cm
1 Freitreppe
MANN IM MATSCH
17.1.1994
Th. Schütte

19
Mann im Matsch (I. Version) (*Man in Mud [1st Version]*). 1982/2014. Aluminum and steel, 9 ⅝ × 52 ¾ × 50" (24.4 × 134 × 127 cm). Edition 2 of 5

Opposite page:
Two drawings of *Mann im Matsch* for *Großer Respekt* (*Large Respect*). 1994. Pencil, pen, and crayon on paper, 19 ¹¹⁄₁₆ × 27 ⁹⁄₁₆" (50 × 70 cm). Collection Niels Dietrich

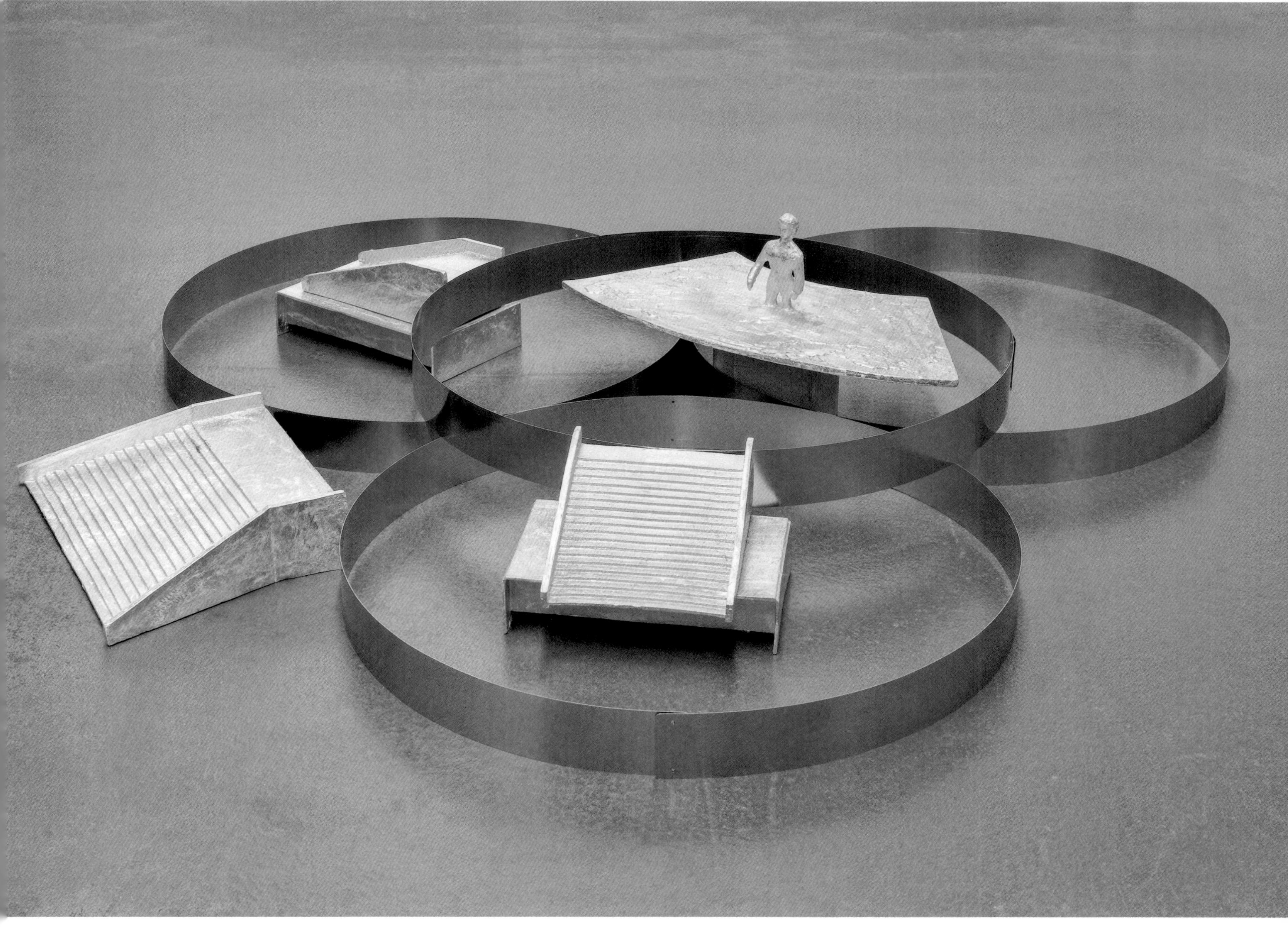

19

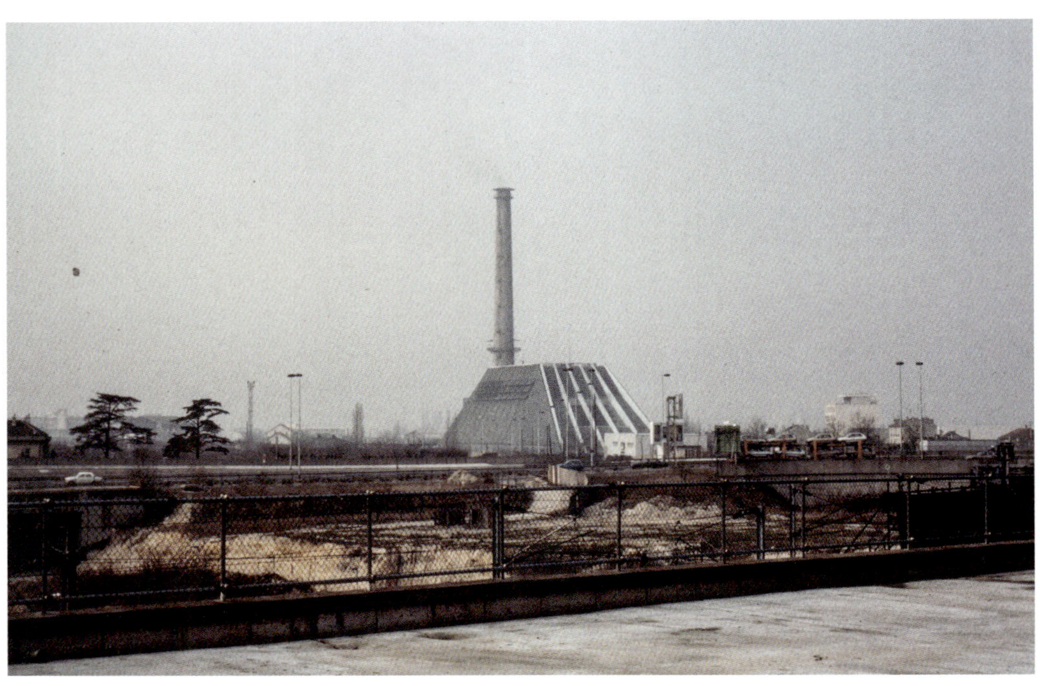

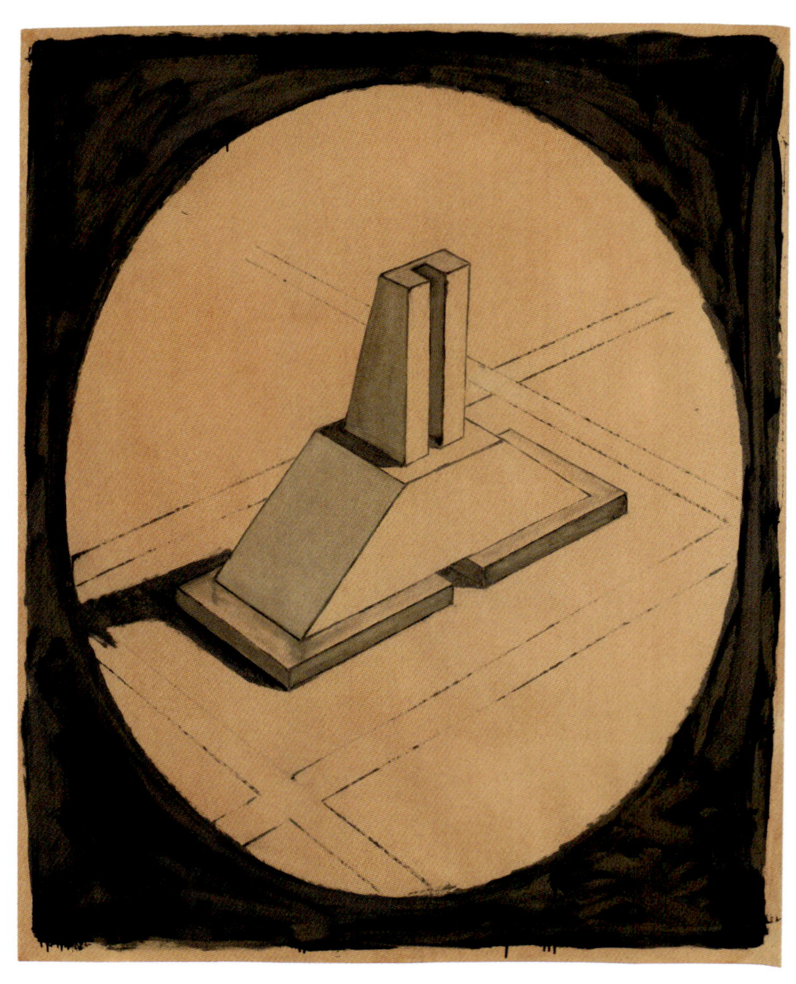

20
Modell für ein Museum (*Model for a Museum*). 1982. Paint on wood with felt on tables and two lacquer-on-paper drawings on easels, model: 7' 8 ½" × 6' 6 ¾" × 1' 11 ⅝" (235 × 200 × 60 cm), easels: each 6' 6 ¾" × 4' 11 1/16" × 2' 3 9/16" (200 × 150 × 70 cm). Installation dimensions variable. Installation view, *Thomas Schütte*, Haus der Kunst, Munich, June 7–September 6, 2009

Above:
Courbevoie thermal power station in La Défense, Paris, c. 1981–82

Right:
Hauptstadt (*Capital*). 1981. Lacquer on paper, one of seven sheets, each 53 ⅛ × 43 5/16" (135 × 110 cm). The Museum of Modern Art, New York. Gift of Jan Christiaan Braun in honor of Konrad Fischer

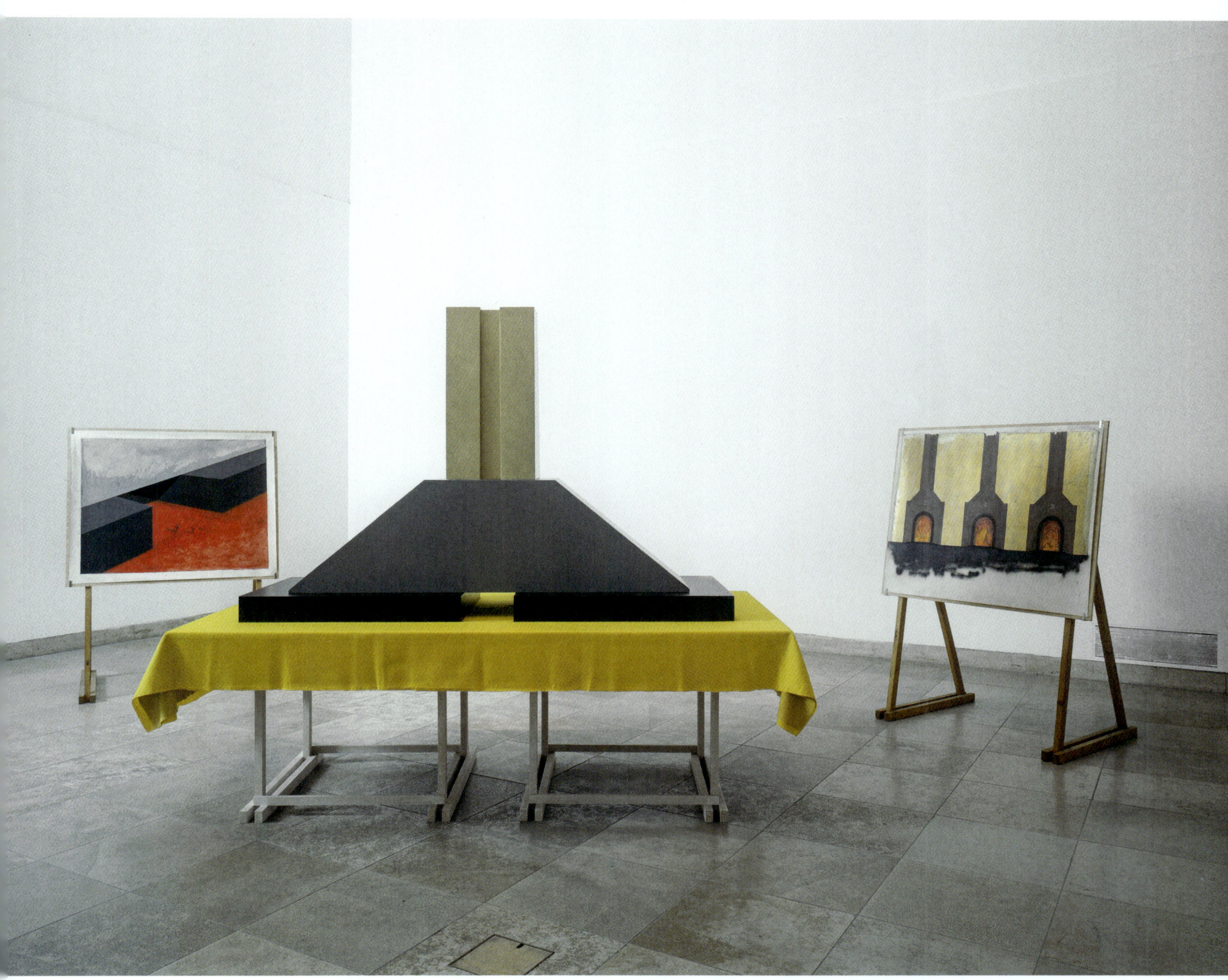

20

21
Studio I. 1983. Paint on wood, model: 34 ¼ × 16 ⅛ × 50 ⅜" (87 × 41 × 128 cm), table: 36 7⁄16 × 33 7⁄16 × 68 ⅞" (92.5 × 85 × 175 cm)

Below:
Installation view of (left to right) *Landhaus 4* (*Country House 4*, 1986), *Studio II* (1983), and *Studio I* (1983), Herbert Foundation, Ghent, 1989

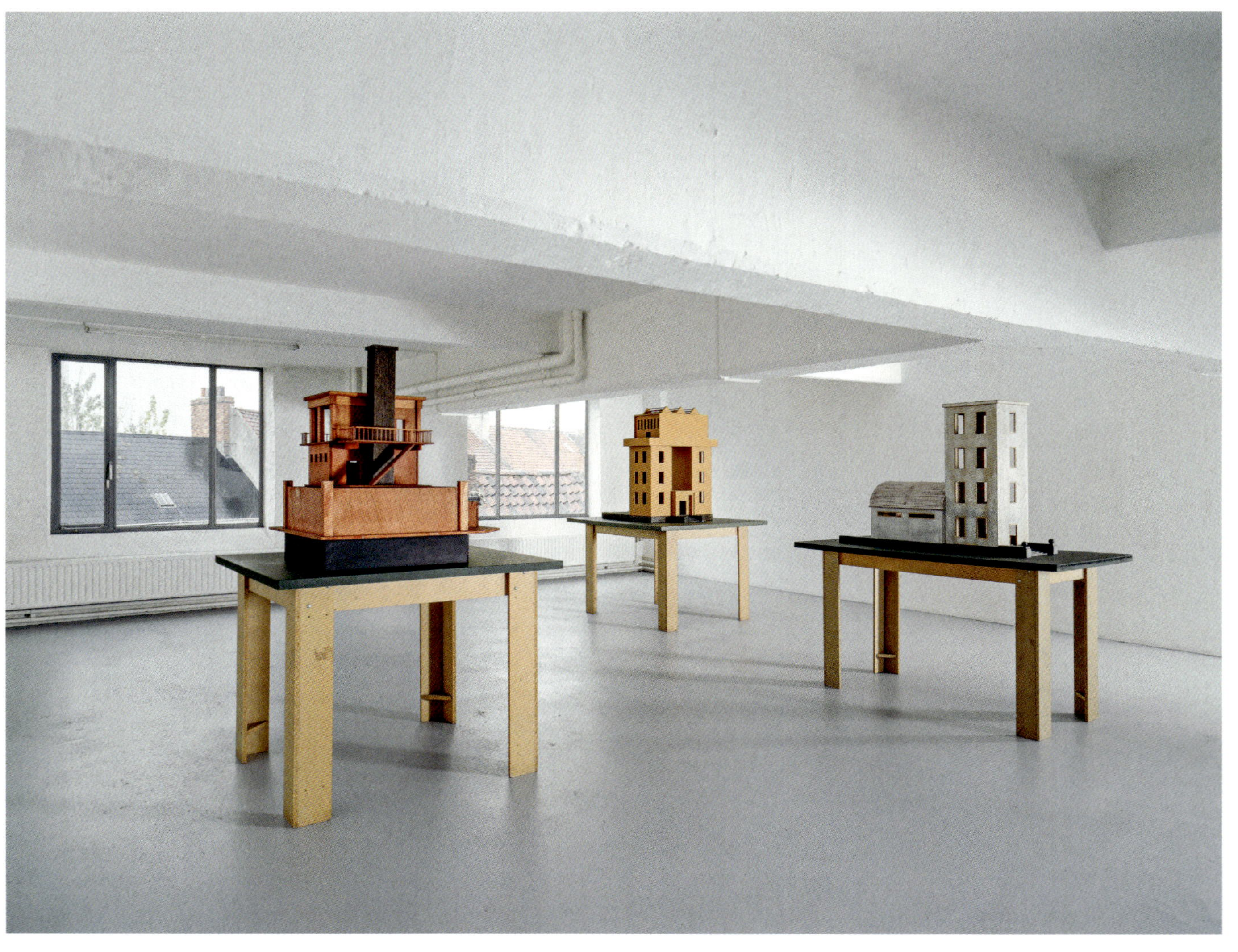

21>

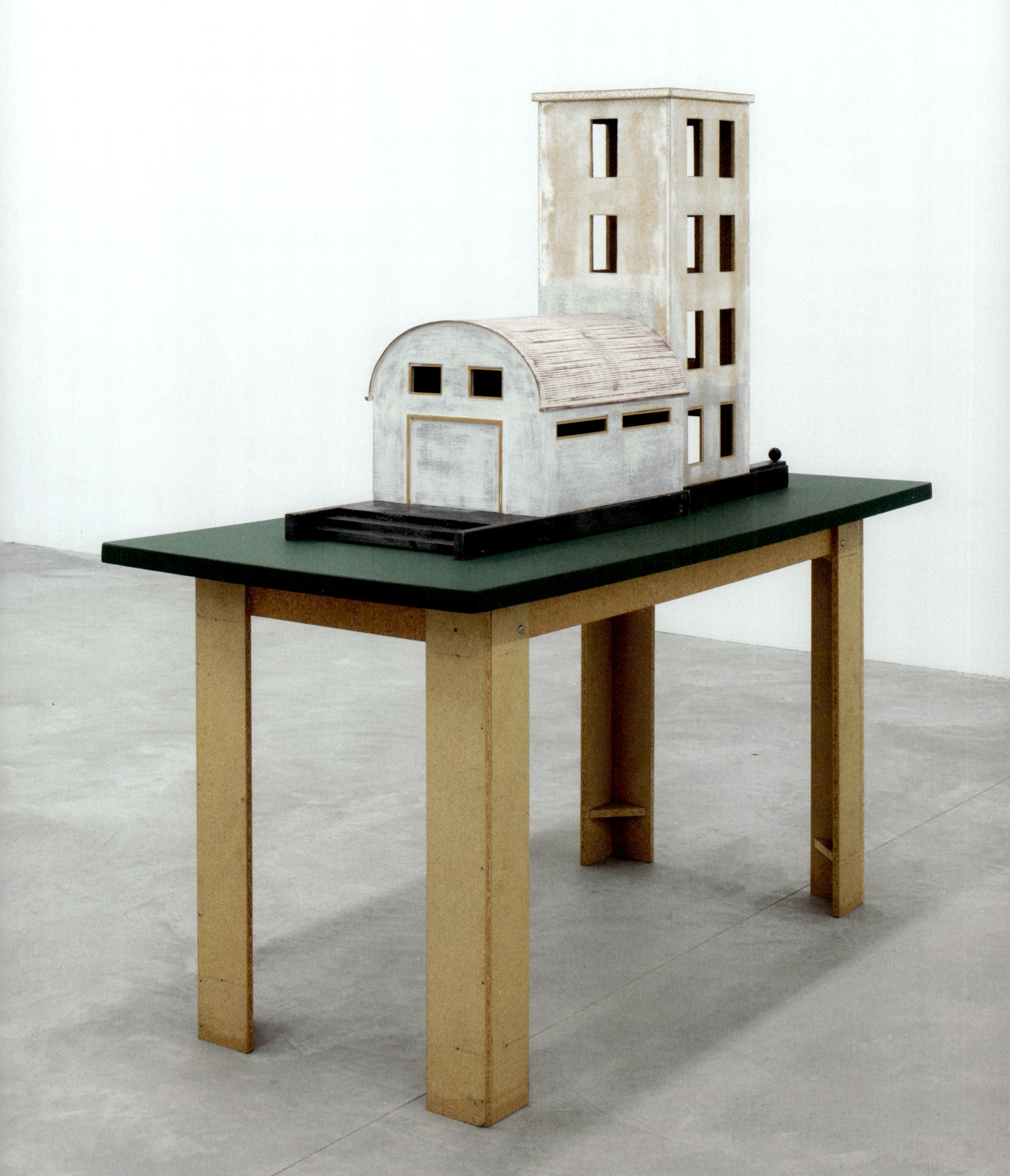

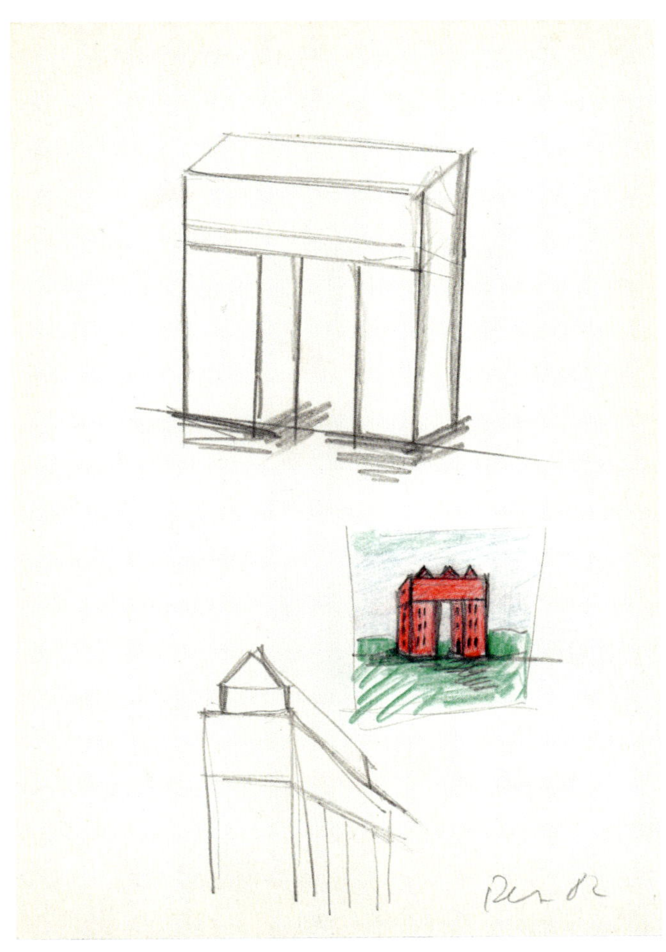

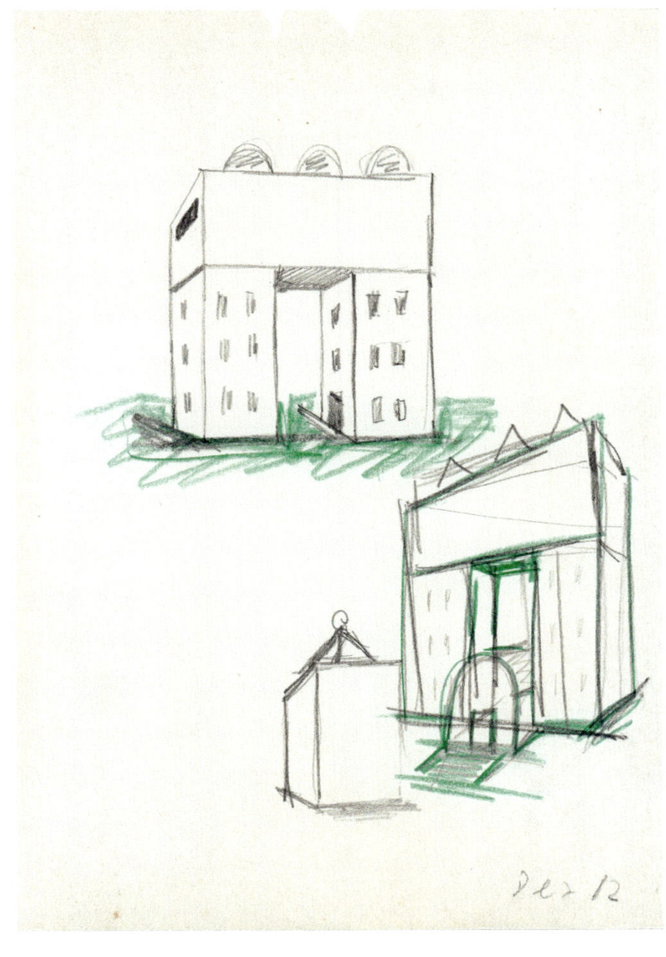

22
Studio II. 1983. Paint on wood, model: 42 ⅛ × 42 ½ × 30 5⁄16" (107 × 108 × 77 cm), table: 37 × 51 ¼ × 59 1⁄16" (94 × 130.2 × 150 cm)

Above:
Two drawings for *Studio II*. 1982. Pencil and crayon on paper, 11 11⁄16 × 8 ¼" (29.7 × 21 cm). Collection the artist, Düsseldorf

22>

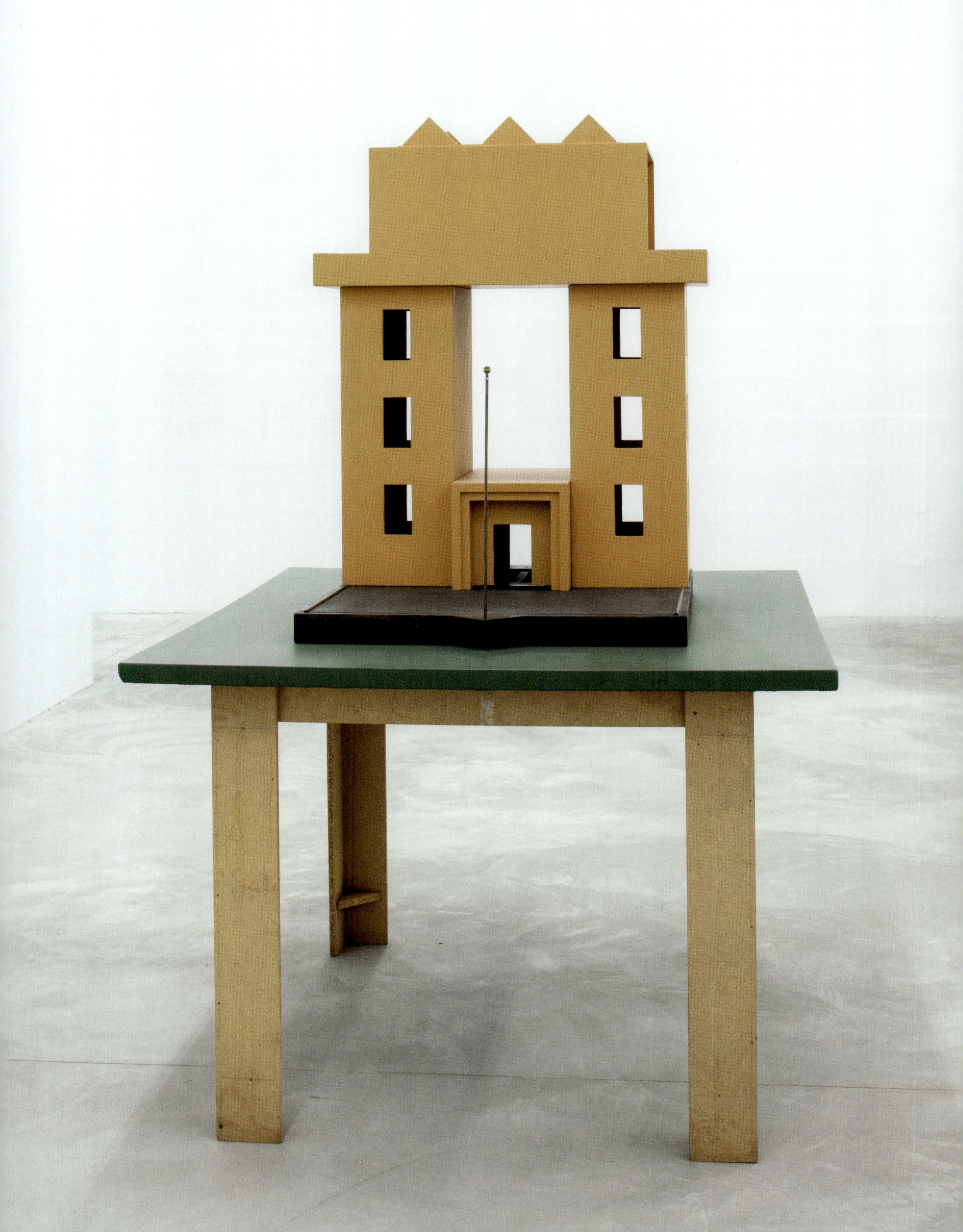

23
Landhaus 4 (*Country House 4*). 1986. Paint on wood with model car, model: 39 ¾ × 35 ¹³⁄₁₆ × 33 ⅞" (101 × 91 × 86 cm), table: 37 ¹³⁄₁₆ × 51 ³⁄₁₆ × 47 ¼" (96 × 130 × 120 cm)

Right:
Drawing for *Landhaus 4.* 1982. Pen on paper, 11 ¹¹⁄₁₆ × 8 ¼" (29.7 × 21 cm). Collection the artist, Düsseldorf

Below:
Schütte installing *Landhaus 4* with gallerist Philip Nelson and curator Bart Cassiman at Herbert Foundation, Ghent, 1989

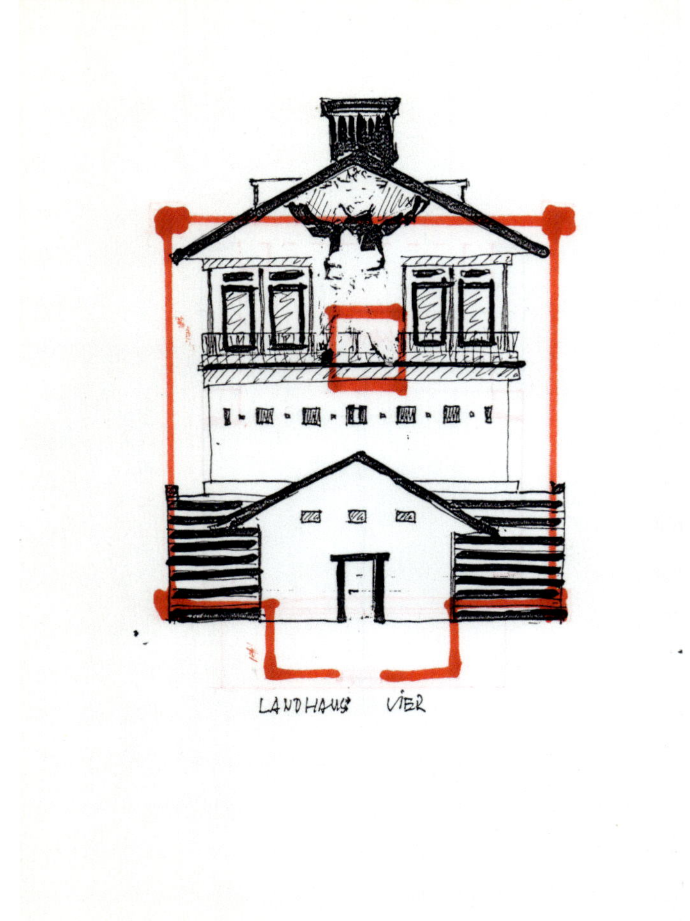

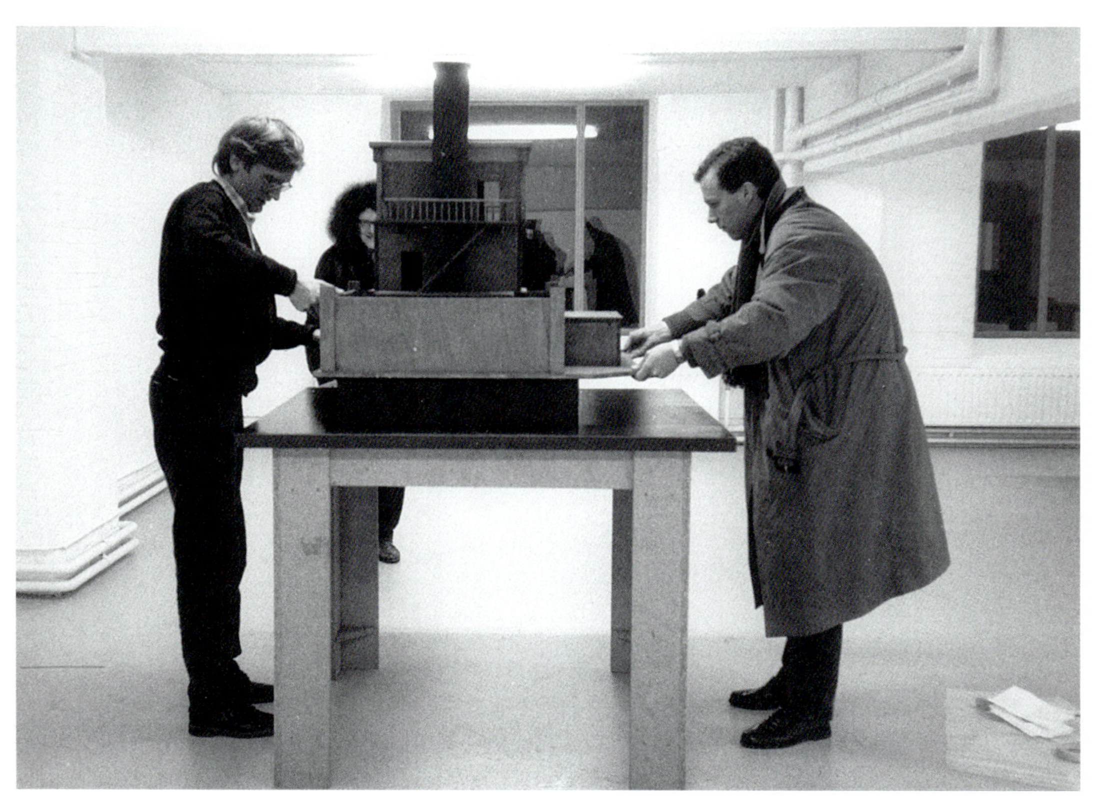

23>

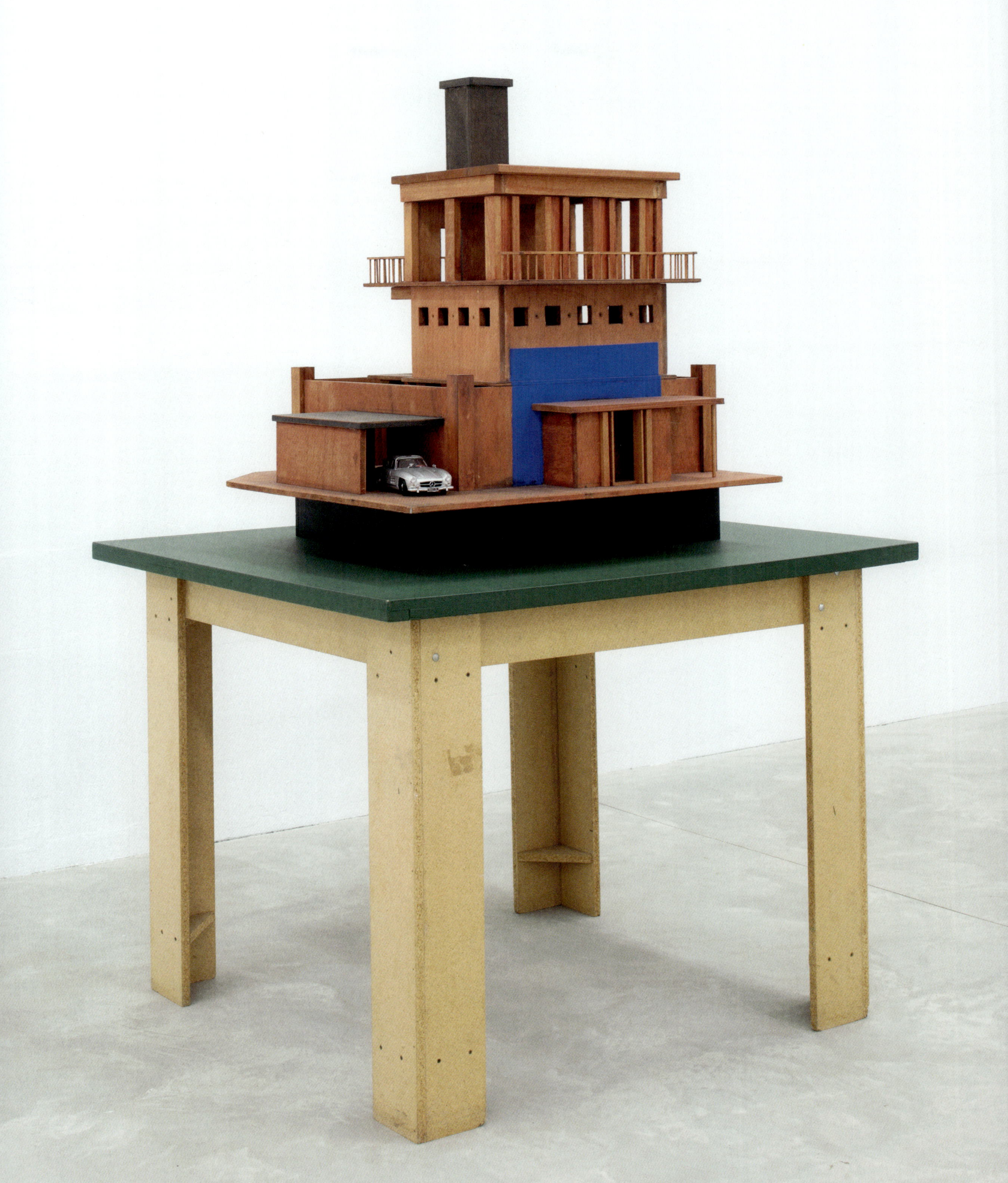

This spread and pages 106–9:

24
Melonely. 1986. Paint on wood, 11 parts, and gouache and watercolor on paper, 14 sheets, each wooden part 39 ⅜ × 19 ¹¹⁄₁₆ × 7' 6 ⁹⁄₁₆" (100 × 50 × 230 cm), each sheet 25 ⁹⁄₁₆ × 19 ¹¹⁄₁₆" (65 × 50 cm). Installation dimensions variable. Installation view, *Thomas Schütte*, Haus der Kunst, Munich, Germany, June 7–September 6, 2009

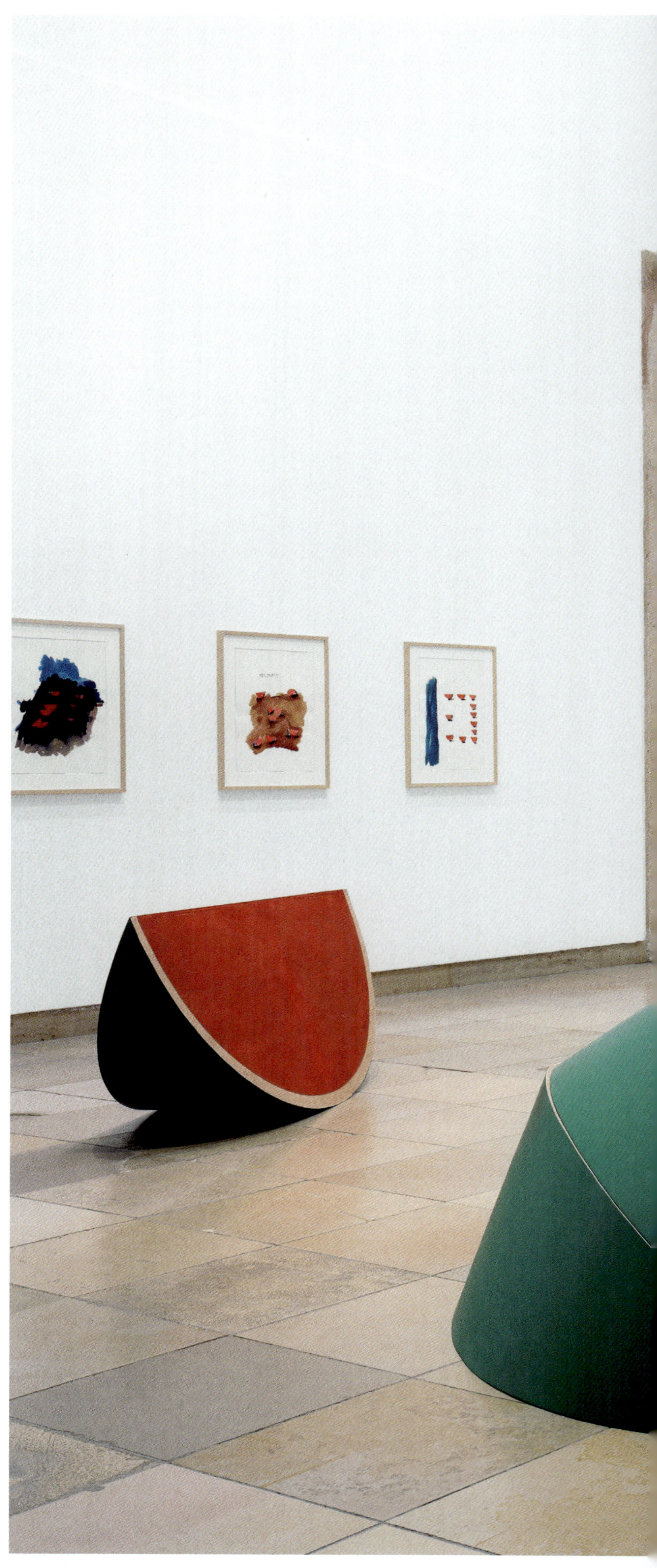

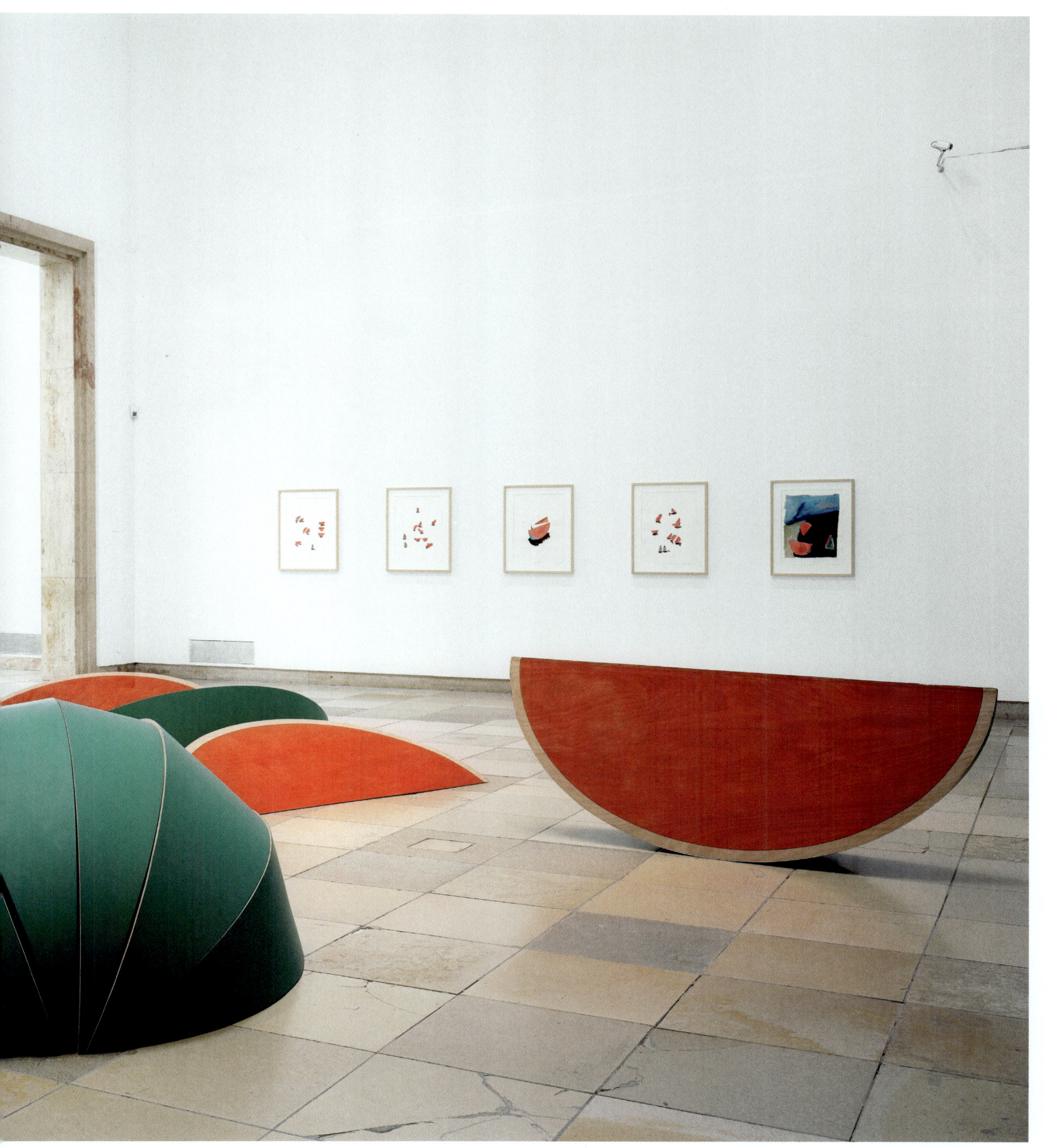

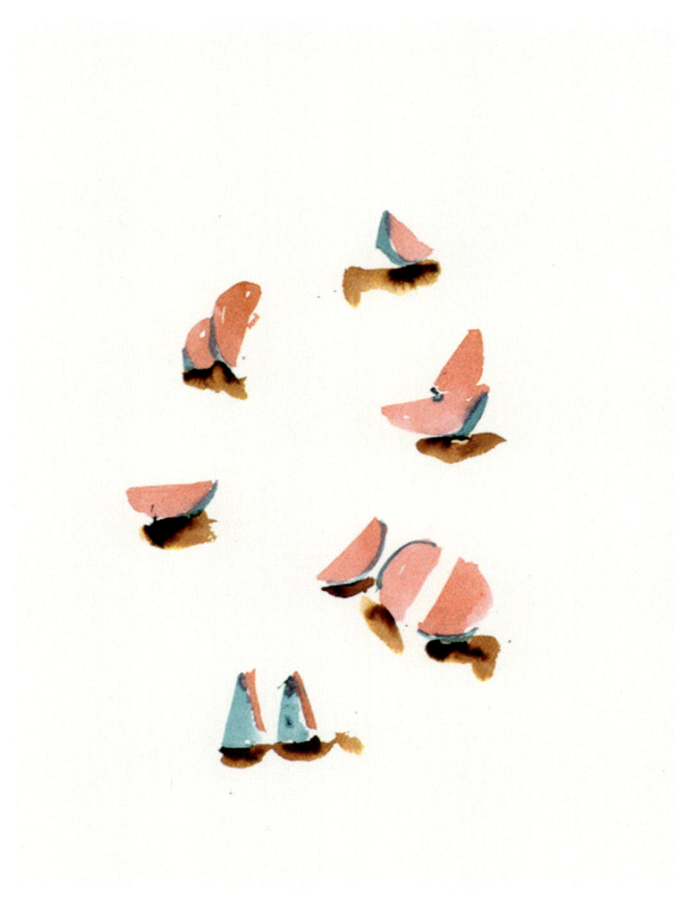

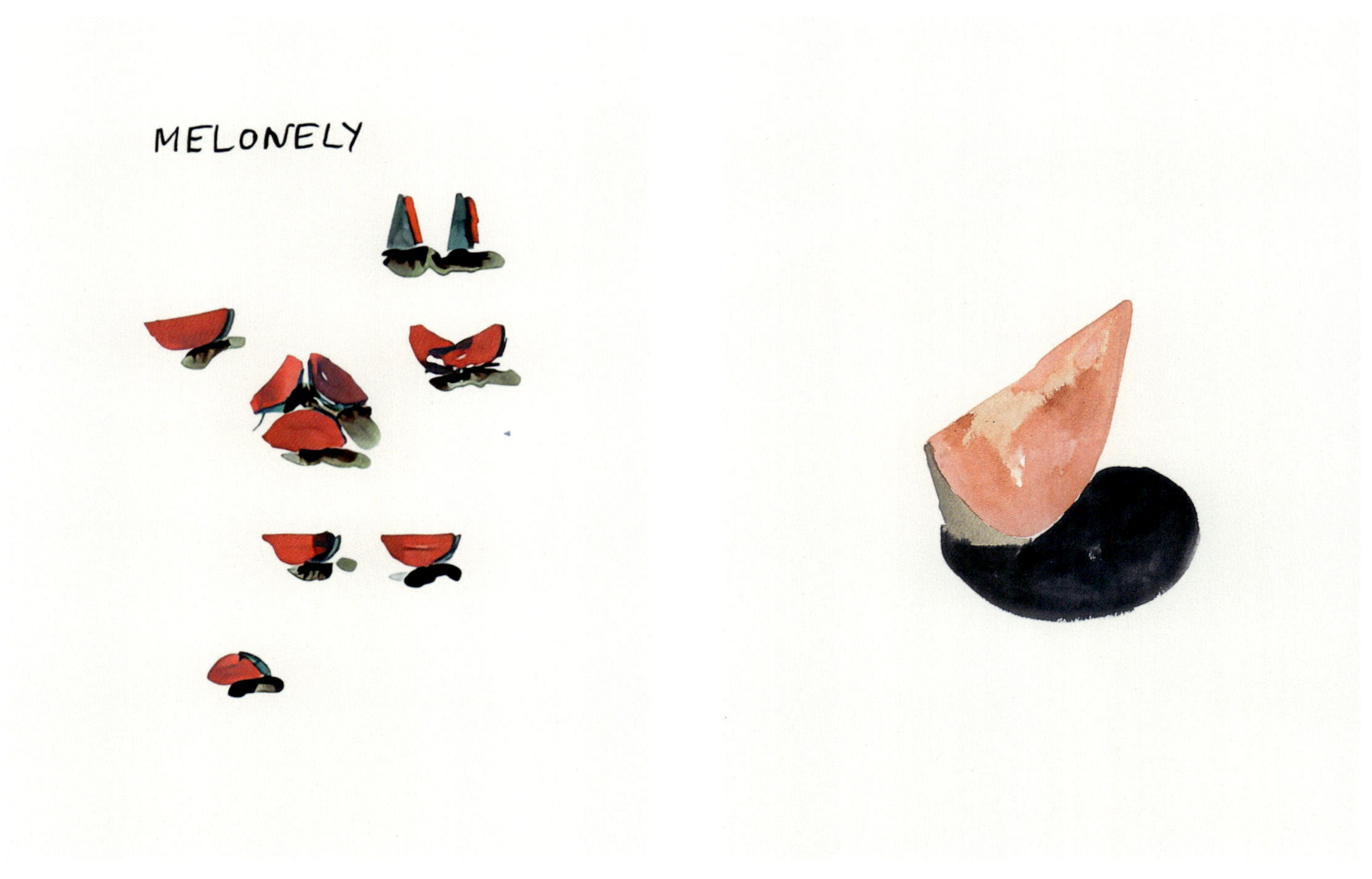
MELONELY

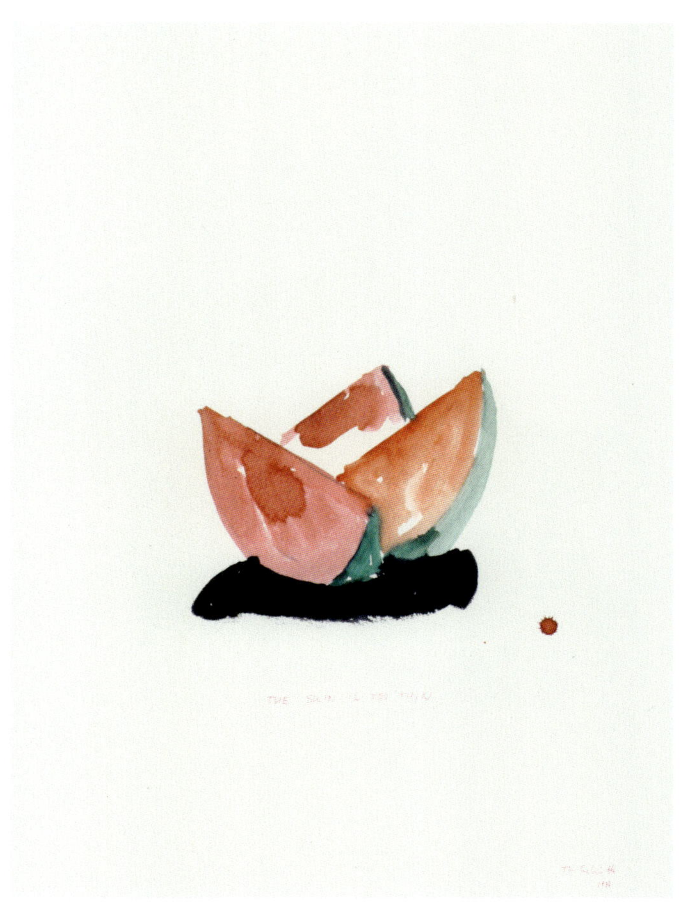

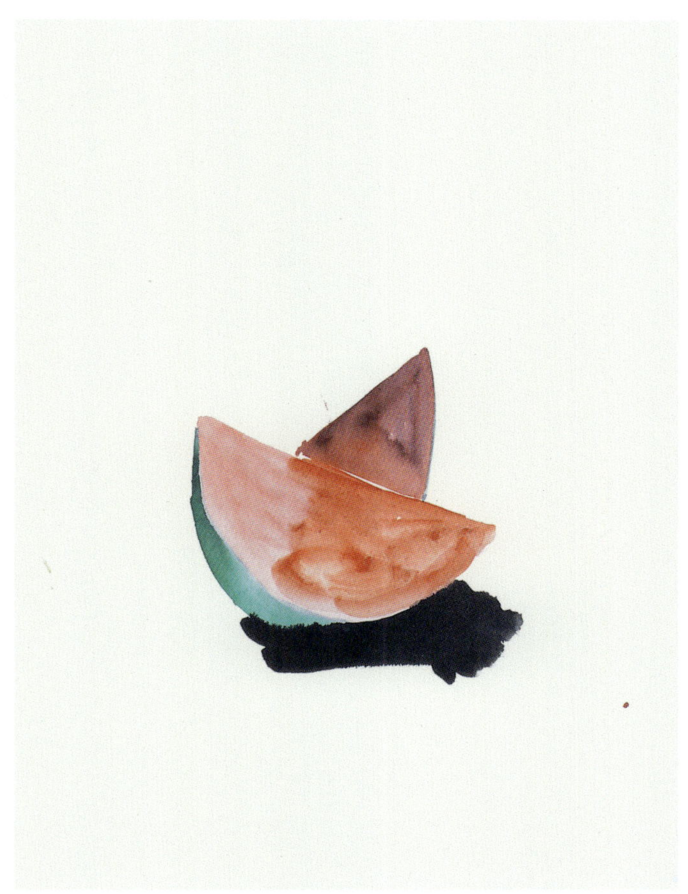

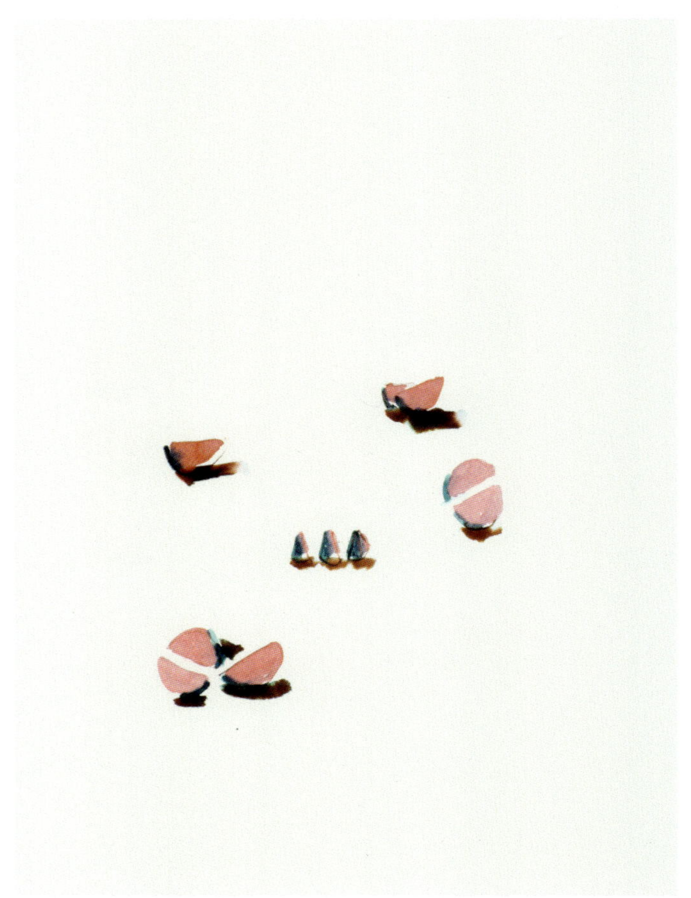

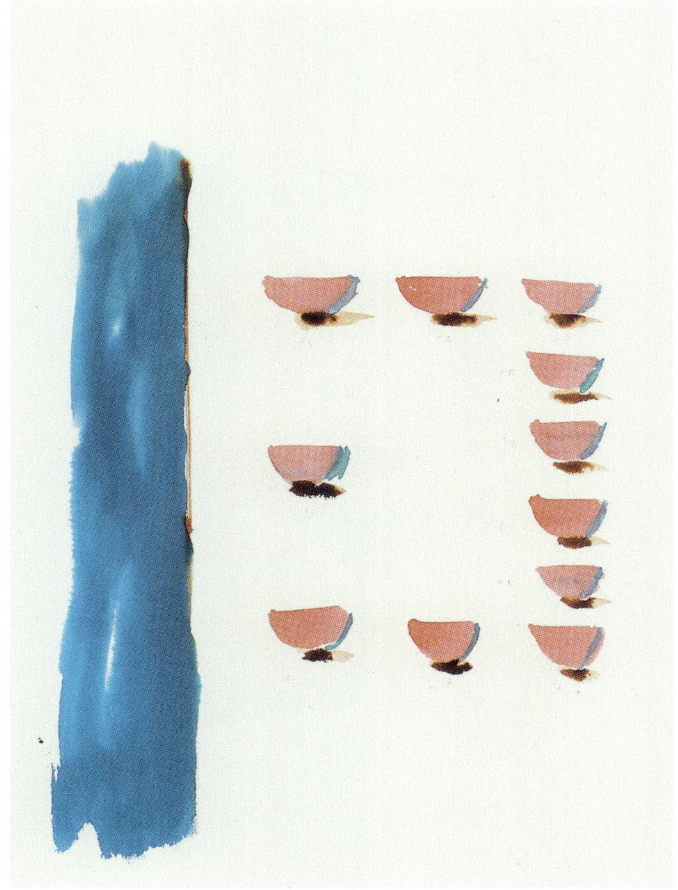

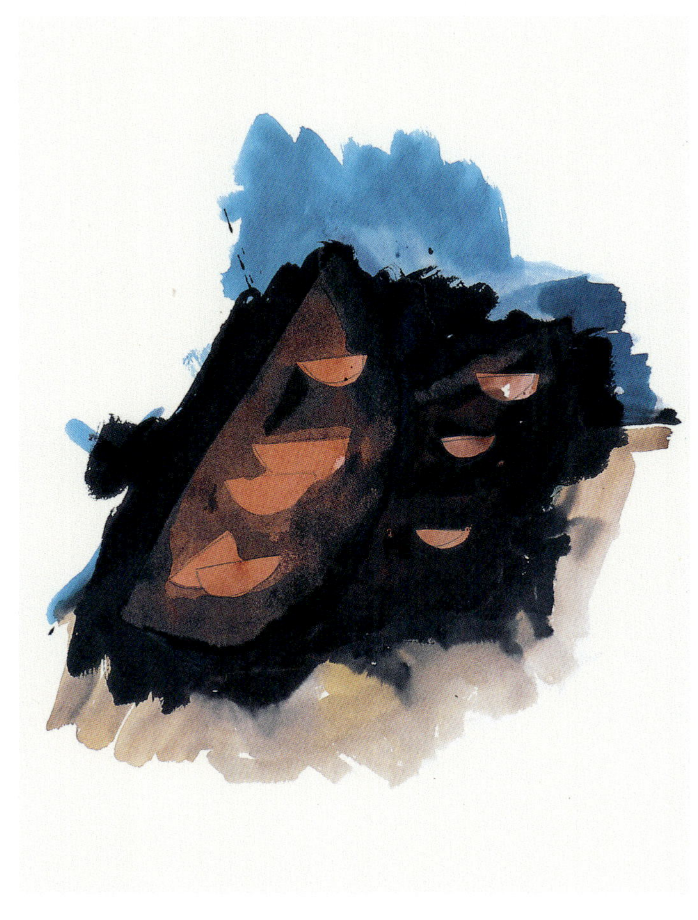

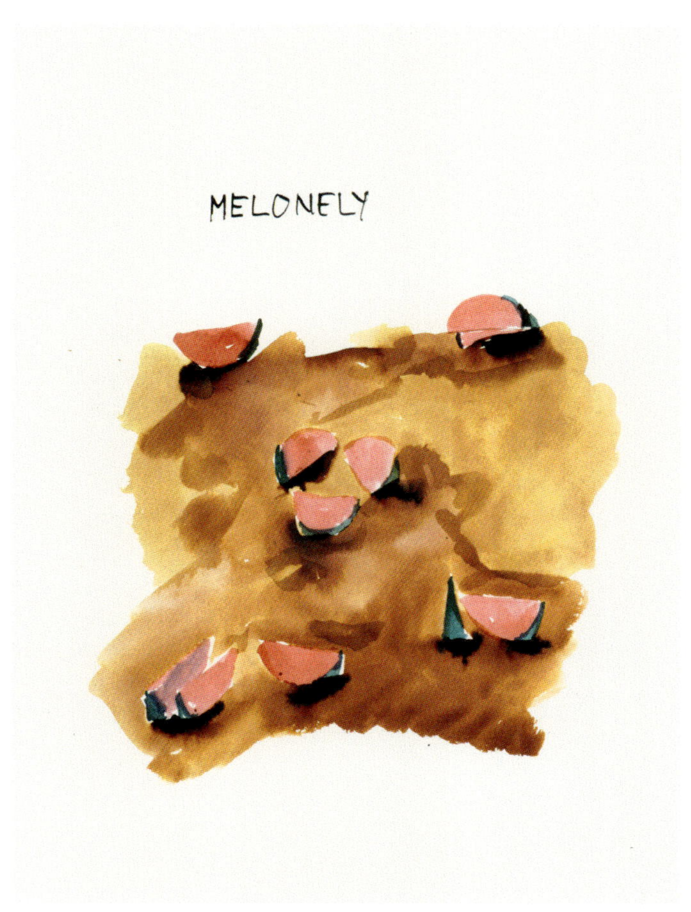
MELONELY

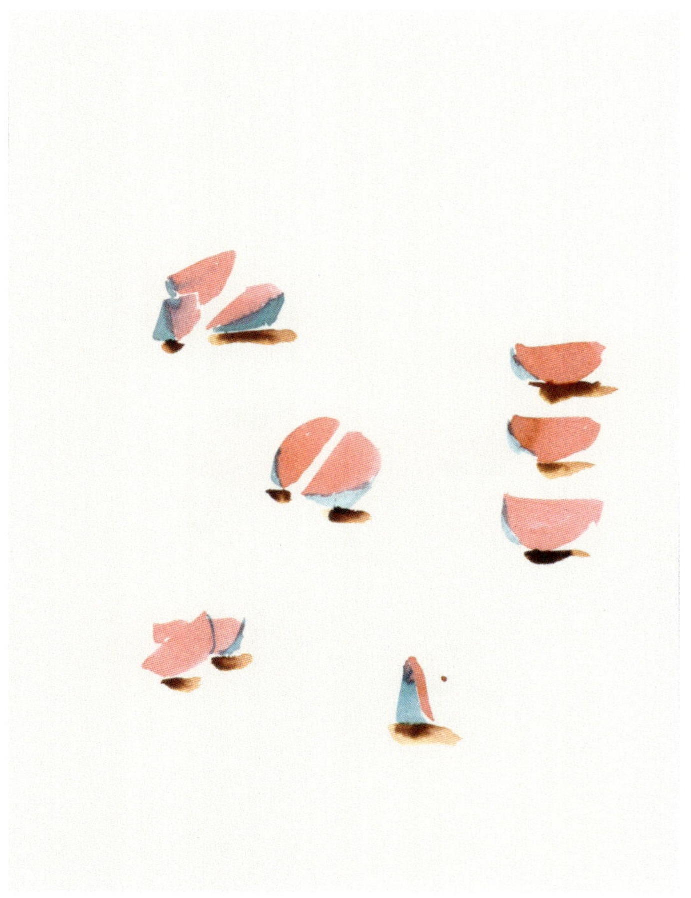

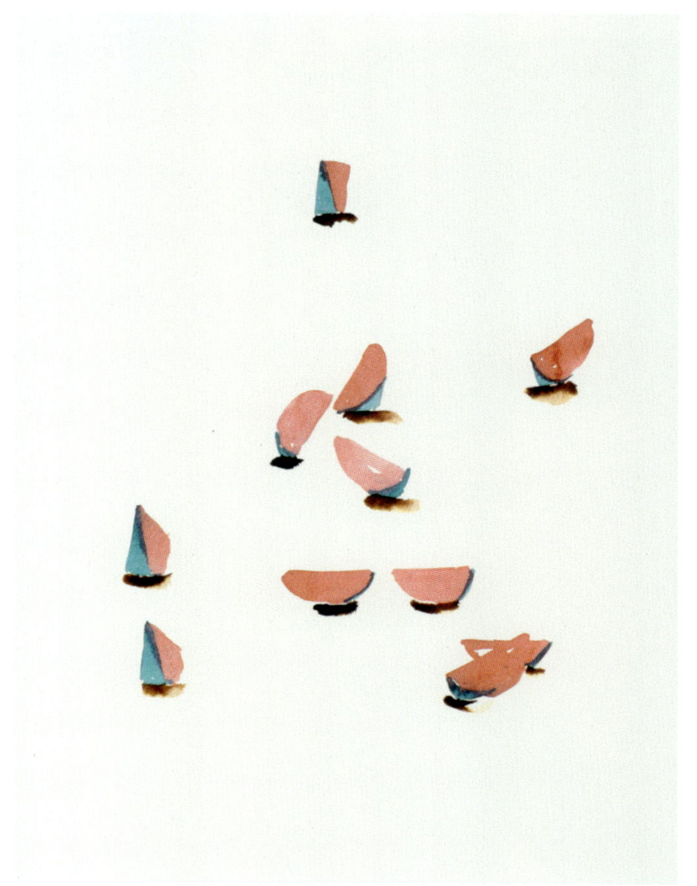

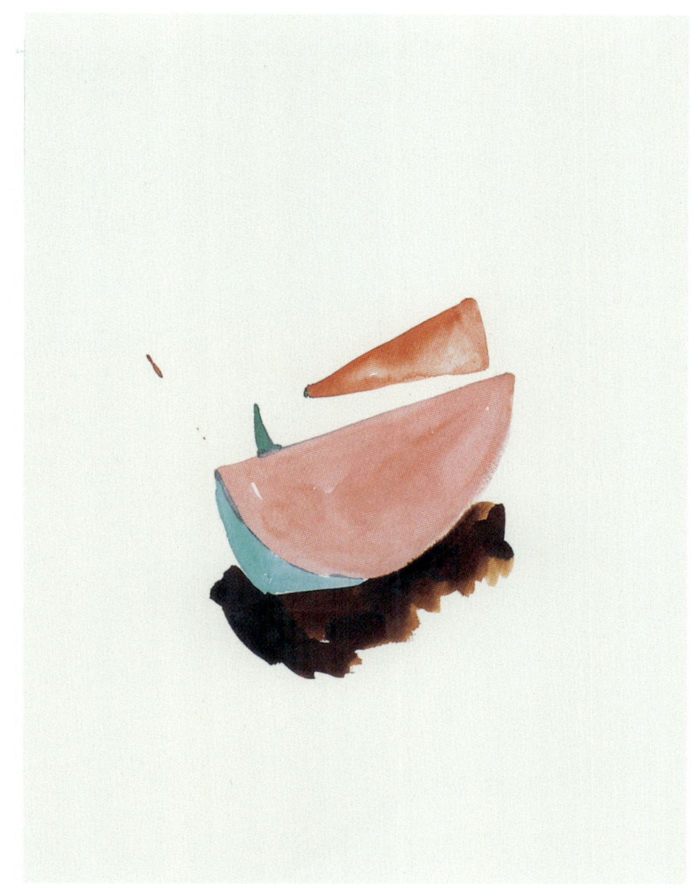

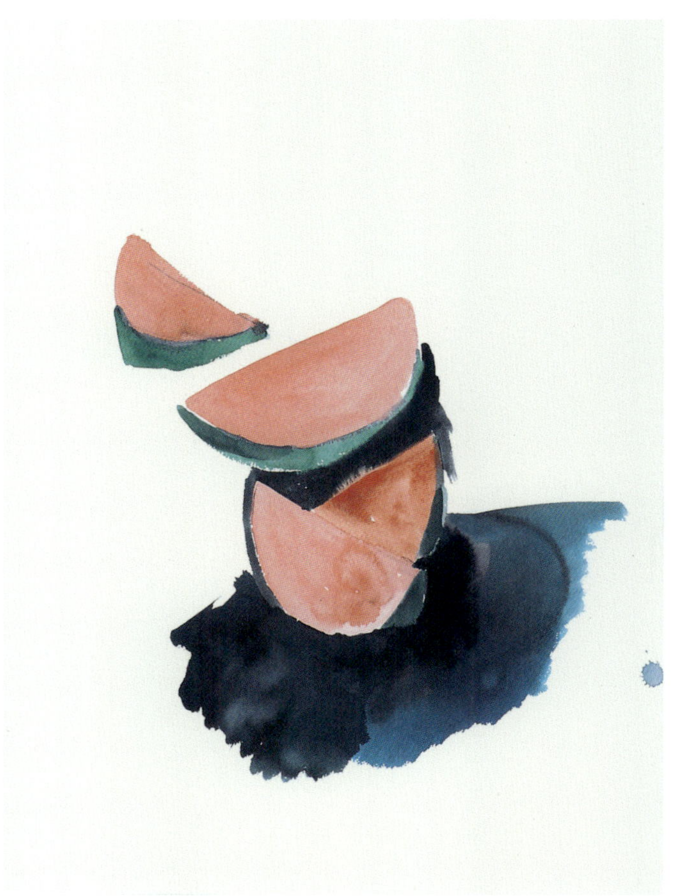

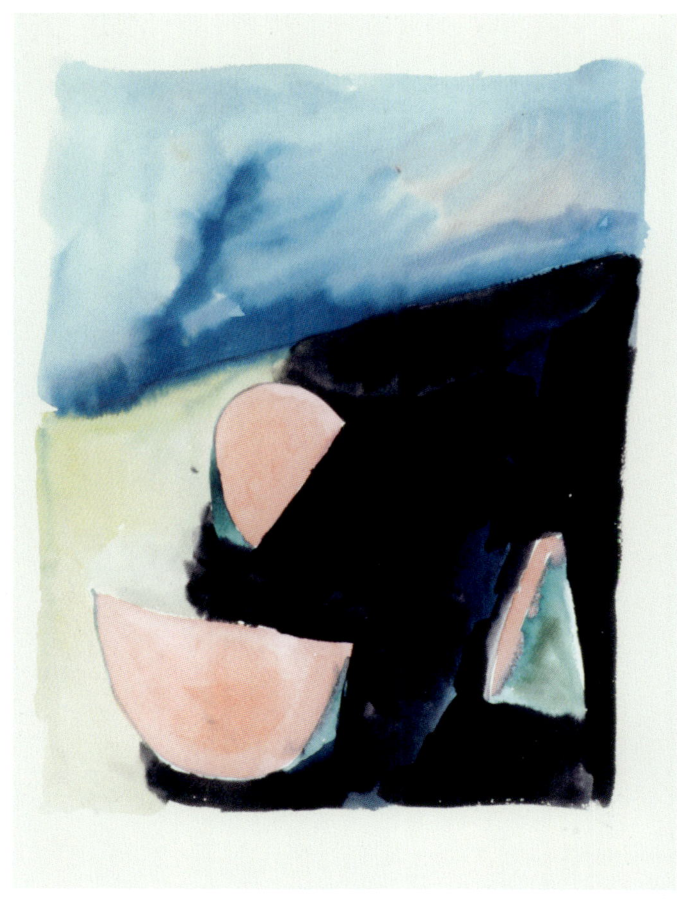

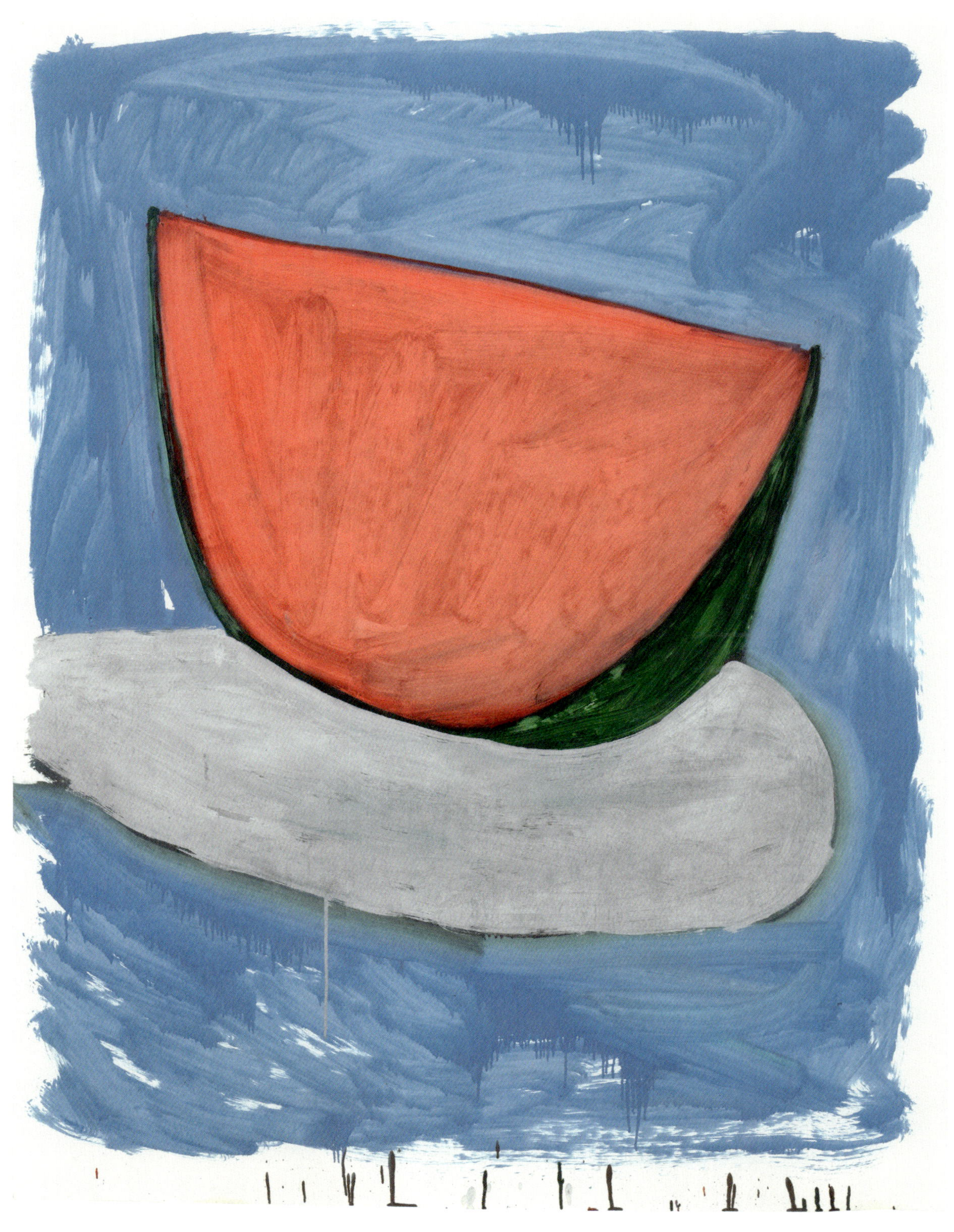

25
Melone (*Melon*). 1985. Lacquer on paper, 55 ⅛ × 43 5⁄16" (140 × 110 cm)

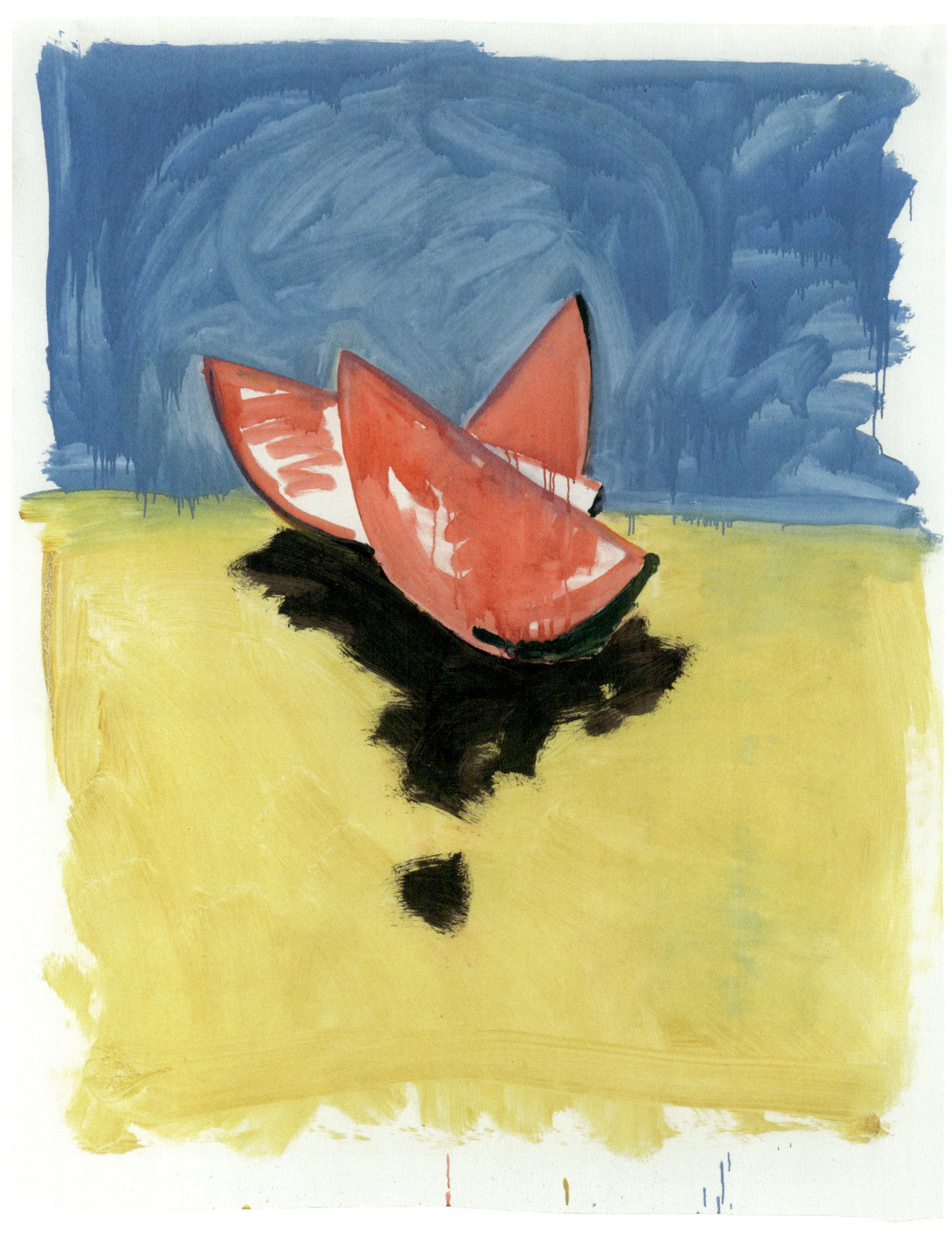

26
Melonen (*Melons*). 1986. Lacquer on paper, 55 ½ × 43 5⁄16" (141 × 110 cm)

27
Pentagon. 1986. Fiberboard with stain, 4' 11 1/16" × 10' 6" × 10' 6" (150 × 320 × 320 cm)

Right:
Hauptstadt (*Capital*). 1981. Lacquer on paper, one of seven sheets, each 53 1/8 × 43 5/16" (135 × 100 cm). The Museum of Modern Art, New York. Gift of Jan Christiaan Braun in honor of Konrad Fischer

Below:
Installation view of *Pentagon*, *Thomas Schütte*, Krefelder Kunstmuseen Museum Haus Lange, Krefeld, Germany, January 26–March 16, 1986

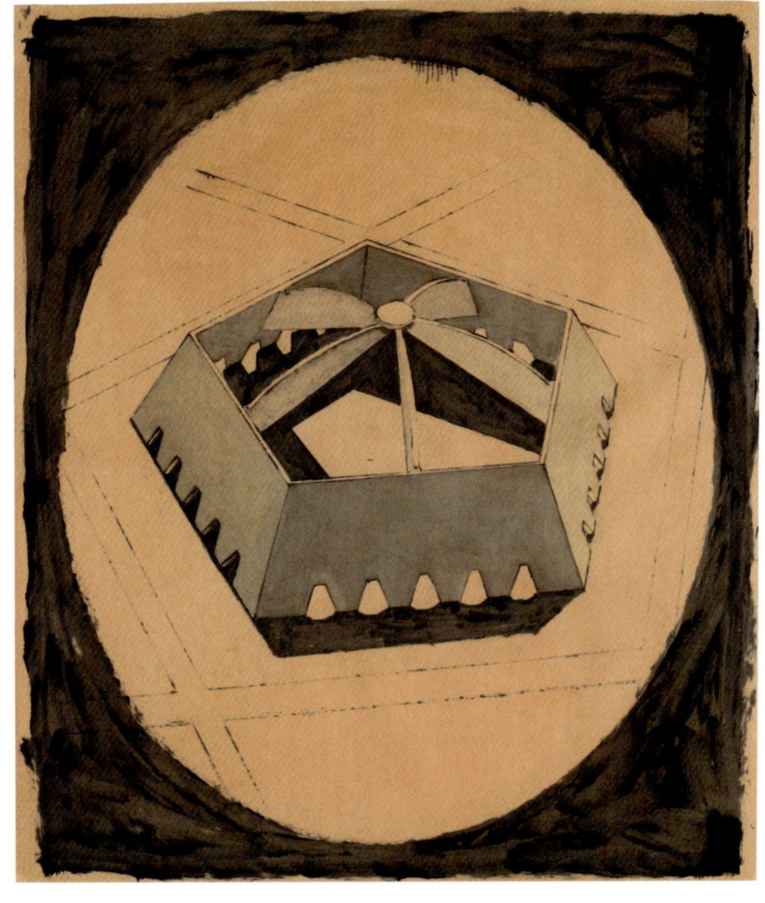

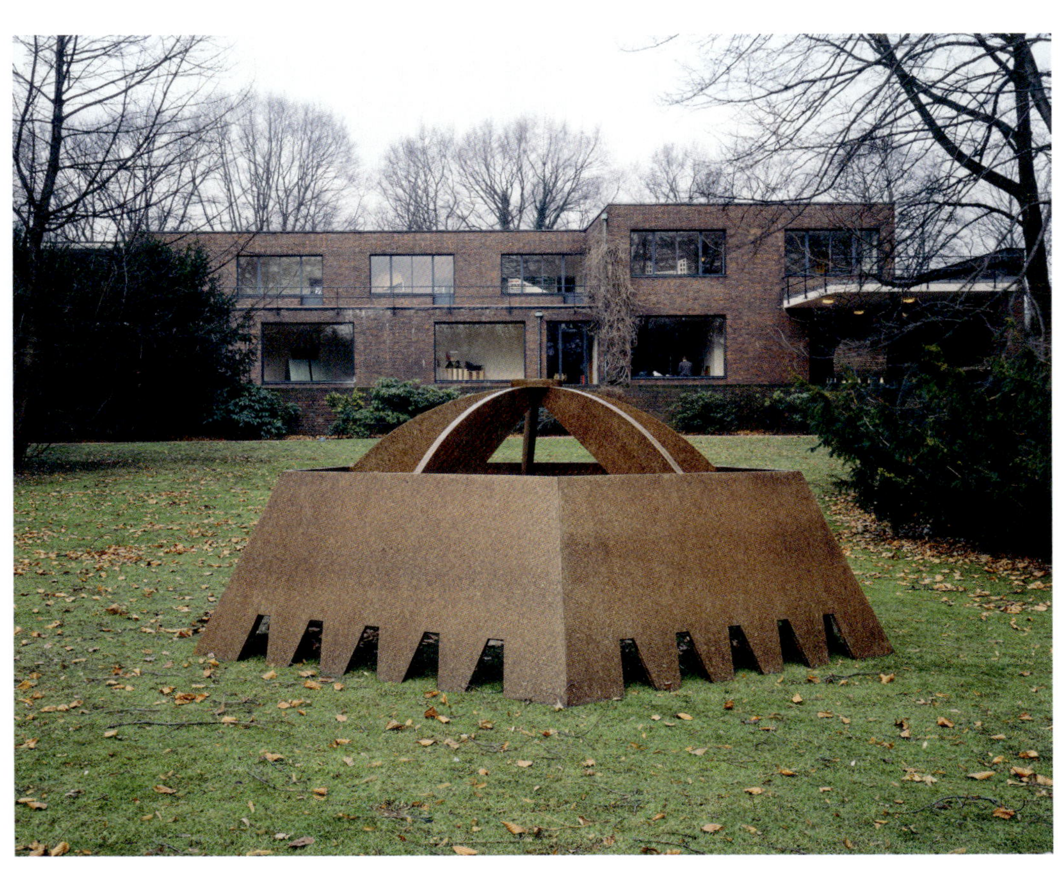

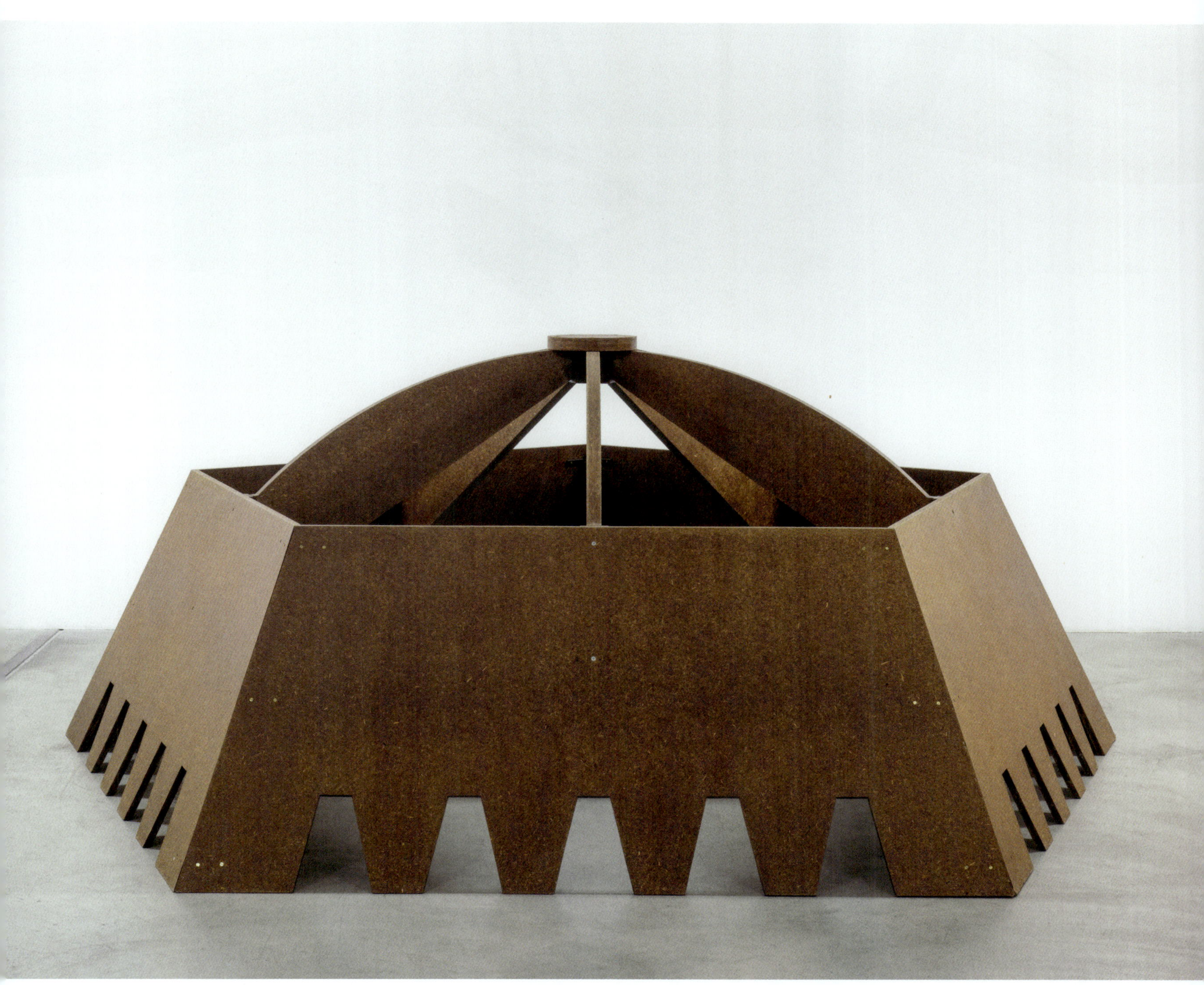

27

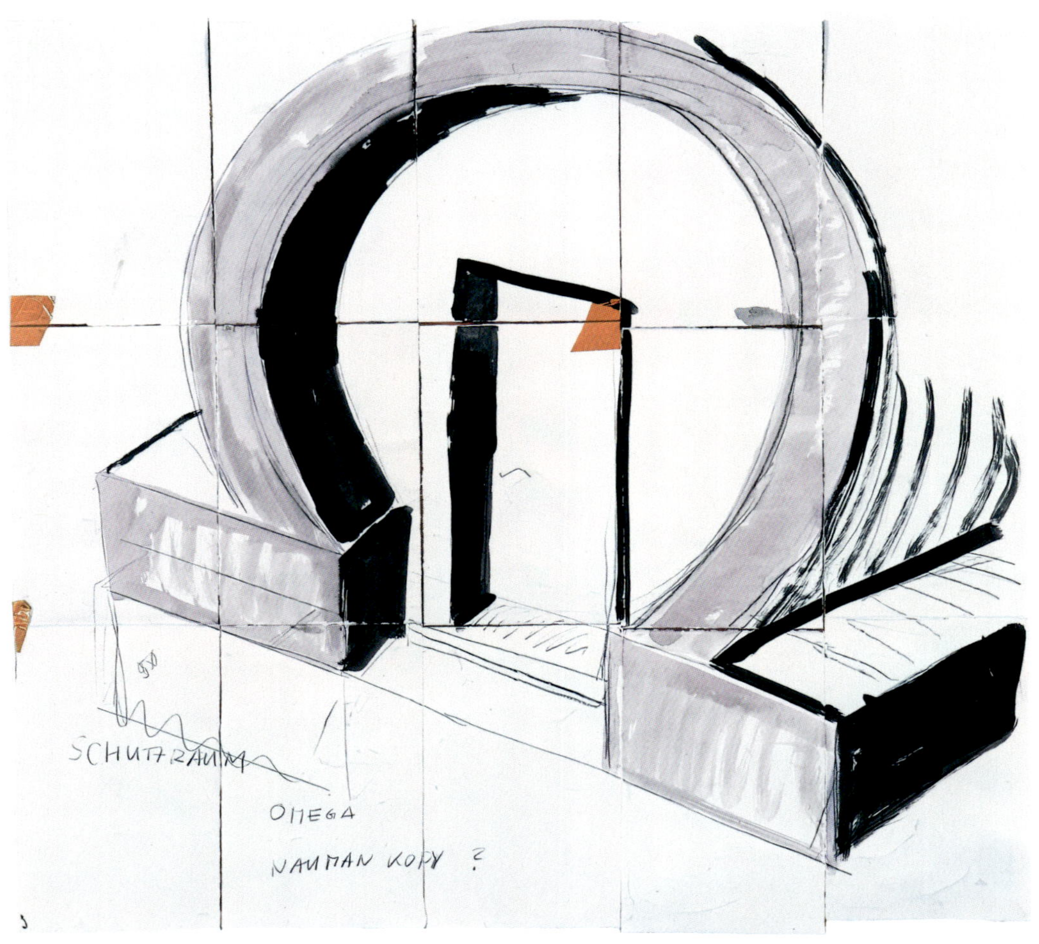

28
Schutzraum (*Shelter*). 1986. Wood, paint, and cardboard, 4 ½ × 4 5⁄16 × 8 1⁄16" (11.5 × 11 × 20.5 cm)

29
Schutzraum (*Shelter*). 1986. Steel and sprayed concrete with steel door, 10' 9 15⁄16" × 8' 8 ¾" × 14' 2 ½" (330 × 266 × 433 cm). Installation view, Sonsbeek '86, Arnhem, Netherlands, June 18–September 15, 1986

Above:
Ohne Titel (Schutzraum) (*Untitled [Shelter]*). 1996. Ink, varnish, tape, and pencil on paper, one of five sheets, various dimensions, this sheet 34 1⁄16 × 37 13⁄16" (86.5 × 96 cm). Sammlung Goetz, Munich

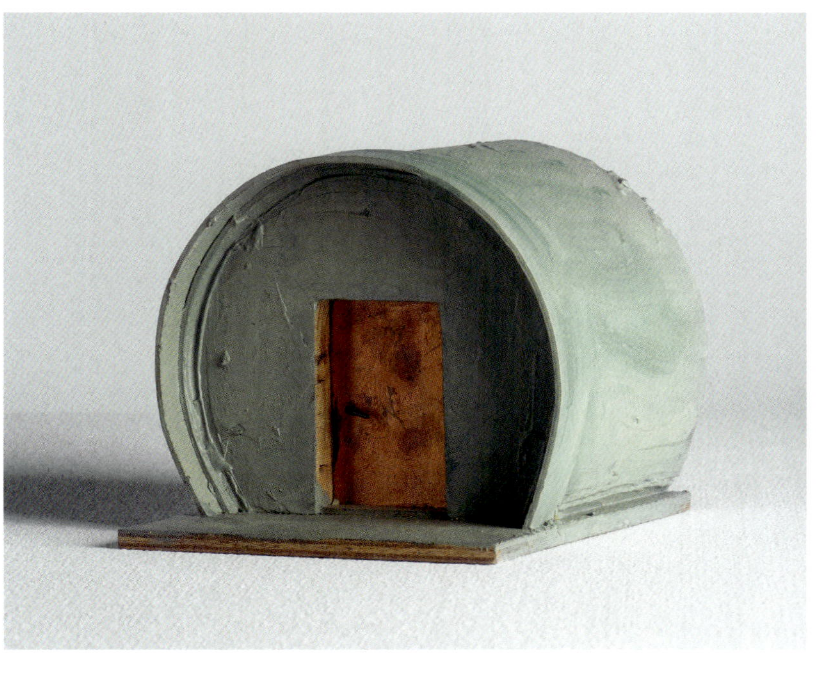

28

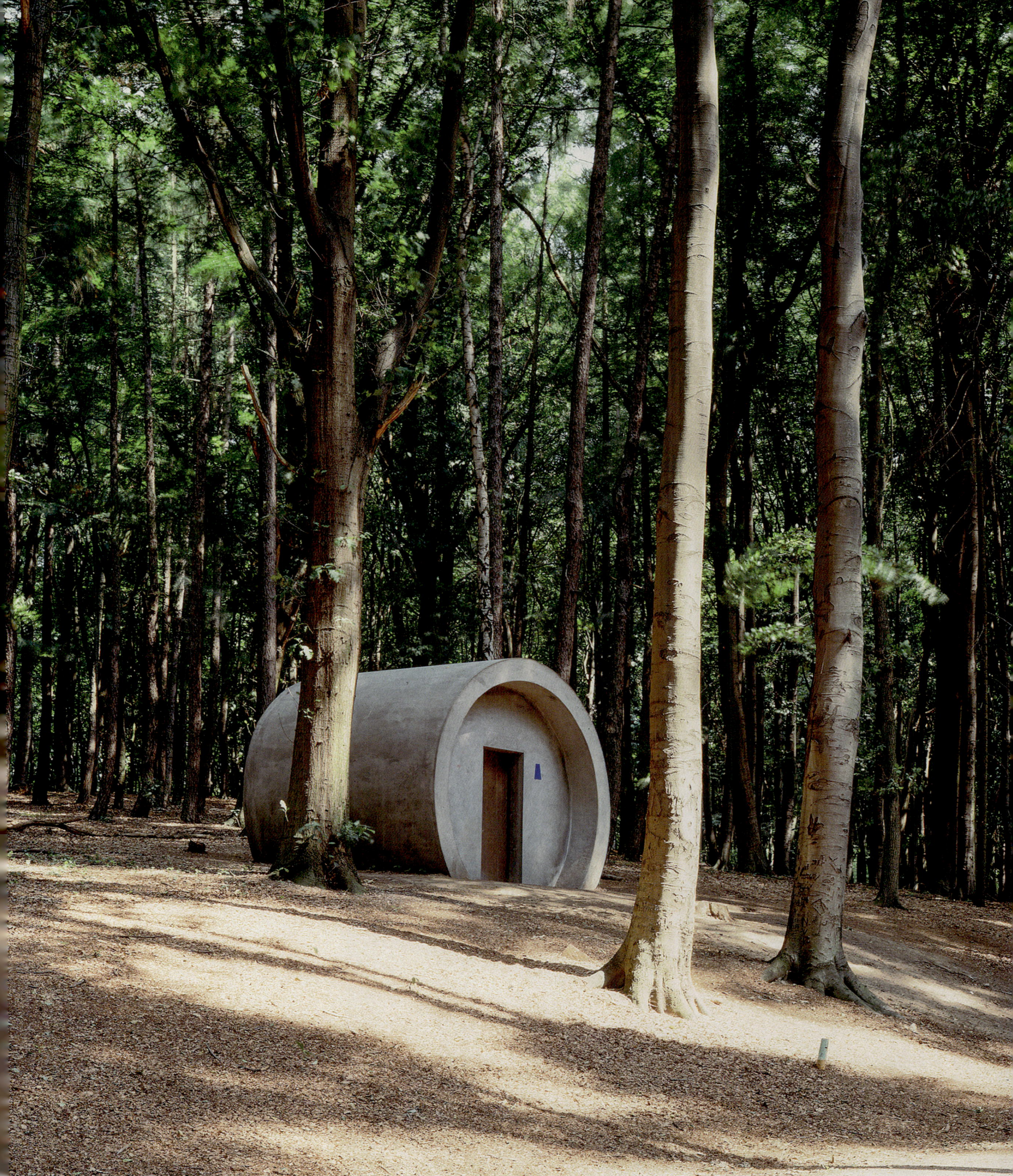

29

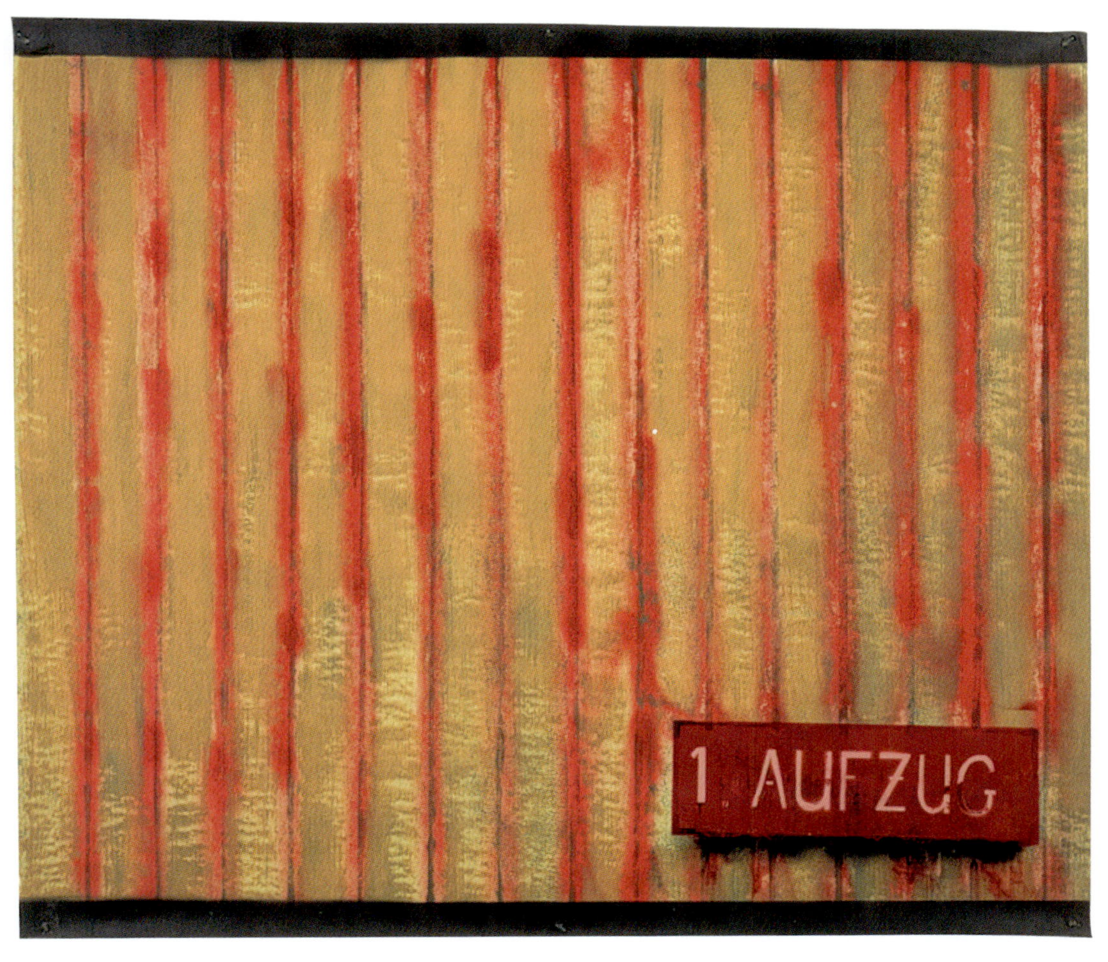
1. AUFZUG

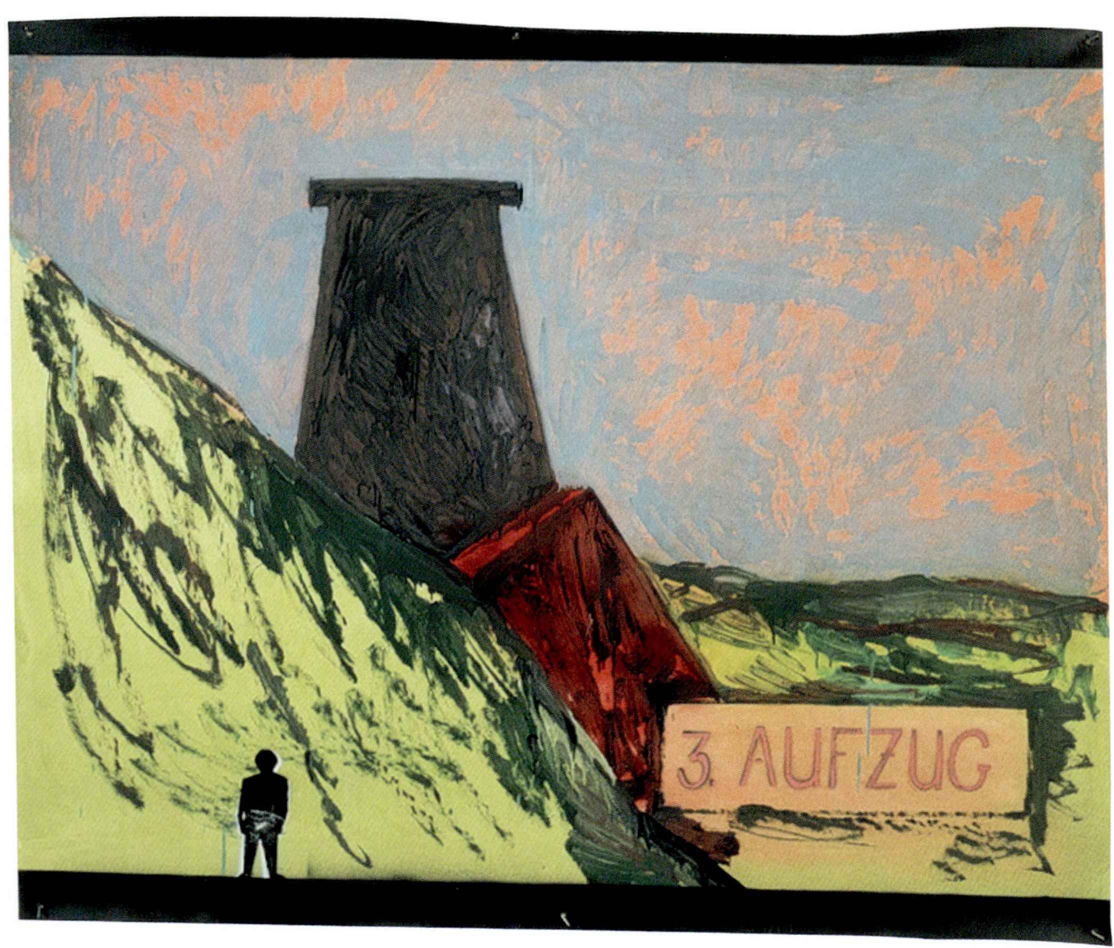
3. AUFZUG

This spread and pages 118–21:

30
Ein Stück mit 12 Aufzügen (*A Play with 12 Acts*).
1987. Lacquer on paper, 12 sheets, each approx.
51 3/16 × 61 13/16" (130 × 157 cm)

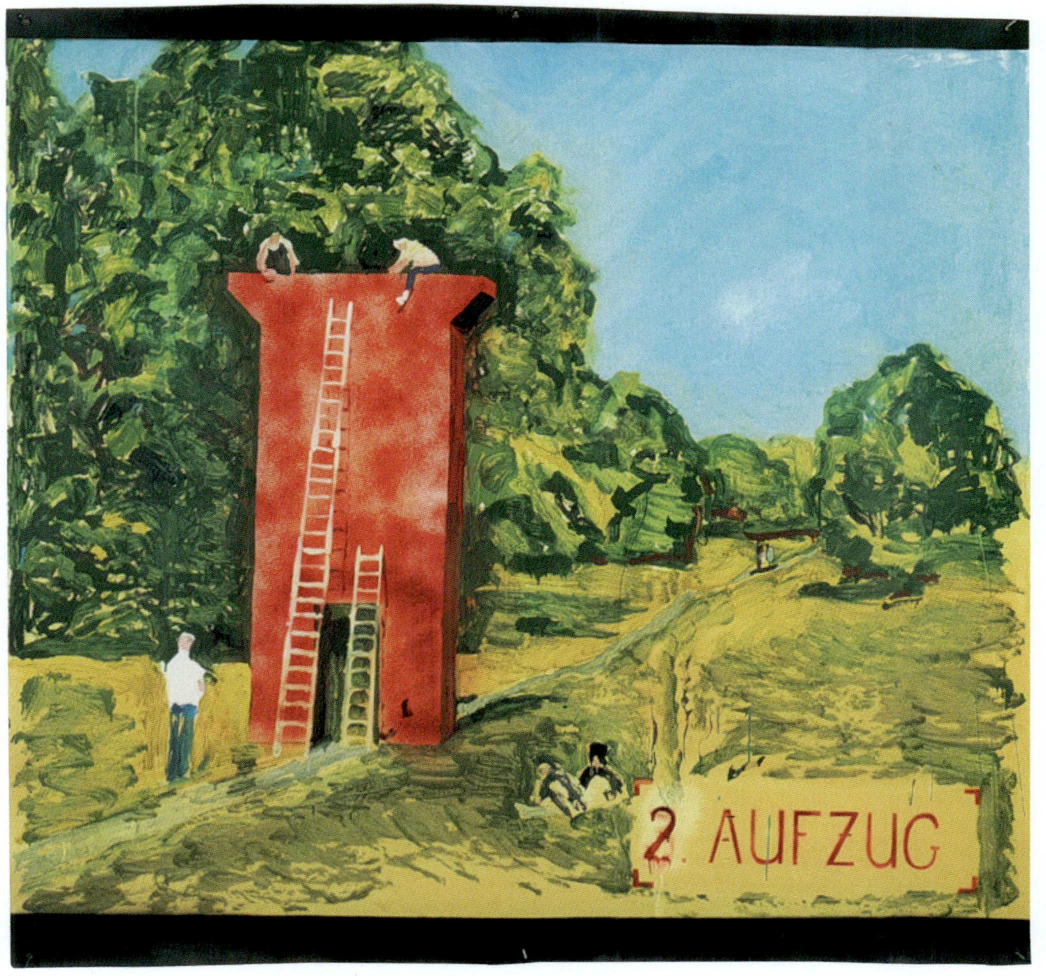

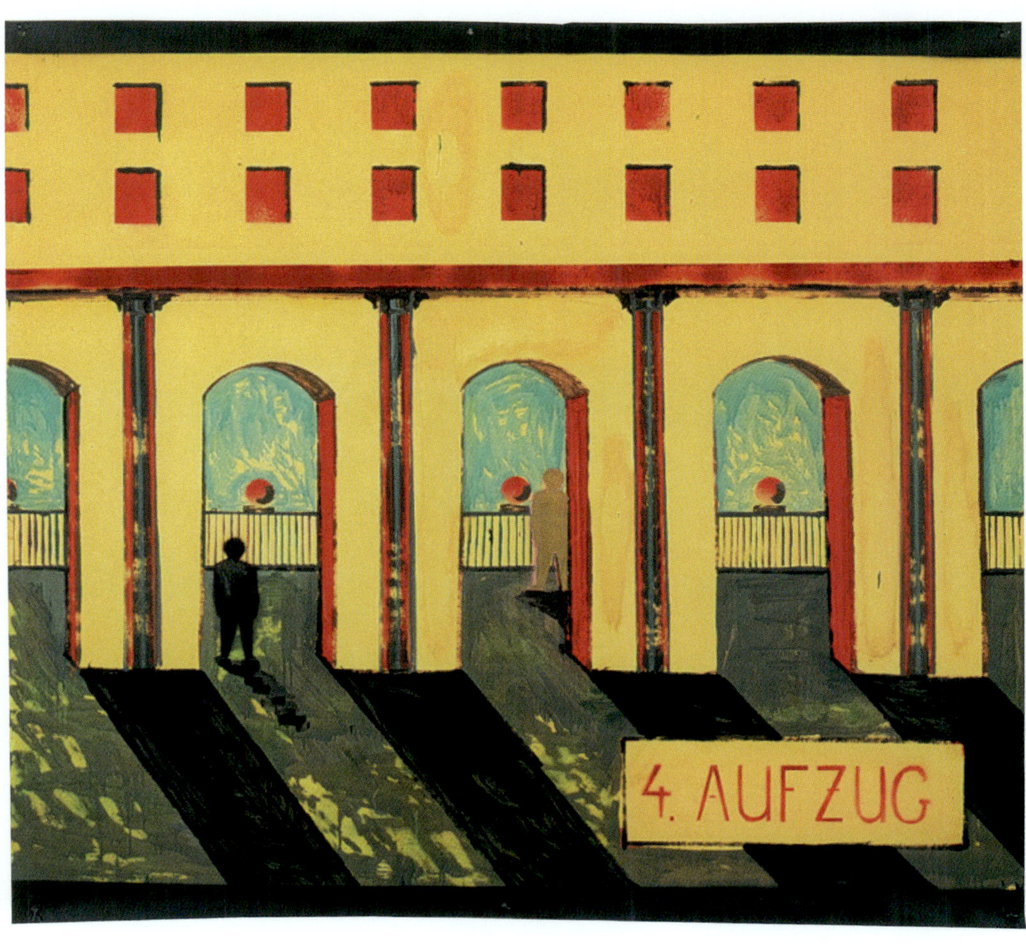

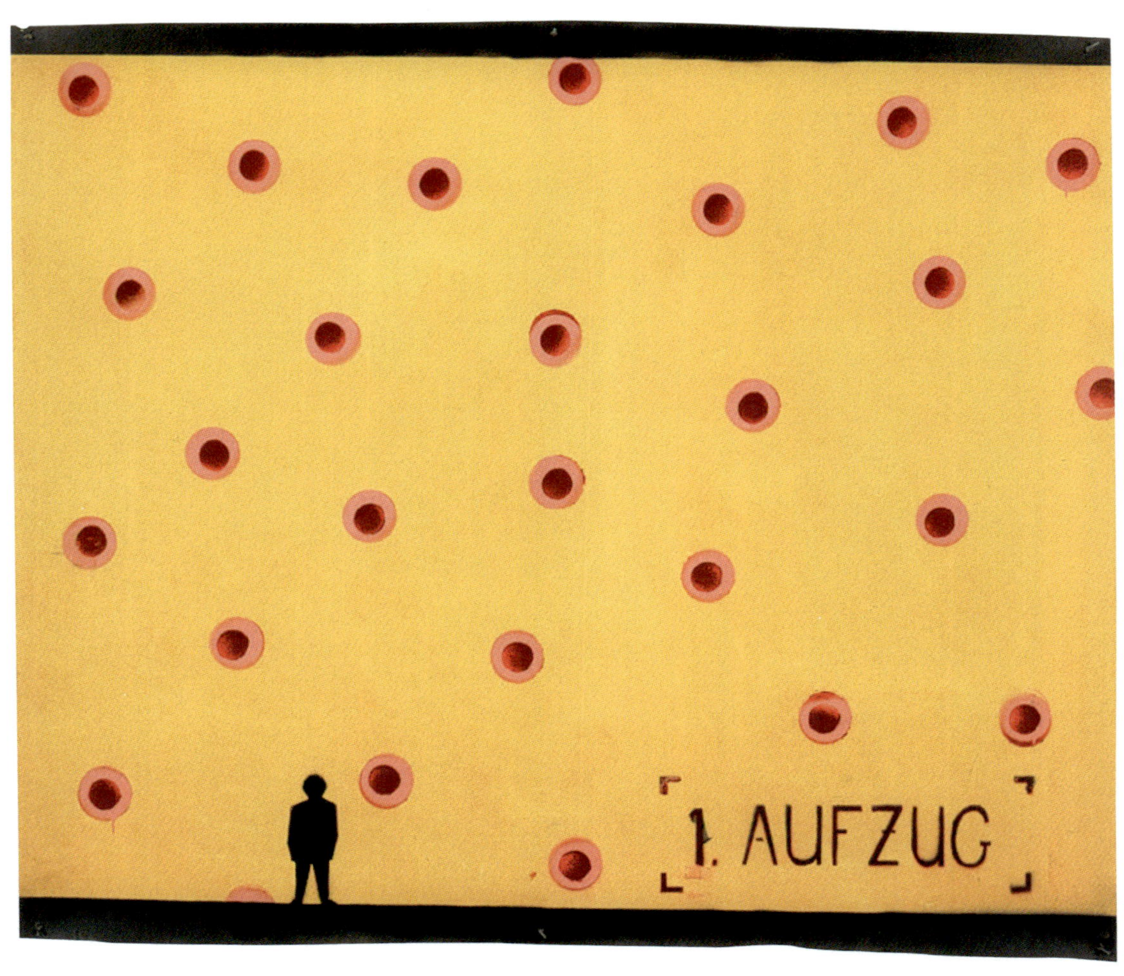
1. AUFZUG

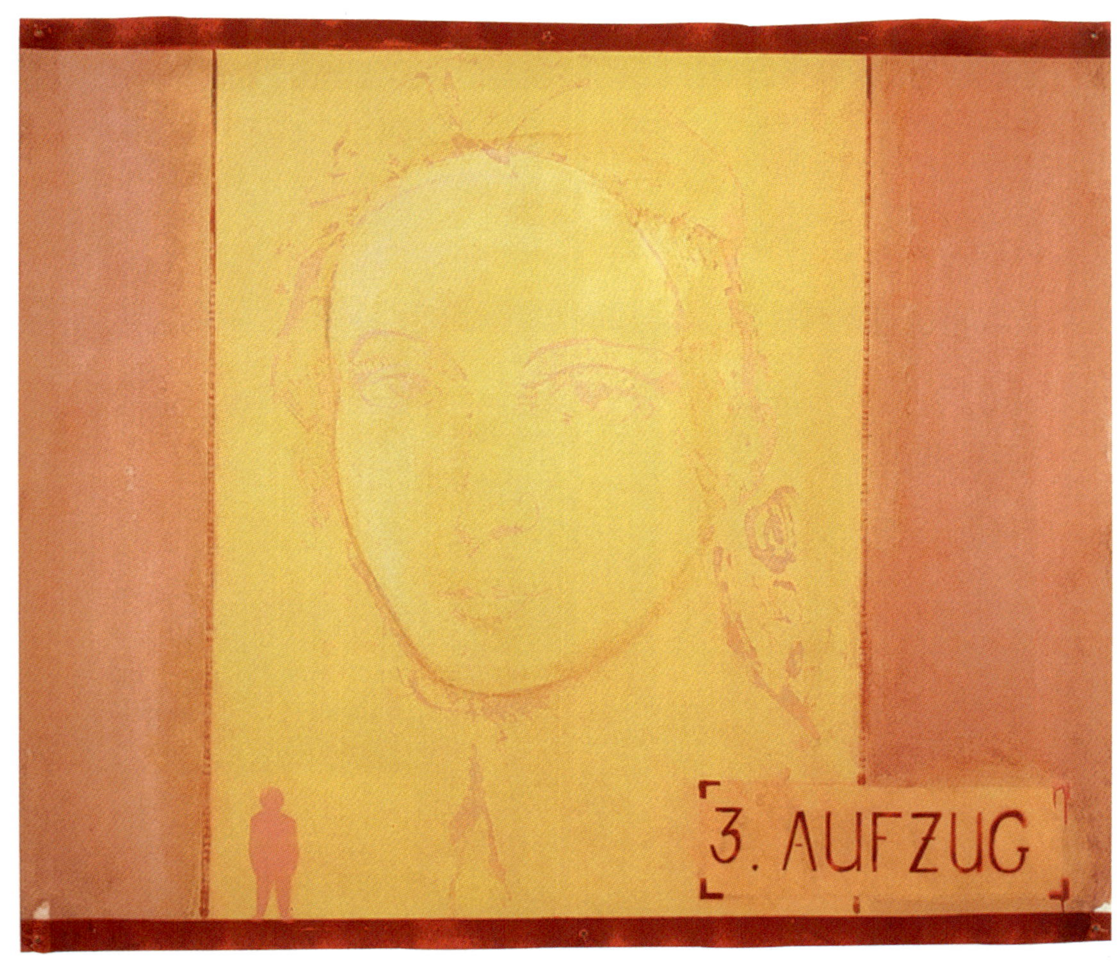
3. AUFZUG

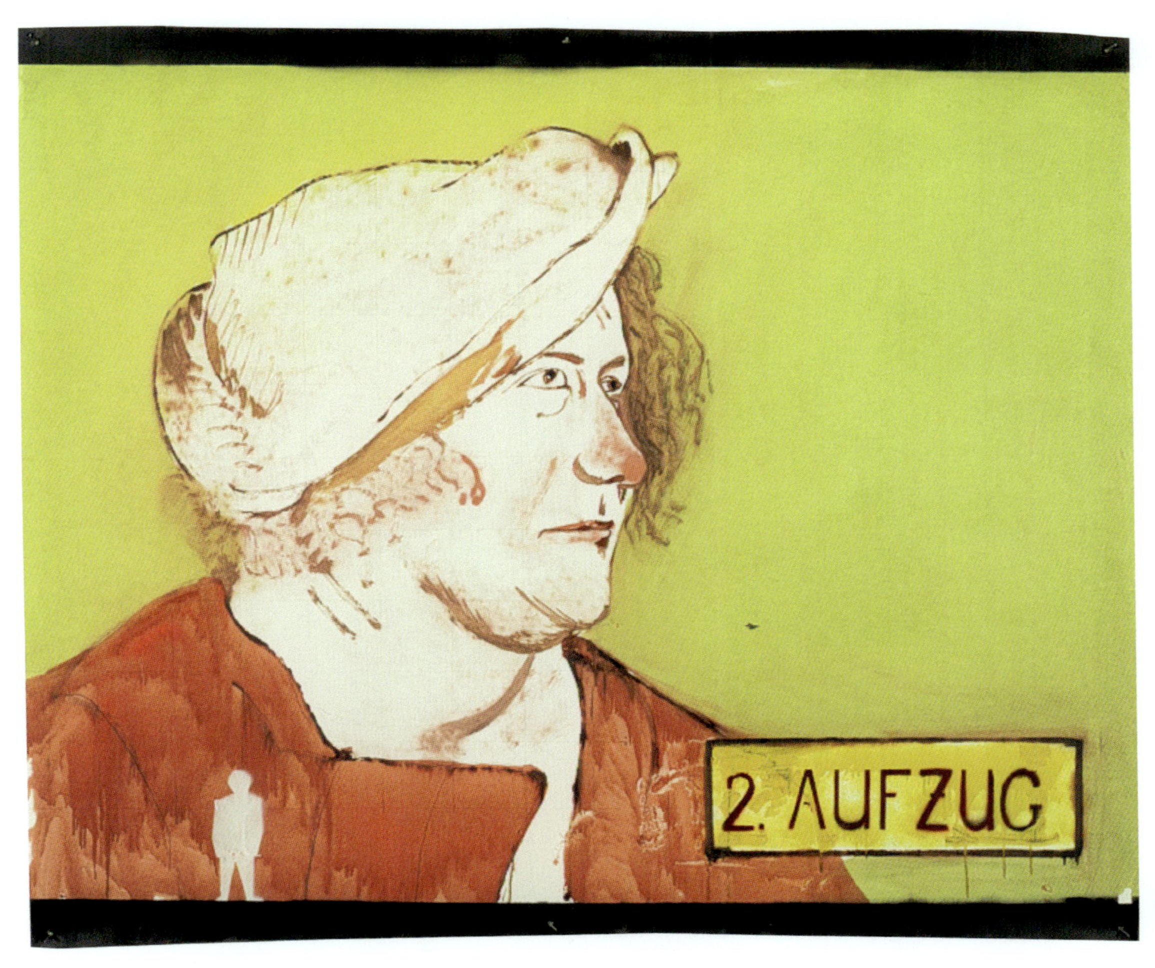
2. AUFZUG

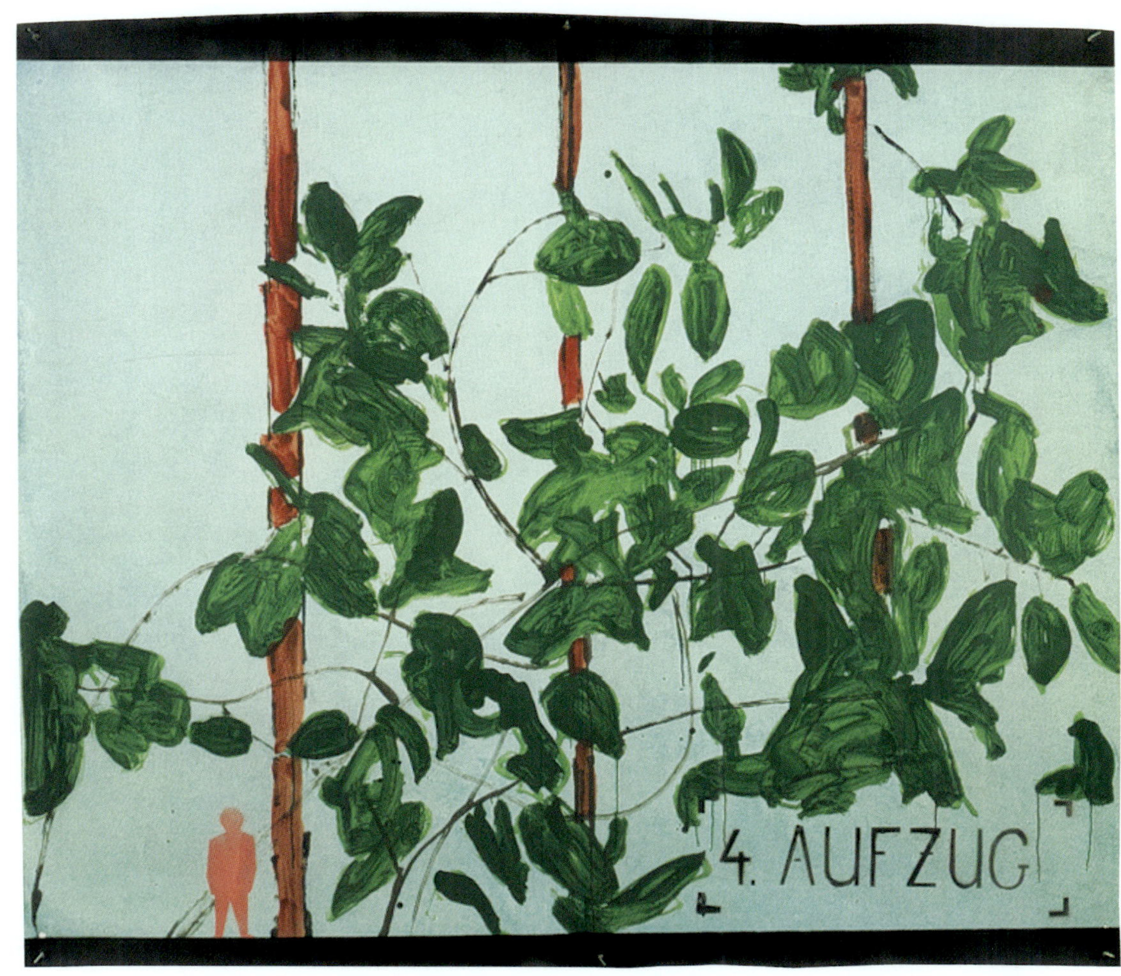
4. AUFZUG

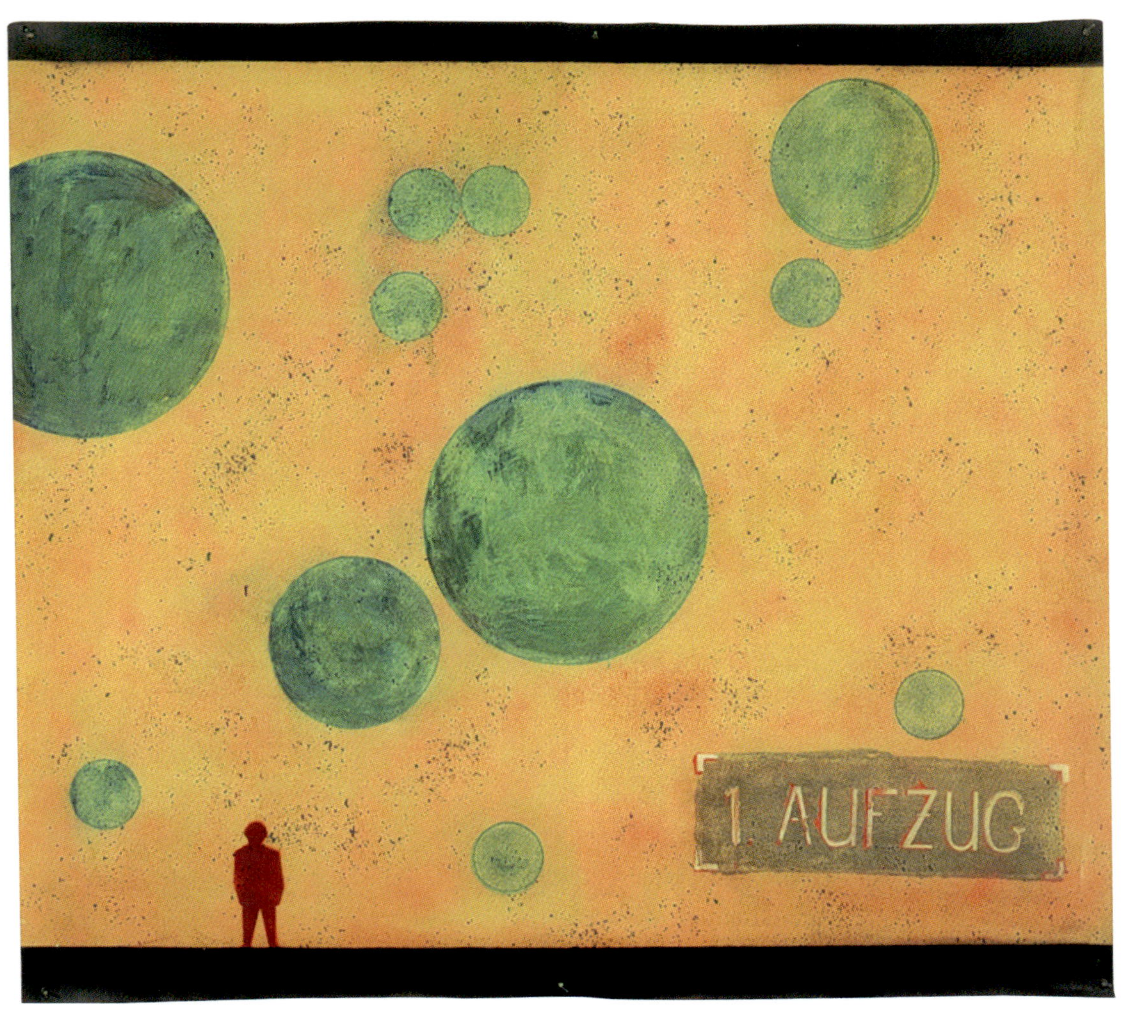
1. AUFZUG

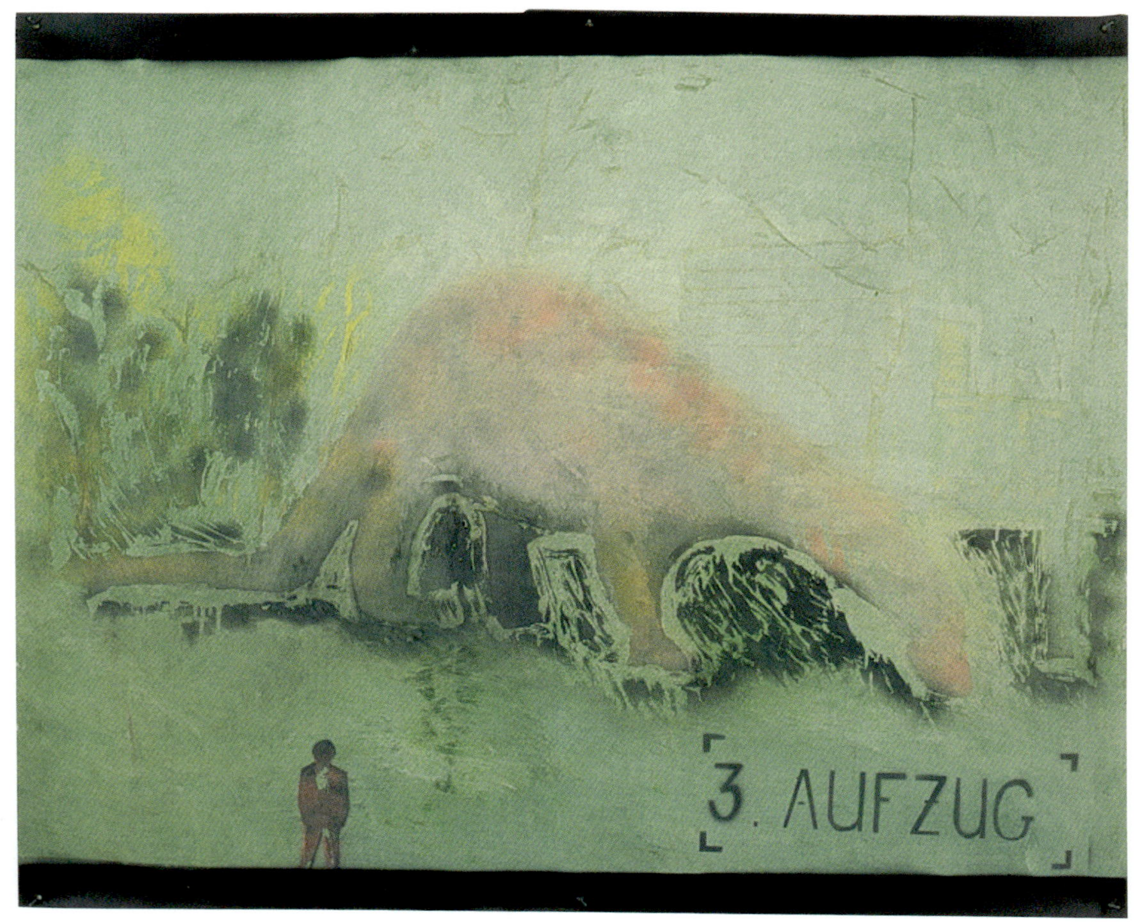
3. AUFZUG

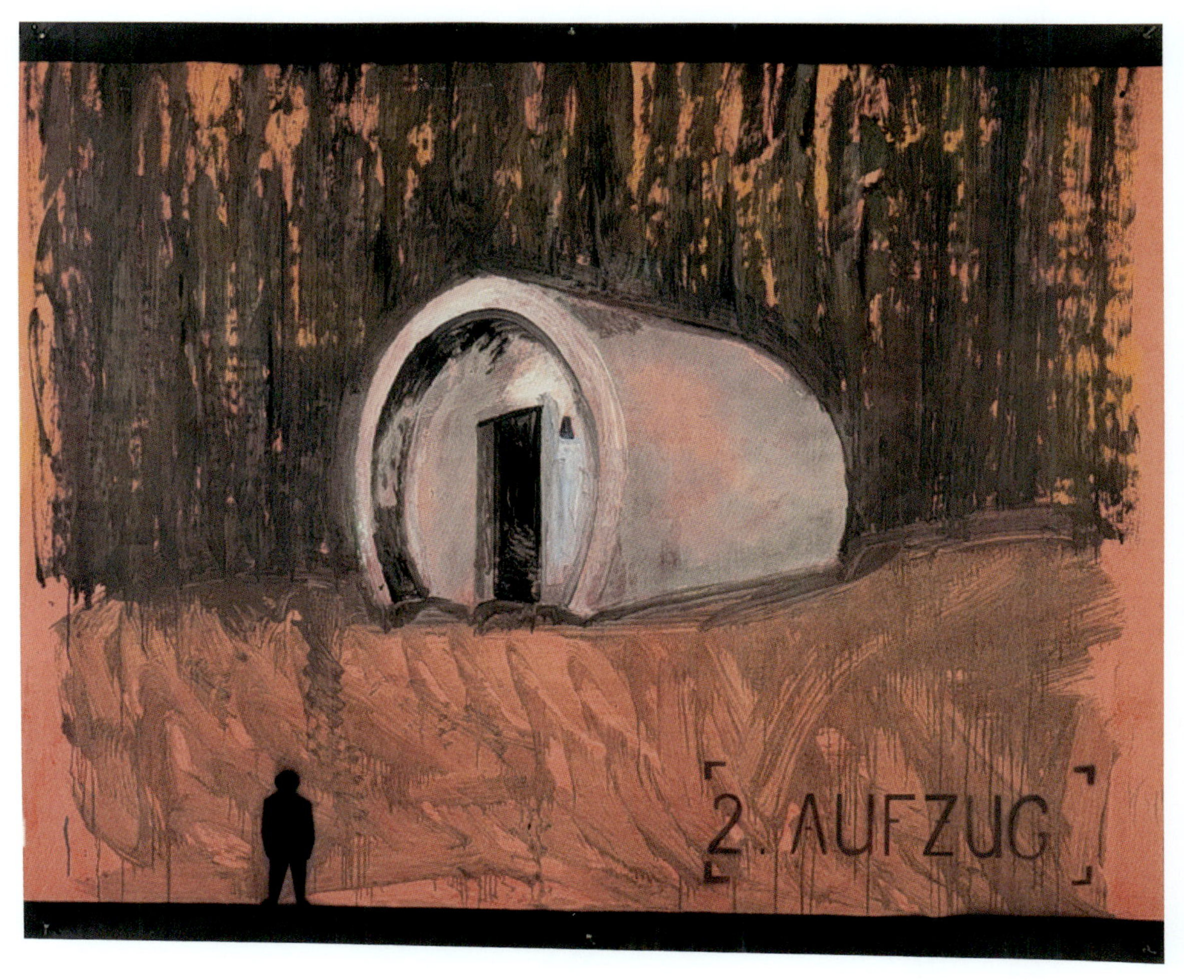
2. AUFZUG

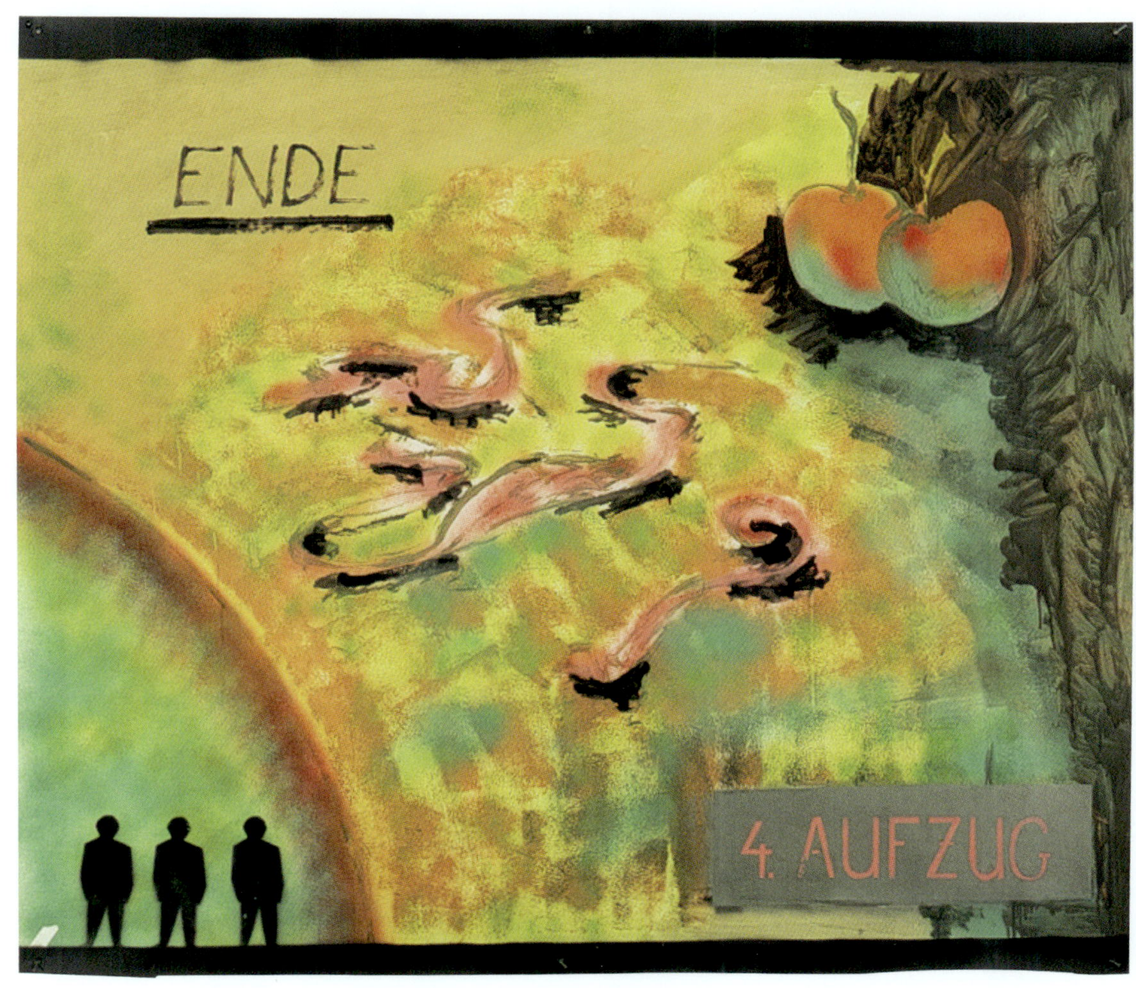
ENDE
4. AUFZUG

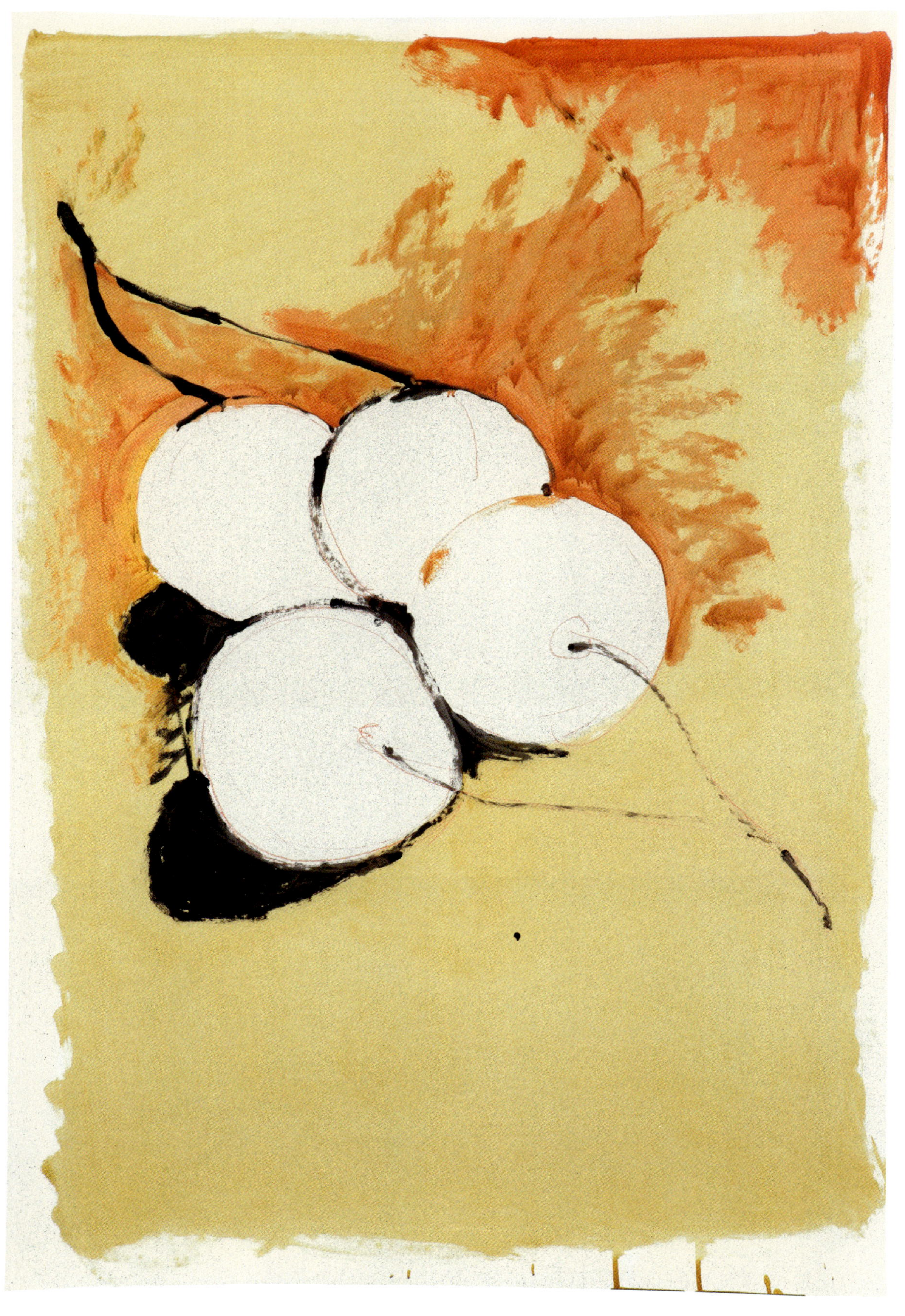

31
Kirschen (*Cherries*). 1986. Lacquer on paper,
59 13⁄16 × 43 5⁄16" (152 × 110 cm)

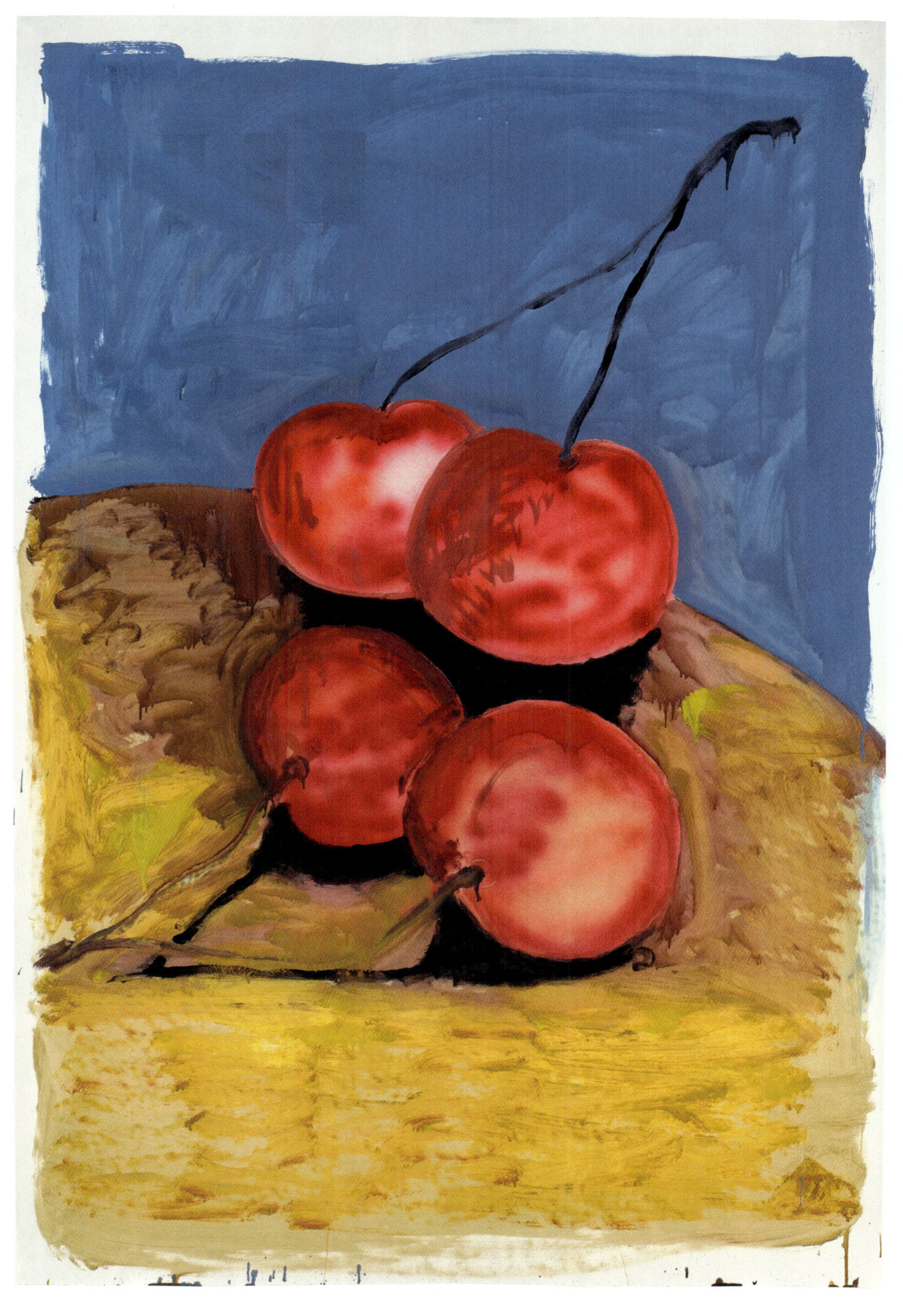

32
Kirschen (*Cherries*). 1987. Lacquer on paper,
62 ¾ × 43 ¼" (159.4 × 109.8 cm)

33
Sheet from *Projekt "Monument Alain Colas"* (*Alain Colas Monument Project*). 1989. Photocopy, 11 ⅝ × 16 ⁹⁄₁₆" (29.5 × 42 cm)

34
Alain Colas. 1989. Clay, polystyrene, paint, foam, cardboard, wood, and wire on two wooden pallets, 45 ⅞ × 47 ⁷⁄₁₆ × 31 ½" (116.5 × 120.5 × 80 cm)

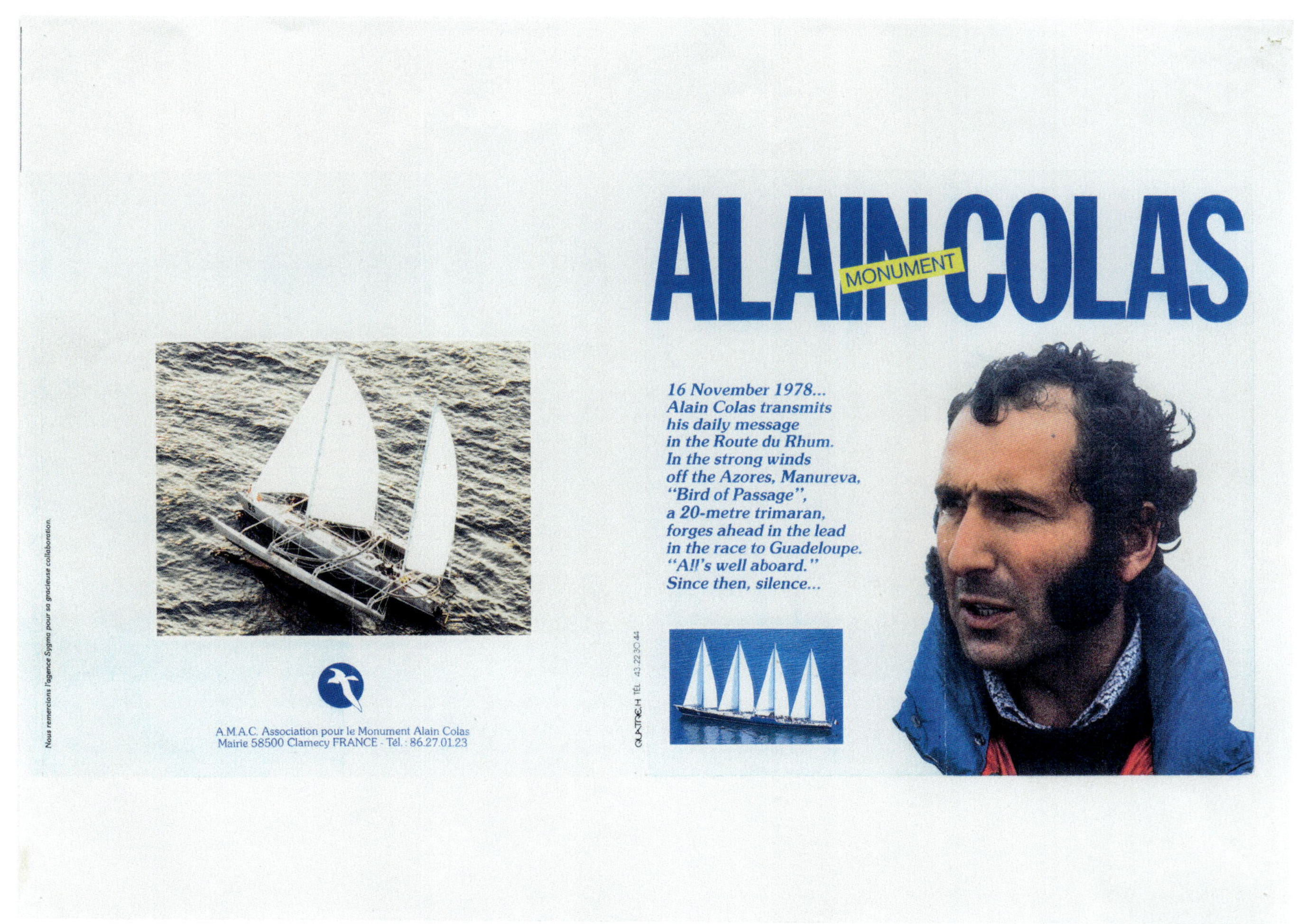

33

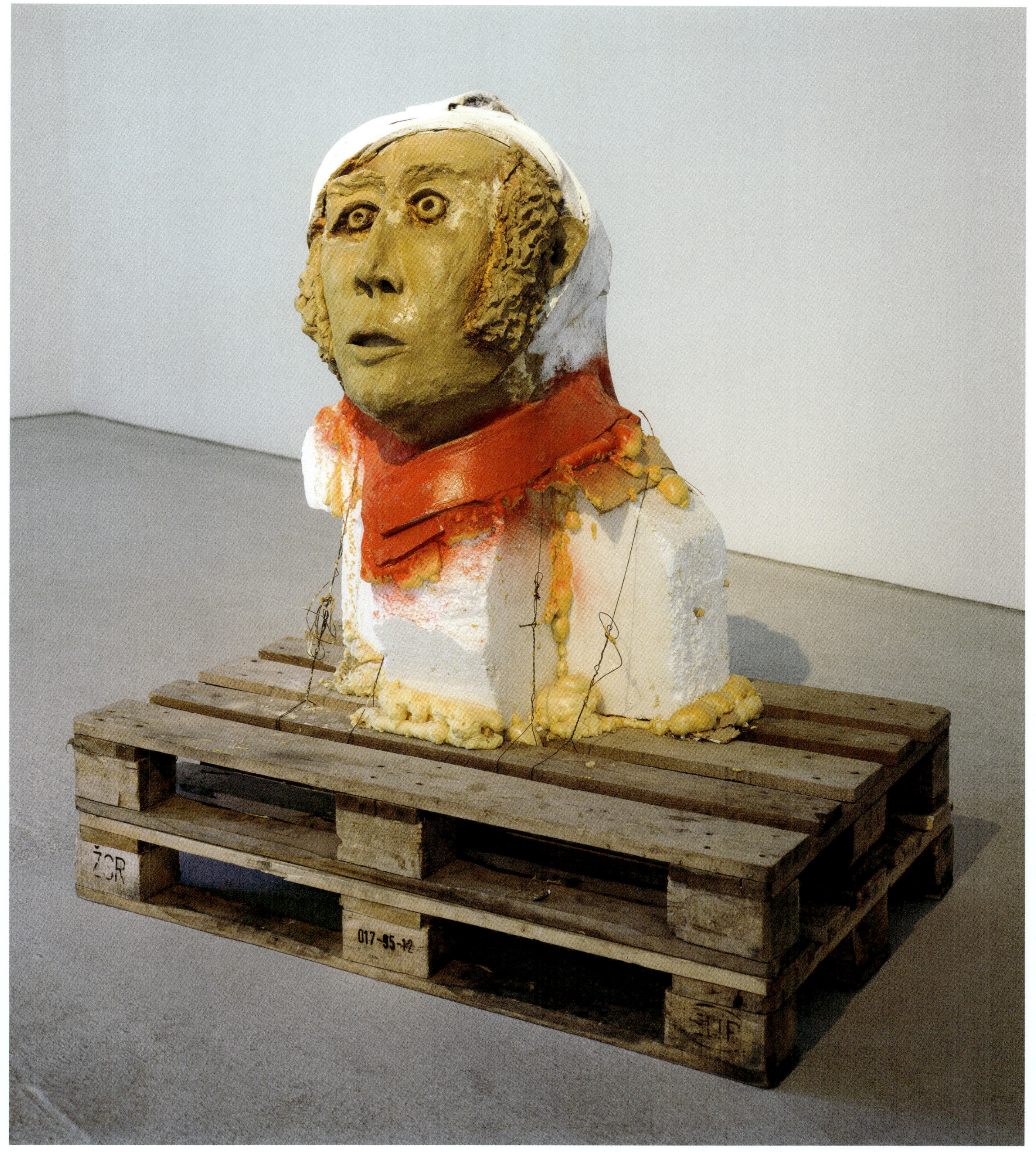

34

35
Zeichnung für Alain Colas (*Drawing for Alain Colas*). 1989. Collage with ink on paper, 23 ⅝ × 31 ½" (60 × 80 cm)

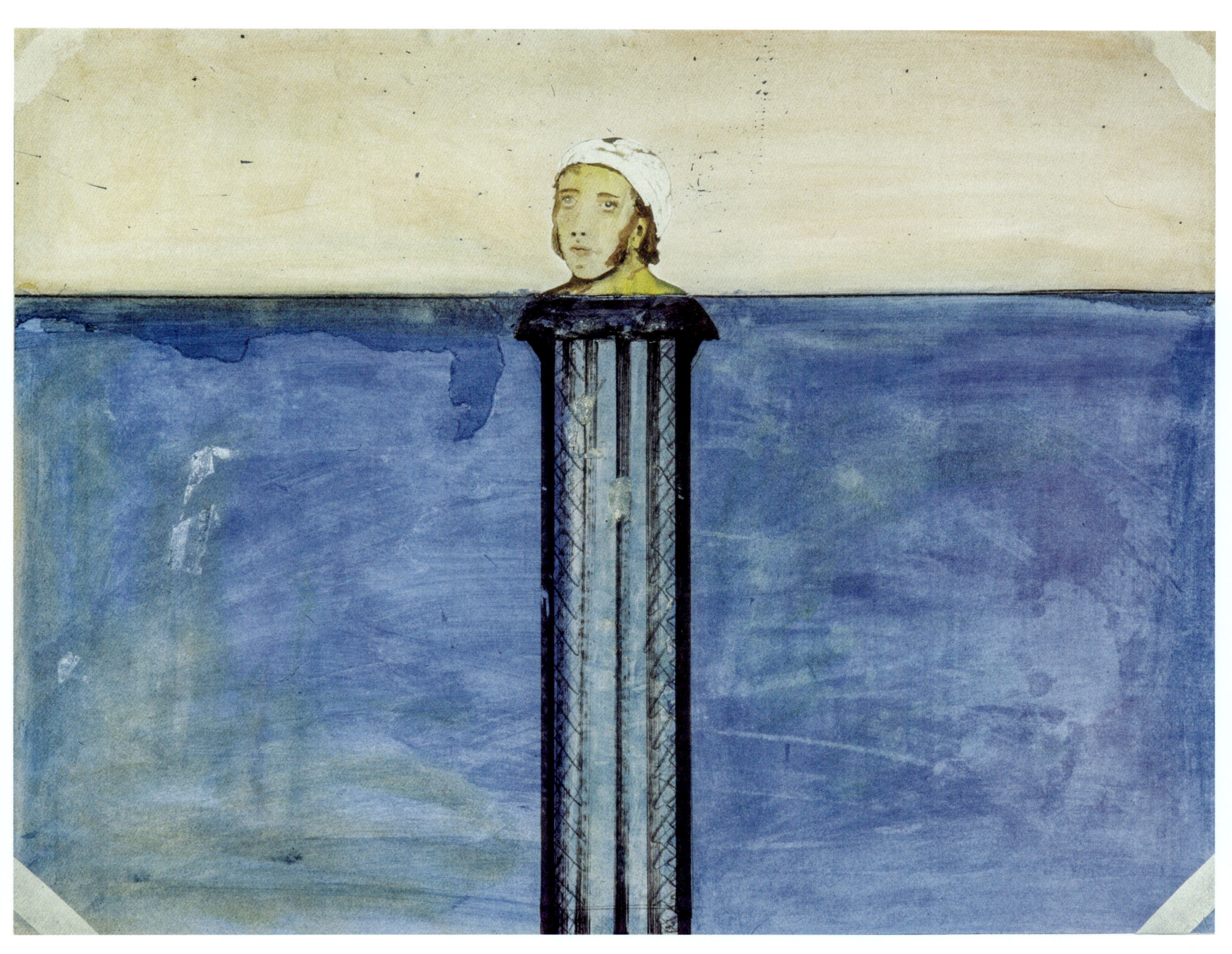

36
Mohr's Life. 1988. Two figures of modeling clay with fabric, string, and wooden dowels; four oil paintings on easels; two painted tin cans; and iron rack with socks, 5' 10 ⅞" × 11' 5 ¹³⁄₁₆" × 11' 5 ¹³⁄₁₆" (180 × 350 × 350 cm). Installation view, *Moving Is in Every Direction*, Hamburger Bahnhof, Berlin, March 17–September 24, 2017

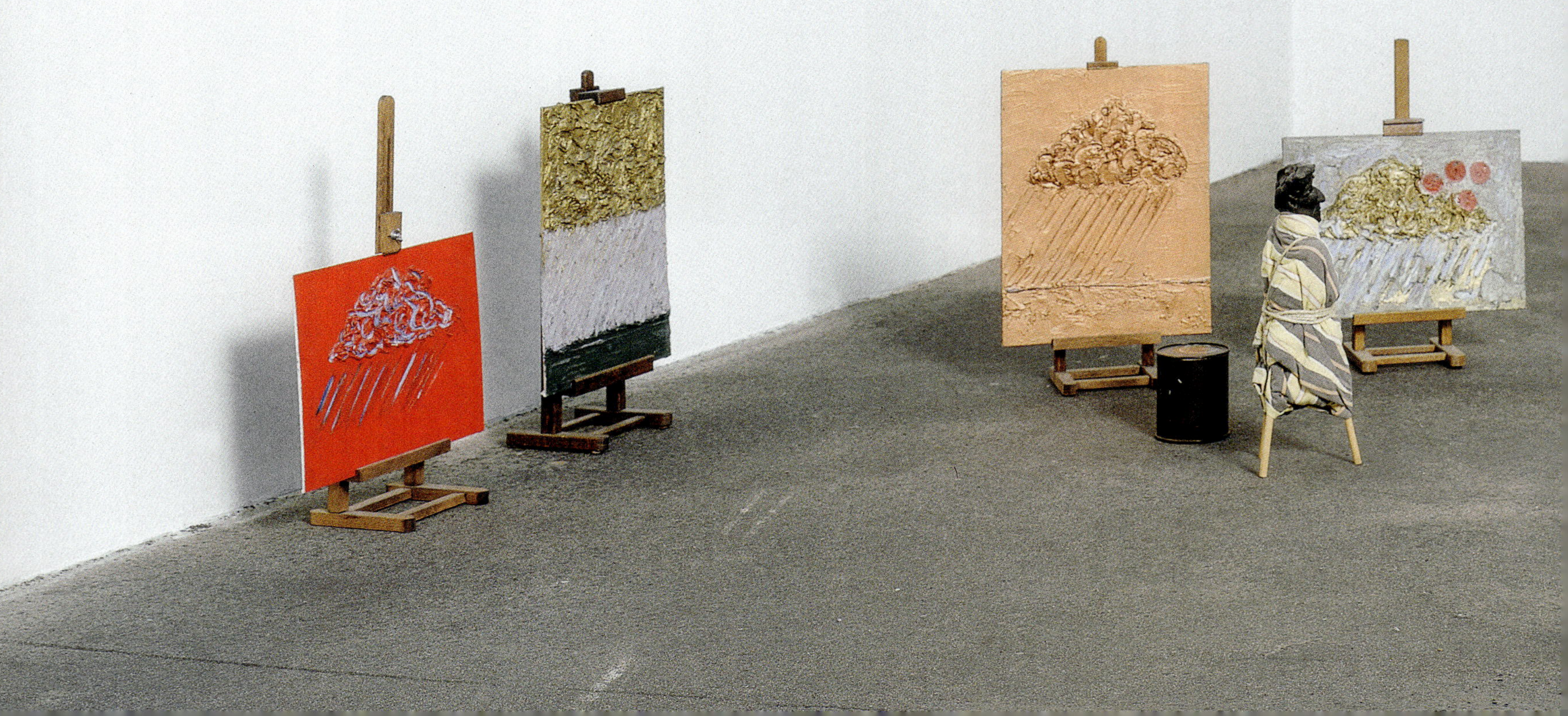

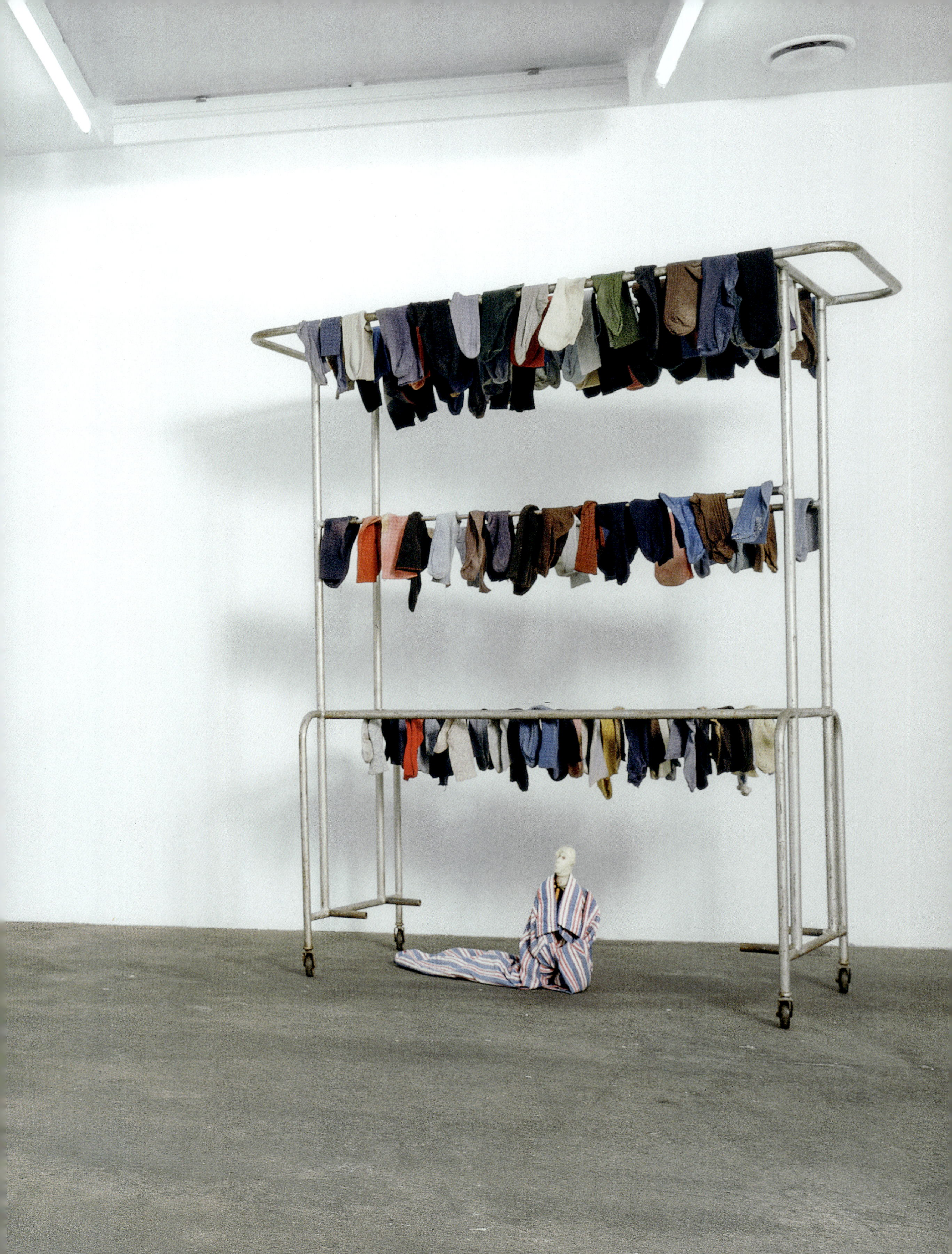

37
Mohr's Life: The Collectors. 1988–99. Figure of cast resin; seven figures of modeling clay with fabric, string, and wooden dowels; taped cardboard wardrobe moving box with clothes on hangers; and clamp lamp and cable reel, 5' 3" × 6' 6 ¾" × 6' 6 ¾" (160 × 200 × 200 cm)

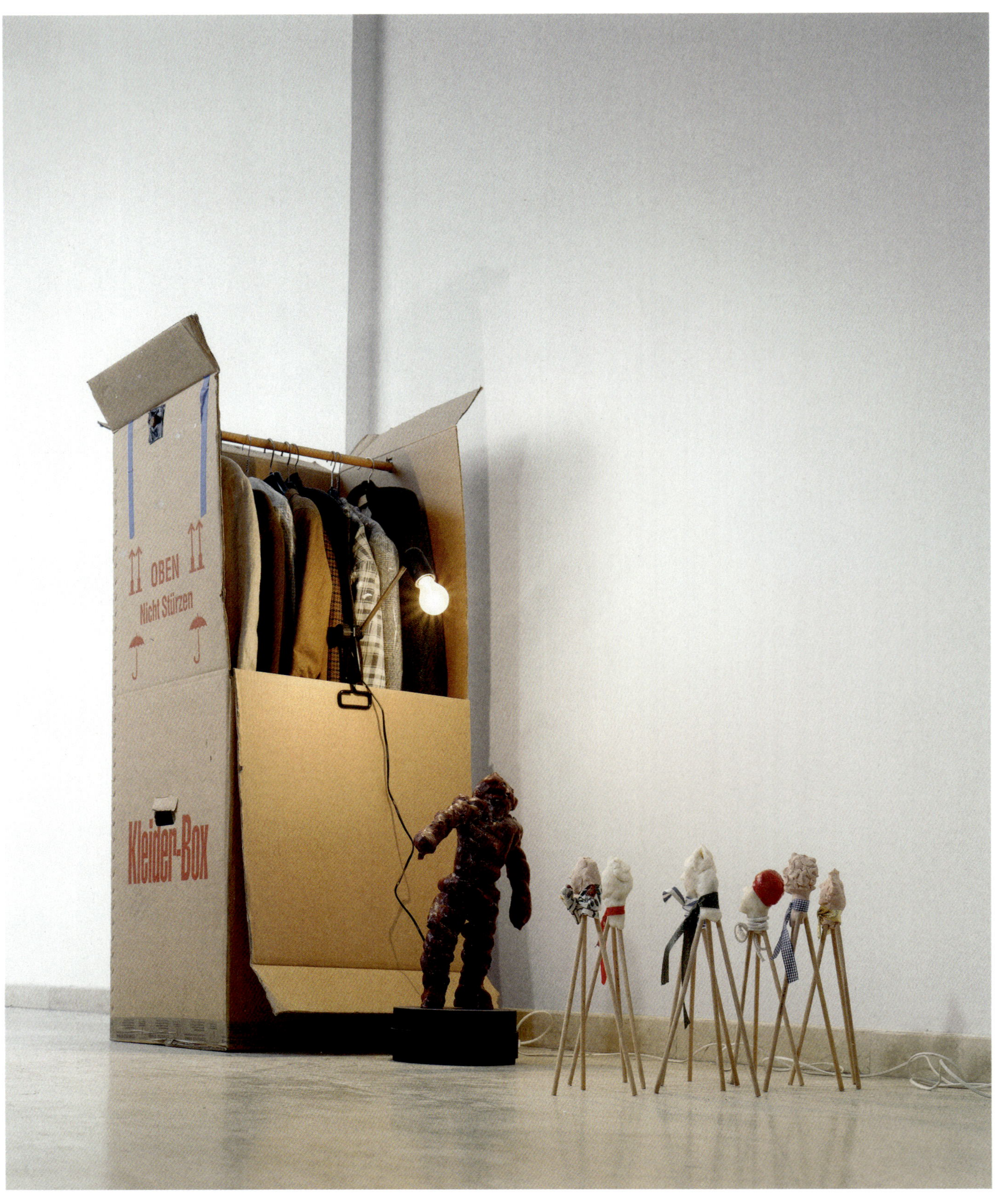

38

Mohr's Life: The Sculptor. 1988–99. Figure of modeling clay with fabric, string, hat, nail, and wooden dowels; unfired painted clay on brick on wooden table; raffia basket with nails; reading lamp on paint can; and metal shelving with shoes and unfired clay bust, 5' 3" × 6' 10 11⁄16" × 5' 10 7⁄8" (160 × 210 × 180 cm)

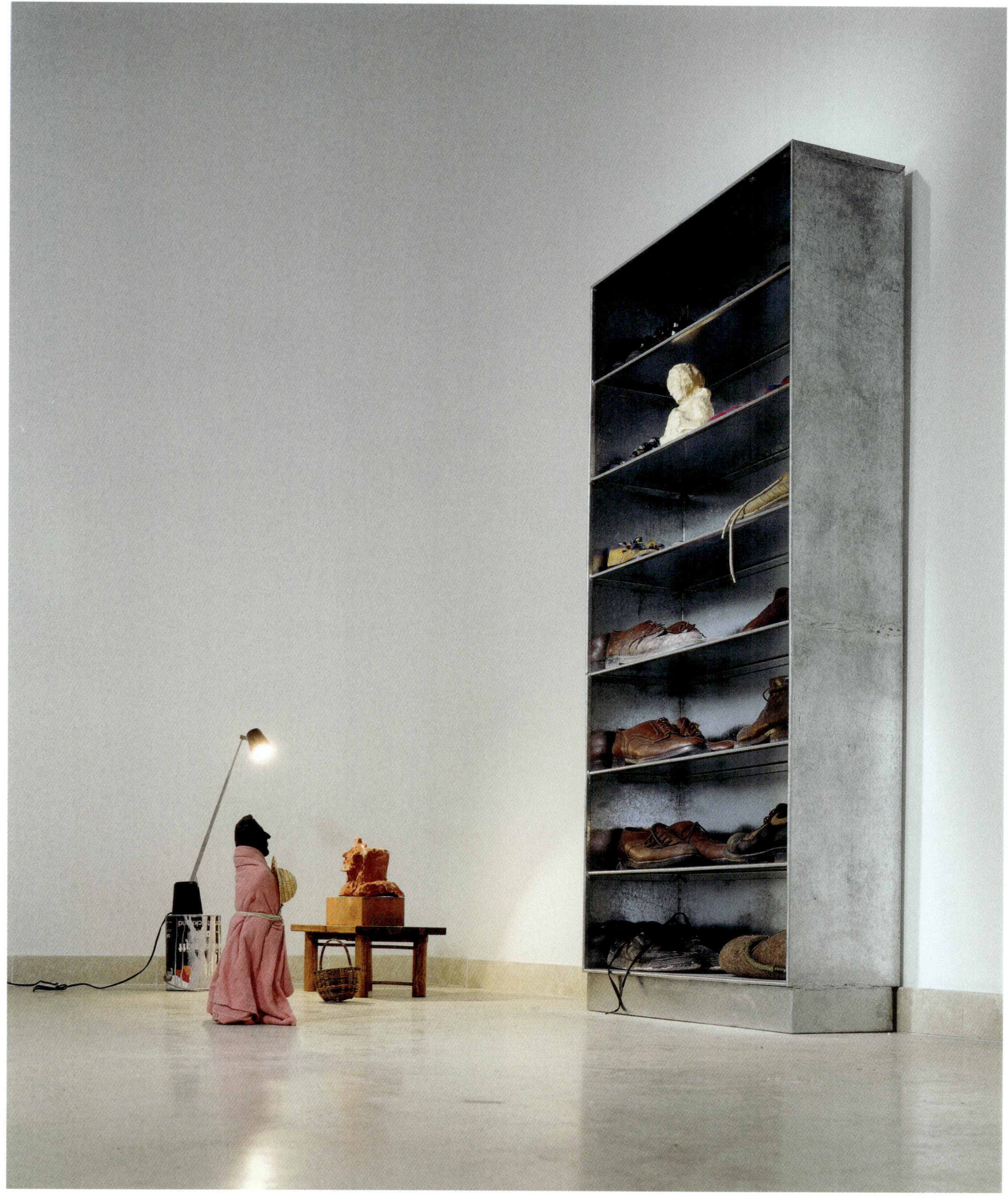

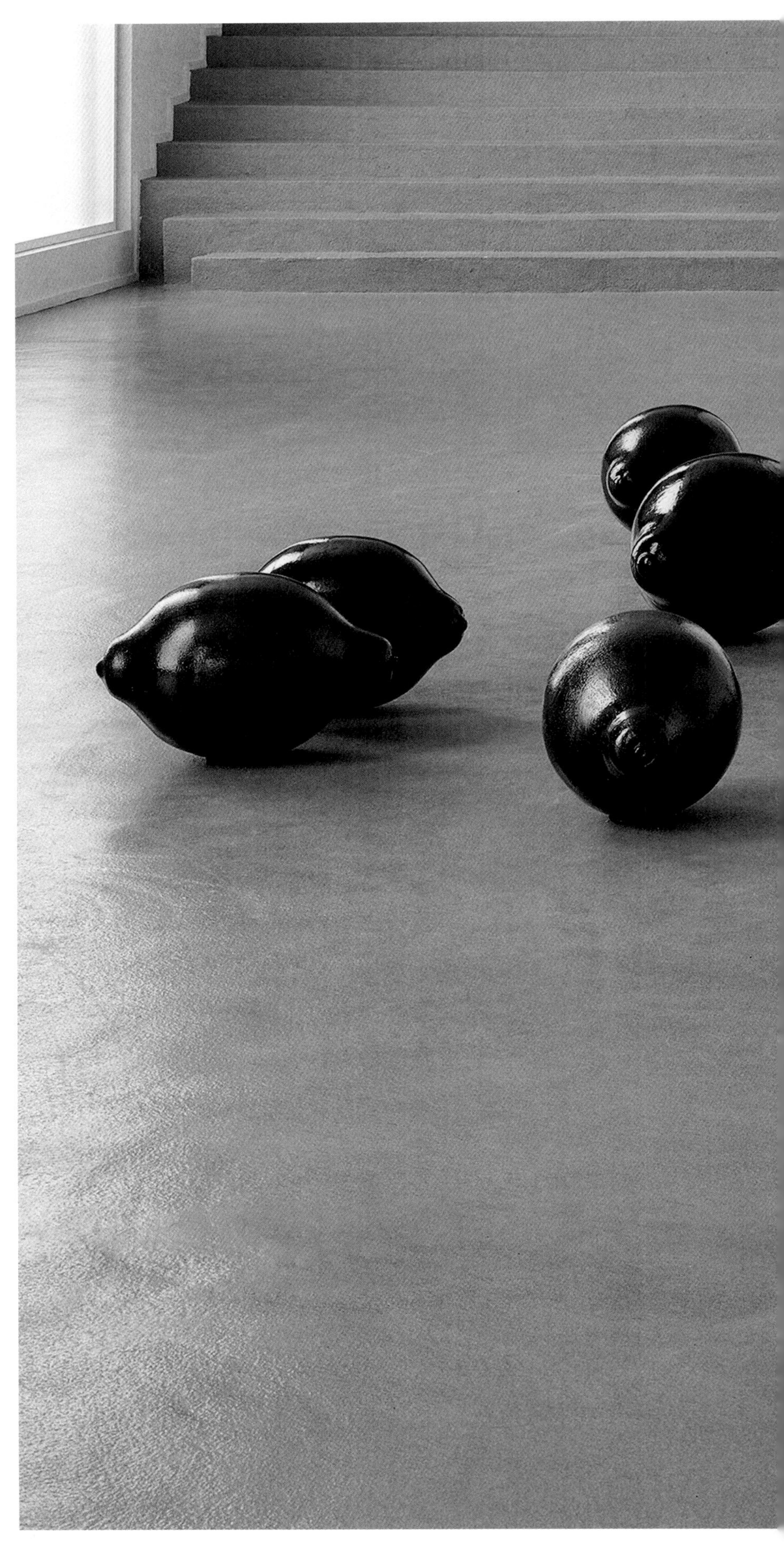

39
Schwarze Zitronen (*Black Lemons*). 1990. Glazed ceramic, 20 parts; ten parts 21 ⅝ × 14 $^{3}/_{16}$" (55 × 36 cm), ten parts 27 $^{3}/_{16}$ × 16 ⅛" (69 × 41 cm). Installation view, *Les flammes: L'âge de la céramique*, Musée d'Art Moderne de Paris, October 15, 2021–February 6, 2022

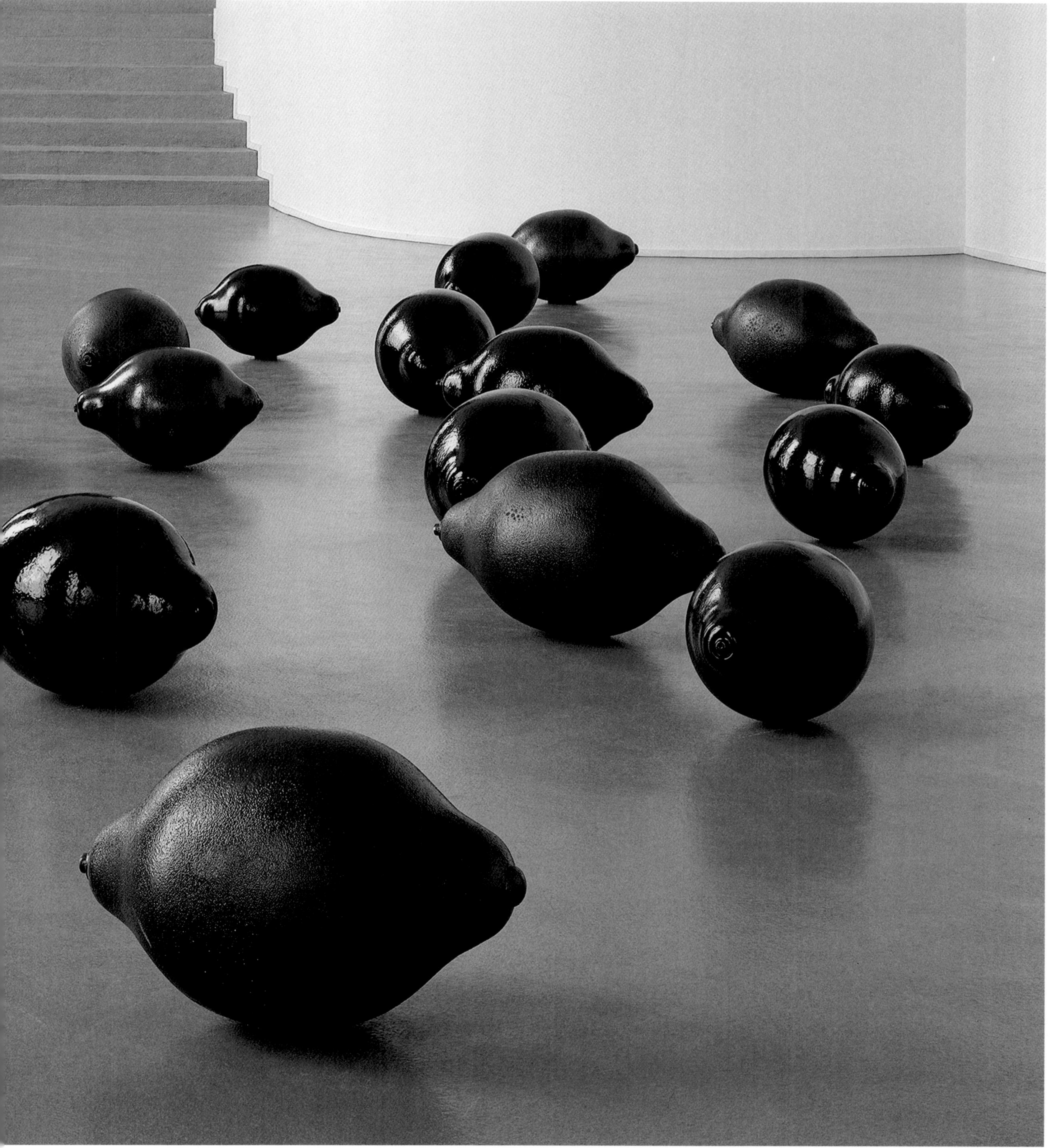

40
Die Fremden (*The Strangers*). 1992. Glazed ceramic and steel, nine parts, various dimensions from 41 ¼ × 18 ³⁄₁₆ × 19 ⅞" (104.8 × 46.2 × 50.5 cm) to 74 ¾ × 26 ¹⁄₁₆ × 20 ¹⁵⁄₁₆" (189.8 × 66.2 × 53.2 cm)

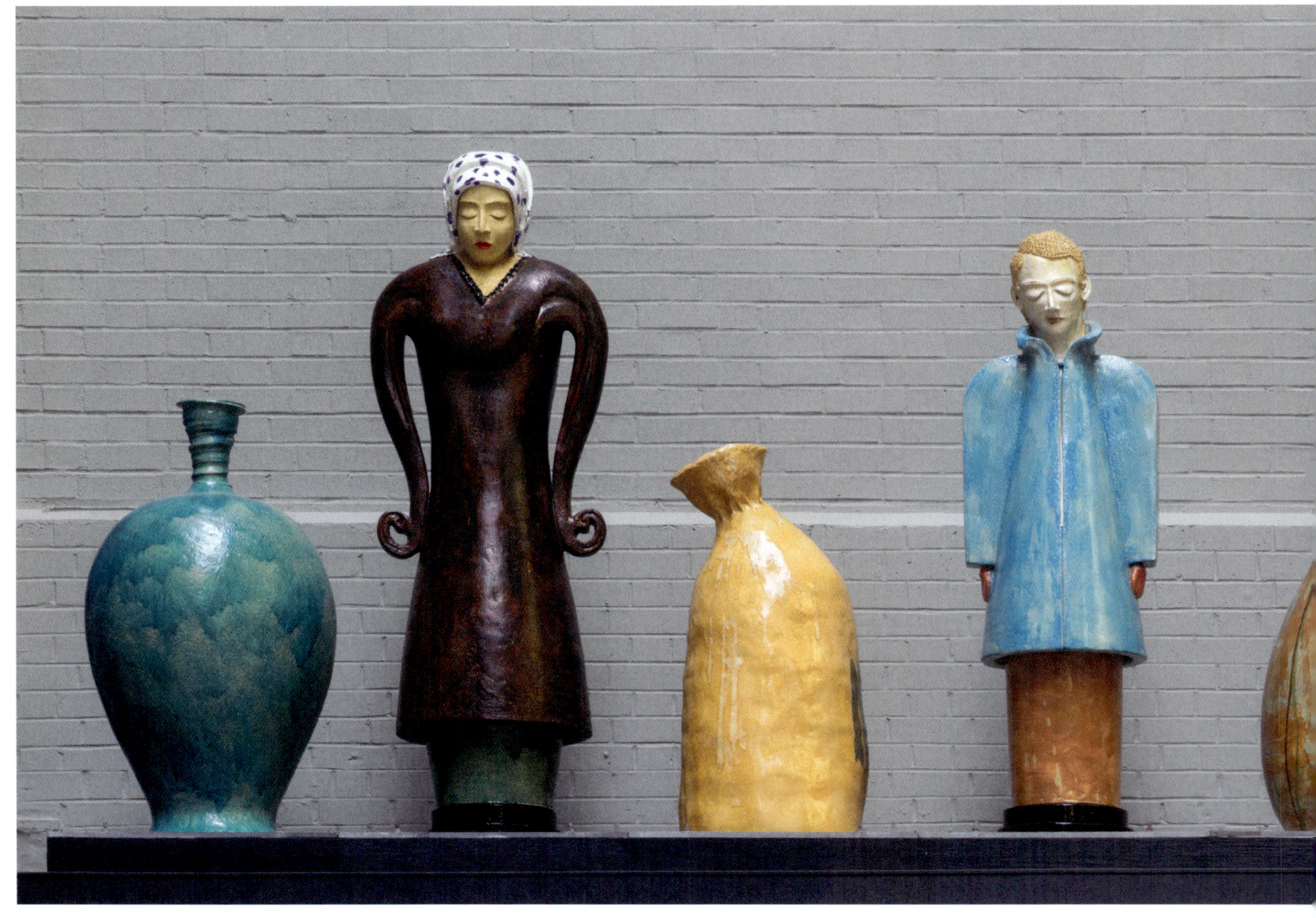

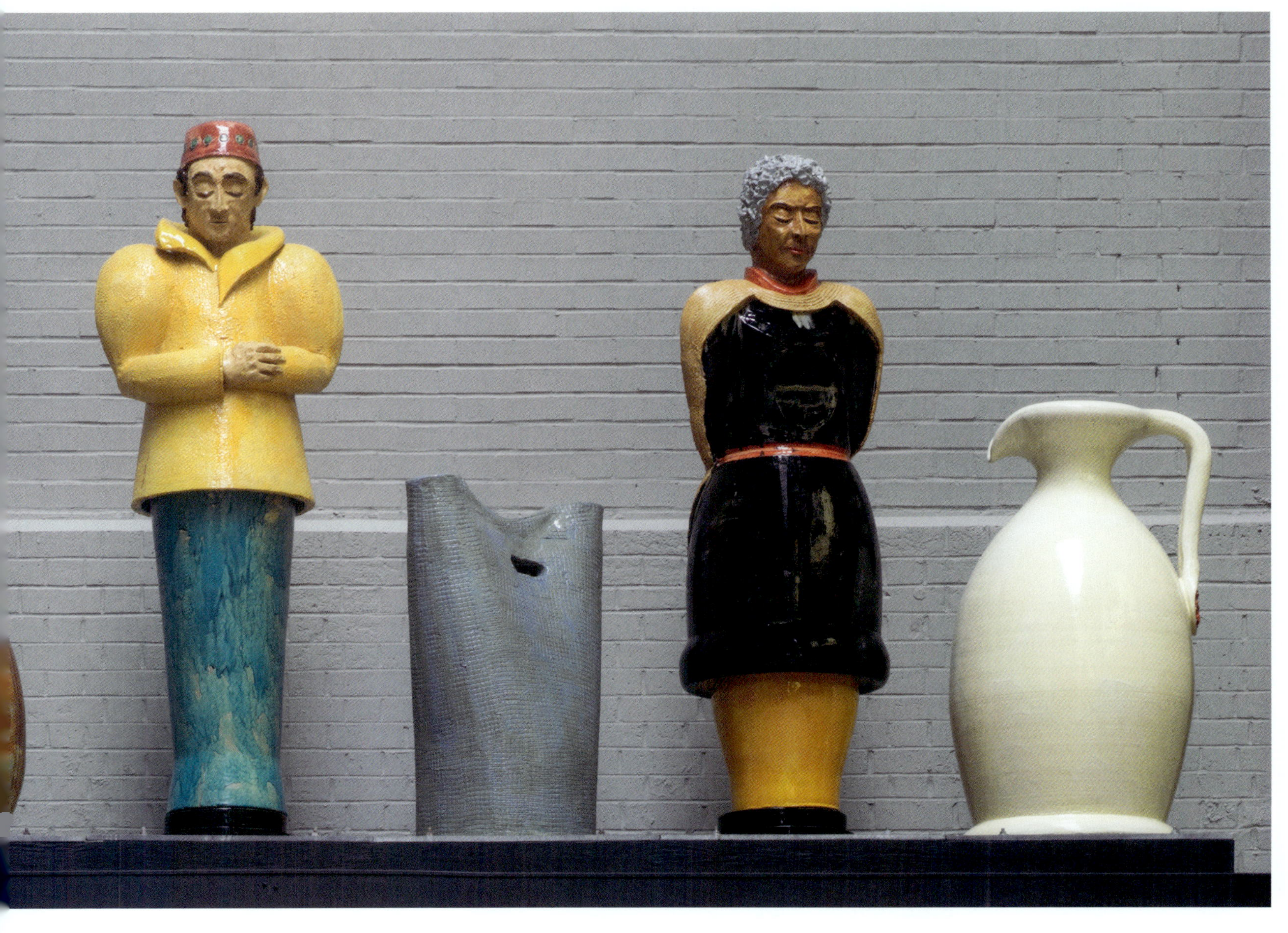

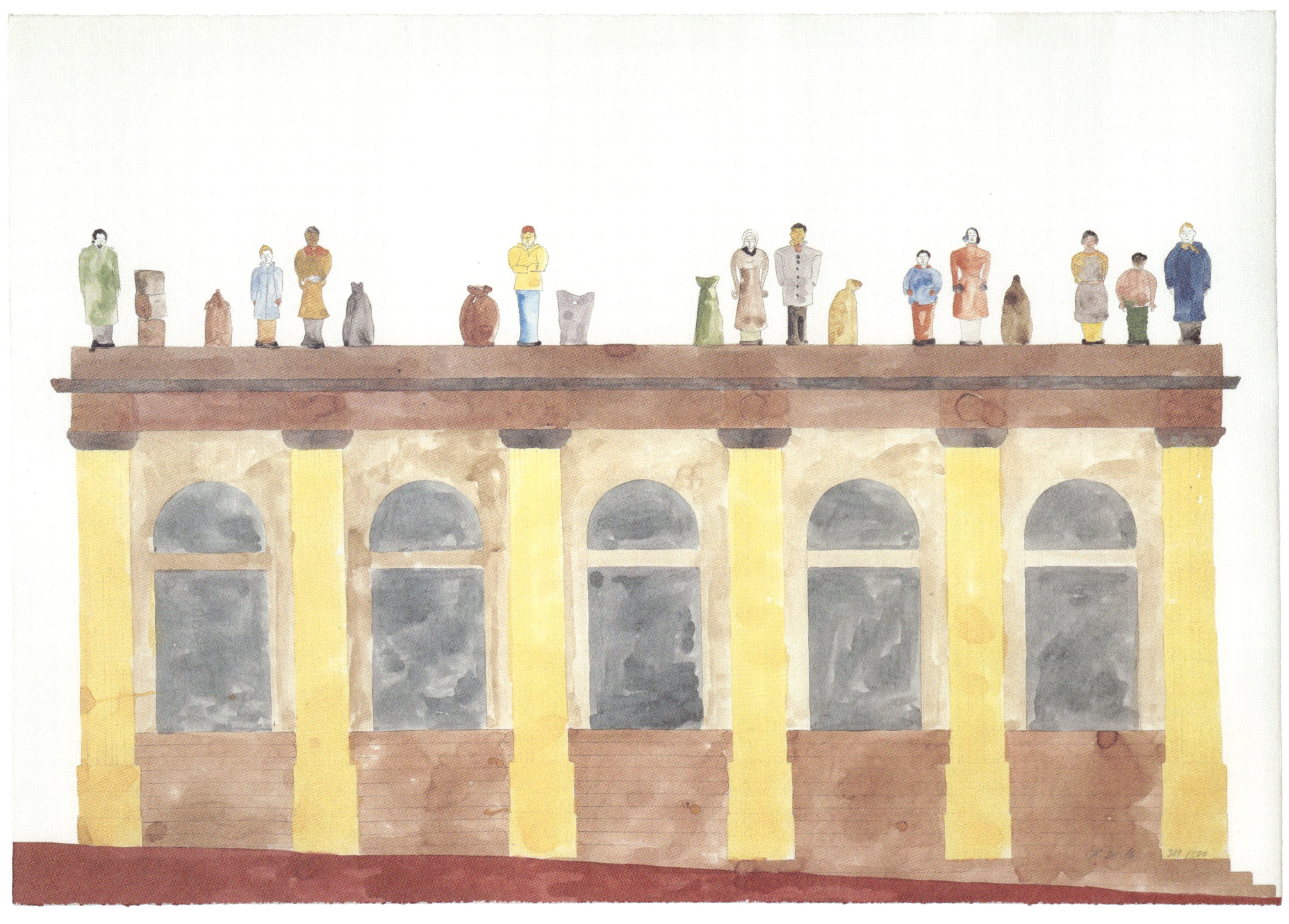

Above:
Die Fremden (*The Strangers*). 1992. Screenprint on paper, 21 × 30" (53.3 × 76.2 cm). De Pont Museum, Tilburg, Netherlands

Opposite page, top:
Die Fremden (*The Strangers*). 1991. Lacquer on paper, left sheet 8' 9 ½" × 57 1⁄16" (268 × 145 cm), center and right sheets 8' 11 7⁄8" × 43 5⁄16" (274 × 110 cm). Collection the artist, Düsseldorf

Opposite page, bottom:
Die Fremden (10 Skizzen für Figuren—Keramik) (*The Strangers [10 Sketches for Figures—Ceramic]*). 1991. Ink on paper, two of ten sheets, each 25 9⁄16 × 19 11⁄16" (65 × 50 cm). Collection Niels Dietrich

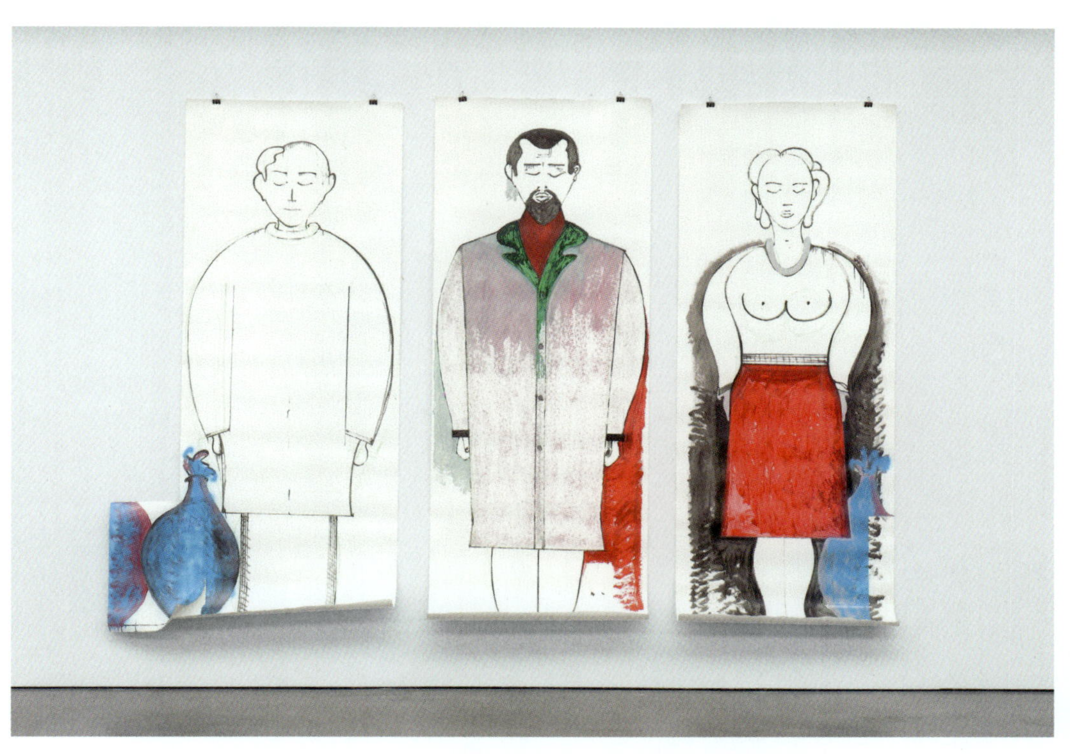

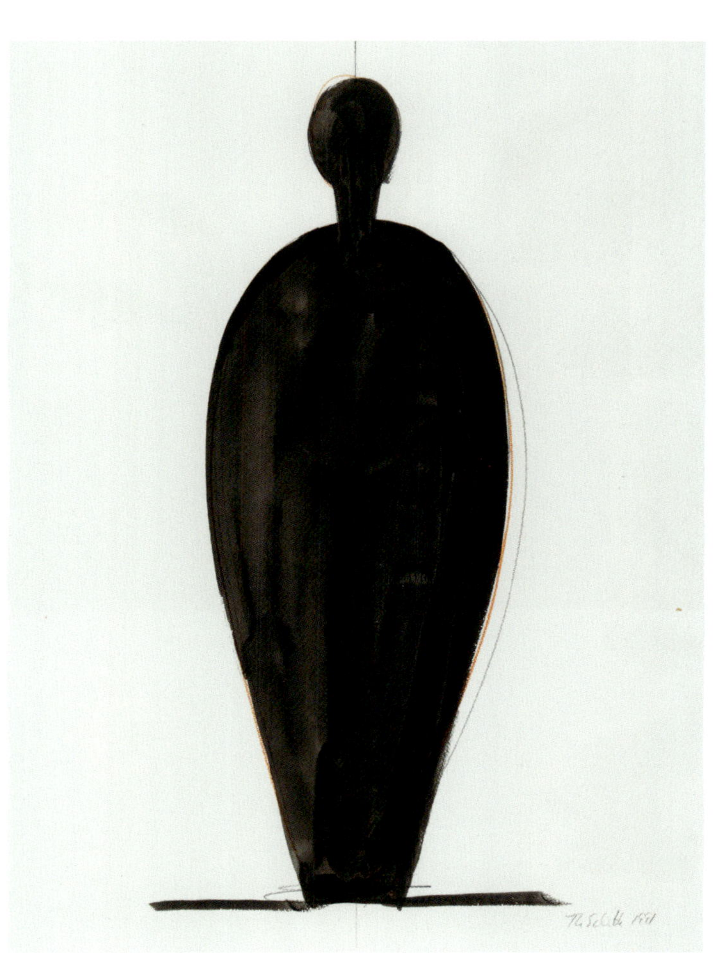

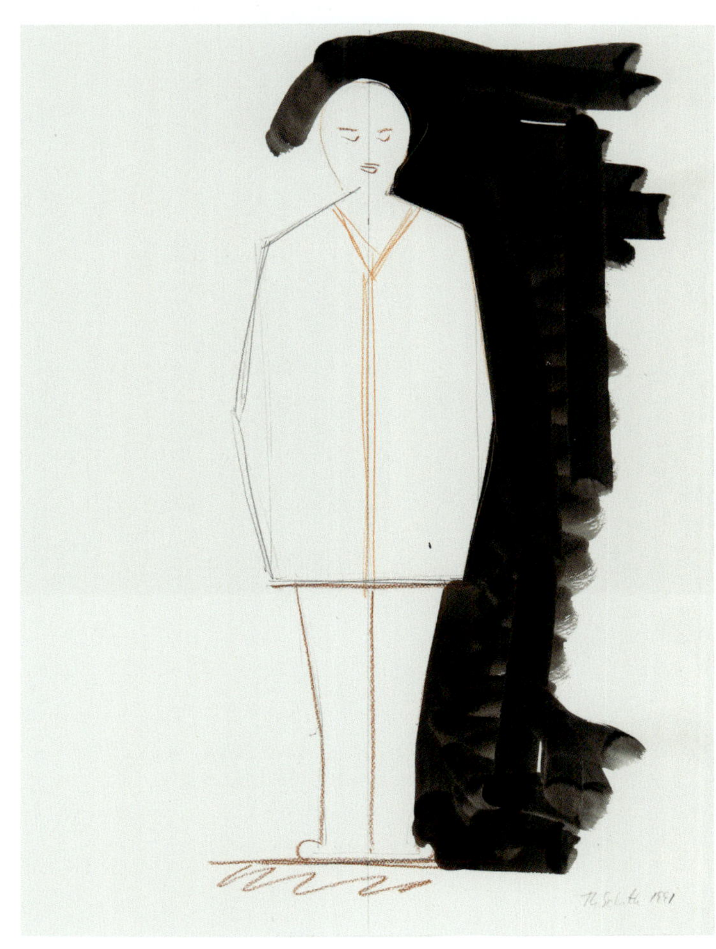

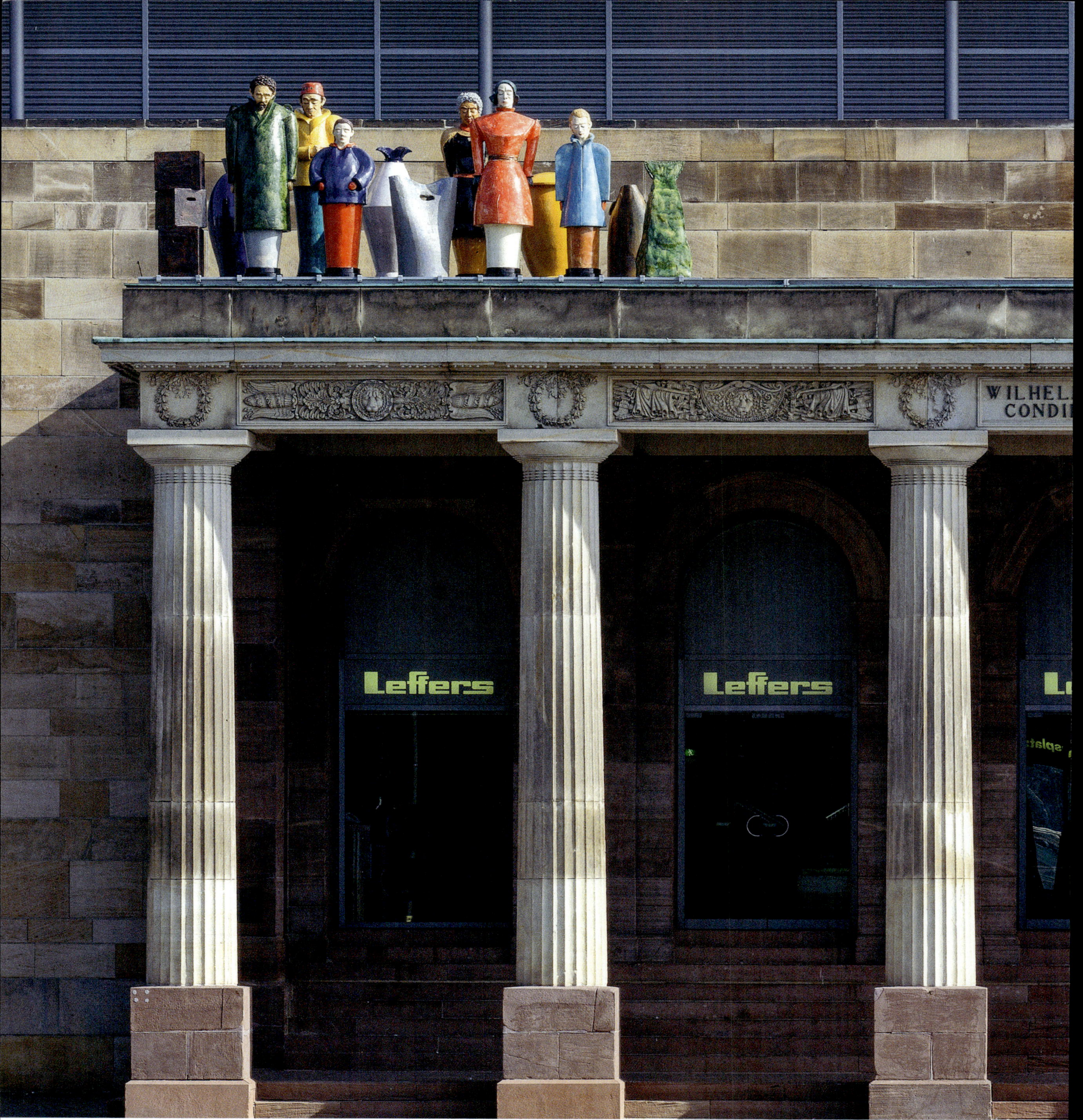

Installation view of *Die Fremden* (*The Strangers*), SinnLeffers department store, Friedrichsplatz, Kassel, 1992

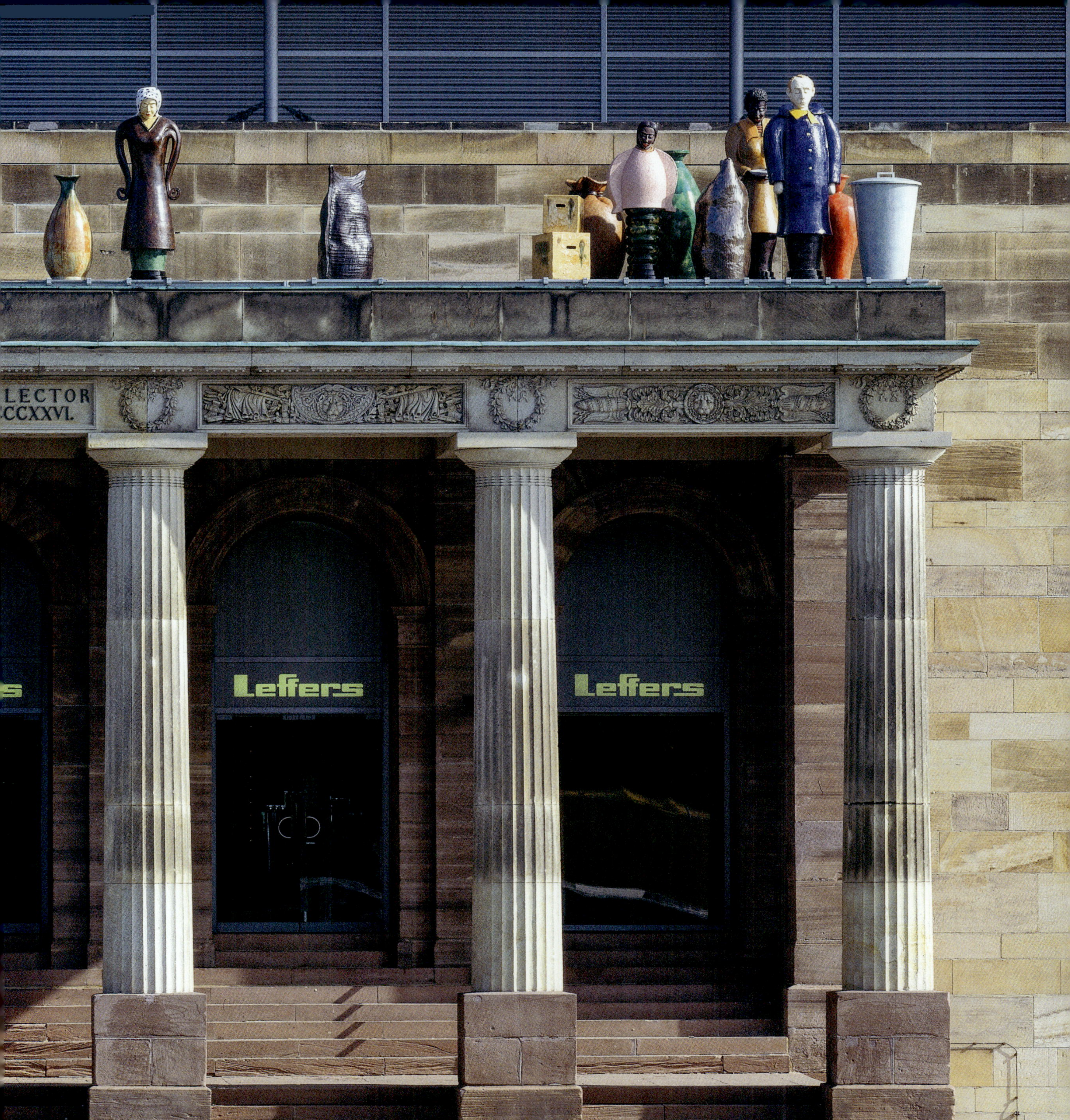
LECTOR
CCXXVI.
Leffers
Leffers

41
Basement II. 1993. Wood and sawdust, 3' 6" × 4' 11" × 6' 8 ¾" (106.7 × 149.9 × 205.1 cm)

42
Basement III. 1993. Wood and sawdust, 3' 4 ³⁄₁₆" × 4' 11 ¹⁄₁₆" × 6' 8 ¹¹⁄₁₆" (102 × 150 × 205 cm)

Right:
Detail of *Basement III*

41

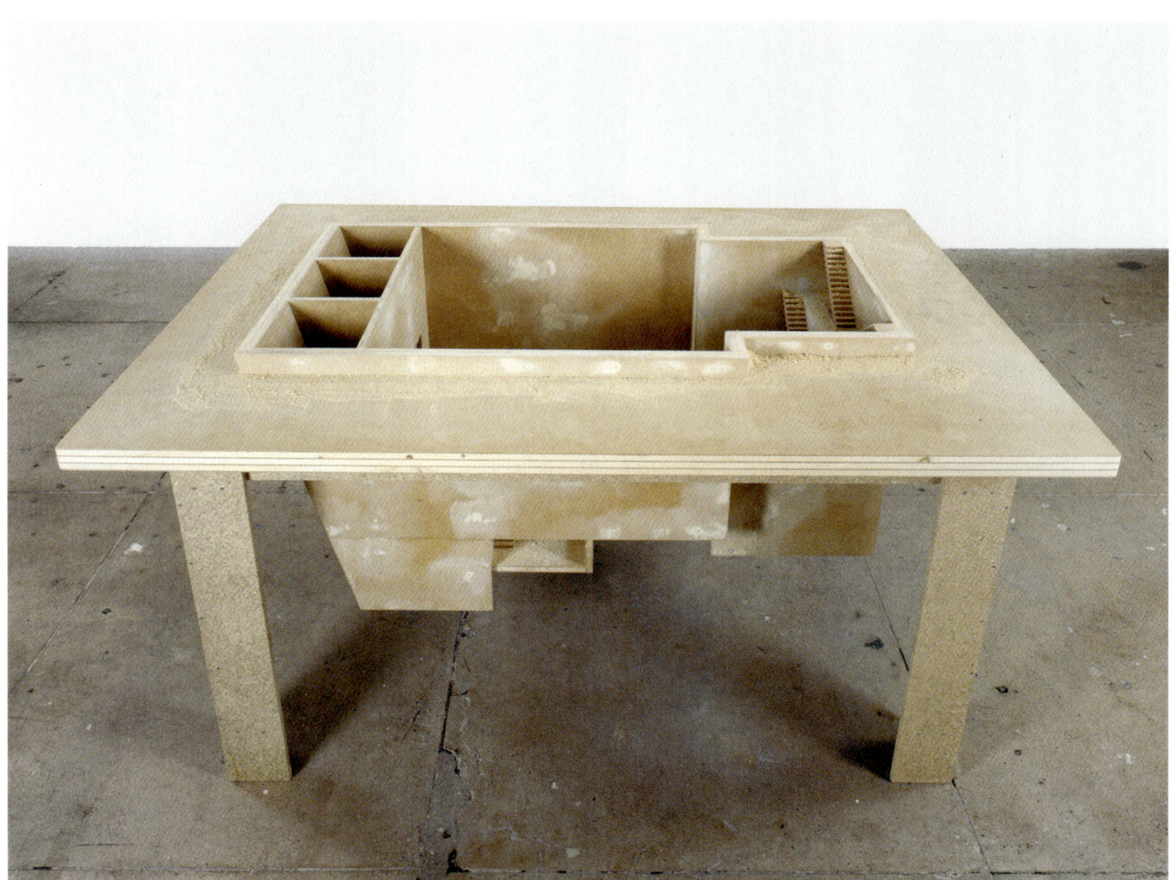

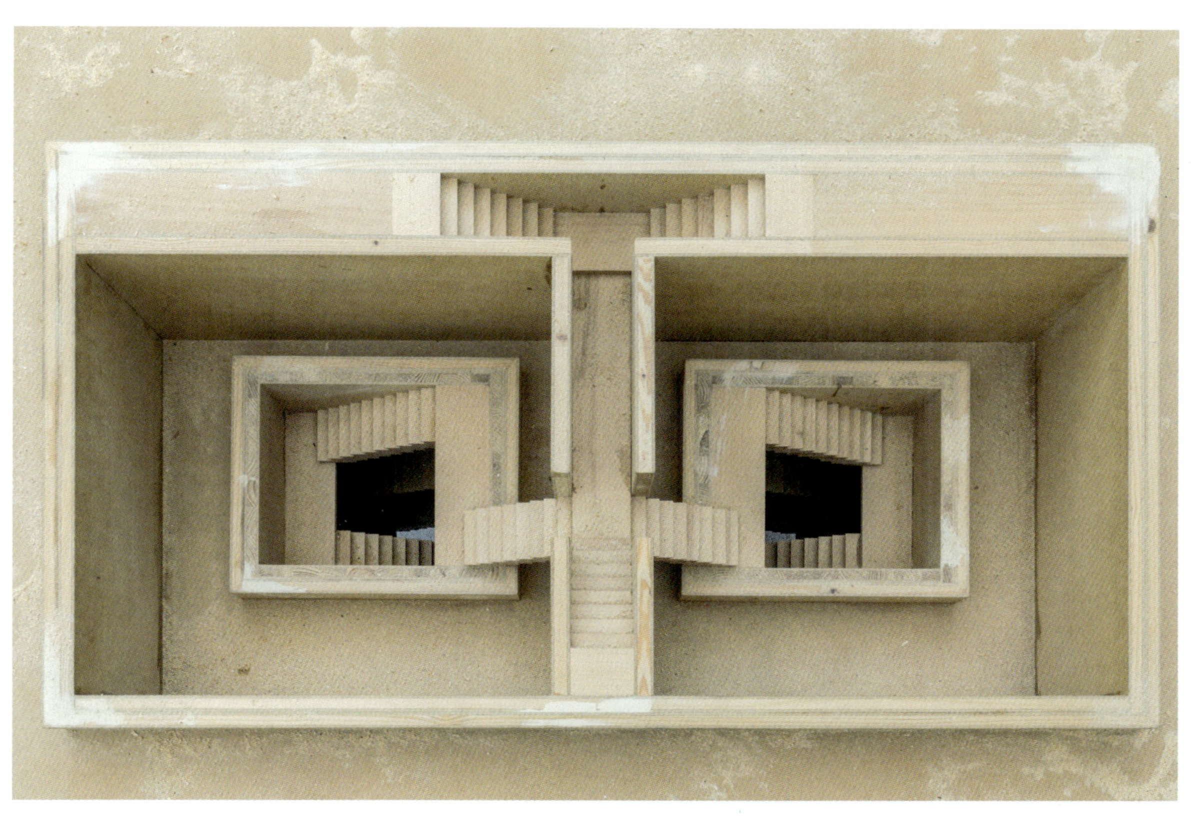

42

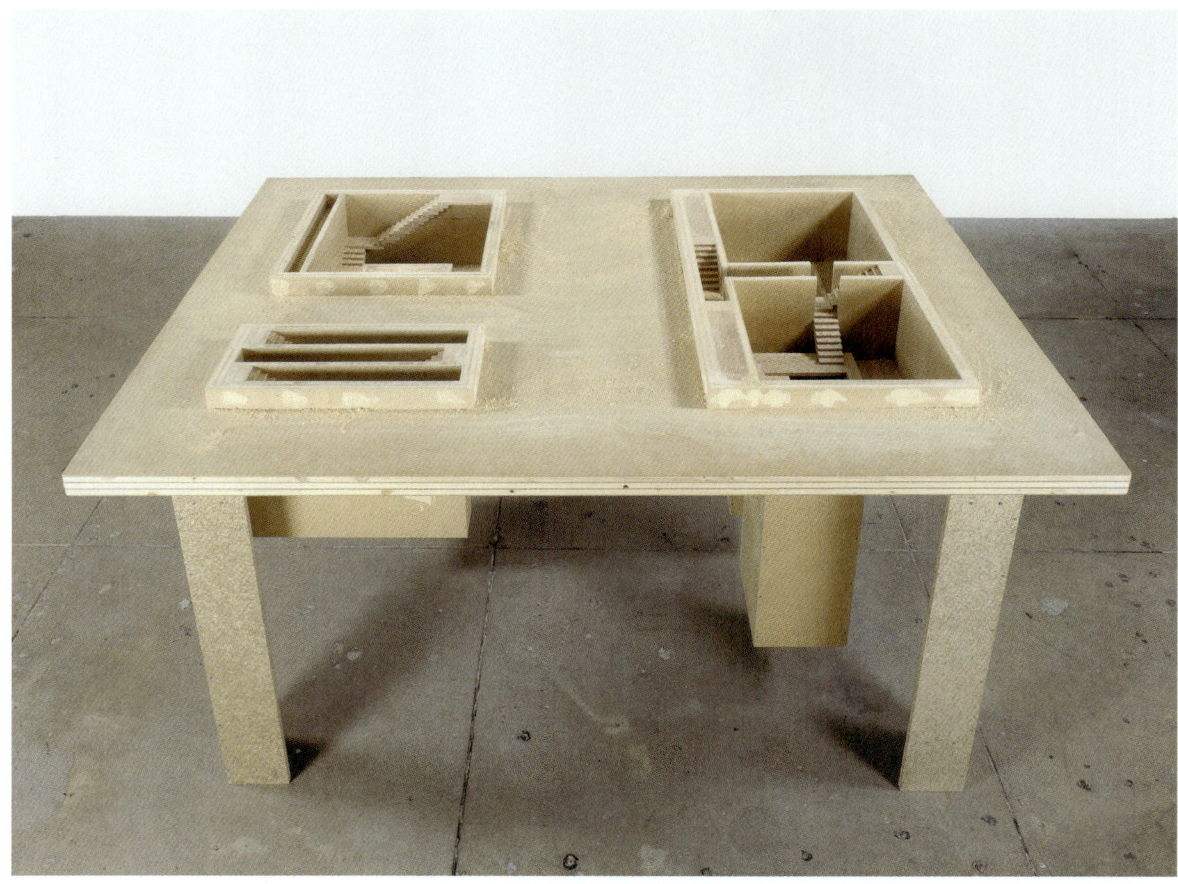

All works this spread:

43–45
United Enemies. 1993. Two figures of modeling clay, fabric, string, and wood on plastic pedestal with glass bell jar (not pictured), 6' 3 3⁄16" × 10 ¼" × 10 ¼" (191 × 26 × 26 cm)

43

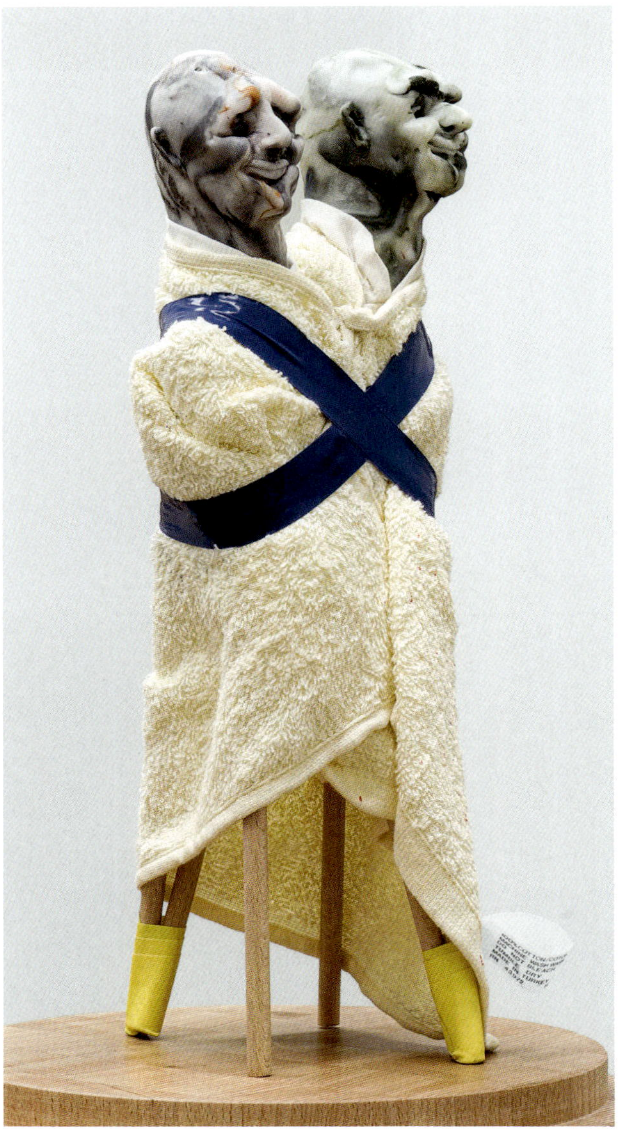

44

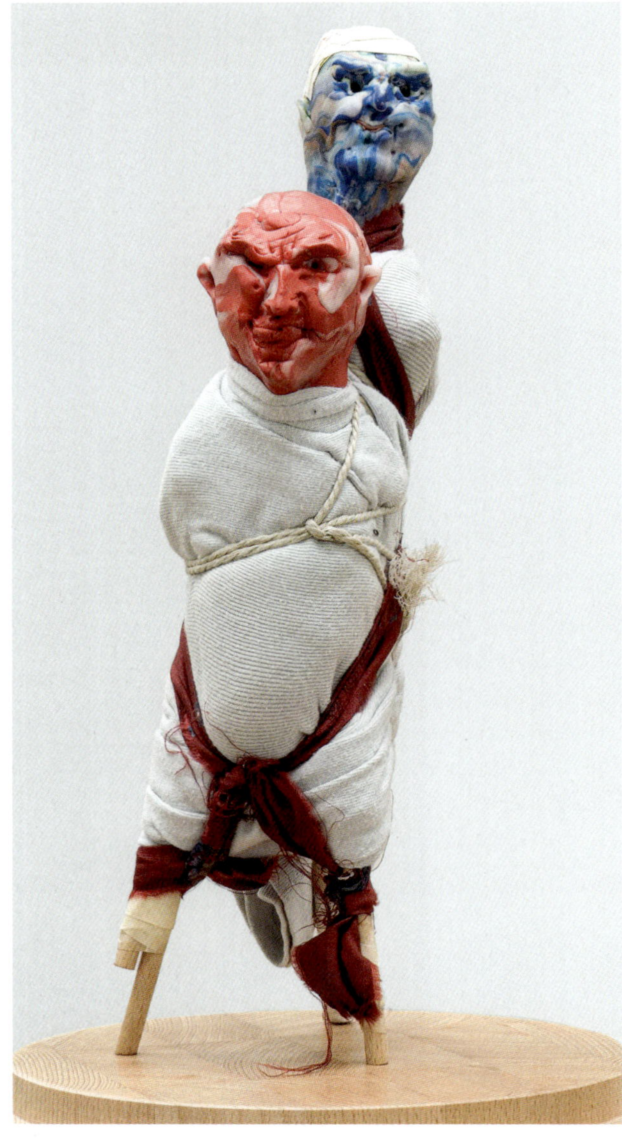

45>

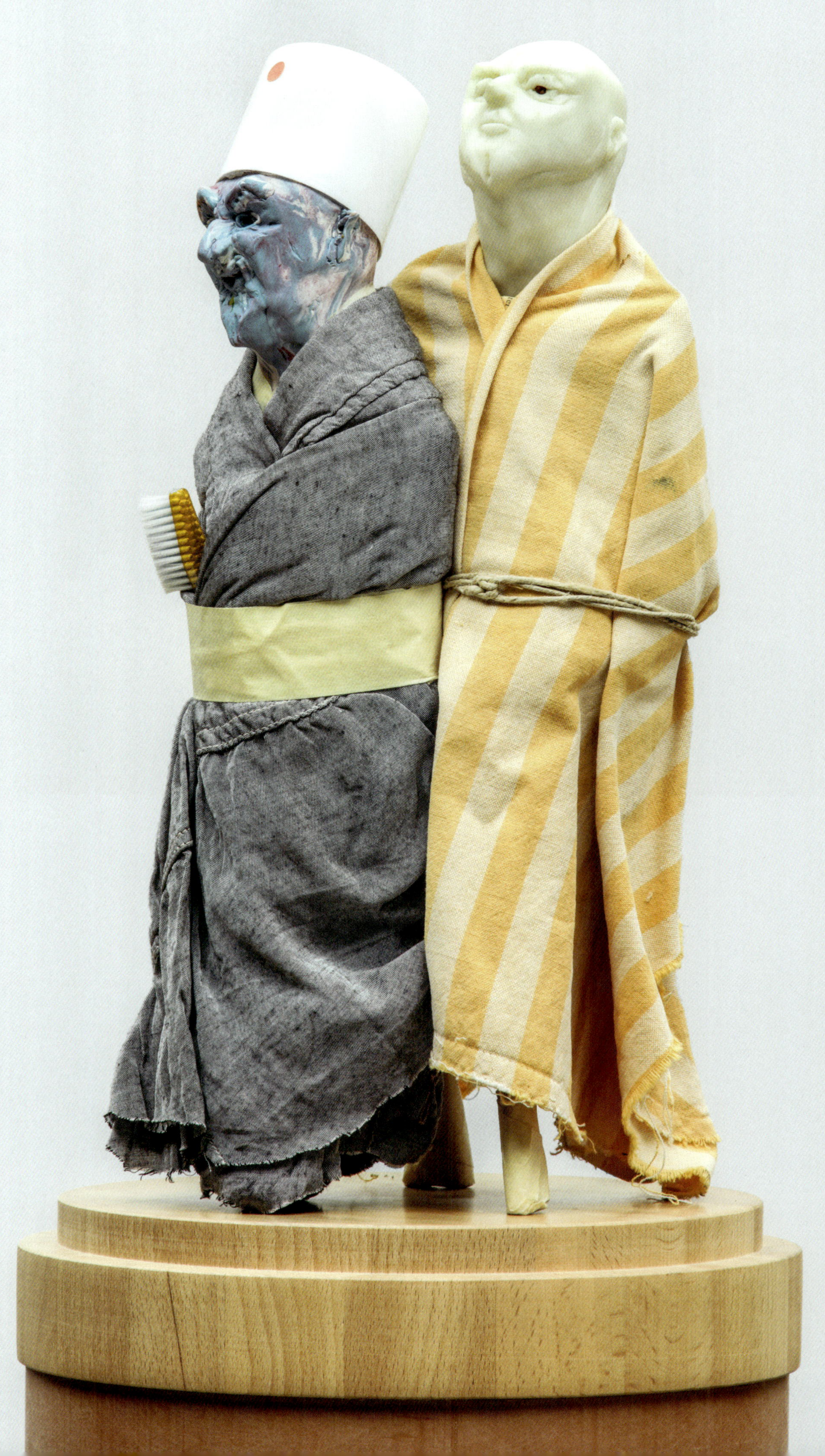

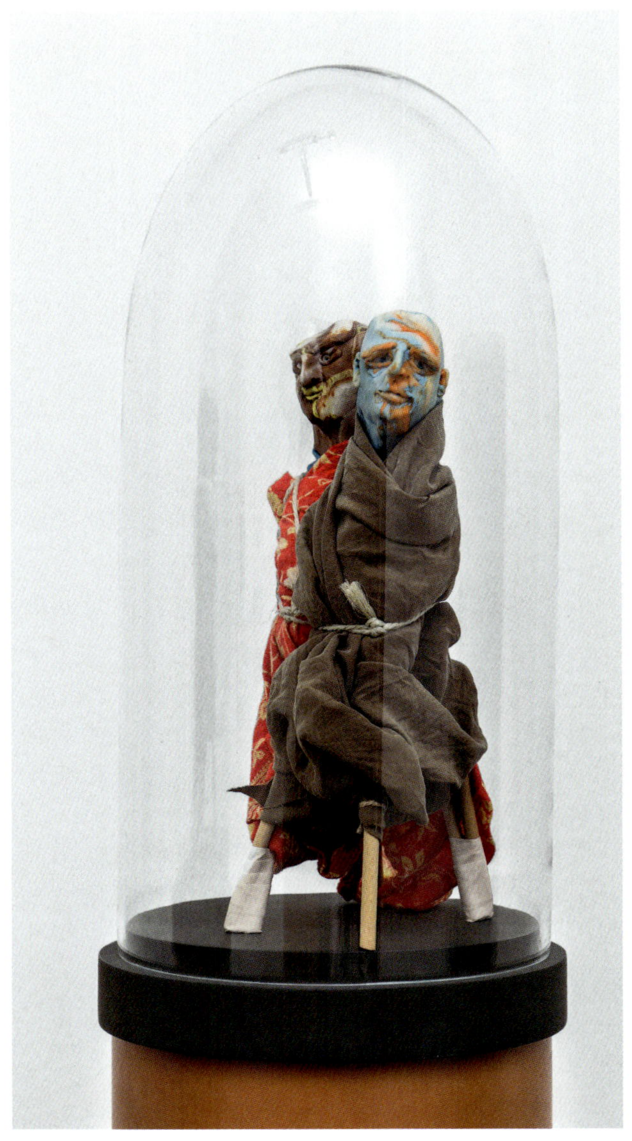

46

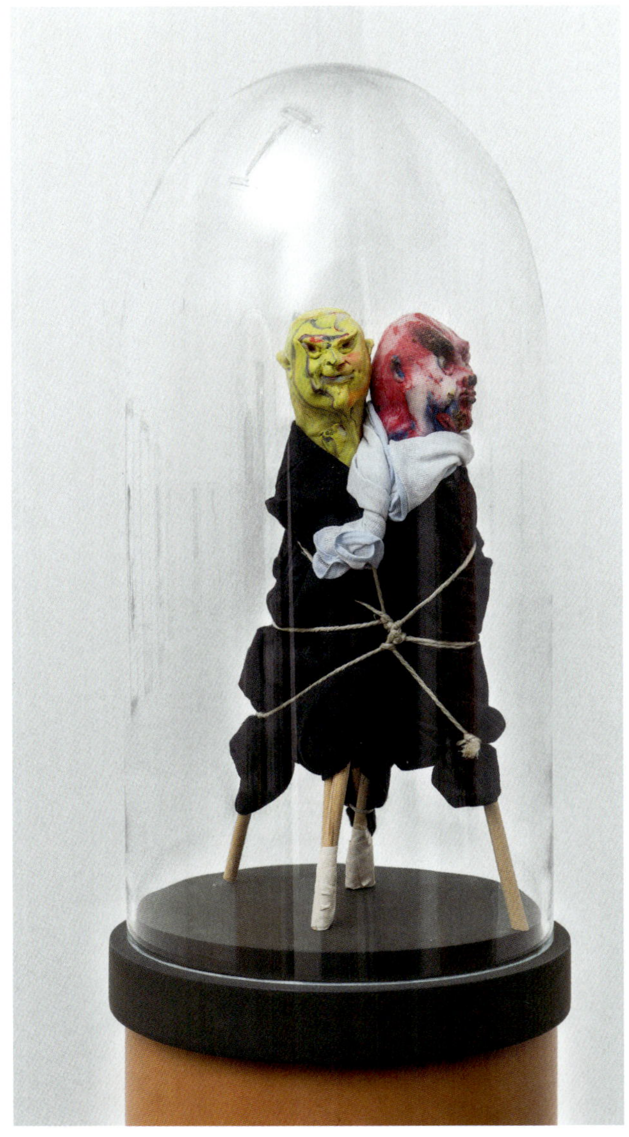

47

All works this spread:

46–48
United Enemies. 1994. Two figures of modeling clay, fabric, string, and wood on plastic pedestal with glass bell jar, 6' 2" × 9 13⁄16" × 9 13⁄16" (188 × 25 × 25 cm)

48>

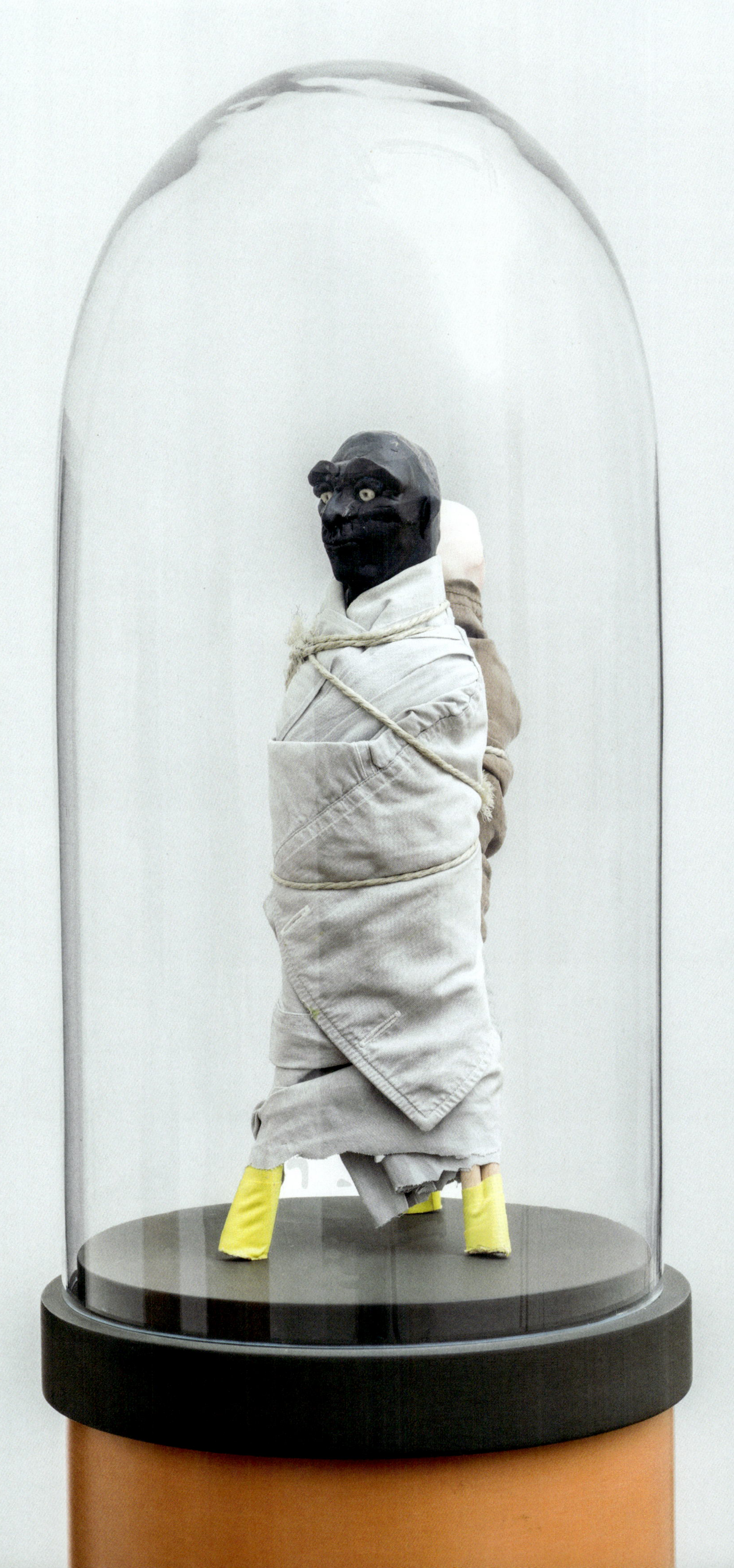

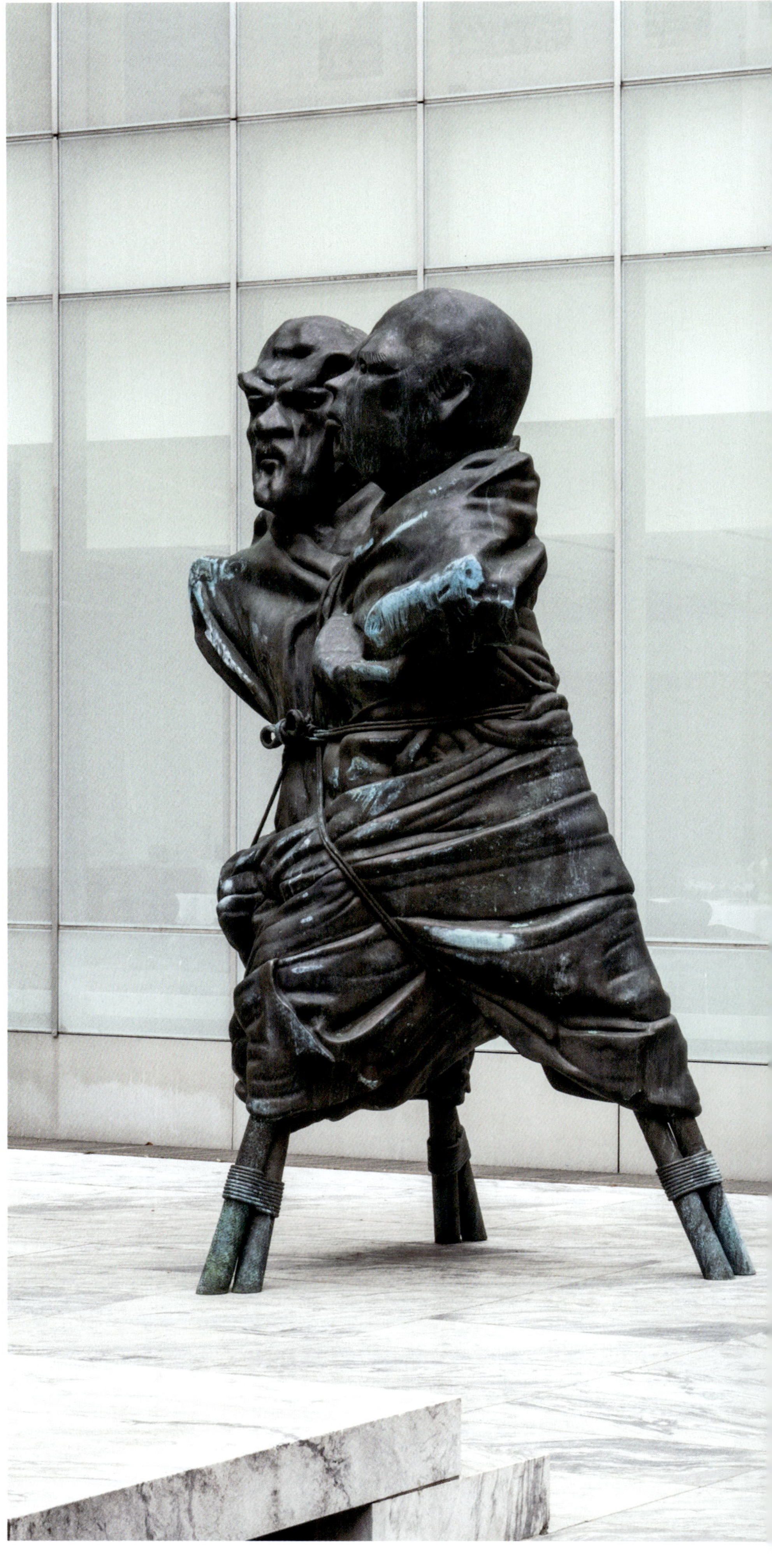

United Enemies I. 2011. Patinated bronze, two parts, 13' 3" × 6' 8" × 7' 5" (406.4 × 203.2 × 226.1 cm) and 12' 8" × 6' 8 ¾" × 6' 11" (391.2 × 205.1 × 201.8 cm). The Museum of Modern Art, New York. Margot Gottlieb Bequest (by exchange). Installation view, Abby Aldrich Rockefeller Sculpture Garden, The Museum of Modern Art, New York, January 1–December 31, 2014

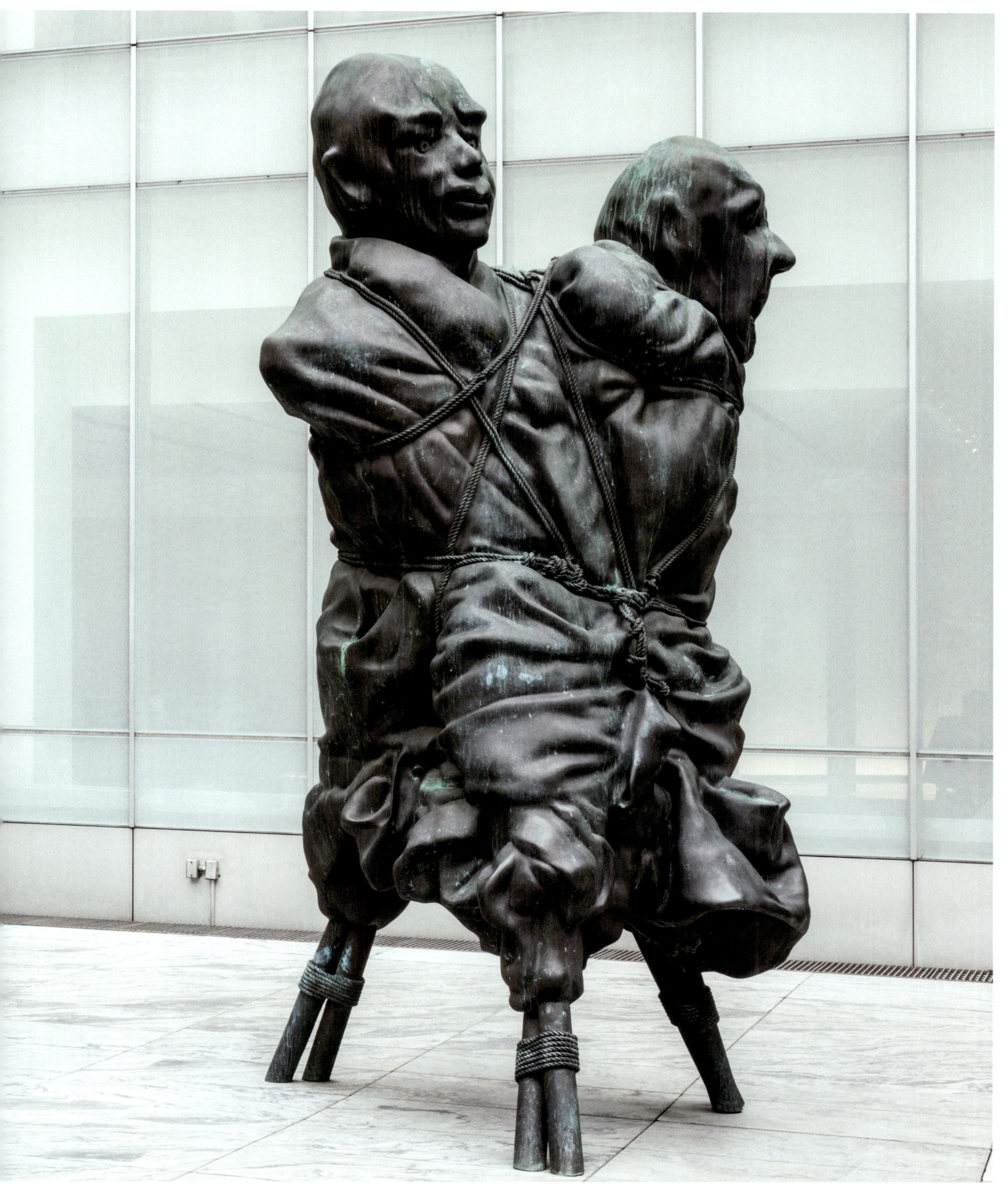

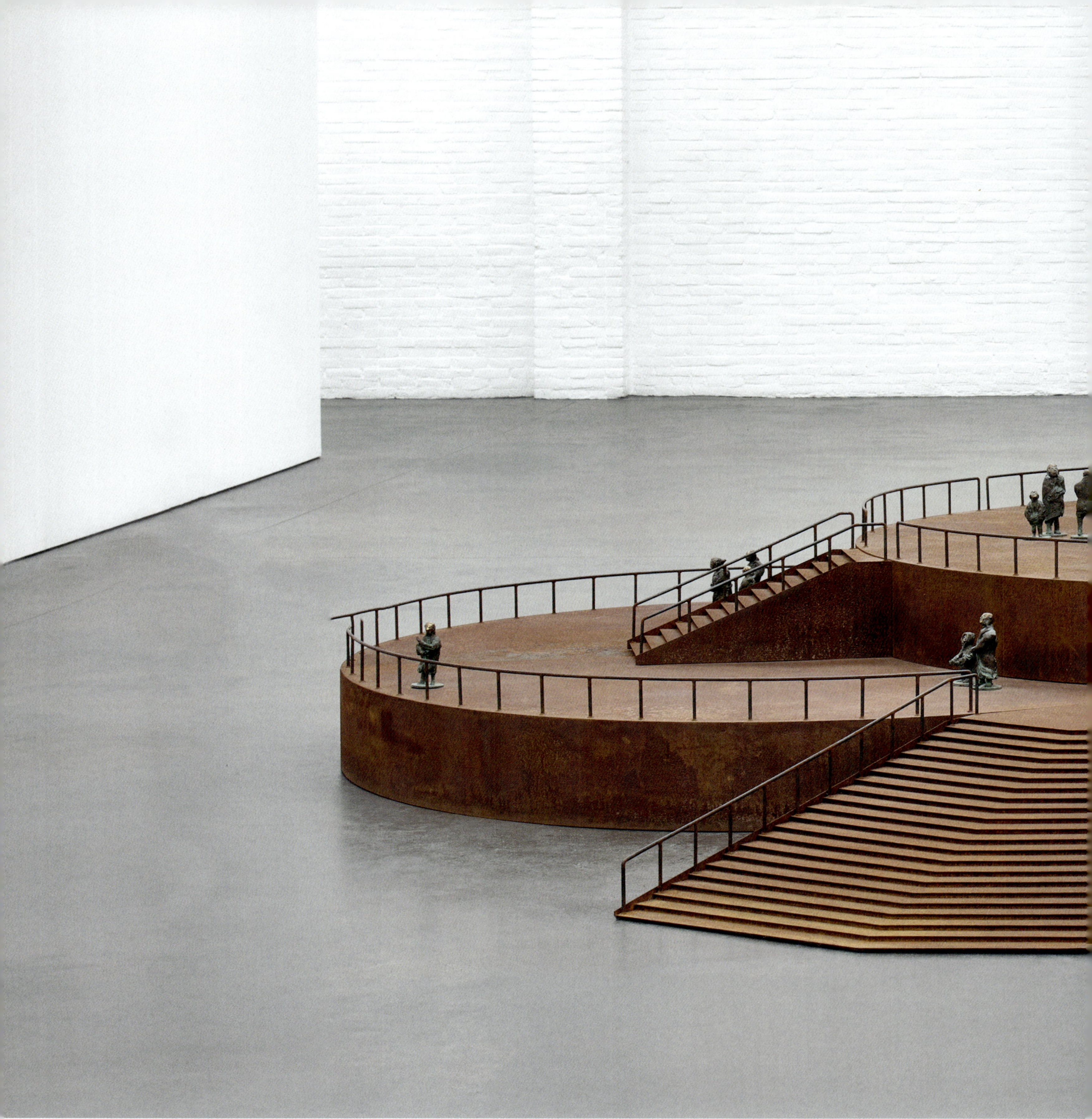

49
Großer Respekt (*Large Respect*). 1994. Steel and patinated bronze, 2' × 14' 9 3⁄16" × 18' 9⁄16" (61 × 450 × 550 cm)

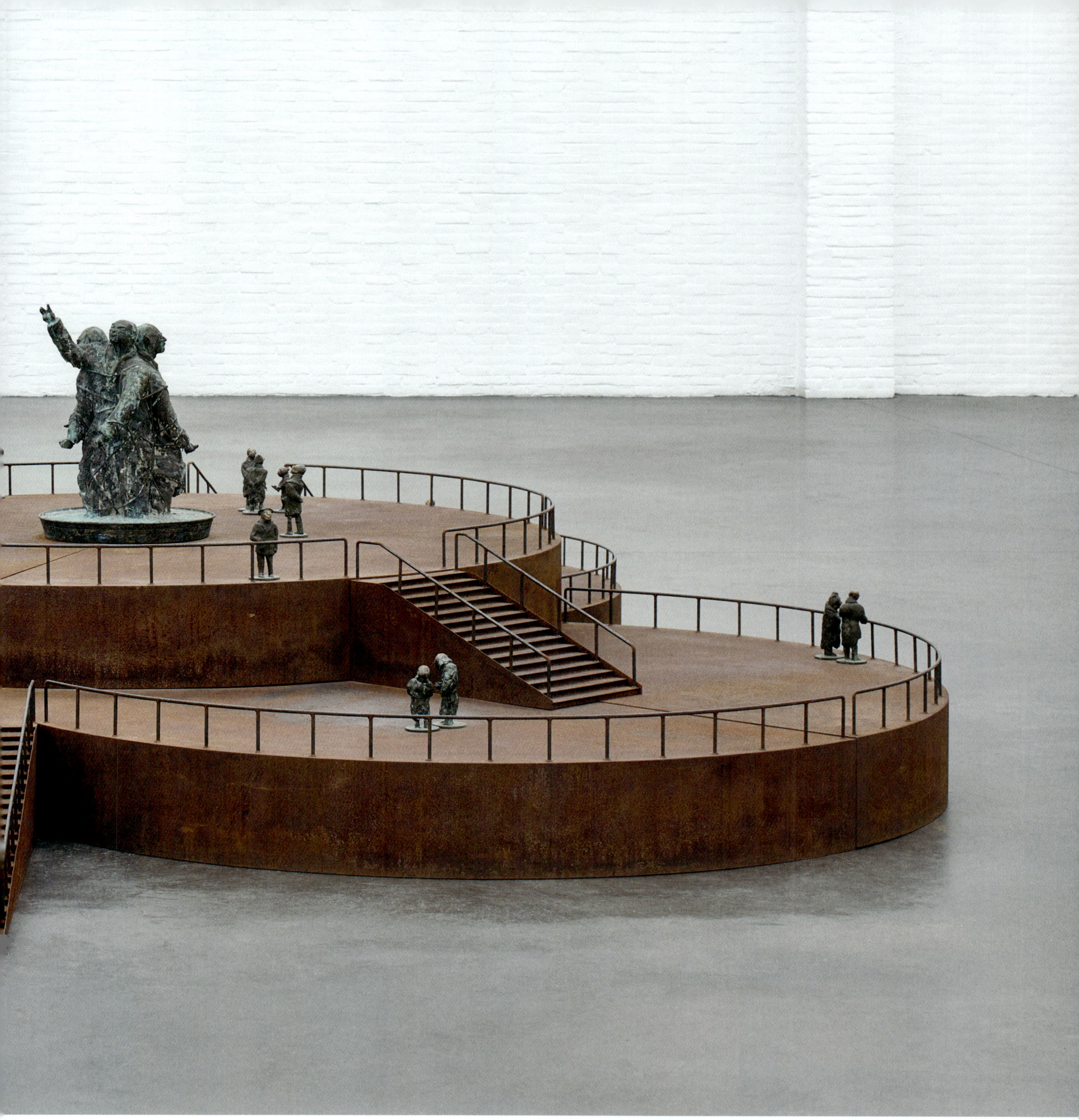

50
Left to right:

Großer Geist Nr. 6 (*Large Spirit No. 6*). 1996.
Polished aluminum, 9' 6 3⁄16" × 4' 7 1⁄8" × 2' 7 1⁄2"
(290 × 140 × 80 cm)

Großer Geist Nr. 8 (*Large Spirit No. 8*). 1997.
Polished aluminum, 8' 2 7⁄16" × 4' 11 1⁄16" × 3' 3 3⁄8"
(250 × 150 × 100 cm)

Großer Geist Nr. 17 (*Large Spirit No. 17*). 2000.
Polished aluminum, 68 7⁄8 × 66 15⁄16 × 47 1⁄4"
(175 × 170 × 120 cm)

Below, from left:
Installation views of *Großer Geist Nr. 17*, *6*, and *8*, *Thomas Schütte: Werkstatt*, Kunstmuseum Wolfsburg, Germany, February 26–April 24, 2000

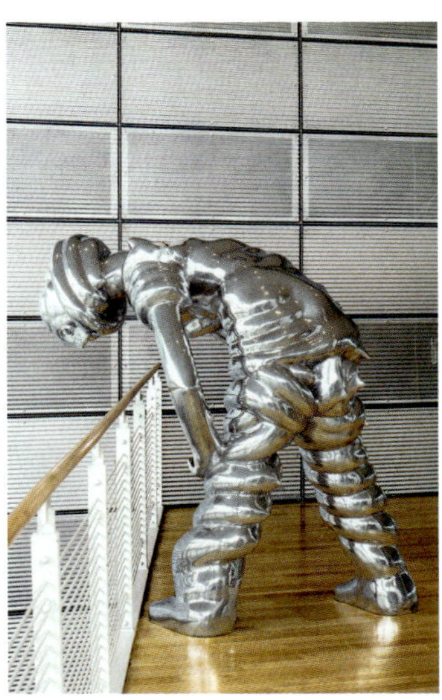

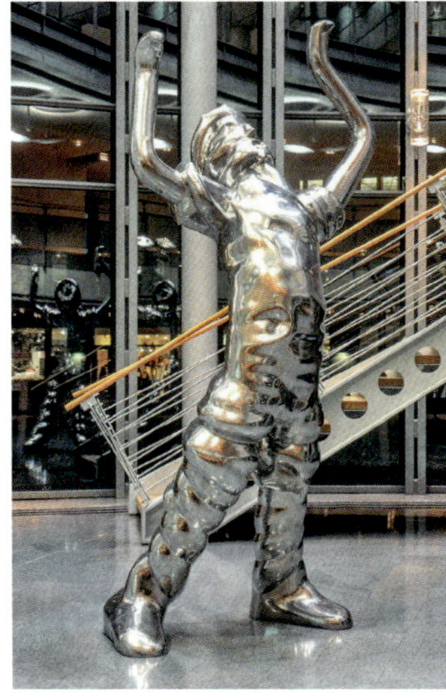

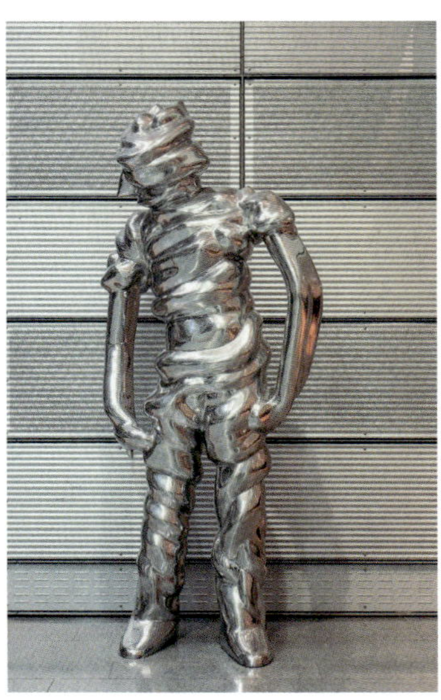

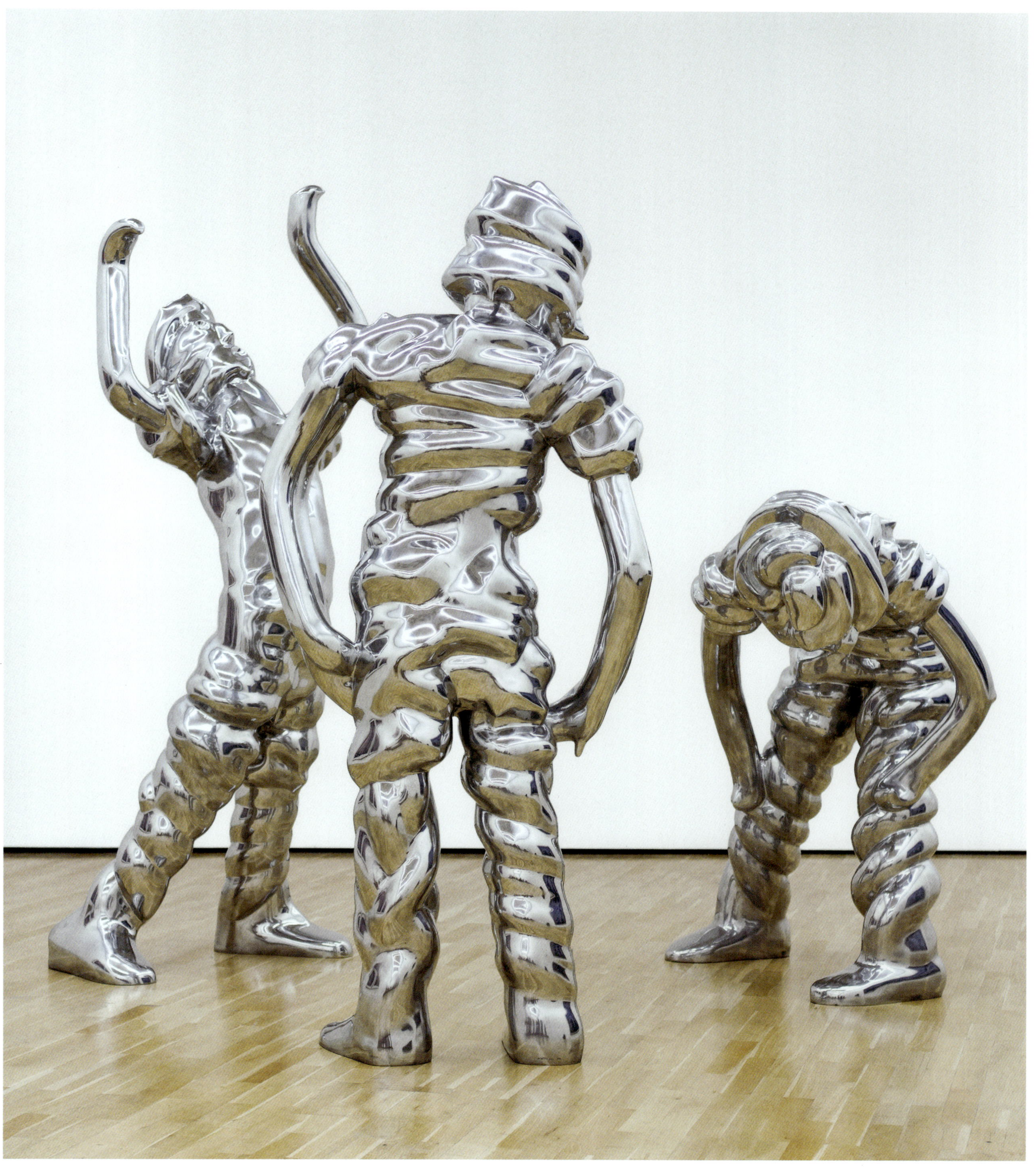

50

This spread and next:

51
Blumen für Konrad (*Flowers for Konrad*). 1997–98.
Watercolor on paper, 12 sheets, each 15 ⅜ × 11 7⁄16"
(39 × 29 cm)

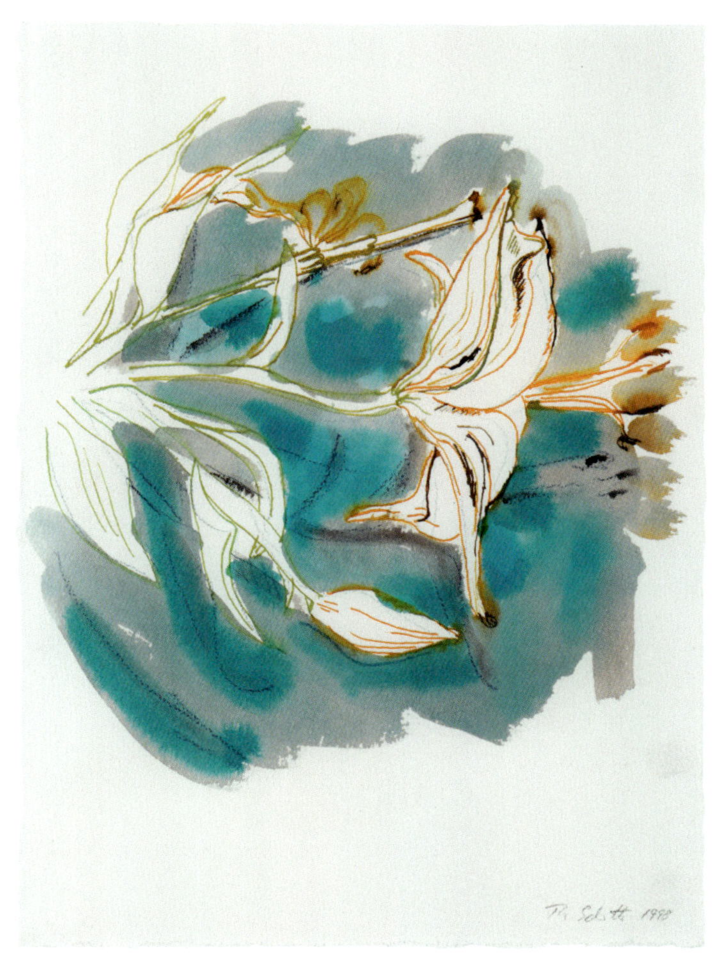

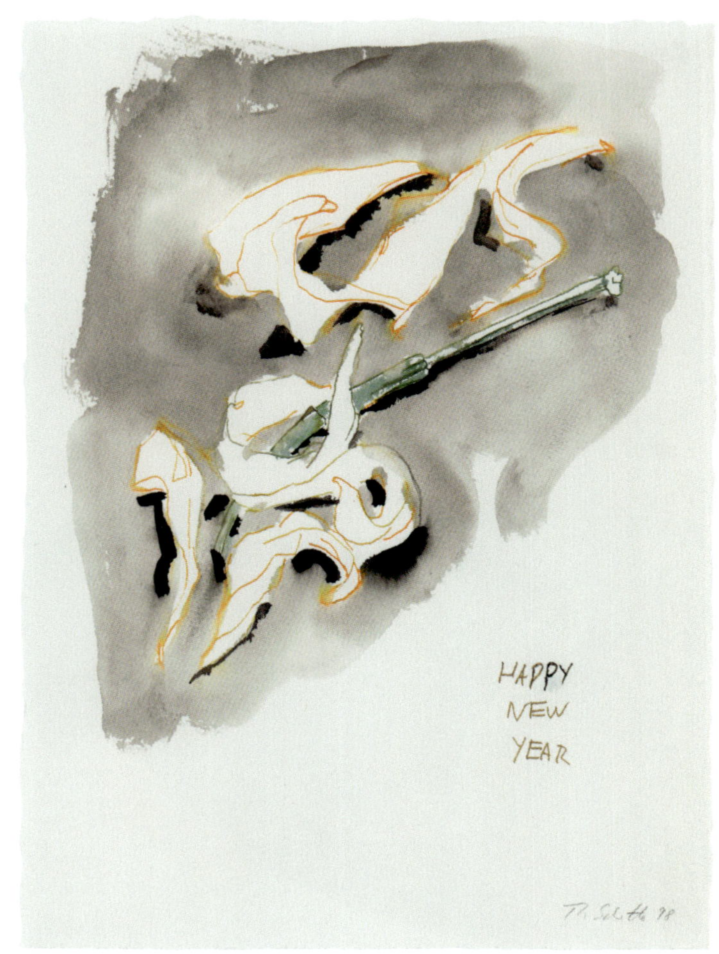
HAPPY
NEW
YEAR

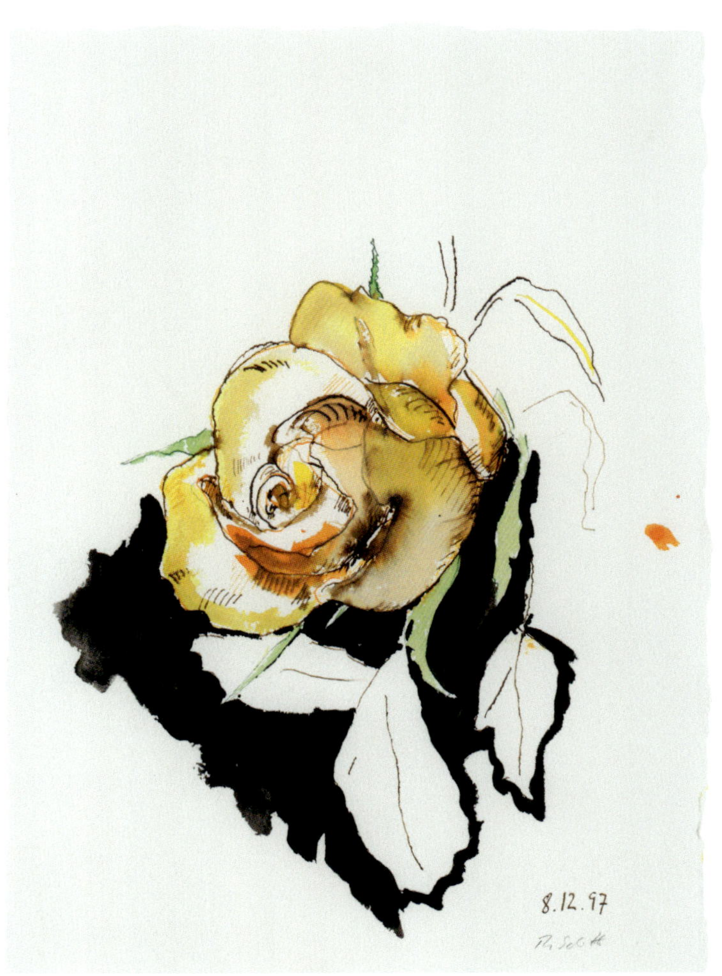
8.12.97

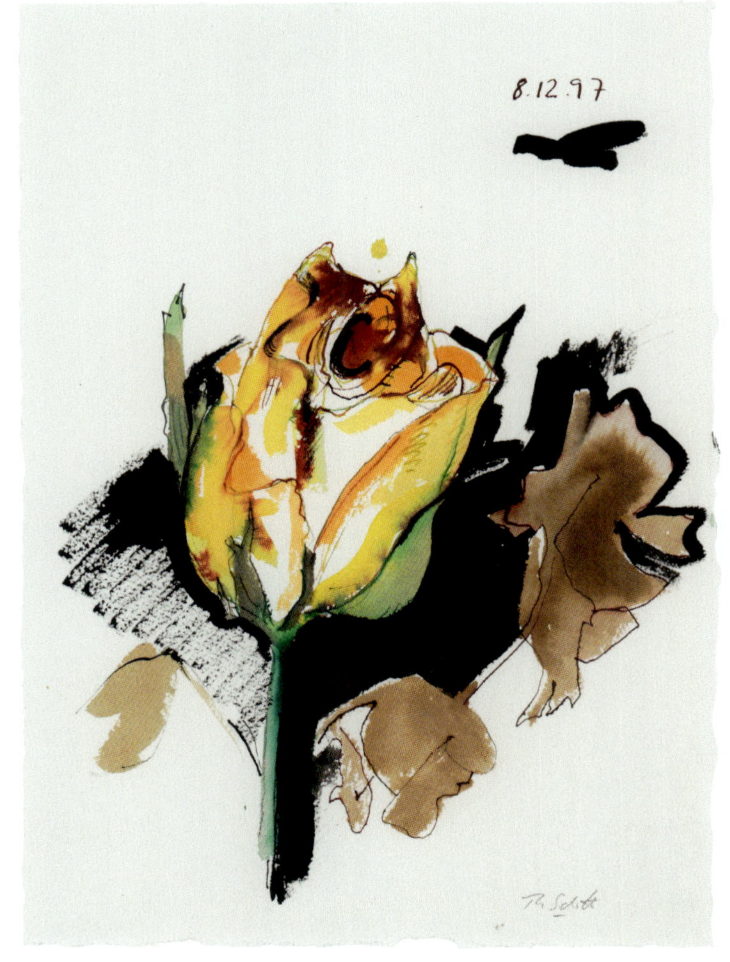
8.12.97

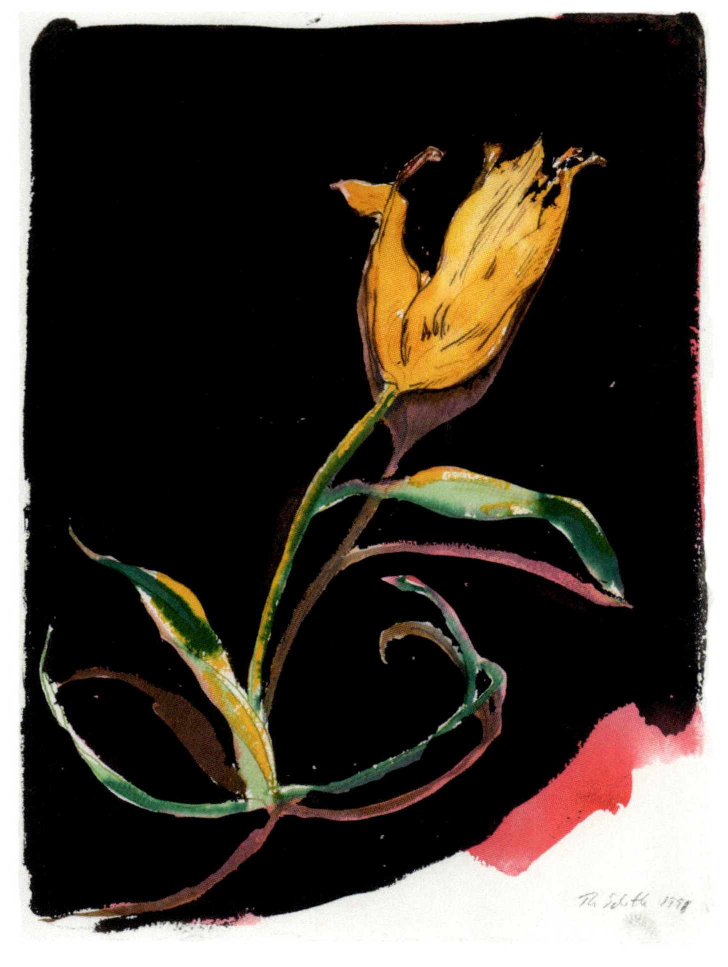

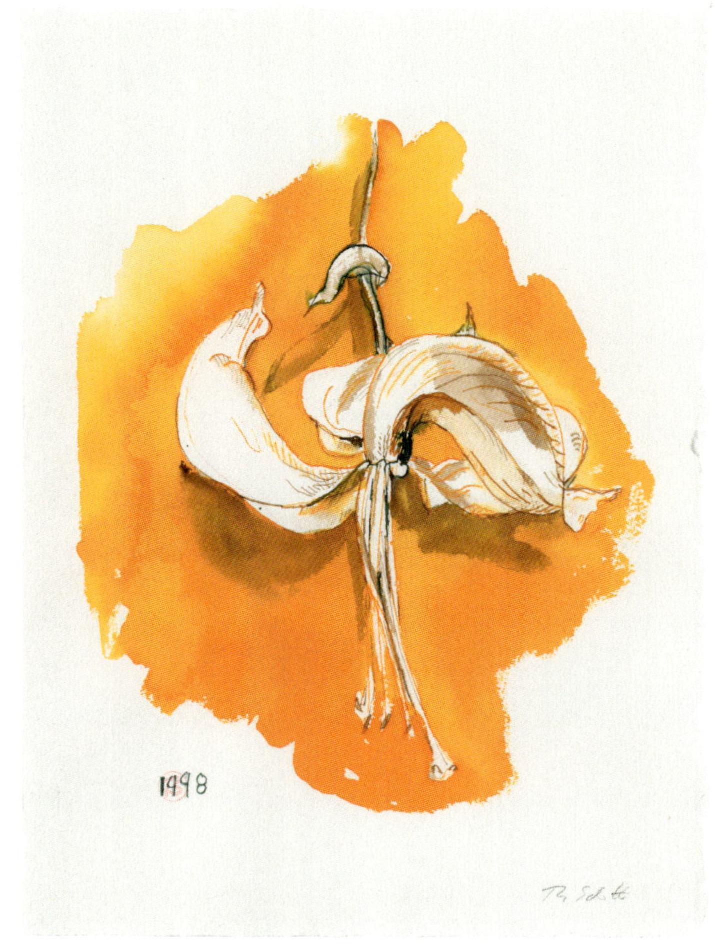
1998

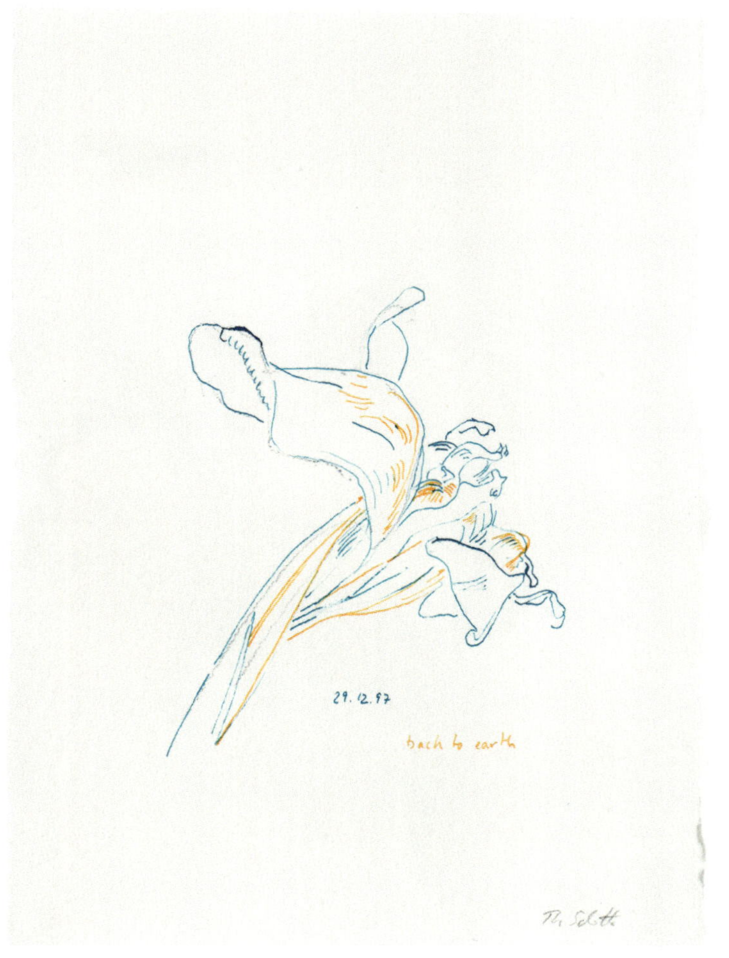
29.12.97
back to earth

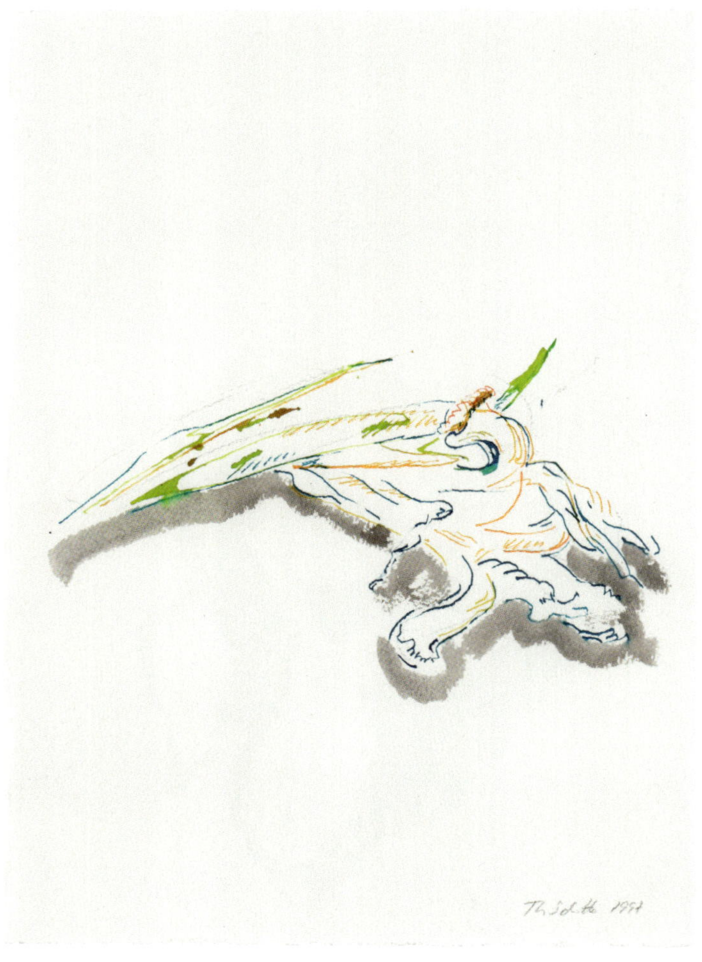

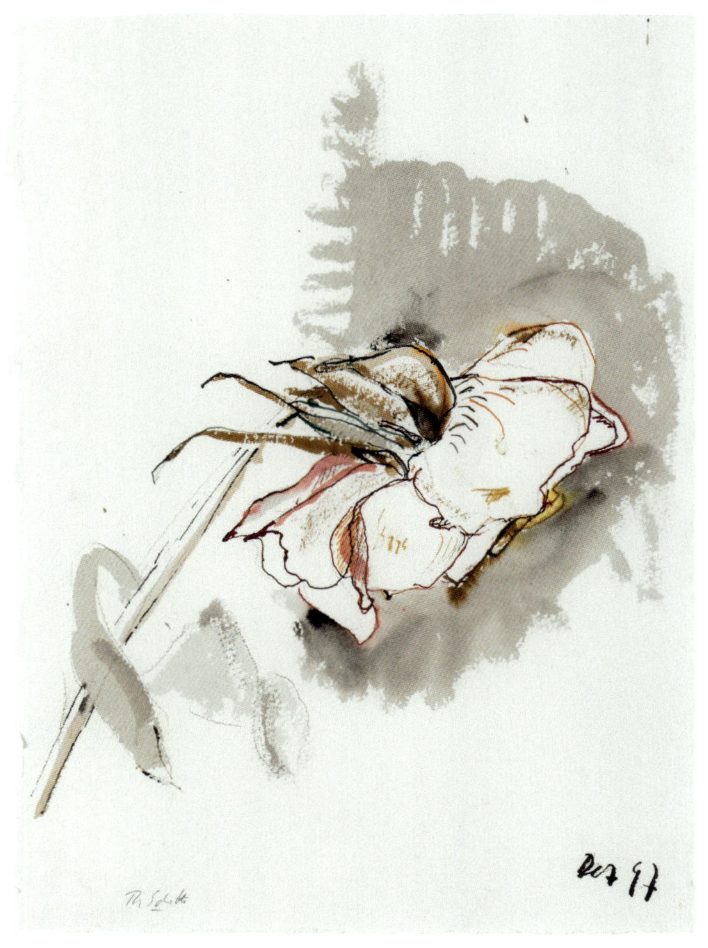
Dez 97

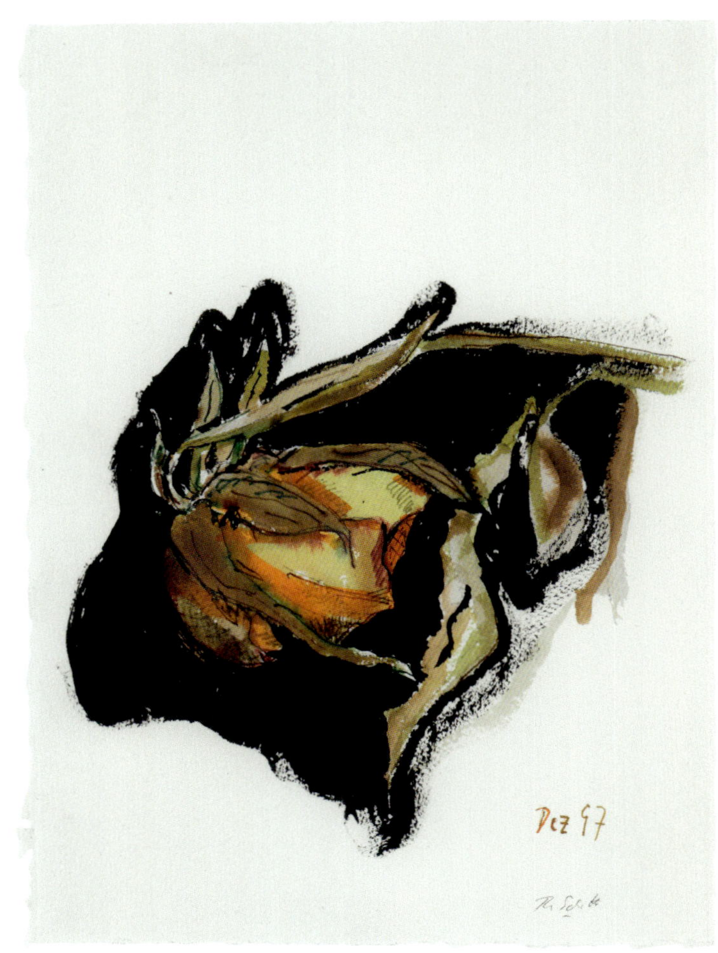
Dez 97

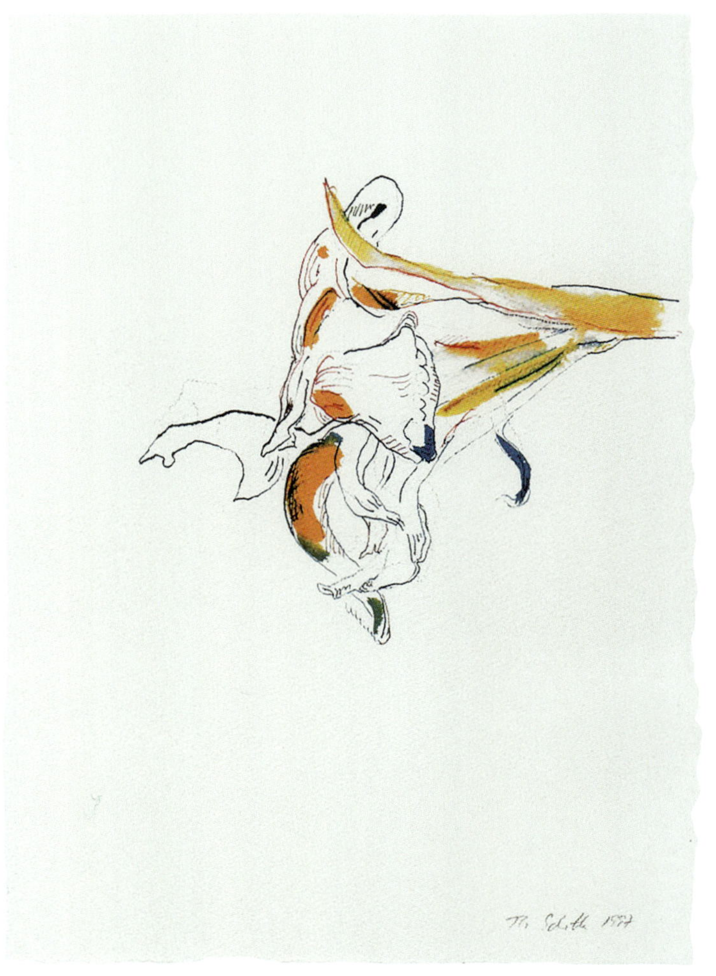

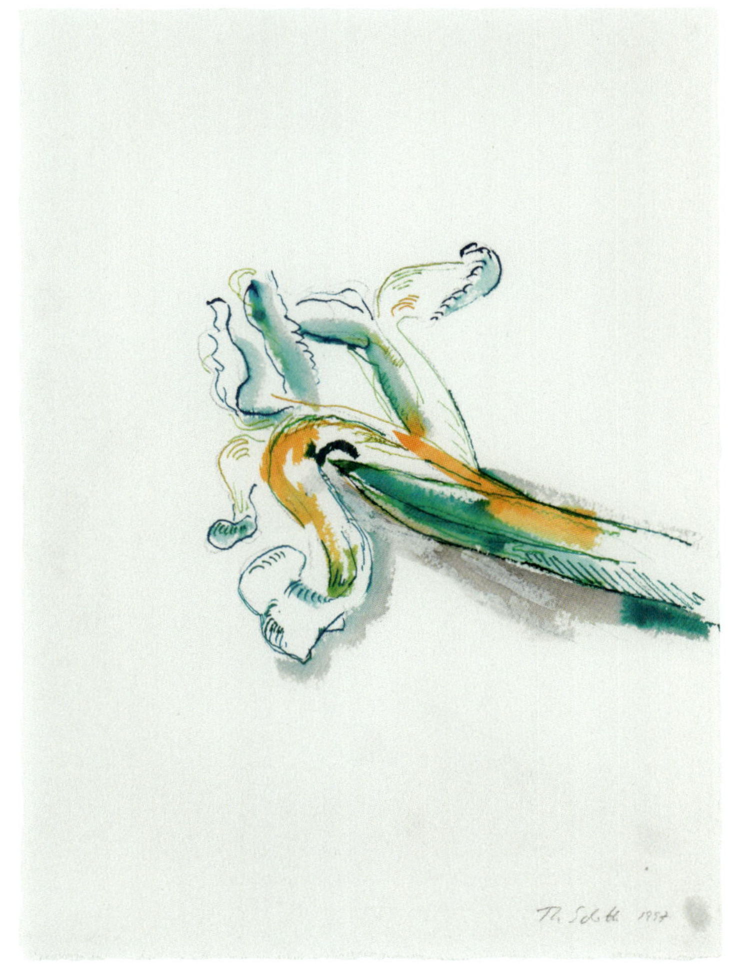

52
Grüner Kopf (Konrad) (*Green Head [Konrad]*). 1997. Glazed ceramic and blanket on wood pedestal, ceramic and blanket: 14 ¾ × 29 ½ × 16 ¾" (37.5 × 75 × 42.5 cm), pedestal: 45 ¼ × 25 $\frac{9}{16}$ × 19 $\frac{11}{16}$" (115 × 65 × 50 cm)

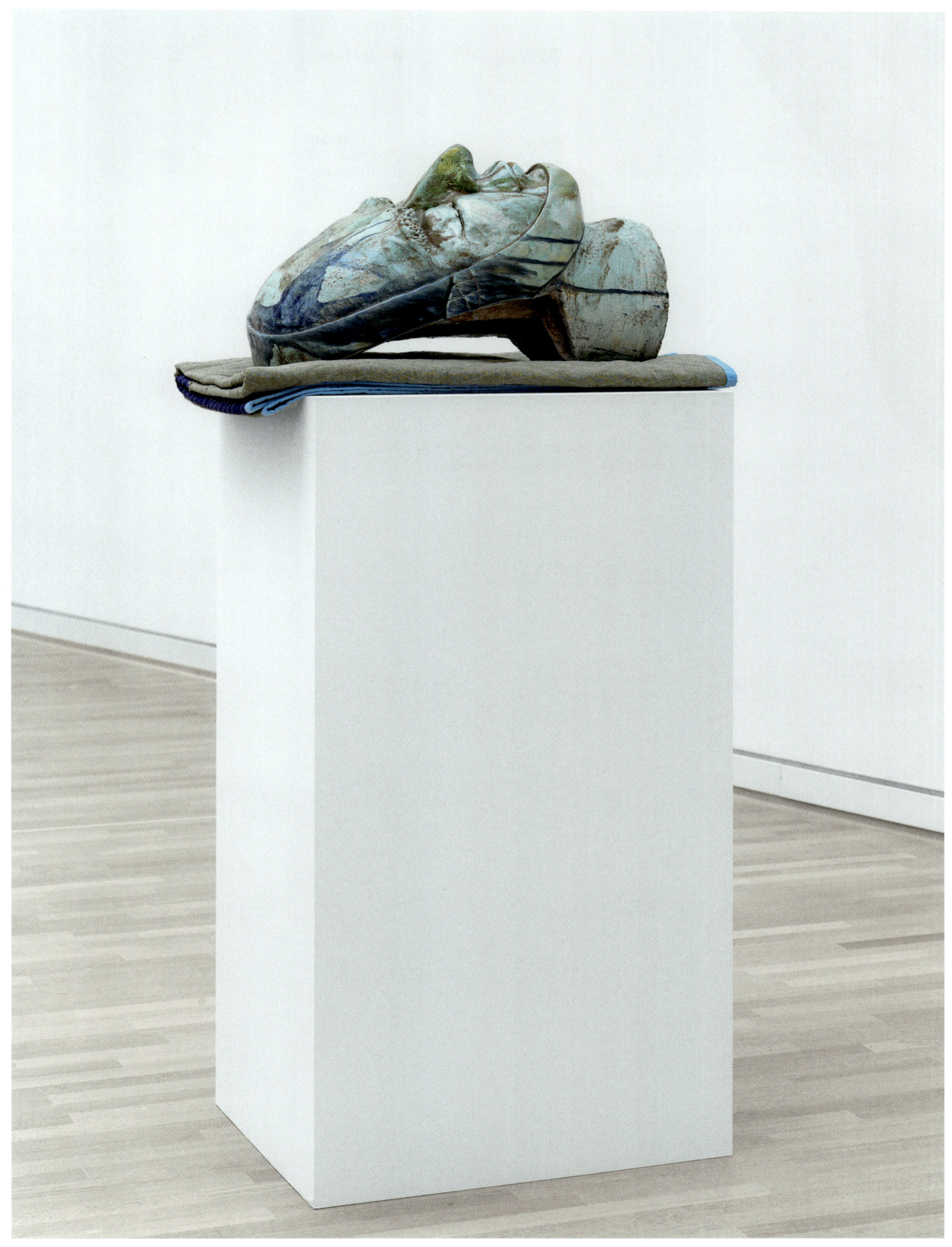

This spread and next:

53
Mirror Drawing. 1998–99. Watercolor, ink, and pencil on paper, 14 15⁄16 × 11" (38 × 28 cm)

54
Mirror Drawing 16-6-98. 1998. Watercolor and ink on paper, 14 15⁄16 × 11" (38 × 28 cm)

55
Mirror Drawing 16-6-98. 1998. Watercolor, ink, and pencil on paper, 14 15⁄16 × 11" (38 × 28 cm)

56
Mirror Drawing 6-8-98. 1998. Watercolor, ink, and crayon on paper, 14 15⁄16 × 11" (38 × 28 cm)

57
Mirror Drawing 20-10-98. 1998. Watercolor, ink, and pencil on paper, 14 15⁄16 × 11" (38 × 28 cm)

58
Mirror Drawing 20-10-98. 1998. Watercolor, ink, and pencil on paper, 14 15⁄16 × 11" (38 × 28 cm)

59
Mirror Drawing 15-11-98. 1998. Watercolor, ink, and pencil on paper, 14 15⁄16 × 11" (38 × 28 cm)

60
Mirror Drawing 16-2-99. 1999. Ink and crayon on paper, 14 15⁄16 × 11" (38 × 28 cm)

61
Mirror Drawing 16-2-99. 1999. Ink and crayon on paper, 14 15⁄16 × 11" (38 × 28 cm)

62
Mirror Drawing 16-2-99. 1999. Watercolor, ink, and crayon on paper, 14 15⁄16 × 11" (38 × 28 cm)

63
Mirror Drawing 14-3-99. 1999. Ink and pencil on paper, 14 15⁄16 × 11" (38 × 28 cm)

64
Mirror Drawing 29-3-99. 1999. Ink and crayon on paper, 14 15⁄16 × 11" (38 × 28 cm)

65
Mirror Drawing 23-5-99. 1999. Watercolor, ink, and crayon on paper, 14 15⁄16 × 11" (38 × 28 cm)

66
Mirror Drawing 3-6-99. 1999. Ink and crayon on paper, 14 15⁄16 × 11" (38 × 28 cm)

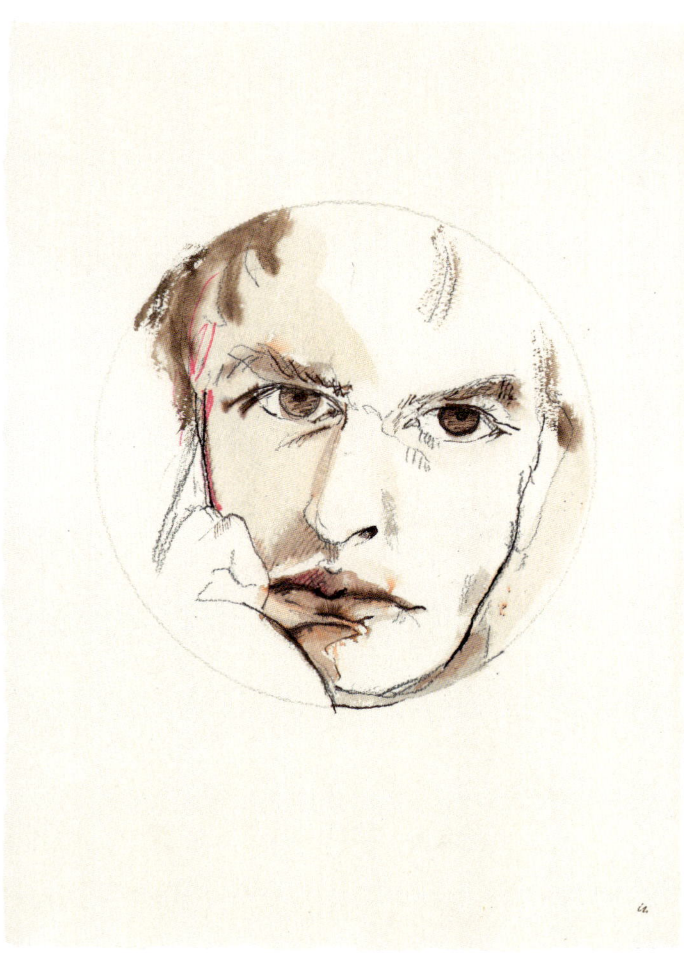

53

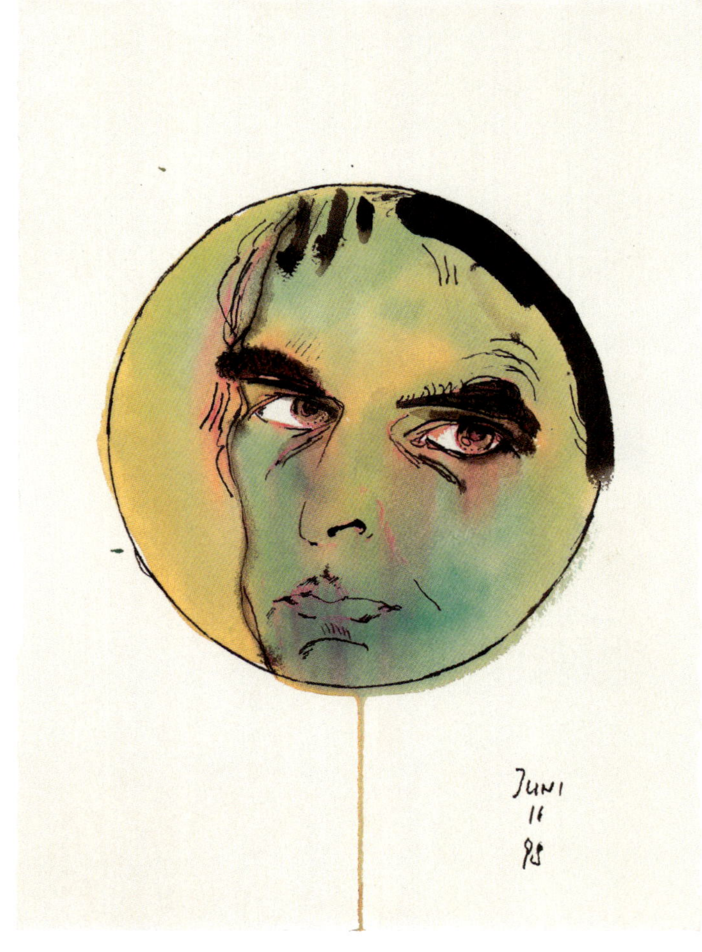

54

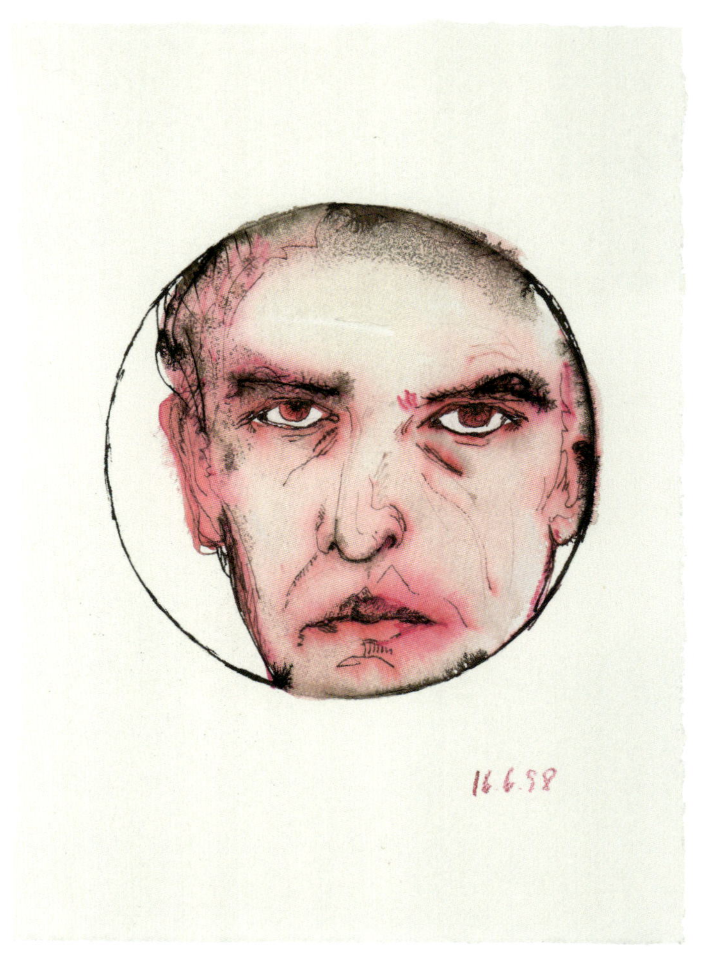

55

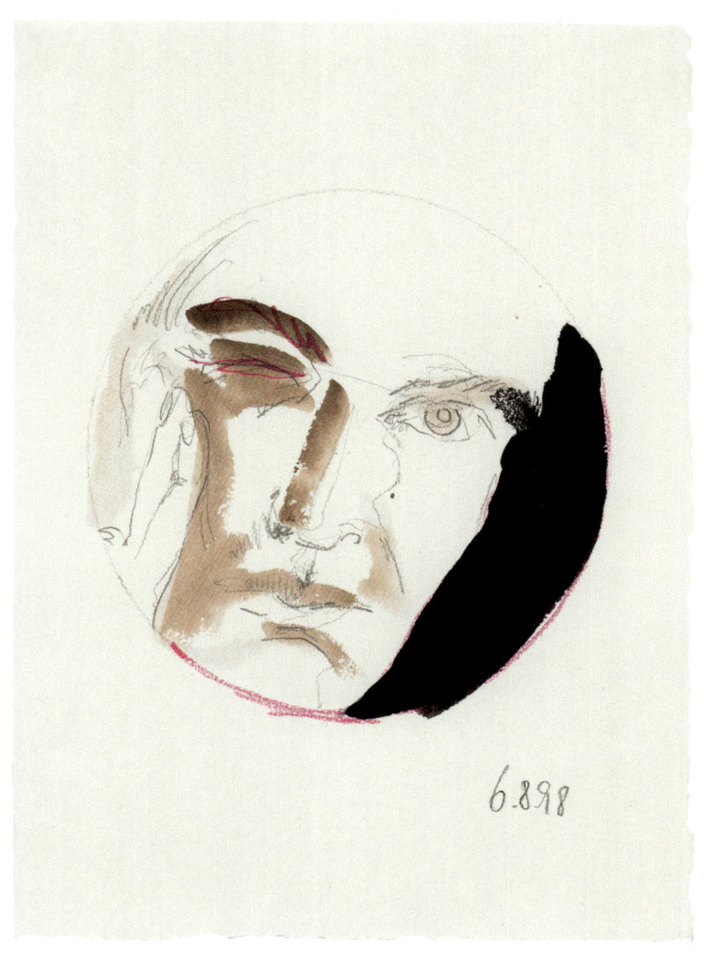

56

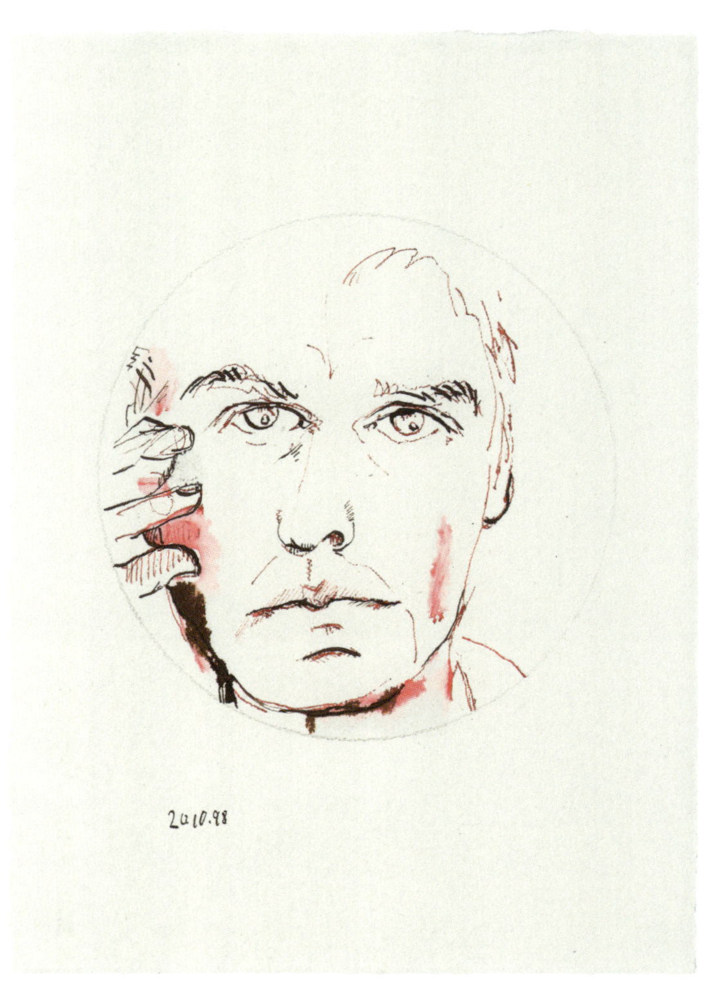

57

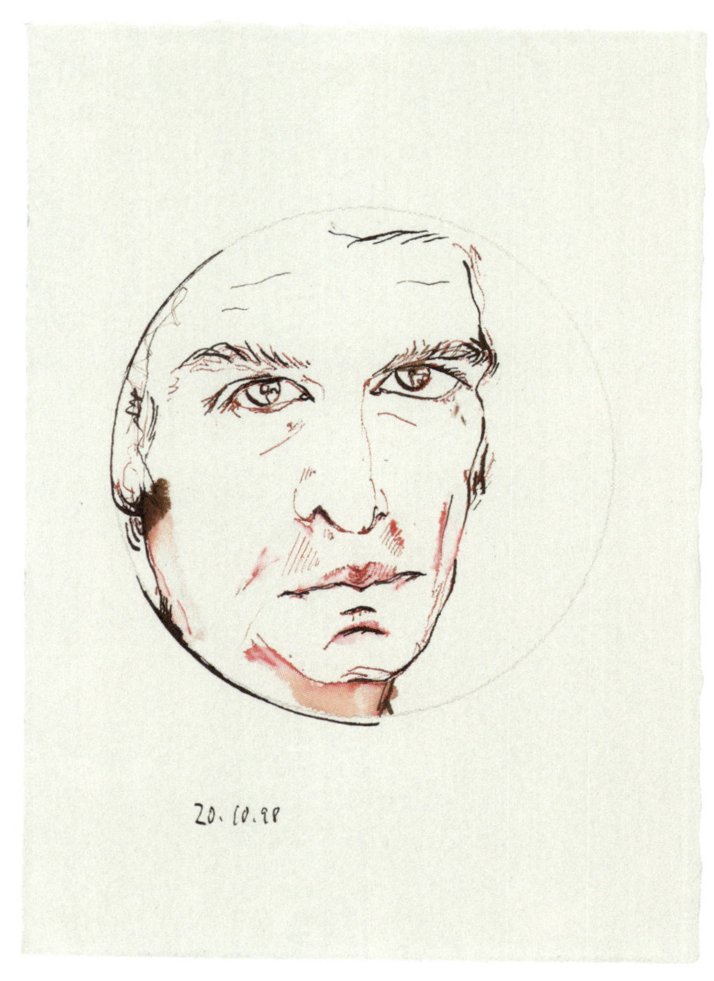

58

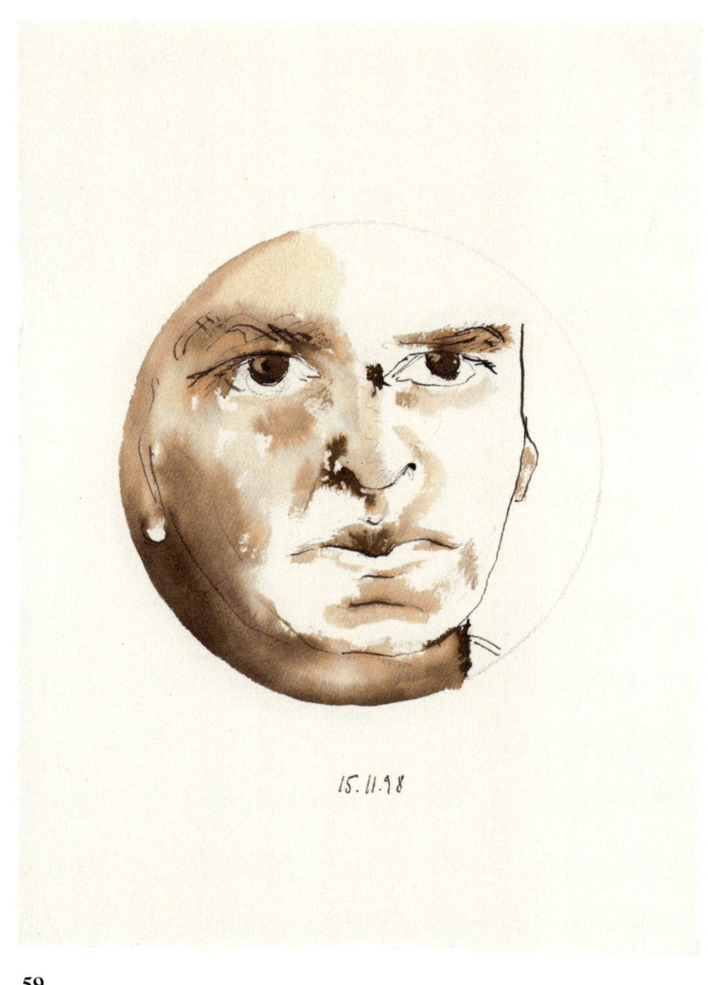

59

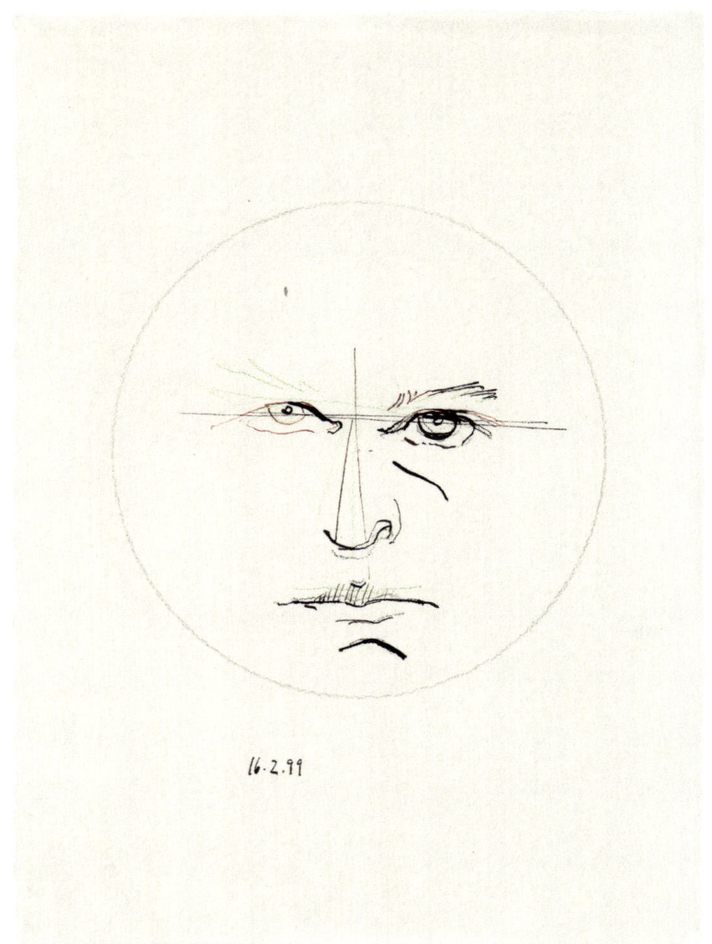

60

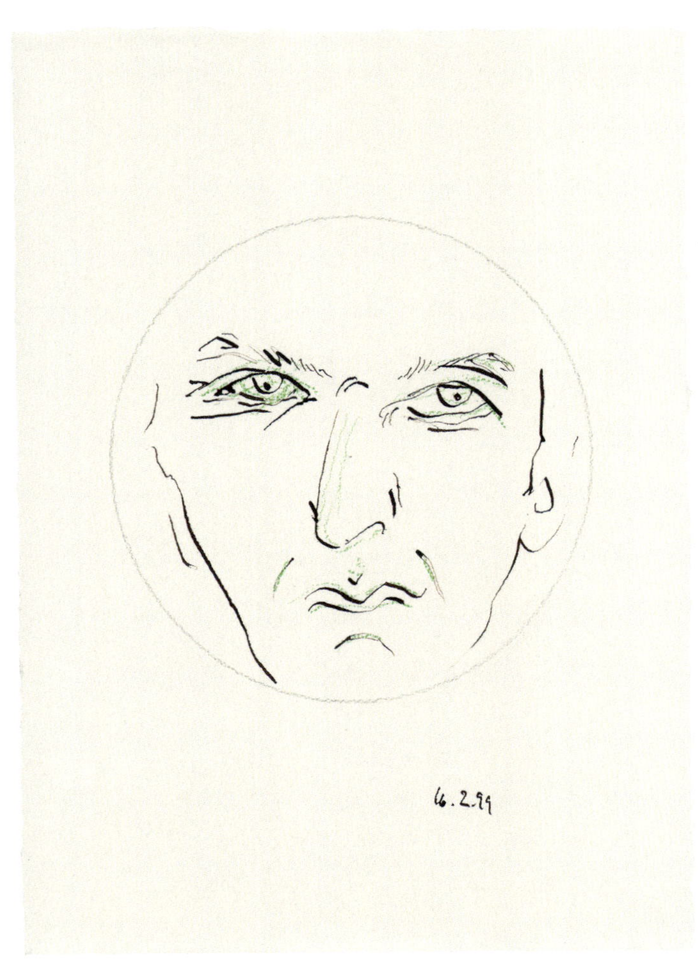

61

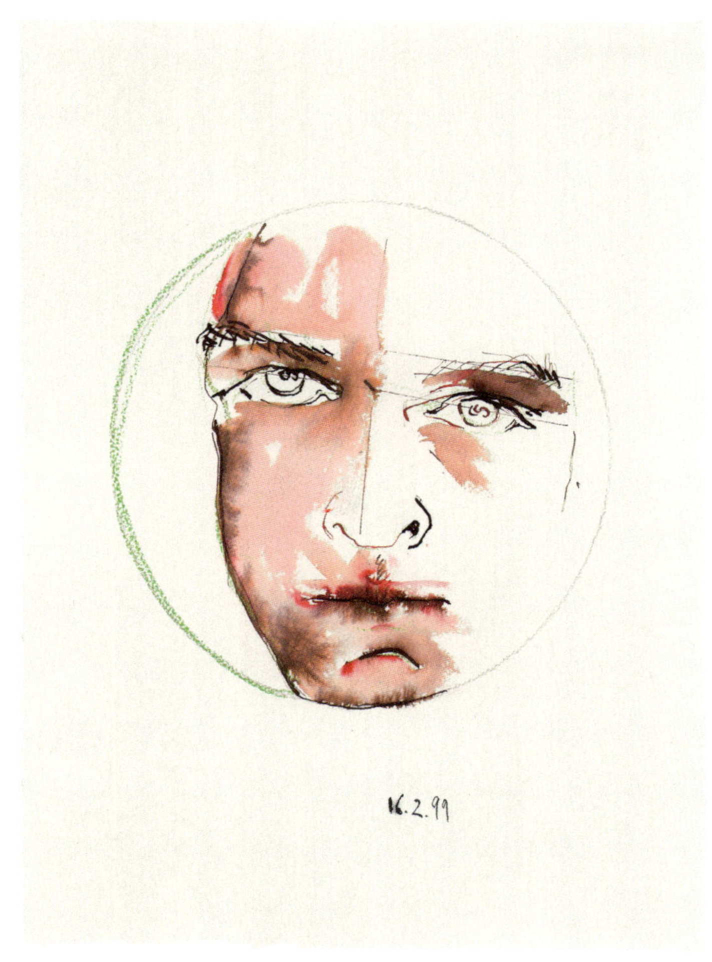

62

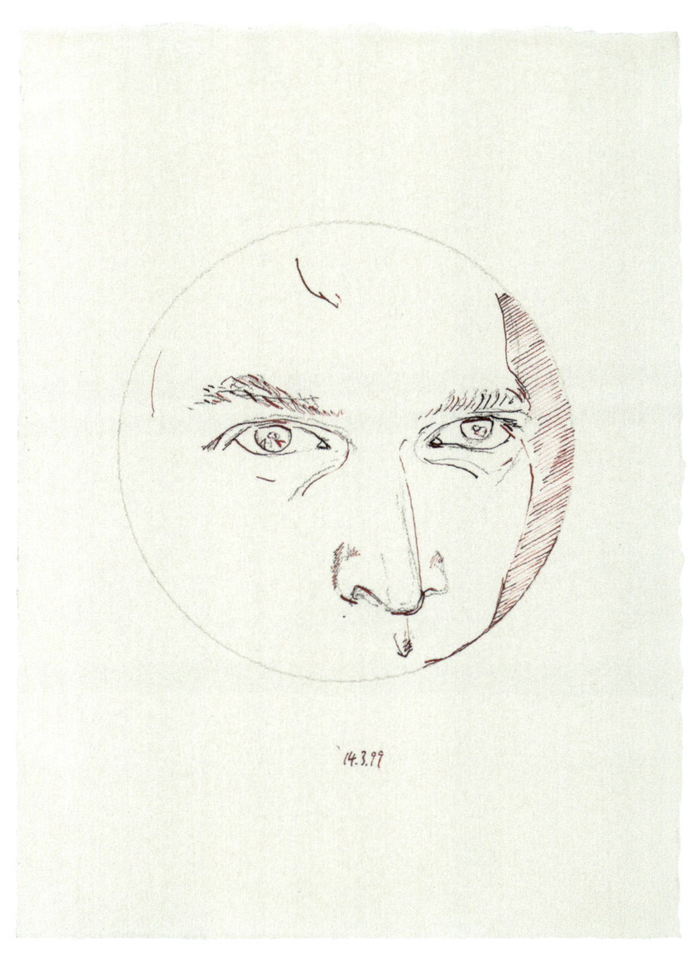

63

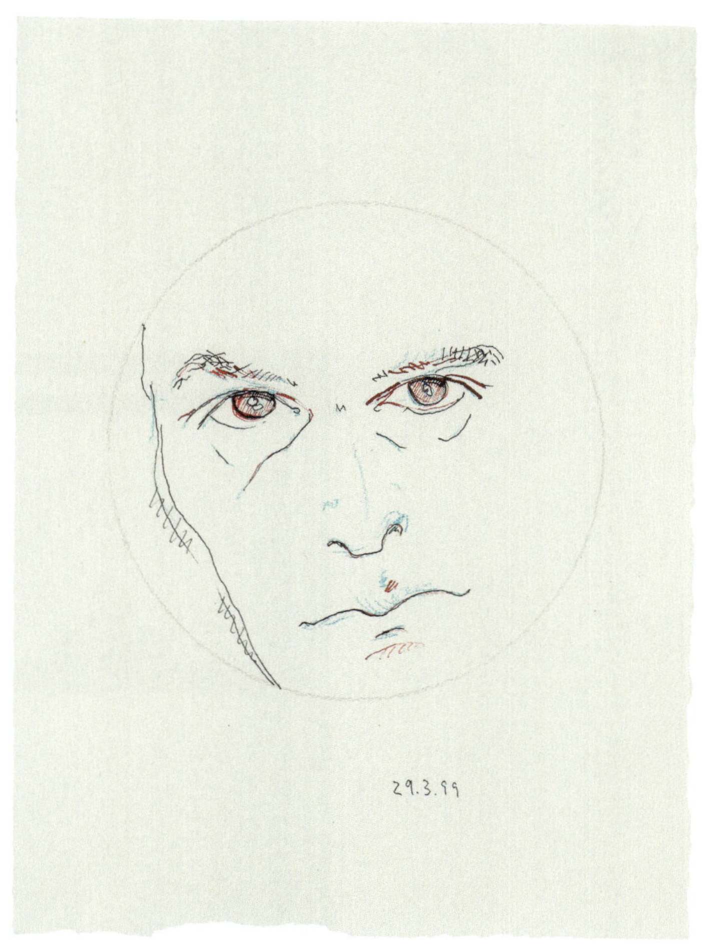

64

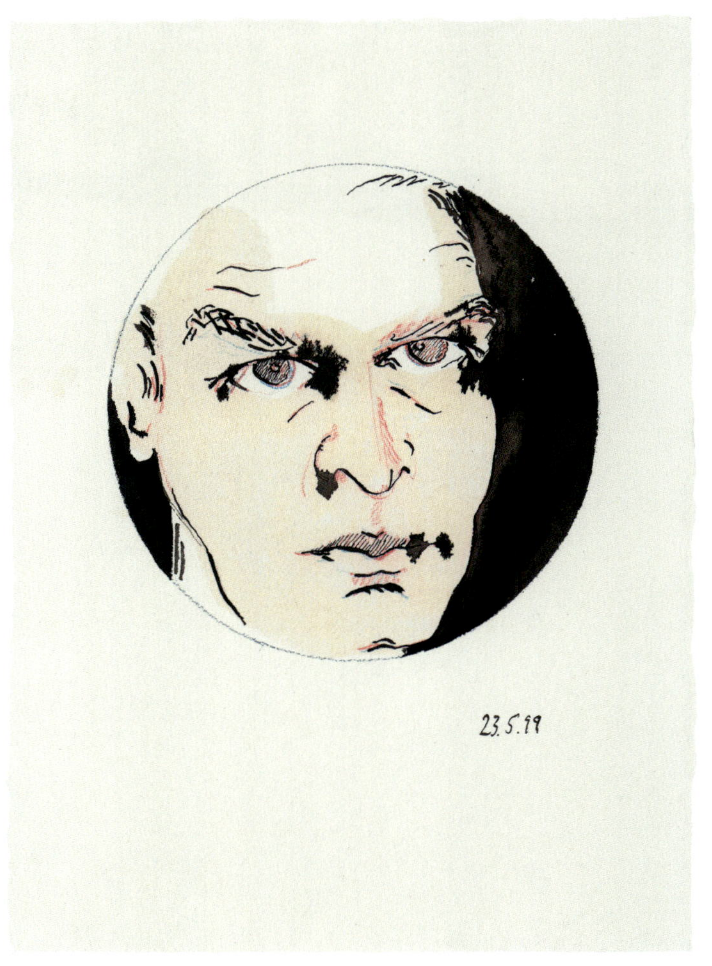

65

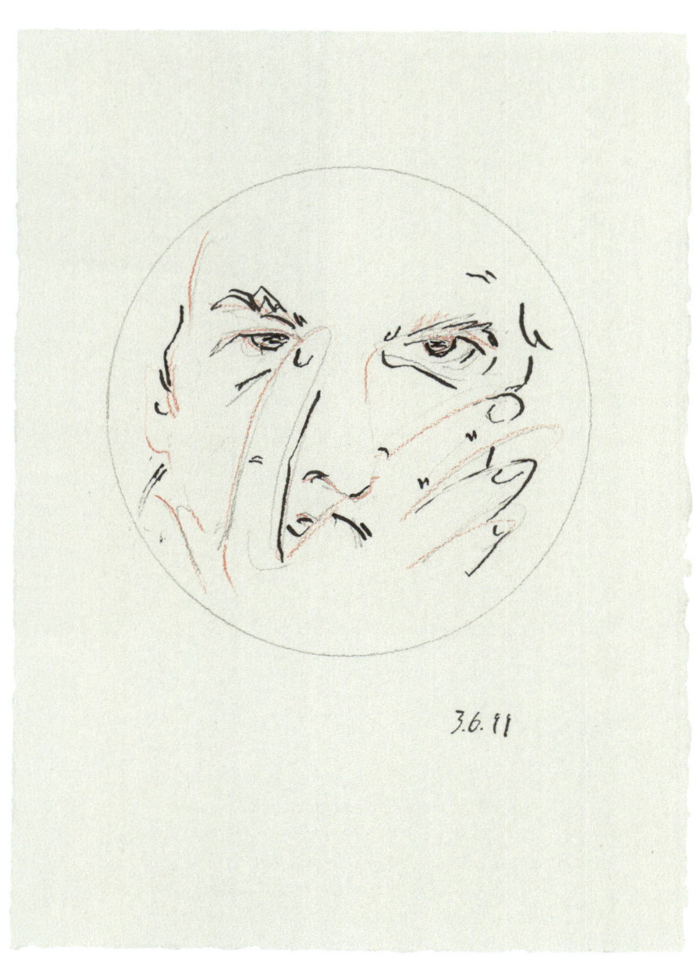

66

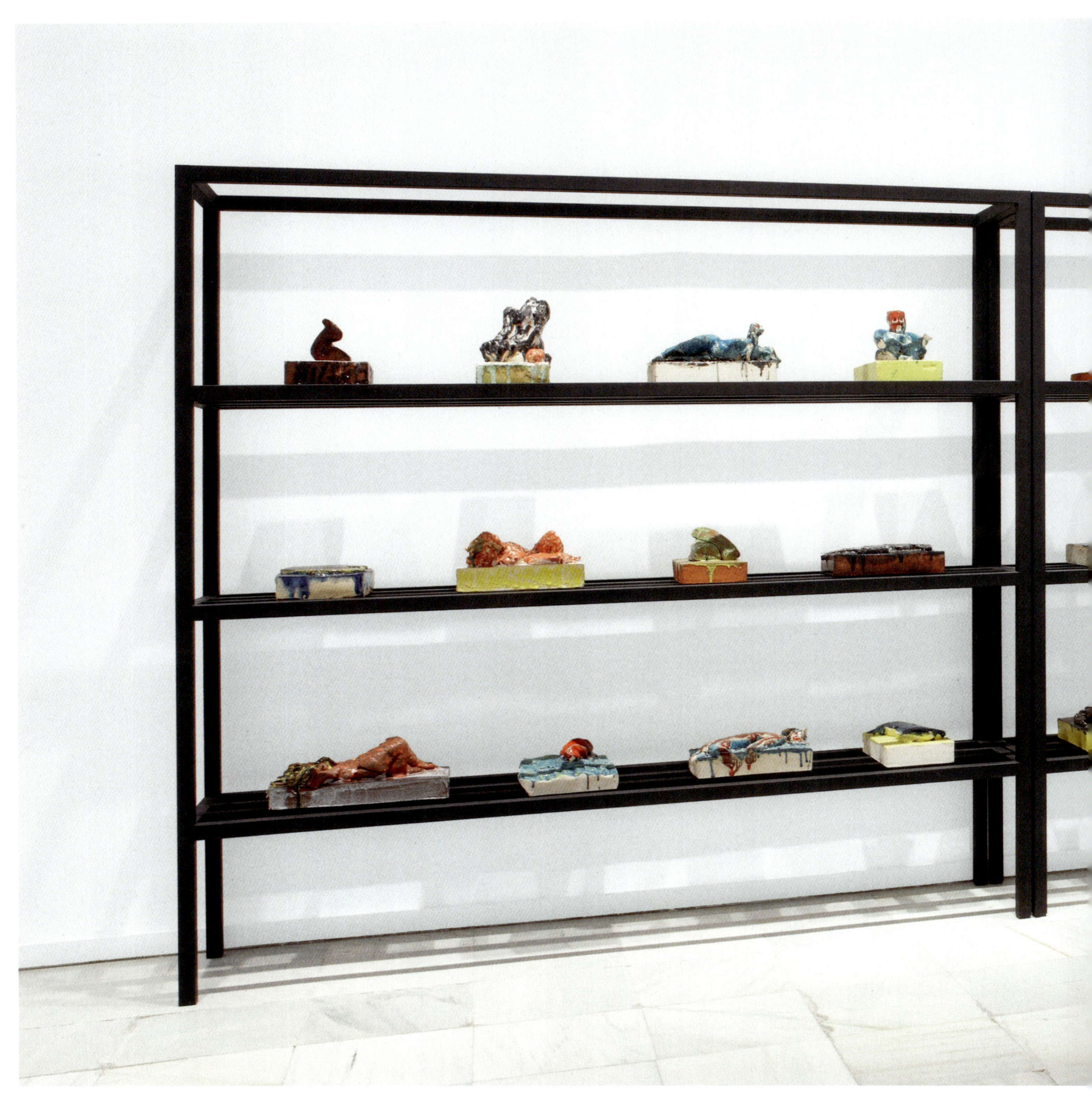

67
Ceramic Sketches. 1997–99. Three steel shelving units with 36 glazed ceramics, each unit 7' ¼" × 7' 6 ⁹⁄₁₆" × 1' 7 ¹¹⁄₁₆" (214 × 230 × 50 cm), each ceramic approx. 9 ¹³⁄₁₆ × 13 × 7 ⅞ (25 × 33 × 20 cm). Installation view, *Thomas Schütte: Hindsight*, Museo Nacional Centro de Arte Reina Sofía, Madrid, February 17–May 17, 2010

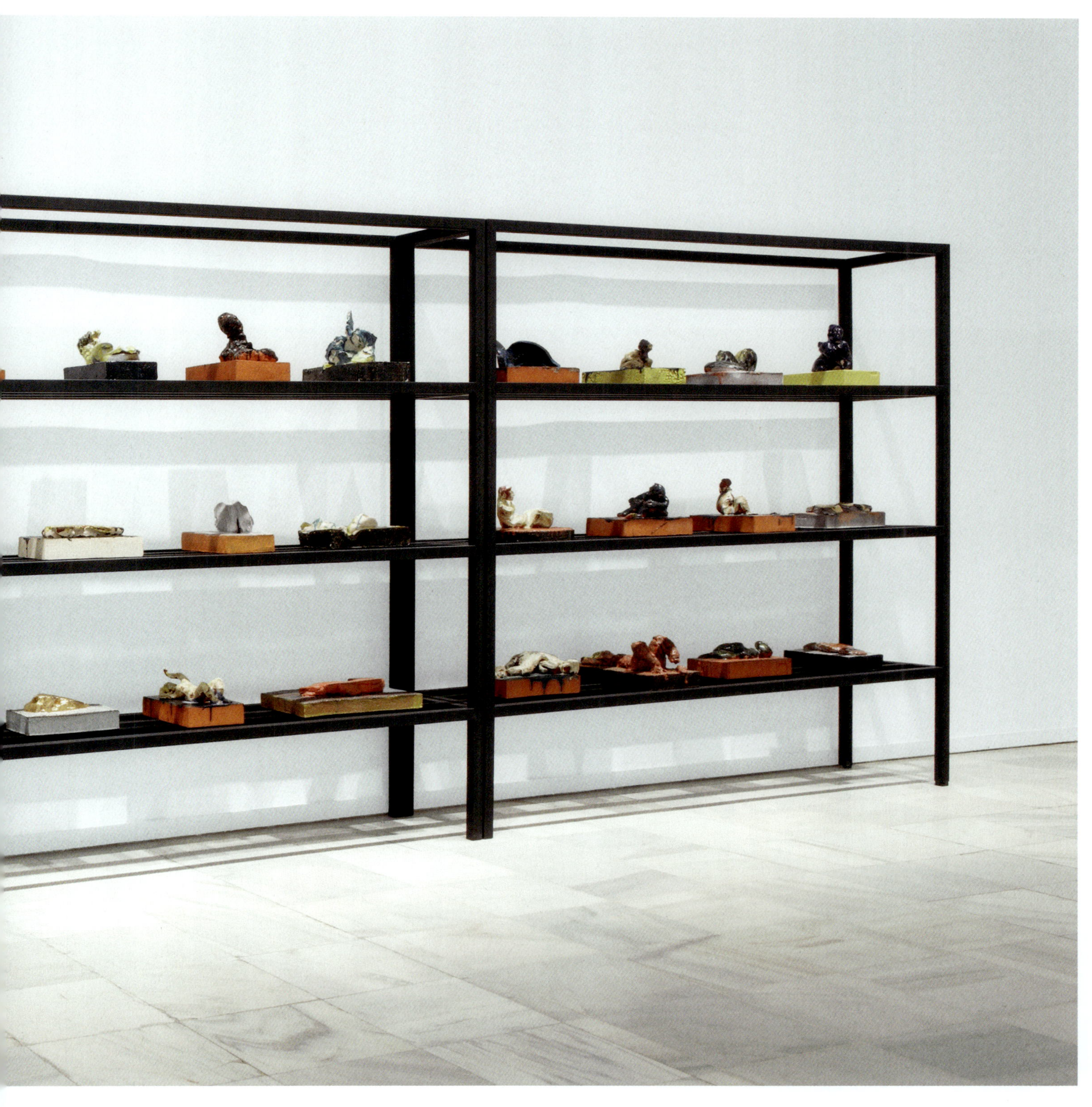

68
Stahlfrau Nr. 1 (*Steel Woman No. 1*). 1998. Steel on steel table, 5' 3" × 8' 2 7⁄16" × 4' 1 3⁄16" (160 × 250 × 125 cm). Installation view, *Body and Void: Echoes of Henry Moore in Contemporary Art*, Henry Moore Institute, Perry Green, United Kingdom, May 1–October 26, 2014

Right:
Aluminiumfrau Nr. 1 (*Aluminum Woman No. 1*). 2001. Aluminum and lacquer on steel table, 5' 3" × 8' 2 7⁄16" × 4' 1 3⁄16" (160 × 250 × 125 cm). Thomas Schütte Stiftung, Neuss, Germany. Installation view, *Thomas Schütte: Frauen*, Castello di Rivoli, Rivoli/Turin, May 22–September 23, 2012

68

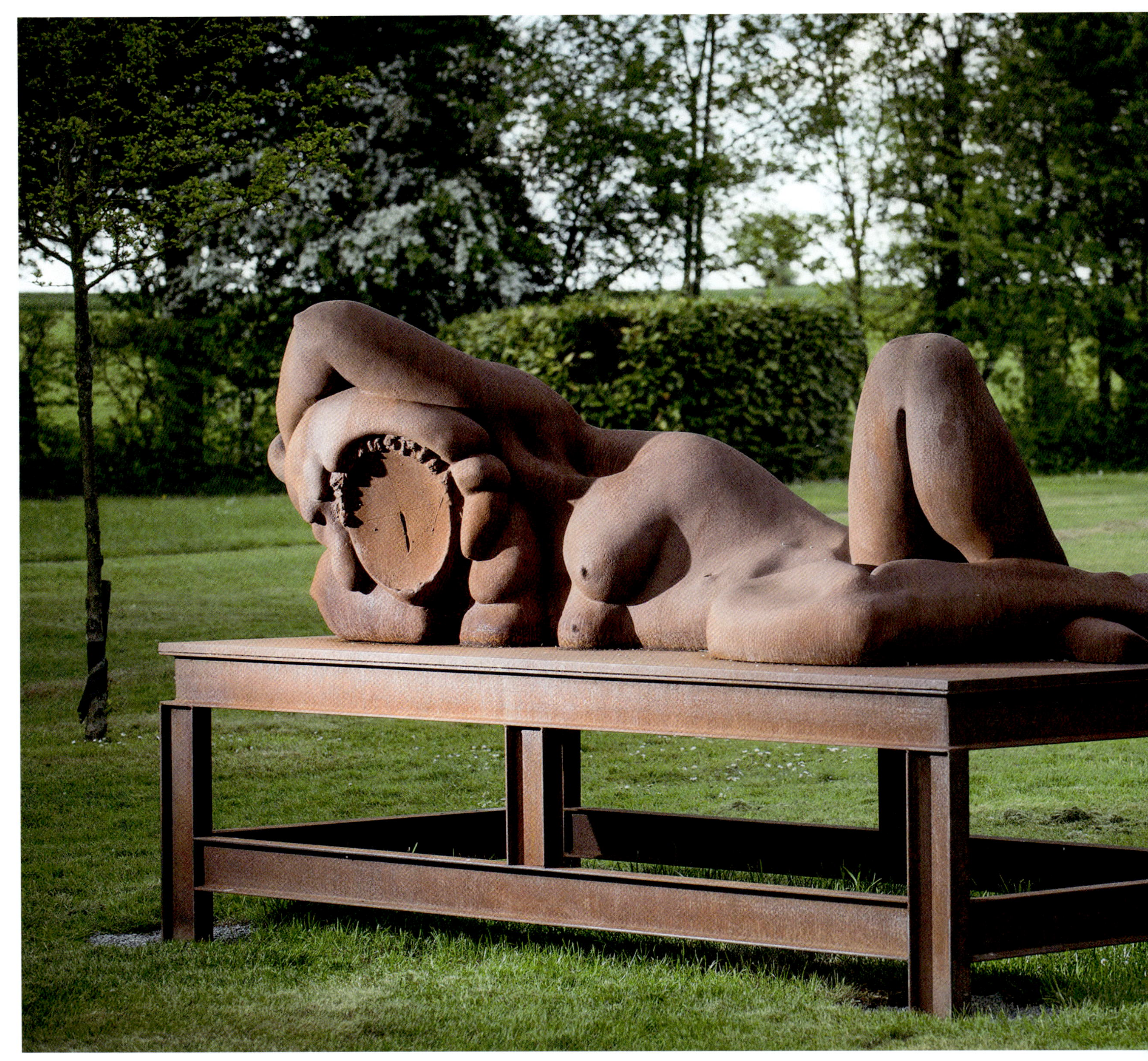

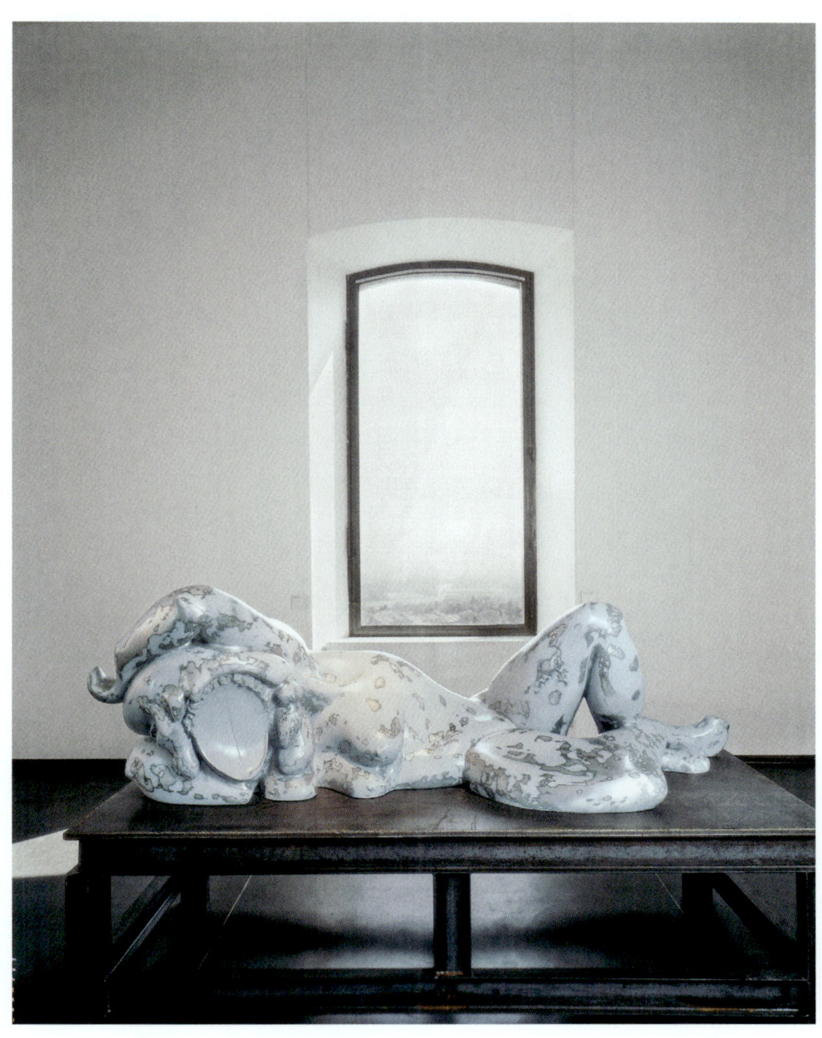

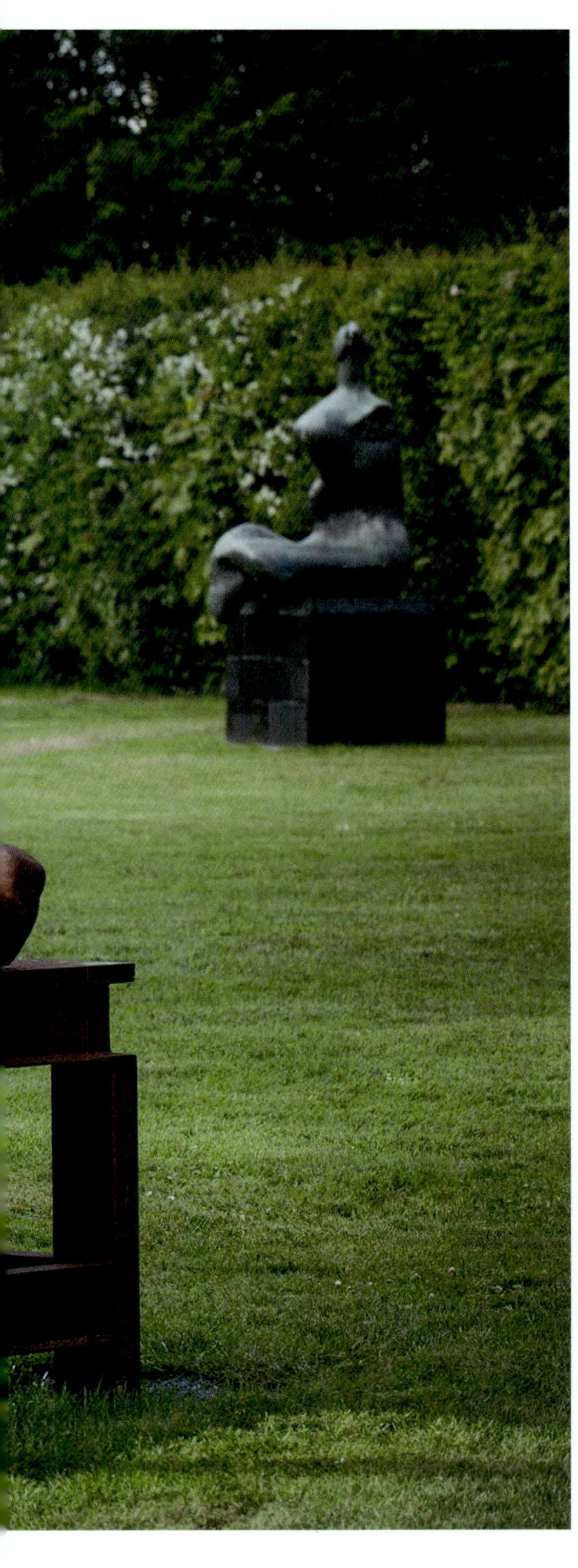

69
Aluminiumfrau Nr. 6 (*Aluminum Woman No. 6*). 2001. Aluminum and lacquer on steel table, 5' 4 3/16" × 8' 2 7/16" × 4' 1 3/16" (163 × 250 × 125 cm). Installation view, *Thomas Schütte*, Kunsthaus Bregenz, Austria, July 13–October 6, 2019. Background: *Fake Flag E* and *Fake Flag C* (both 2018)

Right:
Stahlfrau Nr. 6 (*Steel Woman Nr. 6*). 2003. Steel on steel table, 5' 4 3/16" × 8' 2 7/16" × 4' 1 3/16" (163 × 250 × 125 cm). Private collection

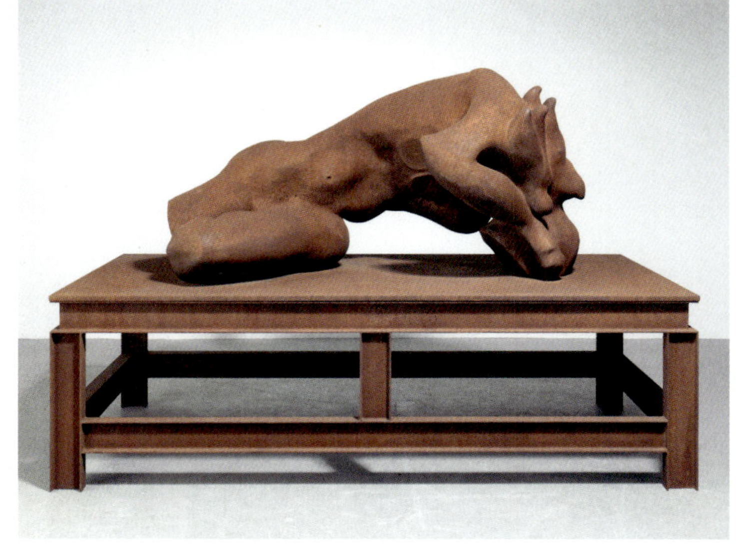

69

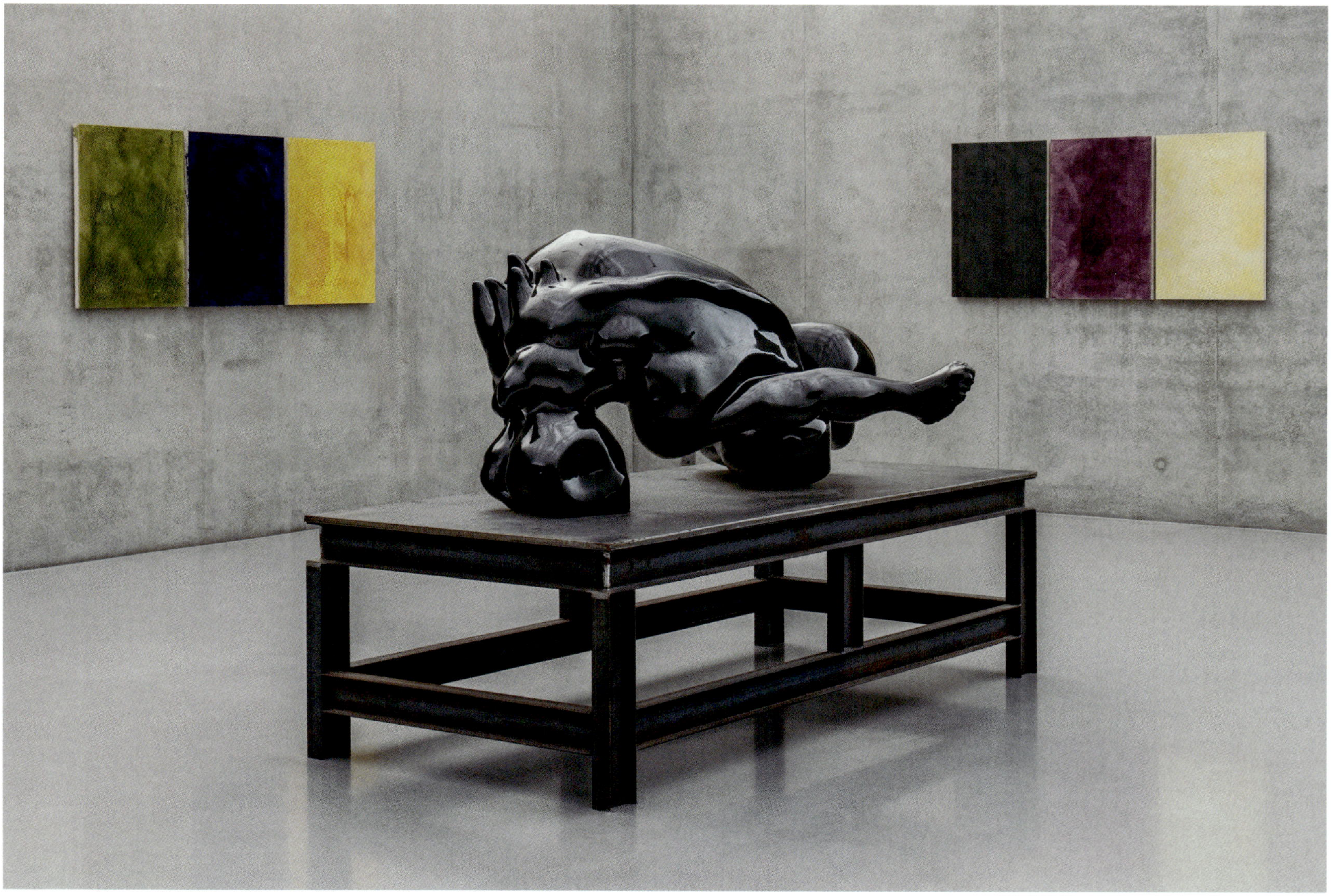

70
Aluminiumfrau Nr. 16 (*Aluminum Woman No. 16*). 2005. Aluminum on steel table, 5' 10 ⅞" × 8' 2 7⁄16" × 4' 1 3⁄16" (180 × 250 × 125 cm). Installation view, *Thomas Schütte: Frauen*, Sara Hildénin Taidemuseo, Tampere, Finland, February 9–May 12, 2013

Right:
Untitled (Ceramic Sketch). 1997–99. Glazed ceramic, approx. 9 13⁄16 × 13 × 7 ⅞" (25 × 33 × 20 cm). Kunstsammlung Nordrhein-Westfalen, Düsseldorf

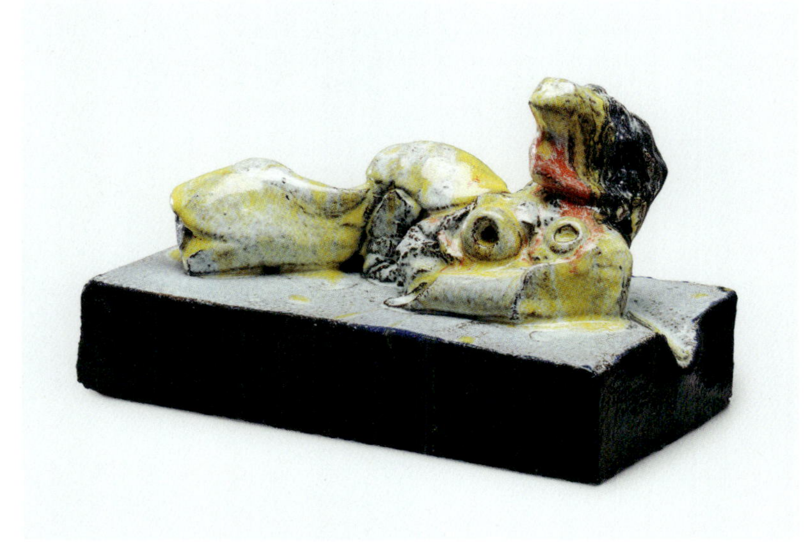

70

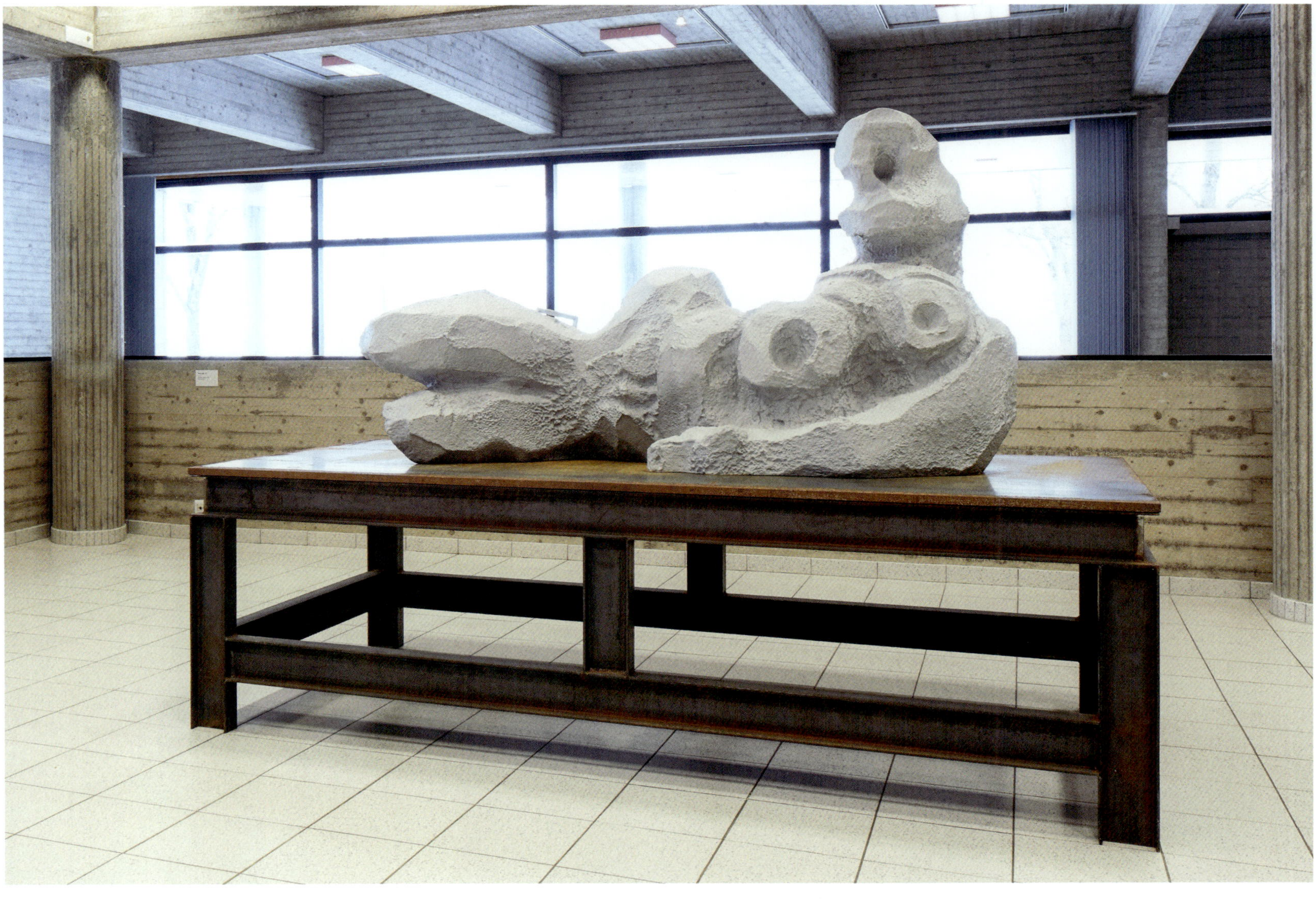

71
Bronzefrau Nr. 17 (*Bronze Woman No. 17*). 2006. Patinated bronze on steel table, 6' 8 3/8" × 8' 2 7/16" × 4' 1 3/16" (204 × 250 × 125 cm)

Right:
Frauenkopf mit Blume (*Woman's Head with Flower*). 2006. Aluminum and lacquer on steel pedestal, aluminum: 13 × 25 9/16 × 19 11/16" (33 × 65 × 50 cm), pedestal: 47 1/4 × 17 11/16 × 17 11/16" (120 × 45 × 45 cm). Collection the artist, Düsseldorf

Below:
Untitled (Ceramic Sketch). 1997–99. Glazed ceramic, approx. 9 13/16 × 13 × 13" (25 × 33 × 33 cm). Kunstsammlung Nordrhein-Westfalen, Düsseldorf

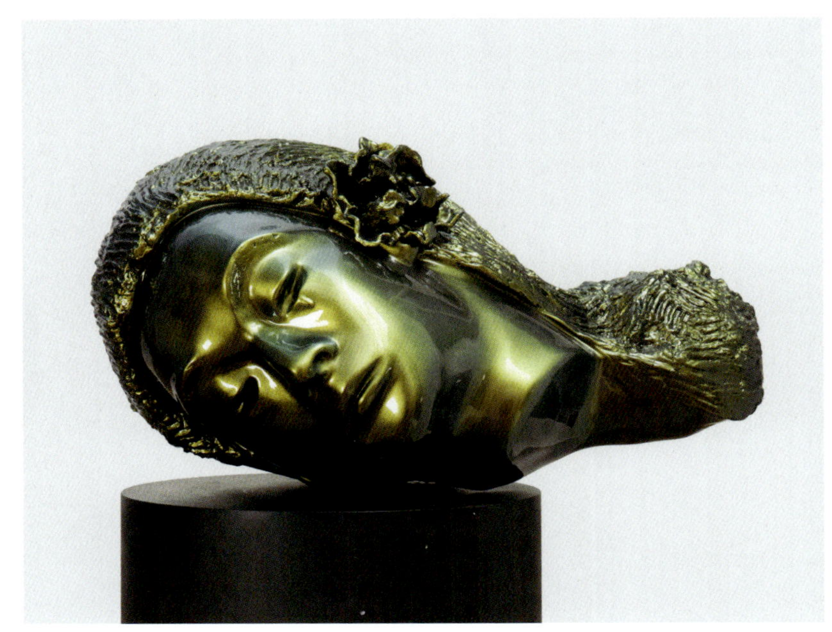

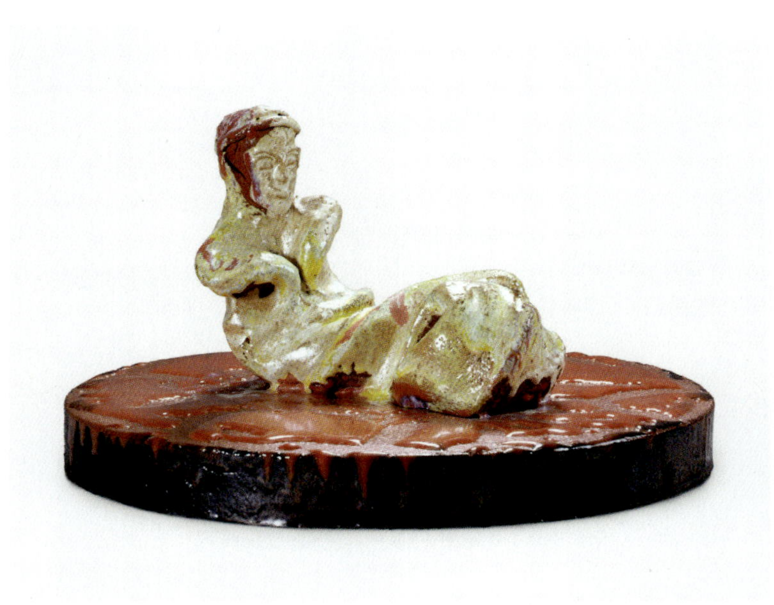

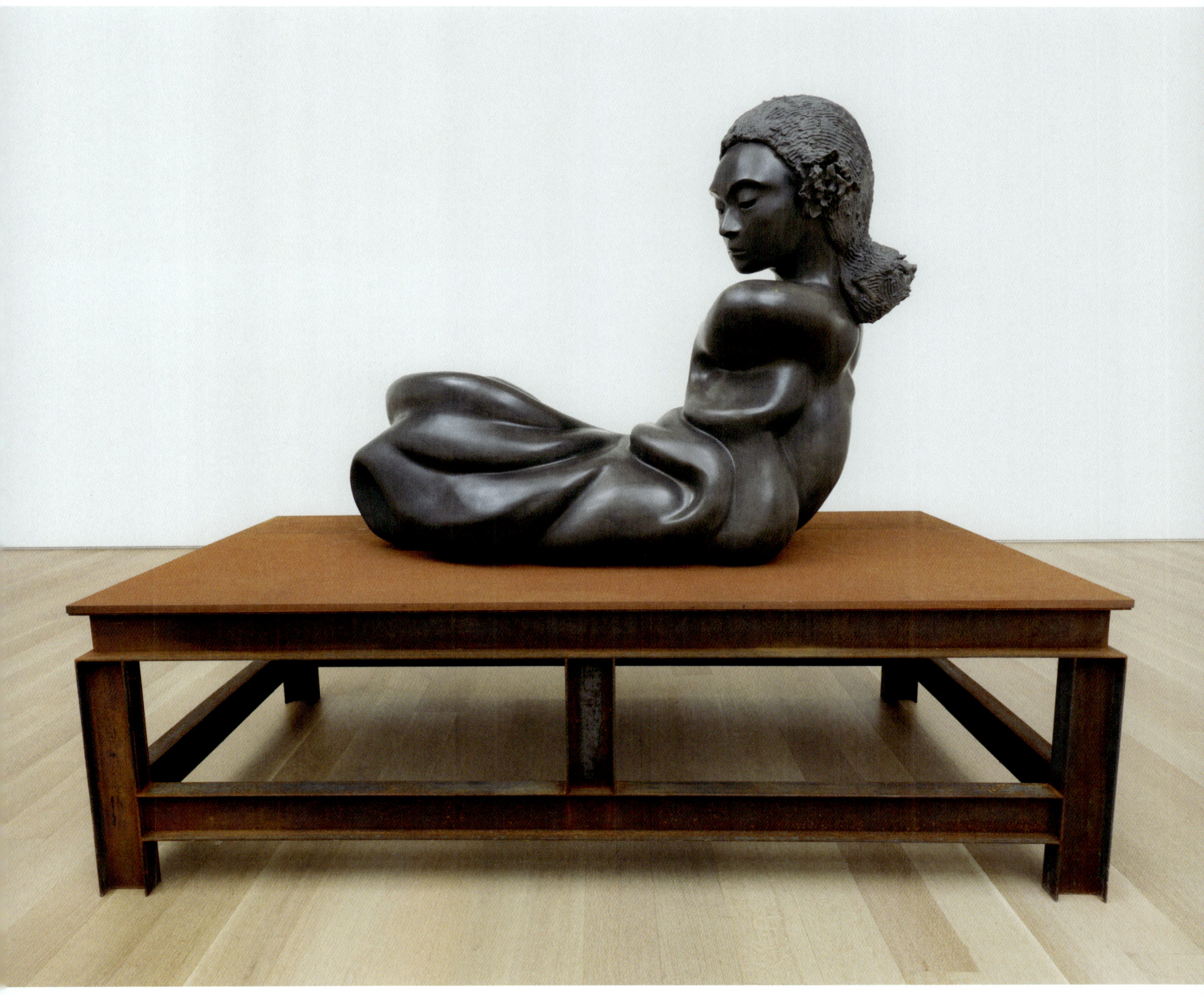

71

This spread and next:

72
Frauen Series A. 2006. Etching on paper with chine collé, 18 sheets, each 27 ¼ × 36" (69.2 × 91.4 cm). Edition 9 of 12 with 5 APs

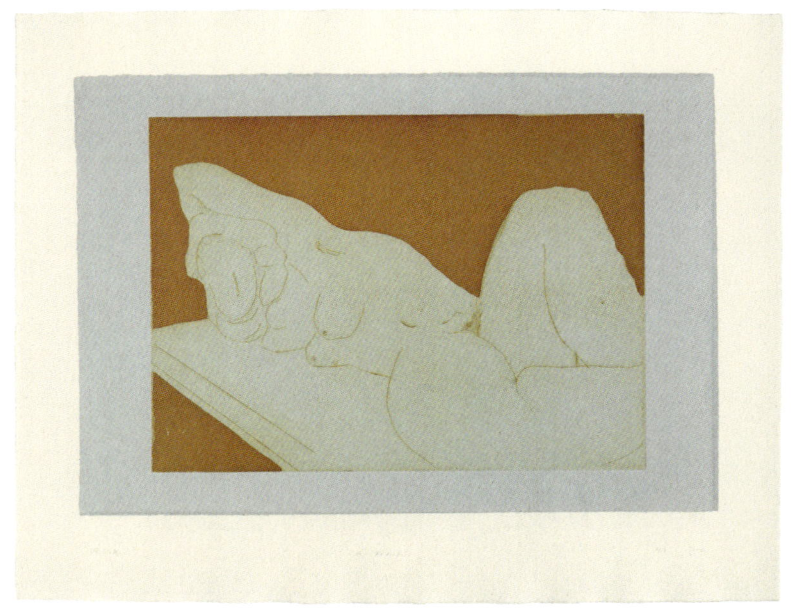

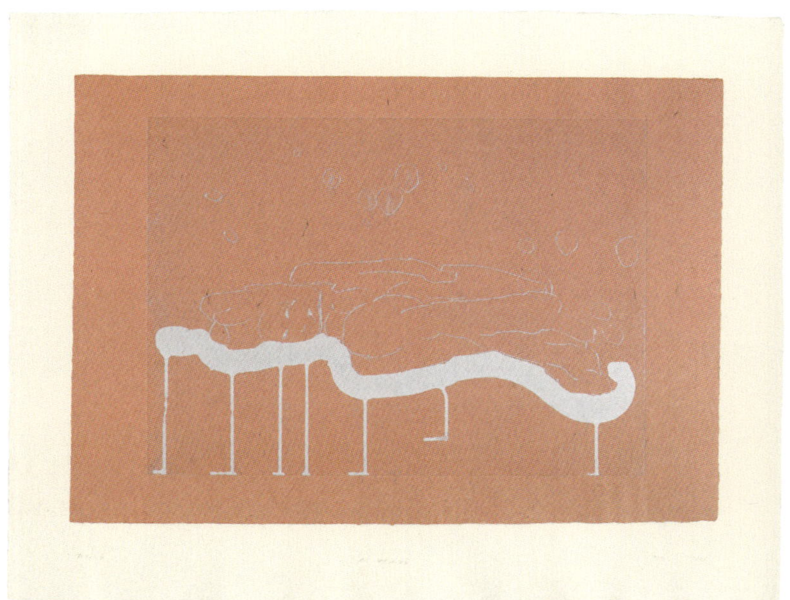

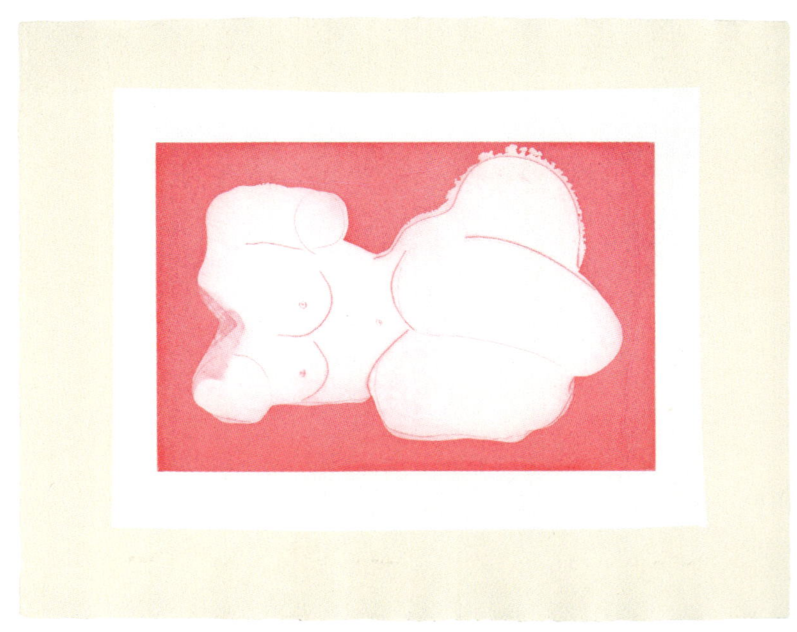

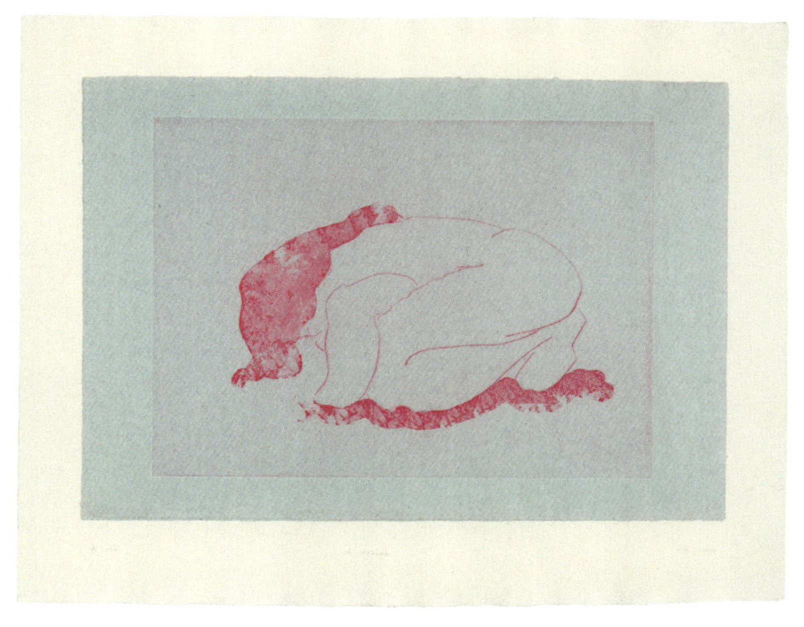
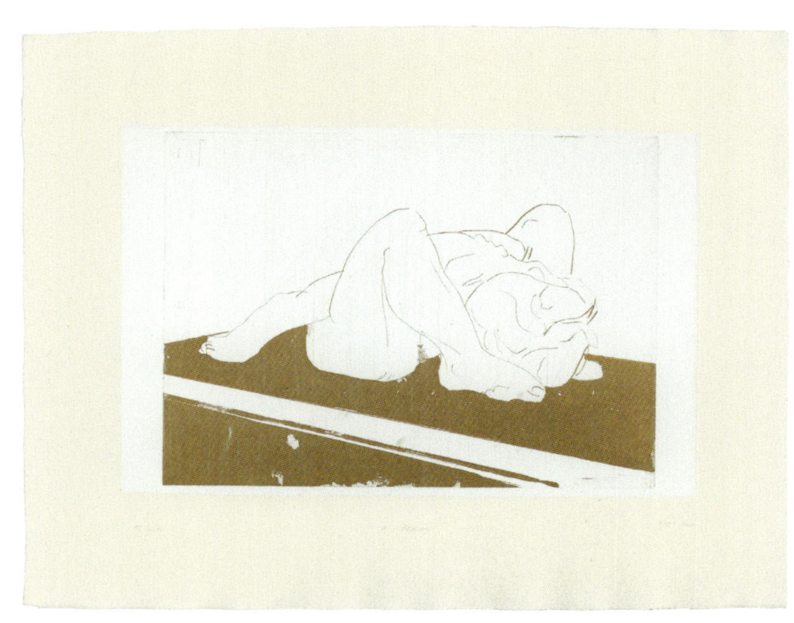
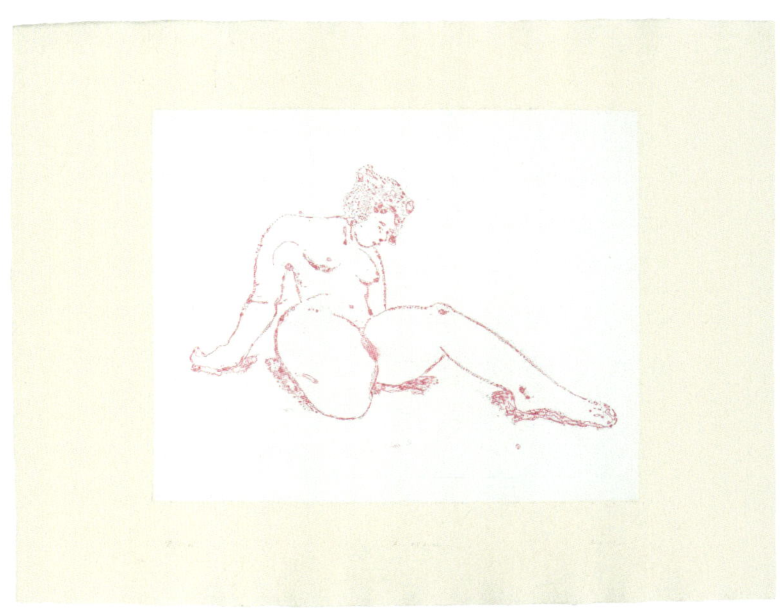
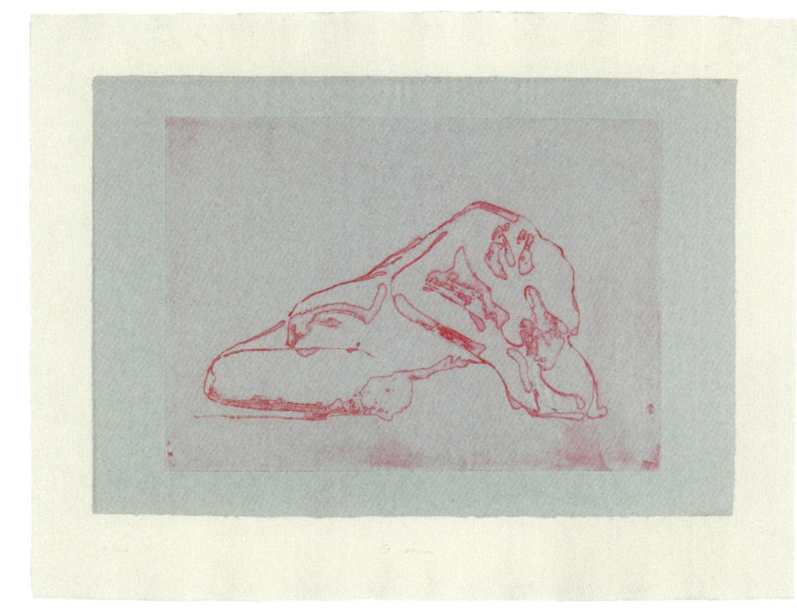
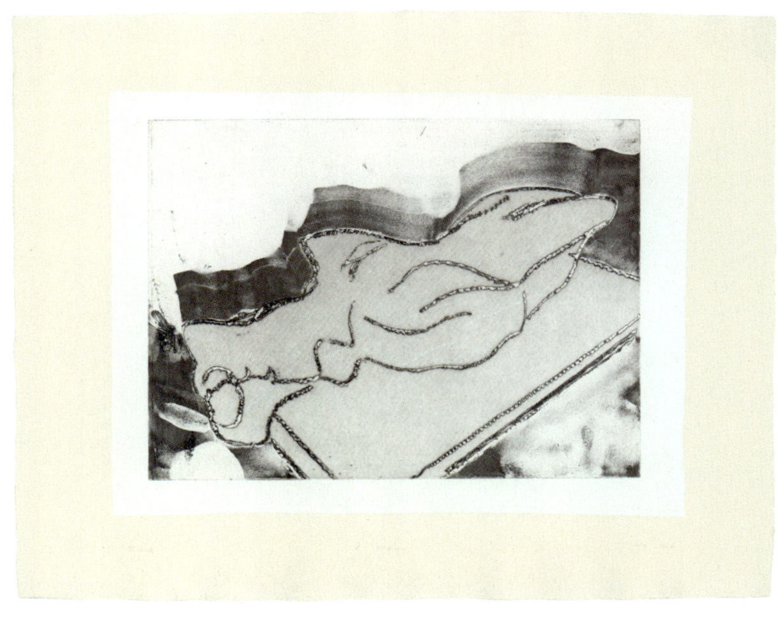
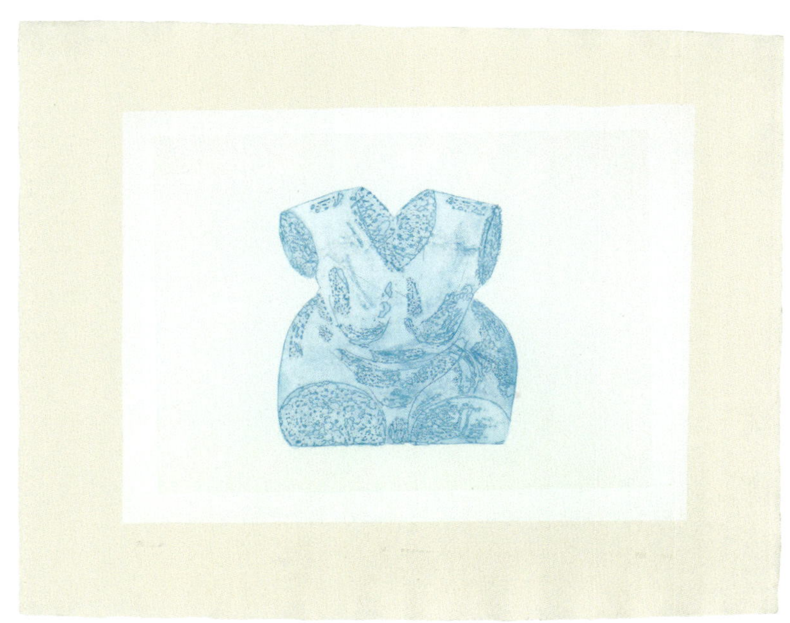

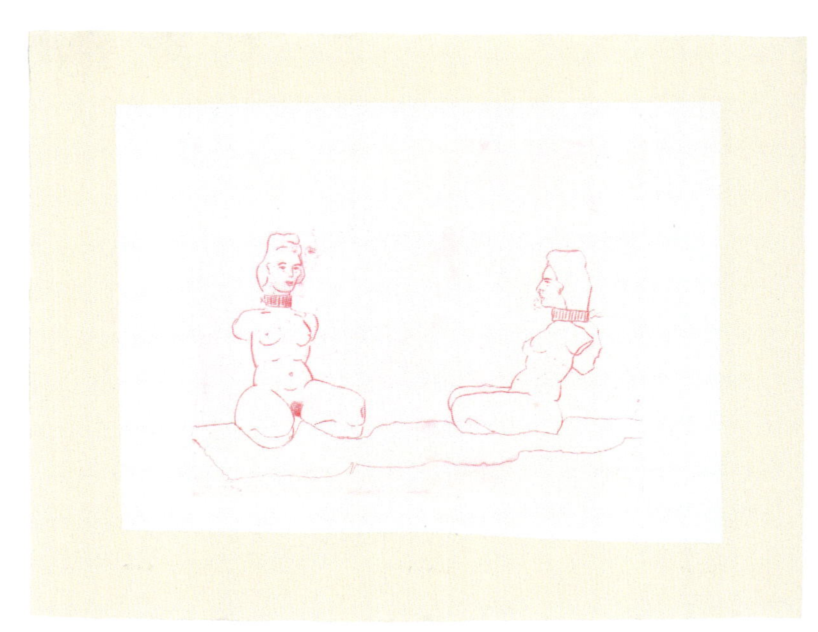

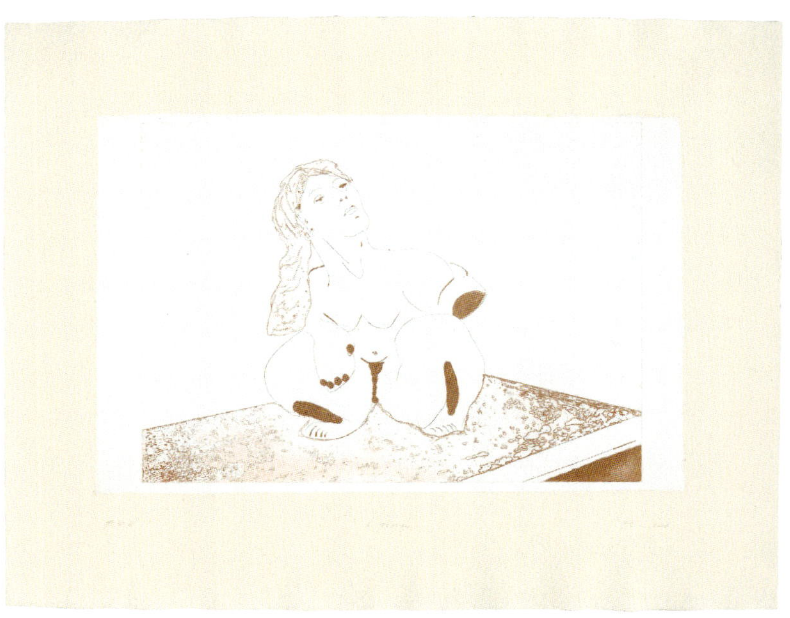

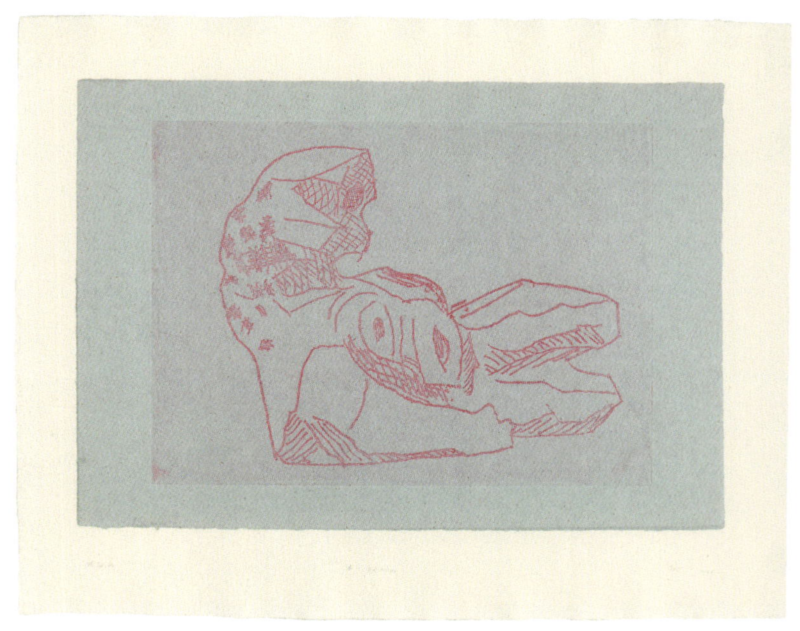

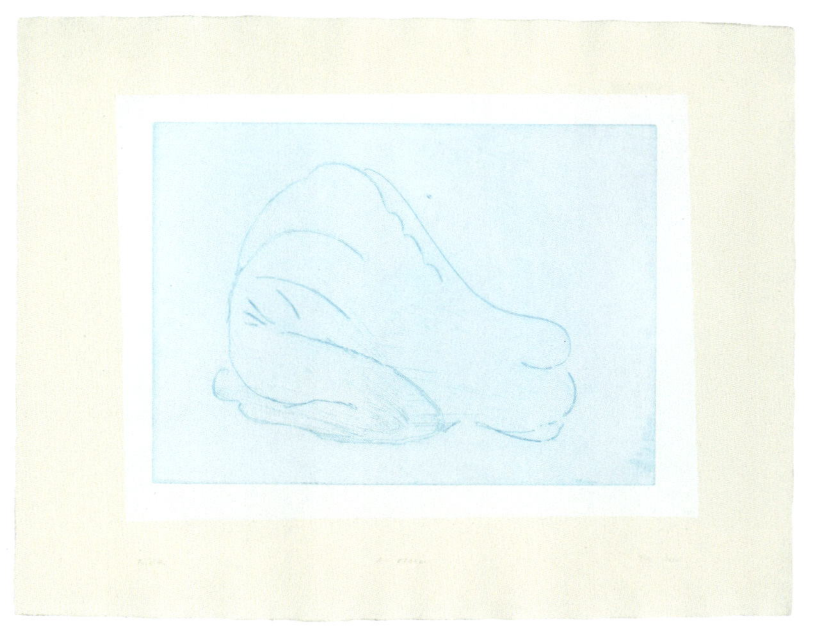
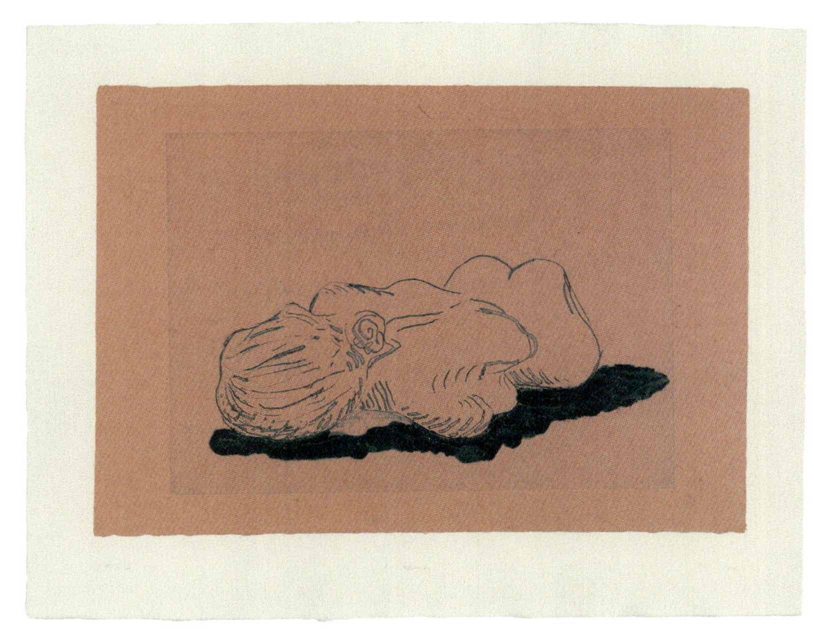
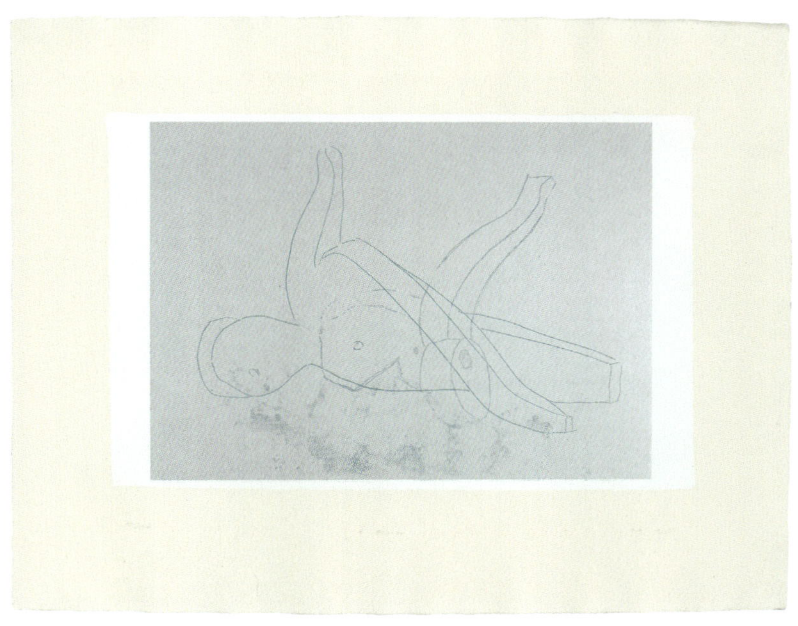
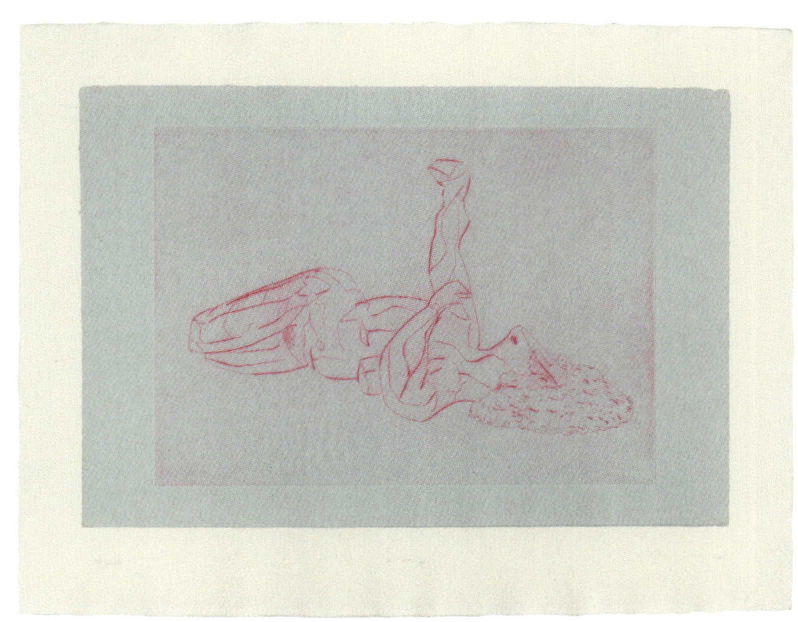
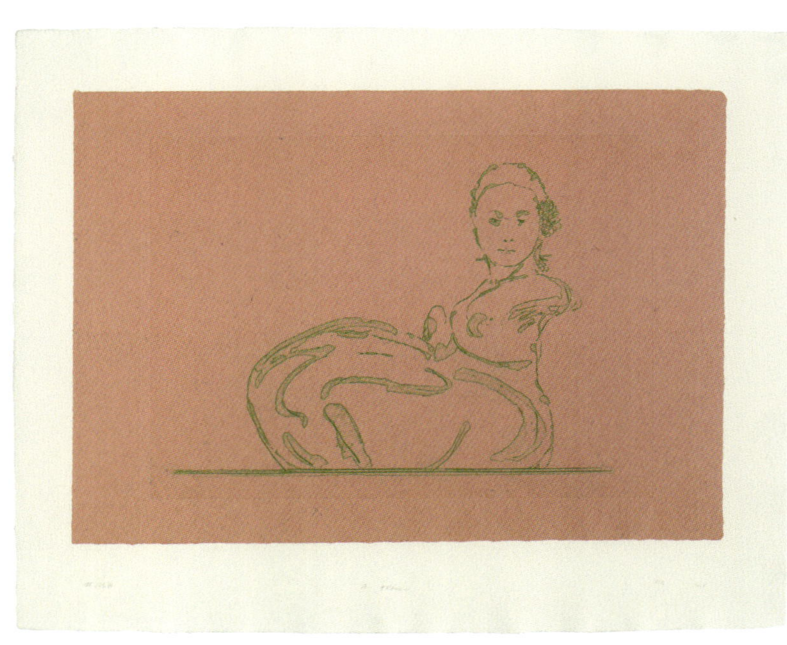
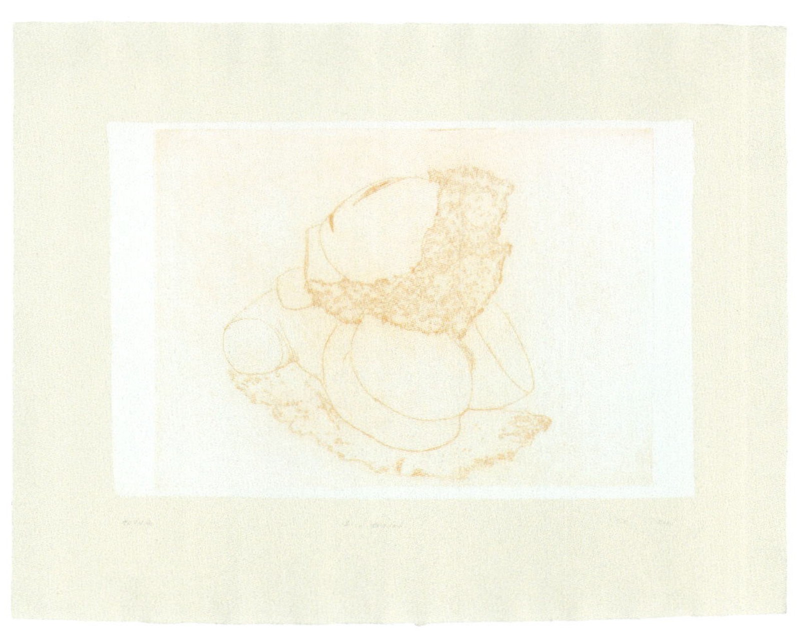

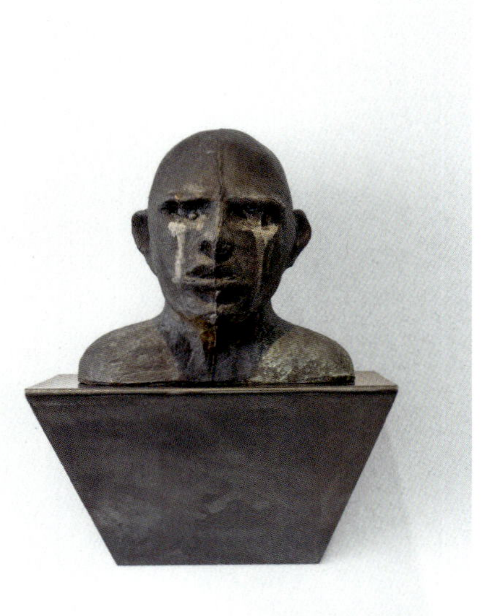

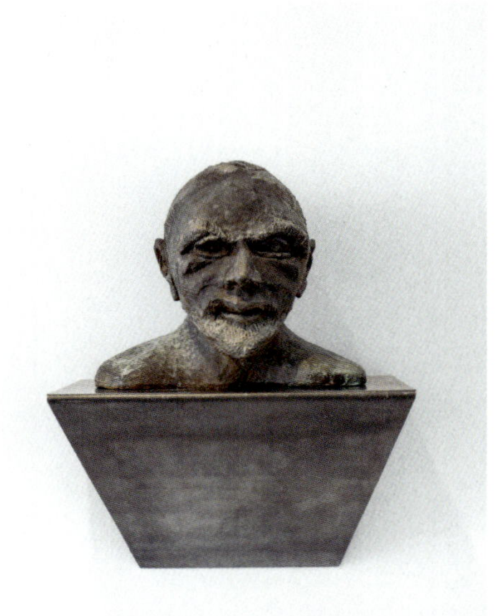

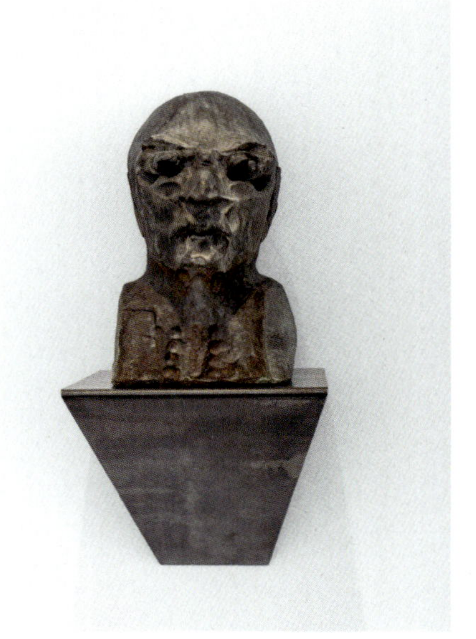

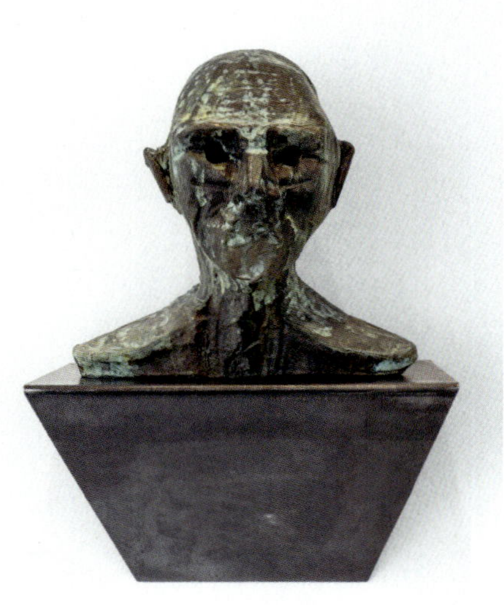

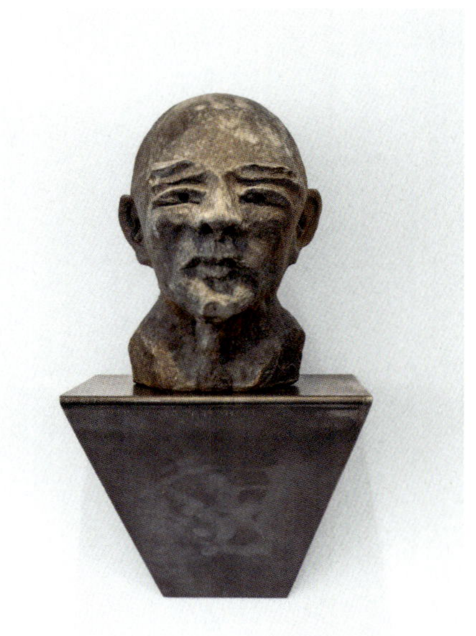

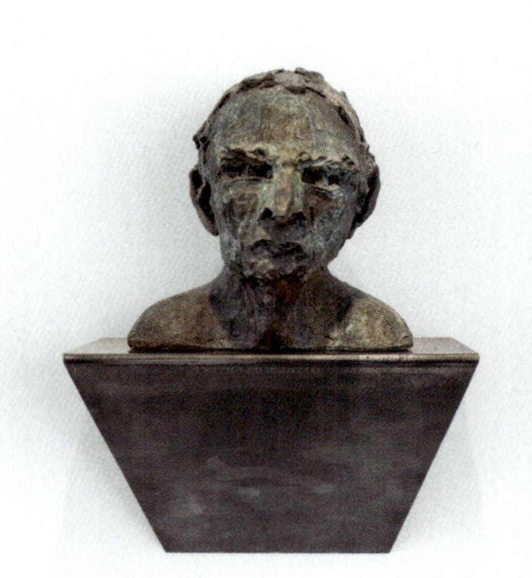

73
Wichte (*Jerks*). 2006. Twelve patinated bronzes on steel shelves, bronzes: each approx. 13 ¾ × 13 ¾ × 11 ¹³⁄₁₆" (35 × 35 × 30 cm), shelves: two sizes, 11 ¹³⁄₁₆ × 13 ¾ × 12 ⅝" (30 × 35 × 32 cm) and 11 ¹³⁄₁₆ × 19 ¹¹⁄₁₆ × 12 ⅝" (30 × 50 × 32 cm). Edition of 6

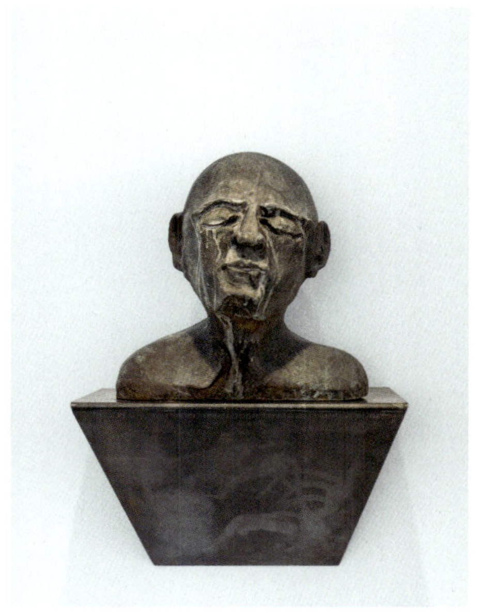

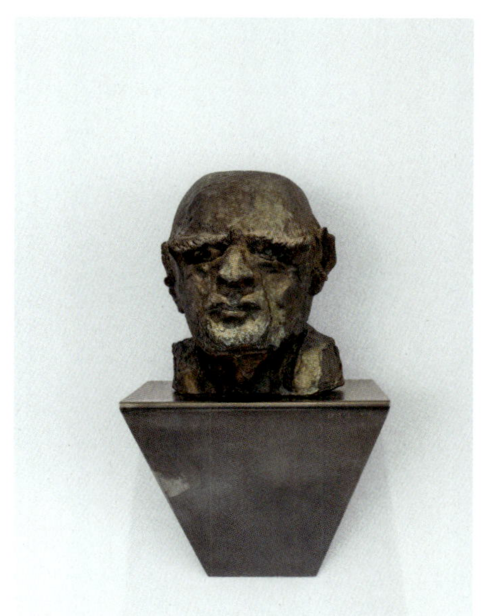

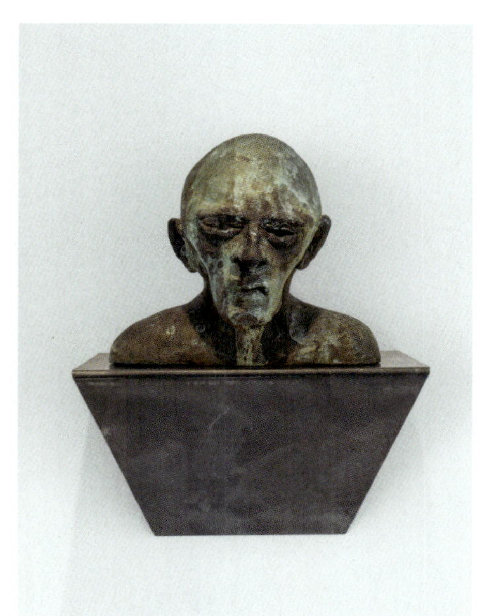

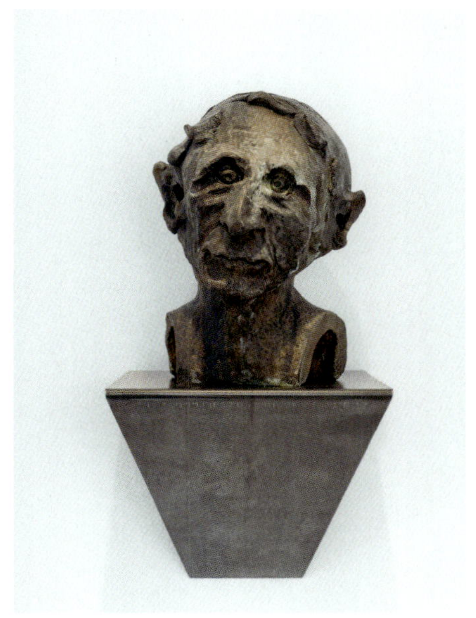

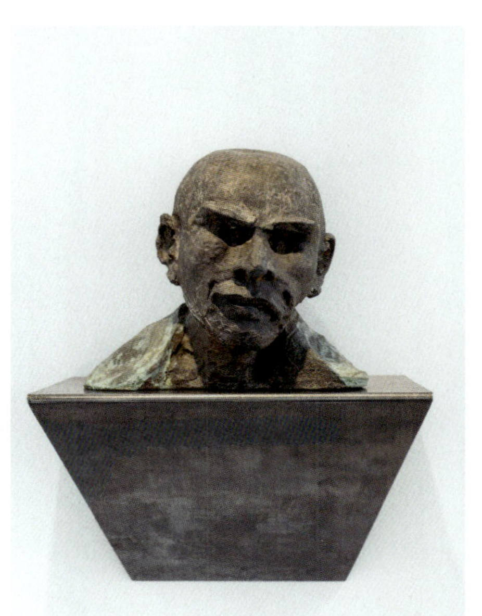

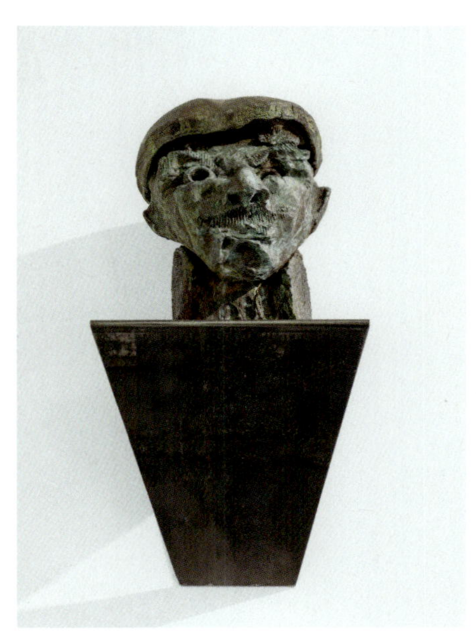

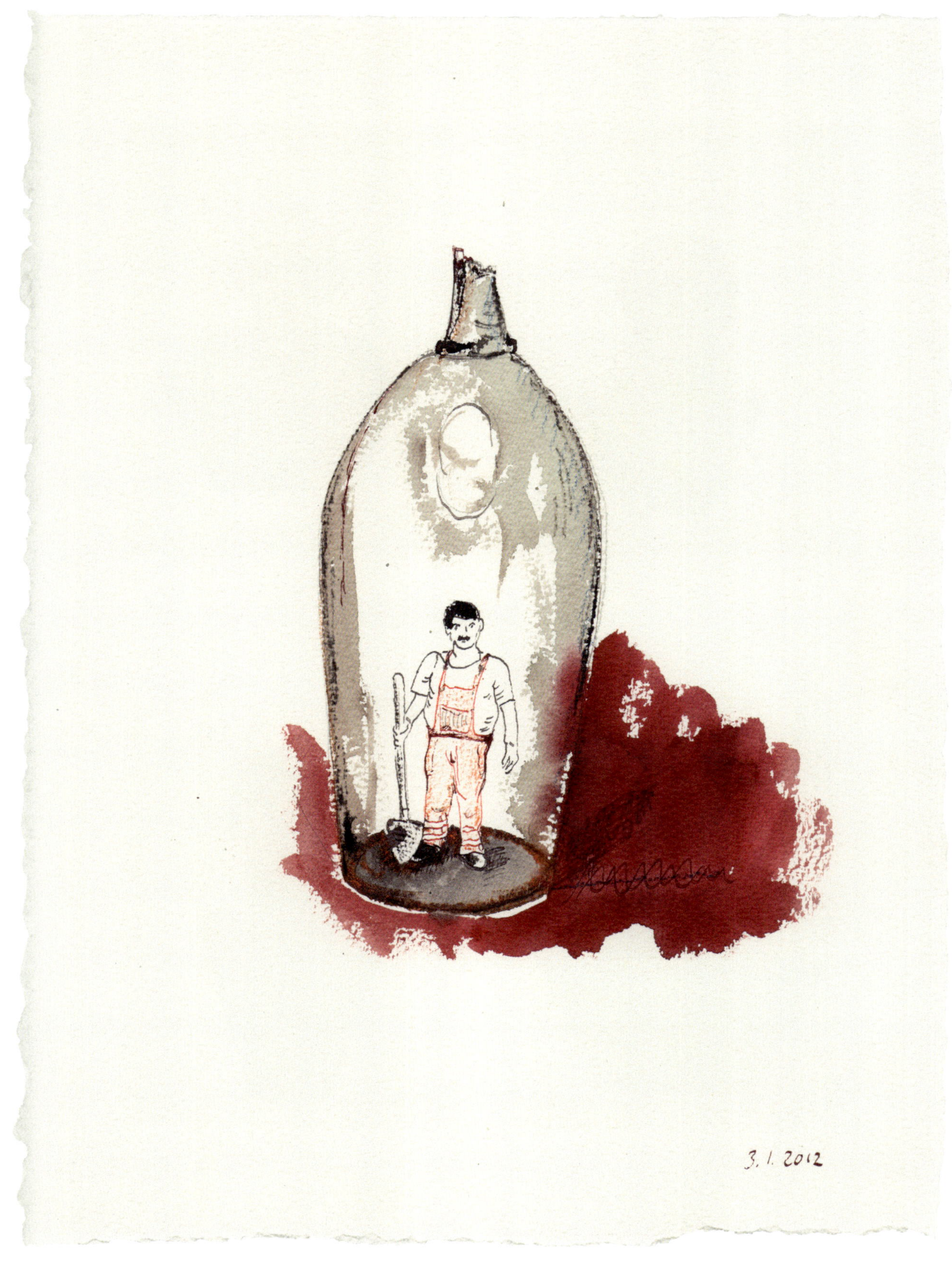

74
Untitled from *Walser Drawings*. 2012. Watercolor, ink, and crayon on paper, 14 15/16 × 11" (38 × 28 cm)

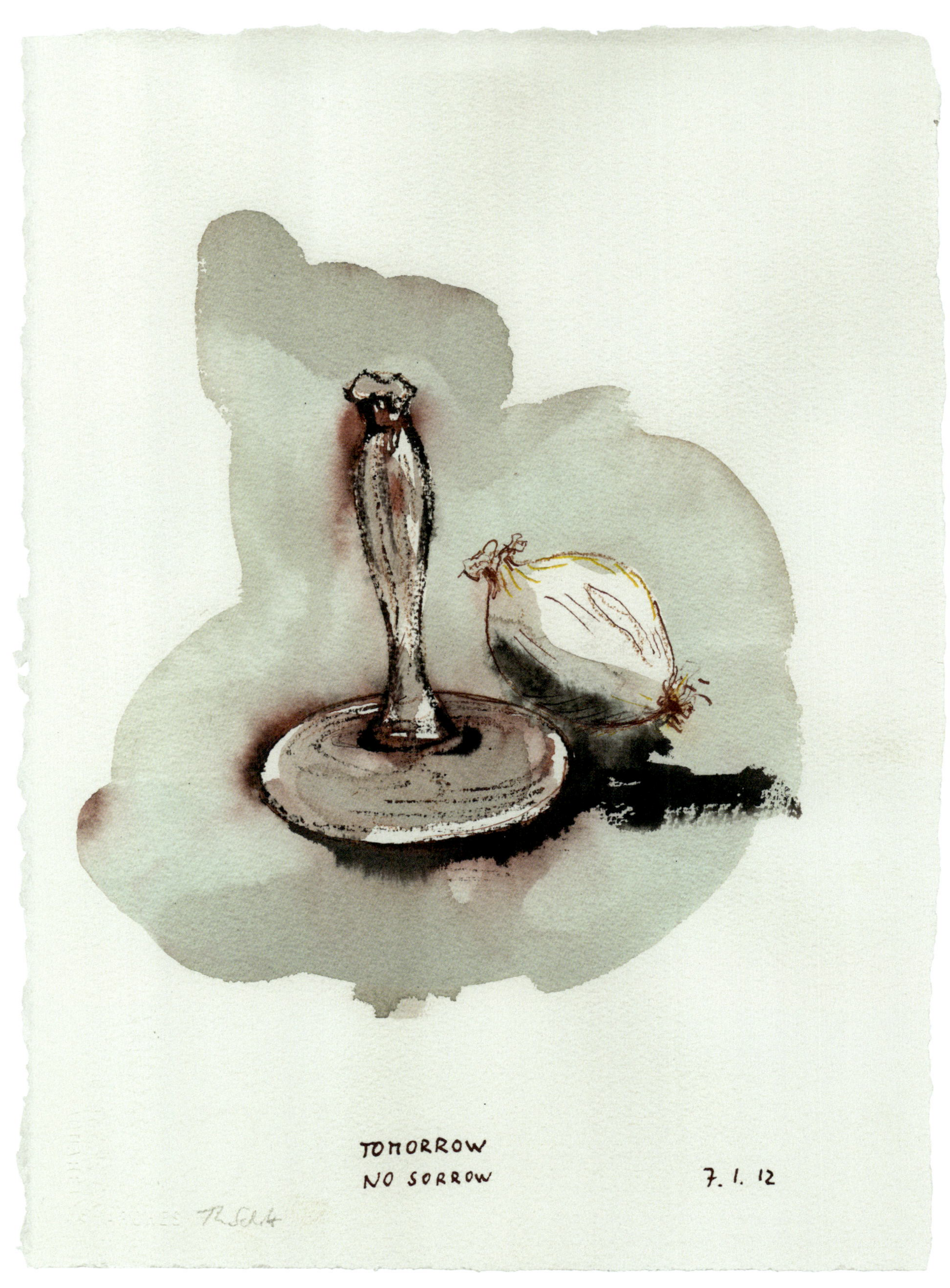

75
Tomorrow No Sorrow from *Walser Drawings*. 2012.
Watercolor, ink, and crayon on paper, 14 15⁄16 × 11" (38 × 28 cm)

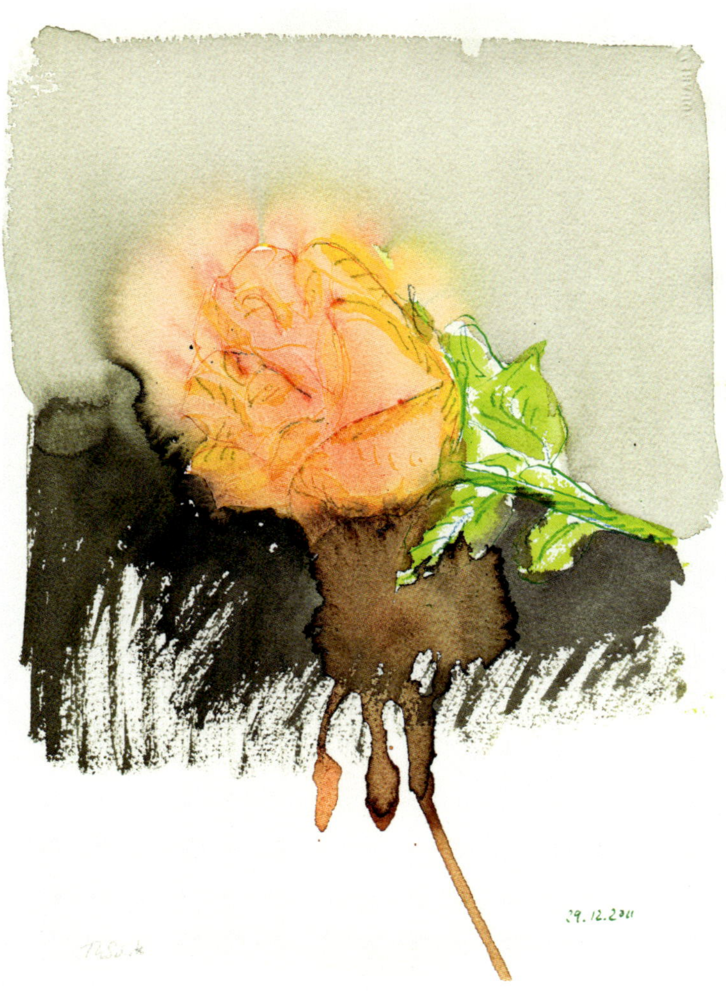

76

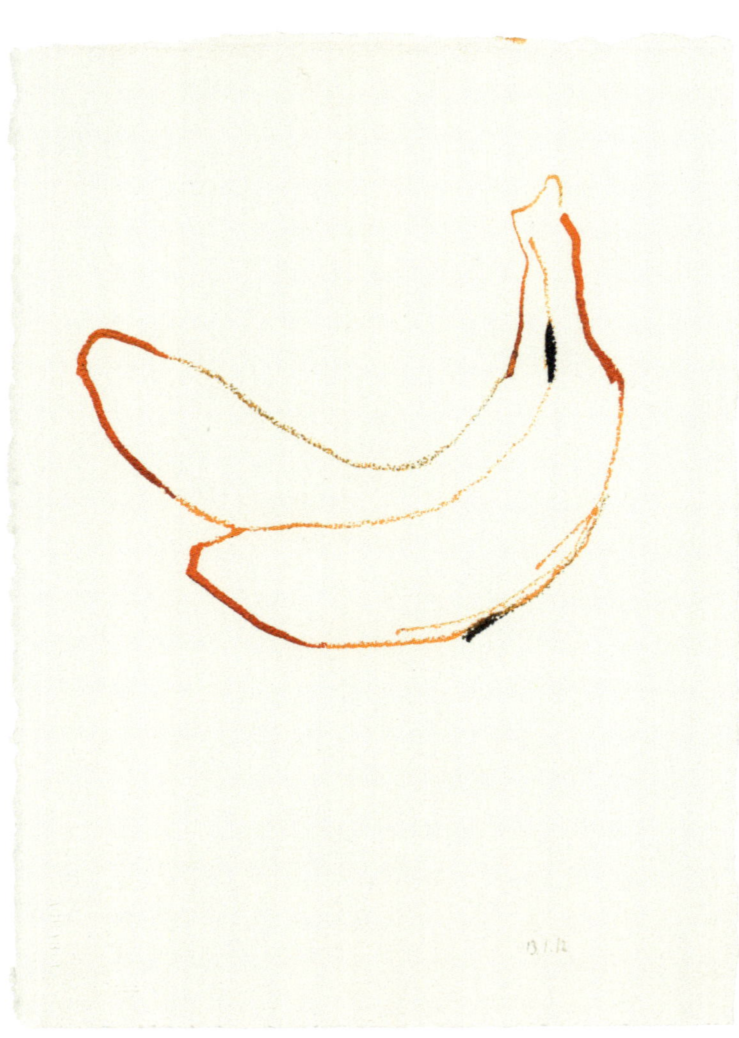

79

76
Untitled from *Walser Drawings*. 2011. Watercolor, ink, and crayon on paper, 14 15⁄16 × 11" (38 × 28 cm)

77
Good Loock from *Walser Drawings*. 2011. Watercolor, ink, and crayon on paper, 14 15⁄16 × 11" (38 × 28 cm)

78
Untitled from *Walser Drawings*. 2011. Watercolor, ink, and crayon on paper, 14 15⁄16 × 11" (38 × 28 cm)

79
Untitled from *Walser Drawings*. 2012. Ink on paper, 14 15⁄16 × 11" (38 × 28 cm)

80
two tomatoes in the dark from *Walser Drawings*. 2012. Watercolor and ink on paper, 14 15⁄16 × 11" (38 × 28 cm)

81
Memory = Gravety => from *Walser Drawings*. 2011. Watercolor, ink, and crayon on paper, 14 15⁄16 × 11" (38 × 28 cm)

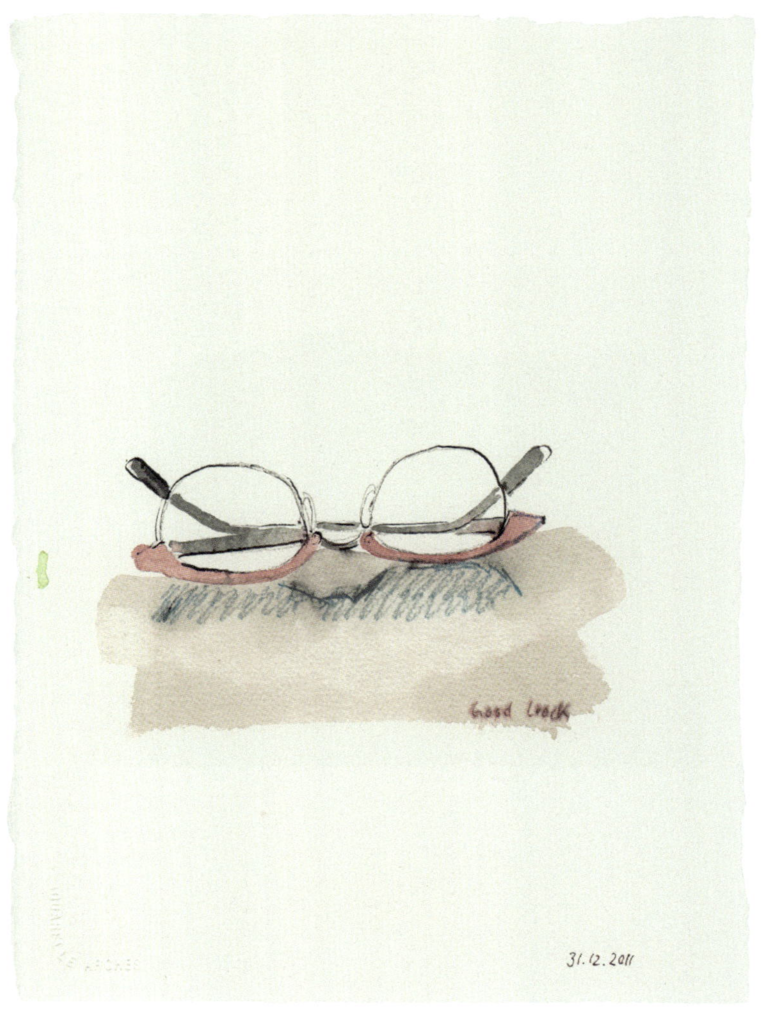

77

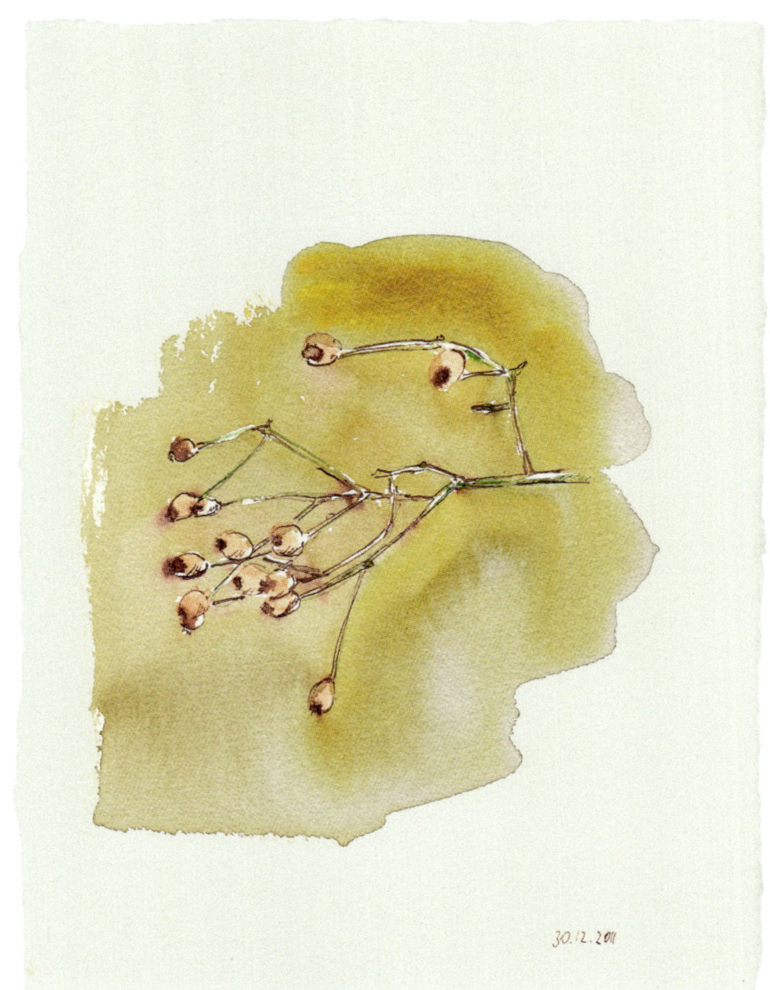

78

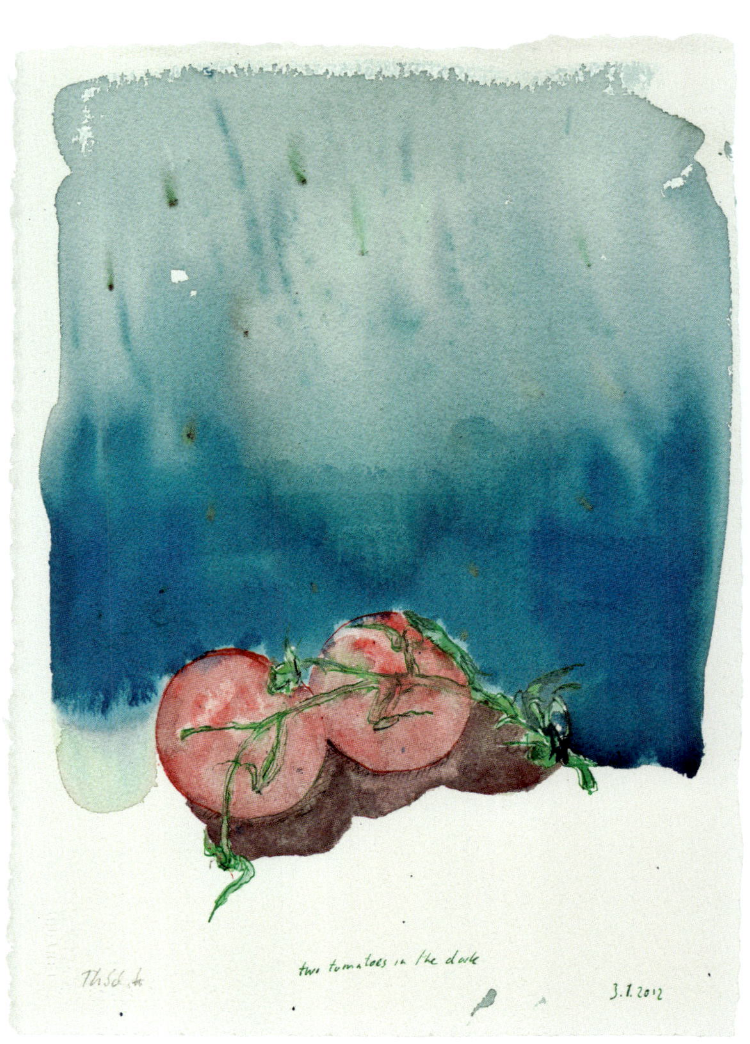

80

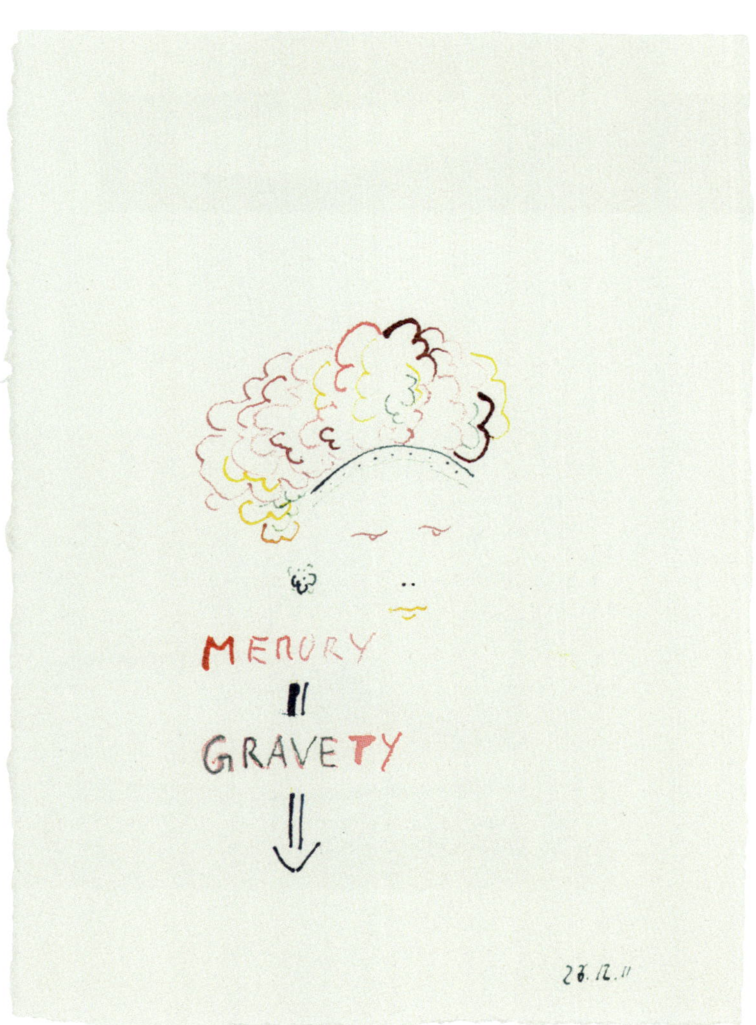

81

82
Ackermans Tempel III (Modell 1:10) (*Ackerman's Temple III [Model 1:10]*). 2011. Lego bricks, wood, and aluminum, 19 1/8 × 17 5/8 × 23 1/16" (48.5 × 44.8 × 58.5 cm)

83
Pommesbude (Modell 1:10) (*Chip Shop [Model 1:10]*). 2015. Wood, 17 5/16 × 18 1/2 × 27 3/16" (44 × 47 × 69 cm)

84
Modell für ein Museum (1:10) (*Model for a Museum [1:10]*). 2007. Wood, fiberboard, paint, and acrylic sheeting, 18 7/8 × 27 3/4 × 20 11/16" (48 × 70.5 × 52.5 cm)

85
Pringles. 2011. Potato chip on matchbox, 1 3/8 × 1 7/8 × 2 3/4" (3.5 × 4.8 × 7 cm)

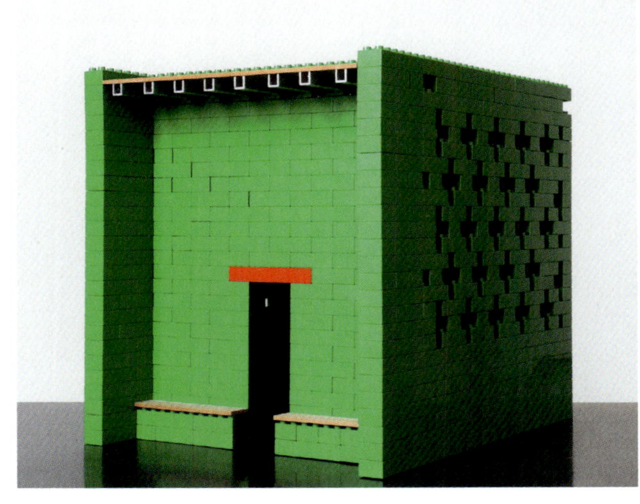

82

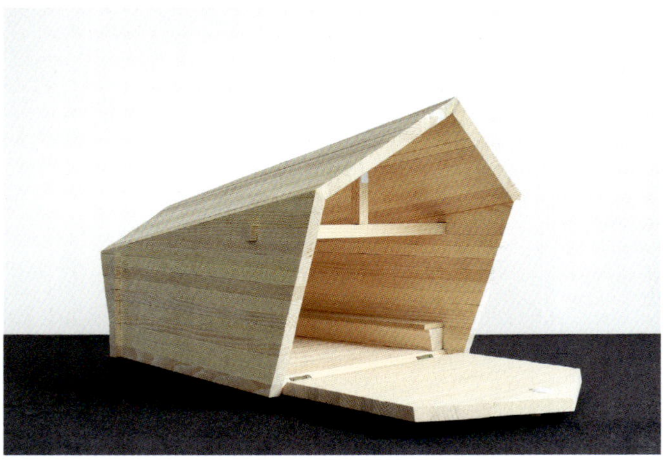

83

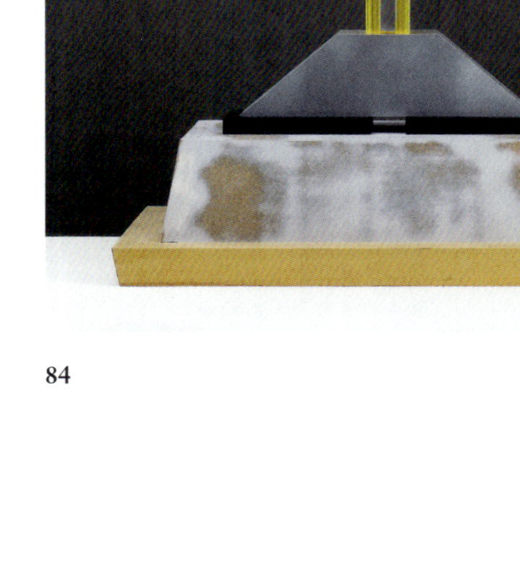

84

85

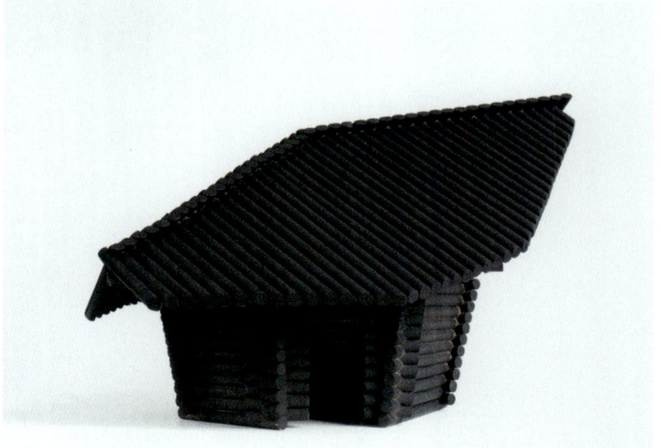

86

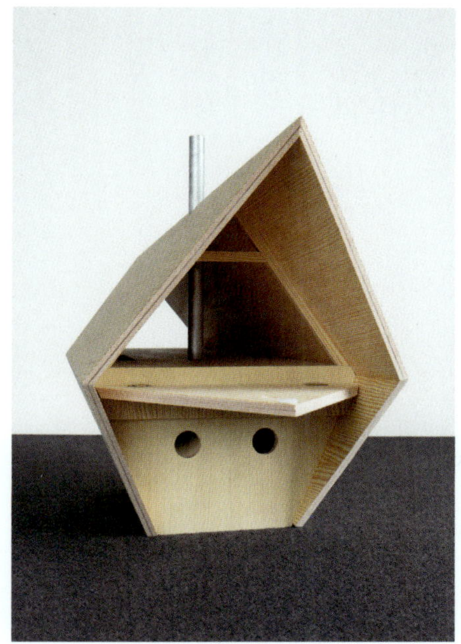

87

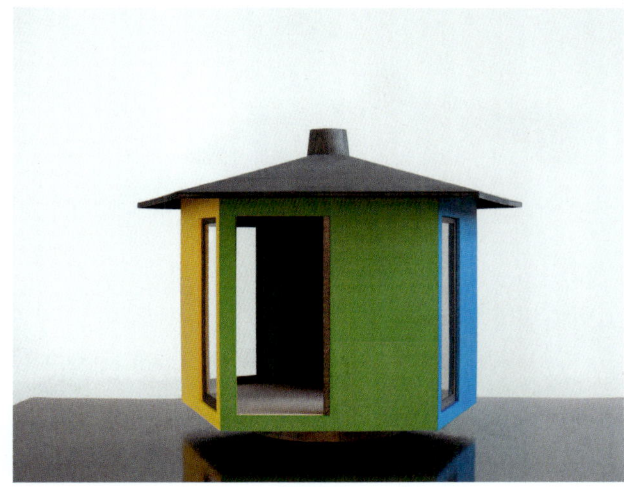

88

86
Blockhaus (Modell 1:15) (*Log House [Model 1:15]*). 2013. Spray paint on wood, 18 ⅛ × 26 ¾ × 22 ⁷⁄₁₆" (46 × 68 × 57 cm)

87
Eifelhütte (Modell 1:20) (*Eifel Hut [Model 1:20]*). 2015. Wood and aluminum, 18 ½ × 14 × 29 ⁵⁄₁₆" (47 × 35.5 × 74.5 cm)

88
Teehaus (Modell 1:10) (*Tea House [Model 1:10]*). 2012/2013. Paint on wood with acrylic sheeting, 14 × 14 ³⁄₁₆ × 14 ³⁄₁₆" (35.5 × 36 × 36 cm)

89
Ferienhaus für Terroristen (Modell 1:20) (*Vacation Home for Terrorists [Model 1:20]*). 2007. Steel and acrylic sheeting, 9 ¾ × 35 ⁷⁄₁₆ × 17 ¹¹⁄₁₆" (24.8 × 90 × 45 cm)

90
Krefeld Pavillon (Modell 1:25) (*Krefeld Pavilion [Model 1:25]*). 2016. Copper, fiberboard, and wood, 14 ⁹⁄₁₆ × 31 ½ × 31 ½" (37 × 80 × 80 cm)

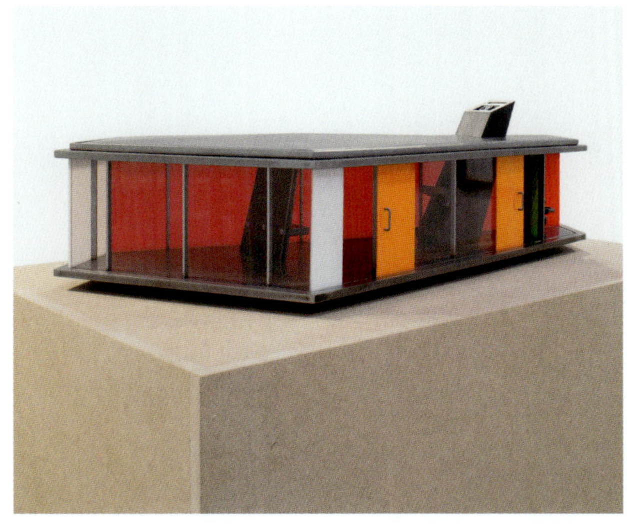

89

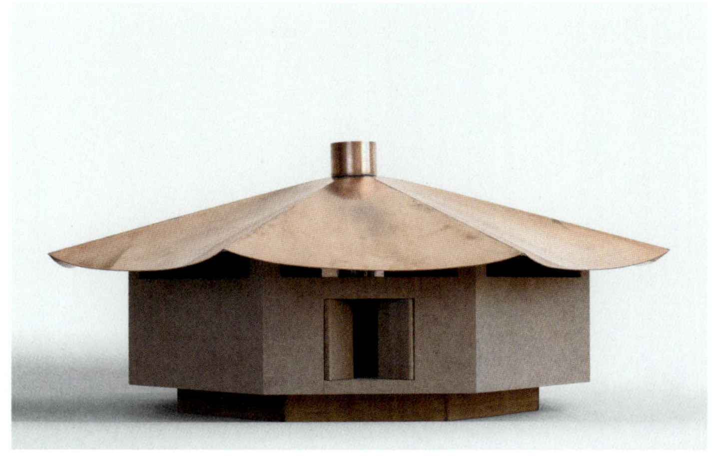

90

91
Vater Staat (*Father State*). 2010. Patinated bronze, 12' 5 ⅝" × 5' 1" × 4' 7" (380 × 155 × 139.7 cm). Installation view, Art Institute of Chicago, 2011

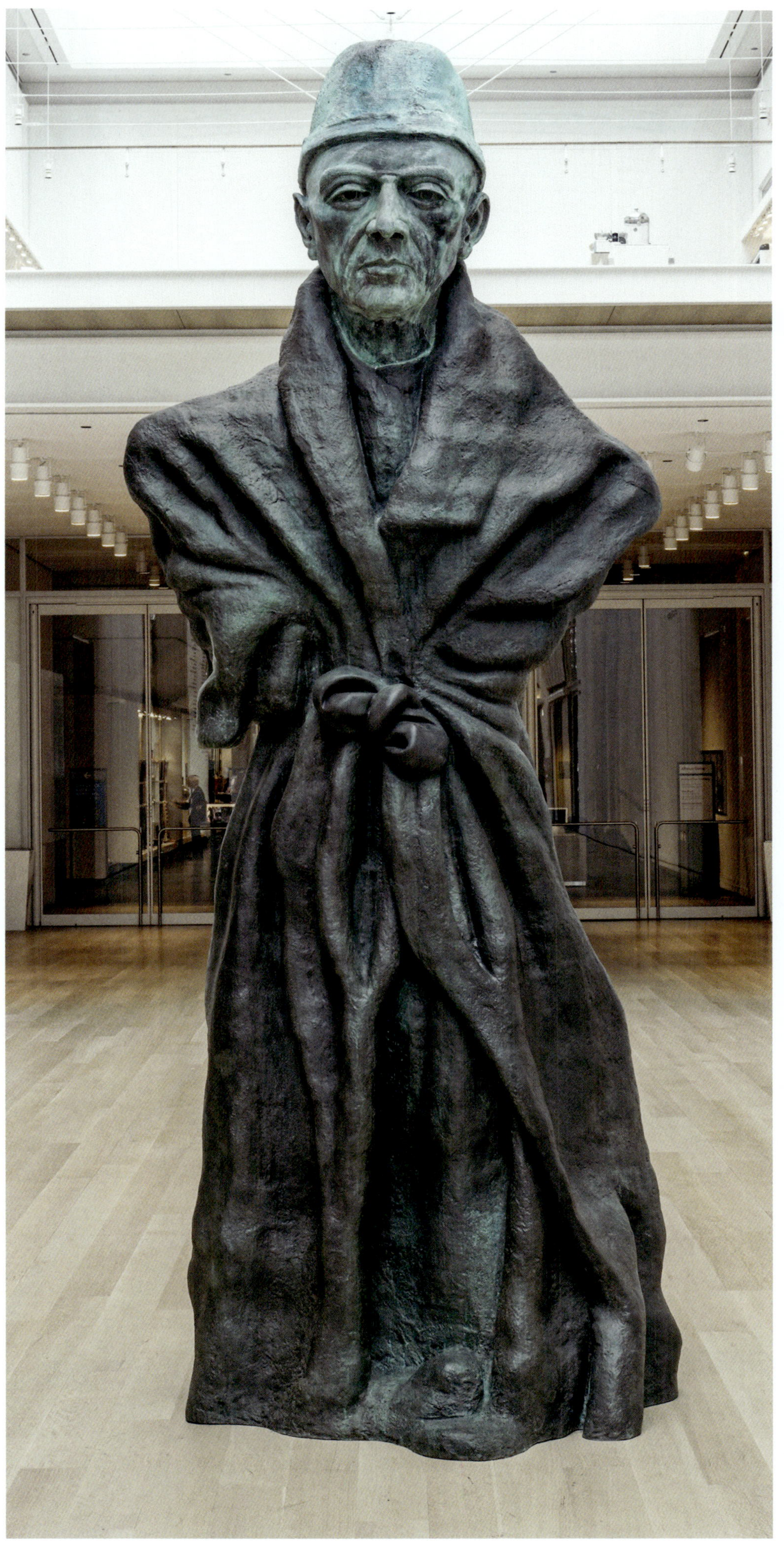

92
Mann im Matsch (Modell 1:10) (*Man in Mud [Model 1:10]*). 2009. Patinated bronze on steel pedestal, bronze: 23 5/8 × 14 3/16 × 11 7/16" (60 × 36 × 29 cm), pedestal: 47 1/4 × 17 11/16 × 14 3/16" (120 × 45 × 36 cm). Artist's proof, edition of 6 with 4 APs

Below:
Installation view, *Skulpturen* (*Sculptures*), Skulpturenhalle, Neuss, Germany, January 13–July 30, 2023

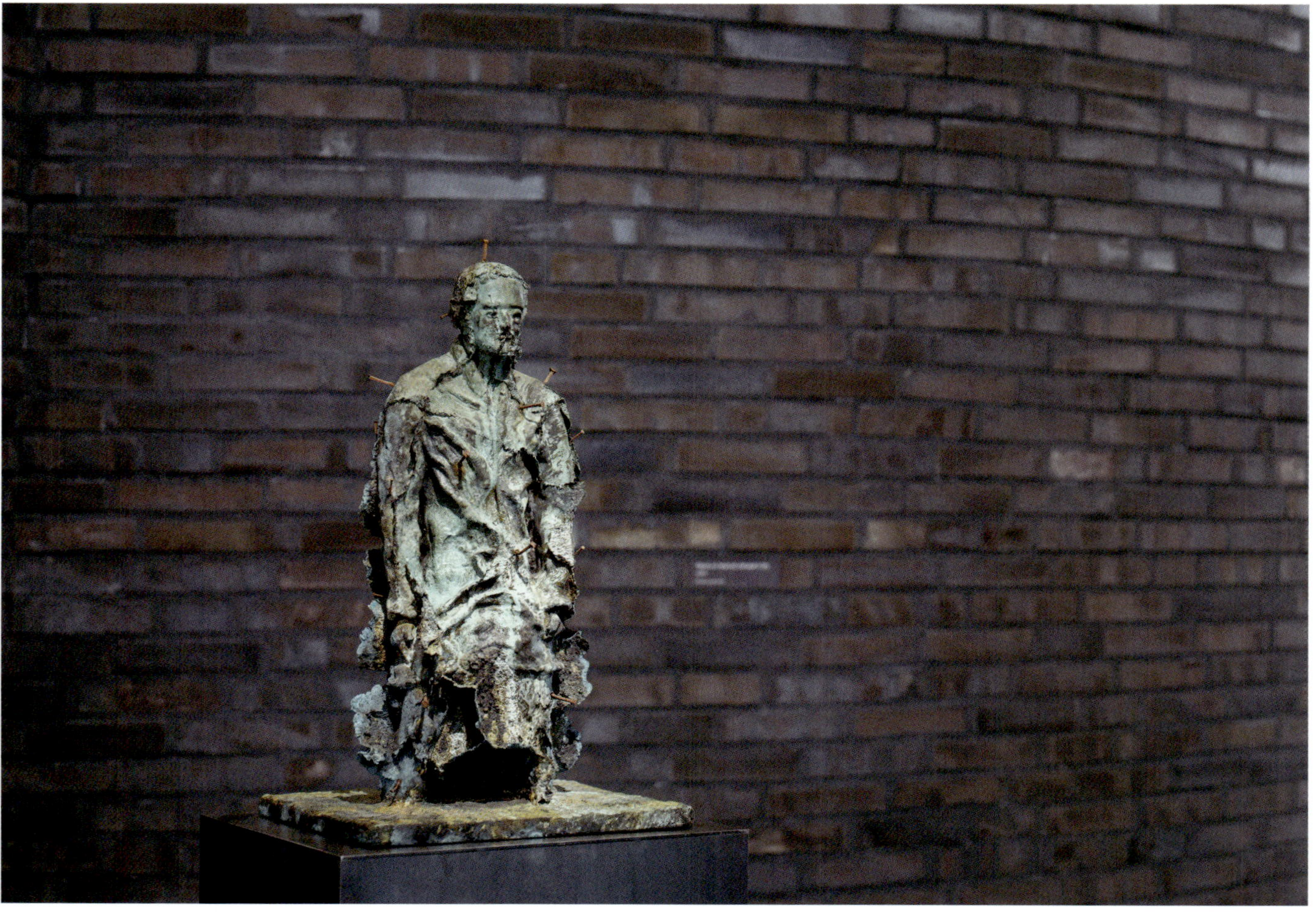

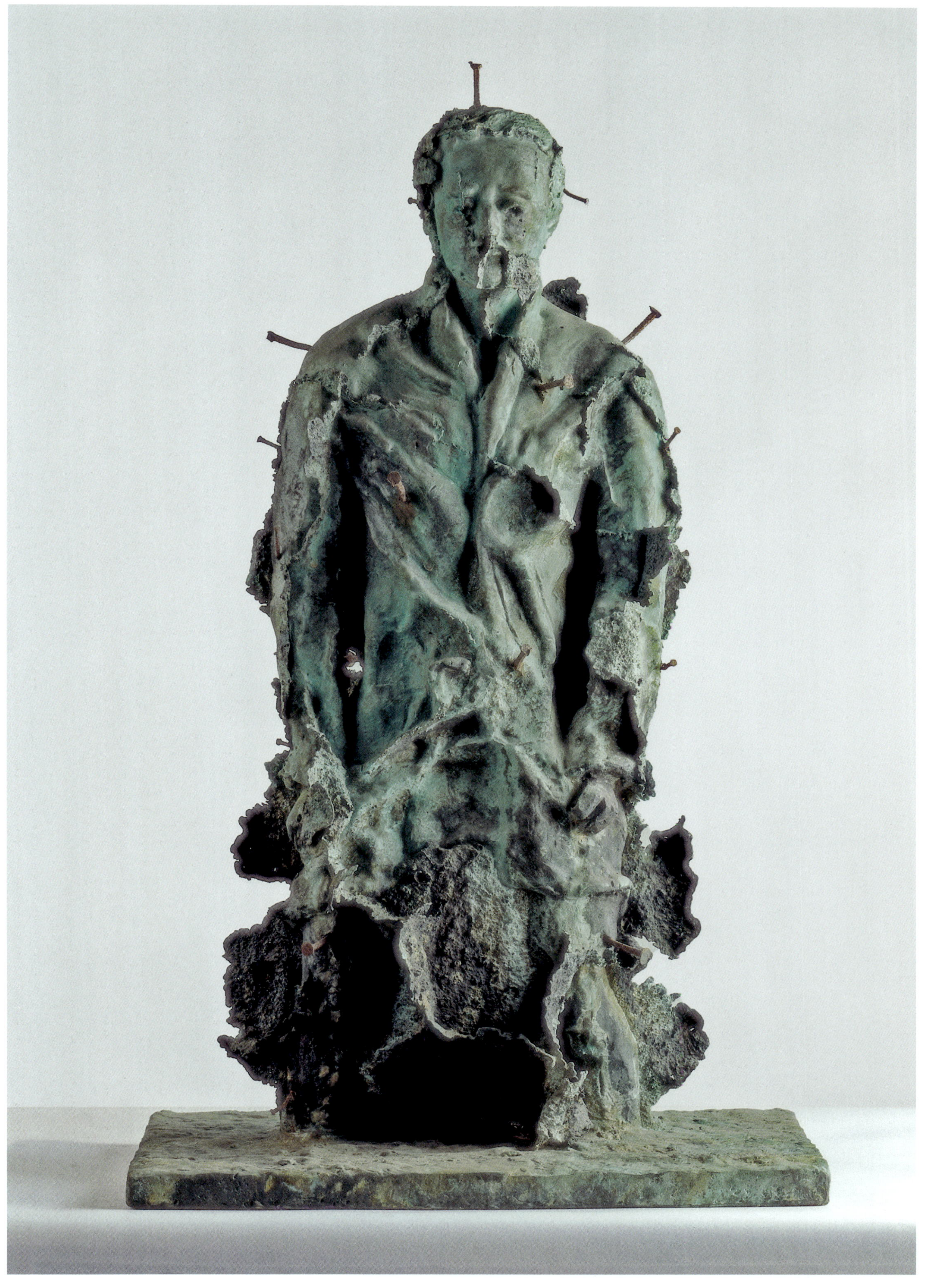

92

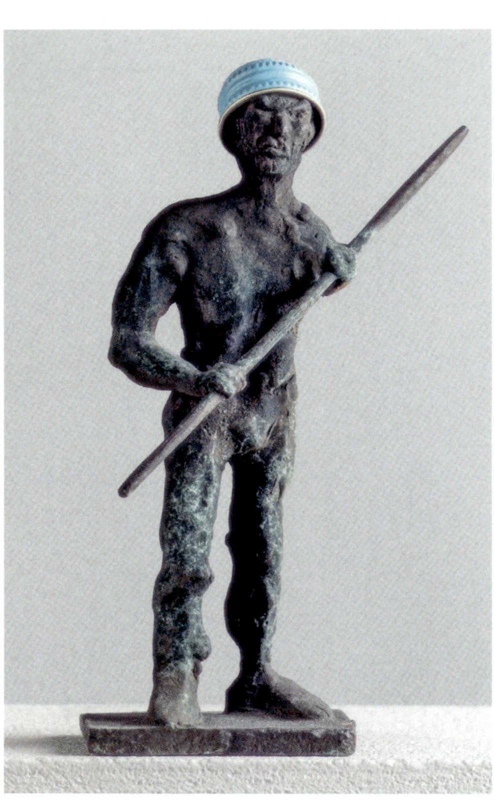

93
Krieger (*Warriors*). 2012. Charred wood with pigment and oil, two parts, 9' 11 ¼" × 4' 1 ½" × 3' 9 ⅛" (302.9 × 125.7 × 114.6 cm) and 9' 9 ½" × 4' 1 ½" × 3' 9 ⅛" (298.5 × 125.7 × 114.6 cm)

Above:
Krieger (*Warrior*). 1994. Patinated bronze, 7 ½ × 4 ¾ × 4 5/16" (19 × 12 × 11 cm). Collection the artist, Düsseldorf

93

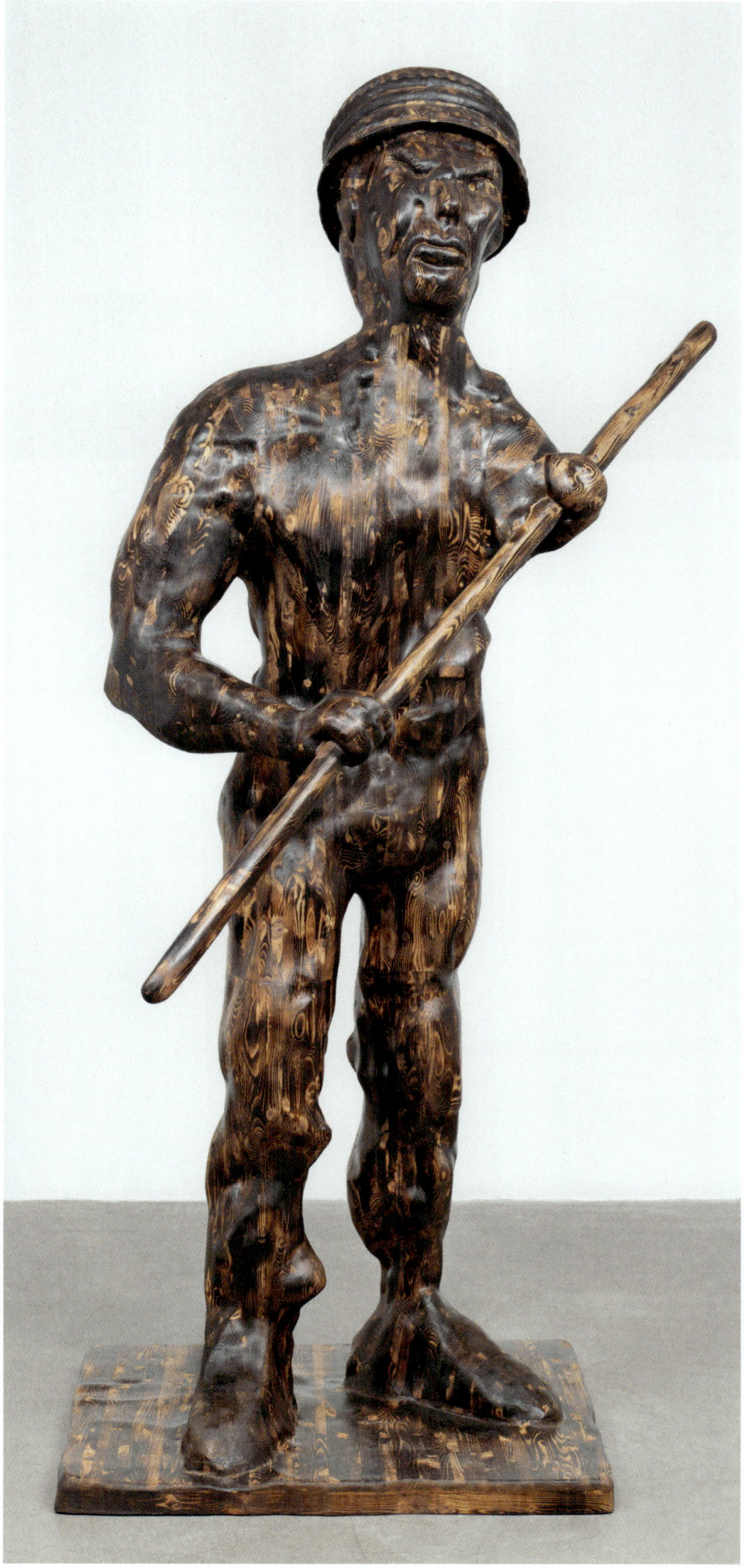

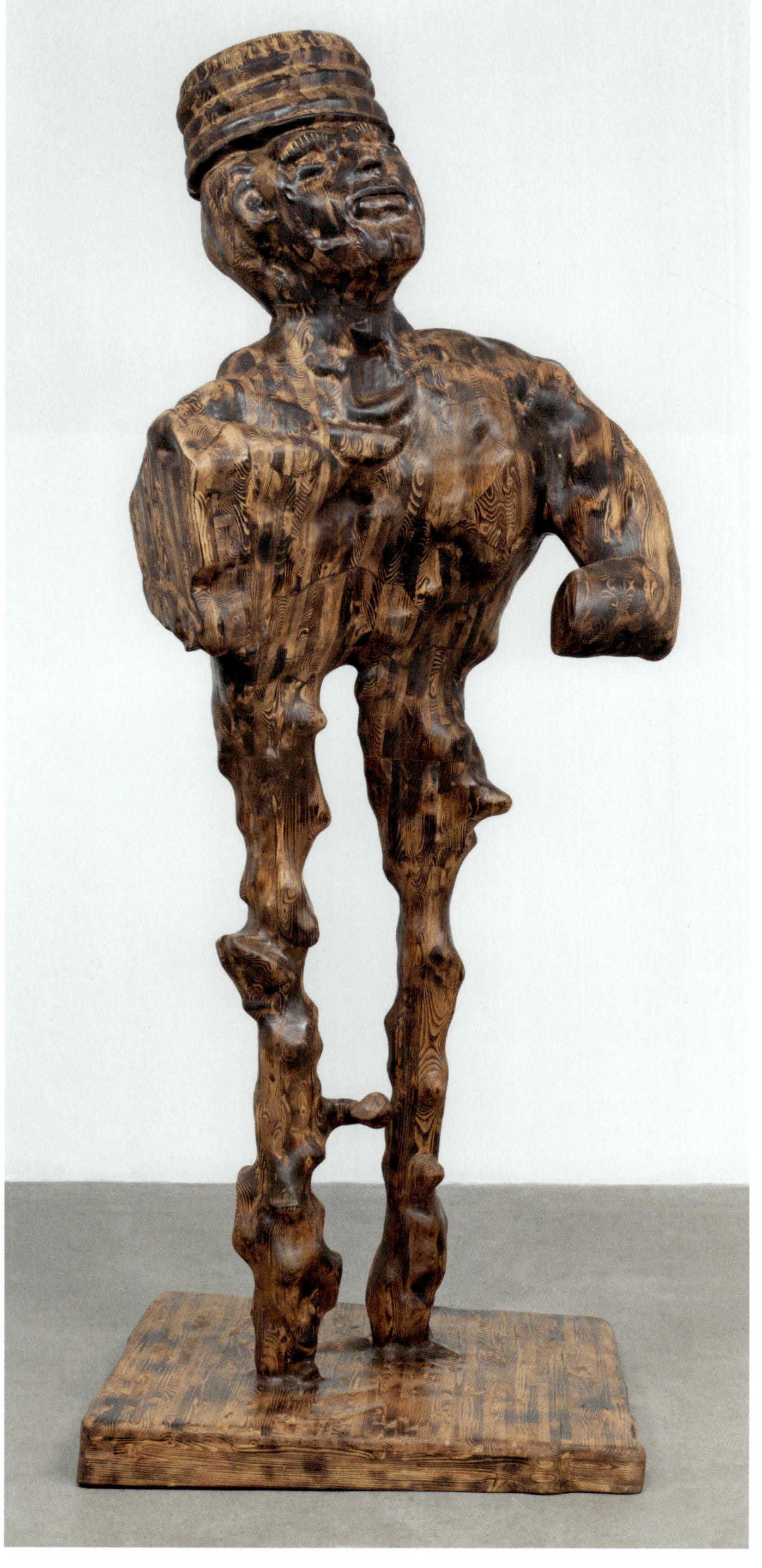

94
Fake Flag H. 2018. Glazed ceramic, three parts,
3' 1 ¾" × 6' 9 ½" × 1 ½" (95.9 × 207 × 3.8 cm)

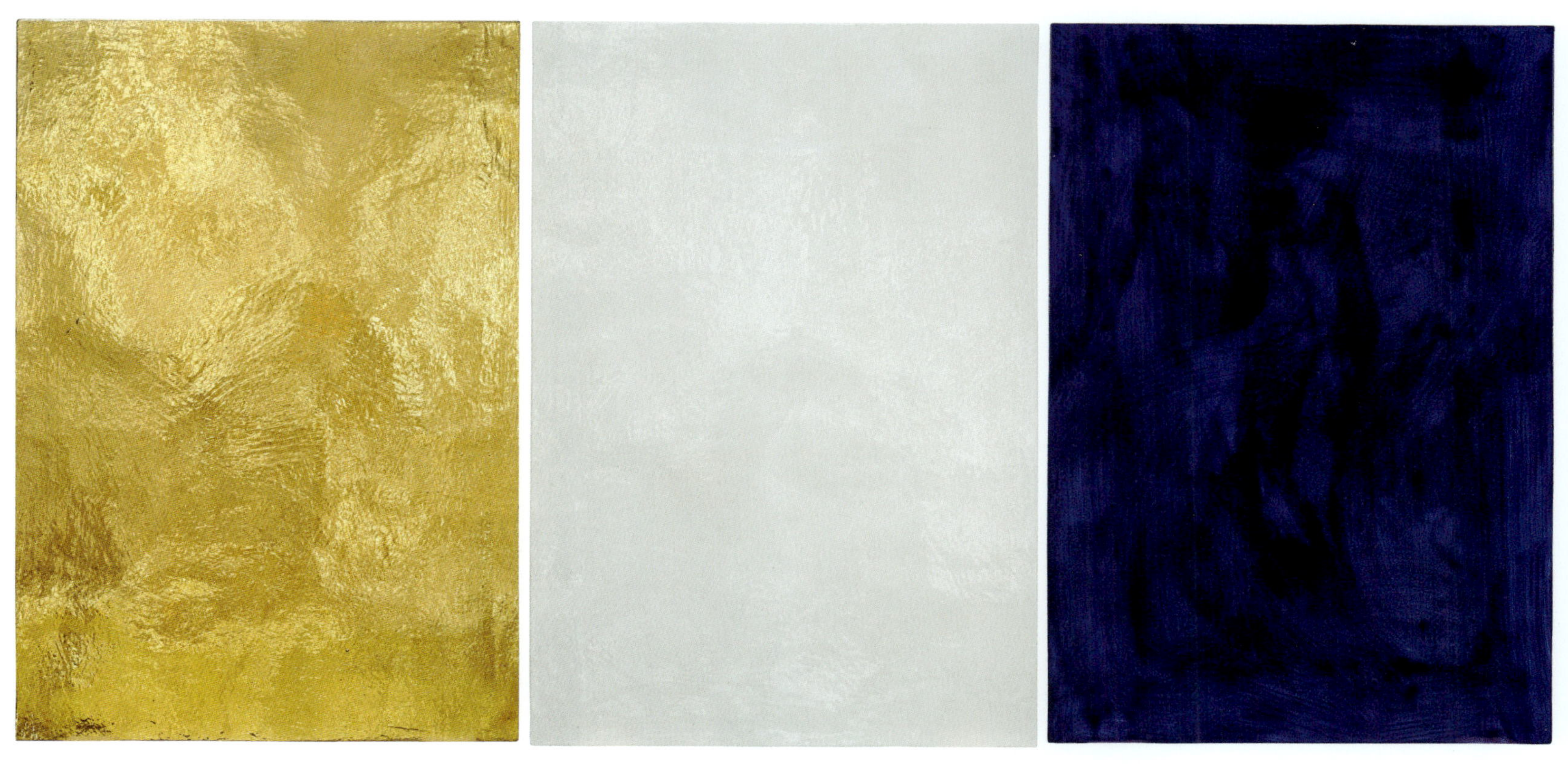

95
Fake Flag I. 2018. Glazed ceramic, three parts,
3' 1 13/16" × 6' 9 1/2" × 1 9/16" (96 × 207 × 4 cm)

96
Old Friend Revisited No. 18. 2021. Glazed ceramic on steel pedestal, ceramic: 18 ½ × 14 9⁄16 × 13 3⁄16" (47 × 37 × 33.5 cm), pedestal: 47 ¼ × 17 11⁄16 × 17 11⁄16" (120 × 45 × 45 cm)

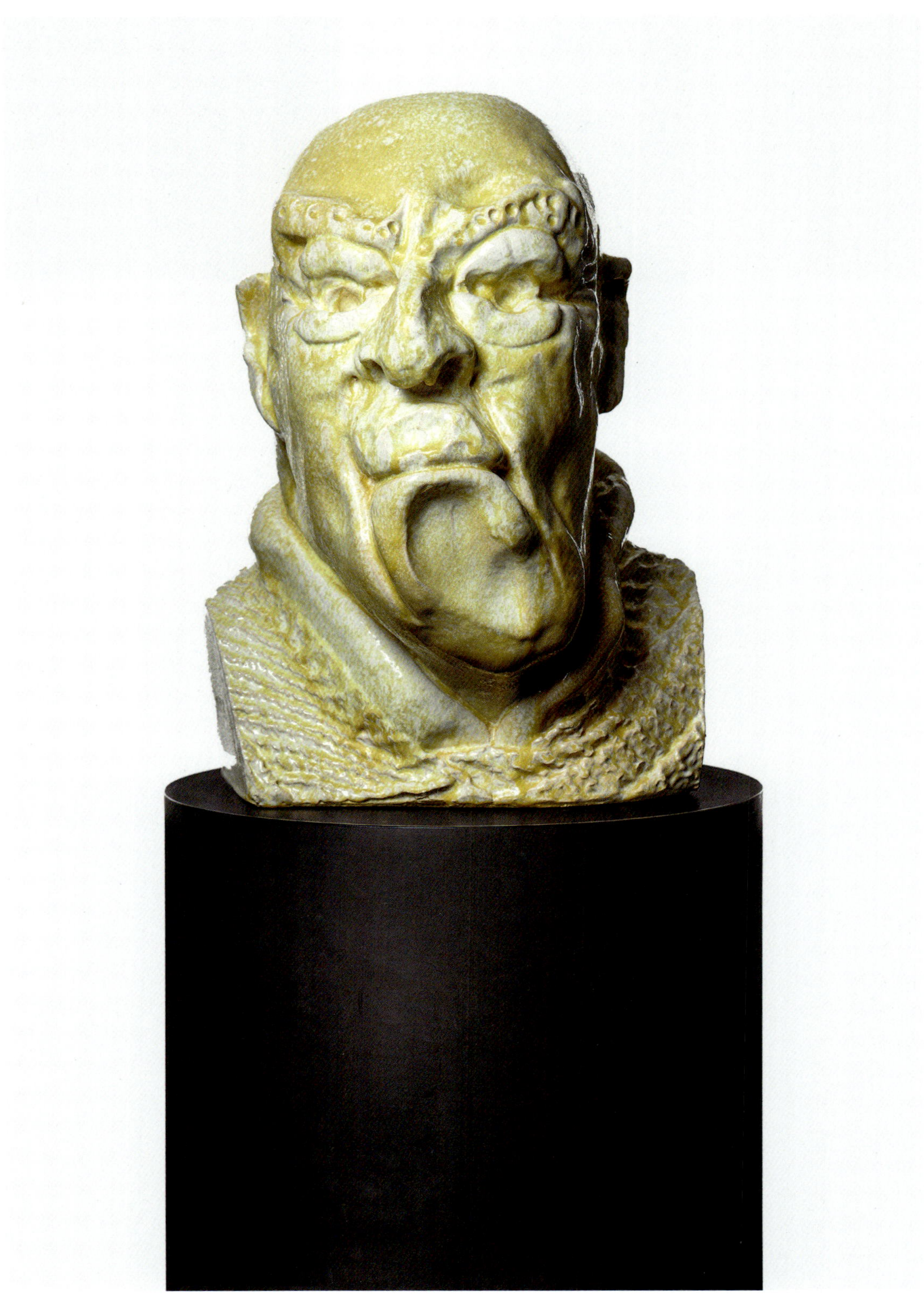

97
Old Friend Revisited No. 27. 2021. Glazed ceramic on steel pedestal, ceramic: 19 11⁄16 × 12 3⁄16 × 13 3⁄8" (50 × 31 × 34 cm), pedestal: 47 1⁄4 × 17 11⁄16 × 17 11⁄16" (120 × 45 × 45 cm)

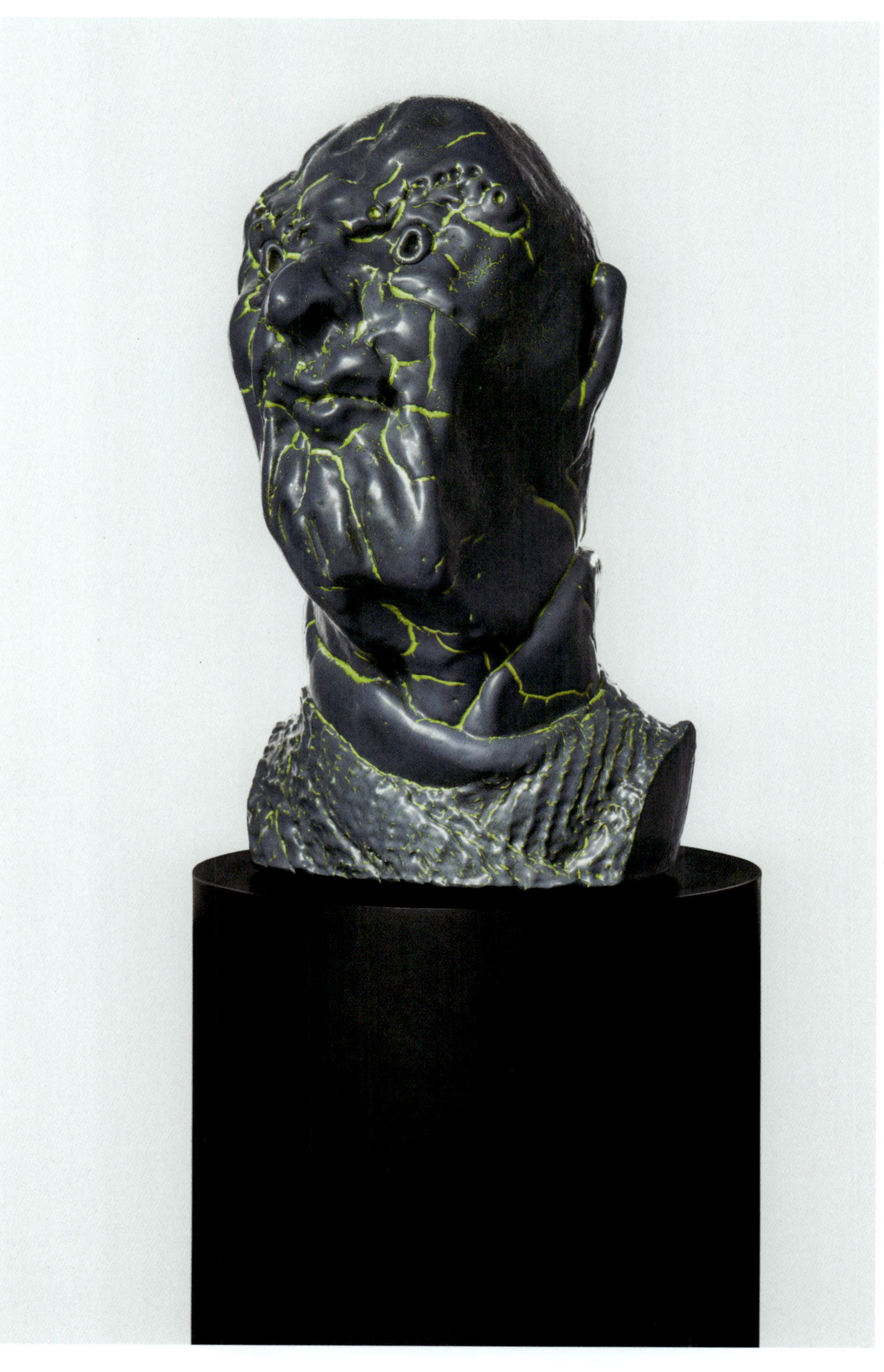

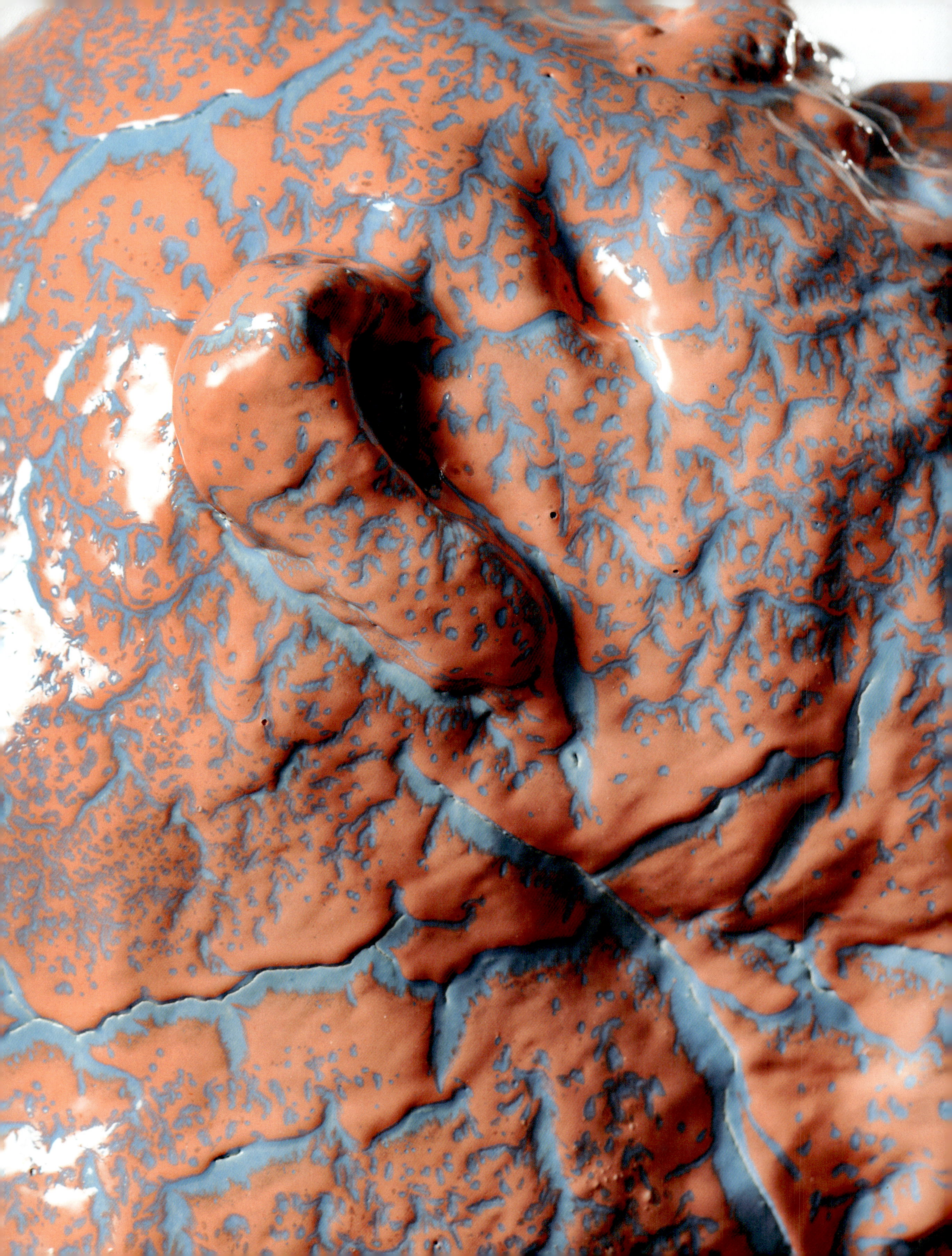

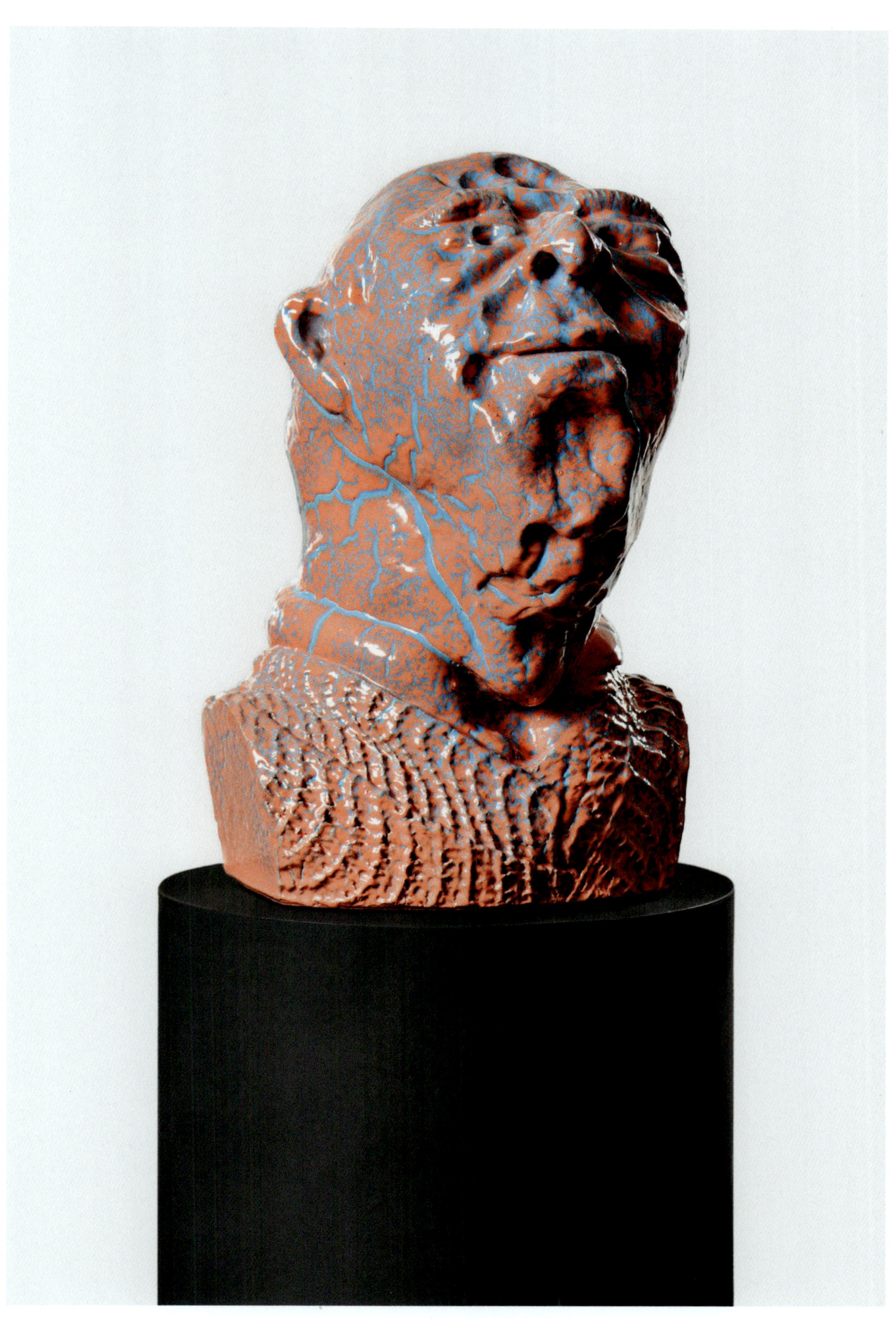

98

98
Old Friend Revisited No. 8. 2021. Glazed ceramic on steel pedestal, ceramic: 18 ⅛ × 12 ⅝ × 15 ¹⁵⁄₁₆" (46 × 32 × 40.5 cm), pedestal: 47 ¼ × 17 ¹¹⁄₁₆ × 17 ¹¹⁄₁₆" (120 × 45 × 45 cm)

Left:
Detail of *Old Friend Revisited No. 8*

99
Frauenkopf (*Woman's Head*). 2020. Glazed ceramic on steel pedestal, ceramic: 22 13⁄16 × 13 3⁄8 × 19 5⁄16" (58 × 34 × 49 cm), pedestal: 47 1⁄4 × 15 3⁄4 × 23 5⁄8" (120 × 40 × 60 cm)

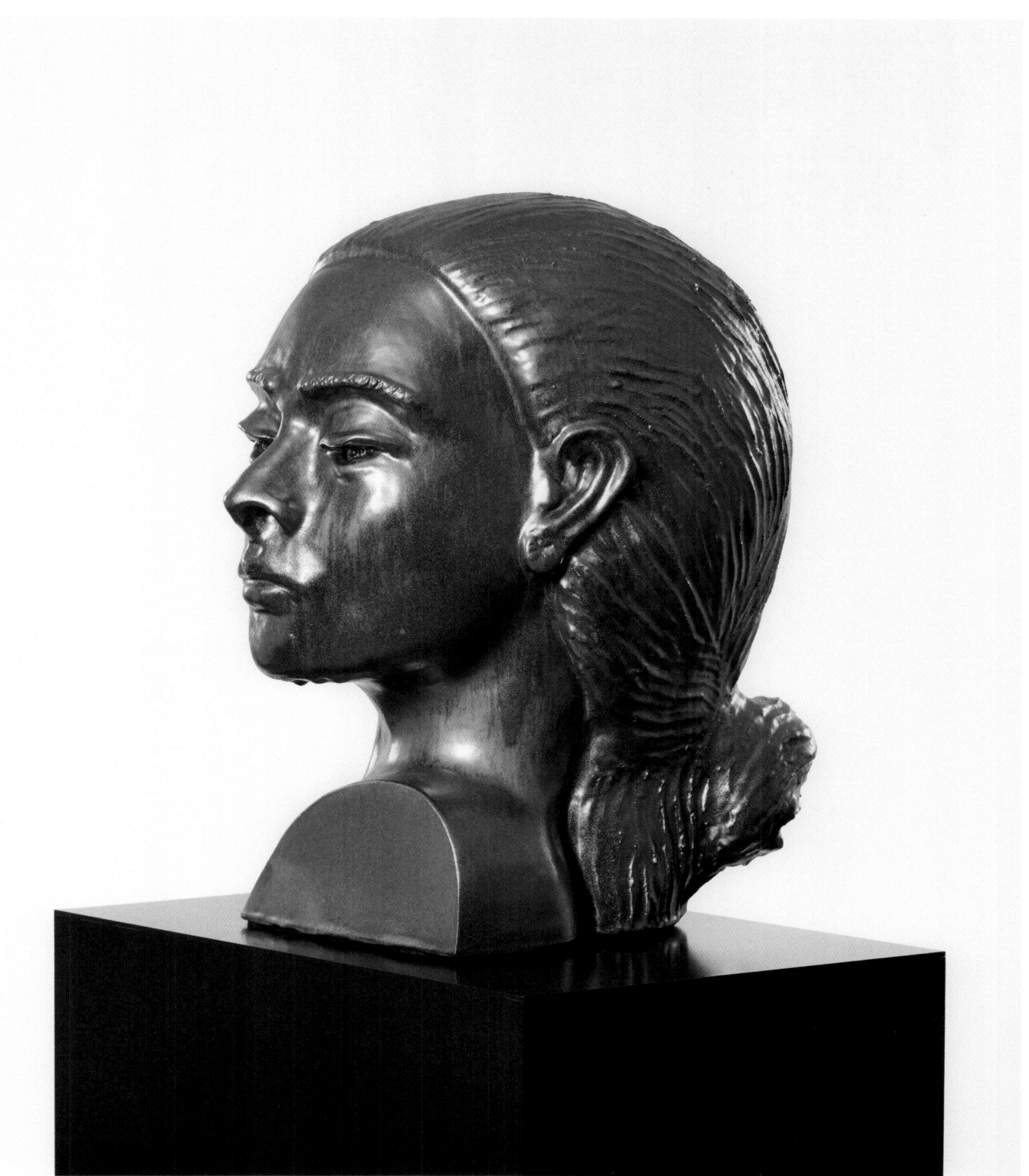

100
Frauenkopf (implodiert) (*Woman's Head [Imploded]*). 2020. Glazed ceramic and steel on steel pedestal, ceramic: 12 ⅛ × 20 ½ × 22 ½" (30.8 × 52.1 × 57.2 cm), pedestal: 47 ¼ × 15 ¾ × 23 ⅝" (120 × 40 × 60 cm)

Below:
Frauenkopf (*Woman's Head*). 2020. Glazed ceramic on steel pedestal, ceramic: 22 ⅜ × 14 3/16 × 18 5/16" (56.8 × 36 × 46.5 cm), pedestal: 47 ¼ × 15 ¾ × 23 ⅝" (120 × 40 × 60 cm). Collection Lonti Ebers, New York

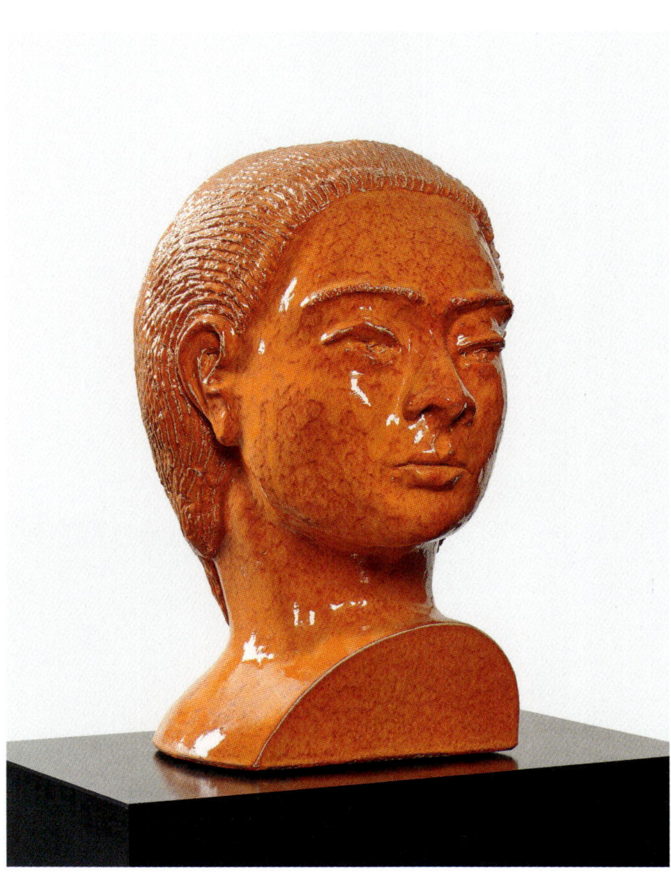

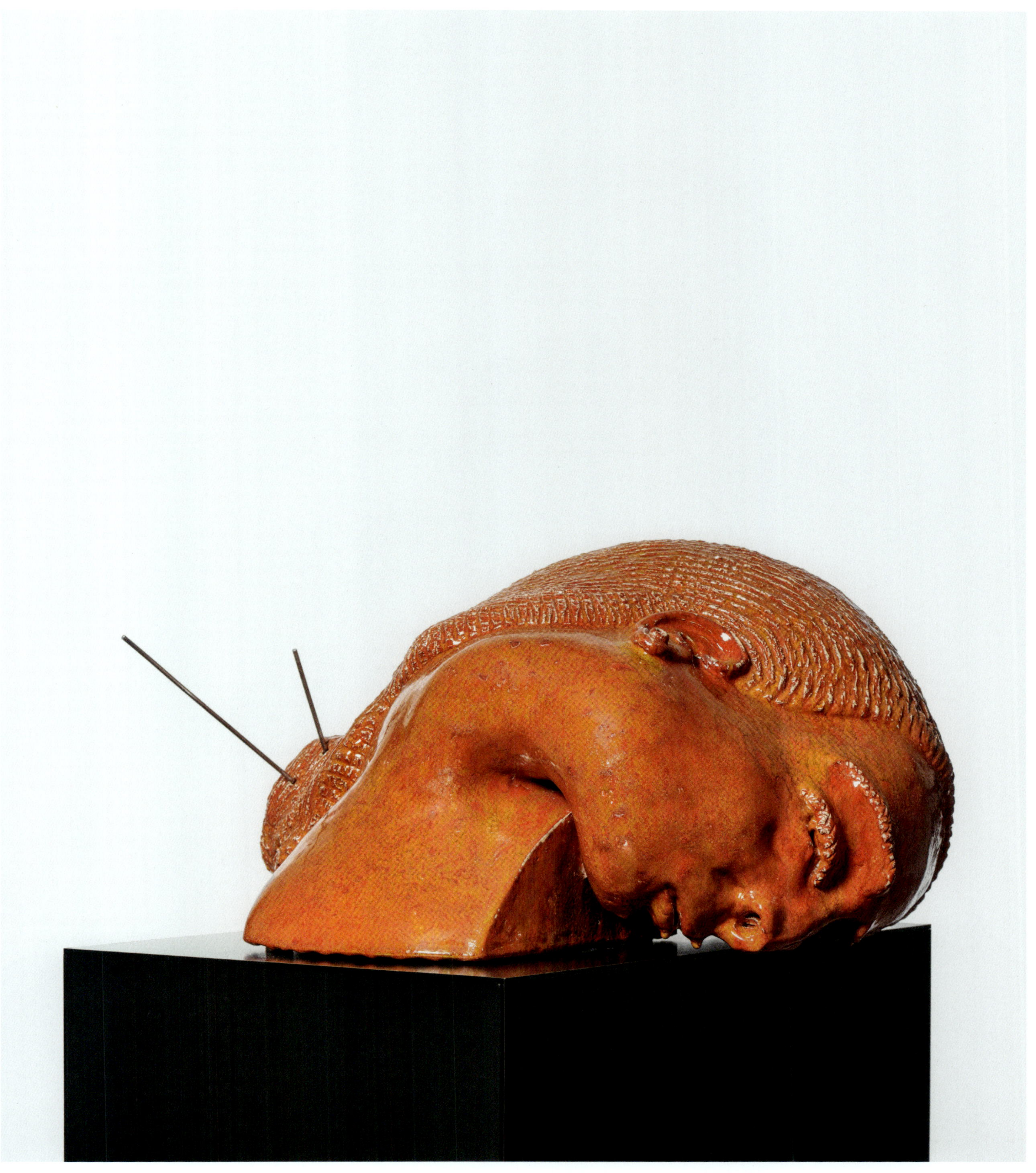

100

Chronology

Caitlin Chaisson and Lydia Mullin

1954

Thomas Schütte is born November 16 in Oldenburg, West Germany (Federal Republic of Germany, or FRG). He is the second of five children. His father is an engineer, and the family moves frequently.

1955

West Germany joins the North Atlantic Treaty Organization (NATO). East Germany (German Democratic Republic, or GDR) joins the Warsaw Pact.

1961

The East German government seals its border with the construction of the Berlin Wall, making it difficult and dangerous to leave the country.

1970

Schütte competes on his high-school's coxed four rowing team as a coxswain, winning local, regional, and national championships between 1970 and 1971.

In the summer, he hitchhikes through Europe, which he will continue to do annually for the next five years.

1972

Visits Documenta 5 in Kassel, West Germany, twice over the course of the summer.

He starts to draw.

1973

Finishes high school in Osnabrück, West Germany.

Enters the Kunstakademie Düsseldorf for the winter semester. Begins his orientation studies with artist Fritz Schwegler.

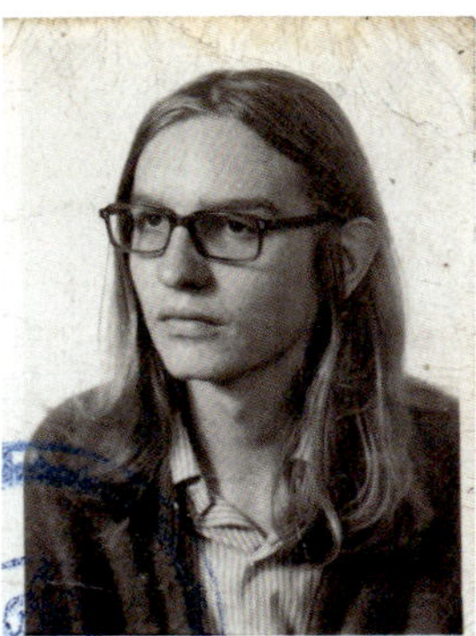

Portrait of Schütte for his student ID at Kunstakademie Düsseldorf, 1973

In October, an oil crisis plunges the world's economy into recession.

1974

Schütte visits *Caspar David Friedrich, 1774–1840* at Kunsthalle Hamburg, the first comprehensive exhibition of Friedrich's paintings in postwar Germany.

1975

At the Kunstakademie Düsseldorf, Schütte transfers to Gerhard Richter's studio class in the summer semester. His connections across the school's departments expand to include students in the photography program led by Bernd and Hilla Becher, as well as those in the stage-design program led by Karl Kneidl. In the course of his education, Schütte's peers will include Katharina Fritsch, Thomas Ruff, and Thomas Struth.

In September, he begins a one-year term of *Zivildienst*, or civilian service, in lieu of conscription into the German armed forces. He volunteers at a home for the elderly in the countryside.

Schütte meets Konrad Fischer and begins to regularly visit Fischer's gallery in Düsseldorf, whose program at the time includes exhibitions by Hanne Darboven, Candida Höfer, Bruce Nauman, Robert Ryman, and Lawrence Weiner.

1976

In the winter semester spanning 1976 and 1977, Schütte attends art historian Benjamin H. D. Buchloh's lectures. The seminar is titled Mythological and Phenomenological Aspects of Art in the Present.

1977

On April 7, Siegfried Buback, the attorney general of West Germany, is murdered by members of the Red Army Faction (RAF), a militant far-left group. The crime initiates a national crisis during which the RAF commits kidnappings, robberies, and assassinations, including the hijacking of Lufthansa Flight 181 in concert with the Popular Front for the Liberation of Palestine on October 13.

Schütte produces *Große Mauer* (*Large Wall*), which he comes to regard as his most significant early work and the start of his mature artistic practice. In a summer student exhibition, he presents the installation in a hallway at the Kunstakademie Düsseldorf.

1978

Schütte receives a grant from the Kunstakademie Düsseldorf and travels for the first time to New York, where he stays for three months.

1979

Schütte is awarded a six-month scholarship and residency at Cité des Arts, Paris. While there, he has an exhibition at Vitrine pour l'Art Actuel, an alternative bookstore and café run by Anka Ptaszkowska, Brigitte Nigel, and Michel Claura that hosts exhibitions and performances from 1977 to 1980. Schütte modifies the shop's electrical wiring so the lights go out for one second every thirty seconds.

Schütte meets curator Kasper König in Düsseldorf and Munich.

In September, Schütte creates *Gelbe Türen* (*Yellow Doors*), a site-specific installation at Konrad Fischer Galerie's space on Platanenstraße in Düsseldorf. He paints two of the doors at the bottom of a stairwell yellow.

On December 12, NATO announces its Double-Track Decision, establishing a plan to deploy 572 nuclear missiles in Central Europe in response to a military buildup by the Warsaw Pact countries. In West Germany, opposition to the arms race and public calls for disarmament are fueled by a growing peace movement.

1980

In January, Die Grünen (The Greens) officially become a national political party in West Germany. Their platform promotes environmentalism, social justice, and nonviolence. One of the founding members is artist Joseph Beuys, who taught at the Kunstakademie Düsseldorf from 1961 to 1972.

Kasper König nominates Schütte for the Jürgen Ponto-Stiftung prize, an award named in honor of the spokesman of the managing board of the Dresdner Bank who was murdered by the RAF in 1977. Schütte and artist Wolfgang Laib win the prize, and Schütte participates in a group exhibition where he presents *Lager* (*Storage*) at a museum housed in a thirteenth-century Carmelite monastery in Frankfurt.

In May, Schütte has his first commercial solo exhibition at Galerie Rüdiger Schöttle in Munich, titled *Arbeiten 1977–1980* (*Work 1977–1980*).

1981

Completes his studies at the Kunstakademie Düsseldorf early in the year.

Kasper König invites Schütte to participate in *Westkunst: Zeitgenössische Kunst seit 1939* (*Art of the West: Contemporary Art since 1939*), which opens in May in Cologne. Schütte produces his first models and ends up exhibiting them instead of his larger proposed architectural structures because of a lack of funds.

Walther König—the brother of Kasper König—commissions Schütte to paint *Alles in Ordnung* (*All in Order*) on the ceiling of his postcard shop in Cologne, where it remains as a permanent installation today.

In October, Schütte exhibits a series of paintings at Konrad Fischer Galerie titled *Pläne I–XXX* (*Plans I–XXX*) that depict architectural and urban motifs such as factories, bridges, bunkers, and towers.

1982

Schütte models his first figure by hand using wax—unsuccessfully. The failed attempt initiates the *Mann im Matsch* (*Man in Mud*) series.

1983

Schütte moves into a studio building on Hildebrandtstraße in Düsseldorf with fellow artists Klaus Jung, Ludger Gerdes, and Wolfgang Luy, with whom he shares the space for five years. Although not a formal group, these artists, along with Reinhard Mucha and Harald Klingelhöller, become known as the Düsseldorfer Modellbauer (Düsseldorf Model Makers).

1984

Solo exhibitions at Galerie Gaston-Nelson, Villeurbanne, France, and Jean Bernier, Athens.

1985

The local cultural authority Kulturbehörde Hamburg commissions Schütte to create an outdoor public artwork. *Tisch* (*Table*), a memorial for eleven resistance fighters killed by the Nazis, is permanently installed.

Teaches as a guest professor at the state college Hochschule für Bildende Künste in Hamburg during the winter term.

1986

Schütte's first major solo museum exhibition, curated by Julian Heynen, opens in January at Kunstmuseen Krefeld Museum Haus Lange. The site is a residence designed by Ludwig Mies van der Rohe in the Bauhaus style, built between 1928 and 1930.

On April 26, the unit 4 reactor of the Chernobyl Nuclear Power Plant in Pripyat, Ukraine (then part of the Soviet Union), melts down.

Schütte is invited to exhibit work in the outdoor sculpture exhibition Sonsbeek '86 in Arnhem, Netherlands, which opens in June. In the park, he installs a steel and concrete bunker, *Schutzraum* (*Shelter*), and welds the door shut.

1987

Schütte is invited to participate in Documenta 8, which opens in June. He builds *Eis* (*Ice Cream*), a functional ice cream shop with a neon artwork by artist Mario Merz installed inside.

Also in June, Schütte creates *Kirschensäule* (*Cherry Column*) for Skulptur Projekte Münster. The tall sandstone column with a pair of lacquered aluminum cherries on top is permanently installed at Harsewinkelplatz, in a parking lot.

1988

Solo exhibitions at Galleria Tucci Russo, Turin, and Galleria Christian Stein, Milan, in the spring.

In December, Schütte's solo exhibition *Mohr's Life & The Laundry* opens at Galerie Nelson's location in Lyon. The gallery is housed in a former furrier's workshop, and Schütte uses an approximate anagram of the original name of the building, H. Morel & Fils, to title the artwork.

1989

First solo exhibition in the United States opens at Marian Goodman Gallery, New York, in March.

Schütte begins working with master ceramicist Niels Dietrich in Cologne.

Soviet reforms and mass protests contribute to a weakening of the Iron Curtain across Europe and propel migration out of East Germany. On November 9, a new travel law allows transit across the border for the first time in thirty years, leading swiftly to the fall of the Berlin Wall.

1990

Curator Ulrich Loock organizes a survey of Schütte's work, *Sieben Felder* (*Seven Fields*), at Kunsthalle Bern, Switzerland, which opens in January and later travels to the Musée d'Art Moderne de la Ville de Paris and the Stedelijk van Abbemuseum, Eindhoven, Netherlands.

On August 2, Iraqi president Saddam Hussein launches an invasion of Kuwait, leading to the Gulf War. The offense is condemned internationally, and a coalition of forty-two countries, led by the United States, enters the conflict. During this time, Schütte keeps a diary of drawings that will become *Aufzeichnungen aus der 2. Reihe* (*Notes from the 2nd Row*). He later recalls, "The first Gulf War caused a huge furor here even before the Americans marched into Iraq. Flags were hung from the windows as if it were the Germans who were being attacked. They hung out peace flags, as I did."[1]

On October 3, the GDR is dissolved and its states become part of the Federal Republic of Germany.

1991

The federation of Yugoslavia breaks apart as states secede and the Yugoslav Wars begin. Between 1990 and 1992, nearly nine hundred thousand people from the region seek asylum in the recently united Germany.

Mikhail Gorbachev, president of the USSR, delivers a farewell address on December 25. His resignation leads to the termination of the Soviet Union as a sovereign state.

1992

Participates in a residency at the Deutsche Akademie Rom Villa Massimo in Rome. There, he starts to model the puppetlike figures that will become *United Enemies*.

Schütte's first group of life-size ceramic figures, *Die Fremden* (*The Strangers*), is installed on the roof of a department store in Kassel, a display that coincides with Documenta 9. The presentation comprises ten figures reminiscent of work by Oskar Schlemmer and fifteen objects that variously resemble bags, parcels, and other containers.

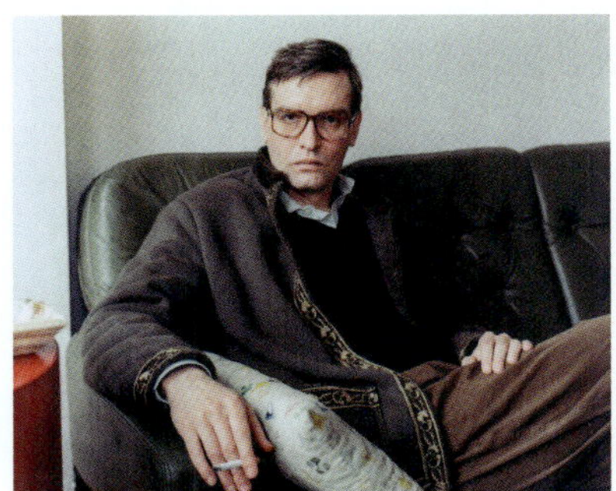

Thomas Schütte, Düsseldorf, 1992. Portrait by Thomas Struth

1994

Birth of daughter Carla.

In May, a solo exhibition curated by Frank Barth, Martin Hentschel, and Annelie Lütgens, *Thomas Schütte: [Figur]*, opens at Hamburger Kunsthalle and travels to Württembergischer Kunstverein Stuttgart.

1995

Begins making *Kleine Geister* (*Little Spirits*) for an exhibition with artist Richard Deacon that opens at Lisson Gallery, London, in May. To cast the sculptures for the show, Schütte collaborates with Rolf Kayser at the Kunstgiesserei Kittl foundry, where Kayser rose from apprentice to manager. In 1999, the business becomes Werkstatt für Metallbildhauerei Rolf Kayser.

Schütte is commissioned to create *Haus des Gedenkens* (*House of Remembrance*) by Kulturbehörde Hamburg to commemorate the fiftieth anniversary of the end of World War II. The work is installed at the former SS-run concentration camp Neuengamme.

1996

Birth of son, Henri.

Gallerist and friend Konrad Fischer dies on November 24.

1997

Participates in Skulptur Projekte Münster and Documenta 10.

1998

A solo exhibition curated by James Lingwood and James Peto opens in January at Whitechapel Art Gallery, London, and later travels to the De Pont Museum, Tilburg, Netherlands, and Fundação de Serralves, Porto.

The first of a trilogy of solo exhibitions, curated by Lynne Cooke, begins at Dia Center for the Arts, New York, in September. In the final installation, the majority of the 120 *Ceramic Sketches* are presented, as well as the first four *Frauen* figures, cast in steel.

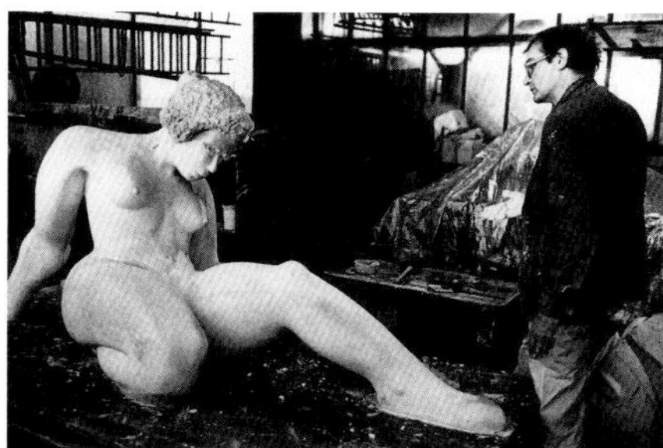

Thomas Schütte working in the foundry on the Frauen *series, c. 1998*

2001

Begins printmaking with the printer Till Verclas in Hamburg.

On September 11, four coordinated terrorist attacks are carried out by al-Qaeda in multiple locations in the United States using hijacked planes. Two planes hit the North and South Towers of the World Trade Center in New York, another plane hits the Pentagon in Arlington, Virginia, and the fourth plane crashes in a field in western Pennsylvania.

2002

The Euro replaces the Deutsche Mark as the official German currency.

Schütte visits New York and sees architectural models for the new World Trade Center on display. Critical of these proposals, which "pepped things up with pathos,"[2] he responds to the experience with his series *Kreuzzug Modelle* (*Crusade Models*, 2002–6) and, eventually, his series *Ferienhaus für Terroristen* (*Vacation Home for Terrorists*, 2006–21).

2003

On March 19, the United States invades Iraq on a spurious hunt for weapons of mass destruction under the leadership of President George W. Bush.

Solo exhibition *Kreuzzug* (*Crusade*), curated by Dieter Schwarz, opens at Kunstmuseum Winterthur, Switzerland, in June, before traveling to Musée de Grenoble, France, and Kunstsammlung Nordrhein-Westfalen K21, Düsseldorf.

2005

Schütte is awarded the Golden Lion at the Venice Biennale.

2006

In March, a retrospective devoted to Schütte's works on paper, curated by Matthias Winzen, opens at Staatliche Kunsthalle Baden-Baden, Germany, before traveling to the De Pont Museum and the Neues Museum Nürnberg in Nuremberg.

Participates in the 4th Berlin Biennale, which opens later in March.

2007

Gallerist and friend Phillip Nelson dies on April 3.

Begins construction of *One Man House II* in the countryside of Roanne, France. It is the first time one of Schütte's architectural models is realized as a private residence.

A solo exhibition of early work, curated by Penelope Curtis, opens at the Henry Moore Institute, Leeds, United Kingdom, in September, before traveling to Kunstmuseum Liechtenstein, Vaduz.

Schütte is awarded the Fourth Plinth Commission for Trafalgar Square, London, and builds *Model for a Hotel*. The work is unveiled November 4.

2008

Birth of daughter Katharina.

The global financial crisis hits Germany's banking sector.

2009

In June, a solo exhibition opens at Haus der Kunst, Munich, curated by Patrizia Dander and Thomas Weski.

Schütte completes *Mann im Matsch—Der Suchende* (*Man in Mud—The Seeker*), a commission for Landessparkasse zu Oldenburg, Germany. In an interview in 2011, he describes how "really amazing" it was for a bank to be building during a financial crisis.[3]

2010

In February, a major retrospective curated by Lynne Cooke opens at Museo Nacional Centro de Arte Reina Sofía in Madrid, titled *Hindsight*.

In July, *Thomas Schütte: Big Buildings* opens at Kunst- und Ausstellungshalle der Bundesrepublik Deutschland in Bonn, curated by Rainald Schumacher.

Revolutions, prodemocracy uprisings, coups, and civil wars spread across countries in North Africa and the Middle East, beginning in Tunisia.

2011

Builds *Ferienhaus T* (*Vacation Home T*) in the Austrian Alps, based on his *Ferienhaus für Terroristen* (*Vacation Home for Terrorists*) models. Schütte abbreviates the name to placate the concerns of local politicians. He contends, "Terrorism is not about war but a communications strategy. It is a closed effort to scare millions of people with very small means."[4]

Schütte creates *Pringles*, a matchbox with a potato chip on top, which later serves as the model for the design of his private museum, Skulpturenhalle.

Begins working with Murano glass, using mouth-blowing and lost-wax casting techniques.

2012

One of each of the eighteen *Frauen* forms, variously fabricated in aluminum, bronze, or steel, are exhibited together for the first time at Castello di Rivoli in Turin in May, in a display curated by Andrea Bellini and Dieter Schwarz.

Thomas Schütte: Faces and Figures, curated by Julia Peyton-Jones, Hans Ulrich Obrist, and Sophie O'Brien, opens at Serpentine Gallery, London, in September, highlighting the artist's longstanding relationship to portraiture.

2013

United Enemies bronze sculptures are installed in Central Park in New York in March for a solo presentation organized by Nicholas Baume for Public Art Fund.

Schütte purchases a piece of land near Neuss and establishes his own art foundation, Thomas Schütte Stiftung.

Solo exhibition opens in October at Fondation Beyeler, Riehen/Basel, curated by Theodora Vischer.

2014

In Neuss, Schütte begins construction of Skulpturenhalle, which offers an exhibition space for artists who make sculpture and alleviates problems with his long-term artwork storage.

2015

Father dies.

First architectural commission in the United States, *Clarks Kristall* (*Clark's Crystal*), opens at the Clark Institute in a meadow near the top of Stone Hill in Williamstown, Massachusetts.

2016

Skulpturenhalle opens in April with an inaugural exhibition of works by Mario Merz, curated by Dieter Schwarz.

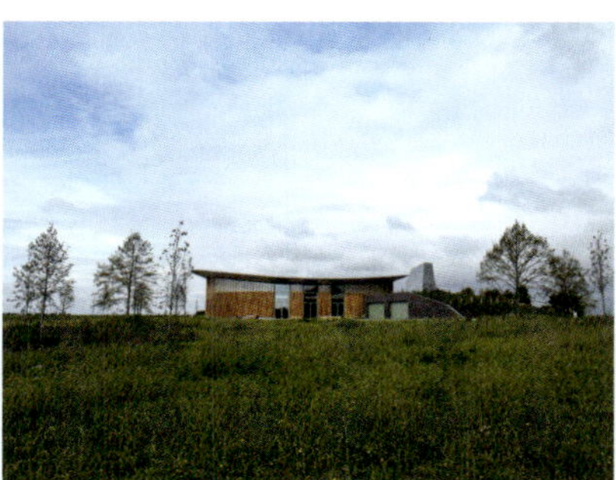

Skulpturenhalle, Neuss, Germany

Thomas Schütte: United Enemies opens in October at Moderna Museet, Stockholm, curated by Matilda Olof-Ors.

2019

Thomas Schütte: Trois Actes (*Three Acts*), curated by Camille Morineau, opens at Monnaie de Paris in March.

In July, another solo show opens at Kunsthaus Bregenz, Austria, curated by Thomas D. Trummer and Rudolf Sagmeister. The exhibition program extends into several of the city's public spaces, with *Drittes Tier* (*Third Beast*) installed at Karl-Tizian-Platz and several billboards appearing on the major thoroughfare Seestraße.

2021

Solo exhibition opens in November at Georg Kolbe Museum, Berlin, curated by Julia Wallner.

2022

In January, a solo exhibition featuring some of Schütte's earliest artworks, made between 1975 and 1981, opens at Skulpturenhalle.

2023

Mother dies.

The documentary film *Thomas Schütte: Ich bin nicht allein* (*Thomas Schütte: I Am Not Alone*), directed by Corinna Belz, is released in June.

Solo exhibition *Westkunstmodelle 1:1* opens at the De Pont Museum in September. Schütte realizes three sculptures from the 1981 Westkunst exhibition, *Shiff* (*Ship*), *Bühne* (*Stage*), and *Kiste* (*Box*), at their originally intended full scale for the first time.

2024

Retrospective opens at The Museum of Modern Art, New York, in September, curated by Paulina Pobocha.

Thomas Schütte lives and works in Düsseldorf, Germany.

---

1 Ulrich Loock, "Illustrations with Comments by the Artist in Conversation with the Author," in *Thomas Schütte*, ed. Dorothea Zwirner (Berlin: Friedrich Christian Flick Collection; Cologne: DuMont Literatur und Kunst, 2004), 198.
2 Hans Ulrich Obrist, "Reality Production: An Interview with Thomas Schütte," *Mousse* 28 (April–May 2011), 72.
3 Hans Ulrich Obrist, "Reality Production: An Interview with Thomas Schütte—Part II," *Mousse* 29 (Summer 2011), 79.
4 Robert Stasinski, "Ten Questions: Thomas Schütte," interview, *Kunstkritikk: Nordic Art Review,* October 7, 2016, https://kunstkritikk.com/ten-questions-thomas-schutte/.

Checklist of the Exhibition

This checklist is organized chronologically, then alphabetically within each year. It comprises works understood to be included in the exhibition at the time of publication. The *Mirror Drawings* and *Walser Drawings* included in the exhibition may differ slightly from those listed here.

Amerika (*America*). 1975
Pencil on paper
6' 10 11/16" × 7' 10 1/2" (210 × 240 cm)
Collection the artist, Düsseldorf
2

Große Tapeten (*Large Wallpapers*). 1975
Emulsion paint on packing paper, seven parts
Each 12' 7 9/16" × 3' 1" (385 × 94 cm)
Collection the artist, Düsseldorf
1

Selbstportrait. 29.5.75 (*Self-portrait: 5/29/75*). 1975
Oil on nettle cloth
23 5/8 × 17 11/16" (60 × 45 cm)
Private collection, Germany
4

Selbstportrait. 30/31.5.75 (*Self-portrait: 5/30–31/75*). 1975
Oil on nettle cloth
23 5/8 × 17 11/16" (60 × 45 cm)
Collection the artist, Düsseldorf
3

Valium. 1975
Crayon on paper
11 13/16 × 23 5/8" (30 × 60 cm)
Collection the artist, Düsseldorf
5

Valium. 1975
Watercolor and pencil on paper
22 13/16 × 15 3/4" (58 × 40 cm)
Collection the artist, Düsseldorf
6

Große Mauer (*Large Wall*). 1977
Oil on hardboard, 1,200 parts
Each 3 15/16 × 7 7/8" (10 × 20 cm)
Installation dimensions variable
Collection the artist, Düsseldorf
7

Lager (*Storage*). 1978
Paint and varnish on wood, 144 parts
Various dimensions from 11 7/8 × 6 7/8" (30 × 17.5 cm) to 53 15/16 × 26 5/8" (137 × 67.7 cm)
Installation dimensions variable
Collection the artist, Düsseldorf
9

Hysterie (*Hysteria*). 1979
Lacquer on paper, 105 sheets
Each 27 15/16 × 20 1/16" (71 × 51 cm)
Collection the artist, Düsseldorf
10

In Arbeit seit Juli 74 (*In Progress since July '74*). 1980
Pencil and primer on nettle cloth
23 5/8 × 23 5/8" (60 × 60 cm)
Collection the artist, Düsseldorf
11

Kollektion (*Collection*). 1980
Fabric, eight parts
Various lengths from 6' 11" (211 cm) to 10' 7 3/8" (323.5 cm)
Overall 10' 4" × 10' 7 9/16" (315 × 324 cm)
Herbert Foundation, Ghent
12

Postkarten, München (*Postcards, Munich*). 1980
Postcards mounted on paper, four sheets
Each 22 × 32" (55.9 × 81.3 cm)
Collection the artist, Düsseldorf
15

Schwäbisch Hall. 1980
Lacquer on plastic, four parts
Each 3 15/16 × 7 7/8" (10 × 20 cm)
Overall 13 3/8 × 16 9/16" (34 × 42 cm)
Courtesy Konrad Fischer Galerie, Düsseldorf
8

Schwarze Girlande (*Black Garland*). 1980
Fabric, seven parts
Various lengths from 11' 9 3/4" (360 cm) to 13' 3 7/16" (405 cm)
Installation dimensions variable
Courtesy Konrad Fischer Galerie, Düsseldorf
14

Skizzen zum Projekt Großes Theater (*Sketches for the Large Theater Project*). 1980
Chromogenic color prints, 14 sheets
Each 15 3/4 × 19 11/16" (40 × 50 cm)
Collection the artist, Düsseldorf
13

Alles in Ordnung (*All in Order*). 1981
Paint on wall
Installation dimensions variable
Collection the artist, Düsseldorf
16

Mein Grab (*My Grave*). 1981
Lacquer on paper
51 3/16 × 43 5/16" (130 × 110 cm)
Collection the artist, Düsseldorf
18

Mein Grab (*My Grave*). 1981
Lacquer on wood on fiberboard pedestal
Model: 20 1/2 × 24 13/16 × 9 13/16" (52 × 63 × 25 cm)
Pedestal: 45 11/16 × 29 1/2 × 13 3/4" (116 × 75 × 35 cm)
Collection the artist, Düsseldorf
18

Silberne Ringe (*Silver Rings*). 1981
Adhesive vinyl
Each ring 4 1/8" (10.5 cm) diam.
Installation dimensions variable
Collection the artist, Düsseldorf
17
Illustrated: *Goldene Ringe* (*Golden Rings*). 1981

Mann im Matsch (I. Version) (*Man in Mud [1st Version]*). 1982/2014
Aluminum and steel
9 5/8 × 52 3/4 × 50" (24.4 × 134 × 127 cm)
Edition 2 of 5
Courtesy the artist and Peter Freeman, Inc., New York/Paris
19

Modell für ein Museum (*Model for a Museum*). 1982
Paint on wood, on felt on tables, and two lacquer-on-paper drawings on easels
Model: 7' 8 1/2" × 6' 6 3/4" × 1' 11 5/8" (235 × 200 × 60 cm)
Easels: each 6' 6 3/4" × 4' 11 1/16" × 2' 3 9/16" (200 × 150 × 70 cm)
Kunstmuseum Bern, Stiftung Kunsthalle Bern
20

Studio I. 1983
Paint on wood
Model: 34 1/4 × 16 1/8 × 50 3/8" (87 × 41 × 128 cm)
Table: 36 7/16 × 33 7/16 × 68 7/8" (92.5 × 85 × 175 cm)
Herbert Foundation, Ghent
21

Studio II. 1983
Paint on wood
Model: 42 1/8 × 42 1/2 × 30 5/16" (107 × 108 × 77 cm)
Table: 37 × 51 1/4 × 59 1/16" (94 × 130.2 × 150 cm)
Herbert Foundation, Ghent
22

Melone (*Melon*). 1985
Lacquer on paper
55 1/8 × 43 5/16" (140 × 110 cm)
Private collection
25

Kirschen (*Cherries*). 1986
Lacquer on paper
59 13/16 × 43 5/16" (152 × 110 cm)
Collection the artist, Düsseldorf
31

Landhaus 4 (*Country House 4*). 1986
Paint on wood with model car
Model: 39 3/4 × 35 13/16 × 33 7/8" (101 × 91 × 86 cm)
Table: 37 13/16 × 51 3/16 × 47 1/4" (96 × 130 × 120 cm)
Herbert Foundation, Ghent
23

Melonely. 1986
Paint on wood, 11 parts, and gouache and watercolor on paper, 14 sheets
Each wooden part 39 3/8" × 19 11/16" × 7' 6" (100 × 50 × 230 cm)
Each sheet 25 9/16 × 19 11/16" (65 × 50 cm)
Installation dimensions variable
Private collection
24

Melonen (*Melons*). 1986
Lacquer on paper
55 1/2 × 43 5/16" (141 × 110 cm)
De Pont Museum, Tilburg, Netherlands
26

Pentagon. 1986
Fiberboard with stain
4' 11 1/16" × 10' 6" × 10' 6" (150 × 320 × 320 cm)
Panza Collection, Mendrisio, Switzerland
27

Schutzraum (*Shelter*). 1986
Wood, paint, and cardboard
4 1/2 × 4 5/16 × 8 1/16" (11.5 × 11 × 20.5 cm)
Collection the artist, Düsseldorf
28

Schutzraum (*Shelter*). 1986
Steel and sprayed concrete with steel door
10' 9 15/16" × 8' 8 3/4" × 14' 2 1/2" (330 × 266 × 433 cm)
29

Ein Stück mit 12 Aufzügen (*A Play with 12 Acts*). 1987
Lacquer on paper, 12 sheets
Each approx. 51 3/16 × 61 13/16" (130 × 157 cm)
Herbert Foundation, Ghent
30

Kirschen (*Cherries*). 1987
Lacquer on paper
62 3/4 × 43 1/4" (159.4 × 109.8 cm)
The Museum of Modern Art, New York. Gift of Jan Christiaan Braun in honor of Christophe Cherix
32

Mohr's Life. 1988
Two figures of modeling clay with fabric, string, and wooden dowels; four oil paintings on easels; two painted tin cans; and iron rack with socks
5' 10 7/8" × 11' 5 13/16" × 11' 5 13/16" (180 × 350 × 350 cm)
Private collection
36

Mohr's Life: The Collectors. 1988–99
Figure of cast resin; seven figures of modeling clay with fabric, string, and wooden dowels; taped cardboard wardrobe moving box with clothes on hangers; and clamp lamp and cable reel
5' 3" × 6' 6 3/4" × 6' 6 3/4" (160 × 200 × 200 cm)
Private collection
37

Mohr's Life: The Sculptor. 1988–99
Figure of modeling clay with fabric, string, hat, nail, and wooden dowels; unfired painted clay on brick on wooden table; raffia basket with nails; reading lamp on paint can; and metal shelving with shoes and unfired clay bust
5' 3" × 6' 10 11/16" × 5' 10 7/8" (160 × 210 × 180 cm)
Private collection
38

Alain Colas. 1989
Clay, polystyrene, paint, foam, cardboard, wood, and wire on two wooden pallets
45 7/8 × 47 7/16 × 31 1/2" (116.5 × 120.5 × 80 cm)
Museo d'Arte della Svizzera Italiana, Lugano, Switzerland. Collection Cantone Ticino. Donation Panza di Biumo
34

Projekt "Monument Alain Colas" (*Alain Colas Monument Project*). 1989
Figure of modeling clay and painted wood with chain and fishing hook; watercolor, pencil, and felt-tipped pen on paper; collage with watercolor, ink, paint, varnish, and felt-tipped pen on paper; and three photocopies
Figure: 20 1/2 × 4 1/8 × 3 1/8" (52 × 10.5 × 8 cm)
Each sheet various dimensions from 7 7/8 × 10 1/2" (20 × 26.7 cm) to 11 5/8 × 16 9/16" (29.5 × 42 cm)
Private collection
33
Illustrated: one photocopy

Zeichnung für Alain Colas (*Drawing for Alain Colas*). 1989
Collage with ink on paper
23 5/8 × 31 1/2" (60 × 80 cm)
Private collection, Berlin
35

Schwarze Zitronen (*Black Lemons*). 1990
Glazed ceramic, 20 parts
Ten parts 21 5/8 × 14 3/16" (55 × 36 cm), ten parts 27 3/16 × 16 1/8" (69 × 41 cm)
Paris Musées / Musée d'Art Moderne
39

Die Fremden (*The Strangers*). 1992
Glazed ceramic and steel, nine parts
Various dimensions from 41 1/4 × 18 3/16 × 19 7/8" (104.8 × 46.2 × 50.5 cm) to 74 3/4 × 26 1/16 × 20 15/16" (189.8 × 66.2 × 53.2 cm)
Seven parts: Tate
Two parts (at right of image): Collection the artist, Düsseldorf
40

Basement II. 1993
Wood and sawdust
3' 6" × 4' 11" × 6' 8 3/4" (106.7 × 149.9 × 205.1 cm)
Glenstone Museum, Potomac, Maryland
41

Basement III. 1993
Wood and sawdust
3' 4 3/16" × 4' 11 1/16" × 6' 8 11/16" (102 × 150 × 205 cm)
Collection the artist, Düsseldorf
42

United Enemies. 1993
Two figures of modeling clay, fabric, string, and wood on plastic pedestal with glass bell jar
6' 3 3/16" × 10 1/4" × 10 1/4" (191 × 26 × 26 cm)
Tate
43

United Enemies. 1993
Two figures of modeling clay, fabric, string, and wood on plastic pedestal with glass bell jar
6' 3 3/16" × 10 1/4" × 10 1/4" (191 × 26 × 26 cm)
Tate
44

United Enemies. 1993
Two figures of modeling clay, fabric, string, and wood on plastic pedestal with glass bell jar
6' 3 3/16" × 10 1/4" × 10 1/4" (191 × 26 × 26 cm)
Tate
45

Großer Respekt (*Large Respect*). 1994
Steel and patinated bronze
2' × 14' 9 3/16" × 18' 9/16" (61 × 450 × 550 cm)
De Pont Museum, Tilburg, Netherlands
49

United Enemies. 1994
Two figures of modeling clay, fabric, string, and wood on plastic pedestal with glass bell jar
6' 2" × 9 13/16" × 9 13/16" (188 × 25 × 25 cm)
De Pont Museum, Tilburg, Netherlands
46

United Enemies. 1994
Two figures of modeling clay, fabric, string, and wood on plastic pedestal with glass bell jar
6' 2" × 9 13/16" × 9 13/16" (188 × 25 × 25 cm)
De Pont Museum, Tilburg, Netherlands
47

United Enemies. 1994
Two figures of modeling clay, fabric, string, and wood on plastic pedestal with glass bell jar
6' 2" × 9 13/16" × 9 13/16" (188 × 25 × 25 cm)
De Pont Museum, Tilburg, Netherlands
48

Großer Geist Nr. 6 (*Large Spirit No. 6*). 1996
Polished aluminum
9' 6 3/16" × 4' 7 1/8" × 2' 7 1/2" (290 × 140 × 80 cm)
Kunstmuseum Wolfsburg, Germany. Donation from the Freundeskreis des Kunstmuseums Wolfsburg e.V.
50

Großer Geist Nr. 8 (*Large Spirit No. 8*). 1997
Polished aluminum
8' 2 7/16" × 4' 11 1/16" × 3' 3 3/8" (250 × 150 × 100 cm)
Kunstmuseum Wolfsburg, Germany. Donation from the Freundeskreis des Kunstmuseums Wolfsburg e.V.
50

Grüner Kopf (Konrad) (*Green Head [Konrad]*). 1997
Glazed ceramic and blanket on wood pedestal
Ceramic and blanket: 14 3/4 × 29 1/2 × 16 3/4" (37.5 × 75 × 42.5 cm)
Pedestal: 45 1/4 × 25 9/16 × 19 11/16" (115 × 65 × 50 cm)
Kunstsammlung Nordrhein-Westfalen, Düsseldorf. Donation of Dorothee and Konrad Fischer 2015
52

Blumen für Konrad (*Flowers for Konrad*). 1997–98
Watercolor on paper, 12 sheets
Each 15 3/8 × 11 7/16" (39 × 29 cm)
Kunstsammlung Nordrhein-Westfalen, Düsseldorf. Donation of Dorothee and Konrad Fischer 2015
51

Ceramic Sketches. 1997–99
Three steel shelving units with 36 glazed ceramics
Each unit 7' 1/4" × 7' 6 9/16" × 1' 7 11/16" (214 × 230 × 50 cm)
Each ceramic approx. 9 13/16 × 13 × 7 7/8" (25 × 33 × 20 cm)
Kunstsammlung Nordrhein-Westfalen, Düsseldorf
67

Mirror Drawing 16-6-98. 1998
Watercolor and ink on paper
14 15/16 × 11" (38 × 28 cm)
Collection the artist, Düsseldorf
54

Mirror Drawing 16-6-98. 1998
Watercolor, ink, and pencil on paper
14 15/16 × 11" (38 × 28 cm)
Collection the artist, Düsseldorf
55

Mirror Drawing 6-8-98. 1998
Watercolor, ink, and crayon on paper
14 15/16 × 11" (38 × 28 cm)
Collection the artist, Düsseldorf
56

Mirror Drawing 20-10-98. 1998
Watercolor, ink, and pencil on paper
14 15/16 × 11" (38 × 28 cm)
Collection the artist, Düsseldorf
57

Mirror Drawing 20-10-98. 1998
Watercolor, ink, and pencil on paper
14 15/16 × 11" (38 × 28 cm)
Collection the artist, Düsseldorf
58

Mirror Drawing 15-11-98. 1998
Watercolor, ink, and pencil on paper
14 15/16 × 11" (38 × 28 cm)
Collection the artist, Düsseldorf
59

Stahlfrau Nr. 1 (*Steel Woman No. 1*). 1998
Steel on steel table
5' 3" × 8' 2 7/16" × 4' 1 3/16" (160 × 250 × 125 cm)
The Museum of Modern Art, New York. Promised gift of Eva and Glenn Dubin
68

Mirror Drawing. 1998–99
Watercolor, ink, and pencil on paper
14 15/16 × 11" (38 × 28 cm)
Collection the artist, Düsseldorf
53

Mirror Drawing 16-2-99. 1999
Ink and crayon on paper
14 15/16 × 11" (38 × 28 cm)
Collection the artist, Düsseldorf
60

Mirror Drawing 16-2-99. 1999
Ink and crayon on paper
14 15/16 × 11" (38 × 28 cm)
Collection the artist, Düsseldorf
61

Mirror Drawing 16-2-99. 1999
Watercolor, ink, and crayon on paper
14 15/16 × 11" (38 × 28 cm)
Collection the artist, Düsseldorf
62

Mirror Drawing 14-3-99. 1999
Ink and pencil on paper
14 15/16 × 11" (38 × 28 cm)
Collection the artist, Düsseldorf
63

Mirror Drawing 29-3-99. 1999
Ink and crayon on paper
14 15/16 × 11" (38 × 28 cm)
Collection the artist, Düsseldorf
64

Mirror Drawing 23-5-99. 1999
Watercolor, ink, and crayon on paper
14 15/16 × 11" (38 × 28 cm)
Collection the artist, Düsseldorf
65

Mirror Drawing 3-6-99. 1999
Ink and crayon on paper
14 15/16 × 11" (38 × 28 cm)
Collection the artist, Düsseldorf
66

Großer Geist Nr. 17 (*Large Spirit No. 17*). 2000
Polished aluminum
68 7/8 × 66 15/16 × 47 1/4" (175 × 170 × 120 cm)
Kunstmuseum Wolfsburg, Germany. Donation from the Freundeskreis des Kunstmuseums Wolfsburg e.V.
50

Aluminiumfrau Nr. 6 (*Aluminum Woman No. 6*). 2001
Aluminum and lacquer on steel table
5' 4 3/16" × 8' 2 7/16" × 4' 1 3/16" (163 × 250 × 125 cm)
Thomas Schütte Stiftung, Neuss, Germany
69

Aluminiumfrau Nr. 16 (*Aluminum Woman No. 16*). 2005
Aluminum on steel table
5' 10 7/8" × 8' 2 7/16" × 4' 1 3/16" (180 × 250 × 125 cm)
Thomas Schütte Stiftung, Neuss, Germany
70

Bronzefrau Nr. 17 (*Bronze Woman No. 17*). 2006
Patinated bronze on steel table
6' 8 3/8" × 8' 2 7/16" × 4' 1 3/16" (204 × 250 × 125 cm)
The Art Institute of Chicago. Through prior gifts or bequests of Leo S. Guthman, Fowler McCormick, Albert A. Robin, Marguerita S. Ritman, Emily Crane Chadbourne, Florence S. McCormick, and Judith Neisser; purchased with funds provided by Per Skarstedt; 20th Century Purchase and Robert and Marlene Baumgarten funds
71

Frauen Series A. 2006
Etching on paper with chine collé, 18 sheets
Each 27 1/4 × 36" (69.2 × 91.4 cm)
Edition 9 of 12 with 5 APs
Collection Peter Freeman and Lluïsa Sàrries Zgonc, New York
72

Wichte (*Jerks*). 2006
Twelve patinated bronzes on steel shelves
Bronzes: Each approx. 13 3/4 × 13 3/4 × 11 13/16" (35 × 35 × 30 cm)
Shelves: two sizes, 11 13/16 × 13 3/4 × 12 5/8" (30 × 35 × 32 cm) and 11 13/16 × 19 11/16 × 12 5/8" (30 × 50 × 32 cm)
Edition of 6
Thomas Schütte Stiftung, Neuss, Germany
73
Illustrated: Private collection

Ferienhaus für Terroristen (Modell 1:20) (*Vacation Home for Terrorists [Model 1:20]*). 2007
Steel and acrylic sheeting
9 3/4 × 35 7/16 × 17 11/16" (24.8 × 90 × 45 cm)
Collection the artist, Düsseldorf
89

Modell für ein Museum (1:10) (*Model for a Museum [1:10]*). 2007
Wood, fiberboard, paint, and acrylic sheeting
18 7/8 × 27 3/4 × 20 11/16" (48 × 70.5 × 52.5 cm)
Collection the artist, Düsseldorf
84

Mann im Matsch (Modell 1:10) (*Man in Mud [Model 1:10]*). 2009
Patinated bronze on steel pedestal
Bronze: 23 5/8 × 14 3/16 × 11 7/16" (60 × 36 × 29 cm)
Pedestal: 47 1/4 × 17 11/16 × 14 3/16" (120 × 45 × 36 cm)
Artist's proof, edition of 6 with 4 APs
Collection the artist, Düsseldorf
92

Vater Staat (*Father State*). 2010
Patinated bronze
12' 5 5/8" × 5' 1" × 4' 7" (380 × 155 × 139.7 cm)
Collection Anne Dias Griffin
91

Ackermans Tempel III (Modell 1:10) (*Ackerman's Temple III [Model 1:10]*). 2011
Lego bricks, wood, and aluminum
19 1/8 × 17 5/8 × 23 1/16" (48.5 × 44.8 × 58.5 cm)
Collection the artist, Düsseldorf
82

Good Loock from *Walser Drawings*. 2011
Watercolor, ink, and crayon on paper
14 15/16 × 11" (38 × 28 cm)
Collection the artist, Düsseldorf
77

Memory = Gravety => from *Walser Drawings*. 2011
Watercolor, ink, and crayon on paper
14 15/16 × 11" (38 × 28 cm)
Collection the artist, Düsseldorf
81

Pringles. 2011
Potato chip on matchbox
1 ⅜ × 1 ⅞ × 2 ¾" (3.5 × 4.8 × 7 cm)
Collection the artist, Düsseldorf
85

Skulpturenhalle I (Modell 1:100) (*Skulpturenhalle I [Model 1:100]*). 2011
Steel and fabric
9 ¼ × 16 7/16 × 19 ¾" (23.5 × 41.8 × 50.2 cm)
Collection the artist, Düsseldorf

Untitled from *Walser Drawings*. 2011
Watercolor, ink, and crayon on paper
14 15/16 × 11" (38 × 28 cm)
Collection the artist, Düsseldorf
76

Untitled from *Walser Drawings*. 2011
Watercolor, ink, and crayon on paper
14 15/16 × 11" (38 × 28 cm)
Collection the artist, Düsseldorf
78

Holzturm (Modell 1:20) (*Wooden Tower [Model 1:20]*). 2012
Wood and glass
22 13/16 × 23 13/16 × 23 13/16" (58 × 60.5 × 60.5 cm)
Collection the artist, Düsseldorf

Krieger (*Warriors*). 2012
Charred wood with pigment and oil, two parts
9' 11 ¼" × 4' 1 ½" × 3' 9 ⅛" (302.9 × 125.7 × 114.6 cm) and
9' 9 ½" × 4' 1 ½" × 3' 9 ⅛" (298.5 × 125.7 × 114.6 cm)
The Museum of Modern Art, New York. Acquired through the generosity of Glenn Dubin, Donald B. Marron, Jerry I. Speyer, Marlene Hess, Anne Dias Griffin, Mimi Haas, Gary Winnick, Edgar Wachenheim III, and Committee on Painting and Sculpture Funds
93

Tempel Robelin (Modell 1:20) (*Robelin Temple [Model 1:20]*). 2012
Styrofoam, porcelain, metal, and wood
14 × 14 3/16 × 14 3/16" (35.5 × 36 × 36 cm)
Collection the artist, Düsseldorf

Tomorrow No Sorrow from *Walser Drawings*. 2012
Watercolor, ink, and crayon on paper
14 15/16 × 11" (38 × 28 cm)
Collection the artist, Düsseldorf
75

two tomatoes in the dark from *Walser Drawings*. 2012
Watercolor and ink on paper
14 15/16 × 11" (38 × 28 cm)
Collection the artist, Düsseldorf
80

Untitled from *Walser Drawings*. 2012
Ink on paper
14 15/16 × 11" (38 × 28 cm)
Collection the artist, Düsseldorf
79

Untitled from *Walser Drawings*. 2012
Watercolor, ink, and crayon on paper
14 15/16 × 11" (38 × 28 cm)
Collection the artist, Düsseldorf
74

Teehaus (Modell 1:10) (*Tea House [Model 1:10]*). 2012/2013
Paint on wood with acrylic sheeting
14 × 14 3/16 × 14 3/16" (35.5 × 36 × 36 cm)
Collection the artist, Düsseldorf
88

Blockhaus (Modell 1:15) (*Log House [Model 1:15]*). 2013
Spray paint on wood
18 ⅛ × 26 ¾ × 22 7/16" (46 × 68 × 57 cm)
Collection the artist, Düsseldorf
86

Golfhalle (Modell 1:100) (*Golf Hall [Model 1:100]*). 2013
Acrylic sheeting, fiberboard, plaster, and cardboard
4 ¾ × 13 ¾ × 9 13/16" (12 × 35 × 25 cm)
Collection the artist, Düsseldorf

Kristall I (Modell 1:10) (*Crystal I [Model 1:10]*). 2013
Wood, cardboard, and paint
15 ¾ × 16 ¾ × 15 ⅜" (40 × 42.5 × 39 cm)
Collection the artist, Düsseldorf

Bibliothek (Modell 1:10) (*Library [Model 1:10]*). 2014
Wood
23 ¼ × 43 5/16 × 23 ⅝" (59 × 110 × 60 cm)
Collection the artist, Düsseldorf

Bootshaus (Modell 1:20) (*Boat House [Model 1:20]*). 2015
Fiberboard
12 × 27 15/16 × 19 15/16" (30.5 × 71 × 50.7 cm)
Collection the artist, Düsseldorf

Eifelhütte (Modell 1:20) (*Eifel Hut [Model 1:20]*). 2015
Wood and aluminum
18 ½ × 14 × 29 5/16" (47 × 35.5 × 74.5 cm)
Collection the artist, Düsseldorf
87

Pommesbude (Modell 1:10) (*Chip Shop [Model 1:10]*). 2015
Wood
17 5/16 × 18 ½ × 27 3/16" (44 × 47 × 69 cm)
Collection the artist, Düsseldorf
83

Hütte (Modell 1:15) (*Hut [Model 1:15]*). 2016
Fiberboard, spray paint, and wood
14 ¾ × 23 ⅝ × 22 1/16" (37.5 × 60 × 56 cm)
Collection the artist, Düsseldorf

Krefeld Pavillon (Modell 1:25) (*Krefeld Pavilion [Model 1:25]*). 2016
Copper, fiberboard, and wood
14 9/16 × 31 ½ × 31 ½" (37 × 80 × 80 cm)
Collection the artist, Düsseldorf
90

Spartà Hut (Model 1:10). 2016/2019
Wood
12 3/16 × 13 ¾ × 23 ⅜" (31 × 35 × 59.3 cm)
Collection the artist, Düsseldorf

Fake Flag H. 2018
Glazed ceramic, three parts
3' 1 ¾" × 6' 9 ½" × 1 ½" (95.9 × 207 × 3.8 cm)
Collection Peter Freeman and Lluïsa Sàrries Zgonc, New York
94

Fake Flag I. 2018
Glazed ceramic, three parts
3' 1 13/16" × 6' 9 ½" × 1 9/16" (96 × 207 × 4 cm)
Collection Niels Dietrich
95

Skulpturenhalle Erweiterungsbau II (Modell 1:50) (*Skulpturenhalle Expansion II [Model 1:50]*). 2018
Wood, fiberboard, and aluminum
9 ¼ × 23 ⅝ × 23 ⅝" (23.5 × 60 × 60 cm)
Collection the artist, Düsseldorf

Frauenkopf (*Woman's Head*). 2020
Glazed ceramic on steel pedestal
Ceramic: 22 13/16 × 13 ⅜ × 19 5/16" (58 × 34 × 49 cm)
Pedestal: 47 ¼ × 15 ¾ × 23 ⅝" (120 × 40 × 60 cm)
Collection the artist, Düsseldorf
99

Frauenkopf (implodiert) (*Woman's Head [Imploded]*). 2020
Glazed ceramic and steel on steel pedestal
Ceramic: 12 ⅛ × 20 ½ × 22 ½" (30.8 × 52.1 × 57.2 cm)
Pedestal: 47 ¼ × 15 ¾ × 23 ⅝" (120 × 40 × 60 cm)
Collection Eleanor Heyman Propp
100

Old Friend Revisited No. 6. 2021
Glazed ceramic on steel pedestal
Ceramic: 18 ⅛ × 12 3/16 × 13 ¾" (46 × 31 × 35 cm)
Pedestal: 47 ¼ × 17 11/16 × 17 11/16" (120 × 45 × 45 cm)
Collection the artist, Düsseldorf

Old Friend Revisited No. 8. 2021
Glazed ceramic on steel pedestal
Ceramic: 18 ⅛ × 12 ⅝ × 15 15/16" (46 × 32 × 40.5 cm)
Pedestal: 47 ¼ × 17 11/16 × 17 11/16" (120 × 45 × 45 cm)
Collection the artist, Düsseldorf
98

Old Friend Revisited No. 18. 2021
Glazed ceramic on steel pedestal
Ceramic: 18 ½ × 14 9/16 × 13 3/16" (47 × 37 × 33.5 cm)
Pedestal: 47 ¼ × 17 11/16 × 17 11/16" (120 × 45 × 45 cm)
Collection the artist, Düsseldorf
96

Old Friend Revisited No. 21. 2021
Glazed ceramic on steel pedestal
Ceramic: 21 1/16 × 15 ⅜ × 14" (53.5 × 39 × 35.5 cm)
Pedestal: 47 ¼ × 17 11/16 × 17 11/16" (120 × 45 × 45 cm)
Collection the artist, Düsseldorf

Old Friend Revisited No. 27. 2021
Glazed ceramic on steel pedestal
Ceramic: 19 11/16 × 12 3/16 × 13 ⅜" (50 × 31 × 34 cm)
Pedestal: 47 ¼ × 17 11/16 × 17 11/16" (120 × 45 × 45 cm)
Collection the artist, Düsseldorf
97

Pilz (Modell 1:10) (*Mushroom [Model 1:10]*). 2021
Steel, copper, and wood
15 ¾ × 20 1/16 × 20 1/16" (40 × 51 × 51 cm)
Collection the artist, Düsseldorf

Sketchbooks. 2022
Sketchbooks in metal frames
Various dimensions from 13 × 11 7/16 × 1 ⅜" (33 × 29 × 3.5 cm) to 16 ⅛ × 19 11/16 × 1 ⅜" (41 × 50 × 3.5 cm)
Collection the artist, Düsseldorf

Mother Earth. 2024
Glazed ceramic on steel pedestal
Ceramic: 49 × 12 3/16 × 15 15/16" (124.5 × 31 × 40.5 cm)
Pedestal: 39 ⅜ × 23 ⅝ × 17 11/16" (100 × 60 × 45 cm)
Collection the artist, Düsseldorf

Selected Exhibition History

Compiled by Caitlin Chaisson and Lydia Mullin

SOLO EXHIBITIONS

1979

Relais. Vitrine pour l'Art Actuel, Paris. Opened September.
Gelbe Türen. Konrad Fischer Galerie, Düsseldorf. Opened September 20.
Drucksache. Galerie Arno Kohnen, Düsseldorf. December 8–29.

1980

Arbeiten 1977–1980. Galerie Rüdiger Schöttle, Munich. May 10–June 10.

1981

Pläne I–XXX. Produzentengalerie Hamburg. May 22–June 13.
Pläne I–XXX. Konrad Fischer Galerie, Düsseldorf. October 17–November 14.

1982

Skizzen zum Projekt "Großes Theater," 1980–82. Galerie Rüdiger Schöttle, Munich. April 17–May 17.

1984

Thomas Schütte: Oeuvres récentes. Galerie Gaston-Nelson, Villeurbanne, France. January 26–April 1 (cat.).
HCH. Jean Bernier, Athens. December 12, 1984–January 26, 1985.

1985

Thomas Schütte. Galerij Micheline Szwajcer, Antwerp. June 22–July 19.
Thomas Schütte. Konrad Fischer Galerie, Düsseldorf. October 19–November 21.
Pläne I–XXX, 1981 / Skizzen zu Skulpturen. Produzentengalerie Hamburg. November 29, 1985–January 11, 1986 (cat.).
Thomas Schütte. Raum für Kunst, Hamburg. December 2, 1985–January 11, 1986.

1986

Thomas Schütte. Kunstmuseen Krefeld Museum Haus Lange, West Germany. January 26–March 16 (cat.).
Skulpturen. Galerie Rüdiger Schöttle, Munich. April 4–May 31.
Thomas Schütte. Galerie Philip Nelson, Villeurbanne, France. June 16–August 27.
Quartier d'hiver. Galerie Crousel-Hussenot, Paris. September 13–October 20.
Thomas Schütte. Galleria Tucci Russo, Turin. October 24–December 6 (cat.).

1987

Two Blue Boats. Jean Bernier Gallery, Athens. January 15–February 21.
Obst und Gemüse. Westfälisches Landesmuseum Münster, West Germany. March 29–May 31 (cat.).
Thomas Schütte. Galerij Micheline Szwajcer, Antwerp. May 2–31.
Thomas Schütte. Konrad Fischer Galerie, Düsseldorf. September 18–October 16.
Thomas Schütte. Museum Overholland, Amsterdam. October 10–November 29 (cat.).

1988

Thomas Schütte. Staatliche Kunsthalle Baden-Baden, West Germany. February 13–March 20 (cat.).
My Eye—Your Eye: Controllo. Galleria Tucci Russo, Turin. March 25–May 21.
Thomas Schütte. Galleria Christian Stein, Milan. Opened May 4.
Mohr's Life & The Laundry. Galerie Nelson, Lyon. December 16, 1988–February 19, 1989.

1989

Big Buildings. Marian Goodman Gallery, New York. March 10–April 8.
Fête de tête. Galerie Pietro Spartà, Chagny, France. Opened April 1.
The Laundry–Mohr's Life. Portikus, Frankfurt. June 17–July 30. Traveled as *Mohr's Life & The Laundry* to Stichting de Appel, Amsterdam, August 26–September 23 (cat.).
Thomas Schütte: Projet pour un monument et autres oeuvres. Musée de Clamecy, France. June 30–August 21.
HQ im Bau. Konrad Fischer Galerie, Düsseldorf. Opened November 25.
Simple Stories. Galerie Ute Parduhn, Düsseldorf. November 25, 1989–January 13, 1990 (cat.).

1990

Sieben Felder. Kunsthalle Bern. January 26–March 11. Traveled to Musée d'Art Moderne de la Ville de Paris, May 4–June 24, and Stedelijk van Abbemuseum, Eindhoven, Netherlands, October 20–December 2 (cat.).
Thomas Schütte: Notes. Marian Goodman Gallery, New York. April 4–28 (cat.).
Aquarelles. Galerie Crousel-Robelin, Paris. May 5–June 16.
Summer Will Show. Galerie Nelson, Lyon. July 21–September 15.
Casino. Konrad Fischer Galerie, Düsseldorf. August 19–September 14.
Jokes. Galerie Rüdiger Schöttle, Munich. December 11, 1990–January 31, 1991.

1991

Harem. Galerie Nelson, Lyon. Opened November 3.
Thomas Schütte. Kasseler Kunstverein, Kassel, Germany. November 30–December 22.

1992

Tomatensalat. Raum für Kunst, Hamburg. February 3–22.
Thomas Schütte. Vereniging voor het Museum van Hedendaagse Kunst, Ghent. May 22–June 28.
Thomas Schütte. Galleria Tucci Russo, Turin. May 29–September 19 (cat.).
Die Fremden. Public installation, SinnLeffers department store, Friedrichsplatz, Kassel, Germany. Opened June 1992.
Thomas Schütte. Konrad Fischer Galerie, Düsseldorf. September 5–24.
Requiem. Jean Bernier Gallery, Athens. November 22, 1992–January 15, 1993.

1993

Thomas Schütte. Marian Goodman Gallery, New York. March 24–April 24.
Alte Freunde—Neue Arbeiten. Produzentengalerie Hamburg. September 20–October 30 (cat.).

1994

Nobody Knows. Galerie Nelson, Paris. March 12–April 16.
Thomas Schütte: [Figur]. Hamburger Kunsthalle, Hamburg. May 6–June 26. Traveled to Württembergischer Kunstverein Stuttgart, September 3–October 16 (cat.).
Thomas Schütte: Requiem. Carré d'Art—Musée d'Art Contemporain, Nîmes, France. October 28, 1994–January 15, 1995 (cat.).

1995

Thomas Schütte. Jean Bernier Gallery, Athens. February 6–March 15.
Neue Arbeiten. Konrad Fischer Galerie, Düsseldorf. March 18–April 20.
Können Lilien lügen? Württembergischer Kunstverein Stuttgart. April 6–30.
Thomas Schütte. Galleria Tucci Russo, Torre Pellice, Italy. May 27–October 15.
Thomas Schütte: 80 Skizzenblöcke (1990–1995). Kunstraum München, Munich. September 8–October 28. Traveled to Oldenburger Kunstverein, Oldenburg, Germany, November 4–December 30; Leopold-Hoesch-Museum, Düren, Germany, January 21–March 17, 1996; and Daadgalerie, Berlin, March 25–May 5, 1996 (cat.).
Thomas Schütte. Wako Works of Art, Tokyo. October 11–November 18 (cat.).

1996

Thomas Schütte. Marian Goodman Gallery, New York. March 8–April 20.
Thomas Schütte. Galerie Gebauer und Günther, Berlin. March 30–April 27.
Thomas Schütte. Museum Fridericianum, Kassel, Germany. May 22–July 21 (cat.).
Reserve. Stella Lohaus Gallery, Antwerp. Opened July 6.
Blumen mit Luise. Galerie Erika + Otto Friedrich, Bern. September 13–October 19 (cat.).
Drawings. Janice Guy, New York. September 21–November 2.
Thomas Schütte: Fucking Flowers. Galerie Nelson, Paris. September 21–November 2.
Thomas Schütte. Städtische Galerie Wolfsburg, Germany. December 15, 1996–February 9, 1997 (cat.).

1997

Die Fremden. Marian Goodman Gallery, New York. April 11–May 10.
Neue Arbeiten. Konrad Fischer Galerie, Düsseldorf. September 27–November 15.

1998

Thomas Schütte. Whitechapel Art Gallery, London. January 16–March 15. Traveled to De Pont Foundation for Contemporary Art, Tilburg, Netherlands, March 28–June 21, and Museu de Arte Contemporânea, Fundação de Serralves, Porto, July 9–September 6 (cat.).
Scenewright. Dia Center for the Arts, New York. September 24, 1998–January 18, 1999 (cat.).
Thomas Schütte. Galerie Nelson, Paris. November 28, 1998–January 30, 1999.

1999

Thomas Schütte. Bernier/Eliades Gallery, Athens. January 16–February 25.
Gloria in Memoria. Dia Center for the Arts, New York. February 4–June 13 (cat.).
Thomas Schütte. Marian Goodman Gallery, New York. February 26–April 3.
Urnen. Produzentengalerie Hamburg. May 1–June 30.
In Medias Res. Dia Center for the Arts, New York. September 16, 1999–June 18, 2000 (cat.).
New Works. Wako Works of Art, Tokyo. December 10, 1999–January 22, 2000.

2000

Thomas Schütte: Werkstatt. Kunstmuseum Wolfsburg, Germany. February 26–April 24.
5 Frauen. Garten Landschaft OWL, Schlosspark Wendlinghausen, Dörentrup, Germany. June 10–October 3 (cat.).

2001

Thomas Schütte. Sammlung Goetz, Munich. March 19–August 11 (cat.).
Thomas Schütte. Konrad Fischer Galerie, Düsseldorf. May 12–June 30.

2002

Selected Works. Faggionato Fine Arts, London. January 24–March 1.
Low Tide Wandering. Frith Street Gallery, London. March 16–April 26.
Neue Arbeiten. Galleria Tucci Russo, Torre Pellice, Italy. April 20–September 15.
Thomas Schütte. Produzentengalerie Hamburg. June 1–July 31 (cat.).
Thomas Schütte. Marian Goodman Gallery, New York. June 21–August 30.
Große Geister. Museum Folkwang, Essen, Germany. September 8–December 1 (cat.).
Dürer. Galerie Nelson, Paris. September 21–November 8.

2003

Thomas Schütte. Marian Goodman Gallery, New York. May 15–June 28.
Thomas Schütte. Galerie Friedrich, Basel. June 5–July 12.
Kreuzzug. Kunstmuseum Winterthur, Switzerland. June 7–August 24. Traveled as *Croisade/Kreuzzug* to Musée de Grenoble, France, October 24, 2003–January 25, 2004, and Kunstsammlung Nordrhein-Westfalen K21, Düsseldorf, April 3–August 7, 2004 (cat.).
Thomas Schütte. Galerie Rüdiger Schöttle, Munich. September 6–October 25.
Thomas Schütte. Bernier/Eliades Gallery, Athens. October 7–November 29.

2004

Quengelware. Hamburger Kunsthalle, Hamburg. June 20–October 10.
Thomas Schütte. Carlier | Gebauer, Berlin. September 22–October 16.
Wision Impossible. Galerie Nelson, Paris. October 23–December 23.

2005

One Man Houses. Marian Goodman Gallery, New York. May 12–July 2.
Thomas Schütte. Galerie Friedrich, Basel. June 13–August 20.
Obras politicas / Political Works. Fundação de Serralves, Porto. July 23–September 25 (cat.).

2006

Thomas Schütte: Ringe (Rings). Faggionato Fine Arts, London. February 6–April 7.
Thomas Schütte—Zeichnungen. Staatliche Kunsthalle Baden-Baden, Germany. March 11–April 30. Traveled to De Pont Museum of Contemporary Art, Tilburg, Netherlands, May 20–September 17, and Neues Museum, Staatliches Museum für Kunst und Design Nürnberg, Nuremberg, Germany, October 20, 2006–January 21, 2007 (cat.).
Krankenhaus. Kabinett für Aktuelle Kunst Bremerhaven, Germany. July 2–August 27.
Thomas Schütte. Konrad Fischer Galerie, Düsseldorf. September 1–October 21.
Thomas Schütte. Produzentengalerie Hamburg. September 9–October 21.
Thomas Schütte. Jarla Partilager, Stockholm. October 28, 2006–March 2, 2007 (cat.).

2007

Thomas Schütte. Galerie Nelson-Freeman, Paris. April 28–June 21.
Thomas Schütte: Last Casts, New Etchings, Some Watercolours. Frith Street Gallery, London. May 17–June 21.
Thomas Schütte: Fake/Function. Henry Moore Institute, Leeds, United Kingdom. September 22, 2007–January 6, 2008. Traveled as *Thomas Schütte: Early Works* to Kunstmuseum Liechtenstein, Vaduz, February 1–April 20, 2008 (cat.).

2008

Thomas Schütte: 18 Women. Margarete Roeder Gallery and Editions, New York. October 4–November 1.

2009

United Enemies. Faggionato Fine Arts, London. May 8–July 8.
Thomas Schütte: Radierungen. Horst-Janssen-Museum, Oldenburg, Germany. May 16–August 16.
Thomas Schütte. Haus der Kunst, Munich. June 7–September 6 (cat.).
Thomas Schütte. Galerie Pietro Spartà, Chagny, France. November 20, 2009–January 19, 2010.

2010

Thomas Schütte. Portalakis Collection, Athens. February 15–June 30 (cat.).
Thomas Schütte: Hindsight. Museo Nacional Centro de Arte Reina Sofía, Madrid. February 17–May 17 (cat.).
Thomas Schütte: Kleine Geister. Donald Young Gallery, Chicago. May 21–July 3.
Thomas Schütte: Big Buildings—Modelle und Ansichten. Kunst- und Ausstellungshalle der Bundesrepublik Deutschland, Bonn. July 15–November 1 (cat.).
Selected Work. Skarstedt Gallery, New York. September 30–October 20.

2012

In the Spirit of Walser: Thomas Schütte. Donald Young Gallery, Chicago. February 4–March 9 (cat.).
Woodcuts 2011. Galerie Nelson-Freeman, Paris. February 17–March 31.
Thomas Schütte: New Work / New Watercolors. Peter Freeman, Inc., New York (two locations). February 23–April 7.
Thomas Schütte: Alte Freunde. Carolina Nitsch, New York. March 1–April 28.
Thomas Schütte: Frauen. Castello di Rivoli, Rivoli/Turin. May 22–September 23. Traveled to Sara Hildénin Taidemuseo, Tampere, Finland, February 9–May 12, 2013, and Museum Folkwang, Essen, September 21, 2013–January 12, 2014 (cat.).
Thomas Schütte. Middelheimmuseum, Antwerp. May 26, 2012–January 13, 2013 (cat.).

Wattwanderung. Kunstsammlung Nordrhein-Westfalen K21, Düsseldorf. June 16–September 9.
Thomas Schütte: Houses. Nouveau Musée National de Monaco, Villa Paloma, France. July 7–November 11. Traveled to Kunstmuseum Luzern, Lucerne, Switzerland, October 26, 2013–February 16, 2014 (cat.).
With Tears in My Ears. Jarla Partilager, Berlin. September 12, 2012–June 16, 2013.
Thomas Schütte: Faces and Figures. Serpentine Gallery, London. September 25–November 18 (cat.).
Thomas Schütte: New Works. Frith Street Gallery, London. September 28–November 15.

2013

United Enemies. Public Art Fund, Central Park, New York. March 5–August 25.
Schöne Grüsse Thomas Schütte. Me Collectors Room / Stiftung Olbricht, Berlin. September 14, 2013–April 6, 2014.
Thomas Schütte. Fondation Beyeler, Riehen/Basel. October 6, 2013–February 2, 2014 (cat.).

2014

Thomas Schütte: Ernst Franz Vogelmann-Preis 2014. Kunsthalle Vogelmann, Heilbronn, Germany. July 12–October 12 (cat.).
Thomas Schütte. Cahiers d'Art, Paris. September 4, 2014–January 31, 2015.
Thomas Schütte. Galerie Pietro Spartà, Chagny, France. Opened September 5.

2015

Thomas Schütte. Peter Freeman, Inc., New York. April 16–May 30.
Thomas Schütte. Bernier/Eliades Gallery, Athens. May 20–July 15 (cat.).

2016

Thomas Schütte. Konrad Fischer Galerie, Düsseldorf. September 2–October 29.
Thomas Schütte: Frauen. Skarstedt Gallery, New York. September 15–December 17.
Thomas Schütte: United Enemies. Moderna Museet, Stockholm. October 8, 2016–January 15, 2017 (cat.).

2017

Thomas Schütte. Skulpturenhalle, Neuss, Germany. January 28–March 12.
Thomas Schütte. Carlier | Gebauer, Berlin. April 28–June 7.
Thomas Schütte. Galerie Pietro Spartà, Chagny, France. Opened July 1.
Thomas Schütte. Frith Street Gallery, London. September 15–November 11.

2018

Thomas Schütte. Skulpturenhalle, Neuss, Germany. January 12–March 18.
Thomas Schütte. Oldenburger Kunstverein, Oldenburg, Germany. January 21–April 15.
New Work. Peter Freeman, Inc., New York. September 13–October 31.
Thomas Schütte. Galleria Tucci Russo Chambres d'Art, Turin. October 4, 2018–February 23, 2019.

2019

Thomas Schütte. Skulpturenhalle, Neuss, Germany. January 11–March 3.
Thomas Schütte: Trois Actes. 11 Conti—Monnaie de Paris. March 15–June 16 (cat.).
Thomas Schütte: Architekturmodelle 2007–2016. Galerie Inselspitze, Heilbronn, Germany. April 27–September 22 (cat.).
Thomas Schütte. Kunsthaus Bregenz, Austria. July 13–October 6 (cat.).

2020

Köpfe. Skulpturenhalle, Neuss, Germany. January 10–March 15.
Thomas Schütte. Konrad Fischer Galerie, Berlin. May 2–September 30.
Thomas Schütte: Keramik. Hetjens—Deutsches Keramikmuseum, Düsseldorf. May 30–August 23 (cat.).
ETWAS FEHLT. Krefeld Pavilion, Germany. June 7–September 13 (cat.).
Thomas Schütte. Kunstforum Baloise Park, Basel. September 17, 2020–January 30, 2021 (cat.).

2021

Skizzen zum Projekt Großes Theater. Skulpturenhalle, Neuss, Germany. April 30–August 1.
Old Friends Revisited. Cahiers d'Art, Paris. June 17–July 31.
Thomas Schütte. Peter Freeman, Inc., New York. September 16–November 6.
Thomas Schütte. Galerie Pietro Spartà, Chagny, France. Opened October 8.
Thomas Schütte. Georg Kolbe Museum, Berlin. November 19, 2021–February 20, 2022 (cat.).

2022

Arbeiten 1975–1981. Skulpturenhalle, Neuss, Germany. January 14–March 13.
Thomas Schütte. Carlier | Gebauer, Madrid. February 25–April 23.
Thomas Schütte. Frith Street Gallery, London. April 29–June 25.
Thomas Schütte. Gallery of Contemporary Art and Architecture—House of Art České Budějovice, Budweis, Czech Republic. May 5–June 5.
Works in Glass. Tucci Russo, Turin. October 27, 2022–January 28, 2023.

2023

Skulpturen. Skulpturenhalle, Neuss, Germany. January 13–July 30.
Westkunstmodelle 1:1. De Pont Museum, Tilburg, Netherlands. September 16, 2023–February 4, 2024 (cat.).

2024

Prints. Skulpturenhalle, Neuss, Germany. March 22–July 28.
Thomas Schütte. The Museum of Modern Art, New York. September 29, 2024–January 18, 2025 (cat.).

GROUP EXHIBITIONS

1979

Schlaglichter: Eine Bestandsaufnahme aktueller Kunst im Rheinland. Rheinisches Landesmuseum, Bonn. September 20–November 4 (cat.).
Perspektiven 1. Kunstverein für die Rheinlande und Westfalen, Düsseldorf. December 14, 1979–February 10, 1980 (cat.).

1980

1. Ausstellung der Jürgen Ponto Stiftung zur Förderung junger Künstler 1980. Jürgen Ponto Stiftung, Karmeliterkloster, Frankfurt, West Germany. January 25–February 17.

1981

Art allemagne aujourd'hui. Musée d'Art Moderne de la Ville de Paris. January 17–March 8 (cat.).
Westkunst: Zeitgenössiche Kunst seit 1939. Rheinhallen Messegelände, Cologne. May 28–August 16 (cat.).

1982

(0211): 22 Künstler in Düsseldorf. Stiftung Museum Kunstpalast, Düsseldorf. March 21–May 9 (cat.).
Halle 6. Kampnagel-Fabrik, Hamburg. May 12–June 30 (cat.).
Gegen das Kriegsrecht in Polen—Für Solidarność. Kunstpalast, Düsseldorf. October 22–November 13 (cat.).

1983

Gerdes, Klingelhöller, Luy, Mucha, Schütte: C 83 Nr. 29. Konrad Fischer Galerie, Düsseldorf. April 9–May 7 (cat.).
Standort Düsseldorf. Städtische Kunsthalle Düsseldorf. October 8–23 (cat.).
Konstruierte Orte 6 × D + 1 × NY. Kunsthalle Bern. October 29–November 27 (cat.).
Sculpture from Germany. Organized by Independent Curators Inc., New York. San Francisco Museum of Modern Art. December 9, 1983–February 5, 1984. Traveled to Sarah Campbell Blaffer Gallery, University of Houston, Texas, March 4–April 8, 1984; Winnipeg Art Gallery, Canada, May 3–June 17, 1984; Art Gallery of Hamilton, Canada, September 13–October 14, 1984; Archer M. Huntington Gallery, University of Texas, Austin, January 13–February 24, 1985; and Queens Museum, Flushing, New York, May 4–June 16, 1985 (cat.).

1984

De Verzegelte Bron. Rotterdamse Kunststichting, Rotterdam. February 3–March 12 (cat.).
Ludger Gerdes / Thomas Schütte: Weiter/Warten. Produzentengalerie Hamburg. April 29–May 27 (cat.).
Ludger Gerdes, Harald Klingelhöller, Wolfgang Luy, Reinhard Mucha, Thomas Schütte. Kunstmuseen Krefeld Museum Haus Esters, West Germany. May 20–July 1 (cat.).
Von hier aus. Gesellschaft für Aktuelle Kunst Düsseldorf. September 29–December 2 (cat.).
Ouverture. Museo d'Arte Contemporanea, Castello di Rivoli, Rivoli/Turin. December 18, 1984–June 15, 1985 (cat.).

1985

The European Iceberg: Creativity in Germany and Italy Today. Art Gallery of Ontario, Toronto. February 8–April 7 (cat.).
Nouvelle Biennale de Paris. Grande Halle de la Villette, Paris. March 21–May 21.
Ludger Gerdes, Thomas Schütte. Galerie Philip Nelson, Lyon. May 16–June 16.
Rheingold: 40 Künstler aus Köln und Düsseldorf / 40 artisti da Colonia e Düsseldorf. Palazzo della Società Promotrice delle Belle Arti, Turin. May 25–June 30 (cat.).
Dreißig Jahre durch die Kunst: Museum Haus Lange 1955–1985. Kunstmuseen Krefeld Museum Haus Lange and Haus Esters, West Germany. September 15–December 1 (cat.).
1945–1985: Kunst in der Bundesrepublik Deutschland. Neue Nationalgalerie, Staatliche Museen zu Berlin. September 27, 1985–January 21, 1986 (cat.).

Aldo Rossi, Thomas Schütte. Galerie Johnen und Schöttle, Cologne. September 29–December 1.
Dispositif-sculpture. Musée d'Art Moderne de la Ville de Paris. December 19, 1985–February 16, 1986 (cat.).

1986

Sieben Skulpturen. Kölnischer Kunstverein, Cologne. April 26–June 1 (cat.).
Origins, Originality and Beyond. 6th Biennale of Sydney. May 16–July 6 (cat.)
Jenisch-Park: Skulptur. Kulturbehörde Hamburg. June 1–November 30 (cat.).
Sonsbeek '86 International Sculpture Exhibition. Arnhem, Netherlands. June 18–September 15 (cat.).
3. Triennale Fellbach: Kleinplastik. Fellbach, West Germany. June 28–August 10 (cat.).
Correspondentie Europa. Stedelijk Museum, Amsterdam. September 20–November 2 (cat.).
Il cangiante. Padiglione d'Arte Contemporanea, Milan. December 3, 1986–January 25, 1987 (cat.).

1987

Tekenen '87. Museum Boijmans–van Beuningen, Rotterdam. March 14–April 27.
Raumbilder: Cinco escultores alemanes en Madrid. Centro de Arte Reina Sofía, Madrid. April 8–June 22 (cat.).
Juxtapositions: Recent Sculpture from England and Germany. Institute for Art and Urban Resources, P.S. 1, Long Island City, New York. April 26–June 21 (cat.).
L'époque, la mode, la morale, la passion: Aspects de l'art d'aujourd'hui, 1977–1987. Centre Georges Pompidou, Paris. May 21–August 17 (cat.).
Bildhauerzeichnungen. Grazer Kunstverein, Graz, Austria. Opened June 1987 (cat.).
Documenta 8. Museum Fridericianum, Kassel, West Germany. June 12–September 20 (cat.).
Skulptur Projekte Münster. Münster, West Germany. June 14–October 4 (cat.).
Das andere Medium: Zeichnungen von Bildhauern. Museum Ostwall, Dortmund, West Germany, August 30–October 11 (cat.).
Musée St. Pierre. Frankfurter Kunstverein, Frankfurt. September 12–October 11 (cat.).
Die große Oper oder die Sehnsucht nach dem Erhabenen. Bonner Kunstverein, Bonn. December 3, 1987–January 20, 1988. Traveled to Frankfurter Kunstverein, Frankfurt, January 29–February 28, 1988 (cat.).
Nachtvuur. De Appel, Amsterdam. December 20, 1987–January 31, 1988 (cat.).

1988

Europa oggi: Arte contemporanea nell'Europa Occidentale. Centro per l'Arte Contemporanea Luigi Pecci, Prato, Italy. June 26–October 20 (cat.).

1989

Periodi di marmo: Arte verso l'inespressionismo. Palazzo di Città, Acireale, Italy. September 2–30 (cat.).
Skulpturen für Krefeld I. Kunstmuseen Krefeld Museum Haus Esters, West Germany. September 3–October 22 (cat.).
Blickpunkte. Musée d'Art Contemporain de Montréal. September 13, 1989–January 14, 1990 (cat.).
Zeitzeichen: Stationen Bildender Kunst in Nordrhein-Westfalen. Museum der bildenden Künste Leipzig und Hochschule für Grafik und Buchkunst, Leipzig, East Germany. November 10, 1989–January 7, 1990 (cat.).

1990

Hacia el paisaje / Towards Landscape. Centro Atlántico de Arte Moderno, Las Palmas, Spain. October 16–November 30 (cat.).
Possible Worlds: Sculpture from Europe. Institute of Contemporary Arts and Serpentine Gallery, London. November 9, 1990–January 6, 1991 (cat.).

1991

Espacio mental. Instituto Valenciano de Arte Moderno Centre del Carme, Valencia. May 10–July 21 (cat.).
Inscapes. De Appel, Amsterdam. June 1–July 14 (cat.).
Zeit-Rausch. Bonner Kunstverein, Bonn. October 30–November 24 (cat.).
In anderen Räumen. Kunstmuseen Krefeld Museum Haus Lange and Haus Esters, Germany. December 1, 1991–January 9, 1992.

1992

Like Nothing Else in Tennessee. Serpentine Gallery, London. March 17–April 26 (cat.).
Tišina / Silence. Moderna Galerija, Ljubljana, Slovenia. May 19–June 21 (cat.).
Art Meets Ads. Kunsthalle Düsseldorf. September 18–27 (cat.).

1993

Tutte le strade portano a Roma? Palazzo delle Esposizioni, Rome. March 11–April 26 (cat.).
New Sculptures. Middelheimmusuem, Antwerp. Opened March 27 (cat.).
Nachtschattengewächse. Museum Fridericianum, Kassel, Germany. May 16–August 8 (cat.).
The Sublime Void: On the Memory of the Imagination. Koninklijk Museum voor Schone Kunsten, Antwerp. July 25–October 10 (cat.).
Viaggio verso Citera. Arte e poesia. Casino Municipale, 45th Venice Biennale. September 30–November 30 (cat.).

1994

Young German Art of the 1990s: The Generation after Beuys, Becher, Polke, Richter. Sonje Museum of Contemporary Art, Kyongju, South Korea, October 7, 1994–January 10, 1995. Traveled to Pao Galleries, Hong Kong Arts Centre, May 6–21, 1995; Taipei Fine Arts Centre, June 3–August 6, 1995; Goethe-Institut Singapore, August 30–September 2, 1995; International Art Gallery, Beijing, October 23–November 5, 1995; and National Museum of Modern Art, Osaka, December 14, 1995–February 27, 1996. (cat.).
Figur. Natur. Sprengel Museum Hannover, Hanover, Germany. October 9, 1994–January 15, 1995 (cat.).
Drawings: Marlene Dumas, Juan Muñoz, Thomas Schütte. Frith Street Gallery, London. November 25, 1994–January 21, 1995.

1995

Der Janustempel. Kunstmuseen Krefeld Kaiser Wilhelm Museum, Germany. February 19–September 3 (cat.).
Micromegas. American Center, Paris. March 9–June 4. Traveled to Israel Museum, Jerusalem, July 18–October 18 (cat.).
Them and Us. Lisson Gallery, London. May 5–July 1.
Artistes, architectes. Institut d'Art Contemporain, Villeurbanne, France. October 7, 1995–January 20, 1996 (cat.).

1996

Beuys and After: Contemporary German Drawings from the Collection. The Museum of Modern Art, New York. February 1–May 14 (cat.).
Private View: A Temporary Exhibition of Contemporary British and German Art. Organized by Henry Moore Institute. Bowes Museum, Barnard Castle, United Kingdom. May 4–July 28 (cat.).
Quo Vadis? Museum Fridericianum, Kassel, Germany. May 22–July 21.
Distemper: Dissonant Themes in the Art of the 1990s. Hirshhorn Museum and Sculpture Garden, Washington, DC. June 20–September 15 (cat.).

1997

Erstbezug: Künstler richten die Galerie der Gegenwart ein. Hamburger Kunsthalle, Hamburg. Opened February (cat.).
Das neue Gesicht. Kunstverein Konstanz, Germany. February 8–April 6 (cat.).
Documenta X. Museum Fridericianum, Kassel, Germany. June 21–September 28 (cat.).
Skulptur Projekte Münster. Münster, Germany. June 22–September 28 (cat.).
Young German Artists 2. Saatchi Gallery, London. September–November (cat.).
A Decade of Collecting: Recent Acquisitions in Contemporary Drawing. The Museum of Modern Art, New York. September 8, 1997–January 20, 1998.
Zuspiel: Thomas Schütte und Henrik Wolff. Kunstverein für die Rheinlande und Westfalen, Düsseldorf. September 27–November 16 (cat.).

1998

Wounds: Between Democracy and Redemption in Contemporary Art. Moderna Museet, Stockholm. February 14–April 19 (cat.).
The House in the Woods: Five Contemporary German Sculptors. Centre for Contemporary Arts Glasgow. April 3–April 27. Traveled to Aberdeen Art Gallery, Scotland, June 6–July 11, and Ormeau Baths Gallery, Belfast, August 20–October 3 (cat.).
Jardin d'artiste: De mémoire d'arbre. Musée Zadkine, Paris. June 11–October 11 (cat.).
Im Reich der Phantome: Fotografie des Unsichtbaren. Fotomuseum Winterthur, Switzerland. June 13–August 16 (cat.).
Mise en scène: Theater und Kunst. Grazer Kunstverein, Graz, Austria. September 27–October 31 (cat.).
A Portrait of Our Times: An Introduction to the Logan Collection. San Francisco Museum of Modern Art. September 29, 1998–January 3, 1999 (cat.).
Unfinished History. Walker Art Center, Minneapolis, Minnesota. October 18, 1998–January 10, 1999 (cat.).

1999

Dream City. Kunstraum München, Kunstverein München, and Museum Villa Stuck, Munich. March 25–June 20 (cat.).
Gesammelte Werke 1. Zeitgenössische Kunst seit 1968. Kunstmuseum Wolfsburg, Germany. July 17–October 3 (cat.).
La realitat i el desig. Fundació Joan Miró, Barcelona. September 23–November 7 (cat.).
Am horizont. Kunstmuseen Krefeld Kaiser Wilhelm Museum, Germany. November 21, 1999–February 27, 2000 (cat.).

Zeitwenden. Kunstmuseum Bonn. December 4, 1999–June 4, 2000. Traveled to Museum moderner Kunst Stiftung Ludwig Wien, Künstlerhaus Wien, Vienna, July 5, 1999–October 1, 2000 (cat.).
Zoom: Ansichten zur deutschen Gegenwartskunst. Württembergischer Kunstverein, Stuttgart, May 20–June 13, Sammlung Landesbank Baden-Württemberg, Stuttgart, May 20–June 20, Galerie Landesbank Baden-Württemberg, May 20–June 27, Galerie der Stadt Stuttgart, May 20–June 27, and Galerie der Stadt Esslingen, Villa Merkel und Bähnwärterhaus, Esslingen, May 20–June 27. Traveled to Städtische Museum Abteiberg, Mönchengladbach, June 11–August 29, and Kunsthalle zu Kiel, Germany, November 14, 1999–January 9, 2000 (cat.).

2000

Das fünfte Element. Geld oder Kunst. Städtische Kunsthalle Düsseldorf. January 28–May 14 (cat.).
Dein Wille geschehe . . . Das Bild des Vaters in der zeitgenössischen Kunst. Haus am Waldsee, Berlin. February 19–April 2 (cat.).
HausSchau. Deichtorhallen Hamburg. May 12–September 17 (cat.).
Between Cinema and a Hard Place. Tate Modern, London. May 12–December 3 (cat.).
How You Look at It: Fotografien des 20. Jahrhunderts. Sprengel Museum Hannover, Hanover, Germany. May 14–August 6 (cat.).
Around 1984: A Look at Art in the Eighties. MoMA PS1, Long Island City, New York. May 21–September 30.
Von Edgar Degas bis Gerhard Richter: Arbeiten auf Papier aus der Sammlung des Kunstmuseums Winterthur. Kunstmuseum Winterthur, Switzerland. August 25–November 19. Traveled to Palác Kinských, Prague, December 15, 2000–March 25, 2001; Museum der Moderne, Salzburg, Austria, April 7–May 20, 2001; Westfälisches Landesmuseum für Kunst und Kulturgeschichte, Münster, Germany, June 3–August 26, 2001; and Neues Museum Nürnberg, Nuremberg, Germany, December 7, 2001–February 24, 2002 (cat.).
Many Colored Objects Placed Side by Side to Form a Row of Many Colored Objects: Works from the Collection of Annick and Anton Herbert. Casino Luxembourg. October 29, 2000–February 11, 2001 (cat.).

2001

Painting at the Edge of the World. Walker Art Center, Minneapolis, Minnesota. February 7–May 6 (cat.).
Between Earth and Heaven. New Classical Movements in the Art of Today. Provinciaal Museum voor Moderne Kunst, Ostend, Belgium. February 23–September 2 (cat.).
Collaborations with Parkett: 1984 to Now. The Museum of Modern Art, New York. April 5–June 5 (cat.).
Sonsbeek 9: Locus Focus. Arnhem, Netherlands. July 2–August 29.
Beautiful Productions: Art to Play, Art to Wear, Art to Own. Whitechapel Art Gallery, London. July 6–August 19, 2001.
Dialogue ininterrompu. Musée des Beaux-Arts, Nantes. July 7–November 19 (cat.).
Ex(o)dus. Haifa Museum of Art, Israel. Opened September 15 (cat.).
Inmensidad íntima: Una selección de obras del Museo de Arte Contemporáneo de Gante. Museo Tamayo, Mexico City. December 13, 2001–April 14, 2002 (cat.).

2002

De Gustibus: Collezione Privata Italia. Palazzo delle Papesse, Siena, Italy. March 2–May 12 (cat.).
Startkapital. Kunstsammlung Nordrhein-Westfalen K21, Düsseldorf. April 20–September 8 (cat.).
Pop! Die Pop Art und die zeitgenössische Bildhauerkunst. Gerhard Marcks Haus, Bremen, Germany. April 28–July 21 (cat.).
The Object Sculpture. Henry Moore Institute, Leeds, United Kingdom. May 30–August 30 (cat.).

2003

Grotesk! 130 Jahre Kunst der Frechheit. Schirn Kunsthalle Frankfurt. March 27–June 9. Traveled to Haus der Kunst, Munich, June 27–September 14 (cat.).
Sculpture de Derain à Séchas: Collection du Centre Pompidou. Carré d'Art—Musée d'Art Contemporain, Nîmes. May 6–August 31 (cat.).
Warum! Bilder diesseits und jenseits des Menschen. Martin-Gropius-Bau, Berlin. May 27–August 3 (cat.).
Durchgehend geöffnet. Staatliche Kunsthalle Baden-Baden, Germany. July 5–September 7 (cat.).
Berlin Moskau / Moskau Berlin: 1950–2000. Martin-Gropius-Bau, Berlin. September 28, 2003–January 5, 2004. Traveled to State Tretyakov Gallery, Moscow, March 21–June 15, 2004. (cat.).

2004

Treasure Island. Kunstmuseum Wolfsburg, Germany. February 7–April 18.
Multiple Räume (1): Seele. Konstruktionen des Innerlichen in der Kunst. Staatliche Kunsthalle Baden-Baden, Germany. February 14–April 18 (cat.).
Sammlung Plum. Museum Kurhaus Kleve, Germany. May 23–September 5 (cat.).
Étrangement proche. Saarland Museum, Saarbrücken, Germany. June 11–August 8 (cat.).
Interior View: Artists Explore the Language of Architecture. De Zonnehof Centrum voor Moderne Kunst, Amersfoort, Netherlands. June 29–September 26. Traveled to Firstsite, Colchester, United Kingdom, December 17, 2004–February 26, 2005, and Friart Centre d'Art Contemporain, Fribourg, Switzerland, July 2–September 11, 2005 (cat.).
Disparities and Deformations: Our Grotesque. SITE Santa Fe 5th International Biennale, New Mexico. July 18, 2004–January 9, 2005.
See History 2004: Der demokratische Blick. Kunsthalle zu Kiel, Germany. July 24, 2004–June 19, 2005 (cat.).
Dependent Objects. Busch-Reisinger Museum, Harvard University Art Museums, Cambridge, Massachusetts. September 18, 2004–January 2, 2005 (cat.).
Friedrich Christian Flick Collection im Hamburger Bahnhof. Hamburger Bahnhof, Berlin. September 22, 2004–August 7, 2005 (cat.).
Reanimation: Hermann Gerber. Kunstmuseum Thun, Switzerland. September 24–November 21 (cat.).
ArchiSkulptur. Fondation Beyeler, Basel. October 3, 2004–January 30, 2005. Traveled to Museo Guggenheim Bilbao, Spain, October 28, 2005–February 19, 2006, and Kunstmuseum Wolfsburg, Germany, April 1–September 10, 2006 (cat.)
Skulptur: Prekärer Realismus zwischen Melancholie und Komik. Kunsthalle Wien, Vienna. October 15, 2004–February 20, 2005 (cat.).
Faces in the Crowd: Picturing Modern Life from Manet to Today. Whitechapel Gallery, London. December 3, 2004–March 6, 2005. Traveled to Castello di Rivoli, Rivoli/Turin, April 6–July 10, 2005 (cat.).

2005

Regarding Terror: The RAF-Exhibition. KW Institute for Contemporary Art, Berlin. January 30–May 16. Traveled to Neue Galerie Graz am Landesmuseum Joanneum, Austria. June 26–August 28 (cat.).
Universal Experience: Art, Life, and the Tourist's Eye. Museum of Contemporary Art Chicago. February 12–June 5. Traveled to Hayward Gallery, London, October 6–December 11 (cat.).
An Aside: Selected by Tacita Dean. Camden Arts Centre, London. February 18–May 1. Traveled to Fruitmarket Gallery, Edinburgh, May 14–July 12, and Glynn Vivian Art Gallery, Swansea, United Kingdom, October 1–November 27 (cat.).
Kunst in Schokolade. Museum Ludwig, Cologne. March 17–June 19 (cat.).
(My Private) Heroes. MARTa Herford, Germany. May 7–August 14 (cat.).
Bilanz in zwei Akten. Kunstverein Hannover, Hanover, Germany. June 11–August 21 (cat.).
The Experience of Art. 51st Venice Biennale. June 12–November 6.
Big Bang: Déstruction et création dans l'art du 20e siècle. Centre Pompidou, Paris. June 15, 2005–April 3, 2006 (cat.).
In the Middle of the Night: Die Neuerwerbungen seit 1996. Kunsthalle Bielefeld, Germany. August 28–November 6 (cat.).
Drawing from the Modern, 1975–2005. The Museum of Modern Art, New York. September 14, 2005–January 9, 2006 (cat.).
Flashback: Eine Revision der Kunst der 80er Jahre. Kunstmuseum Basel. September 29, 2005–February 11, 2006 (cat.).

2006

Public Space / Two Audiences. Obras y documentos de la Colección Herbert. Inventaire. Museu d'Art Contemporani de Barcelona, February 8–May 1. Traveled to Kunsthaus Graz am Landesmuseum Joanneum, Austria, June 10–September 3 (cat.).
Von Mäusen und Menschen. 4th Berlin Biennale. March 25–June 5 (cat.).
Long Live Sculpture! Middelheimmuseum, Antwerp. June 1–September 3, 2006 (cat.).
Radar: Selections from the Collection of Vicki and Kent Logan. Denver Art Museum. October 7, 2006–July 15, 2007 (cat.).
The Unhomely: Phantom Scenes of Global Society. 2nd Bienal Internacional de Arte Contemporáneo de Sevilla, Seville. October 26, 2006–January 15, 2007 (cat.).
The 80s: A Topology. Museu de Arte Contemporânea de Serralves, Porto. November 11, 2006–March 25, 2007 (cat.).

2007

Die Kunst zu sammeln: Das 20./21. Jahrhundert in Düsseldorfer Privat- und Unternehmensbesitz. Museum Kunstpalast, Düsseldorf. April 21–July 22 (cat.).
Rockers Island. Olbricht Collection. Museum Folkwang, Essen, Germany. May 5–July 1 (cat.).
The Present: The Monique Zajfen Collection. Stedelijk Museum, Amsterdam. June 2–September 16.
Artempo: Where Time Becomes Art. Museo Fortuny, Venice. June 9–October 7 (cat.).
Skulptur Projekte Münster. Westfälisches Landesmuseum, Münster, Germany. June 17–September 30.

2008

Out of Shape: Stylistic Distortions of the Human Form in Art from the Logan Collection. Frances Lehman Loeb Art Center, Vassar College, Poughkeepsie, New York. March 14–June 8 (cat.).
La collection de Pont à Paris. Institut Néerlandais, Paris. April 9–June 8 (cat.).

Kavalierstart 1978–1982. Museum Morsbroich, Leverkusen, Germany. April 20–July 20 (cat.).
Life on Mars. 55th Carnegie International, Carnegie Museum of Art, Pittsburgh. May 3, 2008–January 11, 2009 (cat.).
The Immediate Touch: German, Austrian, and Swiss Drawings from Saint Louis Collections, 1946–2007. Saint Louis Art Museum, Missouri. June 29–September 7 (cat.).
After Nature. New Museum, New York. July 17–October 5 (cat.).
Order. Desire. Light. An Exhibition of Contemporary Drawings. Irish Museum of Modern Art, Dublin. July 25–November 23 (cat.).
Nient'altro che scultura. 13th Biennale Internazionale di Scultura di Carrara, Centro Arti Plastiche Internazionali e Contemporanee, Italy. July 27–September 28 (cat.).
Heavy Metal: Vor der unerklärliche Leichtigkeit eines Materials. Kunsthalle zu Kiel, Germany. December 7, 2008–August 30, 2009 (cat.).

2009

Art of Two Germanys / Cold War Cultures. Los Angeles County Museum of Art. January 25–April 19. Traveled to Germanisches Nationalmuseum, Nuremberg, Germany, May 23–September 6, and Deutsches Historisches Museum, Berlin, October 3, 2009–January 10, 2010 (cat.).
Compass in Hand: Selections from The Judith Rothschild Foundation Contemporary Drawings Collection. The Museum of Modern Art, New York. April 22, 2009–January 4, 2010 (cat.).
Gipfeltreffen der Moderne: Das Kunstmuseum Winterthur. Kunst- und Ausstellungshalle der Bundesrepublik Deutschland, Bonn. April 24–August 23. Traveled to Museo de Arte Contemporanea di Trento e Roverto, Italy, September 19, 2009–January 10, 2010, and Museum der Moderne, Salzburg, Austria, February 27–May 30, 2010 (cat.).
60 Jahre. 60 Werke: Kunst aus der Bundesrepublik Deutschland 1949–2009. Martin-Gropius-Bau, Berlin. May 1–June 14 (cat.).
Heidi au pays de Martin Kippenberger. Frac Nouvelle-Aquitaine MÉCA, Bordeaux. May 28–September 5 (cat.).
Locus Oculi. Château de la Batie d'Urfé, Saint Étienne-le-Molard, France. June 21–October 4 (cat.).
Abstraktion und Einfühlung. Deutsche Guggenheim Berlin. August 15–October 16.
Das Fundament der Kunst. Die Skulptur und ihr Sockel in der Moderne. Städtische Museen Heilbronn, Germany. October 24, 2009–January 31, 2010. Traveled to Gerhard Marcks Haus, Bremen, Germany, February 28–May 23, 2010, and Arp Museum Bahnhof Rolandseck, Remagen, Germany, June 25–October 24, 2010 (cat.).

2010

Visceral Bodies. Vancouver Art Gallery. February 6–May 16 (cat.).
With a Probability of Being Seen: Dorothee and Konrad Fischer; Archives of an Attitude. Museu d'Art Contemporani de Barcelona. May 15–October 12. Traveled to Museum Kurhaus Kleve, Germany, November 14, 2010–March 20, 2011 (cat.).
Der Westen leuchtet. Kunstmuseum Bonn. July 10–October 24 (cat.).
Intensif-Station. Kunstsammlung Nordrhein-Westfalen K21, Düsseldorf. July 10, 2010–September 4, 2011.
Auswertung der Flugdaten, Kunst der 80er. Eine Düsseldorfer Retrospektive. Kunstsammlung Nordrhein-Westfalen K21, Düsseldorf. September 11, 2010–January 30, 2011.
Die Natur der Kunst: Begegnungen mit der Natur vom 19. Jahrhundert bis in die Gegenwart. Kunstmuseum Winterthur, Switzerland. October 31, 2010–February 27, 2011 (cat.).

2011

Vollendet das ewige Werk: Sammlung Rheingold in Schloss Dyck 2011. Stiftung Schloss Dyck, Jüchen, Germany. April 10–October 30 (cat.).
KölnSkulptur #6. Skulpturenpark Köln, Cologne. May 15, 2011–May 1, 2013 (cat.).
Living: Frontiers of Architecture III–IV. Louisiana Museum of Modern Art, Humlebæk, Denmark. June 1–October 2 (cat.).
Ostalgia. New Museum, New York. July 6–October 2 (cat.).
Heinz und Marianne Ebers-Stiftung: Eine Sammlung von Format. Kunstmuseen Krefeld Museum Haus Lange, Germany. July 17–September 25 (cat.).
Architektonika. Hamburger Bahnhof, Berlin. September 15, 2011–February 12, 2012 (cat.).
Wunder: Kunst, Wissenschaft und Religion vom 4. Jahrhundert bis zur Gegenwart. Deichtorhallen Hamburg. September 23, 2011–February 5, 2012 (cat.).
Mit Feuer und Flamme. Museum Villa Rot, Burgrieden, Germany. October 2, 2011–February 5, 2012 (cat.)
Vor dem Gesetz: Skulpturen der Nachkriegszeit und Räume der Gegenwartskunst. Museum Ludwig, Cologne. December 17, 2011–April 22, 2012 (cat.).

2012

Glasstress New York: New Art from the Venice Biennales. Museum of Arts and Design, New York. February 14–June 10 (cat.).
Print/Out. The Museum of Modern Art, New York. February 19–May 14 (cat.).
New to the Print Collection: Matisse to Bourgeois. The Museum of Modern Art, New York. June 13, 2012–January 7, 2013.
El factor grotesco. Fundación Museo Picasso, Málaga, Spain. October 21, 2012–February 9, 2013 (cat.).

2013

Die Bildhauer: Kunstakademie Düsseldorf, 1945 bis heute. Kunstsammlung Nordrhein-Westfalen K20, Düsseldorf. February 20–July 28 (cat.).
KölnSkulptur #7. Skulpturenpark Köln, Cologne. May 5, 2013–May 2015 (cat.).
Back to Earth: Von Picasso bis Ai Weiwei—Die Wiederentdeckung der Keramik in der Kunst. Herbert Gerisch-Stiftung, Neumünster, Germany. May 25–October 27 (cat.).
Glasstress: White Light / White Heat. Istituto Veneto di Scienze, Lettere ed Arti, Berengo Centre for Contemporary Art and Glass, and Scuola Grande de the Confraternity of San Teodoro, Venice. June 1–November 24 (cat.).
As If It Could: Works and Documents from the Herbert Foundation, Ouverture. Herbert Foundation, Ghent. June 20–October 26 (cat.).
Thomas Schütte, Danh Vo: Das Reich ohne Mitte. Kunsthalle Mainz, Germany. July 5–October 6 (cat.).
Auf Zeit / For the Time Being. Kunsthalle Bielefeld, Germany. August 4–October 20 (cat.).

2014

Unter der Erde: Von Kafka bis Kippenberger. Kunstsammlung Nordrhein-Westfalen K21, Düsseldorf. April 5–August 10.
Body and Void: Echoes of Moore in Contemporary Art. Henry Moore Institute, Perry Green, United Kingdom. May 1–October 26 (cat.).
Keramische Räume. Museum Morsbroich, Leverkusen, Germany. May 25–August 31 (cat.).
Vanitas: Ewig ist eh nichts. Georg Kolbe Museum, Berlin. June 15–August 31 (cat.).
The Human Factor: The Figure in Contemporary Sculpture. Hayward Gallery, London. June 17–September 7 (cat.).
Branching Out: Positionen zur Natur von Achenbach, Schütte, Schwenk und Struth. Museum Ratingen, Germany. September 26, 2014–February 8, 2015 (cat.).
Ohne Achtsamkeit beachte ich alles. Robert Walser und die bildende Kunst. Aargauer Kunsthaus, Aarau, Switzerland. May 10–July 27, 2014 (cat.).
Some Artists' Artists. Marian Goodman Gallery, New York. June 26–August 22.
Genuine Conceptualism. Herbert Foundation, Ghent. July 4–November 8 (cat.).
Bad Thoughts: Collectie Martijn en Jeanette Sanders. Stedelijk Museum, Amsterdam. July 20, 2014–January 10, 2015 (cat.).
Intenzione manifesta: Il disegno in tutte le sue forme. Castello di Rivoli, Rivoli/Turin. October 11, 2014–January 25, 2015.

2015

Model. Galerie Rudolfinum, Prague. January 29–May 3 (cat.).
(Un)möglich! Künstler als Architekten. MARTa Herford, Germany. February 21–May 31 (cat.).
Gesichter: Ein Motiv zwischen Figur, Porträt und Maske. Neues Museum Nürnberg, Nuremburg, Germany. March 20–June 21 (cat.).
Bare Wunder: Sigmar Polke—100 Years of Mediumistic and Phantasmagorical Photography. Sies + Höke Gallery, Düsseldorf. March 26–May 2 (cat.).
Andy Warhol sul comò. Museo d'Arte Contemporanea di Villa Croce, Genoa. April 2–July 5 (cat.).
Artzuid 2015. Stichting Art Zuid, Amsterdam. May 22–September 22 (cat.).
Formes biographiques. Carré d'Art—Musée d'Art Contemporain de Nîmes, France. May 29–September 20 (cat.).
Beyond Borders. 5th Beaufort Triennial, Belgium. June 21–September 21.
Endless House: Intersections of Art and Architecture. The Museum of Modern Art, New York. June 27, 2015–March 6, 2016.
Avatar und Atavismus / Outside der Avantgarde. Kunsthalle Düsseldorf. August 22–November 8 (cat.).
The Great Mother. Fondazione Nicola Trussardi, Palazzo Reale, Milan. August 26–November 15 (cat.).
Ruhe vor dem Sturm: Postminimalistische Kunst aus dem Rheinland. Museum Morsbroich, Leverkusen, Germany. September 13, 2015–January 10, 2016 (cat.).
Artistes et architecture, Dimensions variables. Pavillon de l'Arsenal, Paris. October 16, 2015–January 17, 2016 (cat.).
Ceramix: Keramiek in de kunst van Rodin tot Schütte. Bonnefanten, Maastricht, Netherlands. October 16, 2015–January 30, 2016. Traveled to Sèvres–Cité de la Céramique and La Maison Rouge, Sèvres, France, March 9–June 12, 2016 (cat.).
A Few Free Years: Von Absalon bis Zobernig. Hamburger Bahnhof, Berlin. November 28, 2015–March 13, 2016 (cat.).

2016

Terra provocata: Percezione della materia e concetto nella materia. Fondazione del Monte, Bologna. January 23–March 20 (cat.).

Von Lucio Fontana bis Thomas Schütte: Erwerbungen 2000–2016 und ausgewählte ältere Bestände. Kunstmuseum Winterthur, Switzerland. January 30–May 22 (cat.).
Accrochage. Palazzo Grassi, Punta della Dogana, Venice. April 17–November 20 (cat.).
Mir ist das Leben lieber: Sammlung Reydan Weiss. Weserburg Museum für Moderne Kunst, Bremen, Germany. May 21, 2016–February 26, 2017 (cat.).
With a Touch of Pink / With a Bit of Violet / With a Hint of Green—Dorothee Fischer in Memoriam. Konrad Fischer Galerie, Düsseldorf. June 3–July 23.
Elective Affinities: German Art since the Late 1960s. Latvian National Museum of Art, Riga. June 17–August 21 (cat.).
Wolke und Kristall: Die Sammlung Dorothee und Konrad Fischer. Kunstsammlung Nordrhein-Westfalen K20, Düsseldorf. September 24, 2016–January 8, 2017 (cat.).
Geliebte Feinde—Symbolismus heute von Peter Doig bis Thomas Schütte. Clemens Sels Museum Neuss, Germany. October 23, 2016–February 19, 2017.

2017

Moving Is in Every Direction. Environments—Installationen—Narrative Räume. Hamburger Bahnhof, Berlin. March 17–September 24 (cat.).
Skulptur Projekte Münster 2017. Münster, Germany. June 10–October 1 (cat.).
The Long Run. The Museum of Modern Art, New York. November 11, 2017–May 5, 2019.

2018

The Playground Project. Bundeskunsthalle, Bonn. May 31–October 28 (cat.).
Zéro de conduite. Fundação de Serralves, Porto. June 1–September 9 (cat.).
L'Almanach 18. Consortium Museum, Dijon, France. June 22–October 14.
Debout! Musée des Beaux-Arts, Rennes, France. June 23–September 9 (cat.).

2019

A Cool Breeze. Galerie Rudolfinum, Prague. April 25–August 11 (cat.).
Homo Faber: Craft in Contemporary Sculpture. Asia Culture Center, Gwangju, South Korea. September 5, 2019–February 23, 2020 (cat.).

2020

Strand: Isa Genzken, Blinky Palermo, Sigmar Polke, Gerhard Richter, Thomas Schütte. Sies + Höke, Düsseldorf. January 24–March 7 (cat.).
KölnSkulptur #10: ÜberNatur—Natural Takeover. Skulpturenpark Köln, Cologne. August 1, 2020–July 31, 2022 (cat.).
Wände / Walls. Kunstmuseum Stuttgart. September 26, 2020–May 30, 2021.

2021

Serien: Druckgraphik von Warhol bis Wool. Hamburger Kunsthalle, Hamburg. April 16–August 15 (cat.).
Moment. Monument. Kunst Museum Winterthur, Switzerland. May 8–August 15 (cat.).
Closer to Life: Drawings and Works on Paper in the Marieluise Hessel Collection. Center for Curatorial Studies, Bard College, Annandale-on-Hudson, New York. June 26–October 17 (cat.).
Au rendez-vous des amis: Klassische Moderne im Dialog mit Gegenwartskunst aus der Sammlung Goetz Teil 2. Pinakothek der Moderne, Munich. August 6, 2021–January 16, 2022 (cat.).
Les flames: L'âge de la céramique. Musée d'Art Moderne de Paris. October 15, 2021–February 6, 2022 (cat.).
Fragile! Alles aus Glas. Kunsthalle Vogelmann, Heilbronn, Germany. December 18, 2021–May 5, 2022. Traveled to Kunstmuseum Ahlen, Germany, June 19–October 16, 2022 (cat.).

2022

Schatzhaus und Labor: 25 Jahre Museum Kurhaus Kleve. Museum Kurhaus Kleve, Germany. July 23, 2022–January 29, 2023 (cat.).

2023

Reaching for the Stars: From Maurizio Cattelan to Lynette Yiadom-Boakye. Fondazione Palazzo Strozzi, Florence. March 4–June 18 (cat.).
Nord-Süd: Perspektiven auf die Sammlung. Kunst Museum Winterthur, Switzerland. March 12–October 30.

Selected Bibliography

Compiled by Caitlin Chaisson and Lydia Mullin

MONOGRAPHS AND SOLO EXHIBITION CATALOGUES

Fifteen Monuments by Thomas Schütte. Villeurbanne, France: Galerie Philip Nelson, 1984. Exhibition catalogue.

Thomas Schütte: Pläne I–XXX, 1981. Hamburg: Produzentengalerie Hamburg, 1985. Exhibition catalogue.

Thomas Schütte: Skizzen zu Skulpturen, 1985. Hamburg: Produzentengalerie Hamburg, 1985. Exhibition catalogue.

Thomas Schütte. Krefeld, West Germany: Krefelder Kunstmuseen, 1986. Exhibition catalogue.

Thomas Schütte. Turin: Galleria Tucci Russo, 1986. Exhibition catalogue.

Thomas Schütte: Aquarellen. Amsterdam: Museum Overholland, 1987. Exhibition catalogue.

Wilmes, Ulrich, ed. *Thomas Schütte: Obst und Gemüse.* Münster: Landschaftsverband Westfalen-Lippe, Westfälisches Landesmuseum für Kunst und Kulturgeschichte, 1987. Exhibition catalogue.

Poetter, Jochen, ed. *Thomas Schütte.* Baden-Baden, West Germany: Staatliche Kunsthalle Baden-Baden, 1988. Exhibition catalogue.

Simple Stories. Düsseldorf: Galerie Ute Parduhn, 1989. Exhibition catalogue.

Wilmes, Ulrich, ed. *Thomas Schütte: The Laundry and Mohr's Life.* Frankfurt: Portikus; Amsterdam: De Appel, 1989. Exhibition catalogue.

Thomas Schütte: Notes. New York: Marian Goodman Gallery, 1990.

Loock, Ulrich, ed. *Thomas Schütte*. Bern: Kunsthalle Bern, 1990. Exhibition catalogue.

Thomas Schütte. Turin: Galleria Tucci Russo, 1992. Exhibition catalogue.

Requiem. Nîmes, France: Carré d'Art—Musée d'Art Contemporain, 1994.

Thomas Schütte: Alte Freunde—Neue Arbeiten. Hamburg: Produzentengalerie Hamburg, 1994. Exhibition catalogue.

Thomas Schütte: [Figur]. Hamburg: Hamburger Kunsthalle, 1994. Exhibition catalogue.

Skizzen und Geschichten 1990–1995. Düsseldorf: Richter Verlag; Munich: Kunstraum München, 1995. Exhibition catalogue.

Thomas Schütte: 1995, Tokio. Tokyo: Wako Works of Art, 1995. Exhibition catalogue.

Thomas Schütte. Stuttgart: Institut für Auslandsbeziehungen, 1996. Exhibition catalogue.

Thomas Schütte: Blumen mit Luise. Bern: Galerie Erika + Otto Friedrich, 1996. Exhibition catalogue.

Thomas Schütte: Kunstpreisträger der Stadt Wolfsburg 1996 "Junge Stadt sieht Junge Kunst." Wolfsburg, Germany: Städtische Galerie und Kunstverein, 1996. Exhibition catalogue.

Könnecke, Achim, ed. *Haus des Gedenkens in der KZ-Gedenkstätte Neuengamme*. Hamburg: Kellner Verlag, 1996.

Heynen, Julian, James Lingwood, and Angela Vettese. *Thomas Schütte.* London: Phaidon, 1998. Exhibition catalogue.

Thomas Schütte: 5 Frauen; Schlosspark Wendlinghausen, Garten Landschaft OWL. Munich: Landschaftsverband Westfalen-Lippe, 2000. Exhibition catalogue.

Schumacher, Rainald, ed. *Thomas Schütte*. Munich: Kunstverlag Ingvild Goetz, Sammlung Goetz, 2001. Exhibition catalogue.

Thomas Schütte. Hamburg: Produzentengalerie Hamburg, 2002. Exhibition catalogue.

Thomas Schütte: Stahlfrauen / Große Geister. Essen, Germany: Museum Folkwang, 2002. Exhibition catalogue.

Wattwanderung, 2001: In 30 Serien; 138 Copper Plate Prints. Düsseldorf: self-published, 2002.

Cooke, Lynne, and Karen Kelly, eds. *Thomas Schütte: Scenewright, Gloria in Memoria, In Medias Res*. New York: Dia Art Foundation; Düsseldorf: Richter Verlag, 2002. Exhibition catalogue.

Schwarz, Dieter, ed. *Thomas Schütte: Kreuzzug, 2003–2004.* Winterthur, Switzerland: Kunstmuseum Winterthur; Grenoble, France: Musée de Grenoble; Düsseldorf: K21 Kunstsammlung Nordrhein-Westfalen, 2003. Exhibition catalogue.

Zwirner, Dorothea, ed. *Thomas Schütte*. Berlin: Friedrich Christian Flick Collection; Cologne: DuMont Literatur und Kunst Verlag, 2004.

Thomas Schütte. Stockholm: Jarla Partilager, 2006. Exhibition catalogue.

Thomas Schütte: Architektur Modelle 1980–2006. Munich: Sabine Knust Maximilian Verlag, 2006.

Winzen, Matthias, ed. *Thomas Schütte: Zeichnungen/ Drawings*. Baden-Baden, Germany: Staatliche Kunsthalle Baden-Baden; Cologne: Snoeck Verlagsgesellschaft, 2006. Exhibition catalogue.

Thomas Schütte: Frauen and Blumen, 1997–2007. Munich: Sabine Knust Maximilian Verlag, 2007.

Curtis, Penelope. *Thomas Schütte: Early Work.* Leeds, United Kingdom: Henry Moore Institute, 2007. Exhibition catalogue.

Friedrich, Julia, ed. *Thomas Schütte: Bücher.* Cologne: Strzelecki Books, 2008.

Mann im Matsch. Düsseldorf: self-published, 2009.

Cooke, Lynne, ed. *Thomas Schütte: Hindsight.* Madrid: Museo Nacional Centro de Arte Reina Sofía, 2009. Exhibition catalogue.

Dander, Patrizia, ed. *Thomas Schütte: Deprinotes, 2006–2008.* Munich: Haus der Kunst; Düsseldorf: Richter Verlag, 2009. Exhibition catalogue.

Thomas Schütte: Big Buildings; Modelle und Ansichten / Models and Views, 1980–2010. Bonn: Kunst- und Ausstellungshalle der Bundesrepublik Deutschland; Cologne: Snoeck Verlagsgesellschaft, 2010. Exhibition catalogue.

Thomas Schütte: Works from the Portalakis Collection. Athens: Portalakis Collection, 2010.

Het Huis: Thomas Schütte Sculpturen / Robbrecht en Daem Architecten. Antwerp: Ludion and Middelheimmuseum, 2012. Exhibition catalogue.

Loock, Ulrich, ed. *Thomas Schütte: Public/Political.* Cologne: Walther König, 2012. Exhibition catalogue.

O'Brien, Sophie, ed. *Thomas Schütte: Faces and Figures*. London: Serpentine Gallery and Koenig Books, 2012. Exhibition catalogue.

Vecellio, Marianna, and Elodie Biancheri, eds. *Thomas Schütte: Frauen*. Rivoli/Turin: Castello di Rivoli; Monaco: Nouveau Musée National de Monaco; Düsseldorf: Richter | Fey Verlag, 2012. Exhibition catalogue.

Wester, Anders, ed. *Thomas Schütte: With Tears in My Ears.* Stockholm: Jarla Partilager, 2012. Exhibition catalogue.

Vecellio, Marianna, Elodie Biancheri, and Catherine Macchi, eds. *Thomas Schütte: Houses*. Lucerne, Switzerland: Kunstmuseum Luzern; Monaco: Nouveau Musée National de Monaco; Düsseldorf: Richter | Fey Verlag, 2013. Exhibition catalogue.

Vischer, Theodora, ed. *Thomas Schütte: Figur*. Riehen/ Basel: Beyeler Museum; Cologne: Walther König, 2013. Exhibition catalogue.

Thomas Schütte: Watercolors for Robert Walser and Donald Young, 2011–2012. Paris: Éditions Cahiers d'Art, 2014.

Gundel, Marc, and Rita E. Täuber, eds. *Thomas Schütte.* Heilbronn, Germany: Kunsthalle Vogelmann, Städtische Museen Heilbronn; Munich: Hirmer Verlag, 2014. Exhibition catalogue.

Jablonka, Rafael, and Teresa Jablonka, eds. *Thomas Schütte: Ferienhaus T.* Cologne: 2014.

Thomas Schütte. Athens: Bernier/Eliades Gallery and Agra Publications, 2015. Exhibition catalogue.

Olof-Ors, Matilda, ed. *Thomas Schütte: United Enemies.* London: Koenig Books; Stockholm: Moderna Museet, 2016. Exhibition catalogue.
Thomas Schütte. Paris: 11 Conti—Monnaie de Paris; Ghent: Éditions Snoeck, 2019. Exhibition catalogue.
Gundel, Marc, ed. *Thomas Schütte: One Man House.* Heilbronn, Germany: Städtische Museen Heilbronn und Künstler, 2019. Exhibition catalogue.
Trummer, Thomas D., ed. *Thomas Schütte.* Bregenz, Austria: Kunsthaus Bregenz, 2019. Exhibition catalogue.
Thomas Schütte. Basel: Kunstforum Baloise Park, 2020.
Bonnet, Anne-Marie, ed. *Thomas Schütte: Keramik.* Düsseldorf: Hetjens—Deutsches Keramikmuseum, 2020. Exhibition catalogue.
Lange, Christiane, and Julian Heynen, eds. *Thomas Schütte: Krefeld Pavillon.* Ostfildern-Ruit, Germany: Hatje Cantz, 2020. Exhibition catalogue.
Walther, Linda. *Schwebezustände: "Frauen" von Thomas Schütte.* Berlin: Walter de Gruyter, 2020.
Wallner, Julia, ed. *Thomas Schütte.* Berlin: Georg Kolbe Museum, 2021. Exhibition catalogue.
de Chassey, Éric, ed. *Thomas Schütte: Old Friends Revisited.* Paris: Édition Cahiers d'Art, 2023.
Schwarz, Dieter. *Thomas Schütte: Houses II.* Berlin: Jovis Verlag, 2023. Exhibition catalogue.

GROUP EXHIBITION CATALOGUES

Heidt Heller, Renate, ed. *Schlaglichter: Eine Bestandsaufnahme aktueller Kunst im Rheinland.* Cologne: Rheinland-Verlag, 1979.
Hering, Karl Heinz, ed. *Perspektiven 1: Aus den Klassen der Professoren: Rolf Crummenauer, Gerhard Hoehme, Alfonso Hüppi, Dieter Krieg, Christian Megert, Ellen Neumann, Gerhard Richter, Rissa, Fritz Schwegler. Schüler der Düsseldorfer Kunstakademie stellen ihre Arbeiten vor.* Düsseldorf: Kunstverein für die Rheinlande und Westfalen, 1979.
Glozer, Laszlo. *Westkunst: Zeitgenössische Kunst seit 1939.* Cologne: DuMont Buchverlag, 1981.
Art allemagne aujourd'hui: Différents aspects de l'art actuel en République Fédérale d'Allemagne. Paris: ARC / Musée d'Art Moderne de la Ville de Paris, 1981.
Gegen das Kriegsrecht in Polen: Für Solidarność. Düsseldorf: Künstlerinitiative gegen das Kriegsrecht in Polen, 1982.
Halle 6. Hamburg: Halle 6 Organisationsbüro, 1982.
von Wiese, Stephan, ed. *(0211) 22 Künstler in Düsseldorf.* Düsseldorf: Kunstmuseum Düsseldorf, 1982.
Gerdes, Klingelhöller, Luy, Mucha, Schütte: C 83 Nr. 29. Düsseldorf: Galerie Konrad Fischer, 1983.
Sculpture from Germany. New York: Independent Curators Incorporated, 1983.
Standort Düsseldorf. Düsseldorf: Städtische Kunsthalle Düsseldorf, 1983.
Martin, Jean-Hubert, ed. *Burton, Gerdes, Huber, Klingelhöller, Luy, Mucha, Schütte: Konstruierte Orte; 6 × D + 1 × NY.* Bern: Kunsthalle Bern, 1983.
De verzegelde Bron. Rotterdam: Rotterdamse Kunststichting, 1984.
Ludger Gerdes / Thomas Schütte: Weiter/Warten. Hamburg: Produzentengalerie Hamburg, 1984. Exhibition catalogue.
Ouverture: Arte contemporanea. Turin: Castello di Rivoli, 1984.
Heynen, Julian, ed. *Ludger Gerdes, Harald Klingelhöller, Wolfgang Luy, Reinhard Mucha, Thomas Schütte.* Krefeld, West Germany: Krefelder Kunstmuseen, 1984.
König, Kasper, ed. *Von hier aus.* Cologne: DuMont Buchverlag, 1984.
Dispositif-Sculpture: Jürgen Drescher, Harald Klingelhöller, Reinhard Mucha, Thomas Schütte. Paris: ARC—Musée d'Art Moderne de la Ville de Paris, 1985.
Dreißig Jahre durch die Kunst: Museum Haus Lange, 1955–1985. Krefeld, West Germany: Krefelder Kunstmuseen, 1985.
1945–1985: Kunst in der Bundesrepublik Deutschland. Berlin: Neue Nationalgalerie Berlin, 1985.
Siméon et les flamants roses: Jeune sculpture européenne, été 85. Albi, France: Centre Culturel d'Albi, 1985.
Anderson, Sascha, ed. *Tiefe Blicke: Kunst der achtziger Jahre aus der Bundesrepublik Deutschland, der DDR, Österreich und der Schweiz.* Cologne: DuMont, 1985.
Celant, Germano. *The European Iceberg: Creativity in Germany and Italy Today.* Milan: Nuove Edizioni Gabriele Mazzotta; Toronto: Art Gallery of Ontario, 1985.
Herzogenrath, Wulf, and Stephan von Wiese, eds. *Rheingold: 40 Künstler aus Köln und Düsseldorf / 40 artisti da Colonia e Düsseldorf.* Cologne: Wienand Verlag, 1985.
Correspondentie Europa. Amsterdam: Het Museum, 1986.
Il cangiante. Milan: Nuova Prearo Editore, 1986.
Kleinplastik. Fellbach, West Germany: Stadt Fellbach, 1986.
Sieben Skulpturen. Cologne: Kölnischer Kunstverein, 1986.
Bos, Saskia, Jan Brand, and Hans Brand. *Sonsbeek '86: Internationale beelden tentoonstelling.* Utrecht: Veen/Reflex, 1986.
Heitter, Josephine, ed. *Origins, Originality and Beyond.* Sydney: Biennale of Sydney, 1986.
Schmidt-Wulffen, Stephan, ed. *Jenisch-Park: Skulptur.* Hamburg: Kulturbehörde Hamburg, 1986.
Das andere Medium: Zeichnungen von Bildhauern. Dortmund, West Germany: Museum am Ostwall, 1987.
Die Grosse Oper, oder, Die Sehnsucht nach dem Erhabenen. Bonn: Bonner Kunstverein, 1987.
Documenta 8. Kassel, West Germany: Weber und Weidemeyer, 1987.
Juxtapositions: Recent Sculpture from England and Germany. Long Island City, NY: P.S. 1, Institute for Art and Urban Resources, 1987.
L'époque, la mode, la morale, la passion: Aspects de l'art d'aujourd'hui 1977–1987. Paris: Centre Georges Pompidou, 1987.
Musée St. Pierre Art Contemporain Lyon. Frankfurt: Frankfurter Kunstverein, 1987.
Raumbilder: Cinco escultores alemanes en Madrid. Madrid: Ministerio de Cultura; Dirección General de Bellas Artes y Archivos; Centro Nacional de Exposiciones, 1987.
Tekenen '87. Rotterdam: Museum Boymans–van Beuningen, 1987.
Bußmann, Klaus, Kasper König, and Florian Matzner, eds. *Skulptur Projekte in Münster 1987.* Cologne: DuMont Buchverlag, 1987.
Pakesch, Peter, ed. *Bildhauerzeichnungen.* Graz: Grazer Kunstverein, 1987.
Barzel, Amnon, and Giorgio Maragliano, eds. *Europa oggi: Arte contemporanea nell'Europa Occidentale.* Florence: Centro di Electa, 1988.
Van Duyn, Edna, and Saskia Bos, eds. *Nightfire.* Amsterdam: De Appel, 1988.
Blickpunkte. Montreal: Musée d'Art Contemporaine de Montréal and Goethe-Institut Montreal, 1989.
Skulpturen für Krefeld I. Krefeld, West Germany: Krefelder Kunstmuseen Museum Haus Esters, 1989.
Zeitzeichen: Stationen Bildender Kunst in Nordrhein-Westfalen. Cologne: DuMont, 1989.
Celant, Germano. *Periodi di marmo: Arte verso l'inespressionismo.* Milan: Electa, 1989.
Hacia el paisaje / Towards landscape. Madrid: Centro Atlántico de Arte Moderno, 1990.
Possible Worlds: Sculpture from Europe. London: ICA and Serpentine Gallery, 1990.
Espacio mental. Valencia: Institut Valencià d'Art Modern, Centre del Carme, 1991.
Zeit-Rausch: Künstlerwettbewerb zur Magnetschnellbahn. Bonn: Bonner Kunstverein, 1991.
Like Nothing Else in Tennessee. London: Serpentine Gallery, 1992.
Tišina: Protislovne oblike resnice / Silence: Contradictory Shapes of Truth. Ljubljana: Moderna Galerija, 1992.
Bos, Saskia. *Inscapes.* Amsterdam: De Appel, 1992.
Nachtschattengewächse. Kassel, Germany: Museum Fridericianum, 1993.
Tutte le strade portano a Roma? Rome: Edizioni Carte Segrete, 1993.
Viaggio verso Citera: Arte e Poesia. Venice: Edizioni Marpesia, 1993.
Cassiman, Bart, Menno Meewis, and Barbara Vanderlinden, eds. *New Sculptures.* Antwerp: Open Air Museum of Sculpture Middelheim, 1993.
Cassiman, Bart, Greet Ramael, and Frank Vande, eds. *The Sublime Void: On the Memory of Imagination.* Antwerp: Koninklijk Museum voor Schone Kunsten, 1993.
Harten, Jürgen, and Michael Schirner. *Art Meets Ads.* Ostfildern-Ruit, Germany: Hatje Cantz, 1993.
Engelking, Gerhard, and Jost Reinert, eds. *Junge deutsche Kunst der 90er Jahre aus NRW: Die Generation nach Becher, Beuys, Polke, Richter, Ruthenbeck.* Ostfildern-Ruit, Germany: Hatje Cantz, 1994.
Krempel, Ulrich, and Susanne Meyer-Büser. *Figur. Natur.* Hanover, Germany: Landeshauptstadt Hannover and Sprengel Museum Hannover, 1994.
Der Janustempel. Krefeld, Germany: Krefelder Kunstmuseen, 1995.
Micromegas. Paris: American Center, 1995.
Private View. Leeds, United Kingdom: Henry Moore Foundation, 1996.
Benezra, Neal, and Olga M. Viso. *Distemper: Dissonant Themes in the Art of the 1990s.* Washington, DC: Smithsonian Institution, 1996.
Dabrowski, Magdalena. *Beuys and After: Contemporary German Drawing from the Collection.* New York: The Museum of Modern Art, 1996.
Artistes, architectes. Villeurbanne, France: Nouveau Musée / Institut d'Art Contemporain, 1997.
Documenta X. Kassel: Documenta and Museum Fridericianum, 1997.
Im Reich der Phantome: Fotografie des Unsichtbaren. Ostfildern-Ruit, Germany: Hatje Cantz, 1997.
Young German Artists 2. London: Saatchi Gallery, 1997.
Bußmann, Klaus, Kasper König, and Florian Matzner, eds. *Contemporary Sculpture. Projects in Münster.* Ostfildern-Ruit, Germany: Verlag Gerd Hatje, 1997.
Lehmann, Ulrike, ed. *Das neue Gesicht.* Konstanz, Germany: Kunstverein Konstanz, 1997.
Schneede, Uwe M., ed. *Erstbezug: Künstler richten die Galerie der Gegenwart ein.* Hamburg: Hamburger Kunsthalle, 1997.
Stecker, Raimund, ed. *Thomas Schütte und Henrik Wolff.* Düsseldorf: Verlag des Kunstvereins für die Rheinlande und Westfalen, 1997. Exhibition catalogue.
Artist's Proof: Grafische/fotografische Arbeiten aus den letzten dreissig Jahren. Cologne: Oktagon, 1998.
The House in the Woods. Glasgow: Centre for Contemporary Arts, 1998.
Jardin d'artiste: De mémoire d'arbre. Paris: Paris-Musées, 1998.
A Portrait of Our Times: An Introduction to the Logan Collection. San Francisco: San Francisco Museum of Art, 1998.
Bonami, Francesco. *Unfinished History.* Minneapolis, MN: Walker Art Center, 1998.
Elliott, David, and Pier Luigi Tazzi, eds. *Wounds: Between Democracy and Redemption in Contemporary Art.* Stockholm: Moderna Museet, 1998.
Huber, Sebastian, Eva Maria Stadler, and Thomas Trummer, eds. *Mise en scène: Theater und Kunst.* Graz: Grazer Kunstverein, 1998.
Am Horizont. Krefeld, Germany: Krefelder Kunstmuseen, 1999.

Dream City. Munich: Kunstraum München, Kunstverein München, and Museum Villa Stuck, 1999.
La realitat i el desig. Barcelona: Fundació Joan Miró, 1999.
Zoom: Ansichten zur deutschen Gegenwartskunst, Sammlung Landesbank Baden-Württemberg. Ostfildern-Ruit, Germany: Hatje Cantz, 1999.
Broeker, Holger, ed. *Gesammelte Werke 1. Zeitgenössische Kunst seit 1968*. Ostfildern-Ruit, Germany: Hatje Cantz, 1999.
Ronte, Dieter, and Walter Smerling, eds. *Zeitwenden: Ausblick*. Bonn: Stiftung für Kunst und Kultur, Kunstmuseum Bonn; Cologne: DuMont Buchverlag, 1999.
HausSchau: Das Haus in der Kunst. Ostfildern-Ruit, Germany: Hatje Cantz, 2000.
Bilstein, Johannes, ed. *Dein Wille geschehe. Das Bild des Vaters in zeitgenössischer Kunst und Wissenschaft*. Stuttgart: Oktagon, 2000.
Burton, Jane, ed. *Between Cinema and a Hard Place*. London: Tate Modern, 2000.
Gevaert, Yves, ed. *Many Colored Objects Placed Side by Side to Form a Row of Many Colored Objects: Works from the Collection of Annick and Anton Herbert*. Luxembourg: Casino Luxembourg, 2000.
Harten, Jürgen, ed. *Das fünfte Element—Geld oder Kunst*. Cologne: DuMont, 2000.
Schwarz, Dieter, ed. *Von Edgar Degas bis Gerhard Richter: Arbeiten auf Papier aus der Sammlung des Kunstmuseums Winterthur*. Winterthur, Switzerland: Kunstmuseum Winterthur; Düsseldorf: Richter Verlag, 2000.
Weski, Thomas, and Heinz Liesbrock. *How You Look at It. Fotografien des 20. Jahrhunderts*. Hanover, Germany: Sprengel Museum, 2000.
Between Earth and Heaven: New Classical Movements in the Art of Today. Oostende, Belgium: Provinciaal Museum voor Moderne Kunst, 2001.
Dialogue ininterrompu. Nantes: Musée des Beaux-Arts de Nantes, Éditions MeMo, 2001.
Ex(o)dus. Haifa: Haifa Museum, 2001.
Fogle, Douglas, ed. *Painting at the Edge of the World*. Minneapolis, MN: Walker Art Center, 2001.
Ostrander, Tobias. *Inmensidad íntima: Una selección de obras de la colección del Museo de Arte Contemporáneo de Gante*. Mexico City: Instituto Nacional de Bellas Artes, Museo Tamayo, 2001.
Wye, Deborah, and Susan Tallman. *Parkett Collaborations and Editions since 1984: A Small Museum and a Large Library of Contemporary Art*. Zurich: Parkett Publishers, 2001.
Die Pop Art und die zeitgenössische Bildhauerkunst. Bremen: Gerhard Marcks Haus, 2002.
Curtis, Penelope, ed. *The Object Sculpture*. Leeds, United Kingdom: Henry Moore Foundation, 2002.
Heynen, Julian, ed. *Startkapital*. Düsseldorf: Kunstsammlung Nordrhein-Westfalen K21; Ostfildern-Ruit, Germany: Hatje Cantz, 2002.
Risaliti, Sergio, and Achille Bonito Oliva. *De Gustibus: Collezione Privata Italia*. Pistoia, Italy: Maschietteo e Musolino, 2002.
Choroschilow, Pawel, ed. *Berlin-Moskau / Moskau-Berlin 1950–2000*. Berlin: Nicolai, 2003.
Cohen, Françoise, and Marielle Tabart. *Sculpture de Derain à Séchas: Collection du Centre Pompidou, Musée National d'Art Moderne*. Paris: Éditions du Centre Pompidou; Nîmes, France: Carré d'Art—Musée d'Art Contemporain, 2003.
Flügge, Matthias, and Friedrich Meschede, eds. *Warum! Bilder diesseits und jenseits des Menschen*. Ostfildern-Ruit, Germany: Hatje Cantz, 2003.
Kort, Pamela, ed. *Grotesk! 130 Jahre Kunst der Frechheit*. Munich: Prestel Verlag, 2003.
Winzen, Matthias, and Isabel Greschat, eds. *Durchgehend geöffnet: Skulpturensommer in Baden-Baden*. Baden-Baden, Germany: Staatliche Kunsthalle Baden-Baden, Sammlung Frieder Burda; Cologne: DuMont, 2003.
ArchiSkulptur. Riehen/Basel: Fondation Beyeler, 2004.
Faces in the Crowd: Picturing Modern Life from Manet to Today. Rivoli/Turin: Castello di Rivoli Museo d'Arte Contemporanea; London: Whitechapel Gallery; Milan: Skira Editore, 2004.
Interior View: Artists Explore the Langauge of Architecture. Amersfoort, Netherlands: De Zonnehof, Centrum voor Moderne Kunst, 2004.
Sammlung Plum: Museum Kurhaus Kleve. Kleve, Germany: Freundeskreis Museum Kurhaus und Koekkoek-Haus, 2004.
Seltsam vertraut. Saarbrücken, Germany: Saarlandmuseum, 2004.
Bilstein, Johannes, and Matthias Winzen. *Seele: Konstruktionen des Innerlichen in der Kunst*. Baden-Baden, Germany: Staatliche Kunsthalle Baden-Baden and Verlag für Moderne Kunst Baden-Baden, 2004.
Binder, Ulrich, and Madeleine Schuppli, eds. *Reanimation: Hermann Gerber*. Thun, Switzerland: Kunstmuseum Thun, 2004.
Blume, Eugen, Joachim Jäger, and Gabriele Knapstein, eds. *Friedrich Christian Flick Collection im Hamburger Bahnhof*. Cologne: SMB DuMont, 2004.
Folie, Sabine. *Skulpture: Prekärer Realismus zwischen Melancholie und Komik*. Vienna: Kunsthalle Wien, 2004.
Luckow, Dirk, ed. *See History 2004: Der Demokratische Blick*. Kiel, Germany: Kunsthalle zu Kiel, Schleswig-Holsteinischer Kunstverein, 2004.
Weiss, Kirsten. *Dependent Objects*. Cambridge, MA: Harvard University Art Museums, 2004.
An Aside: Selected by Tacita Dean. London: Hayward Gallery Publishing, 2005.
Big Bang: Creation and Destruction in 20th Century Art. Paris: Éditions du Centre Pompidou, 2005.
Kunst in Schokolade / Chocolate Art. Ostfildern-Ruit, Germany: Hatje Cantz Verlag; Cologne: Museum Ludwig and Imhoff-Stollwerck-Museum, 2005.
Regarding Terror: The RAF-Exhibition Volume 1 and 2. Göttingen, Germany: Steidl Verlag, 2005.
Universal Experience: Art, Life, and the Tourist's Eye. Chicago: Museum of Contemporary Art; New York: Distributed Art Publishers, 2005.
Kaiser, Philipp, ed. *Flashback: Eine Revision der Kunst der 80er Jahre*. Berlin: Hatje Cantz, 2005.
Kantor, Jordan. *Drawing from the Modern, 1975–2005*. New York: The Museum of Modern Art, 2005.
Kellein, Thomas. *In the Middle of the Night: Die Neuerwerbungen seit 1996*. Bielefeld, Germany: Kerber Verlag, 2005.
Souben, Véronique. *(My Private) Heroes*. Herford, Germany: MARTa Herford, 2005.
Lang leve Beeldhouwkunst! / Long Live Sculpture! Antwerp: Middelheimmuseum, 2006.
Public Space / Two Audiences. Works and Documents from the Herbert Collection. Barcelona: Museu d'Art Contemporani de Barcelona, 2006.
Radar: Selections from the Collection of Vicki and Kent Logan. Denver: Denver Art Museum, 2006.
Cattelan, Maurizio, Massimiliano Gioni, and Ali Subotnick. *Of Mice and Men: 4th Berlin Biennial for Contemporary Art*. Berlin: KW Institute for Contemporary Art, 2006.
Enwezor, Okwui, ed. *The Unhomely: Phantom Scenes in Global Society*. Seville: Fundación Bienal Internacional de Arte Contemporáneo de Sevilla, 2006.
Loock, Ulrich. *The 80s: A Topology*. Porto: Museu de Arte Contemporânea de Serralves, 2006.
Die Kunst zu sammeln: Das 20./21. Jahrhundert in Düsseldorfer Privat- und Unternehmensbesitz. Düsseldorf: Stiftung Museum Kunst Palast, 2007.
Rockers Island: Olbricht Collection. Göttingen, Germany: Steidl, 2007.
Franzen, Brigitte, Kasper König, and Carina Plath, eds. *Skulptur Projekte Münster 07*. Cologne: Walther König, 2007.
Vervoordt, Axel, and Mattijs Visser, eds. *Artempo: Where Time Becomes Art*. Ghent: Axel Vervoordt in association with Mer. Paper Kunsthalle, 2007.
After Nature. New York: New Museum, 2008.
La collection de Pont à Paris. Paris: Institut Néerlandais, 2008.
Consagra, Francesca. *The Immediate Touch: German, Austrian, and Swiss Drawings from the Saint Louis Collections 1946–2007*. Saint Louis, MO: Saint Louis Art Museum, 2008.
Fogle, Douglas. *Life on Mars: 55th Carnegie International*. Pittsburgh: Carnegie Museum of Art, 2008.
Juncosa, Enrique. *Order. Desire. Light: Contemporary Drawing*. Dublin: Irish Museum of Modern Art, 2008.
Kreuzer, Stefanie. *Kavalierstart 1978–1982: Aufbruch in die Kunst der 80er*. Cologne: Dumont, 2008.
Lombino, Mary-Kay. *Out of Shape: Stylistic Distortions of the Human Form in Art from the Logan Collection*. Poughkeepsie, NY: Frances Lehman Loeb Art Center, 2008.
Luckow, Dirk. *Heavy Metal: Die unerklärbare Leichtigkeit eines Materials*. Ostfildern-Ruit, Germany: Hatje Cantz, 2008.
Poli, Francesco, Gabriella Serusi, and Sandra Botti, eds. *Nient'altro che scultura: Nothing but Sculpture*. Milan: Silvana Editoriale, 2008.
Barron, Stephanie, and Sabine Eckmann, eds. *Art of Two Germanys: Cold War Cultures*. New York: Abrams; Los Angeles: Los Angeles County Museum of Art, 2009.
Bayrle, Thomas, ed. *Heidi au pays de Martin Kippenberger*. Blou, France: Monografik, 2009.
Brunner, Dieter. *Das Fundament der Kunst: Die Skulptur und ihr Sockel in der Moderne*. Heidelberg: Edition Braus, 2009.
Rattemeyer, Christian, ed. *Compass in Hand: Selections from The Judith Rothschild Foundation Contemporary Drawings Collection*. New York: The Museum of Modern Art, 2009.
Rüdiger, Bernhard. *Locus Oculi*. Loire: Musée d'Art Moderne et Contemporain Saint-Étienne, 2009.
Smerling, Walter, ed. *60 Jahre 60 Werke: Kunst aus der Bundesrepublik Deutschland 1949–2009*. Cologne: Wienand Verlag, 2009.
Der Western leuchtet. Bielefeld, Germany: Kerber Verlag, 2010.
Die Natur der Kunst: Begegnungen mit der Natur vom 19. Jahrhundert bis in die Gegenwart. Düsseldorf: Richter Verlag, 2010.
Augaitis, Daina, ed. *Visceral Bodies*. Vancouver: Vancouver Art Gallery, 2010.
Meschede, Friedrich, and Guido de Werd, eds. *With a Probability of Being Seen: Dorothee and Konrad Fischer; Archives of an Attitude*. Barcelona: Museu d'Art Contemporani de Barcelona; Kleve, Germany: Museum Kurhaus Kleve; Düsseldorf: Richer Verlag, 2010.
Living: Frontiers of Architecture III–IV. Humlebæk, Denmark: Louisiana Museum of Modern Art, 2011.
Mit Feuer und Flamme: Keramik in der Gegenwartskunst. Burgrieden, Germany: Museum Villa Rot, 2011.
Vollendet das ewige Werk: Sammlung Rheingold in Schloss Dyck 2011. Düsseldorf: Feymedia, 2011.
Gregory, Jarrett, and Sarah Valdez. *Ostalgia*. New York: New Museum, 2011.
Hentschel, Martin, ed. *Heinz and Marianne Ebers Foundation: A Collection with Stature*. Bielefeld, Germany: Kerber Verlag, 2011.
König, Kasper, and Thomas Trummer, eds. *Vor dem Gesetz: Skulpturen der Nachkriegszeit und Räume der Gegenwartskunst*. Cologne: Walther König, 2011.
Meschede, Friedrich. *KölnSkulptur #6*. Cologne: Walther König, 2011.
Tyradellis, Daniel, Beate Hentschel, and Dirk Luckow, eds. *Wunder*. Cologne: Snoeck Verlagsgesellschaft, 2011.
Berengo, Adriano. *Glasstress New York: New Art from the Venice Biennales*. Milan: Skira Editore, 2012.
Cherix, Christophe, ed. *Print/Out: 20 Years in Print*. New York: The Museum of Modern Art, 2012.

Fernández, Valeriano Bozal, ed. *The Grotesque Factor*. Málaga: Fundación Museo Picasso Málaga, 2012.
Knapstein, Gabriele, and Matilda Felix. *Architektonika*. Berlin: Nationalgalerie Staatliche Museen zu Berlin, 2012.
As If It Could: Works and Documents from the Herbert Foundation. Ghent: Herbert Foundation, 2013.
Die Bildhauer: Kunstakademie Düsseldorf, 1945 bis heute. Bielefeld, Germany: Kerber Verlag, 2013.
Berengo, Adriano, and James Putnam. *Glasstress: White Light / White Heat*. London: London College of Fashion, 2013.
Henatsch, Martin, ed. *Back to Earth: Von Picasso bis Ai Weiwei—Die Wiederentdeckung der Keramik in der Kunst*. Neumünster, Germany: Wachholtz, 2013.
Holten, Johan, and Friedrich Meschede, eds. *Auf Zeit*. Cologne: Walther König, 2013.
Meschede, Freidrich. *KölnSkulptur #7*. Cologne: Walther König, 2013.
Bad Thoughts: Collective Martijn en Jeannette Sanders. Amsterdam: Stedelijk Museum, 2014.
Body and Void: Echoes of Moore in Contemporary Art. Perry Green, United Kingdom: Henry Moore Foundation, 2014.
Branching Out: Positionen zur Natur. Bielefeld, Germany: Kerber Verlag, 2014.
The Human Factor: The Figure in Contemporary Sculpture. London: Hayward Publishing, 2014.
Keramische Räume. Dortmund, Germany: Verlag Kettler, 2014.
Vanitas—Ewig ist eh nichts. Berlin: Georg Kolbe Museum, 2014.
Merz, Beatrice, and Marianna Vecellio. *Intenzione manifesta: Il disegno in tutte le sue forme*. Mantua, Italy: Corraini Edizioni, 2014.
Morris, Lynda. *Genuine Conceptualism*. Ghent: Herbert Foundation, 2014.
Schuppli, Madeleine, Thomas Schmutz, and Recto Sorg, eds. *Paying No Attention I Notice Everything: Robert Walser and the Visual Arts*. Aarau, Switzerland: Aargauer Kunsthaus; Sulgen, Switzerland: Benteli Verlag, 2014.
Andy Warhol sul comò: Opera dalla collezione Rosetta Barabino. Genoa: Museo d'Arte Contemporanea Villa Croce, 2015.
Artistes et architecture. Paris: Pavillon de l'Arsenal, 2015.
Artzuid 2015. Amsterdam: Stichting Art Zuid, 2015.
Avatar und Atavismus: Outside der Avantgarde. Heidelberg: Kehrer Verlag, 2015.
A Few Free Years: Schenkungen von Friedrich Christian Flick an die Nationalgalerie. Berlin: Staatliche Museen zu Berlin, 2015.
Ceramix: From Rodin to Schütte. Cologne: Snoeck Verlagsgesellschaft, 2015.
Gesichter: Ein Motiv zwischen Figur, Porträt und Maske. Vienna: Verlag für Moderne Kunst, 2015.
Ruhe vor dem Sturm: Postminimalistische Kunst aus dem Rheinland. Dortmund, Germany: Verlag Kettler, 2015.
Chevrier, Jean-François. *Formes biographiques*. Vanves, Switzerland: Éditions Hazan, 2015.
Gioni, Massimiliano, and Roberta Tenconi, eds. *The Great Mother: Women, Maternity, and Power in Art and Visual Culture, 1900–2015*. Milan: Skira Editore, 2015.
Kesner, Ladislav, ed. *Model*. Prague: Galerie Rudolfinum, 2015.
Schwarz, Dieter, ed. *Von Lucio Fontana bis Thomas Schütte*. Winterthur, Switzerland: Kunstmuseum Winterthur, 2016.
Zeman, Bettina, and Michael Stoeber. *Geliebte Feinde—Symbolismus heute von Peter Doig bis Thomas Schütte*. Dortmund, Germany: Verlag Kettler, 2016.
Gebbers, Anna-Catharina, and Gabriele Knapstein, eds. *Moving Is in Every Direction: Environments, Installations, Narrative Spaces*. Berlin: Staatliche Museen zu Berlin and Preußischer Kulturbesitz, 2017.
König, Kasper, Britta Peters, and Marianne Wagner, eds. *Skulptur Projekte Münster 2017*. Leipzig: Spector Books, 2017.
Schoppmann, Wolfgang, Peter Friese, and Guido Boulboullé, eds. *Mir ist das Leben lieber: Sammlung Reydan Weiss*. Heidelberg: Keher Verlag; Bremen, Germany: Weserburg Museum für Moderne Kunst, 2017.
Trummer, Thomas D., ed. *Das Reich ohne Mitte*. Translated by Matthew Harris. Vienna: Verlag für Moderne Kunst, 2017.
Debout! Paris: Éditions Dilecta, 2018.
Burkhalter, Gabriela ed. *The Playground Project*. Bonn: Kunst- und Ausstellungshalle der Bundesrepublik Deutschland; Zurich: JRP/Ringier, 2018.
Ribas, João, and Ricardo Nicolau. *Zéro de conduite*. Porto: Fundação de Serralves, 2018.
Homo Faber: Craft in Contemporary Sculpture. Gwangju: Asia Culture Center, 2019.
Nedoma, Petr. *A Cool Breeze*. Prague: Galerie Rudolfinum, 2019.
Berger, Tobias. *KölnSkulptur #10—ÜberNatur*. Cologne: Skulpturenpark Köln, 2020.
Eccles, Tom, and Amy Zion, eds. *Closer to Life: Drawings and Works on Paper in the Marieluise Hessel Collection*. Annandale-on-Hudson, NY: Center for Curatorial Studies, Bard College, 2020.
Strand: Isa Genzken, Blinky Palermo, Sigmar Polke, Gerhard Richter, Thomas Schütte. Düsseldorf: Sies + Höke, 2020.
Moment. Monument. Cologne: Snoeck Verlagsgesellschaft, 2021.
Dresser, Anne, ed. *Les flammes: L'âge de la céramique*. Paris: Musée d'Art Moderne de Paris, 2021.
Kase, Oliver, and Karsten Löckemann, eds. *Au rendez-vous des amis: Klassische Moderne im Dialog mit Gegenwartskunst aus der Sammlung Goetz*. Munich: Hirmer Verlag, 2021.
Padberg, Marc, Martina Padberg, and Rita G. Täuber, eds. *Fragile: Alles aus Glas!* Cologne: Snoeck Verlagsgesellschaft, 2021.
Roettig, Petra, ed. *Serien: Druckgraphik von Warhol bis Wool*. Hamburg: Hamburger Kunsthalle; Berlin: Dr. Cantz'sche Verlagsgesellschaft, 2021.
Schatzhaus und Labor—25 Jahre Museum Kurhaus Kleve 1997–2022. Kleve, Germany: Freundeskreis Museum Kurhaus and Koekkoek Haus Kleve, 2022.
Galansino, Arturo, ed. *Reaching for the Stars: From Maurizio Cattelan to Lynette Yiadom-Boakye*. Venice: Marsilio, 2023.

ARTICLES AND REVIEWS

Weskott, Hanne. "Wolfgang Laib und Thomas Schütte, Preisträger der Jürgen Ponto-Stiftung 1980." *Kunstforum International*, no. 37 (January 1980): 243–45.
Weskott, Hanne. "Flatz und Thomas Schütte bei Rüdiger Schöttle." *Kunstforum International*, no. 40 (April 1980): 224–25.
Johnen, Jörg. "Retten, was zu retten ist oder: Weiter mit Verstand." *Kunstforum International*, no. 48 (February/March 1982): 124–33.
Weskott, Hanne. "Thomas Schütte: Skizzen zum Projekt 'Großes Theater': Galerie Schöttle, München." *Kunstforum International*, no. 51 (July 1982): 171.
Johnen, Jörg. "Abdankung des Hier und Jetzt: 'Ausstellung B' in der Lothringerstraße." *Kunstforum International*, no. 56 (December 1982): 152–63.
Loock, Ulrich. "Sculpture ou mise en condition? Allemagne 1982, aspects d'une problématique." Translated by Denys Zacharopoulos. *Artistes*, no. 14 (January/February 1983): 21–25.
Johnen, Jörg. "Tribüne mit Ausblick (Manchmal)." *Kunstforum International*, no. 62 (June 1983): 164–67.
Galloway, David. "Report from Germany: Totems without Taboos." *Art in America* 72, no. 9 (October 1984): 29–37.
Galloway, David. "Report from Germany." *Art in America*, no. 3 (March 1985): 23–29.
Javault, Patrick. "Les états du lieu: Thomas Schütte, Reinhard Mucha, Harald Klingelhöller, Wolfgang Luy." *Art Press* 90 (March 1985): 37–41.
Schmidt-Wulffen, Stephan. "Models." *Flash Art*, no. 121 (March 1985): 70–73.
Johnen, Jörg. "Beispiel Hamburg: Erfahrungsbericht über Kunst im öffentlichen Raum." *Kunstforum International*, no. 81 (April 1985): 120–33.
Puvogel, Renate. "Pflicht und Kür: Denk-Modelle zwischen Skulptur und Architektur." *Das Kunstwerk* 38, no. 6 (December 1985): 12–21 and 44–58.
Kipphoff, Petra. "Gestellte Bilder und gebaute Szenen." *Die Zeit*, February 7, 1986.
Catoir, Barbara. "Ein Heimwerker." *Frankfurter Allgemeine Zeitung*, February 8, 1986.
Locker, Ludwig. "Architektonische Aspekte in der Düsseldorfer Gegenwartskunst (2)." *Artefactum* 2, no. 12 (February/March 1986): 2–9.
Hentschel, Martin. "Thomas Schütte im Museum Haus Lange." *NIKE*, no. 12 (March/April 1986): 20–21.
Schmidt-Wulffen, Stephan. "Vom Stand der Dinge." *Kunstforum International*, no. 83 (March–May 1986): 260–62.
Arghir, Anca. "Thomas Schütte: Museum Haus Lange, Krefeld." *Das Kunstwerk* 2, no. 39 (April 1986): 64, 85.
Taylor, Paul. "Café Deutschland." *Art News* 85, no. 4 (April 1986): 68–76.
Dreher, Thomas. "Thomas Schütte: Skulpturen." *Das Kunstwerk* 4–5, no. 39 (September 1986): 193–94.
Dank, Ralph. "Sonsbeek '86." *Kunstforum International*, no. 85 (September/October 1986): 247–55.
Pohlen, Annelie. "On the Rhetoric of Forms and the Vividness of Blueprints: Aspects of New German Sculpture." *Artscribe International*, no. 59 (September/October 1986): 38–43.
von Drateln, Doris. "Skulpturen in Hamburg." *Kunstforum International*, no. 85 (September/October 1986): 272–85.
Tazzi, Pier Luigi. "Thomas Schütte: Tucci Russo Studio per l'Arte Contemporanea." *Artforum* 25, no. 6 (February 1987): 127–28.
Dimitrijevic, Nena. "Meanwhile, In the Real World." *Flash Art*, no. 134 (May 1987): 44–49.
Christov-Bakargiev, Carolyn. "Förg, Kiecol, Mucha, Schütte." *Flash Art*, no. 135 (Summer 1987): 94.
Heynen, Julian. "Kunst für den öffentlichen Raum? Öffentlicher Raum für die Kunst?" *Kunstforum International*, no. 90 (July–September 1987): 268–81.
Meinhardt, Johannes. "Präambel und Promenade." *Kunstforum International*, no. 90 (July–September 1987): 250–67.
Hueck-Ehmer, Britta. "Skulptur/Projekte/Münster/1987." *Das Kunstwerk* 4–5, no. 40 (September 1987): 52–55, 94–96.
Tazzi, Pier Luigi. "Skulptur Projekte Münster." *Wolkenkratzer Art Journal*, no. 5 (September/October 1987): 52–57 and 108–9.
Christov-Bakargiev, Carolyn. "Thomas Schütte: Micheline Szwajczer, Antwerpen." *Flash Art*, no. 136 (October 1987): 116–17.
Schmidt-Wulffen, Stephan. "Enzyklopädie der Skulptur." *Kunstforum International*, no. 91 (October/November 1987): 288–301.
Schmidt-Wulffen, Stephan. "Krise des Erzählens?" *Noema*, no. 15 (November/December 1987): 41–45.
Grasskamp, Walter. "Kleinmut: Hinweise zum Modell / Faint of Heart: Guidelines for the Model." Translated by Christian Caryl. *Daidalos*, no. 26 (December 1987): 62–71.
Schmidt-Wulffen, Stephan. "Fit for the Postmodern." *Flash Art*, no. 138 (January/February 1988): 96–99.

Oliva, Achille Bonito. "Neo-Europe (West)." *Flash Art*, no. 139 (March/April 1988): 67–71.
Hettig, Frank-Alexander. "Nachtfeuer." *Kunstforum International*, no. 94 (April/May 1988): 322–23.
Schwarze, Dirk. "Schlaf der Vernunft." *Kunstforum International*, no. 94 (April/May 1988): 248–51.
Stahl, Johannes. "Neue Collectionen: Kaiser Wilhelm Museum Krefeld, Gemeentemuseum Helmond." *Kunstforum International*, no. 94 (April/May 1988): 319–21.
Braxmeier, Rainer. "'Hier 88' (Mic Enneper, Gerald Domenig, Stefan Demary, Thomas Schütte): Kunsthalle Baden-Baden." *Das Kunstwerk* 41 (May 1988): 90–91.
Franzke, Andreas. "New German Sculpture." *Art and Design* 5, nos. 9–10 (1989): 28–34.
Heynen, Julian. "Thomas Schütte." *Das Kunstwerk* 4–5, no. 41 (January 1989): 145.
Levitte Harten, Doreet. "We Androids." *Artforum* 27, no. 5 (January 1989): 100–106.
Brenson, Michael. "A Show's Instructive Provocation." *New York Times*, March 17, 1989.
Christov-Bakargiev, Carolyn. "Thomas Schütte: Nelson, Lyon." *Flash Art*, no. 145 (March/April 1989): 124.
Gookin, Kirby. "Thomas Schütte: Marian Goodman Gallery." *Artforum* 27, no. 10 (Summer 1989): 138.
Heartney, Eleanor. "Thomas Schütte: Marian Goodman." *Art News* 88, no. 6 (Summer 1989): 170, 172.
Morgan, Robert C. "New York in Review." *Arts Magazine* 63 (July 1989): 99.
Roskam, Mathilde. "Performing Poet." *De Appel Bulletin*, no. 2 (August/September 1989): 2–7.
Klaus, Petra. "Mein wunderbarer Waschsalon." *Wolkenkratzer Art Journal*, no. 5 (September/October 1989): 79.
Piguet, Philippe. "Thomas Schütte: Musée de Clamecy." *Art Press*, no. 140 (October 1989): 108.
Princenthal, Nancy. "Thomas Schütte at Marian Goodman." *Art in America* 77, no. 10 (October 1989): 207–8.
Schmitz, Rudolf. "Thomas Schütte: Portikus, Frankfurt." *Flash Art*, no. 148 (October 1989): 135–36.
Suermann, Marie-Theres. "Thomas Schütte: Portikus, Frankfurt am Main." *NIKE*, no. 30 (October/November 1989): 44.
Loock, Ulrich. "Sculpture Places—Sculpture as Place." *Kunst en Museumjournaal* 2, no. 1, (January 1990): 7–18.
Bochynek, Martin. "Thomas Schütte: Galerie Konrad Fischer, Düsseldorf." *Artis* 42, no. 2 (February 1990): 48.
Bosquet, Oscarine. "Thomas Schütte: Le théâtre de l'oeil." *Galeries Magazine*, no. 36 (April 1990): 110–13 and 184.
Hermes, Manfred. "Thomas Schütte: Konrad Fischer." *Artscribe*, no. 81 (May 1990): 85–86.
Grout, Catherine. "Schütte o el arte de vivir." *El Guía* (June 1990): 64–65.
Piguet, Philippe. "Jean-Marc Bustamante, Thomas Schütte: Musée d'Art Moderne de la Ville de Paris, ARC." *Art Press*, no. 149 (July 1990): 90.
Gintz, Claude. "Thomas Schütte: Retour aux 'fonctions iconiques de l'art.'" *Art Press*, no. 150 (September 1990): 32–35.
Cueff, Alain. "Thomas Schütte: ARC, Galerie Crousel-Robelin/BAMA." *Artforum* 29, no. 1 (September 1990): 170.
Van Giersbergen, Marieke. "Architektur als levensontwerp: Het werk van Thomas Schütte." *Archis*, no. 10 (October 1990): 43–46.
Reust, Hans Rudolf. "Man in the Mud." Translated by Ted Gang. *Artscribe*, no. 84 (November/December 1990): 75–78.
Heynen, Julian. "Arte Povera: Waiting for a Wonder. Fragmenten bij het werk van Thomas Schütte." *Metropolis M* 12, no. 1 (1991): 20–25.
Schneede, Marina. "Gebaute Bilder: Zur Skulptur in den achtziger Jahren." *Kunst und Antiquitäten*, no. 6 (1991): 20–27.
Vanderlinden, Barbara. "Towards Landscape." *Artefactum*, no. 37 (February/March 1991): 47.
Tazzi, Pier Luigi. "Outside in the Storms of Springtime: Thomas Schütte." *Artforum* 29, no. 9 (May 1991): 130–35.
Lebovici, Élisabeth. "En Belgique, l'art en privé." *Art Press*, no. 162 (October 1991): 49–57.
Hoet, Jan. "Documenta als Motor." *Kunstforum International*, no. 119 (1992): 238–43.
Hübl, Michael. "Deutschland: Ein Fragment mit 24 Künstlern." *Kunstforum International*, no. 119 (1992): 158–63.
Donaldson, Andrew. "Thomas Schütte / Günther Förg." *Art and Text*, no. 41 (January 1992): 82–89.
Archer, Michael. "Documenta IX." *Art Monthly*, no. 158 (July/August 1992): 7–9.
Huitorel, Jean-Marc. "C'est pas la fin du monde." *Art Press*, no. 172 (September 1992): 82–83.
Pasini, Francesca. "Thomas Schütte: Galleria Tucci Rosso." *Artforum* 31, no. 2 (October 1992): 116–17.
Stegeman, Elly. "The Sublime Void." *Kunst en Museumjournaal* 5, no. 2 (1993): 53–58.
Sinkovits, Péter. "Minőség helyett koncepció: Documenta IX Kasselban / Conception Instead of Quality: Documenta IX in Kassel." Translated by Éva Polgár. *Új művészet* 4, no. 3 (March 1993): 4–12, 69.
Smith, Roberta. "German Art Still Breathes the Air of Ideas." *New York Times*, April 23, 1993.
Puvogel, Renate. "Thomas Schütte." *Artis* 45 (June 1993): 18–23.
Smolik, Noemi. "Thomas Schütte: Produzentengalerie, Hamburg." *Artforum* 32, no. 4 (December 1993): 92.
Clauss, Gunder. "Thomas Schütte: Schöne Träume, Böse Satiren." *Art: Das Kunstmagazin*, no. 5 (May 1994): 78–85.
Hoffmann, Gabriele. "Geringer Materialaufwand." *Taz: Die Tageszeitung*, May 31, 1994.
Wagner, Thomas. "Finsterer Udo, gelber Erhard." *Frankfurter Allgemeine Zeitung*, June 10, 1994.
Müller, Silke. "Kunsthalle, Hamburg; exhibit." *Flash Art*, no. 177 (July 1994): 130.
Reust, Hans Rudolf. "Old Friends and All Houses" and "Distant Neighbours." Translated by Chris Hodder. *Arti* 16 (August–October 1993): 48–81, 82–93.
Ermen, Reinhard. "Thomas Schütte: Figur." *Kunstforum International*, no. 128 (October–December 1994): 375–77.
Rudolph, Karen. "Thomas Schütte." *Beaux Arts Magazine*, no. 128 (November 1994): 108–9.
Vogel, Sabine B. "Thomas Schütte: Kunsthalle Hamburg." Translated by Charles V. Miller. *Artforum* 33, no. 3 (November 1994): 97–98.
Janus, Elizabeth. "Thomas Schütte: Carré d'art, Nîmes." *Frieze*, no. 20 (January/February 1995): 52.
Rochette, Anne, and Wade Saunders. "Figures of Estrangement." *Art in America* 83, no. 5 (May 1995): 102–7.
Sanderson, Philip. "Richard Deacon and Thomas Schütte." *Art Monthly*, no. 188 (July/August 1995): 34–35.
Janus, Elisabeth. "Schütte's Innocents." *Parkett*, no. 47 (September 1996): 129–37.
Loock, Ulrich. "Installations." *Parkett*, no. 47 (September 1996): 124–28.
Mari, Bartomeu. "A Public for the Space." *Parkett*, no. 47 (September 1996): 104–9.
Reust, Hans Rudolf. "Lily Lies." *Parkett*, no. 47 (September 1996): 110–15.
Searle, Adrian. "Thomas Schütte." *Parkett*, no. 47 (September 1996): 97–103.
Wakefield, Neville. "Lost at Sea." *Parkett*, no. 47 (September 1996): 116–21.
Hilty, Greg. "Men in the Mud: Thomas Schütte's Figures." *Modern Painters* 10, no. 4 (Winter 1997): 97–98.
Benezra, Neal. "Thomas Schütte: Ironic Outdoor Monuments." *Flash Art*, no. 192 (January/February 1997): 80–83.
Kuspit, Donald. "Thomas Schütte: Marian Goodman Gallery." *Artforum* 36, no. 1 (September 1997): 123.
Meister, Helga. "Zuspiel: Thomas Schütte und Henrik Wolff." *Kunstforum International*, no. 139 (December 1997): 355–56.
Berk, Anne. "Thomas Schütte en het bestaansrecht van de kunstenaar." *Kunstbeeld* 22, no. 4 (1998): 19–21.
Alberro, Alexander. "No Place Like Home." *Frieze* 38 (January/February 1998): 64–67.
"In the Realm of the Senseless." *Blueprint (02684926)*, no. 147 (February 1998): 42.
Burton, Jane. "Sci-Fi Storm Troopers." *Art Newspaper* 9 (February 1998): 20.
Suto, Wilma. "Een vrolijke maskerade van kinderklei." *De Volkskrant*, February 12, 1998.
Thorn-Prikker, Jan. "Extremisten der Normalität." *Frankfurter Allgemeine Zeitung*, May 29, 1998.
Bindman, Catherine. "Thomas Schütte: Whitechapel Art Gallery, London." *On Paper* 2, no. 5 (May/June 1998): 44–45.
Schwarz, Dieter. "Thomas Schütte: Modelle und Blumen." *Neue Zürcher Zeitung*, November 14, 1998.
Gropp, Rose-Maria. "Brit-pack in der Fabrikhalle." *Frankfurter Allgemeine Zeitung*, December 12, 1998.
Smith, Roberta. "Shortcomings of Art in the Realm of Tragedy." *New York Times*, March 26, 1999.
Johnson, Ken. "Thomas Schütte: In Medias Res, Dia Center for the Arts." *New York Times*, December 3, 1999.
Altmann, Susanne. "Akt auf Pritsch." *Taz: Die Tageszeitung*, January 10, 2000.
Princenthal, Nancy. "Thomas Schütte: Heroic Measures." *Art in America* 88, no. 5 (May 2000): 122–27.
Röder, Sabine. "Krefelder Kunstmuseen." *Wallraf-Richartz-Jahrbuch* 62 (2001): 385–87.
Clauss, Gunder. "Mit nackter Schönheit gegen den Zeitgeist: Thomas Schütte." *Art: Das Kunstmagazin*, no. 3 (March 2001): 44–48.
Filser, Hubert. "Die Auflösung ist das Problem." *Süddeutsche Zeitung*, March 19, 2001.
Sachs, Brita. "Luise zeichnen und an das Nashorn denken." *Frankfurter Allgemeine Zeitung*, May 29, 2001.
Hartmann, Kathrin. "Zitronen anbieten, Bananen verkaufen." *Frankfurter Rundschau*, June 29, 2001.
Searle, Adrian. "The Wanderer." *Guardian*, April 2, 2002.
Hunt, Ian. "Thomas Schütte: Frith Street Gallery." *Art Monthly*, no. 256 (May 2002): 36–37.
Kinsman, Chloé. "Thomas Schütte: Frith Street Gallery, London." *Tema Celeste*, no. 91 (May/June 2002): 98.
Colin, Anne. "Richard Deacon, Thomas Schutte: Frith Street Gallery." *Art Press*, no. 280 (June 2002): 72–73.
Sausset, Damien. "Thomas Schütte, de la modernité à la tradition." *Connaissance des Arts*, no. 597 (September 2002): 74–79.
Fricke, Christiane. "Große, böse Geister." *Süddeutsche Zeitung*, September 14, 2002.
Posca, Claudia. "Thomas Schütte—Grosse Geister." *Kunstforum International*, no. 162 (November 2002): 321–22.
Hoffmann, Gabriele. "Bitte kein Fotto!" *Frankfurter Rundschau*, July 17, 2003.
Eliard, Astrid. "Schütte, un Allemand à Grenoble." *Connaissance des Arts*, no. 609 (October 2003): 24.
Farine, Manou. "Thomas Schütte: Petits et grands monuments." *L'Oeil*, no. 553 (December 2003): 35.
Ezard, John. "An Eye-Opener with Nods to Bob Dylan, Overambitious Architects and Pigeons." *Guardian*, December 12, 2003.
Guillerm, Martine. "Thomas Schütte: Musée de Grenoble." *Art Press*, no. 298 (February 2004): 76–77.
Schwarz, Manfred. "Der Berg ruft." *Süddeutsche Zeitung*, July 6, 2004.
Searle, Adrian. "Is That Allowed?" *Guardian*, July 27, 2004.
Meister, Helga. "Thomas Schütte—Kreuzzug: K21, Kunstsammlung NRW, Düsseldorf." *Kunstforum International*, no. 171 (July/August 2004): 328–30.

Goodman, Jonathan. "Thomas Schutte: Marian Goodman Gallery." *Sculpture* 23, no. 7 (September 2004): 71–72.
Ruthe, Ingeborg. "Die Kängurusiedlung." *Berliner Zeitung*, September 14, 2004.
Müller, Katrin Bettina. "Sackgassen aufschließen." *Taz: Die Tageszeitung*, September 17, 2004.
Piguet, Philippe. "Schütte, la solitude mise en scène." *L'Oeil*, no. 564 (December 2004): 32.
Prince, Mark. "On Sculpture." *Art Monthly*, no. 282 (December 2004): 7–10.
Sausset, Damien. "Thomas Schütte: Galerie Nelson." Translated by L. S. Torgoff. *Art Press*, no. 308 (January 2005): 76–77.
Heiser, Jörg. "Heroes and Villains." *Frieze*, no. 89 (March 2005): 98–103.
Cork, Richard. "Bizarre Encounters." *New Statesman*, March 21, 2005: 43–44.
Johnson, Ken. "Thomas Schütte: Marian Goodman." *New York Times*, June 3, 2005.
Jürgens, Sandra Vieira. "Consciência cívica." *L+Arte*, no. 16 (September 2005): 64–65.
Amado, Miguel. "Thomas Schütte: Museu Serralves." *Flash Art*, no. 8 (October 2005): 128.
Heartney, Eleanor. "Thomas Schütte at Marian Goodman." *Art in America* 93, no. 10 (November 2005): 173–74.
Braun, Adrienne. "In der Notlösung steckt wenigstens noch Not." *Süddeutsche Zeitung*, March 24, 2006.
Meinhardt, Johannes. "Thomas Schütte: Zeichnungen: 'Modelle für Zeichnungen': Staatliche Kunsthalle Baden-Baden." *Kunstforum International*, no. 180 (May 2006): 352–54.
Pohlen, Annelie. "Thomas Schütte: Konrad Fischer Galerie." *Kunstforum International*, no. 183 (December 2006–February 2007): 325–26.
Mayer, Gabriele. "Das Auge des Malers im Rasierspiegel." *Frankfurter Allgemeine Zeitung*, January 5, 2007.
de Maulmin, Valérie. "Thomas Schütte toujours grinçant." *Connaissance des Arts*, no. 649 (May 2007): 134.
Williams, Gilda. "Thomas Schütte: Frith Street Gallery." *Artforum* 46, no. 1 (September 2007): 480.
Buckell, Gareth. "Thomas Schütte—Early Works at The Henry Moore Institute, Leeds." *Culture* 24, October 9, 2007.
Fusco, Maria. "Fourth Plinth's Latest Is a Failure." *Architects' Journal* 226, no. 18 (November 2007): 49.
Searle, Adrian. "It Is Like a Jewel." *Guardian*, November 8, 2007.
Kent, Pam. "Dressing Up Trafalgar Square?" *New York Times*, November 10, 2007.
Hubbard, Sue. "Art for the People." *New Statesman*, November 19, 2007, 44.
Cooke, Lynne. "Thomas Schütte: Leeds." *Burlington Magazine* 149, no. 1257 (December 2007): 875–77.
Gleadowe, Teresa. "Fake/Function: Thomas Schütte: Early Work; Henry Moore Institute, Leeds." *Art Monthly*, no. 312 (December 2007): 22–23.
Gronlund, Melissa. "I Would Play Piano If I Could—Each Time You Play a Piece, It's Slightly Different." *Art Review*, no. 17 (December 2007): 66–71.
Sausset, Damien. "Thomas Schütte: Les choses doivent être faites." *Art Press*, no. 340 (December 2007): 46–52.
Martin, Courtney. "Thomas Schütte: Henry Moore Institute." *Artforum*, December 22, 2007. https://www.artforum.com/picks/thomas-schuette-19120.
Weaver, Thomas. "Observations on the Fourth Plinth." *Log*, no. 11 (Winter 2008): 130.
Williams, Eliza. "Thomas Schütte." *Flash Art*, no. 41 (January 2008): 78.
Cole, Ina. "Model Figures." *Sculpture* 27, no. 5 (June 2008): 34–39.
McElheny, Josiah. "Now on Display: Sculpture." *Yale University Art Gallery Bulletin* (2009): 59–69.
Sachs, Brita. "Metallfrauen und Matschmänner." *Frankfurter Allgemeine Zeitung*, June 15, 2009.
Latimer, Quinn. "Thomas Schütte: Haus der Kunst, Munich, Germany." *Frieze* 126 (October 2009): 212–13.
Herbert, Martin. "The Modern Dance: Thomas Schütte Stays One Step Ahead." *Kaleidoscope*, no. 4 (November/December 2009): 146–49.
Spies, Werner. "Wie man Sparkassen bloßstellt." *Frankfurter Allgemeine Zeitung*, March 9, 2010.
Krohn, Carsten. "Das Haus als Skulptur." *Neue Zürcher Zeitung*, March 24, 2010.
"Thomas Schütte, en Madrid." *Lapiz* 29, no. 261 (April/May 2010): 20.
Sinaga, Fernando. "Thomas Schütte: Los pies en la ciénaga." *Arte y Parte*, no. 86 (April/May 2010): 28–41.
Cueff, Alain. "Thomas Schütte: Galerie Pietro Sparta." Translated by Charles Penwarden. *Art Press*, no. 367 (May 2010): 82–83.
Stech, Fabian. "Thomas Schütte: 'Ferienhaus für Terroristen.'" *Kunstforum International*, no. 202 (May/June 2010): 376–78.
Wolff, Rachel. "Thomas Schütte: Reina Sofía." *Modern Painters* 22, no. 5 (Summer 2010): 74.
Nössig, Franziska. "Wo Terroristen Urlaub machen." *Thüringische Landeszeitung*, July 15, 2010.
Hoffmans, Christiane. "Ohne Arbeit kriegt man den Tag nicht rum." *Welt am Sonntag*, August 1, 2010.
Kröner, Magdalena. "Musterhaus Deutschland." *Frankfurter Allgemeine Zeitung*, October 4, 2010.
Raap, Jürgen. "Thomas Schütte: 'Big Buildings—Modelle und Ansichten, Kunst- und Ausstellungshalle der BRD, Bonn.'" *Kunstforum International*, no. 204 (October/November 2010): 301–3.
Wege, Astrid. "Thomas Schütte." Translated by Oliver E. Dryfuss. *Artforum* 49, no. 3 (November 2010): 259.
Capper, Beth. "Thomas Schütte: Donald Young Gallery." *Modern Painters* 24, no. 4 (May 2012): 70.
Salsbury, Britany. "The Serial Drama of the Serial Format: Tradition, Revision and the Print Portfolio 'Print/Out' and 'Printin.'" *Art in Print* 2, no. 1 (May/June 2012): 10–16.
Boutoulle, Myriam. "Middelheim, un musée à ciel ouvert." *Connaissance des Arts* (July/August 2012): 135–40.
Rainò, Marco. "Thomas Schütte: Houses." *Domus*, August 8, 2012. https://domusweb.it/en/art/2012/08/08/thomas-schutte-houses.html.
Searle, Adrian. "Thomas Schütte: Men, Monsters and Self-Portraits." *Guardian*, September 24, 2012.
Cumming, Laura. "Thomas Schütte: Faces and Figures—Review." *Guardian*, September 29, 2012.
Hamilton, Adrian. "Thomas Schütte—Ahead of the Rest." *Independent*, October 1, 2012.
Wright, Karen. "In the Studio: Thomas Schütte, Sculptor." *Independent*, October 25, 2012.
Barillà, Silvia Anna. "Disciplined Multidisciplinarity: The Ways of Thomas Schütte." *Damn°* 41 (November/December 2013): 120–22.
Meister-Klaiber, Dagmar. "Was von der Kunst bleibt, wenn sie Architektur wird: Thomas Schüttes Häuser im Kunstmuseum Luzern." *Stadt Bauwelt* 200, no. 48 (2013): 3.
Vogel, Carol. "Struggling in Bronze: Figures Visit Central Park." *New York Times*, January 24, 2013.
Valjakka, Timo. "Thomas Schütte: Sara Hildén Art Museum." *Artforum*, April 22, 2013. https://artforum.com/picks/thomas-schuette-40418.
Messmer, Martin. "Kunstmuseum zeigt 'Houses.'" *20 Minuten—Luzern*, October 16, 2013.
Bellet, Harry. "Thomas Schütte, même pas peur!" *Le Monde*, November 28, 2013.
Herzog, Andres. "Architekturmodelle des Künstlers Thomas Schütte." *Tages-Anzeiger*, November 28, 2013.
Spagnesi, Licia. "Lo scultore che venne dal dubbio." *Arte*, no. 485 (2014): 78–83.
Duchesne, Virginie. "La création selon Thomas Schütte: Fondation Beyeler." *L'Oeil*, no. 664 (January 2014): 109.
Gerling, Heike. "'Houses'—Eine Ausstellung von Thomas Schütte im Kunstmuseum Luzern," *Ensuite*, January 2014. https://www.ensuite.ch/houses-eine-ausstellung-von-thomas-schuette-im-kunstmuseum-luzern/.
Duponchelle, Valérie. "Thomas Schütte se risque aux rictus." *Le Figaro*, January 8, 2014.
Schmitz, Edgar. "The Human Factor: The Figure in Contemporary Sculpture; Hayward Gallery, London." *Kunstforum International*, no. 229 (October/November 2014): 314–15.
Vervoort, Stefaan. "'Iets Ontbreekt': Neoavant-Garde en Traditie in het Vroege Werk van Thomas Schütte." *De Witte Raaf*, no. 178 (November/December 2015): 11–16.
Bosetti, Annette. "Kunst-Raumschiff im Acker." *Rheinische Post*, March 19, 2016. rp-online.de/kultur/kunst-raumschiff-im-acker_aid-22344659.
Hoffmans, Christiane. "Ein begehbares Kunstwerk für die Nachwelt." *Welt*, April 21, 2016.
Bosetti, Annette. "Schütte stellt Schütte aus." *Rheinische Post*, January 31, 2017.
Lloyd, Joe. "Thomas Schütte: Frith Street Gallery, London." *Studio International*, February 10, 2017.
Speed, Mitch. "Thomas Schütte: carlier | gebauer, Berlin, Germany." *Frieze*, no. 189 (September 2017): 170.
Rakow, Reinhard. "Helden der etwas anderen Art." *Nordwest Zeitung*, January 19, 2018. nwzonline.de/kultur/oldenburg-schau-helden-der-etwas-anderen-art_a_50,0,2784400456.html.
Krolczyk, Radek. "Der ungeheure Reiz der fiesen alten Männer." *Taz: Die Tageszeitung*, March 7, 2018.
"Thomas Schütte stellt in seiner Geburtsstadt Oldenburg aus." *Kreiszeitung*, March 22, 2018.
Detterer, Gabriele. "Mach mal Pause!" *Frankfurter Allgemeine Zeitung*, July 19, 2018.
Korff Sausse, Simone. "Thomas Schütte: Trois Actes." *Le Carnet Psy*, no. 223 (April 5, 2019): 17.
Laster, Paul. "Thomas Schütte: Monnaie de Paris." *Sculpture*, June 14, 2019. sculpturemagazine.art/thomas-schutte/.

INTERVIEWS

Johnen, Jörg. "Ich lebe hier in Deutschland und muß mich dazu stellen." *Badische Zeitung Magazin*, January 15–16, 1983.
Hentschel, Martin. "Ein Gespräch mit Thomas Schütte." In *Rheingold: 40 Künstler aus Köln und Düsseldorf / 40 artisti da Colonia e Düsseldorf*. Edited by Wulf Herzogenrath and Stephan von Wiese, 226–28. Cologne: Wienand Verlag, 1985. Exhibition catalogue.
Loock, Ulrich. "Interview avec Thomas Schütte / Interview mit Thomas Schütte." In *Dispositif-Sculpture: Jürgen Drescher, Harald Klingelhöller, Reinhard Mucha, Thomas Schütte,* 86–91. Paris: ARC—Musée d'Art Moderne de la Ville de Paris, 1985. Exhibition catalogue.
Hentschel, Martin. "Vergessen macht glücklich: Ein Gespräch mit Thomas Schütte." *NIKE*, no. 6 (January/February 1985): 10–12. Reprinted in Spanish as "Olvidar hace feliz: Una conversación con Thomas Schütte." In *Thomas Schütte*, in *Raumbilder: Cinco escultores alemanes en Madrid*, 7–10. Madrid: Ministerio de Cultura, Dirección General de Bellas Artes y Archivos, and Centro Nacional de Exposiciones, 1987. Exhibition catalogue.
Hentschel, Martin. "Grande y pequeño: Thomas Schütte en conversación con Martin Hentschel." In *Thomas Schütte*, in *Raumbilder: Cinco escultores alemanes en Madrid*, 11–12. Madrid: Ministerio de Cultura, Dirección General de Bellas Artes y Archivos, and Centro Nacional de Exposiciones, 1987. Exhibition catalogue.

Blazwick, Iwona, and Andrea Schlieker. Interview with Thomas Schütte. In *Possible Worlds: Sculpture from Europe*, 70–72. London: ICA and Serpentine Gallery, 1990. Exhibition catalogue.

Morell, Lars. "Architecture Creates Space." *Skala*, no. 23 (1990): 24–29.

Badovinac, Zdenka. Interview with Thomas Schütte. In *Tišina: Protislovne oblike resnice / Silence: Contradictory Shapes of Truth*, 59. Ljubljana: Moderna Galerija, 1992. Exhibition catalogue.

Balkenhol, Stephan. "Gespräch Stephan Balkenhol—Thomas Schütte, September 1992." In *Stephan Balkenhol: Über Menschen und Skulpturen / About Men and Sculpture*, 72–79. Stuttgart: Edition Cantz, 1992. Exhibition catalogue.

Gould, Trevor. "'It Is Difficult to Arrange an Earthquake': An Interview with Thomas Schütte." *Parachute*, no. 68 (October–December 1992): 38–41.

Jocks, Heinz-Norbert. "Thomas Schütte: Man kann auch schattenboxen oder weiter stochern im Nebel." *Kunstforum International*, no. 128 (October–December 1994): 244–61.

Winzen, Matthias. "Collect Yourself: Ein Gespräch mit Thomas Schütte." In *Zuspiel*, 105–12. Ostfildern-Ruit, Germany: Hatje Cantz; Siemens Kulturprogramm, 1997.

Lingwood, James. "In Conversation with Thomas Schütte." In *Thomas Schütte*, by Julian Heynen, Lingwood, and Angela Vetese, 8–37. London: Phaidon, 1998.

Den Hartog Jager, Hans. "Schizofreen en grimmig: Gesprek met de Duitse kunstenaar Thomas Schütte." *NRC Handelsblad*, April 2, 1998.

Lingwood, James. "Gespräch mit Thomas Schütte in Düsseldorf und London. Juli/Dezember 2000 / Conversation with Thomas Schütte in Düsseldorf and London. July/December 2000." In *Thomas Schütte*, edited by Rainald Schumacher, 76–88. Munich: Kunstverlag Ingvild Goetz, Sammlung Goetz, 2001. Exhibition catalogue.

Buckner, Swen. Interview with Thomas Schütte. *Site*, no. 6 (May 2002): 36–47.

Loock, Ulrich. "Illustrations with Comments by the Artist in Conversation with the Author." In *Thomas Schütte*, edited by Dorothea Zwirner, 71–210. Berlin: Friedrich Christian Flick Collection; Cologne: DuMont Literatur und Kunst Verlag, 2004.

Hoffmans, Christiane. "'Schlag in die Magengrube.'" *Welt am Sonntag*, April 25, 2004.

Kölle, Brigitte. "Er hat ganz viel Sinn mit ins Spiel gebracht: Ein Gespräch mit Thomas Schütte / He Always Brought a Lot of Sense into Play: A Conversation with Thomas Schütte." In *Okey Dokey Konrad Fischer*, edited by Kölle, 225–46. Cologne: Walther König, 2007.

Krohn, Carsten. "Signs, Basements, Monument." *Archithese* 39, no. 6 (November 2009): 14–19.

Buck, Louisa. "Something Old, Something New: Interview with Thomas Schütte on His Works in London and Leeds." *Art Newspaper*, November 30, 2007.

Jarque, Fietta. "El dinero diseña hoy las carreras de los artistas." *El País*, February 6, 2010.

Liebs, Holger. "Matsch und Quatsch: Thomas Schütte in München." *Süddeutsche Zeitung*, May 17, 2010.

Gnyp, Marta. "Where There's Will, There's a Way." *Zoo*, no. 27 (Summer 2010): 66–75.

Wallner, Julia. "Giacometti Always Wanted Something Else: An Interview with Thomas Schütte." In *Alberto Giacometti: The Origin of Space*, edited by Markus Brüderlin and Toni Stooss, 208–11. Wolfsburg: Kunstmuseum Wolfsburg; Salzburg: Museum der Moderne Mönchberg; Ostfildern-Ruit, Germany: Hatje Cantz, 2011. Exhibition catalogue.

Obrist, Hans Ulrich. "Reality Production: An Interview with Thomas Schütte." *Mousse*, no. 28 (April/May 2011): 62–75.

Obrist, Hans Ulrich. "Reality Production: An Interview with Thomas Schütte—Part II." *Mousse*, no. 29 (Summer 2011): 68–79.

Heynen, Julian. "Through the Flower: A Conversation between Thomas Schütte and Julian Heynen." In *Het Huis: Thomas Schütte Sculpturen / Robbrecht en Daem Architecten.* Antwerp: Ludion and Middelheimmuseum, 2012. Exhibition catalogue.

Loock, Ulrich. "Gespräch: Ulrich Loock mit Thomas Schütte / Conversation: Ulrich Loock with Thomas Schütte." In *Thomas Schütte: Public/Political*, edited by Loock, 196–211. Cologne: Walther König, 2012. Exhibition catalogue.

Loock, Ulrich. "Tierisches Theater / Public Figures." Translated by Nicholas Grindell. *Frieze d/e*, no. 8 (February/March 2013): 84–93.

Liebs, Holger. "Gefangen im Neuland." *Monopol*, no. 9 (September 2013): 51–60.

Sorg, Reto. "Clint Eastwood and Robert Walser—The Two Have Something in Common." In *Paying No Attention I Notice Everything: Robert Walser and the Visual Arts*, edited by Madeleine Schuppli, Thomas Schmutz, and Reto Sorg, 135–142. Aarau, Switzerland: Aargauer Kunsthaus; Sulgen, Switzerland: Benteli Verlag, 2014. Exhibition catalogue.

Stasinski, Robert. "Ten Questions: Thomas Schütte." *Kunstkritikk*, October 7, 2016.

Fehlbaum, Rolf. "'It's Not about Entertainment': Thomas Schütte on the Blockhaus." *Vitra,* July 26, 2018. vitra.com /en-us/magazine/details its-not-about-entertainment.

Drnek, Angelika. "'Die digitale Kunst ist total uninteressant. Davor bleibe ich nie lange stehen.'" *Neue Zürcher Zeitung*, September 9, 2019.

"For me it's always about spaces. I don't care about the single sheet." In *Serien: Druckgraphik von Warhol bis Wool*, ed. Petra Roettig, 233–35. Hamburg: Hamburger Kunsthalle; Berlin: Dr. Cantz'sche Verlagsgesellschaft, 2021.

ARTIST WRITINGS AND PROJECTS

"Lieber Jean-Hubert Martin!" In *Burton, Gerdes, Huber, Klingelhöller, Luy, Mucha, Schütte: Konstruierte Orte; 6 × D + 1 × NY*, edited by Jean-Hubert Martin, 80–81. Bern: Kunsthalle Bern, 1983. Exhibition catalogue.

"One Ninety Nine (. . . And Here . . . A Project for *Artforum*)." *Artforum* 25, no. 10 (Summer 1987): 100–101.

"Gute-Nacht-Geschichte nr. 5: Der Maler." In *Jahresring 38: Der öffentliche Blick*, edited by Kasper König and Hans Ulrich Obrist, 319–28. Munich: Verlag Silke Schreiber, 1991.

"Gute-Nacht-Geschichten nr. 6: Der Streik—Das Leben ging weiter." In *Alte Freunde—Neue Arbeiten*, 25–28. Hamburg: Produzentengalerie Hamburg, 1993. Exhibition catalogue.

"Medardo Rosso." In *Medardo Rosso*, by Gloria Moure, 252. Santiago de Compostela, Spain: Centro Galego de Arte Contemporánea, 1996. Exhibition catalogue.

"Bedtime Story No. 6" and "Letter from Bilka." In *Thomas Schütte*, by Julian Heynen, James Lingwood, and Angela Vettese, 136–40, 142–43. London: Phaidon, 1998.

"La grève—mais la vie continue . . ." *Cahiers du Musée National d'Art Moderne* 67 (Spring 1999): 89–91.

"Heart and Mouth Disease." In *Thomas Schütte: Scenewright, Gloria in Memoria, In Medias Res*, edited by Lynne Cooke and Karen Kelly, 150–51. New York: Dia Art Foundation; Düsseldorf: Richter Verlag, 2002. Exhibition catalogue.

"Quengelware 2002: Ein Tagebuch mit 104 Radierungen." *Diamondpaper*, no. 4 (2003).

"Take a Day Off." In *Do It*, edited by Hans Ulrich Obrist, 322–23. New York: E-flux; Frankfurt: Revolver, 2004.

"Judgment Days: Gerhard Richter II." *Tate Etc.*, no. 23 (Fall 2011): 62–63.

"Arte di abitare / Inhabitable Art." *Domus*, no. 976 (January 2014): 110–19.

FILMS

Tomatensalat. VHS, directed by Martin Kreyssig, 1991, 40 min.

Thomas Schütte. Viele Spiele Grosse Kleine. 16mm film, directed by Martin Kreyssig, 1994, 15 min.

Richard Deacon—Thomas Schütte. Them and Us. VHS, directed by Martin Kreyssig, 1996, 5:25 min.

Thomas Schütte: Ich bin nicht allein. DVD, directed by Corinna Belz, 2023, 95 min.

Acknowledgments

The exhibition *Thomas Schütte* and this accompanying publication are Odyssean. I blame my own fixation on the siren call of Schütte's work; only the most dedicated and ambitious had the humor to undertake this journey with me. I began working on this project in 2015, and over the course of nearly a decade I have had the honor of collaborating with no fewer than a hundred people. Their contributions to the manifestation of what for so long was only an idea reverberate across this catalogue and throughout the Museum's galleries. I'd like to think that I stumbled into good luck, but everyone was just doing their job—when "doing their job" meant adhering to a standard of excellence that is truly inimitable. Thank you.

Glenn D. Lowry, Director of The Museum of Modern Art, supported this project through a global, generationally defining cataclysm. No volume can contain my gratitude for Glenn's profound belief in the importance and urgency of Schütte's art and his commitment to this presentation.

This show would not have moved forward without the wholehearted support of Kathy Halbreich, MoMA's former Associate Director, who was an advocate for Schütte's work from the beginning. Christy Thompson, Senior Deputy Director of Exhibitions and Collections, and her predecessor, Ramona Bronkar Bannayan, championed this undertaking despite the many obstacles it presented. Sarah Suzuki, the Museum's Associate Director, and Peter Reed, former Associate Director of Curatorial Affairs, similarly offered steadfast support. I relied on the wisdom and friendship of Jan Postma, Chief Financial Officer, throughout the planning of this exhibition and beyond. I also thank Diana Pulling, Chief of Staff; James Gara, Chief Operating Officer and Assistant Treasurer to the Board of Trustees; and Beverly Morgan-Welch, Senior Deputy Director of External Affairs.

The Museum's Board of Trustees is without equal. Its unwavering commitment to this institution makes ambitious exhibitions such as this one possible. Marie-Josée Kravis, Chair, and Ronnie F. Heyman, President Emerita, led the board during the preparation of *Thomas Schütte*; I relied on their insight and encouragement throughout. I thank Sarah Arison, President, an ardent proponent of contemporary art. Anne Dias Griffin has a keen understanding of Schütte's work in all its complexity, and I have valued her counsel. I also thank Lonti Ebers and Bruce Flatt, Eva and Glenn Dubin, and Glenn and Amanda Fuhrman, who have been passionate advocates of Schütte's work for many years.

I gratefully acknowledge the largesse of our donors. Major support for this publication was provided by Jo Carole and Ronald S. Lauder through The International Council of The Museum of Modern Art and the Dale S. and Norman Mills Leff Publication Fund. The exhibition was made possible by MoMA's partner Hyundai Card, with leadership support by the Eyal and Marilyn Ofer Family Foundation, the Xin Zhang and Shiyi Pan Endowment Fund, Eva and Glenn Dubin, and The International Council of The Museum of Modern Art. Together they have enabled the exploration of Schütte's richly textured and tentacular body of work both on these pages and in the Museum's galleries.

Generosity of spirit and great trust distinguish the lenders to this exhibition, both private individuals and public institutions and foundations throughout the United States and Europe. By agreeing to temporarily part with beloved works from their collections, they made this presentation possible. To them I express my most profound appreciation. I especially recognize the contributions of the Herbert Foundation and the Kunstsammlung Nordrhein-Westfalen, whose loans were essential. Their long-standing relationships with the artist make this collaboration particularly meaningful. The Art Institute of Chicago, De Pont Museum, Glenstone Museum, Kunstmuseum Bern, Kunstmuseum Wolfsburg, Paris Musées / Musée d'Art Moderne, Panza Collection, and Tate approved our requests without hesitation. Loans from private individuals, including Niels Dietrich, Eva and Glenn Dubin, Peter Freeman and Lluïsa Sàrries Zgonc, Anne Dias Griffin, Eleanor Heyman Propp, and others who wish to remain anonymous, were just as crucial. Like many artists, Schütte has held onto objects of particular significance. He has been the most hospitable of all, entrusting us with the care of dozens of delicate works.

Without Konrad and Dorothee Fischer, today's presentation would not be possible. Beginning in the 1960s, Konrad Fischer Galerie in Düsseldorf has exhibited the most challenging art of its time and acted as a hub for artists visiting the city. The Fischers and their gallery offered Schütte first a real-world education and then a place to show his work. We are immensely grateful to Berta Fischer, who in addition to being an artist is now the owner of Konrad Fischer Galerie, and to Thomas W. Rieger, its Senior Director. They offered unfaltering support and facilitated much of the scholarly research necessary for this retrospective. Peter Freeman, whose eponymous gallery exhibits Schütte's work in New York, and his partner, the conservator Lluïsa Sàrries Zgonc, have approached this project with unmatched attention and devotion. I consider them partners in the making of this exhibition and true friends whose kindness and generosity extend far beyond professional parameters. The staff at Peter Freeman, Inc., especially Katie Rashid, Senior Director; Jessica Heerten, Head Registrar; and Anna Lustberg, Head of Communications, fielded countless detailed questions and pressing requests, sympathetically understanding their urgency.

My appreciation extends to all the galleries Schütte works with. They opened their doors, answered their phones, and always pointed me in the right direction. Thanks are due to the staffs of Frith Street Gallery, Pietro Spartà, Bernier/Eliades Gallery, and Carlier | Gebauer. Although Marian Goodman Gallery does not currently represent the artist, its staff generously shared information from its archive on more than one occasion.

In the Department of Painting and Sculpture, my greatest thanks are due to Ann Temkin, The Marie-Josée and Henry R. Kravis Chief Curator. In 2008, Ann hired me as a curatorial assistant. Since then, we have spent countless hours working side by side on special exhibitions and with the Museum's unrivaled collection. Her vast knowledge of art history, her carefully attuned eye, and her exceptional sensitivity to space have shaped each of her many installations. Ann taught me how to be a curator; I have had the extraordinary good fortune to have learned from the best. As I embarked on this project, her support was essential, and I turned to her for advice and sought her opinion on matters large and small. Her wisdom and measured judgment course through this show. Thank you, Ann.

I would also like to thank the other members of the Department of Painting and Sculpture, past and present. Anne Umland, the former Blanchette Hooker Rockefeller Senior Curator, is a scholar who places art at the center. Her passion for her profession is as rare as her dedication to it, and she has inspired me to follow suit. Leah Dickerman, Director of Research Programs, is a fearless curator and capacious thinker whose exhibitions are nothing short of revelatory. Without Leah's example, this would be a very different show. Michelle Kuo, Chief Curator at Large and Publisher, formerly the Marlene Hess Curator, is a friend and trusted colleague. Her capacity for critical thinking knows no end and is buttressed by her emotional intelligence. I have leaned on her in times of doubt and looked to her for guidance. Finally, it is my great privilege to thank Cara Manes, Associate Curator. Cara has read every sentence in this book and seen all the iterations of the model for this exhibition. Her intelligence and creativity impact nearly every collection presentation at The Museum of Modern Art. This undertaking has benefitted from her many talents—her understanding, her sense of humor, and, above all, her empathy.

Across the Museum's curatorial departments, the institution's commitment to Schütte is apparent, particularly in the extensive holdings of his work in the Department of Drawings and Prints. Christophe Cherix, The Robert Lehman Foundation Chief Curator, and his colleagues have supported this exhibition with key interdepartmental loans. I also thank Stuart Comer, The Lonti Ebers Chief Curator of Media and Performance, and Roxana Marcoci, The David Dechman Senior Curator and Acting Chief Curator, Department of Photography. We have worked together with the Museum's collection of contemporary art for many years, and they have been supportive friends and important interlocutors throughout the planning of *Thomas Schütte*.

Designing an exhibition with an artist for whom the principles of space and architecture are paramount requires an extraordinarily talented and flexible team. In the Department of Exhibition Design and Production, I am endlessly grateful to Lana Hum, Director, along with LJ McNerney, Exhibition Designer, and Boris Chesakov, Temporary Production Manager. Their knowledge, sensitivity, and creativity resulted in a lively and sophisticated floor plan, ideal for the display of Schütte's complex body of work. Their former colleague Matthew Cox was an inspired collaborator early in the process.

The advocacy and acumen of Rachel Kim, Associate Director of Exhibition Planning and Collections, and Maya Taylor, Exhibition Manager, were wholly indispensable to this presentation. Sacha Eaton and Carla Hernandez, Associate Registrars, shouldered every challenge and intricacy of this project with seeming ease and uncompromising attention. I thank Stefanii Ruta Atkins, Director of Collection Management and Exhibition Registration, for her leadership. The limitless expertise of Lynda Zycherman, Sculpture Conservator, and Caitlin Richeson, Assistant Objects Conservator, was on full display throughout the planning stages of this exhibition. I am grateful to them and to Annie Wilker, Paper Conservator, for her diligent care of Schütte's works on paper.

This exhibition presented us with the unique opportunity to realize a number of Schütte's key works in situ, an achievement that belongs to a league of essential staff and contractors. I thank Allan Smith, Foreman, Carpenter Shop, for his charge in realizing a 1:1 scale model of *Schutzraum* (*Shelter*), which was shown only in 1986 and destroyed thereafter. Claire Corey, Senior Production Manager, Design, and scenic painter Paulette Giguere expertly recreated a pivotal text-based work that Schütte has displayed on just two other occasions. I am indebted to all MoMA's carpenters, painters, framers, and mechanics. Their expert handiwork is immediately apparent in every facet of this show.

Across the many branches of the Museum, my gratitude extends to the talented staff of the departments and divisions of Art Handling and Preparation, Collection Management and Exhibition Registration, Communications and Public Affairs, Learning and Engagement, External Affairs, Design, Imaging and Visual Resources, Marketing, Special Events, and Security. Too many to name, these colleagues have worked with determination and creativity to meet the many unusual demands presented by this exhibition.

The achievements of this catalogue are the product of collective brilliance. First, I offer my profound thanks to the authors of the illuminating texts this publication contains. Jennifer L. Allen, Associate Professor of History, Yale University, provides invaluable historical context for the art reproduced in these pages. André Rottmann, Professor of Art and Media Theory, Europa-Universität Viadrina Frankfurt (Oder), considers Schütte's work within the framework of theoretical discourse, an approach previously absent from the literature. Artists Marlene Dumas and Charles Ray accepted my invitation to contribute to this publication with enthusiasm. Dumas clearly and persuasively communicates the significance of the community and conversation that art making engenders, while Ray speaks as only a sculptor can: his essay offers a vivid and tangible understanding of where the physicality and form of a sculpture can lead the eye and mind. My essay would not have been possible without the invaluable contributions of Corinna Belz, Benjamin H. D. Buchloh, Katharina Fritsch, Janice Guy, Kasper König, Camille Morineau, Rüdiger Schöttle, Dieter Schwarz, and Thomas Struth, each of whom gamely agreed to join me in conversation and whose thoughts helped shape my own. I also thank the many outstanding curators, historians, and critics who have considered Schütte's art at length, especially Lynne Cooke, Senior Curator, Department of Modern and Contemporary Art, National Gallery of Art, Washington, DC, the foremost expert on Schütte's work and organizer of not one but two retrospective exhibitions devoted to it. Domenick Ammirati, the editor of this volume, has been an essential collaborator. His critical mind and dexterous command of language can be detected in every sentence. The book's designer, Joseph Logan, brought a puzzling array of materials into clear focus. His elegant design responds to and reflects the art it presents.

Alongside Michelle Kuo, in the Department of Publications I thank Rebecca Roberts, Editor, whose expert skills are matched only by her unflappable disposition and patience. Joseph Mohan, Production Director, coordinated countless moving parts; Curtis R. Scott, Associate Publisher, provided essential guidance; Matthew Pimm, Production Manager, ensured the superlative quality of the printed volume; and Hannah Kim, Business and Marketing Director, secured its bilingual release. These were no small feats. Ava Childers, Associate General Counsel, and Lena Saltos, Deputy General Counsel, provided crucial legal guidance, and Anne Levine, Rights Coordinator, deftly oversaw image permissions. For research assistance we are indebted to our colleagues in MoMA's Archives, Library, and Research Collections, especially Jillian Suarez, Head of Library Services, and Sophie Cianfarani, Library Assistant, and to interns Nora Chapman, Athina Fili, and Max Langefeld.

In January 2024, I joined the Hammer Museum, Los Angeles, as Robert Soros Senior Curator. In easing the enormous pressures of this transition, Ann Philbin, Director of the Hammer, displayed a superhuman level of patience. Annie's unflagging generosity enabled me to see this project across the finish line. I thank the entire staff of the Hammer Museum for their warm welcome and continued flexibility as I navigate this new terrain.

I would be remiss not to extend thanks to the many friends who indulged me in conversations about Schütte's work and art in general. Their probing questions and generous insights, reflections, and criticism have been invaluable to the organization of my thoughts and to the construction of this show. I have relied on Ian Alteveer, Nairy Baghramian, Eric Banks, Thea Djordjadze, Darby English, Rachel Harrison, Jane Panetta, Paloma Varga Weisz, and Michel Ziegler at many critical junctures. I would also like to thank Robert Gober. Together with Ann Temkin, we organized his 2014 MoMA retrospective, *The Heart Is Not a Metaphor*. I have returned time and again to that exhibition and the many lessons it still confers. My husband, Greg, and my daughter, Matilda, kept me tethered to the ground so my thoughts could roam. I love them beyond limit.

Little more than one year before the opening of this exhibition, Caitlin Chaisson joined the team as Curatorial Assistant. When I decamped for Los Angeles, she took the wheel. Her efforts have been nothing short of heroic and her accomplishments astonishing. Caitlin possesses an exceptional combination of grace and grit that she deploys in perfect measure to navigate every challenge thrown her way and to ensure that, as the subject of this exhibition might say, "all is in order." By turns prudent, intrepid, shrewd, and broad-minded, Caitlin has far surpassed all bars of excellence. I can say with confidence that without her, order of any sort would have been elusive. Caitlin's predecessor, Lydia Mullin, now Manager of Collection Galleries at MoMA, got the project off the ground. She has remained a dear friend of the show and a valued contributor.

Schütte's work is by necessity a collaborative endeavor; bronze sculpture requires a foundry, ceramics a kiln, architecture a licensed practitioner. Over the course of many years, I have become acquainted with Rolf Kayser of Kunstgiesserei Kayser and Niels Dietrich of Werkstatt Niels Dietrich, both masters of their trades. Each gave me a front-row seat from which to observe the impossible made real. The sculptures on view in this exhibition result from centuries of cumulative knowledge as well as up-to-the-moment innovation. Architect Lars Klatte has worked with Schütte to realize his many experiments in brick and mortar. With Heinrich Heinemann, Klatte oversaw the construction of Skulpturenhalle, Schütte's museum in Neuss, Germany, and the artist's most ambitious project to date. For this exhibition, Klatte's architectural renderings and material specifications enabled the construction of *Schutzraum*. We are in his debt.

In his studio, Schütte has worked with Luise Heuter since 2003 and Rupert Huber since 2007. They know his work best, and they were unsparing in sharing their time and knowledge. More significant even than that, their warmth, good will, and ready laughter set the tone for our relationship from the start. They have my boundless praise and appreciation.

I admired Schütte's work from afar long before embarking on this project. All he did was utterly beguiling. Mysterious and multifaceted, it didn't add up; it couldn't be explained in a few simple sentences. It set up residence in my mind and refused to leave. When MoMA approached the artist with the prospect of a retrospective exhibition, he agreed despite being well aware that the journey would be long and demanding. Though no one was prepared for what was to come, his commitment never wavered and his generosity only grew. In fact, the delays created by the COVID-19 pandemic enriched this presentation beyond measure, as he and I scoured through forgotten drawings, notes, and notebooks. We drove from the foundry to the ceramics workshop, from his storage facility to an exhibition in a neighboring city or nearby country. In his studio and over dinner, we talked about things of extreme urgency and things that were significantly less so. I've had the privilege of seeing him patinate bronze, shape a ceramic, and install his work in at least a dozen museums. Cumulatively these experiences fed this exhibition and engendered the depth of understanding evident in all aspects of this publication. He and I share an unstinting belief in the importance of art and the urge to present its profundity to audiences with clarity and precision—no filler, no fat. That's the goal. Thank you, Thomas, for guiding the way.

Paulina Pobocha
Robert Soros Senior Curator, Hammer Museum,
Los Angeles, and former Associate Curator,
Department of Painting and Sculpture, MoMA

Major support for this publication is provided by Jo Carole and Ronald S. Lauder through The International Council of The Museum of Modern Art. Additional funding is provided by the Dale S. and Norman Mills Leff Publication Fund.

Hyundai Card

The exhibition is made possible by MoMA's partner Hyundai Card.

Leadership support is provided by the Eyal and Marilyn Ofer Family Foundation, the Xin Zhang and Shiyi Pan Endowment Fund, Eva and Glenn Dubin, and The International Council of The Museum of Modern Art.

Published in conjunction with the exhibition *Thomas Schütte*, at The Museum of Modern Art, New York, September 29, 2024–January 18, 2025. Organized by Paulina Pobocha, Robert Soros Senior Curator, Hammer Museum, Los Angeles, and former Associate Curator, MoMA; and Caitlin Chaisson, Curatorial Assistant, Department of Painting and Sculpture, MoMA.

Major support for this publication is provided by Jo Carole and Ronald S. Lauder through The International Council of The Museum of Modern Art. Additional funding is provided by the Dale S. and Norman Mills Leff Publication Fund.

Hyundai Card

The exhibition is made possible by MoMA's partner Hyundai Card.

Leadership support is provided by the Eyal and Marilyn Ofer Family Foundation, the Xin Zhang and Shiyi Pan Endowment Fund, Eva and Glenn Dubin, and The International Council of The Museum of Modern Art.

Produced by the Department of Publications, The Museum of Modern Art, New York

Michelle Kuo, Chief Curator at Large and Publisher
Curtis R. Scott, Associate Publisher
Joseph Mohan, Production Director
Hannah Kim, Business and Marketing Director

Edited by Domenick Ammirati
Design by Joseph Logan, assisted by Anamaria Morris and Sam Pearson
Production by Matthew Pimm
Proofread by Jeffrey Castle
Color separations by t'ink, Brussels
Printed and bound by Graphius, Belgium

This book is typeset in Jjannon by Optimo. The paper is 135 gsm Magno Volume.

Published by The Museum of Modern Art
11 West 53 Street
New York, NY 10019-5497
www.moma.org

Library of Congress Control Number: 2024940427
ISBN: 978-1-63345-163-6

Distributed in the United States and Canada by
ARTBOOK | D.A.P.
75 Broad Street, Suite 630
New York, NY 10004
www.artbook.com

Distributed outside the United States and Canada by
Thames & Hudson
181A High Holborn
London WC1V 7QX
www.thamesandhudson.com

Printed in Belgium

PHOTOGRAPH CREDITS

In reproducing the images contained in this publication, the Museum obtained the permission of the rights holders whenever possible. If the Museum could not locate the rights holders, notwithstanding good-faith efforts, it requests that any contact information concerning such rights holders be forwarded so that they may be contacted for future editions.

All works by Thomas Schütte © 2024 Thomas Schütte / Artists Rights Society (ARS), New York / VG Bild-Kunst, Bonn. Unless otherwise noted, images of works by Thomas Schütte were provided by the artist's studio.

Photograph by Roland Aellig © 2024 Artists Rights Society (ARS), New York / ProLitteris, Zurich: p. 127. Photograph by Stefan Altenburger, Zurich: pp. 110, 124. © The Art Institute of Chicago: p. 183. The Art Institute of Chicago / Art Resource, NY; photograph by Elyse Allen: p. 169. Photograph by Walther Benser, https://creativecommons.org/licenses/by-sa/4.0/: p. 19 (fig. 20). bpk Bildagentur / Kunstsammlung Nordrhein-Westfalen / Achim Kukulies / Art Resource, NY: pp. 153–55, 157. © The Estate of James Lee Byars, courtesy Michael Werner Gallery, New York, London, and Berlin: p. 10. Photograph by Cathy Carver: pp. 64 (bottom), 125. Courtesy Castello di Rivoli Museo d'Arte Contemporanea; photograph by Paolo Pellion: p. 33 (fig. 13). Photograph by Leon Chew: p. 26. © 2017 Christie's Images Limited: p. 166 (top). Cnap; photograph © Fabrice Lindor: p. 30. Photograph by Peter Cox © 2024 Artists Rights Society (ARS), New York / c/o Pictoright Amsterdam: pp. 27 (fig. 2), 137 (top), 144 (left and right), 145. © DB–ADAGP, Paris / Artists Rights Society (ARS), New York 2024: p. 12 (fig. 6). Herbert Foundation, Ghent: pp. 116–21; photograph by Philippe De Gobert, 1989: p. 98; photograph by Yuri van der Hoeven, 2019: pp. 77, 99, 101, 103. Photograph by Luise Heuter © 2024 Artists Rights Society (ARS), New York / VG Bild-Kunst, Bonn: pp. 12 (fig. 7), 38, 50 (top), 51, 57, 59, 70–73, 71 (top), 75, 76, 78 (top left and right), 84–85, 90–91, 91 (top), 180 (top right, center left, and bottom left), 181 (top left and right, center left, and bottom right), 184. Photograph by Candida Höfer © 2024 Artists Rights Society (ARS), New York / VG Bild-Kunst, Bonn: p. 31. Photograph by Florian Holzherr: pp. 104–5. Photograph by Axel Hütte: p. 115. © 2024 Jasper Johns / Licensed by VAGA at Artists Rights Society (ARS), NY: pp. 14 (fig. 11), 15. Photograph by Jürgen Weller Fotografie: p. 66 (bottom). Photograph by Florian Kleinefenn © 2024 Artists Rights Society (ARS), New York / SAIF, Paris: pp. 130, 131. Photograph by Jussi Koivunen / Sara Hildén Art Museum: p. 167 (bottom). Photograph by Marek Kruszewski: p. 151. Photograph by Achim Kukulies, Düsseldorf: pp. 62, 63. Photograph by Michael Meyborg: p. 42 (fig. 5). Photograph © Aurélien Mole 2017: p. 22. Reproduced by permission of The Henry Moore Foundation; photograph by Jonty Wilde: pp. 164–65. Photograph by Helge Mundt: p. 150 (left, center, and right). Photographic Archives Museo Nacional Centro de Arte Reina Sofía; photograph by Joaquín Cortés / Román Lores: pp. 43 (figs. 6 and 7), 68–69, 162–63. Digital image © 2024 The Museum of Modern Art, New York, Department of Imaging and Visual Resources; photograph by Robert Gerhardt: pp. 96 (bottom), 112 (top), 123; photograph by Thomas Griesel: pp. 32 (figs. 10 and 11), 46 (fig. 12), 187; photograph by Jonathan Muzikar: p. 27 (fig. 3); photograph by Martin Parsekian: p. 14 (fig. 11); photograph by Martin Seck: p. 28 (fig. 5); photograph by John Wronn: pp. 146–47. © 2024 Claes Oldenburg: p. 28 (fig. 5). Courtesy Panza Collection, Mendrisio; photograph by Alessandro Zambianchi, Milan: p. 113. Photograph by Tom Powel: pp. 140, 141 (bottom). © Gerhard Richter 2024 (06022024): pp. 11, 18 (figs. 16 and 18), 29 (fig. 7). © Gerhard Richter 2024 (18012024), courtesy Gerhard Richter Archive Dresden: p. 29 (fig. 6). Photograph © RMN-Grand Palais / Art Resource, NY: pp. 132–33; photograph by Herve Lewandowski: p. 23 (fig. 2). © 2024 Estate of Alexander Rodchenko / UPRAVIS, Moscow/ARS, NY: p. 13 (fig. 9). Photograph by Thomas Ruff © 2024 Artists Rights Society (ARS), New York/VG Bild-Kunst, Bonn: pp. 4, 41 (fig. 2), 112 (bottom). Photograph by Tomasz Samek: pp. 106–9, 122. Courtesy Sammlung Goetz, Munich; photograph by Nic Tenwiggenhorn: p. 114 (top). Photograph by Thomas Schütte: pp. 9 (fig. 3), 17, 19 (fig. 19), 41 (fig. 3), 82 (top and bottom), 86 (top and bottom). Courtesy Thomas Schütte and Konrad Fischer Galerie; photograph by Achim Kukulies: pp. 67, 83. Courtesy Thomas Schütte and Peter Freeman, Inc., New York/Paris: p. 95; photograph by Florian Kleinefenn: pp. 170–73, 174–75; photograph by Nicholas Knight Studio: p. 24. © Thomas Struth (*Thomas Schütte, Düsseldorf 1992*): p. 199. Studio Fuis Photographie: p. 87. Tate: pp. 134–35, 142 (left and right), 143. Photograph by Nic Tenwiggenhorn © 2024 Artists Rights Society (ARS), New York / VG Bild-Kunst, Bonn: pp. 33 (fig. 12), 44, 45 (figs. 9 and 10), 97, 114 (bottom), 128–29, 138–39, 165 (top), 167 (top), 168 (top and bottom), 180 (center right), 185, 186, 200, 201. Photograph by Mareike Tocha: pp. 94 (top and bottom), 137 (bottom left and right), 188, 189, 190, 191 (left and right), 192, 193, 195, 196, 197. © 2024 Niele Toroni / Artists Rights Society (ARS), New York / ADAGP, Paris: p. 27 (fig. 3). Photograph by Markus Tretter: pp. 93, 141 (top), 166 (bottom). Photograph by John Tromp: pp. 111, 136. Photographic Archive Tucci Russo: p. 13 (fig. 8). University of California, Berkeley Art Museum and Pacific Film Archive: p. 10. Photograph by Tom Van Eynde: p. 23 (fig. 3). Photograph by Antoine van Kaam: pp. 148–49.

Cover: Thomas Schütte. *Proposal for a Facade in Hamburg* (detail). 1980. Acrylic on paper, 7 ½ × 10 ¾" (19 × 27.3 cm). Collection the artist, Düsseldorf

Endpapers: Thomas Schütte. *Kollege Immendorf* (recto and verso, details). 2022. Ink and crayon on paper, 11 7/16 × 7 ½" (29 × 19 cm). Collection the artist, Düsseldorf

Page 4: Portrait of Thomas Schütte by Thomas Ruff, 2024